Beginning SUSE Linux

Second Edition

Keir Thomas

Apress®

Beginning SUSE Linux, Second Edition

Copyright © 2006 by Keir Thomas

ISBN-13 (pbk): 978-1-59059-674-6

ISBN-10 (pbk): 1-59059-674-9

Printed and bound in the United States of America 9 8 7 6 5 4 3 2 1

Lead Editor: Jason Gilmore
Technical Reviewer: John Hornbeck
Editorial Board: Steve Anglin, Ewan Buckingham, Gary Cornell, Jason Gilmore, Jonathan Gennick, Jonathan Hassell, James Huddleston, Chris Mills, Matthew Moodie, Dominic Shakeshaft, Jim Sumser, Keir Thomas, Matt Wade
Project Manager: Richard Dal Porto
Copy Edit Manager: Nicole LeClerc
Copy Editor: Marilyn Smith
Assistant Production Director: Kari Brooks-Copony
Production Editor: Ellie Fountain
Compositor: Molly Sharp, ContentWorks
Proofreader: Nancy Sixsmith
Indexer: John Collin
Cover Designer: Kurt Krames
Manufacturing Director: Tom Debolski

Distributed to the book trade worldwide by Springer-Verlag New York, Inc., 233 Spring Street, 6th Floor, New York, NY 10013. Phone 1-800-SPRINGER, fax 201-348-4505, e-mail orders-ny@springer-sbm.com, or visit http://www.springeronline.com.

For information on translations, please contact Apress directly at 2560 Ninth Street, Suite 219, Berkeley, CA 94710. Phone 510-549-5930, fax 510-549-5939, e-mail info@apress.com, or visit http://www.apress.com.

Dedicated to my sister, Bethany Collier.

Contents at a Glance

PART I ▪▪▪ Introducing the World of Linux

PART II ▪▪▪ Installing SUSE Linux

PART III ▪▪▪ The No-Nonsense Getting Started Guide

PART IV ▪▪▪ The Shell and Beyond

PART V ■■■ Multimedia

PART VI ■■■ Office Tasks

PART VII ■■■ Keeping Your System Running

Contents

PART I ■ ■ ■ Introducing the World of Linux

PART II ■ ■ ■ Installing SUSE Linux

PART III ■ ■ ■ The No-Nonsense Getting Started Guide

PART IV ■ ■ ■ The Shell and Beyond

PART V ■■■ Multimedia

PART VI ■■■ Office Tasks

PART VII ■ ■ ■ Keeping Your System Running

About the Author

 **KEIR THOMAS** has been writing about computers, operating systems, and software for a decade. He has edited several best-selling computer magazines, including *Linux User & Developer, PC Utilities,* and *PC Extreme.* He has worked as part of the editorial staff on a range of other titles and was formerly Technical Group Editor at a British computer magazine publisher.

In addition to his authoring work, Keir works as a full-time editor for Apress. He lives on the side of a mountain in England, and his pastimes include hill walking and playing musical instruments. *Beginning SUSE Linux, Second Edition* is Keir's third book for Apress, in addition to the first edition and *Beginning Ubuntu Linux.*

About the Technical Reviewer

 **JOHN HORNBECK** has been involved with open source software since 1999. He has used SUSE Linux since version 4 and has helped compile packages for the distribution. His dedication to Linux is so strong that he had the Linux penguin tattooed onto his right forearm. Currently, John owns and operates a software company and is involved with multiple web startups. He also maintains many GNU/Linux servers and instructs GNU/Linux at his local technology school.

Acknowledgments

Books like the one you're holding now take an enormous amount of work by a lot of people to come to fruition. To this end, I'd like to acknowledge the help of the following individuals in the production of this book: Chris Mills, Emily Wolman, Jason Gilmore, Sofia Marchant, Richard Dal Porto, Marilyn Smith, Ellie Fountain, and the many other people at Apress whose work behind the scenes made this book possible.

I'd like to thank the technical editors of this edition and the first edition—John Hornbeck and Frank Pohlmann, respectively—for their insightful comments that helped shape the book into what it is.

Thanks also go to Andreas Jaeger and Michael Loeffler at SUSE.

Introduction

Linux has come a long way in a short time. Computing itself is still relatively young by any standard; if the era of modern computing started with the invention of the microchip, it's still less than 50 years old. But Linux is a youngster compared even to this; it has been around for only 15 of those years.

In that brief time span, a student's personal project has grown to where it now runs many computers throughout the world. It has rampaged through the computing industry, offering an alternative to commercial solutions such as those offered by Microsoft, and toppling long-held beliefs about the way things should be done. This is all by virtue of the fact that Linux is simply better than every other choice out there. Many argue that it's more secure and faster than other operating systems. But here's the kicker—Linux is free of charge. Yes, that's right. It doesn't have to cost a penny. It is one of the computing industry's best-kept secrets.

I was bitten by the Linux bug in the mid-1990s. I was introduced to it by a friend who sold it to me as a kind of alternative to DOS. At that time, I tapped a few commands at the prompt and was greeted by error messages. I must admit that I was put off. But shortly afterward, I revisited Linux and quickly became hooked.

Yet getting used to Linux wasn't easy. I read as many books as I could, but they weren't very helpful to me. They were usually overly complicated or simply irrelevant. To start off, I didn't want to know how to create a program that could parse text files. I just wanted to know how to copy and delete files. I didn't want to set up a web server. I just wanted to know how to play my MP3 tracks and browse the Web.

This book is my answer to the need for a fundamental, authoritative, and down-to-earth guide to Linux, done in the context of one of the most popular flavors of Linux in existence today. It's a book that is desperately needed in our modern world, especially as Linux becomes more and more popular and enters homes and workplaces.

Beginning SUSE Linux, Second Edition purely and simply focuses on what you need to know to use Linux. It's concise and to the point, aiming to re-create under Linux all the stuff you used to do under Windows. But don't think that this means *Beginning SUSE Linux, Second Edition* cuts corners. Wherever justified, this book spends time examining the topics you need to know in order to gain a complete and comprehensive understanding. For example, you'll find a hefty chapter looking at the command-line prompt—arguably the heart of Linux and the element that gives Linux most of its power. There's also an entire chapter discussing (and illustrating) how to initially install SUSE Linux on your computer. *Beginning SUSE Linux, Second Edition* really is a complete guide.

About SUSE Linux

Most versions of Linux are broadly similar, but this book focuses specifically on SUSE Linux. Even more specifically, I focus on SUSE Linux 10.1 and above, including the work of the openSUSE project.

SUSE Linux is one of the premier distributions of Linux available today and is widely used within business and home environments. Some say that it's the absolute best version of Linux around but, whatever the case, it's certainly a professional product that delivers the best of the Linux world to its users.

Novell bought SUSE GmbH in 2003, giving SUSE Linux the kind of push that only a multinational corporation allows. The result is SUSE Linux is being snapped up around the world for use in corporate and home environments alike. SUSE partners with IBM, Hewlett-Packard, and many other computer manufacturers around the world as one of their distributions of choice.

This isn't without reason. SUSE Linux has managed to pull off the seemingly impossible feat of being both easy to use and also extremely powerful. It overcomes one of the standard criticisms of Linux—that it's hard to configure—by providing the YaST tool. Uniquely in the Linux world, this tool offers access to just about every aspect of Linux configuration, from setting up your printer to installing new software, and much more besides. Users of Windows might think of it as being like the Control Panel on steroid-enhancing drugs. But Windows doesn't even come close to providing an alternative.

The comparison with Windows is apt because SUSE Linux manages to pull off another seemingly impossible feat: it's easy to use for those coming from Windows, yet retains its own independent look and feel. Virtually everyone in the Linux world agrees that SUSE Linux has the best user interface around, and this is clearly something SUSE Linux's software engineers spent a long time developing. SUSE Linux is a luxury product in the often rough-and-ready world of Linux. Its hardware support is also excellent, meaning that installing it is a breeze. It's ideal for every level of user, and the desktop user in particular.

What You'll Find in This Book

Beginning SUSE Linux, Second Edition is split into seven parts, each of which contains chapters about a certain aspect of SUSE Linux use. These parts can be read in sequence, or you can dip in and out of them at will. Whenever a technical term is mentioned, a reference is made to the chapter where that term is explained.

Part I examines the history and philosophy behind the Linux operating system. I aim to answer many of the common questions about Linux. Such knowledge is considered to be as important, if not more so, than understanding the technical details of how Linux works. But while these chapters should be read sooner rather than later, they don't contain any technical information that you absolutely require to get started with SUSE Linux.

Part II covers installing SUSE Linux on your computer. An illustrated guide is provided, and all installation choices are explained in depth. Additionally, you'll find a problem-solving chapter to help just in case anything goes wrong.

Part III focuses on getting started with SUSE Linux. It covers setting up the Linux system so that it's ready to use. One chapter is dedicated to setting up common hardware devices, such as printers and modems, and another explains how you can secure your system. Other chapters in this part explore the desktop, explaining what you need to know to begin using SUSE Linux on a daily basis.

In Part IV, we take a look at how the underlying technology behind Linux functions. You'll be introduced to the command-line prompt and learn how the file system works. It's in these chapters that you'll really master controlling Linux!

Part V covers multimedia functions available for SUSE Linux users, which let you watch movies and play back music. We also take a look at the image-editing software built into SUSE Linux.

Part VI moves on to explain how typical office tasks can be accomplished under SUSE Linux. We investigate OpenOffice.org, the complete office suite built into SUSE Linux. After an introduction to OpenOffice.org, separate chapters explore its word processor, spreadsheet, database, and presentation package. You'll also learn how to use the Evolution e-mail and personal information manager program, and how to run Microsoft Office under SUSE Linux.

Part VII carries on from Part IV, taking an even more in-depth look at the underlying technology behind SUSE Linux. This time, the emphasis is on giving you the skills you need to keep your system running smoothly. You'll learn how to install software, manage users, optimize your system, back up essential data, schedule tasks, and access computers remotely.

Finally, at the back of the book, you'll find three appendixes. The first is a glossary of Linux terms used not only in this book, but also in the Linux and Unix world. The second appendix is a quick reference to commands typically used at the command-line prompt under Linux. The final appendix explains how to get further help when using SUSE Linux.

What's New in the Second Edition

This edition of *Beginning SUSE Linux* has been drastically overhauled to take into account new technologies introduced with version 10.1 of SUSE Linux. In addition, this edition covers the GNOME and KDE desktop environments, because SUSE Linux now gives both equal emphasis. The previous edition focused solely on KDE.

The biggest changes are in Chapter 8, which describes how to get your hardware and essential software up and running. It has been completely rewritten to take into account changes in SUSE Linux 10.1 and also to reflect modern hardware use. Other rewritten chapters include Chapter 9, which describes how to secure your computer; Chapters 18 and 19, which cover multimedia; and Chapter 29, which has instructions for installing software. These now cover new and improved technology offered within SUSE Linux 10.1. Part VI has been heavily edited to take into account version 2.0 of OpenOffice.org. Beyond this, all chapters have been revised in some way, shape, or form.

About the DVD-ROM Supplied with This Book

Attached to this book is a DVD-ROM disc featuring the full version of SUSE Linux 10.1. This contains the full hard disk installation of the operating system, as was used during the writing of this book. In addition to being able to install SUSE Linux, the DVD-ROM can run in "live" mode, which means that the entire operating system boots from the disc and doesn't touch your hard disk. This can be useful for those who wish to "try out" SUSE Linux, but there are a handful of caveats, as I explain in Chapter 5.

The DVD-ROM is based on work of the openSUSE project, but has been specially tweaked by SUSE Linux developers to include several items of useful proprietary software, such as Adobe Reader and RealPlayer.

Conventions Used in This Book

The goal when writing *Beginning SUSE Linux* was to make it as readable as possible while providing the facility for readers to learn at their own pace.

Throughout the book, you'll find various types of notes and sidebars complementing the regular text. These are designed to provide handy information to help further your knowledge. They also make reading the book a bit easier.

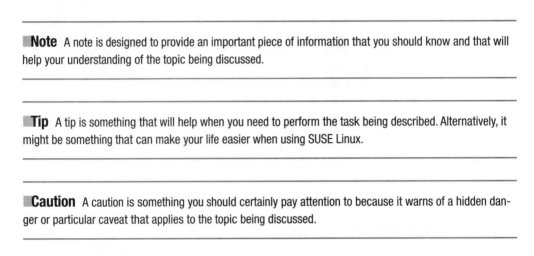

◼**Note** A note is designed to provide an important piece of information that you should know and that will help your understanding of the topic being discussed.

◼**Tip** A tip is something that will help when you need to perform the task being described. Alternatively, it might be something that can make your life easier when using SUSE Linux.

◼**Caution** A caution is something you should certainly pay attention to because it warns of a hidden danger or particular caveat that applies to the topic being discussed.

In the sidebars, I take a moment to explain something that you should know, but that isn't vital to an understanding of the main topic being discussed. You don't need to read the sidebars there and then; you can return to them later if you wish.

PART I

■■■

Introducing the World of Linux

## CHAPTER 1

Welcome!

If you're an avid computer user, there's a good chance that you've heard of Linux. You might have read about it, or perhaps you've seen TV ads that refer to it.

One of the odd things about Linux is that the more you learn about it, the more questions you have. For instance, it's generally thought that Linux is free of charge, but this then raises the question of how, in our modern world, something like an entire computer operating system can cost nothing. Who pays the programmers?

Over the following introductory chapters, I'm going to try to answer some of these questions. In this chapter, I'll explain what Linux is and its benefits compared to Windows.

What Is Linux?

There are two ways of looking at a PC. The first is to see it as a magical box, which lets you do cool stuff like browse the Internet or play games. Seen in this way, it's like a VCR—put in a tape, press a button, and a picture appears on your TV. On your PC, you click the Internet Explorer icon, type a web address, and a web site somehow appears. The astonishing technical complexity behind these simple procedures isn't important to most people.

The other way of looking at a PC is as a collection of components that are made by various manufacturers. You might be familiar with this way of thinking if you're ever tried to upgrade your PC's hardware. In that case, you'll know that your PC consists of a CPU, a hard disk, a graphics card, and so on. You can swap any of these out to put in newer and better components that upgrade your PC's performance or allow more data storage.

What almost no one realizes is that the operating system is just another component of your PC. It, too, can be swapped out for a better replacement. Windows doesn't come free of charge, and Microsoft isn't performing a public service by providing it. Around $50 to $100 of the price you pay for a PC goes straight into Microsoft's pocket. Bearing in mind that hundreds of millions of PCs are made each year, it's not hard to see why Microsoft is one of the world's richest corporations.

It would be difficult to question this state of affairs if Microsoft gave us our money's worth. But it often falls far short. Its products are full of serious security holes, which at best inconvenience us and at worst make us lose data. And that's before we consider the instability of Microsoft products—hardly a day goes by without something unexpected happening. One of the first things people are taught when attending Windows training is how to use the Ctrl+Alt+Delete keyboard combination, which helps you recover after a crash!

Microsoft became rich, and maintains its wealth, by a virtual monopoly over PC manufacturers. While the intelligent computer buyer can choose between components to put together a better PC—deciding between an AMD or Intel processor, for example—you usually have little choice but to buy Windows with a new PC. Try it now. Phone your favorite big-name computer retailer. Say that you want a PC but you *don't* want Windows installed. Then listen as the salesperson on the other end of the phone struggles to understand.

■**Note** Some PC manufacturers actually will sell you a PC without Windows installed on it. All you have to do is ask, although you might need to speak to a senior salesperson to get through to someone who understands your request. Smaller local companies, in particular, will be more than willing to sell you a PC without Windows. Some larger multinational companies, such as Hewlett-Packard, sell workstations with Linux preinstalled instead of Windows. However, these computers are usually aimed at businesses rather than home users.

Wouldn't it be terrific if you could get rid of Windows? Would you like to finally say goodbye to all those security holes and not have to worry about virus infections anymore, yet not lose out on any features or need to make sacrifices or compromises?

There is an alternative. Welcome to the world of Linux.

Linux is an operating system, which is to say that it's a bit like Windows. It's the core software that runs your computer and lets you do stuff on it. By the strictest definition of the term, an *operating system* is the fundamental software that's needed to make your PC work. Without an operating system installed on your PC, it would merely be an expensive doorstop. When you turned it on, it would beep in annoyance—its way of telling you that it can't do much without a whole set of programs to tell it what to do next.

An operating system allows your PC's hardware to communicate with the software you run on it. It's hundreds of programs, system libraries, drivers, and more, all tightly integrated into a whole. In addition, an operating system lets programs talk to other programs and, of course, communicate with you, the user. In other words, the operating system runs everything and allows everything to work.

■**Note** Some companies and individuals, including Microsoft, define an operating system as much more than this fundamental software. They add in the basic tools you run on an operating system, such as web browsers and file management programs.

Linux consists of a central set of programs that run the PC on a low level, referred to as the *kernel*, and hundreds (if not thousands) of additional programs provided by other people and various companies. Technically speaking, the word *Linux* refers explicitly just to the core kernel program. However, most people generally refer to the entire bundle of programs that make up the operating system as *Linux*.

GNU/LINUX

Although most of us refer to Linux as a complete operating system, the title "Linux" hides a lot of confusing but rather important details. Technically speaking, the word Linux refers merely to the kernel file: the central set of programs that lie at the heart of the operating system. Everything else that comes with a typical version of Linux, such as programs to display graphics on the screen or let the user input data, is supplied by other people, organizations, or companies. The Linux operating system is the combination of many disparate projects. (I'll explain how this works in the next chapter.)

The GNU organization, in particular, supplies a lot of vital programs and also system library files, without which Linux wouldn't run. These programs and files were vital to the acceptance of Linux as an operating system in its early days. Because of this, and the fact that Linux completed a long-running goal of the GNU project to create a Unix-like operating system, some people choose to refer to Linux as GNU/Linux.

A fierce debate rages over the correct way to refer to the Linux operating system and whether the GNU prefix should be used. For what it's worth, an equally fierce debate rages over how we should define an operating system. It can all get very confusing. It's also very easy to accidentally offend someone by not using the correct terminology!

It's not the purpose of this book to get involved in this debate. Suffice it to say that I acknowledge the vital input of the GNU project into the operating system many people refer to simply as Linux, as well as that of other vital projects. However, readers should note that when I refer to Linux throughout this book, I mean the entire operating system. If I intend to refer simply to the kernel programs, I will make that clear.

The Age of Linux

At the time of writing this book, Linux is a little more than 14 years old. It has gone from a hobbyist project maintained by just one man to a professional and corporate-sponsored solution for virtually every level of computer user.

Linux has also gone from being a server operating system, designed for central computers that hand out files and other computer resources to other computers, to becoming a full-fledged graphical desktop operating system like Windows. In fact, it's gone even further. Today, it's very likely that you'll find Linux running your digital video recorder and other computerized household gadgets.

Getting technical for a moment, Linux is a 32-bit and 64-bit, multitasking, multiuser operating system. This is a complicated way of saying that it's pretty darn powerful. Linux is as capable of running supercomputers as it is of running a desktop PC. Linux builds on the foundation laid by Unix, which itself was based on Multics, which was one of the first modern computer operating systems. It's not an exaggeration to say that Linux can trace its family tree all the way back to the pioneering days of computing.

CORRECT PRONUNCIATION

What most people refer to as the Linux operating system takes its name from the kernel program, one of its most important system components. This, in turn, was named after its creator, Linus Torvalds.

The name Linus is commonly pronounced "Lie-nus" in many English-speaking countries, but Torvalds speaks Swedish. He pronounces his name "Leen-us" (imagine this spoken with a gentle Scandinavian lilt, and you've got it about right).

Because of this, he pronounces Linux as "Lin-ux" and most people copy this pronunciation. You can hear this spoken by Torvalds himself by visiting `www.paul.sladen.org/pronunciation/`.

Some people refer to the Linux operating system by its full title of GNU/Linux. In this case, GNU is pronounced as in the name of the animal, with a hard G: "G-noo." The full pronunciation is therefore "G-noo Lin-ux."

Finally, the DVD that comes with this book contains a version of Linux called SUSE Linux. SUSE is a German acronym and is normally pronounced "Sooz-eh."

The Problems with Windows

The world's most popular operating system is Windows, which is made by the Microsoft Corporation. Linux has no links with Windows at all. Microsoft doesn't contribute anything to Linux and, in fact, is rather hostile toward it because it threatens Microsoft's market dominance. This means that installing Linux can give you an entirely Microsoft-free PC. How enticing does *that* sound?

Windows is used on 91% of the world's desktop computers. In other words, it must be doing a good job for it to be so popular, right?

Let's face facts. Windows is not without problems, and that's putting it mildly. It's stunningly insecure, and virtually every day a new security hole is uncovered. This leads to the creation of worms by malevolent programmers. *Worms* are small programs that exploit security holes within operating systems, leaping from computer to computer and spreading like wildfire via the Internet. Examples include Sasser (as well as its variations), which causes your computer to crash and shut down as soon as you go online.

Then there are the viruses—hundreds and hundreds of them. This has led to an entire industry that creates antivirus programs, which are additional pieces of software. Antivirus software is vital if you want to use Windows without losing data or running the risk of your files being stolen!

Some argue that Windows is hit by so many viruses merely because it's so popular. But consider that many of these viruses are simple programs that just take advantage of security holes in Windows. For example, one particular virus took advantage of a bug in such a way that just viewing an e-mail message caused the virus to infect your computer! And we're *paying* for this quality of software?

The United States Computer Emergency Readiness Team (`www.us-cert.gov`) reported 812 security vulnerabilities for Microsoft Windows during 2005. That translates to 15 vulnerabilities *per week*! In June 2005, the Sophos computer security company (`www.sophos.com`) advertised that its Windows antivirus program defended against more than 103,000 viruses!

■Note Although I'm being disparaging about Windows here, unlike many books, *Beginning SUSE Linux* doesn't ignore Windows. Throughout its pages, you'll find frequent references to Windows and the software that runs under it. You'll find direct comparisons with actual Windows programs, and you'll learn how to work with Windows files. So, if you have prior experience with Windows, you'll be able to get started with SUSE Linux very quickly.

And how about the speed at which Windows runs? It's just dandy when your PC is brand new. But after just a few months, it seems like someone has opened up the case and poured molasses inside. It takes quite a few seconds for My Computer to open, and there's time for a coffee break while Internet Explorer starts up.

So is Linux the solution to these problems? Most would agree that it's a step in the right direction, at the very least. Linux doesn't need antivirus programs, because there are virtually no Linux-specific viruses. As with all software, security holes are occasionally discovered in Linux, but the way it is built means exploiting those holes is much more difficult.

■Note There have been a couple of viruses for Linux, but they're no longer "in the wild" (that is, they are no longer infecting PCs). This is because the security holes they exploited were quickly patched, causing the viruses to die out. This happened because the majority of Linux users update their systems regularly, so any security holes that viruses might exploit are patched promptly. Compare that to Windows, where most users aren't even aware they can update their systems, even when Microsoft gets around to issuing a patch (which has been known to take months).

There's also the fact that Linux encourages you to take control of your computer, as opposed to treating it like a magical box. As soon as you install Linux, you become a power user. Every aspect of your PC is under your control, unlike with Windows. This means fixing problems is a lot easier, and optimizing your system becomes part and parcel of the user experience. You no longer have to take poor performance lying down. You can do something about it!

WINDOWS COMPATIBLE?

One of the biggest questions asked by most newcomers to Linux is whether it can run Windows software. The answer is yes . . . and no.

Linux is completely different from Windows on a fundamental technical level. Its creators based it on Unix, an industrial-strength operating system, and deliberately steered clear of emulating Windows. This means that Linux isn't a swap-in replacement for Windows. You cannot take the installation CD of a Windows program and use it to install that program on Linux, in the same way that you cannot install an Apple Mac program on Windows.

Continued

However, several current projects let you run Windows programs on Linux. Wine (www.winehq.com) is an example of such a project, and you can download a commercial and easy-to-use variation of it from www.codeweavers.com. You can also use programs like VMware (www.vmware.com) to create a "virtual PC" running on Linux. Then you can install the Windows operating system and, therefore, any Windows software you like.

In most cases, however, you'll find that there's a Linux equivalent of your favorite Windows software. Frequently, you'll find that this Linux version is actually superior to the Windows program you've been using. I'll discuss many of these in Chapter 11.

The Benefits of Linux

People have been known to exaggerate about Linux when singing its praises, and there's certainly some hyperbole around. But there are several cast-iron facts about its benefits.

Crash-Free

A primary benefit of Linux is that it doesn't crash. In years and years of using Linux, you will never experience your mouse cursor freezing on screen. A strange error box won't appear and not go away until you reboot. It's possible to leave a Linux system running for years without ever needing to reboot (although most desktop SUSE Linux users shut down their PC when they won't be using it for a while, just like the rest of us).

Of course, programs that run on top of Linux sometimes crash, but they don't take the rest of the system down with them, as can happen under Windows. Instead, you can clean up after a crash and just carry on.

Note Actually, very few programs under Linux crash. Because Linux programmers use a different method of bug testing than used by Microsoft developers, there are arguably fewer bugs, and those that are discovered are fixed very quickly.

Security

The next benefit is that Linux is far, far more secure than Windows. Linux is based on years of proven computer science research. It works on the principle of users who have permissions to undertake various tasks on the system. If you don't have the correct permission, then you cannot, for example, access a particular piece of hardware. Additionally, privacy can be ensured because the files on the PC are "owned" by individual users, who can permit or deny others access to those files.

Free and Shareable

Another big benefit is that Linux can be obtained free of charge. Once it's installed, the latest updates for all your programs are also free of charge. Not only that, but if you want any new software, it will also usually be free of charge (and normally just a download away). Is this starting to sound attractive yet?

Because the software is free, you can share it with friends. Suppose that you find a really great image editor. You mention it to a friend, and he asks for a copy. Under Windows, copying the program is strictly illegal—to do so turns you into a software pirate! Unless that image editor is freeware, your friend will need to buy the software himself. Under Linux, sharing software is normally entirely legal. In fact, it's encouraged! I'll explain why in Chapter 2.

Compatible with Older Hardware

Another benefit of Linux is that it works well on older hardware and doesn't require a cutting-edge PC system. The latest version of Windows XP requires high-powered hardware, to the extent that upgrading to that operating system usually means buying a new PC, even if your old one still works fine!

In contrast, Linux works on computers dating back as far as the late 1990s. This book was largely written on a five-year-old Pentium II 450 MHz notebook running SUSE Linux. Although it would be an exaggeration to claim that the computer is lightning-fast, there's little waiting around for programs to start. On the same machine, Windows 2000 (which came installed on the computer) grinds and churns, and using it can be a frustrating experience.

Linux encourages an attitude of both recycling and making the most of what you have, rather than constantly upgrading and buying new hardware. You can pull out that "old" PC and bring it back to life by installing Linux. You might even be able to give it away to a family member or friend who does not have a PC. Perhaps it's time for grandma to get online, or perhaps you can give the kids their own PC so they will stop using yours.

Alternatively, you might consider turning old hardware into a server. Linux is capable of just about any task. As well as running desktop computers, it also runs around 60% of the computers that make the Internet work. Linux is extremely flexible. You could turn an old PC into a web server, e-mail server, or firewall that you can attach to a broadband Internet connection. If you were to do this with Microsoft software, it would cost hundreds of dollars, not to mention requiring an advanced computer. It's free with Linux.

The Linux Community

So we've established that Linux is powerful, secure, and flexible. But I've saved the best for last. Linux is more than a computer operating system. It's an entire community of users spread across the globe. When you start to use Linux, you become part of this community (whether you like it or not!).

One of the benefits of membership is that you're never far from finding a solution to a problem. The community likes to congregate online around forums and newsgroups, which you can join in order to find help.

Your placement in the ranks of the community is "newbie." This is a popular way of describing someone who is new to Linux. Although this sounds derisory, it will actually help when you talk to others. Advertising your newbie status will encourage people to take the time to help you. After all, they were newbies once upon a time!

There's another reason not to be disheartened by your newbie tag: you'll outgrow it very quickly. By the time you reach the end of this book, you'll have advanced to the other end of the spectrum—"guru." You'll be one of those giving out the advice to those poor, clueless newbies, and you'll be 100% confident in your skills.

Tip One of the best ways to learn about Linux is under the auspices of a knowledgeable friend. It's very beneficial to have your own guru to help you along when you get stuck—someone who is just an e-mail message or phone call away. If you have a friend who uses Linux, consider taking him or her out for a drink and getting more friendly!

But being part of a community is not just about getting free technical support. It's about sharing knowledge. Linux is as much about a political ideal as it is about software. It was created to be shared among those who want to use it. There are no restrictions, apart from one: any changes you make must also be made available to others.

The spirit of sharing and collaboration has been there since day one. One of the first things Linus Torvalds did when he produced an early version of Linux was to ask for help from others. And he got it. Complete strangers e-mailed him and said they would contribute their time, skills, and effort to help his project. This has been the way Linux has been developed ever since. Hundreds of people around the world contribute their own small pieces, rather than there being one overall company in charge. And the same concept applies to knowledge of Linux. When you learn something, don't be afraid to share this knowledge with others. "Giving something back" is a very important part of the way of Linux.

To understand why Linux is shared, you need to understand its history, as well as the history of what came before it. This is the topic of Chapter 2.

Summary

This chapter provided an introduction to Linux. It explained what Linux can be used for and also its many advantages when compared to Microsoft Windows. It also introduced the community surrounding Linux, which adds to its benefits. You should be starting to realize what makes millions of people around the world use Linux as the operating system of choice.

The next chapter covers the history of Linux. It also discusses another curious aspect: the political scene that drives the operating system forward.

■ ■ ■

## CHAPTER 2

A History and Politics Lesson

Linux is more than just software. It's an entire community of users, and as such, there's a detailed social history behind it. In this chapter, we'll look at the origins of Linux, both in terms of where it came from and the people who make it.

You might be tempted to skip this chapter and move on to the information about installing SUSE Linux. To be fair, nothing of vital technical importance is mentioned here. But it's important that you read this chapter at some stage, because Linux is more than simply the sum of its parts. It's far more than simply a set of computer programs.

If nothing else, this chapter explains the fundamental philosophies behind Linux and attempts to answer some of the often-baffling questions that arise when Linux is considered as a whole.

In the Beginning

Linux was created 15 years ago, in 1991. A period of 15 years is considered a lifetime in the world of computing, but the origins of Linux actually hark back even further, into the early days of modern computing in the mid-1970s.

Linux was created by a Finnish chap named Linus Torvalds. At the time, he was studying in Helsinki and had bought a desktop PC. His new computer needed an operating system, but his choices were limited. There were various versions of DOS and something called Minix. It was the latter that Torvalds decided to use.

Minix was a clone of Unix, a popular operating system used on huge computers in businesses and universities, including those at Torvalds's university. Unix was created in the early 1970s and had evolved since then to become what many considered the cutting edge of computing. Unix brought to fruition a large number of computing concepts in use today and, many agree, got almost everything just right in terms of features and usability.

Note Linux is a pretty faithful clone of Unix. If you were to travel back in time 20 or 30 years, you would find that using Unix on those old mainframe computers, complete with their teletype interfaces, would be similar to using Linux on your home PC. Many of the fundamental concepts of Linux, such as the file system hierarchy and user permissions, are taken directly from Unix.

Torvalds liked Unix because of its power, and he liked Minix because it ran on his computer. Minix was created by Andrew Tanenbaum, a professor of computing, to demonstrate the principles of operating system design to his students. Because Minix was also a learning tool, people could view the *source code* of the program—the original listings that Tanenbaum had entered to create the software.

But Torvalds had a number of issues with Minix. At the time, Minix was only available for a fee (although in many universities, students could obtain free copies from professors who paid a group licensing fee). The copyright issue meant that using Minix in the wider world was difficult, and this, along with a handful of technical issues, inspired Torvalds to create his own version of Unix, just as Tanenbaum had done with Minix. Torvalds managed to produce version 0.01 of Linux in around half a year.

■Note Most clones or implementations of Unix are named so that they end in an *x*. One story has it that Torvalds wanted to call his creation Freax, but a containing directory was accidentally renamed Linux on an Internet server. The name stuck.

From day one, Torvalds intended his creation to be shared among everyone who wanted to use it. He encouraged people to copy it and give it to friends. He didn't charge any money for it, and he also made the source code freely available. The idea was that people could take the code and improve it.

This was a master stroke. Many people contacted Torvalds, offering to help out. Because they could see the program code, they realized he was onto a good thing. Soon, Torvalds wasn't the only person developing Linux. He became the leader of a team that used the fledgling Internet to communicate and share improvements.

■Note The popular conception of Linux is that it is developed by a few hobbyists who work on it in their spare time. This might have been true in the very early days. Nowadays, in addition to these "bedroom programmers," Linux is programmed by hundreds of professionals around the world, many of whom are employed specifically for the task. Torvalds adds to the effort himself and also coordinates the work.

It's important to note that when we talk here about Linux, we're actually talking about the kernel—the central program that runs the PC hardware and keeps the computer ticking. This is all that Torvalds initially produced back in 1991. It was an impressive achievement, but needed a lot of extra add-on programs to take care of even the most basic tasks. Torvalds's kernel needed additional software so that users could enter data, for example. It needed a way for users to be able to enter commands so they could manipulate files, such as deleting or copying them.

Linux itself didn't offer these functions. It simply ran the computer's hardware. Once it booted up, it expected to find other programs. If they weren't present, then all you saw was a blank screen.

LINUS TORVALDS

Linus Benedict Torvalds was born in Helsinki, Finland, in 1969. A member of the minority Swedish-speaking population, he attended the University of Helsinki from 1988 to 1996, graduating with a Masters degree in Computer Science.

He started Linux not through a desire to give the world a first-class operating system, but with other goals in mind. Its inspiration is in part due to Helsinki winters being so cold. Rather than leave his warm flat and trudge through the snow to the university's campus in order to use its powerful minicomputer, he wanted to be able to connect to it from home! He also wanted to have a platform to use to experiment with the properties of the Intel 386, but that's another story. Torvalds needed an operating system capable of such tasks. Linux was born.

Torvalds started his kernel project in 1991 and made the first public release in September of that year. During this initial development period, he worked alone in a darkened room. In the announcement accompanying the first release, he described Linux as "just a hobby," and claimed it would never be big. It wouldn't be until 1994 that it reached version 1.0.

In the early days, Torvalds's creation was fairly primitive. He was passionate that it should be free for everyone to use, and so he released it under a software license that said that no one could ever sell it. However, he quickly changed his mind, adopting the GNU Public License.

Torvalds was made wealthy by his creation, courtesy of the dot.com boom of the late 1990s, even though this was never his intention; he was driven by altruism. Nowadays, he lives in Portland, Oregon, with his wife and children, having moved to the United States from Finland in the late 1990s.

Initially, Torvalds worked for Transmeta, developing CPU architectures as well as overseeing kernel development, although this wasn't part of his official work. He still programs the kernel, but currently he oversees the Open Source Development Lab, an organization created to encourage open source adoption in industry and which is also referred to as the home of Linux.

The GNU Project

Around the time Torvalds created Linux, another project, called GNU, also existed. The GNU project team also hoped to create an operating system that used Unix as its inspiration, while avoiding some of the pitfalls that had blighted that operating system, both technically and in terms of its licensing. GNU is a so-called recursive acronym that stands for "GNU's Not Unix," a play on words favored by computer programmers.

GNU's parent organization, the Free Software Foundation (FSF), had been formed eight years prior to Torvalds's effort, and since that time, had produced the majority of the core software that Linux desperately needed. However, as luck would have it, FSF lacked the essential functionality of the kernel. The developers were in the process of creating their own kernel, but it had not come to fruition.

The GNU software was distributed for free to anyone who wanted it. The source code was also made available so users could adapt and change the programs to meet their own needs (in fact, Torvalds had used the GNU model when deciding how to distribute Linux).

Richard Stallman is the man behind GNU and, along with Linus Torvalds, is the second accidental hero in our story. Stallman had been around since the Dark Ages of computing, back when wardrobe-sized computers were "time-shared" among users who used small desktop terminals to access them. Like Torvalds, Stallman started GNU as a personal project, but then found others who were more than willing to join his cause.

■Note Stallman created the Emacs text editor and the GNU C Compiler (GCC). Together, they allow the creation of yet more software, so it's no surprise that one of the very first programs Torvalds used in the early days to create Linux was Stallman's GCC.

Back in Stallman's day at the legendary Massachusetts Institute of Technology (MIT), computer software was shared. If you came up with a program to perform a particular task, you offered it to practically anyone who wanted it. Alternatively, if you found an existing program wasn't adequate or had a bug, you improved it yourself, and then made the resulting program available to others. People might use your improved version, or they might not; it was up to them.

This way of sharing software was disorganized and done on an ad hoc basis, but came about of its own accord. Nobody questioned it, and it seemed the best way of doing things. There certainly wasn't any money involved, just as there wouldn't be money involved in one friend explaining an idea to another.

RICHARD STALLMAN

Richard Matthew Stallman, usually referred to as RMS, was born in 1953 in Manhattan. He comes from the old school of computing forged during the 1970s and was a member of MIT's legendary Artificial Intelligence Lab.

Seemingly destined for a life in academia, Stallman left MIT in 1984 to found the GNU Project. This was as a reaction to the increasing commercialization of computer software. Whereas once all hackers (that is, programmers) had shared ideas and program code, the trend in the 1980s was toward proprietary, non-shared code, as well as legal contracts, which forced programmers to keep secrets from one another.

Stallman is a very talented programmer and is considered a genius by many observers. He single-handedly created many essential programming tools in his initial efforts to get GNU off the ground. Many of these find a home in Linux.

Stallman is also widely applauded for the creation of the GNU Public License (GPL). This is a legal document that lets people share software. It introduces the concept of *copyleft* and is opposed to the legal concept of copyright, which attempts to limit the freedom of individuals when using a piece of software (or any other creative work). Nowadays, the concept of copyleft has been applied to literature, music, and other arts in an attempt to avoid restricting who can and cannot access various items, as well as to encourage a collaborative working environment.

Proprietary Software and the GPL

In the 1980s, everything changed. The world became more corporate, and with the rise of the desktop PC, the concept of proprietary software became prevalent. More and more companies started to sell software. They reasoned that this was impossible to do if they shared it with everybody else, so they kept it secret. Microsoft led this charge and did very well with its proprietary software.

To Stallman, this "trade secrets" approach to software was anathema. He had nothing against software being sold for a profit, but he hated the fundamental ideas behind software being kept secret. He felt passionately that sharing software and being able to understand how it worked was akin to free speech—necessary and vital for the furthering of technology, and therefore society itself. How could the new generation of programmers improve on the previous generation's work if they were unable to see how it worked? It was absurd to need to create software from scratch each time, rather than taking something that already existed and making it better.

Because of his beliefs, Stallman resigned from his job in the MIT Artificial Intelligence Lab and founded GNU. His aim initially was to produce a complete clone of Unix that would be shared in the ways he knew from the early days of computing. This software would be available for everyone to use, to study, and to adapt. It would be free, in the same sense as free speech—shared and unrestricted. This gave rise to the vital concept of "free software" and soon GNU, and the FSF, became not just a programming venture, but also a political movement.

■**Note** A very common misconception of "free software" is that it is always free of charge. This isn't correct. The word *free* is used here in its political sense, as in "free speech." Many companies and individuals make a healthy profit from selling free software and, in fact, selling free software is encouraged by the GNU Project.

To protect the rights of people to share and adapt the GNU software, Stallman came up with the GNU Public License (GPL). Various drafts of this license were produced over time, until it became a completely watertight legal contract, which furthered the concept of free software.

Most software you buy comes with a license agreement—that big chunk of text you must agree to when installing software (in the case of Windows desktop software, it's frequently referred to as the End-User License Agreement, or EULA). The license agreement usually says that you cannot copy the software or share it with friends. If others want to use the software, they must buy their own version.

The GPL turns this on its head. Rather than restricting what people can do with the software, it gives them permission to share the software with whomever they wish. However, if they modify the program in any way, and then distribute it to others, the program they come up with must also be licensed under the GPL. In other words, people cannot make changes to a program that has a GPL, and then sell the modified program, keeping their improvements secret.

■**Note** An interesting side note is that the actual wording of the GPL says that any changes you make should be shared with others *only if the software is redistributed.* This means that if you modify some GPL software and don't give it to anyone else, there's no need for you to publish your changes or make others aware of those changes.

GNU and Linux Together

The Linux kernel, developed by Torvalds, and the GNU software, developed by Stallman, were a perfect match. It's important to note that this doesn't mean the two projects joined forces. It simply means that the Linux project took some of the GNU software and gave it a good home. This was done with Stallman's blessing, but there wasn't any official union between the two groups. Remember that Stallman had intended everyone to freely share and use the GNU tools. Linux represented a set of people doing just that. GNU is still working on its own kernel, called Hurd, which may provide an alternative to using the Linux kernel.

■**Note** Hurd was first planned back in the 1980s and, at the time of writing, still has yet to see the light of day (although testing versions are available). Hurd is a hugely ambitious project and will set a gold standard when it is released.

GNU and Linux together formed a complete operating system, which mimicked the way Unix operated. Other projects and individuals spotted the success of Linux and came onboard, and it wasn't long before Linux realized the potential for a graphical user interface (GUI), the fundamentals of which were provided by the XFree86 Project. A lot of additional software was also provided by individuals and organizations, all using the same "share and share alike" example set by Stallman with the GNU tools and Torvalds with his kernel.

Many people refer to Linux as GNU/Linux. This gives credit to the GNU Project that provided the majority of tools vital to making Linux into a usable operating system. However, like the majority of people in the computing world, I use the term *Linux* throughout this book to avoid confusion.

Different Flavors of Linux

All the pieces of GNU software were available for free download and were therefore free of charge. But this brought its own problems. Not everyone had the know-how to put all the bits and pieces together into a complete operating system. Those who could do this didn't necessarily have the time for it.

Because of this, a number of companies stepped in to do the hard work. They put together versions of Linux, complete with all the software from the GNU Project, which they then sold for a fee on floppy disks, CDs, or DVDs. They also added in bits of their own software, which made it possible to install Linux easily onto a computer's hard disk, for example. They produced their own manuals and documentation, too, and did other things such as bug testing to ensure it all worked well. What they came up with became known as *distributions* of Linux, or *distros* for short. Examples of these companies include Red Hat, Mandrake, and many others around the world. Additionally, a number of enthusiasts got together and formed organizations to create their own distros, such as Debian and Slackware.

Modern distros are very advanced. They make it easy to install Linux on your PC, and they usually come with everything you need, so you can get started immediately. Additionally, they have their own look and feel, as well as unique ways of working and operating. This means that SUSE Linux is not the same as Red Hat Linux, for example, although they share a lot of common features and, of course, they all share the core GNU software.

Linux Today

Nowadays, Linux is a thoroughly modern and capable operating system, considered cutting-edge by many. It also runs on many different types of computer hardware, including Apple Macintosh computers, Sun SPARC machines, and the ubiquitous desktop PCs equipped with Intel or AMD processors. One of the ironies is that, although Linux was based on Unix, it has slowly come to dominate the computer operating system market. According to industry sources, Linux is on its way to making commercial varieties of Unix redundant. Companies that sell their own versions of Unix, such as Hewlett Packard and IBM, have added Linux to their traditional product range.

Recent innovations in the latest versions of the kernel mean that it finds uses on the smallest computers in the world, as well as on the biggest. Several of the top supercomputers in the world run Linux and, ironically, it can also be used on handheld personal digital assistants (PDAs) or even digital watches! You'll even find it running things like digital video recorders or other household goods, where it sits invisibly in the background and makes everything work. Remember that one of the fundamental principles of Linux is that you can use it for whatever you want. You don't need to ask for permission first or tell anyone what you're doing.

Linux's initial mainstream use was by software developers and on server computers, such as those that run the Internet. However, in recent years, it has become increasingly popular on desktop computers. This is the area where experts suggest it will see massive growth over the coming years.

Modern Linux Development

Nowadays, Linux is developed not only by Torvalds, who remains the project leader, but also by hundreds of volunteers and corporations who contribute resources. Most recently, IBM and Novell have gotten involved and contribute hundreds of people to the effort of creating Linux. Sun contributes the OpenOffice.org office suite and sells its own version of Linux. Corporations like Computer Associates contribute their own software, too.

These companies have realized that the best way of producing software is to share and share alike, rather than develop their own proprietary software and keep it secret. The proprietary ways of the 1980s are starting to seem like an ill-conceived flash in the pan.

Most recently, Novell found that by embracing Linux, it could massively enhance the functions of its aging NetWare product, yet without needing to return to the drawing board and start from scratch. It could just take what it wanted from the pile of Linux software. This shows the philosophy of Linux in action.

Linux has software for just about every need, ranging from simply receiving e-mail to running a huge e-mail server. There are databases, office suites, web browsers, video games, movie players, audio tools, and more, as well as thousands of pieces of specialized software used in various niches of industry (and too boring to mention here). Most of this software is available to anyone who wants it, free of charge.

What more could you want?

Summary

This chapter has detailed the history of Linux and explained its origins. It also explained *why* Linux came into being. We looked at how Linux formed one of the building blocks of a political movement geared toward producing software that can be shared.

We discussed the creator of Linux, Linus Torvalds. We've also looked at the massive input the GNU Project has made and, in particular, that of its philosopher king, Richard Stallman.

In the next chapter, we move on to look at what you can expect from day-to-day use of Linux.

CHAPTER 3

■ ■ ■

The Realities of Running Linux

So now that you've learned about the politics, history, and personalities behind Linux, only one question remains: what's Linux actually like when used on a daily basis? What should the average user expect from the experience? These are the questions I hope to answer in this brief chapter.

Learning to Use Linux

What should you expect from Linux once you've installed it? Well, it's a little like running Windows, except there are no viruses, fewer crashes, and no inexplicable slowdowns.

In addition, you have complete control over the system. This doesn't mean Linux is necessarily complicated. It's just that you have the control if you wish to make use of it. We'll look into this in the later chapters of this book.

Most software you use under Windows has at least one equivalent under SUSE Linux, installed by default. It's unlikely that you'll need to download or install any additional software and, even if you do, you'll probably find it's available for free.

In most cases, the Linux swap-ins are at least as powerful and easy to use as their Windows alternatives. Tabbed browsing in the Mozilla Firefox web browser lets you visit more than one site at once, for example, without needing to have a lot of browser instances running. (Internet Explorer 7 has this feature too, but it's stolen straight from Firefox, which has included it for years.) The Evolution program has a search routine that lets you look through your e-mail messages quickly for a variety of criteria, and it puts the features in a similar Microsoft product to shame.

Does this sound too good to be true? There is just one caveat. Linux isn't a clone of Windows and doesn't aim to be. It has its own way of doing certain things, and sometimes works differently from Windows. This means that many people experience a learning curve when they first begin using Linux.

Note Several Linux distributions aim to mimic Windows pretty faithfully. For example, Xandros, Lycoris/lx, and Linspire copy the look and feel of Windows to the extent that (allegedly) some people are unable to tell the difference.

But in just a few weeks after your move to Linux, everything will start to seem entirely normal. Most of the time, you won't even be aware you're running Linux. Of course, some patience is required during those initial few weeks. Linux can be illogical and frustrating; on the other hand, so can Windows. We simply got used to it.

Who Uses Linux?

Who uses Linux? The modern myth is that it's only for techies and power users. Back in the days when you needed to put everything together by hand, this was clearly true. But modern distributions make Linux accessible to all users. It's no exaggeration to say that you could install Linux on a computer Luddite's PC and have that person use it in preference to Windows.

Up until quite recently, Linux was largely seen as a developer's tool and a server operating system. It was geared toward programmers or was destined for a life running backroom computers, serving data, and making other computer resources available to users.

To this end, Linux continues to run a sizable proportion of the computers that make the Internet work, largely because it provides an ideal platform for the Apache web server, as well as various databases and web-based programming languages. This has lead to the LAMP acronym, which stands for Linux; Apache (a web server); MySQL (a database); and PHP, Python, or Perl (three programming languages that can be used in an online environment).

Despite its technical origins, recent years have seen a strong push for Linux on desktop computers. Linux has stepped out of the dark backrooms, with the goal of pushing aside Microsoft Windows and Mac OS in order to dominate the corporate workstation and home user market. To be clear, running Linux on the desktop has always been possible, but the level of knowledge required was often prohibitively high, putting Linux out of the reach of most ordinary users. It's only relatively recently that the companies behind the distributions of Linux have taken a long, hard look at Windows and attempted to mirror its user-friendly approach. In addition, the configuration software in distributions like SUSE Linux has progressed in leaps and bounds. Now, it's no longer necessary to know arcane commands in order to do something as simple as switch the screen resolution. The situation has also been helped by the development of extremely powerful office software, such as OpenOffice.org and KOffice.

Is Linux for you? There's only one way to find out, and that's to give it a try. Linux doesn't require much of you except an open mind and the will to learn new ways of doing things. You shouldn't see learning to use Linux as a chore. Instead, you should see it as an adventure—a way of finally getting the most from your PC and not having to worry about things going wrong for reasons outside your control.

Linux puts you in charge. You're the mechanic of the car as well as its driver, and you'll be expected to get your hands dirty every now and then. Unlike with Windows, Linux doesn't hide any of its settings or stop you from doing things for your own protection; everything is available to tweak. Using Linux requires commitment and the realization that there are probably going to be problems, and they're going to need to be overcome.

However, using Linux should be enjoyable. In his initial newsgroup posting announcing Linux back in 1991, Linus Torvalds said that he was creating Linux "just for fun." This is what it should be for you.

Getting Hold of Linux

Getting hold of Linux is easy. You'll already have spotted the version of SUSE Linux packaged with this book. SUSE Linux is the main focus of this book, and I consider it to be one of the very best versions of Linux out there. It's ideal for both beginners and power users, and it really does match the functionality offered in Windows. It includes several easy-to-use configuration tools, which make changing your system settings a breeze. For example, the YaST software can automate the download and installation of new software with just a few clicks.

SUSE Linux is also a very good-looking distribution. You'll find your friends and colleagues "wowing" when they happen to pass by and glance at your PC!

Quite a number of Linux distributions are available. If you want to explore other Linux distributions as well as SUSE Linux, by far the most fuss-free method of getting hold of Linux is to pop over to your local computer store (or online retailer) and buy a boxed copy. You can choose from Red Hat, Mandrake, Libranet, TurboLinux (if you want foreign language support, although nearly all commercial distributions do a good job of supporting mainstream languages), and many others. Many distributions come on more than a single CD—typically up to four CDs at the moment. Some versions of Linux come on DVD.

■**Caution** Bearing in mind what I've said about the sharing nature of Linux, you might think it possible to buy a boxed copy of Linux and then create copies for friends, or even sell them for a profit. However, you shouldn't assume this is the case. A minority of distribution companies, such as Xandros and Linspire, incorporate copyrighted corporate logos into their distributions that place restrictions on redistribution. Sometimes they include proprietary software along with the Linux tools, which you cannot copy without prior permission. However, in many cases, reproducing the CDs in small volumes for friends or for use on workstations in a company environment is permitted. You can copy the DVD included with this book as much as you want without restriction!

Many of the Linux distributions are also available to download free of charge. In fact, many community-run distributions—such as Slackware, Debian, Fedora, and Gentoo—are only available this way (although you can often buy "homemade" CDs from smaller retailers, who effectively burn the CDs for you and produce makeshift packaging). If your PC has a CD-R/RW drive and you have some CD-burning software under Windows (such as Nero), you can download an ISO image and make your own installation CD from it.

■**Note** An *ISO image* is a very large file (typically 700MB), which you can burn to CD. This CD is then used to install Linux.

Using SUSE Linux

SUSE Linux is one of the oldest distributions of Linux available, and it was the first version to come out shortly after Linus Torvalds had completed his initial versions of the Linux kernel.

SUSE was originally a German company, but nowadays it is owned by Novell. In addition, SUSE is a distribution partner of many large computer manufacturers, such as Sun Microsystems and IBM.

SUSE is an acronym for *Software und System-Entwicklung*, which translates as software and system development. This refers to the days, long passed, when the SUSE company was also a Unix consultancy.

Like many Linux distributions, SUSE Linux formed its reputation as a server operating system. Its unique YaST and SaX configuration tools made configuring and updating the system easy for those new to Linux and Unix. Recent years have seen the company make a strong push for the desktop market, with the result that SUSE Linux is considered one of the best desktop Linux distributions available, again thanks to its YaST configuration software.

The developers behind SUSE Linux have invested time not only in polishing the user interface, but also in improving hardware compatibility, to the extent that SUSE Linux is frequently considered cutting-edge in terms of the sheer number of items of hardware supported. Considering that a major criticism of Linux has been its poor showing in this area, SUSE is to be applauded in this regard.

Unlike some desktop distributions that abandon fundamental Linux concepts in order to mirror the Windows experience, SUSE Linux retains the robust feel and power of Linux. While technical thoroughness isn't sacrificed, SUSE Linux is nonetheless very easy to use, even for those who are new to computing. It's certainly an ideal distribution for Windows users who are looking for a way into Linux.

Learning how to use SUSE Linux has an added advantage in the corporate workspace. Novell has released its own distribution of Linux, which is largely based on SUSE Linux technology. In addition, Sun Microsystems offers its Java Desktop product, which is again based on SUSE Linux.

In fact, there are several versions of SUSE Linux. The one included with this book is a special edition of openSUSE. This is almost identical to the release of SUSE Linux that's sold in a box, except that it is supported by the openSUSE community, rather than by the Novell SUSE organization.

Summary

This chapter explained what you can realistically expect when using Linux every day. It also discussed the kind of company you'll be keeping in terms of fellow users.

You learned how people usually get hold of Linux. Of course, with this book, you already have a version of Linux, SUSE Linux, which was introduced in this chapter.

This completes the general overview of the world of Linux. In the next part of the book, you'll move on to actually installing Linux on your hard disk. This sounds more daunting than it actually is. The next chapter gets you started by explaining a few basic preinstallation steps.

PART II

Installing SUSE Linux

## CHAPTER 4

Preinstallation Steps

The first part of this book discussed the pros and cons of using Linux as part of your day-to-day life. It was intended to help you evaluate Linux and understand what you're buying into should you decide to make it your operating system of choice. Now, we move on to actually installing Linux and, specifically, SUSE Linux, which is included with this book on a DVD.

Installing any kind of operating system is a big move and can come as something of a shock to your PC. However, SUSE Linux makes this complicated maneuver as easy as it's possible to be. Its installation routines are very advanced compared to previous versions of Linux, and even compared to other current alternative distributions.

What does saying that you're going to install SUSE Linux actually mean? This effectively implies three things:

- Somehow all the files necessary to run SUSE Linux are going to be put onto your hard disk.

- The PC will be configured so that it knows where to find these files when it first boots up.

- The SUSE Linux operating system will be set up so that you can use it.

However, in order to do all this and get SUSE Linux onto your PC, you must undertake some preparatory work, which is the focus of this chapter.

Understanding Partitioning

Chances are, if you're reading this book, your PC already has Windows installed on it. This won't present a problem. In most cases, SUSE Linux can live happily alongside Windows in what's called a *dual-boot setup*, where you can choose at startup which operating system to run. However, installing SUSE Linux means that Windows must make certain compromises. It needs to cohabit your hard disk with another operating system—something Windows isn't designed to do.

The main issue with such a situation is that Windows needs to shrink and make some space available for SUSE Linux (unless you install a second hard disk, which is discussed later in this chapter). SUSE Linux isn't able to use the same file system as Windows, and it needs its own separately defined part of the disk, which is referred to as a *partition*. All of this can be handled by the SUSE Linux installation routine, but it's important that you know what happens.

All hard disks are split into partitions, which are large chunks of the disk created to hold operating systems (just like a large farm is partitioned into separate fields). A partition is usually multiple gigabytes in size, although it can be smaller. You can view your disk's partitions using the Disk Management tool in Windows XP and Windows 2000, as shown in Figure 4-1. You can access this tool by opening Control Panel, clicking the Administrative Tools icon, selecting Computer Management, and then choosing Disk Management.

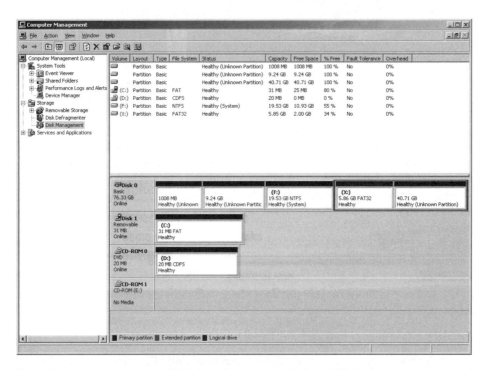

Figure 4-1. *You can view your disk's partitions using Windows XP's Disk Management tool.*

Most desktop PC systems have just one partition, unless the user has specifically created new partitions. As mentioned, SUSE Linux needs a partition of its own. During installation, SUSE Linux needs to shrink the main Windows partition and create a fresh partition alongside it (actually, it creates two partitions; the extra one is used to hold the swap file).

In addition, the SUSE Linux installation routine writes a new *boot sector* (also known as a *boot loader*). The boot sector is located at the very beginning of the disk and contains a small program that then runs another program that lets you choose between operating systems (and therefore partitions) when you first boot up.

■**Note** Not all Linux distributions have the ability to repartition the hard disk. In fact, at the time of writing, it's pretty rare. Most expect to simply take over the entire hard disk, wiping Windows in the process (although they'll always ask the user to confirm this beforehand). The ability to repartition a disk is just one of the reasons that SUSE Linux is among the best Linux distributions currently available.

Of course, SUSE Linux cannot shrink a Windows partition that is packed full of data, because no space is available for it to reclaim.

SUSE LINUX AND WINDOWS FILE SYSTEMS

One of the benefits of dual-booting Linux and Windows is that SUSE Linux lets you access the files on the Windows partition. This is quite handy and facilitates the easy exchange of data.

If the Windows partition is FAT32—used on Windows 95, 98, Me, and (sometimes) 2000 and XP—then SUSE Linux can both read and write files to the partition. However, if the file system is NTFS—used with Windows NT, 2000, and (sometimes) XP—then SUSE Linux will make the file system available as read-only. Because of this, you might consider converting your NTFS Windows partition to FAT32 before you install SUSE Linux (but be aware that doing so means you lose some of the security and performance features of NTFS). Microsoft doesn't include a tool that lets you do this automatically, but you can use third-party disk partitioning programs like Symantec's Partition Magic (www.symantec.com) to convert your file system.

Freeing Up Space

The first step before installing SUSE Linux alongside Windows is to check how much free space you have in your Windows partition. To see the amount of free space you have, double-click My Computer, right-click your boot drive, and select Properties. The free space is usually indicated in purple on a pie-chart diagram, as shown in Figure 4-2.

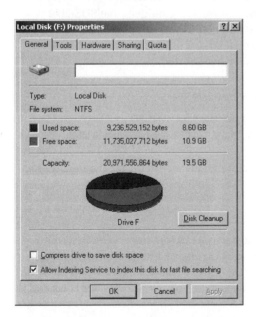

Figure 4-2. *SUSE Linux needs free disk space in which to install, so you might need to clean up your Windows partition.*

You need to have at least 2GB of free space in your Windows partition for SUSE Linux to use. You'll need more space if you wish to install a lot of programs. If you don't have enough free space, you have several options: reclaim space, remove Windows, or use a second hard disk.

Reclaiming Space

On Windows XP, you can run the Disk Cleanup tool to free some space on your hard disk. Click the Disk Cleanup button beneath the pie-chart diagram showing the free disk space (refer to Figure 4-2). Disk Cleanup is also accessible by choosing Start ➤ All Programs ➤ Accessories ➤ System Tools ➤ Disk Cleanup.

You might also consider turning off System Restore. This consumes a lot of disk space, which you can therefore reclaim. However, deactivating System Restore will mean that you lose the possibility of returning your system to a previous state should anything go wrong. To access the System Restore control, right-click My Computer, click Properties, and then click the System Restore tab.

If you still cannot free up enough disk space, consider uninstalling unused software via the Add/Remove Programs applet within Control Panel. If you have any large games installed, consider removing them first, because they usually take up substantial amounts of hard disk space. You might also consider deleting movie and MP3 music files, which are renowned for eating up hard disk space. The average MP3 is around 4MB, for example, and one minute of video typically takes up anywhere between 1MB and 10MB of disk space!

Removing Windows

Some users might prefer a second, more radical option: getting rid of Windows completely and letting SUSE Linux take over the entire hard disk. If you feel confident that SUSE Linux will fulfill your needs, this is undoubtedly the most straightforward solution. You'll be able to do this during installation. However, this will also mean that any personal data you have will be lost, so you should first back up your data (as described shortly).

■**Caution** You should be aware that installing Windows back onto a hard disk that has SUSE Linux on it is troublesome. Windows has a Darwinian desire to wipe out the competition. If you attempt to install Windows on a SUSE Linux hard disk, it will overwrite Linux.

Using Another Hard Disk

A third option for making room for SUSE Linux is attractive and somewhat safer in terms of avoiding the potential for data loss, but also potentially expensive: fitting a second hard disk to your PC. You can then install SUSE Linux on this other hard disk, letting it take up the entire disk. Unlike Windows, SUSE Linux doesn't need to be installed on the primary hard disk and is happy on a secondary drive.

A second hard disk is perhaps the best solution if you're low on disk space and want to retain Windows on your system. However, you'll need to know how to install the new drive or find someone to do it for you (although step-by-step guides can be found on the Web—just search using Google or another search engine). In addition, if your PC is less than 12 months old, there is a possibility that you'll invalidate your guarantee by opening up your PC.

If you have an old PC lying around, you might also consider installing SUSE Linux on it, at least until you're sure that you want to run it on your main PC. As noted in Chapter 1, one of the best features of SUSE Linux is that it runs relatively well on older hardware. For example, a Pentium III with 256MB of memory should allow for very good performance.

NO-INSTALL LINUX

If you want to use the Linux operating system but leave your hard disk untouched, you might consider a number of additional options. Perhaps the most popular is to use a "live" version of Linux. A live version of Linux is one that boots and runs entirely from a CD or DVD; it doesn't touch the user's hard disk. Although it's designed to install to the hard disk, the version of SUSE Linux supplied with this book can run in this way— simply select the LiveCD entry from the boot menu after booting from the DVD-ROM. The pros and cons of using a LiveCD are discussed in the next chapter.

Alternatively, you might consider using virtual PC software. This type of software runs under Windows and re-creates an entire PC hardware system within software—effectively a PC within a PC. The hard disk is contained within one or two Windows files. Linux can then be installed on the virtual PC system. When the program is switched to full-screen mode, it's impossible to tell you're running inside a computer system created in software. Two commercially available examples are considered worthwhile by many: VMware (`www.vmware.com`) and Microsoft's Virtual PC (`www.microsoft.com/windowsxp/virtualpc/`). You should be aware that both are designed to be professional-level tools, so they are quite expensive. You can also obtain open source renditions of virtual PC software, such as QEMU (`http://fabrice.bellard.free.fr/qemu/`) and Bochs (`http://bochs.sourceforge.net/`).

Another option in its infancy at the time of writing is Cooperative Linux, or coLinux for short (`www.colinux.org`). This is a set of Windows programs that aims to let Linux run under Windows using emulation. Unfortunately, setting up and using coLinux requires some expert knowledge, so you might want to wait until you have more experience with Linux.

Backing Up Your Data

Whichever route you decide to take when installing SUSE Linux, you should back up the data currently on your computer beforehand. Possibly the easiest way of doing this is to burn the data to CD-R/RW discs using a program like Nero and a CD-R/RW drive.

If you choose the coexistence route, installing SUSE Linux alongside Windows, backing up your data should be done for insurance purposes. Although the SUSE developers test all their software thoroughly and rely on community reporting of bugs, there's always the chance that something will go wrong. Repartitioning a hard disk is a major operation and carries with it the potential for data loss.

If you intend to erase the hard disk when installing SUSE Linux (thereby removing Windows), you can back up your data, and then import it into SUSE Linux.

Table 4-1 shows a list of common personal data file types, their file extensions, where they can be typically found on a Windows XP system, and notes on importing the data into SUSE

Linux. Note that earlier versions of Windows (95, 98, and Me) may differ when it comes to data storage locations.

Table 4-1. *Data That Should Be Backed Up*

Type of File	File Extensions	Typical Location	Notes
Office files	`.doc`, `.xls`, `.ppt`, `.pdf`, etc.	My Documents	Microsoft Office files can be opened, edited, and saved under SUSE Linux using the OpenOffice.org suite. PDF documents can be viewed within various programs under SUSE Linux.
E-mail files	N/A	N/A	The Evolution mail client used by the GNOME desktop under SUSE Linux cannot import data directly from Microsoft Outlook or Outlook Express. However, there is a convoluted but effective workaround, which is described in the next section. The Kmail email client under KDE can import Outlook Express email.
Digital images	`.jpg`, `.bmp`, `.tif`, `.png`, `.gif`, etc.	My Pictures (within My Documents)	SUSE Linux includes a variety of programs to both view and edit image files.
Multimedia files	`.mp3`, `.mpg`, `.avi`	Various	SUSE Linux can play back MP3s, CDs, and some movie formats. With some additional downloads, discussed in Chapter 19, it can also play a wider range of movie file formats, as well as DVD movie discs.
Internet Explorer Favorites	None	\Documents and Settings\ <*username*>\ Favorites	Your Favorites list cannot be imported into SUSE Linux, but the individual files can be opened in a text editor in order to view their URLs, which can then be opened in the SUSE Linux web browser.
Miscellaneous Internet files	Various	Various	You might also want to back up web site archives or instant messenger chat logs, although hidden data such as cookies cannot be imported.

Backing Up E-mail Files

Microsoft e-mail cannot be easily imported into SUSE Linux because Microsoft prefers to create its own proprietary file formats, rather than use open standards recognized by the rest of industry. Most e-mail programs use the MBOX format, and this is true of SUSE Linux as well as programs created by the Mozilla Foundation (the organization behind the Firefox web browser). However, Microsoft uses its own DBX file format for Outlook Express and PST format for Outlook.

As a workaround, you can download and install the free Mozilla Thunderbird e-mail client (available from `www.mozilla.com`) on your Windows system. In Thunderbird, select

Tools ➤ Import to import your messages from Outlook, Outlook Express, or even the popular Eudora mail client. You will then be able to back up Thunderbird's mail files and import them into Evolution or Kmail under SUSE Linux.

To find where the mail files are stored, in Thunderbird, select Tools ➤ Account Settings, and then look in the Local Directory box. Back up each file that corresponds to a folder within your mail program (for example, Inbox, Sent, and so on). Note that you only need to back up the files *without* file extensions. You can ignore the .sbd folders as well as the .msf files.

Making Notes

When you're backing up data, a pencil and paper come in handy, too. You should write down any important usernames and passwords, such as those for your e-mail account and other online services. You might want to write down the phone number of your dial-up connection, for example, or your DSL/cable modem technical settings. Figure 4-3 shows an example of some information you might want to record.

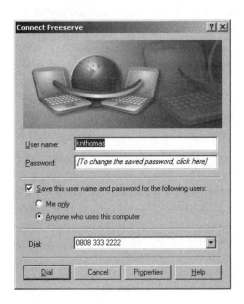

Figure 4-3. *Don't forget to back up "hidden" data, such as Internet passwords.*

In addition, don't forget to jot down essential technical details, such as your IP address if you are part of a network of computers using static addresses (this will usually be relevant only if you work in an office environment).

■**Tip** If you've forgotten any passwords, several freeware/shareware applications are able to "decode" the asterisks that obscure Windows passwords and show what's beneath them. A good example is Asterisk Password Reveal, which you can download from www.paqtool.com/product/pass/pass_001.htm. Sites like www.download.com offer similar applications.

Note that you don't need to write down information such as hardware interrupt (IRQ) or memory addresses, because hardware is configured automatically by SUSE Linux. However, it might be worth making a note of the make and model of some items of internal hardware, such as your graphics card, modem (dial-up, DSL, or cable), and sound card. This will help if SUSE Linux is unable to automatically detect your hardware, although such a situation is fairly unlikely to arise. You can garner this information by right-clicking My Computer on your desktop, selecting Properties, clicking the Hardware tab, and then clicking the Device Manager button. Instead of writing everything down, you might consider taking a screenshot by pressing the Print Scr button and then using your favorite image editor to print it (start a new document and then click Edit ➤ Paste).

■Tip SUSE Linux works with a wide variety of hardware, and in most cases, it will automatically detect your system components. If you want to check on a particular piece of hardware, you can consult the hardware compatibility list at `http://hardwaredb.suse.de/index.php?LANG=en_UK`. If you need more help, consider visiting the official SUSE Linux forums (`http://forums.suselinuxsupport.de/`) and posting a question. Remember that an important element of SUSE Linux is its community of users, many of whom will be very willing to answer any questions you might have.

Once you're certain that all your data is backed up, you can move on to the next chapter, which provides a step-by-step guide to installing the operating system.

Summary

The aim of this chapter has been to prepare both you and your computer for the installation of SUSE Linux. We've looked at how your hard disk will be partitioned prior to installation and the preparations you should make to ensure your hard disk has sufficient free space. You also learned about the types of files you might choose to back up, in addition to vital details you should record, such as usernames and passwords for your online accounts.

In the next chapter, we move on to a full description of the SUSE Linux installation procedure. The chapter guides you through getting SUSE Linux onto your computer.

CHAPTER 5

■■■

Installing SUSE Linux

This chapter details how to install SUSE Linux, as supplied with this book. SUSE uses the YaST program for this purpose.

Installing Linux is a surprisingly quick task to complete and shouldn't take more than 30 minutes on a modern PC. It's also fairly simple, with very few decisions to make throughout. The YaST program automates the task to a high degree. However, you should examine all of the options you're offered to make sure they're correct. Installing an operating system involves a couple of serious maneuvers that, via an incorrect click of the mouse or accidental keystroke, bring with them the possibility of data loss. Be sure to keep your wits about you, and make a backup of your data!

An Overview of the Installation Process

Installing SUSE Linux requires little of the user beyond the ability to use a mouse. The installation program attempts to choose safe default choices in most cases. If it intends to do something that involves deleting data, it will make sure that you're aware of this by highlighting the option in red on the main menu. In nearly all cases, you should be able to accept the default choices.

You can proceed through the installation by clicking the Next button at the bottom right of each page of choices. Wherever a series of options needs to be confirmed, you should click the Accept button if you're happy with the selections. If not, make your changes, and then click Accept.

No changes will be made to your system until you confirm your choices later on, just prior to starting to copy the files onto your hard disk. This means that you can experiment with different partition combinations, for example, without worrying about damaging or otherwise irreversibly affecting your system. It also means that you can cancel installation at any time prior to the file-copying phase. If you find yourself needing to do this, simply click the Abort button at the bottom of the screen.

■**Note** Although you can experiment with partitioning, YaST will suggest choices that I strongly advise you accept. Experimentation with partitioning is only for the knowledgeable, brave, and/or curious!

The installation procedure works through a handful of stages in order to install SUSE Linux. First, just after it starts, it will probe your system to discover the nature of your current PC setup, such as whether you already have Windows installed.

At this stage, you will be shown the hard disk partitioning choices and also the selection of software packages that are to be installed. After this, you'll be asked to confirm that you're satisfied with the installation options, and then the installation program will actually partition the disk and copy the Linux files from the DVD.

At the end of this procedure, your PC will reboot, and the post-installation phase will begin. Your hardware will be probed and configured (usually automatically, with negligible user input). You'll be invited to create users and enter various passwords. After this, setup is complete. Your new system will then be booted, ready for use.

In most cases, the installation of SUSE Linux will run smoothly. If you run into any problems, see Chapter 6, which addresses many of the most common issues and provides solutions.

■**Note** Other Linux installation programs differ from the SUSE Linux routines. However, most involve the same basic steps.

BOOTING SUSE LINUX DIRECTLY FROM THE DVD

If you don't want to install SUSE Linux just yet, you can try it out by booting the operating system straight from the DVD supplied with this book. To do this, simply insert the DVD-ROM disc and then reboot your computer. Make sure the computer is set to boot from CD/DVD (see step 1 of the installation guide in this chapter to learn how), and, at the SUSE Linux boot menu, choose either the LiveCD – GNOME or LiveCD – KDE option. The difference is in which desktop environment you will use. Note that even though this is a DVD, SUSE Linux still refers to it as a "LiveCD." I won't make this mistake here and will refer to it as a "Live DVD."

After a few moments, the SUSE Linux desktop will appear. You can follow most of the chapters in this book using the Live DVD. However, you should be aware of the following issues:

- **Settings:** Any changes you make to the system will be forgotten as soon as you shut down your PC or reboot. In other words, each time you boot the Live DVD, it will be as if Linux had been freshly installed. For example, if you've configured a network card or rearranged the desktop, those changes will be lost. There are ways around losing settings on each reboot, but they involve partitioning your hard disk and, frankly, doing so is as much effort as installing SUSE Linux from scratch. So there's little to be gained by doing so.

- **Performance:** Because the data must be read from DVD-ROM, running SUSE Linux via the Live DVD is a slow and therefore frustrating experience. It can also be noisy if your DVD-ROM is a model that makes a whirring noise as it spins.

- **System:** As strange as it sounds, SUSE Linux is unaware of when it's running in Live DVD mode. If you configure the system to go online, it will prompt you to update the system with new packages, for example, or attempt to save files to the hard disk. Of course, it can't do this because, as far as SUSE Linux is concerned, the DVD-ROM is the hard disk and it's impossible to write data to it. This can create confusing error messages.

- **Root:** When using the Live DVD, you're automatically given root user powers. I explain the significance of this in Step 14 below, but for the moment, it's enough to know that the root user has unlimited control over the system. This means that you could repartition the hard disk, for example, or even wipe the hard disk entirely, all without any password prompt or warning. This can be useful in certain circumstances—you can attempt to "rescue" a hard disk that's having problems using the Live DVD mode of the SUSE Linux disc. But using it for everyday tasks is taking a huge risk, and the potential for accidental damage is high.

In short, I would recommend that you use the Live DVD mode sparingly and only to get a taste of what SUSE Linux is like. If you intend to use SUSE Linux for any significant period of time, you should install it to your hard disk.

Step-by-Step Guide

As outlined in Chapter 4, you shouldn't start the installation process until you've made sure there is enough space for SUSE Linux on your hard disk and you have backed up your data. With those preparations, you're ready to install SUSE Linux. The remainder of this chapter takes you through the process.

Step 1: Boot from the DVD

With your computer booted up, insert the SUSE Linux disc into the DVD-ROM drive. Close the tray, and then reboot your computer.

SUSE Linux is installed by booting the installation program from DVD. Therefore, the first step is to make sure your computer's BIOS is set to boot from the DVD-ROM drive. How this is achieved varies from computer to computer.

Many modern computers let you press a particular key during the initial boot phase of your computer, during the memory testing and drive identification period, to make a boot menu appear. On the boot menu, you can choose to boot from the CD or DVD-ROM drive. On my test PC and also on my notebook computer, hitting the Esc key caused this menu to appear, but your computer may be different. Your computer's boot screen should indicate which key to press.

If you do not have an option to boot from the CD/DVD drive, you'll need to enter the BIOS setup program and change the boot priority of your computer. To do this, press the Delete key just after the computer is first activated. Again, some computers use another key or key combination, and your boot screen should indicate which key to press.

When the BIOS menu appears, look for a menu option such as Boot and select it (you can usually navigate the BIOS menu using the cursor keys and select options by pressing Enter). On the new menu, look for a separate entry that reads something like "Boot Device Priority" or "Boot Sequence." Make sure that the entry for the CD/DVD-ROM is at the top of the list, as shown in the example in Figure 5-1. Arrange the list so that it's followed by the floppy drive and then your main hard disk (which will probably be identified as "IDE-0" or "First hard disk"). You can usually press the F1 key for help on how the menu selection system works.

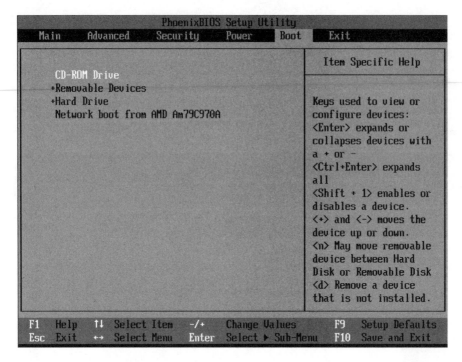

Figure 5-1. *Before starting, you should make sure your computer can boot from the DVD-ROM.*

Once you've made the changes, be sure to select the Exit Saving Changes option. Your PC will then reset and boot from the SUSE Linux DVD-ROM, and you'll be greeted by the blue SUSE Linux DVD boot menu.

■**Note** After SUSE Linux has been installed on your computer, you might choose to repeat this step and rearrange the boot order once more to make the hard disk appear at the top of the list. Then your computer won't waste time checking the CD/DVD-ROM drive for a boot disc every time it starts.

Step 2: Select to Install

After a welcome screen greeting you in several different languages, you should see the DVD-ROM boot menu. From here, you can select to install SUSE Linux (use the cursor keys to move the selection up and down), as shown in Figure 5-2.

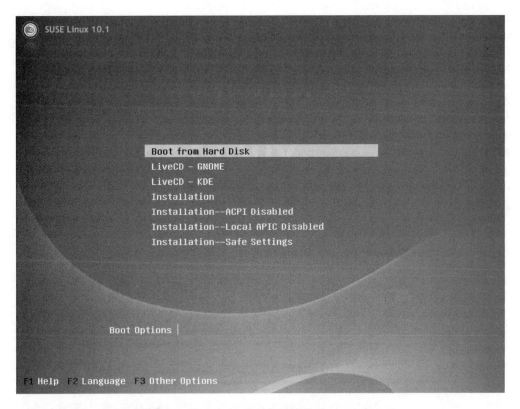

SUSE Linux 10.1

Boot from Hard Disk
LiveCD - GNOME
LiveCD - KDE
Installation
Installation--ACPI Disabled
Installation--Local APIC Disabled
Installation--Safe Settings

Boot Options |

F1 Help   F2 Language   F3 Other Options

Figure 5-2. *Select to install SUSE Linux from the DVD-ROM boot menu.*

Choose the Installation option to install SUSE Linux. You can also choose to boot from the hard disk, avoiding installing Linux, or boot to the "LiveCD" version of SUSE Linux, which lets you run SUSE Linux without installing it to your hard disk.

■**Note** Two more options can be accessed by scrolling down the boot menu using the down arrow key: Rescue System and Memory Test. The Rescue System option is designed for repairing an installed SUSE Linux system, allowing the user to boot to a command prompt and issue commands. The Memory Test option starts MemTest86, a simple program that can be used to rigorously test the computer's RAM for errors.

The Installation--ACPI Disabled, Installation--Local APIC Disabled, and Installation--Safe Settings options are designed to overcome issues with some older computers. The ACPI Disabled option ignores the power-saving features of the PC, and the Local APIC Disabled option turns off the Advanced Programmable Interrupt Controller. The Installation--Safe Settings option is designed to overcome certain hardware incompatibilities. If you find that installation won't work with the standard Installation option, you might try these, starting with the ACPI Disabled option, and then the Safe Settings option if the installation still fails. However, these options are not necessary in the majority of cases.

You should choose the simple Installation option to continue. Then you will have a short wait as SUSE Linux loads the installation software on your computer.

■**Tip** You can hit the Esc key to read the SUSE Linux boot messages and therefore see what SUSE Linux is doing while you're waiting for the next step. It will probably be gibberish to you at this stage of your Linux education, but it can be fun to watch the information fly past!

Step 3: Select Your Language

SUSE Linux is a fully internationalized operating system, and one of the first steps is to select the language you wish to use during installation, as shown in Figure 5-3. Many European and Asian languages are offered. The default is English (US). After you've selected your language, click the Next button at the bottom right.

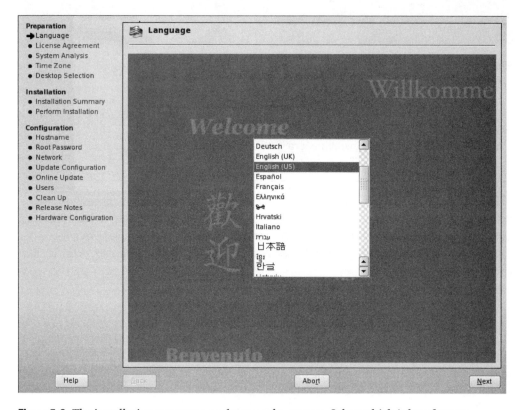

Figure 5-3. *The installation program speaks many languages. Select which is best for you.*

Step 4: Read the SUSE Linux License

Next, you'll see the SUSE Linux end-user license, as shown in Figure 5-4. You should read through this and make sure that you're knowledgeable about, and comfortable with, the points it raises. If so, click the Yes, I Agree to the License Agreement button.

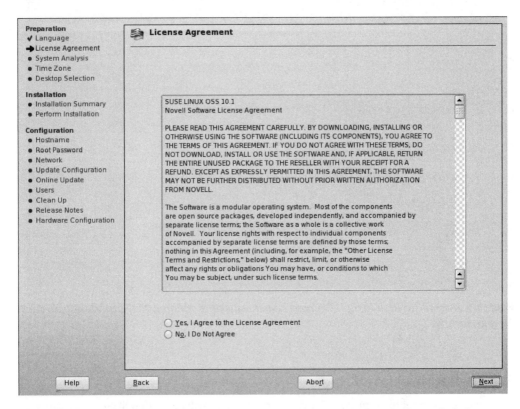

Figure 5-4. *Read the license agreement and choose the appropriate response beneath, before clicking the Next button.*

Step 5: Choose an Installation Mode

You'll need to choose the installation type that you want, as shown in Figure 5-5. The SUSE Linux installation routine can also upgrade an existing Linux setup. However, for new users, the only option here will be New Installation, which is selected by default, so click the Next button to continue.

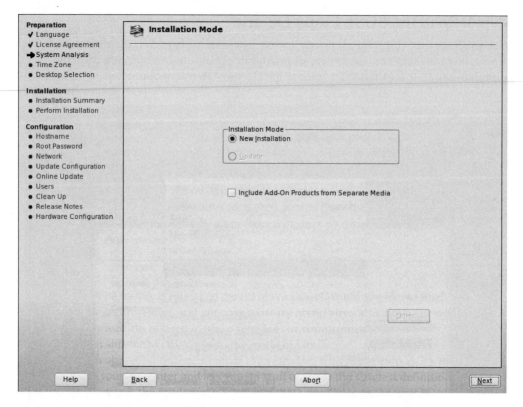

Figure 5-5. *Upgrade or fresh install? On most systems, the only option is New Installation, so click Next to continue.*

Step 6: Set the Time Zone

The next step is to set the time zone for your location. This will mean that SUSE Linux can automatically take into account schemes such as daylight saving time. A list of countries and continents appears on the left side of the screen, and the relevant time zones are listed on the right side, as shown in Figure 5-6.

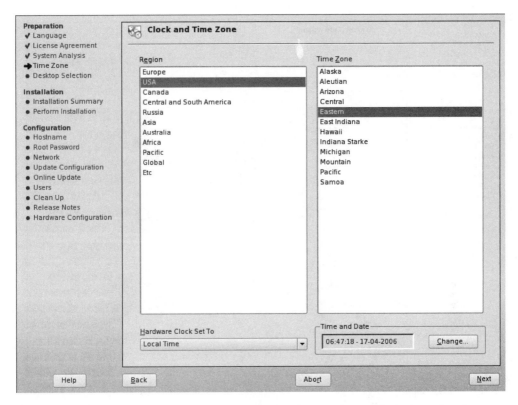

Figure 5-6. *Setting the time zone means that SUSE Linux can adjust to daylight saving time.*

If you're in an area covered by Greenwich Mean Time, also referred to as Universal Time Coordinated (UTC), and *SUSE Linux will be the only operating system on your hard disk,* select the UTC option under the Hardware Clock Set To drop-down list. If you dual-boot with Windows, or live in an area that's in advance of or behind UTC, leave the Hardware Clock Set To option as Local Time.

Step 7: Choose the Default Desktop Environment

You must choose the default desktop environment that you wish to use under SUSE Linux. The two main choices are GNOME and KDE, as shown in Figure 5-7. Both offer a broadly similar desktop experience that's comparable to what you might have had under Windows, but there are some minor although important differences. I explain these differences in Chapter 11.

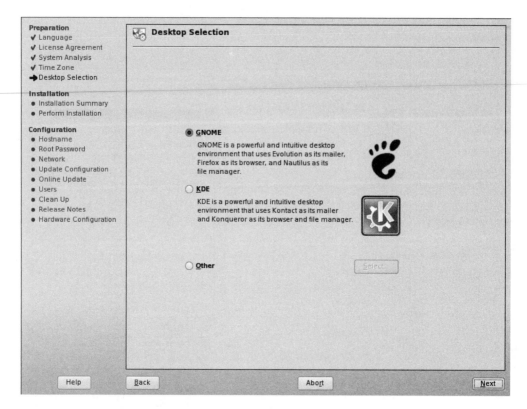

Figure 5-7. *Choose the default desktop you want to use under SUSE Linux. Don't worry—you can change it later.*

Most of SUSE and Novell's desktop Linux products default to the GNOME desktop. In addition, several other prominent Linux distributions, such as Ubuntu and Red Hat, also default to GNOME. However, a large community of SUSE Linux users prefers KDE, and several other Linux distributions default to KDE.

If you use Linux in a workplace environment, there's little doubt that you'll use GNOME. GNOME is genuinely easy to use for newcomers to Linux. It is less complex than KDE, which is arguably better for power users and those who like a feature-rich desktop that contains everything but the proverbial kitchen sink!

I suggest choosing GNOME at this stage. You can always choose to install KDE later and configure it to be your default desktop.

Tip Step 10 in this chapter describes choosing the software packages to install under SUSE Linux, and you can choose to override the defaults and install both KDE and GNOME. This gives you the widest possible range of software choices. However, the desktop you choose in step 7 will be the default that SUSE Linux boots into.

Step 8: Choose Installation Settings

After choosing the desktop environment, the system will work away for a few seconds, examining your system. If you're using an older PC, this might take up to a minute or two. The Installation Settings screen will then appear, as shown in Figure 5-8. This screen describes the default installation choices, such as which software will be installed, how the hard disk will be partitioned, and more. You can click the Expert tab to see complete details of the SUSE Linux installation choices, but this isn't necessary.

■**Tip** You might have noticed the installation progress display on the left side of the screen. This will stay on your screen throughout the installation process.

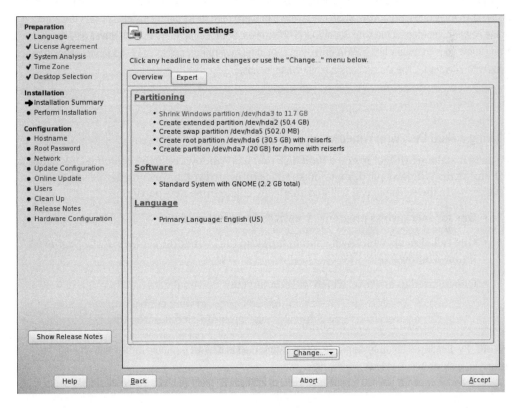

Figure 5-8. *SUSE Linux makes default installation choices, which you can edit if you wish.*

The default installation choices are usually correct, and the user in a hurry can simply click the Accept button at this stage. However, it's a good idea to check through the selections, to be sure that you're happy with the changes that will be made to your system and avoid the possibility of overwriting existing data.

You can click each heading in the list to reveal a fresh page full of details and configurable options. You might want to do this for the partitioning and software selection (steps 9 and 10).

Step 9: Partition the Disk

Partitioning the disk is one of the most important steps during installation, although, unfortunately, it's one that's also couched in difficult terminology. However, SUSE Linux does a good job of making it easy to understand. In most cases, SUSE Linux's default choice of action is appropriate. But you should understand what is happening and check the suggested course of action to make sure it's correct.

As noted in Chapter 4, you have three main options related to disk partitioning: install on a hard disk that also has Windows, install on a second hard disk, or delete the Windows partition.

Note Throughout the instructions relating to partitioning, I assume your computer uses an IDE hard disk, also known as Parallel ATA (PATA). SUSE Linux refers to these hard disks during installation as /dev/hda. Some newer computers come with Serial ATA (SATA) drives. SUSE Linux refers to such drives as /dev/sda. If you know your computer has a SATA drive, you should replace references to /dev/hda in these instructions with /dev/sda. The instructions are otherwise identical.

Sharing a Hard Disk with Windows

If you're installing SUSE Linux on a hard disk that has Windows on it, by default, SUSE Linux will shrink the Windows partition to make space (provided you have enough free space; see Chapter 4). In the free space, it will automatically create three new partitions:

- One for data such as programs, known as the *root partition*

- One called *swap*, which will contain the swap file (sometimes known as the *paging file* under Windows)

- One referred to as /home, which will contain your personal data

---

Note By default, on Linux systems, the swap data is held in its own partition, rather than sharing the main hard disk, as with Windows.

SUSE Linux will attempt to fairly cohabit the hard disk with Windows, by shrinking the Windows partition between 30% to 50%. If you want to alter this, perhaps to shrink the Windows partition even further, you can change the default partitioning choices by clicking the Partitioning menu heading. Then select the Base Partition Setup on This Proposal option. The next screen will show a list of the partitions. Select your Windows partition—it will be marked either FAT32 or HPFS/NTFS—and click the Resize button. You'll see a graphical display along with a slider (see Figure 5-9), which you can click and drag to alter the size of the Windows partition.

■**Note** You might notice that SUSE Linux won't let you shrink the Windows partition beyond a certain size. This is because doing so would leave no room on the Windows partition, making it unusable.

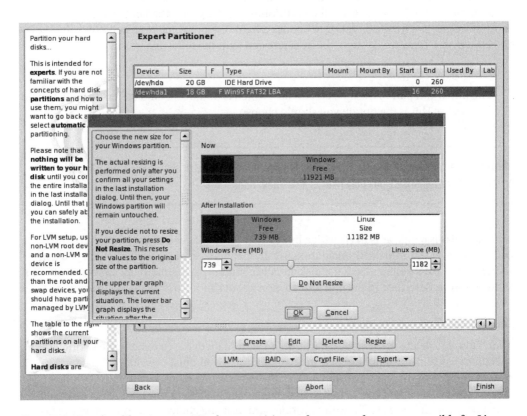

Figure 5-9. *You should resize your Windows partition to free as much space as possible for Linux.*

There's no hard-and-fast rule for the partition sizes, apart from the fact that you should allow at least 6GB of free space for SUSE Linux to use. If you intend to install a lot of software, you should consider giving SUSE Linux 8GB or more.

Once you've resized the Windows partition, YaST will ask if you want to automatically enlarge the SUSE Linux partition to fill the space. This is a good idea, so click Yes. When you're satisfied with the partition setup, click the Finish button.

■**Note** If you've already created some free space using a program like Partition Magic, as mentioned in Chapter 4, SUSE Linux will simply suggest creating its partitions in this free space and not touch the Windows partition.

Installing on a Separate Hard Disk

If you intend to install SUSE Linux on a second hard disk, you must tell SUSE Linux to use it in preference to the first disk. Click the Partitioning heading, and then click Create Custom Partition Setup. You'll then be asked to choose a hard disk on which to install. Click the second hard disk. On my test system, this was referred to in the following way:

```
2:  2. IDE,  40.0 GB, /dev/hdb, Maxtor-84320D4
```

The important part of this line is /dev/hdb, which is how SUSE Linux refers to your second hard disk drive. This is the option you should choose.

■**Note** If the drive was installed as a slave on the secondary channel (it shares the same IDE cable as the CD/DVD-ROM drive), SUSE Linux may refer to it as /dev/hdd.

If the disk is blank, as is likely with a brand-new hard disk, you should find that SUSE Linux takes over the entire disk and automatically creates a set of partitions, which you can accept and use to install Linux. If the disk already contains partitions, SUSE Linux will offer to shrink them, as described in the previous section about sharing a hard disk with Windows.

Deleting the Windows Partition

If you intend to delete the Windows partition on your main disk—to remove the Windows operating system from your hard disk in favor of Linux—you must override SUSE Linux's choices and create your own partitions. Click the Partitioning menu heading, and then click Create Custom Partition Setup. You'll then need to choose the disk on which you wish to install Linux. In the case of a PC with only one hard disk, the choice is simple: select the first hard disk, which will be described something like this:

```
1:  1. IDE, 40GB, /dev/hda, WDC-WD400BB
```

The most important part of this line is /dev/hda, which is how SUSE Linux identifies the first hard disk in a system. The section after that is the make and model of your hard disk, and the section before simply describes how much space the disk has.

Click Next, and then click the Use Entire Hard Disk button. Then click Next. Partitioning will be automatic after this. SUSE Linux will delete everything on the hard disk and create Linux partitions, ready for Linux installation.

Step 10: Choose Software Packages

By default, SUSE Linux installs a fully functional system, which includes a desktop environment, the OpenOffice.org office suite, help and support documents, and many other essential programs. This gives you a system that offers everything you need but isn't too overwhelming. However, if you want to change the selection of software that will be installed, click the Software heading to see the screen shown in Figure 5-10. Here, the software is arranged into groups on the left side, and the right side shows a list of the individual software packages, which will be installed as part of the larger group. Items that will be installed have a check in their check box.

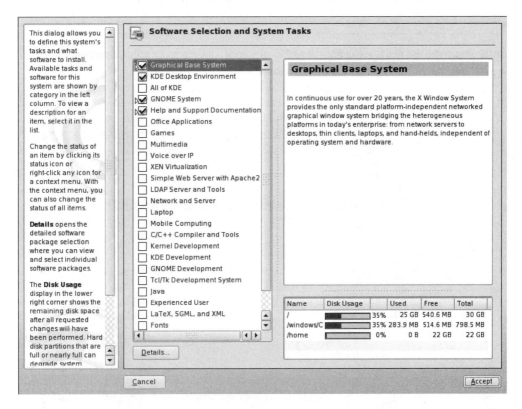

Figure 5-10. *The default software selection is adequate, but you can add more choices manually.*

You might not understand many of the software choices because they require some experience with Linux. Choices worth selecting from the package group listing on the left side of the screen include KDE Desktop Environment and GNOME System, if they aren't already selected. This will install both KDE and GNOME, giving you not only a superb range of software from both desktop environments, but also letting you switch between the two later. But realize that installing both GNOME and KDE will eat up around 4.5GB of your hard disk. Some of the other package selections also are very large.

Keep in mind that you can always add more software later, after you have SUSE Linux up and running, so there's no need to make a definitive choice at this stage.

When you're satisfied with your selection, click the Accept button.

Step 11: Start the Installation

After you've made your partitioning and software choices and clicked the Accept button, you'll see the Confirm Installation dialog box, as shown in Figure 5-11. Clicking the Install button starts the full installation, and the program will copy SUSE Linux files onto your hard disk. Before doing so, take the time for one final check to make sure that all your installation options are set correctly, particularly with regard to hard disk partitioning.

Note You might also need to read through additional license agreements for some components of SUSE Linux, such as the Macromedia Flash Player and Adobe Acrobat.

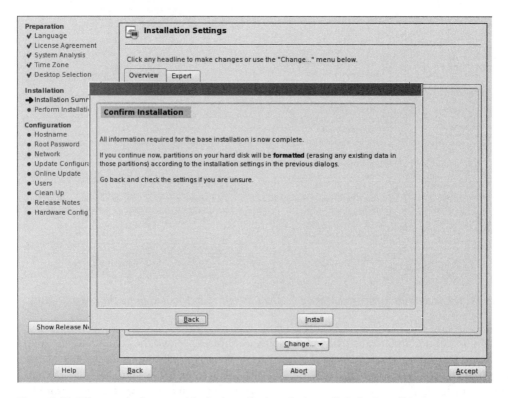

Figure 5-11. *When you're happy with the installation choices, click the Install button to start copying files.*

Installation will take between 30 and 60 minutes, depending on the speed of your PC. If you've opted to shrink your Windows partition, this may add to the installation time.

█Caution Shrinking your Windows partition not only takes a long time but, at certain points, it may look as if your computer has frozen because nothing much will appear on screen. It's very unlikely that your computer will have crashed! What's more, resetting your PC at this stage will in all likelihood destroy your Windows partition and all your data! Be patient and wait for installation to finish.

There are some additional steps to take at the end of the installation, so you should check on the installation progress periodically.

Step 12: Monitor the Installation

Although it is not necessary, you can monitor the installation progress and read the on-screen messages that point out some of SUSE Linux's main features, as shown in Figure 5-12. Click the Details tab to see which packages are being copied across. Don't worry if some of the software packages sound complicated, or even unnecessary. The way Linux works means that some software packages rely on other software packages, so some software that will never be used directly is installed.

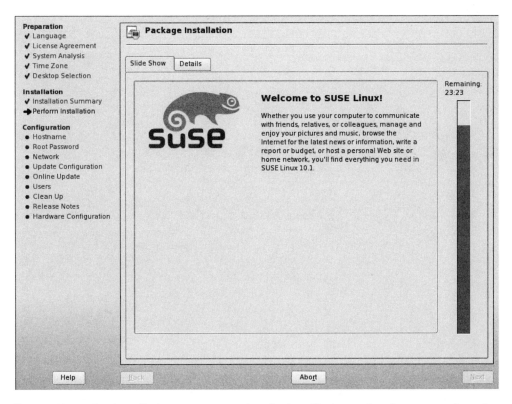

Figure 5-12. *During installation, you can monitor the installation and read messages about the features of SUSE Linux.*

Eventually, after the packages have been installed, the computer will spend a little time reconfiguring itself and then reboot. Following this, opt to boot from the hard disk on the DVD-ROM's boot menu, and choose to boot SUSE Linux when the second boot menu appears.

Step 13: Set the Hostname and Domain Name

The first post-installation step is to set the hostname and the domain name, as shown in Figure 5-13. These identify your computer in a network environment. They're relics of a bygone age when computers worked differently, and most desktop users don't need to pay much attention to these names. However, you might like to enter something descriptive in the Hostname box. Whatever you type here will appear as the second half of the command prompt, which I discuss in Chapter 13. You might choose to type something like **Office_PC** or **Notebook**. A hostname of SUSE is a good default choice that I normally use on my systems.

■**Note** You can't enter spaces in the Hostname box or include certain punctuation characters (you'll be told if you use illegal characters). You should limit the hostname to one or two short words. If it's too long, the command prompt will also be very long, making it difficult to use.

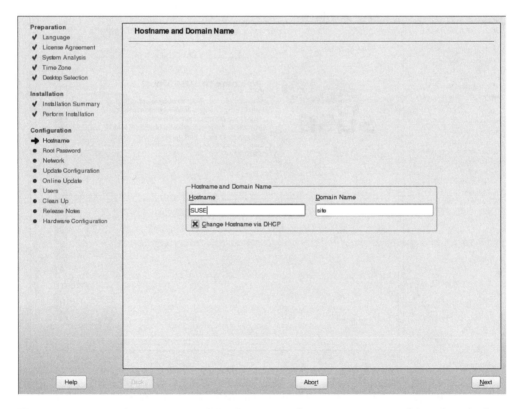

Figure 5-13. *Setting a hostname is useful only in networking environments, although it also lets you personalize your Linux setup.*

Step 14: Set the Root Password

You will be prompted to set a password for the root user, as shown in Figure 5-14. The root user is like the Administrator user on a Windows PC—the user who has complete control over the system. Although we talk of root as being a "user," in reality, you should rarely, if ever, log in to your computer as root. Instead, you should switch into root only when necessary, on a temporary basis. I'll explain how this is done via the GUI and via the command-line prompt in Chapter 9 and Chapter 14, respectively. For day-to-day use, you should create an ordinary user account, and you'll be invited to do this later in the configuration process.

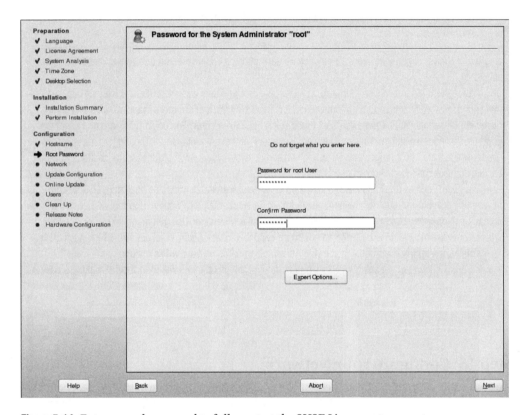

Figure 5-14. *Enter a good password to fully protect the SUSE Linux root account.*

You should choose a password that's secure. SUSE Linux doesn't impose any strict rules regarding the length or quality of passwords, and you can create a password of just a single character if you wish. But that wouldn't be wise, because it would be very easy for a hacker to guess. In fact, any kind of short password is a bad idea because, in addition to the possibility of being guessed, it can be cracked by what's referred to as a *brute-force attack*, where the hacker tries every combination of letters and/or words.

You shouldn't forget the root password. There's a vigorous debate among computer security experts about whether it's a good idea to physically write down passwords. In the case of the root password, I advise that you do so, because forgetting it effectively means you will not be able to change any settings within SUSE Linux, or even perform fundamental system administration tasks, such as install new software and update the system. However, once you have written down the password, make sure that it isn't stored near your computer. You might consider writing it on a card and storing it in your handbag or wallet, for example.

CREATING A STRONG PASSWORD

A good password is referred to as being *strong*. The rules are simple: strong passwords are of a reasonable length and consist of many different types of characters, such as uppercase and lowercase letters, symbols, and so on.

Although SUSE Linux doesn't enforce any rules, the root and user password dialog boxes do suggest that your passwords contain both uppercase and lowercase letters, and are more than five letters long. This makes for reasonably strong passwords, but why stop at just five letters? You could type an entire sentence or phrase, complete with uppercase and lowercase letters, and even punctuation! The longer a password is, generally speaking, the stronger it is. However, you should avoid well-known phrases, such as literary quotes, because crackers are likely to try those first.

Password choices to avoid include the names of your nearest and dearest (too easy to guess), as well as anything else obvious such as the name of your favorite sports team or TV show. Don't think that simply repeating an obvious word twice as your password makes it any stronger. Using numbers in place of certain letters (for example, E=3, I=1, T=7, and so on) isn't a good idea either. Again, crackers are wise to such tricks.

Finally, don't think that choosing your mother's maiden name (or your wife's maiden name if you're a married man) is a watertight solution. That's one of the first things crackers will try if they're making a concerted effort to break into your system!

Step 15: Configure Your Network

The next step is to configure your network devices, as shown in Figure 5-15. The best policy is to configure these devices when SUSE Linux is actually up and running, rather than during installation. That way, you'll be able to alter other vital settings to match, which is impossible to do at this stage. Configuring network devices is covered in Chapter 8.

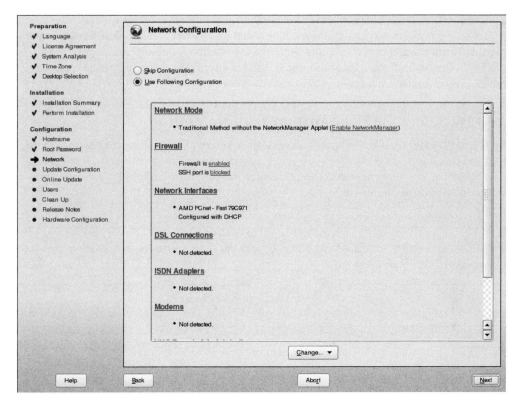

Figure 5-15. *The best policy is to wait until Linux has finished installing and booted up before configuring network devices.*

However, you do need to make one choice at this stage. SUSE Linux offers two methods of network configuration:

YaST: This is the traditional way of network configuration and is good for desktop systems that use a single network connection consistently, such as a wired Ethernet connection or a connection to a wireless DSL router.

NetworkManager Applet: This is a new method that allows users to quickly switch from one network to another. It's designed primarily for users of wireless networks.

SUSE Linux will automatically guess which is best for your system and select it. For example, if you are installing on a notebook computer, you should find that NetworkManager is selected, because SUSE Linux assumes that you will use a wireless network connection.

If you have a computer that uses wireless networking, including a desktop PC with a wireless network card, I suggest you use the NetworkManager Applet option. Click the Enable NetworkManager link if NetworkManager isn't already selected. The Network Mode entry will then read "User-Controlled Interfaces with the NetworkManager Applet."

If you use a wired Ethernet connection, it's best to select the traditional YaST method of configuration. You can do this by clicking the Disable NetworkManager, if it's available, so that the line then reads "Traditional Method without the NetworkManager Applet." Of course, if the line already reads this way, that means the traditional method is already selected.

Once you've made your selection, click Next.

Following network configuration, you'll be asked if you want to test your Internet connection and download updates. You should decline the invitation for now by clicking No, Skip This Test. When everything is up and running, you'll want to download updates as soon as possible, as covered in Chapter 9.

Step 16: Select the User Authentication Method

You'll next be asked what kind of user authentication you require, as shown in Figure 5-16. In nearly all cases, you can select the Local (/etc/passwd) option. This is the choice if your computer is located in a home or small office. It means that your username and password details are stored on your computer's hard disk.

■**Note** Your password is stored in a highly encrypted form that is considered very secure, so no one will be able to read it.

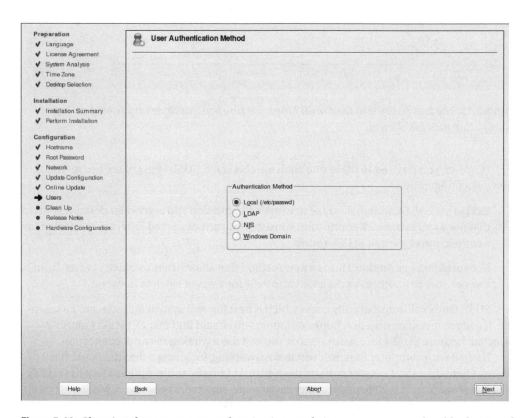

Figure 5-16. *Choosing the correct user authentication mode is easy; most users should select Local (/etc/passwd).*

If your computer is part of a corporate network that uses Network Information System (NIS), Lightweight Directory Access Protocol (LDAP), or Windows Domain (SMB/Samba) authentication, you should choose the relevant option. You'll then need to speak to your system administrator to find out the address of the authentication server, as well as your username and password.

Step 17: Create Users

Assuming that you selected the Local (/etc/passwd) option in the previous step, you'll now be invited to create new user accounts, as shown in Figure 5-17. As mentioned earlier, you should create a simple user account for yourself to use every day, rather than using the root account. The screen has fields for various details. Most important are the username and password, which must be entered twice to ensure accuracy.

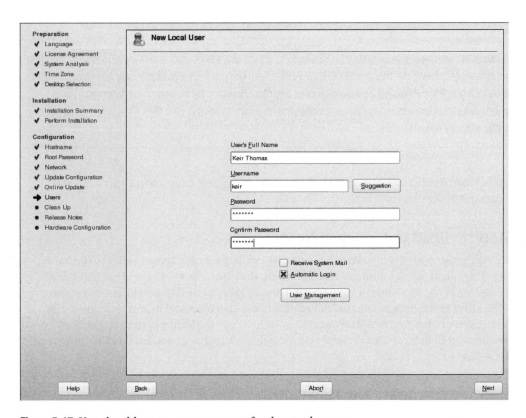

Figure 5-17. *You should create a user account for day-to-day use.*

The username cannot have spaces in it. It can be a mixture of uppercase and lowercase letters. You should avoid using symbols in the username, because this can create problems later on. The password can include numbers, letters, symbols, and spaces.

Notice that the Automatic Login option is selected by default. This means that SUSE Linux will not ask for your username and password when it boots up; it will simply boot straight into the default user account. If you require more security (in other words, your PC is located where strangers can access it), you can deselect the Automatic Login option. In that case, a username and password prompt will appear after SUSE Linux boots, and no one will be able to casually access the PC without the correct username and corresponding password.

Selecting the Receive System Mail option will cause messages created by certain background systems to be forwarded to your system mailbox, rather than the root user. This option is only useful for those running server systems, so you can leave this box unchecked. Note that the system mail account is not linked to the e-mail account you might eventually set up (as described in Chapter 8).

■**Caution** Anyone can access your SUSE Linux PC if they use a boot disc, and there's no way of stopping this (short of removing the floppy and CD/DVD-ROM drive). Using a boot disc in this way automatically gives users root powers, so they will be able to access any files. However, by turning of the Automatic Login option, you can at least stop any casual snoops who might try to access your files. Chapter 9 covers all of your security options.

You can create additional users here, too, but this is best done when Linux is up and running. Adding users is discussed in Chapter 30.

Step 18: Read the Release Notes

After creating users, the installation routine will write your new system setup to the hard disk. This might take a minute or two. Following this, you'll be able to read the SUSE Linux release notes file, as shown in Figure 5-18. This contains some late-breaking news about SUSE Linux at the time of release, including a handful of bugs and incompatibilities. However, much of what it says will be negated as soon as you perform a system upgrade, as described in Chapter 9. This is simply because these bugs have been fixed in the time since the release of SUSE Linux!

Step 19: Configure the Hardware

After clicking Next, you'll be invited to configure your hardware, as shown in Figure 5-19. In reality, this is largely a summary of SUSE's autoprobing of your hardware. Although it's possible to configure your hardware at this point, you should wait until after SUSE Linux is up and running, because you'll have better access to the configuration software. I cover configuring your hardware in Chapter 8.

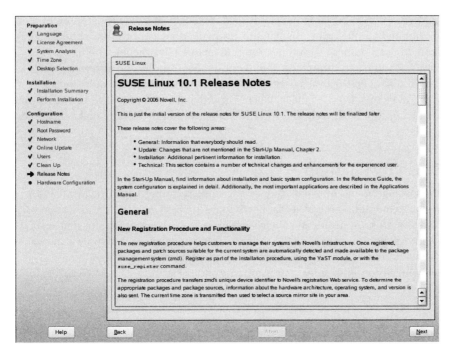

Figure 5-18. *Read through the release notes, but don't be too worried about any bugs it mentions.*

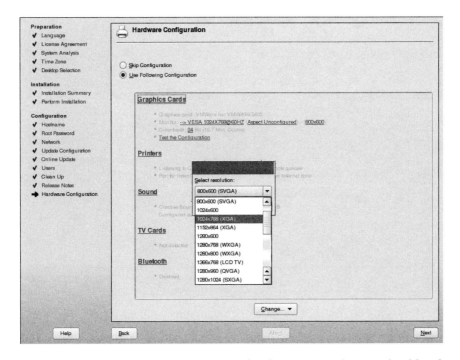

Figure 5-19. *You don't need to configure your hardware just yet, but you should make sure that the graphics card settings are correct.*

However, pay attention to the Graphics Cards section. Ideally, the details here should match your monitor and graphics card. SUSE Linux normally does a good job of choosing the correct resolution, but sometimes it gets that wrong. To fix this, click the relevant link under the Graphics Cards heading and choose a different option. For example, on one of my test PCs, a default resolution of 800×600 was suggested. I knew that the monitor could, in fact, support 1024×768. To fix this, I clicked the 800×600 link and chose a better resolution from the drop-down list that appeared. I also clicked Test the Configuration to check to make sure it all worked.

Step 20: Finish Installation

At this point, the installation has finished. After saving some settings to disk, the installation routine will display a completion message, as shown in Figure 5-20, and then your system will be restarted. Note that this doesn't mean your system will reboot! It simply means that several parts of the system will be shut down and the restarted, after which your desktop will appear if you selected the Automatic Login option when creating a new user account. Alternatively, you'll be greeted with a prompt to enter your username and password.

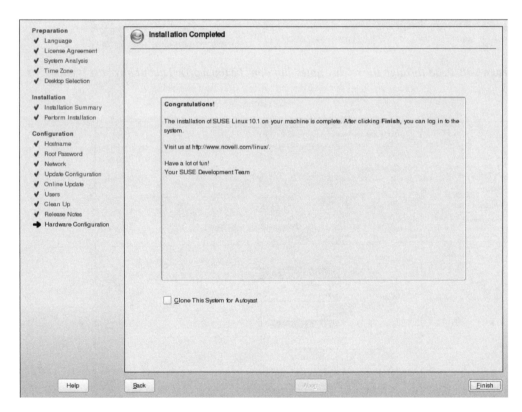

Figure 5-20. *Once installation has finished, you'll see a final message from the SUSE Linux team before your system boots.*

Summary

By following the steps outlined in this chapter, you should now have SUSE Linux installed on your computer. I've tried to provide you with enough information to get around any problems, as well as to explain exactly what's happening every step of the way.

Alas, it's still possible that you encountered hurdles that weren't addressed here. In the next chapter, you'll find solutions to common problems associated with SUSE Linux installation.

■■■

## CHAPTER 6

Solving Installation Problems

Chances are that your installation of SUSE Linux will complete without a hitch, and you'll find yourself with a first-rate operating system up and running within just a few minutes. However, if a problem rears its ugly head, you should be able to find the solution in this chapter, which addresses the most common installation problems. These problems are organized by when they occur: before you begin the installation, during the installation, and after the installation. The final section of the chapter describes how to configure the graphical subsystem, which can be useful if graphical glitches arise.

Preinstallation Problems

Some problems might arise before you even begin the installation process, or very early in the process, before the main installer program starts to run. This section addresses such issues.

Problem

My PC doesn't have a DVD-ROM drive. It has only a CD-ROM drive.

Solution

In this case, you won't be able to install SUSE Linux from the DVD-ROM supplied with this book. However, DVD-ROM drives are relatively inexpensive and you might consider upgrading your hardware.

Sadly, Novell does not produce a CD of the version of SUSE Linux as supplied with this book. However, you can download ISO images of the community-sponsored openSUSE CDs and burn them to CD yourself. The openSUSE CDs are broadly similar to the version of SUSE Linux supplied with this book, except that some proprietary software is omitted.

You'll find the CDs available for download at `http://en.opensuse.org/Released_Version`. At the time of this writing, there are five CD images to download, although only the first three are needed for a standard GNOME/KDE desktop installation as featured in this book.

Once downloaded, the ISO images can be burned to blank CD-R discs using a Windows utility such as Nero (check the program's manual or help file to learn how to burn ISO images).

Problem

When I boot from the DVD-ROM, I see a dialog box warning me that I'm trying to install 32-bit software on a 64-bit computer. I have a computer with an AMD Athlon 64 or recent Intel Pentium IV processor.

Solution

This is simply an informational warning and can be ignored. Installation will proceed correctly.

The warning is to alert you that you are using 32-bit software on a computer containing a processor with 64-bit functionality. A 64-bit processor can run 32-bit software without any problems, so this is not an issue.

However, a special 64-bit version of SUSE Linux is available for optional download. In theory, this will be better able to exploit the functions of a 64-bit processor. For more information, visit `http://en.opensuse.org/Released_Version`.

Problem

When I boot from the DVD-ROM, the first thing I see is graphical corruption. I don't even see the DVD-ROM boot menu offering installation options.

Solution

Hold down the Shift key just before the SUSE Linux DVD starts to boot (just after your PC has finished its boot-time memory testing). Type **n** when asked if you want to load the boot graphic. Then, at the prompt, type **failsafe** and hit Enter.

Problem

The computer boots from the DVD-ROM, but when the initial boot screen appears, hitting Enter doesn't start the installation. I can't move up and down in the menu options using the cursor keys either. The installation starts when the menu delay times out, but my mouse also doesn't respond. It's like my keyboard and mouse have been unplugged!

Solution

If your PC uses a USB keyboard, it might be that it's not being recognized by the SUSE Linux boot loader and/or installation routine. The solution is to make the USB keyboard and mouse pretend to be older PS/2 devices. This is done on a fundamental hardware level and is invisible to the operating system. Here are the steps:

1. Enter the BIOS setup program by pressing Delete during the initial stages of your computer boot routine (while memory testing and drive identification are still taking place). Some computers might use a different key combination to enter BIOS setup, such as Ctrl+Insert; this information will be displayed on the screen.

2. Use the cursor keys to navigate to the Integrated Peripherals section, and then look for an entry along the lines of USB Legacy Support. Set it to Enabled.

3. Press Esc to return to the main menu and opt to save the changes.

4. Reboot the computer.

You should repeat this procedure and deactivate USB Legacy Support once SUSE Linux has been installed. At that stage, SUSE Linux should be able to recognize the USB keyboard properly.

Problem

After I've hit Enter to clear the initial loading screen, the screen fills with text, and then the computer hangs with a message along the lines of "Kernel Panic."

Solution

Kernel Panic errors occur when the operating system cannot continue to load for various reasons. In this context, it's likely that either the DVD is faulty (or dirty) or that your PC has a defective item of hardware.

Check to make sure that the DVD is both clean and not scratched. If possible, try it on a different computer. If it works, then it's clearly not at fault, and your computer most likely has a hardware issue. In particular, bad memory can cause problems. Does the computer already have an operating system installed? Does this run without problems? If not, consider replacing your memory modules.

You can test your computer's memory using the Memtest program that's built into SUSE Linux. To access this program, hold down the Shift key just before the SUSE Linux DVD starts to boot (just after your PC has finished its boot-time memory testing). Type **n** when asked if you want to load the boot graphic. Then, at the prompt, type `memtest` and press Enter (be sure to do this quickly; within five seconds the graphical installer will automatically step in).

Memtest will begin to scan your computer's memory immediately. Look in the Errors column on the right to see the number of errors. Good memory should have no errors. To learn more about how to use Memtest, visit `www.memtest86.com`.

Problem

The installation freezes or reboots almost as soon as it begins.

Solution

It is possible that the power-saving features in your computer are causing problems. Boot from the DVD-ROM and, instead of choosing the Installation option at the boot prompt, choose the Installation--ACPI Disabled option.

If this doesn't fix the problem, boot again from the DVD-ROM, and this time choose the Installation--Safe Settings option. This will start the installation routine so that it will overcome certain hardware incompatibilities.

Problem

When I boot from the DVD, I select to install and everything appears to run smoothly for a few seconds, but then the system freezes before installation starts (alternatively, or in addition, there may be graphical corruption on the screen). I've tried the solutions mentioned in the previous answer and used the Installation--ACPI Disabled and Installation--Safe Settings boot menu options, but neither have fixed the problem.

Solution

Try running the installation routine in text mode. Press F3 and then F2 when the DVD-ROM boot menu appears and select Text Mode from the list (use the up and down cursor keys to navigate the menu, and hit Enter to make a choice). Then highlight Installation on the menu and press Enter.

Using the text-mode installation routine is similar to using YaST's graphical installer, as described in the previous chapter, except that you don't use your mouse. Instead, you use the keyboard's cursor keys to highlight various options, and the Tab key to move from field to field (rather like using an application within MS-DOS). Press Enter or the spacebar to select options.

The main installation options are virtually identical to those offered within the graphical installation. See Chapter 5 for guidance.

Installation Problems

During installation, you may get error messages or experience other difficulties. This section offers some solutions to common installation problems.

Problem

I'm using the same keyboard, mouse, and monitor across several computers, courtesy of a keyboard, video, and monitor (KVM) switch. During installation, it appears that the auto-probing of my video hardware produces the wrong results.

Solution

It's impossible to correctly probe a monitor if a KVM switch is attached to the computer. Consider attaching the monitor directly to the computer for the duration of the installation.

Problem

When I try to install, the partitioning section of the installation program talks about /dev/sda, /dev/sdb, /dev/sdc, and so on, rather than /dev/hda. When I choose to install, I'm told the disk doesn't have enough free space.

Solution

If your system uses SCSI or SATA hard disks, then this is correct. SCSI disks are mostly used on servers and very rarely on desktop computers.

However, if in spite of this you still see this message, it's likely you have a flash memory card inserted into your card reader, or another form of external memory. Unfortunately, SUSE Linux sometimes attempts to install Linux to such devices, which are identified internally by Linux as SCSI devices.

The solution is to disconnect or remove the removable memory device during installation.

Problem

The installation program seems to run smoothly, but then crashes/freezes at a random point before completing.

Solution

In the case of freezes, make sure the computer has actually frozen and isn't simply busy with a task. Check the hard disk light on the computer's case for activity and also look at the DVD-ROM drive light to see if it's flashing.

If the computer genuinely has become unresponsive, reboot, and when the boot menu appears, select the Installation--ACPI Disabled option. This will deactivate the power-saving features of your computer. If the problem persists, choose the Installation--Safe Settings option from the DVD boot menu. This will start the installation program but configure it to overcome certain hardware issues.

If neither solution fixes the problem, see the solution to the last problem in the "Preinstallation Problems" section, which begins, "When I boot from the DVD, I select to install and everything appears to run smoothly . . ." for information about how to start the installation program in text mode.

Problem

Installation fails when a software package called `suse-build-key` is being copied across from the DVD.

Solution

This happens if the PC's clock is set incorrectly to a date in the past (such as a random date in 2002). To fix this problem, ensure the PC's date and time are set correctly and then restart installation. You can set the correct date and time via the computer's BIOS setup program.

During the initial stages of your computer boot routine, enter the BIOS setup program by pressing the specified key (usually the Delete key), and then navigate to the relevant menu option (which depends on the BIOS setup system used on your computer). At the top of the screen, you should see options for setting the time and date.

Problem

In the early stages of installation, SUSE Linux reports that there are no hard disks present (alternatively, the computer might crash). I'm using a computer with an SiS chipset.

Solution

Reboot the computer and, on the DVD boot menu, highlight the Installation option and type the following:

```
insmod=ide-generic
```

Then press Enter to start installation, which should now work properly.

Problem

The installation fails with the following error message: "Usb.3: read info."

Solution

This problem is caused by an incorrectly configured BIOS. Reboot the computer and, before installation starts, enter the BIOS setup program by pressing the specified key (usually the Delete key). In the PNP/PCI Configuration section, make sure the Assign IRQ for USB option is set to Enabled. (You can use the cursor keys to move around the menus in the BIOS program and use the Enter key to change various values.)

Problem

During installation, I see the following error message: "Disk doesn't contain a valid partition table." Yet installation seems to continue normally and, afterward, the system appears to work fine.

Solution

This is simply a glitch in the installation procedure. The error is effectively meaningless and can be ignored.

Postinstallation Problems

Problems might also occur after you install SUSE Linux. This section addresses several possible postinstallation problems. This section covers only problems that appear immediately after installation—those that prevent SUSE Linux from working correctly immediately after its first boot. Issues surrounding the configuration of hardware or software are dealt with in the next part of this book.

Problem

After installation has finished, I find myself with a blank screen (or a screen that's full of corrupted graphics). If I reboot, the computer appears to boot SUSE Linux correctly but, again, it ends with a blank/corrupted screen.

Solution

For some reason, your graphical configuration isn't working. See the "Fixing Graphical Problems" section later in this chapter for the steps to fix this problem.

Problem

When I boot for the first time, the resolution is too low/high!

Solution

If you chose the GNOME desktop during installation, click Desktop ➤ GNOME Control Center. Double-click the Screen Resolution icon in the window that appears, and then select a more suitable resolution from the list. If you find that the maximum resolution offered is not high enough, your graphics card will need to be reconfigured. See the "Fixing Graphical Problems" section later in this chapter.

If you chose the KDE desktop during installation, right-click a blank spot and select Configure Desktop from the menu. In the window that appears, click the Display icon in the panel on the left and select a suitable resolution in the Screen Size drop-down list on the right. Again, if the highest resolution offered isn't suitable, you will need to reconfigure your graphics card. See the "Fixing Graphical Problems" section later in this chapter.

Problem

After booting up, my USB mouse and/or USB keyboard are not recognized.

Solution

Try unplugging the keyboard and/or mouse, and then reattaching them. If you find they now work, log in to SUSE Linux, and then perform an online system upgrade. See Chapter 9 for more information.

If this fails to solve the problem, you can configure your BIOS to pretend your mouse and keyboard are traditional PS/2-style devices, as follows:

1. Enter the BIOS setup program by pressing Delete during the initial stages of your computer boot routine (while memory testing and drive identification are still taking place). Some computers might use a different key combination to enter BIOS setup, such as Ctrl+Insert; this information will be displayed on the screen.

2. Use the cursor keys to navigate to the Integrated Peripherals section, and then look for an entry along the lines of USB Legacy Support. Set it to Enabled.

3. Press Esc to return to the main menu and opt to save the changes.

4. Reboot the computer.

Problem

When I boot for the first time, all I see is a black screen with some text at the top saying, "Welcome to SUSE Linux 10.1 (i586)" and, beneath that, "linux login."

Solution

For some reason, the automatic configuration of your graphics card failed during installation. See the following section for instructions on configuring your GUI manually.

Fixing Graphical Problems

Although SUSE Linux is extremely good at automatically detecting and configuring your PC's graphics hardware, it sometimes gets the configuration wrong. This is characterized by one of the following:

- SUSE Linux freezes when the desktop would normally appear.

- You see on-screen graphical corruption, either of text or graphics.

- You see a message that the X server isn't working.

- You see a black screen with only a text login prompt.

The solution is to use the SaX2 software to reconfigure the system's graphics. SaX2 is a powerful configuration utility provided by SUSE. It's designed to configure X.org, the software that provides the basis for the GUI under SUSE Linux. It aids in setting up the graphics card, monitor, keyboard, and mouse, and it uses autodetection to make the process easier.

Usually, you don't need to use SaX2 because, during setup, the YaST program automatically installs the graphics card, keyboard, mouse, and monitor based on the results of probing your hardware. However, in a minority of cases, YaST gets it wrong, nearly always with regard to the monitor. An incorrect monitor configuration results in a system that boots up but is unable to start the GUI. The screen will usually go blank or flash at the end of the boot procedure, and the user will be taken to a text login prompt.

■**Note** Although the boot procedure features a blue picture background with the SUSE gecko, Linux isn't actually running in GUI mode at that time. This is simply a trick to make the screen look prettier. Effectively, the computer is still in a text mode. GUI mode starts when the bootup has finished and is usually indicated by the appearance of the mouse cursor.

Autoconfiguring Using SaX2

SaX2 needs to be run with administrative powers, because it involves configuring the entire Linux system. Follow these steps to run SaX2:

1. Assuming that you can boot to a login prompt (the words `linux login:` appear alongside a flashing cursor), type `root` as the username and, when prompted, type the root password you entered during setup. If you find that you can only boot to a blank screen without a login prompt, hold down Ctrl+Alt and then press F2. This should bring up a login prompt, from which you can log in as root.

2. SaX2 cannot operate if your system is in run level 5. It needs to be activated in run level 3. The concepts behind run levels are explained in Chapter 31, but for the moment, you should type the following command:

```
init 3
```

3. You might need to wait a few seconds while some commands are processed in the background. Press Enter to return to the command prompt, and then type the following:

   sax2

4. When SaX2 starts, it may show a dialog box claiming that it has worked out the best graphics configuration for your system, as shown in Figure 6-1. You can click OK to exit SaX2 if you wish to try the new configuration.

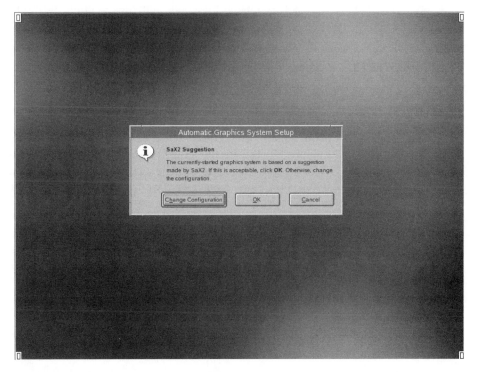

Figure 6-1. *SaX2 will try to autodetect the best settings, and most of the time, it's correct.*

5. Once the program has closed, type the following at the command prompt to switch back to GUI mode:

   init 5

6. If SaX2 has guessed the correct configuration, you should see the desktop or the GUI login prompt appear, complete with a mouse cursor. You can then proceed to use Linux, and no further work with SaX2 is necessary. However, if you return once again to the command prompt, then clearly SaX2 has failed, and some manual configuration is necessary, as described in the next section.

Using SaX2 to Change Your Configuration

If you need to manually configure your GUI, repeat the preceding steps to start SaX2, first switching to run level 3 as described. When you see the dialog box asking if you want to accept the default configuration (Figure 6-1), decline the offer and instead click Change Configuration. This will open a dialog box that lists the various elements you can manually configure. The first step is to configure the monitor because, in the majority of cases, this is what will be causing the problem. Often, SaX2 guesses incorrect vertical and horizontal scan rates.

Here's how to reconfigure the monitor:

1. Ensure the Monitor icon is selected in the left pane, and then examine the properties in the pane on the right. SaX2 should have identified the make and model of both your graphics card and monitor.

2. You can't change the details about the graphics card, but you can alter the monitor details by clicking the Change button. This should display a list of monitor manufacturers and models.

3. If you're lucky, your monitor will be included, and you can select it from the list. However, your monitor might not appear, because there are simply too many different types for SaX2 to list them all. Therefore, often the best solution is to select from the section headed -->VESA, as shown in Figure 6-2. The VESA display is a list of generic monitors based on industry standards, which work with most monitors. This is a good choice if you find that SaX2 selects the right monitor automatically but, for some reason, it just doesn't work correctly.

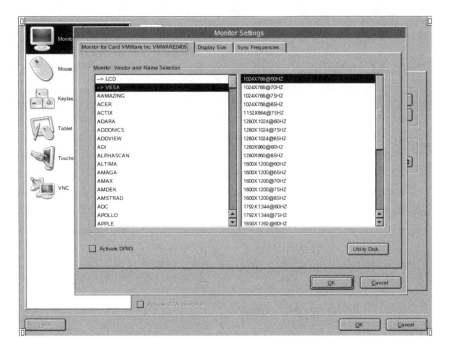

Figure 6-2. *VESA settings are a safe choice because they will work with virtually all monitor makes and models.*

4. At this point, you'll need to know a little about your monitor's technical settings, such as the resolution at which it normally runs, as well as its horizontal refresh rate. See Table 6-1 for a list of standard monitor sizes and resolutions (most monitors work well at 70Hz refresh rates). You can choose one of these if you don't know your monitor's exact details. Note that most monitors sold at the present time are 17-inch models. If your monitor is a widescreen model, it will run at a nonstandard resolution; consult the monitor's documentation for more information.

Table 6-1. *Typical Monitor Resolutions*

Monitor Size	Typical Resolutions
CRT Monitors	
14 inches	800×600, 640×480
15 inches	800×600, 640×480
17 inches	1024×768, 800×600, 640×480
19 inches	1280×1024, 1024×768, 800×600, 640×480
20 inches	1600×1200, 1280×1024, 1024×768, 800×600, 640×480
TFT Screens	
14 inches	1024×768
15 inches	1024×768
17 inches	1280×1024
19 inches	1280×1024

5. Once you've chosen the monitor settings, click the OK button in the dialog box.

6. In the parent window, select from the drop-down list the default resolution you want to use (this will normally automatically match the resolution you selected a moment ago). Also, select the color depth from the Colors drop-down list. Most graphics cards can handle 24-bit color, but if you find there are problems later on, return to this step and select 16-bit color.

■**Note** After setting up the monitor, you can also change the settings for your keyboard and mouse by clicking the icons on the left side of the window. However, in the vast majority of cases, these will have been correctly autodetected and configured. Therefore, there's little need to undertake extra configuration.

7. Click the OK button. You'll be given a chance to test your new configuration. This is highly recommended. If your new configuration is correct, a test screen should appear, as shown in Figure 6-3. The test screen will let you change the screen size and positioning, but this is better done using the controls on your monitor. So, if the picture is too small, too big, or off-center, don't worry too much about it. The most important thing is that you are seeing a picture, which means your configuration has worked. Don't forget to test your mouse, too, to make sure that it's working.

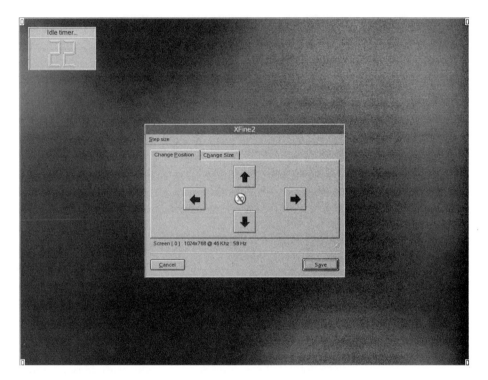

Figure 6-3. *Don't forget to test your new settings before saving them!*

8. If you're happy with the new configuration, click the Save button in the test screen dialog box, and then quit SaX2.

9. Switch back to graphical mode by typing the following:

```
init 5
```

You should boot to the desktop, and everything should work correctly.

Running xf86config

If SaX2 simply won't work, you can try the text-mode xf86config program as a last resort. This isn't particularly user-friendly, but it does have the advantage of writing a simple but usable GUI configuration file at the end. You may find that, after running xf86config, you're able to run SaX2 immediately afterward and create a better configuration file. You should certainly find that you'll be able to boot to the desktop.

In the following steps, I'll explain how to set up a system using "safe" settings, based around VESA compatibility modes offered by all graphics cards and monitors. This means that the instructions should work with all computers. However, the resultant setup will not be optimized.

Using xf86config is relatively straightforward. Answer yes or no to various questions by pressing Y or N. When you need choose an option from a numbered list, simply type the relevant number alongside the entry you want.

1. Follow the earlier instructions in the "Autoconfiguring Using SaX2" section to log in as the root user. Then, at the command prompt, type the following:

   xf86config

2. After reading the instructions, press Enter to continue.

3. For the choice of mouse, type 4. This will install a PS/2 mouse device driver, which is compatible with the majority of mice.

4. Answer N to the question about emulating three mouse buttons.

5. In the mouse device field, type the following, and then press Enter:

   /dev/input/mice

6. Press Enter to continue when the warning about XKB rules appears.

7. Read the instructions about monitor sync rates, and then press Enter again.

8. Choose a resolution and scan rate combination that suits your monitor. If your monitor is a 17-inch model, it will probably run at 1024×768 resolution, and option number 7 is best.

9. Select the option that matches your monitor's vertical sync rate (also known as the refresh rate). You might need to consult your monitor's manual to discover this information. If you can't find this information, choose option 1.

10. You'll be asked to enter a name for your monitor definition. Anything will do; this is merely for your own reference in the future.

11. You'll be asked if you want to look at the graphics card database. Answer Y.

12. Press Enter to move through the list of cards. Try to find a driver that matches your graphics card chipset. Once you find one, type its number at the prompt. However, I strongly advise choosing option 0 – Generic VESA compatible. This is a widely compatible driver that will work with most cards.

13. After choosing your graphics card, press Enter to confirm the details.

14. Select from the list the quantity of video memory that matches your graphics card. Generally speaking, most modern cards have upward of 32MB (32,768KB) of memory. However, a safe choice that will allow 24-bit color depth at 1024×768 resolution, is 8192KB, which is option number 6.

15. You'll need to enter an identifier for the card. As with the monitor, this is purely for your reference, so anything will do.

16. You'll need to set the default resolutions for your monitor. If the resolutions are okay, type 4. If you wish to change them, type 1, 2, or 3, depending on which color depth you wish to alter (you may need to alter all three). If you choose to do this, you'll need to select the range of resolutions you want to be able to choose between in the future. Generally speaking, users of a standard 17-inch monitor can choose option 4 – 1024×768. Users of larger monitors might want to consult Table 6-1 earlier in this chapter. Answer N when asked if you want to create a virtual screen.

17. You'll be asked what color depth you want to use by default. Option number 5 (24 bits) is best, although if you run into problems later, you might wish to repeat these steps and choose option 4 (16 bits).

18. You'll be asked if you want to write your new `xorg.conf` file. Answer Y.

19. You can now test your setup by rebooting. To do this, type the following at the prompt:

```
init 6
```

WHAT IF YOU WANT TO REMOVE LINUX FROM YOUR COMPUTER?

Linux isn't for everyone, and you might find that, after trying it out, it's not for you. In that case, you might wish to return to having a Windows-only PC and reclaim the disk space taken up by the Linux partitions. This is easily done using the Windows installation CD.

Before you do this, please think long and hard about your reasons for deciding to give up on Linux. If you found it too difficult to use compared to Windows, consider giving Linux just a bit longer to prove itself. If you find that Linux doesn't support a particular piece of hardware on your PC, try updating the system to see if support has been added. If you find that a piece of software you need isn't supplied with SUSE Linux, search the Internet to see if you can track down that software. Linux has software for just about every need, but, unfortunately, a particular program might sometimes be difficult to find.

If you're certain you want to remove Linux, you'll be pleased to hear it's relatively easy. Assuming you're using Windows XP, insert your installation CD and boot from it. When you are asked whether you want to install Windows, choose to run the Rescue program. After prompting you for your Administrator password (if you have one; if you don't, leave the password field blank and press Enter), and asking you to choose your keyboard and which Windows partition you wish to work on, you'll be returned to a DOS command prompt. At this point, you should type the following:

```
bootcfg /rebuild
```

Then simply issue the following two commands in sequence. These will rewrite the boot sector with Windows code, making Linux no longer accessible.

```
fixboot
fixmbr
```

These commands will likely ask questions for which the answers are obvious, but this depends on your system.

After running the commands, boot into Windows and use the Disk Management tools to remove the Linux partitions. Open Control Panel, click Administrative Tools, click Computer Management, click Storage, and finally click Disk Management. Your Windows partitions will be identified with drive letters, and the Linux partitions will be referred to as Unknown Partitions. You can safely delete these, which will eradicate Linux entirely from your system.

Summary

This chapter's goal was to address problems that might occur during the installation of SUSE Linux. It discussed preinstallation, installation, and postinstallation issues. It also covered how to use the SaX2 and xf86config configuration utilities to configure the graphics subsystem, which may be necessary if the installation program failed to properly recognize your graphics card or monitor.

You should now have SUSE Linux installed. The next part of this book focuses on helping you get everything up and running. You'll learn essential skills and become a confident Linux user.

PART III

■ ■ ■

The No-Nonsense Getting Started Guide

CHAPTER 7

■■■

Booting Linux for the First Time

Now that you have SUSE Linux on your PC, you'll no doubt want to get started immediately, and that's what Part 3 of this book is all about. In later chapters, we'll examine specific details of using SUSE Linux and getting essential hardware up and running. We'll also look at personalizing SUSE Linux so that it works in a way that's best for you on a day-to-day basis. But right now, the goal of this chapter is to get you doing the same things you did under Windows as quickly as possible.

This chapter explains how to start up SUSE Linux for the first time and work with the desktop. It also looks at how some familiar aspects of your computer, such as using the mouse, are slightly enhanced under SUSE Linux.

Starting Up

The first SUSE Linux screen you will see is the boot loader, which appears shortly after you switch on your PC, as shown in Figure 7-1. This is actually a separate program called GRUB, but you don't need to know that right now. Suffice it to say that this program kicks everything off and starts SUSE Linux.

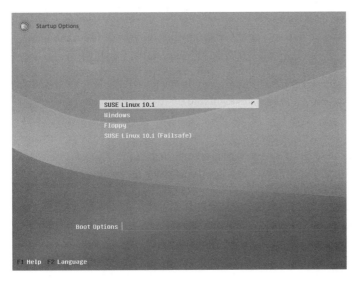

Figure 7-1. *The default choice is fine on the boot menu, so press Enter to start SUSE Linux.*

There are usually three or four choices on the menu, but the default (SUSE Linux) is what you need. You might find that you have an entry for Windows if you've chosen to dual-boot. There's usually an entry called Failsafe, which is a little like Safe Mode within Windows, in that only conservative system settings are used (however, unlike Safe Mode, it's entirely possible to fully utilize SUSE Linux when the Failsafe option is selected, which is to say you can start the GUI in standard resolution, and networking devices should still work).

The SUSE Linux option will be selected automatically within eight seconds, but you can press Enter to start immediately. (To select any option other than SUSE Linux from the boot menu, simply use the arrow keys to move the selection down the list, and then press Enter.)

■**Note** All operating systems need a boot loader—even Windows. However, the Windows boot loader is hidden and simply starts the operating system. Under SUSE Linux, the boot loader usually has a menu, so you can select Linux or perhaps an option that lets you access your PC for troubleshooting problems. When you gain some experience with SUSE Linux, you might choose to install two or more versions of Linux on the same hard disk, and you'll be able to select among them using the boot menu.

Depending on which options you selected during installation, you'll either boot directly to the desktop or you'll see a login screen first. If you boot to the desktop, you can skip the following section and go directly to "Exploring the Desktop."

Logging In

Depending on whether you selected the GNOME or KDE desktop environment during installation, you'll see slightly different types of login screens. However, they're broadly similar.

On the GNOME login screen, shown in Figure 7-2, you can enter the username and password you created toward the end of the installation process. Simply type the username, press Enter, and you'll be prompted for the password.

On the KDE login screen, you can either type the username and password into the fields provided or click the relevant username in the list on the left side of the screen, and then type the password.

From either login screen, you can reboot or shut down the system by clicking the relevant options (on the KDE login screen, these options are available on the System menu).

■**Tip** Clicking Session lets you switch between various desktop environments. So, if you opted to install both GNOME and KDE during installation, you can switch between the two here. To revert back to your original choice, simply reselect it when you log in again.

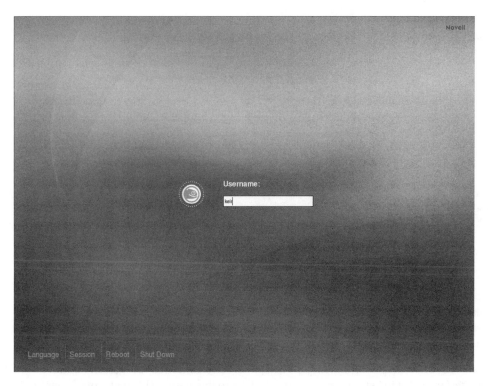

Figure 7-2. *If you did not select to log in automatically, you'll need to enter your username and then your password.*

A common mistake among those who are new to Linux is to use the root account, rather than the standard user account created during setup, to log in on a daily basis. This is certainly possible, but it's not recommended. One of the reasons that Windows XP is so fundamentally insecure is that it allows all users to run with Administrator permissions by default. It is possible to run Windows XP with a limited account, but this must be specially configured by someone who knows what he is doing (you've got to love Microsoft's lackluster approach to security!). This means that any Windows user can change the entire software and hardware settings of the PC.

■**Note** Windows Vista won't allow certain hardware and software configuration without an Administrator password. However, many are critical of how the system is implemented. Compare that to Linux, where the system of restricted versus root users has been in use since day one and has been perfected since that time! In fact, it's been around since the days of Unix in the 1970s and 1980s.

SUSE Linux prefers people to run as ordinary users. This is restrictive in the sense that it lets you run only particular programs and access certain pieces of hardware, but you shouldn't consider it a limitation. Consider it a security feature. In practice, this will not affect your day-to-day work with Linux.

If a situation arises where you need root powers—to run a program that configures hardware, for example—you'll be given the opportunity to switch temporarily to the root user account. You should see an Administrator Password box, into which you can type the root password. Your root powers will apply to only that program, however, and in all other regards, you'll still be running Linux as an ordinary user. In many ways, this practice of borrowing root powers for certain tasks gives you the best of all worlds, with minimal hassle.

Exploring the Desktop

The SUSE Linux desktop is similar to what you might be used to under Windows, but subtly different. It also varies slightly depending on whether you chose the GNOME or KDE desktop environment when installing SUSE Linux, but there are several common elements:

Icons: As with Windows, both KDE and GNOME use desktop icons to represent files and also shortcuts to programs. Under KDE, a single-click is all that's needed to activate icons, whereas GNOME relies on the standard Windows-style double-click. I'll explain how KDE can be configured for double-click icon activation in Chapter 10.

Panel: Both desktop environments have a panel at the bottom of the screen (known as the *taskbar* in Windows), which provides a home to the menus, shortcut icons, clock, and various useful applets.

Notification area/system tray: At the bottom right of the screen is what's known as the notification area in GNOME or the system tray under KDE (and also Windows). This is where various applets run in the background and provide handy functionality or feedback when a particular task requires urgent attention. Examples include the Volume Control applet, as shown in Figure 7-3, and the Software Updater applet, which will indicate when vital updates are available for SUSE Linux (once configured, as explained in Chapter 9).

Figure 7-3. *Both the KDE and GNOME desktops provide a number of handy applets, including one to control the PC's volume level.*

Once the desktop appears, there's nothing stopping you from getting started immediately, so feel free to click around and see what you can discover. Remember that because you're running as a standard user, you can't do any irreversible damage to the system setup. So let yourself go wild!

■**Tip** Although you can't damage the system by messing around, you might find that you delete essential icons or somehow cause programs to work incorrectly. Don't worry if this happens. You can always create a new account for yourself following the instructions in Chapter 30. When using this new account, you should find all the settings are returned to normal, and you'll be back to square one!

The mouse works largely as it does in Windows, in that you can move it around and click on things. You can also right-click virtually everything and everywhere to bring up context menus, which usually let you alter settings. And you should find that the mouse wheel in between the mouse buttons lets you scroll windows.

Table 7-1 indicates where popular Windows desktop features can be found under the GNOME and KDE desktops.

■**Caution** Bear in mind that SUSE Linux isn't a clone of Windows and doesn't try to be. Although it works in a similar way—by providing icons and containing programs within windows—there are various potholes in the road that can trip up the unwary. I would advise you apply a little patience and give yourself some time to get used to SUSE Linux, especially in the first few days of using it.

Table 7-1. *Windows Desktop Features Equivalents Under SUSE Linux*

Windows Function	Description	GNOME Equivalent	KDE Equivalent
My Computer	Gives access to the PC system and lets you browse files	Places ➤ Computer at the bottom of the screen	My Computer on the desktop
Recycle Bin	Repository of recently deleted files	Trash icon on the desktop	Wastebin icon on the desktop
Start menu	Provides access to many computer functions, as well as a list of programs	Applications and Desktop menus at the bottom of the screen	K menu at the bottom left of the screen
Quick launch toolbar	Small icons on the taskbar that allow you to launch popular programs	Icons can be dragged from any menu into the space to the right of the Applications/Places/Desktop menus	Icons to the right of the K menu

Continued

Table 7-1. *Continued*

Windows Function	Description	GNOME Equivalent	KDE Equivalent
My Network Places/Network Neighborhood	Provides access to network services	Places ➤ Network Servers	Click the Konqueror icon at the bottom of the screen, and then click Network Folders
My Documents	Storage space set aside for a user's documents	Double-click the Home icon on the desktop, and then double-click Documents	Click the Home icon at the bottom of the screen, and then click Documents
Control Panel	Lets you change system settings and preferences	Desktop ➤ Control Center for superficial changes or Desktop ➤ YaST to configure hardware/software	K menu ➤ Personal Settings for superficial changes or System ➤ YaST (Control Center) to configure hardware/software
Find Files	Lets you search the file system	Places ➤ Search for Files	K menu ➤ Find Files/Folders
Shutdown/Reboot	Lets you shut down or restart the system	Desktop ➤ Log Out	K menu ➤ Log Out

Quick Desktop Guide: GNOME

The GNOME desktop is very clean compared to Windows. By default, all you'll find is a shortcut to your /home folder, where you can store your personal files, and the Trash icon, which works in an identical way to the Windows Recycle Bin.

Of course, you can fill the desktop with stuff if you want to do that. As with Windows, you can save files to the desktop for easy access, or click and drag them there from file browser windows. In addition, you can click and drag icons from any of the menus onto the desktop in order to create shortcuts to your favorite programs.

Figure 7-4 shows the components of the GNOME desktop, which work as follows:

Home: Double-clicking this icon will open a file browser window displaying the contents of your /home folder, which is your personal area for storing files.

Trash: This is a clone of the Windows Recycle Bin, in that files can be dragged and dropped here to be "deleted," but can also be salvaged later by double-clicking this icon to browse the contents of the Trash.

Applications menu: This menu is similar to the Start menu's Program submenu under Windows, in that it allows quick access to most of the software installed on your system. All the software titles are arranged under submenus relating to what they do. The web browser and e-mail programs are collected under the Internet submenu, for example.

Places menu: This is similar to My Computer under Windows, in that it allows shortcut access to popular locations within the file system. You can also quickly browse the network for file-sharing-enabled computers and search for files on your own computer.

Desktop menu: This is similar to the Windows Control Panel, in that it allows you to change hardware and software settings on your computer. The Control Center icon lets you change superficial aspects of your setup, such as the wallpaper and screensaver, and the YaST icon allows you to change other settings, such as the hardware configuration. I explain how to use YaST to configure your hardware and software settings in Chapter 8.

Tomboy Notes: This applet allows you to create "sticky notes" on the desktop to remind yourself of certain things. To create a new note, click the icon, and then select Create New Note. The benefit of using Tomboy Notes is that the notes stick around, even after the computer has been rebooted, and there's no need to manually save each one.

Window list: This is the GNOME desktop equivalent of the Windows taskbar, in that any programs currently running will be listed here. You can click each to bring it to the top of the desktop, and also right-click each to minimize or maximize it.

Desktop Search: This allows you to search for files, e-mail messages, and even recently visited web pages. The functionality is very similar to the Google Desktop Search that you might have used under Windows, or the Spotlight feature of Apple OS X. Search terms can be formatted in the same way as those on web search engines like Google. For example, use the word *AND* between two words to ensure that both appear in the search results. To learn more, click the Help menu.

Resolution Switcher: Click here to quickly switch resolutions.

Software Updater: When configured correctly, as explained in Chapter 9, this applet will allow you to quickly see what security updates are available for your computer and also download and install them.

Volume: Click to display the volume slider, which you can use to increase or decrease the overall speaker volume of the computer. Double-clicking the icon will display the full Volume Control applet, which allows you to control all aspects of your PC's sound system.

Time and Date: This allows you to see the current time and date. Click this icon to see a monthly calendar. Click it again to make the calendar disappear.

Show Desktop: Clicking this icon will cause all open programs to instantly minimize, showing the desktop underneath. Clicking it again will revert the windows to their previous state.

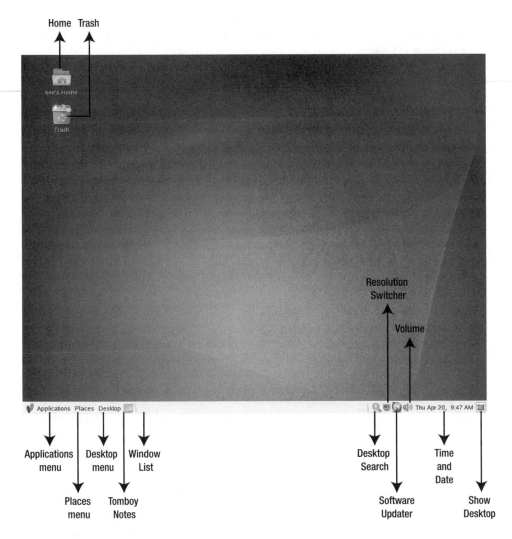

Figure 7-4. *The GNOME desktop is simple and clean, but broadly similar to what you might be used to in Windows.*

Quick Desktop Guide: KDE

The very first time you boot the KDE desktop, a tips screen will appear. Click the Close button at the bottom right to get rid of it. If you want to stop the tips screen from appearing on each boot, you can uncheck the Show Tips on Startup button. However, it will often present handy information about using KDE that you might find useful.

KDE's desktop contains a number of icons, including many that you might be used to under Windows, such as My Computer, which provides access to your file system, and the Wastebin, which is a clone of the Windows Recycle Bin.

Figure 7-5 shows the components of the KDE desktop, which work as follows:

OpenOffice.Org launcher: Clicking this icon will start OpenOffice.org, giving you a choice of templates to start working with the word processor, spreadsheet, presentations, drawing, and database applications. OpenOffice.org is covered in Part 6 of this book.

Firefox: Clicking this icon will start Firefox, the primary web browser offered by SUSE Linux.

SUSE Help: Clicking this icon will launch a brief welcome and help page, prepared by the creators of SUSE Linux, which will help you find useful resources online.

Wastebin: This is a clone of the Recycle Bin on the Windows desktop, in that programs can be dragged and dropped here for temporary deletion. Clicking the icon will open the Wastebin and let you fish out contents that have not yet been permanently deleted.

My Computer: Like its Windows counterpart, this icon lets you quickly access the file system of the SUSE Linux computer. You can see at a glance how much space is free on the various hard disks attached to your computer. The KDE My Computer window also shows technical details about your computer, such as the quantity of free memory and the CPU speed.

Network Browsing: Provided your computer is configured correctly (see "Accessing Windows File Shares and Servers" in Chapter 8), clicking this icon will open a Konqueror window that will display nearby computers or resources on the network.

Printer: This will open KJobViewer, which lets you manage items you've sent to the printer. I explain how to configure a printer in Chapter 8.

K menu: This is the KDE equivalent of the Windows Start menu. It provides access to most of the software installed on the system. In addition, the System submenu provides tools that you can use to configure and monitor the hardware and software in your system. The K menu also lets you log in and out of the system.

Home: Clicking this icon will open a file browser window displaying the contents of your /home directory, which is your personal file storage area on the hard disk.

Konsole: Clicking this icon opens a Konsole terminal window, where you can issue commands directly to SUSE Linux, via the BASH interface. I explain more about BASH in Part 4 of this book.

Help: Clicking this icon will let you access the KDE/SUSE Linux help system, which you can use to learn more about how applications under KDE work, as well as how to use specific SUSE Linux components.

Konqueror: Clicking this icon will launch Konqueror, which is KDE's built-in file and web browser. Once opened, Konqueror displays shortcuts to various popular places within the file system. To browse to a web site, simply enter its address into the Location bar.

■**Note** The KDE desktop under SUSE Linux offers both the Firefox and Konqueror web browsers. It's up to you which you choose. Generally speaking, Firefox is compatible with more web sites, but Konqueror is more tightly integrated into the KDE desktop experience.

Kontact: Clicking this icon will launch Kontact, which is the KDE mail, calendar, and personal information manager.

Pager: This lets you switch between two (or more) virtual desktops. I explain how virtual desktops work in the next section of this chapter.

Taskbar: Here, you can see at a glance which programs are currently running under KDE. As with Windows, clicking each button will bring it "to the top," and right-clicking each button will provide a number of options, including minimizing the window.

Desktop Search: This allows you to search for files, e-mail messages, and even recently visited web pages. The functionality is very similar to the Google Desktop Search, which you might have used under Windows, or the Spotlight feature of Apple OS X. Search terms can be formatted in the same way as those on web search engines like Google. For example, you can use the word *AND* between two words to ensure that both appear in the search results. To learn more, click the Help menu.

Volume: Click this icon to adjust the overall volume of your speakers. Clicking the Mixer button will display more-complicated controls for fine-grained control over the sound system.

KPowersave: If KDE is running on a notebook computer, this icon displays where the power for the current session is being drawn from: battery or an electrical power outlet. In addition, right-clicking the icon may allow you to hibernate or suspend your computer, depending on the capabilities of your computer.

Klipper: This applet is the KDE clipboard manager. It stores the recent history of items that have been cut or copied from documents. Clicking its icon lets you paste the clipboard contents into any document.

Software Updater: When configured correctly, as explained in Chapter 9, this applet will allow you to quickly see what security updates are available for your computer and also download and install them.

Clock: This applet displays the current time and date. Clicking the clock will display a monthly calendar.

BEHIND THE DESKTOPS: KDE AND GNOME

The two primary SUSE Linux desktop environments are based on software produced by the GNOME and KDE projects, respectively. These are two of the most well-established organizations currently producing desktop interfaces for Linux, as well as for other versions of Unix.

Although based on GNOME and KDE, the SUSE Linux's desktops have their own set of individual features and programs, as well as a unique look and feel. That said, they basically work in the same way as versions of GNOME and KDE that are used in other Linux distributions, such as Mandriva in the case of KDE, and Ubuntu in the case of GNOME.

The nature of open source software—whereby anyone can take the source code and create his own version of a program—makes SUSE's reinvention of the KDE and GNOME desktops possible. Unlike with Windows software, there can be more than one current version of a particular program or software suite, and each is usually tailored to the particular needs of one of the various Linux distributions.

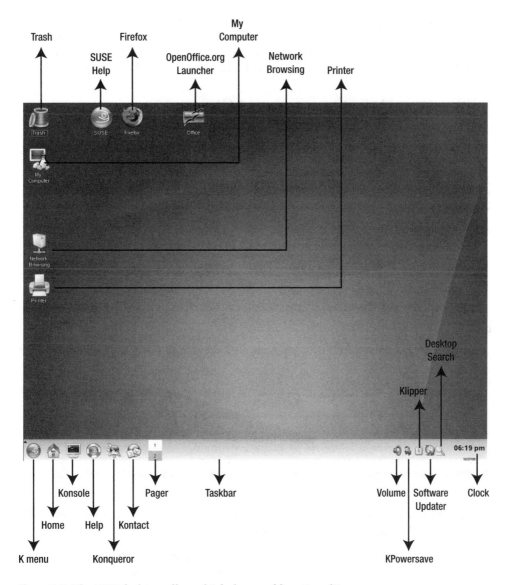

Figure 7-5. *The KDE desktop offers a high degree of functionality.*

Working with Virtual Desktops

Windows works on the premise of everything taking place on top of a "desktop." When you start a new program, that program runs on top of the desktop, effectively covering it up. In fact, all programs are run on this desktop, so it can get a bit confusing when you have more than a couple of programs running at the same time. Which Microsoft Word window contains the document you're working on, rather than the one you've opened to take notes from? Where is that My Computer window you were using to copy files?

SUSE Linux overcomes this problem by offering more than one desktop area, a system known as *virtual desktops*. Under KDE, this is achieved using the Pager tool, which is located to the left of the taskbar. Under the GNOME desktop, virtual desktops aren't activated by default, although you can use the Workspace Switcher applet to manually activate them.

Activating Virtual Desktops in GNOME

Here's how to activate virtual desktops in the GNOME desktop environment:

1. Right-click in a blank spot on the panel and select Add to Panel.

2. From the list, scroll to the bottom and select Workspace Switcher.

3. A new icon will appear on the panel. Right-click it and select Preferences.

4. In the Number of Workspaces box, click the up arrow so that you have more than one workspace. Two gives you a "spare" desktop, but many people find using four desktops is convenient and comfortable.

5. Click Close.

Using Virtual Desktops

Using virtual desktops is easy and is best explained by a demonstration.

1. Make sure that you're currently on the first virtual desktop (make sure that the 1 square is highlighted on the Pager, or the first square selected on the Workspace Switcher) and start up the web browser.

2. Click 2 in the Pager, or the second square on the Workspace Switcher. This will switch you to a clean desktop, where no programs are running—desktop number 2.

3. Start up the file browser (by clicking the Home icon), and you should see that the browser appears on your screen.

4. Click the 1 in the Pager, or the first square on the Workspace Switcher. You should switch back to the desktop that is running the web browser.

5. Click the 2 in the Pager, or the second square on the Workspace Switcher, and you'll switch back to the other desktop, which is running the file browser.

Tip Putting your mouse over the Pager or Workspace Switcher tools and scrolling the mouse wheel switches between the various virtual desktops instantly.

Creating Additional Virtual Desktops

You can create more than 2 virtual desktops—as many as 20 under KDE and 36 under GNOME—if you want to organize your work this way.

- To create more desktops under GNOME, follow the earlier instructions for setting up the Workspace Switcher and simply add more desktops.

- Under KDE, right-click the Pager icon and select Configure Desktops. In the Configure dialog box, drag the Number of Desktops slider until you have the number of desktops you want, as shown in Figure 7-6.

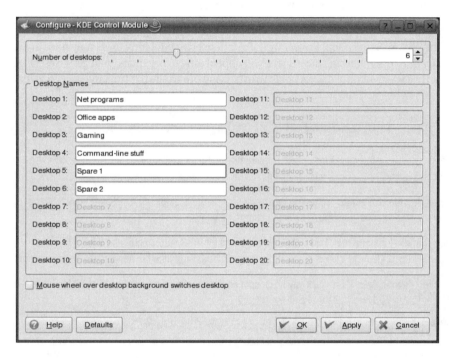

Figure 7-6. *Two virtual desktops are set up by default under KDE, but you can have as many as 20.*

Tip Right-clicking any of the program entries in the taskbar will bring up a menu where you can move a program from one virtual desktop to another. Select Move to Another Workspace under GNOME, or To Desktop under KDE.

Renaming Virtual Desktops

You can also rename each virtual desktop under both KDE and GNOME. This allows you to be even more organized. For example, you might reserve desktop 1 for running Internet programs and give it a name that indicates this, such as Net Programs. You might then use desktop 2 to run office programs, giving it an appropriate title; have a desktop 3 for file browsing; and so on.

These names will appear whenever you right-click and choose to send each program window to a different desktop.

- To rename virtual desktops under KDE, right-click the Pager, select Configure Desktops, and then type a name into each entry field for each desktop within the dialog box.

- Under GNOME, right-click the Workspace Switcher icon, select Preferences, and then double-click each entry in the Workspace Names list.

The Pager and Workspace Switcher provide a way of organizing your programs and also reducing the clutter. Some people swear by it. Experienced SUSE Linux users may have in excess of ten virtual desktops, although clearly this will appeal only to organizational geniuses! Other users think it's a waste of time. It's certainly worth trying out to see if it suits the way you work.

QUICK TIPS FOR PERSONALIZING THE DESKTOP

Chapter 10 is an in-depth explanation of how to customize SUSE Linux to your tastes. However, if you're already itching to tweak, here are some quick tips.

- **Changing the wallpaper:** Right-click any blank spot on the desktop. Under GNOME, select Change Desktop Background. Under KDE, select Configure Desktop.

- **Altering the look and feel:** Under GNOME, click Desktop ➤ Control Center and double-click the Theme icon. Under KDE, click K menu ➤ Personal Settings, and then the Appearance & Themes icon.

- **Adding new applets:** Right-click any blank spot on the panel. Under GNOME, select Add to Panel. Under KDE, select Add Applet to Panel.

- **Altering desktop fonts:** Under GNOME, click Desktop ➤ Control Center and double-click the Fonts icon. Under KDE, click K menu ➤ Personal Settings, and then the Appearance & Themes icon. Then click the Fonts icon.

- **Moving Items on the panel:** Right-click the relevant element and select Move (under GNOME you may have to uncheck Lock to Desktop first). To move items like the notification area/system tray, simply click and drag the grab handle to the left of the element. Under KDE, the grab handle is invisible until the mouse is placed over it.

- **Creating desktop shortcuts:** Click and drag items from the Applications/K menu to the desktop. Under KDE, a menu will appear when you do this. Simply select Link Here.

- **Altering mouse properties (including speed):** Under GNOME, click Desktop ➤ Control Center, and then double-click the Mouse icon. Under KDE, click K menu ➤ Personal Settings, click Peripheral Settings, and then click the Mouse icon.

Using the Mouse

As noted earlier, the mouse works mostly the same under SUSE Linux as it does under Windows: a left-click selects things, and a right-click usually brings up a context menu. Try right-clicking various items, such as icons on the desktop or even the desktop itself.

Tip Under KDE, right-clicking a blank spot on the desktop and selecting the Create New option from the menu lets you create shortcuts to applications, as well as create new folders and even new files. Under GNOME, right-click and select Create Folder, Create Launcher, or Create Document.

You can use the mouse to drag icons on top of other icons. For example, you can drag a file onto a program icon in order to run it. You can also click and drag in certain areas to create an elastic band and, as in Windows, this lets you select more than one icon at once.

SUSE Linux also makes use of the third mouse button for middle-clicking. You might not think your mouse has one of these but, actually, if it's relatively modern, it probably does. Such mice have a scroll wheel between the buttons, as shown in Figure 7-7, and this can act as a third button when pressed. If you're running the KDE desktop, try using the third button to click the desktop. You'll see a second type of context menu, offering the ability to organize your desktop windows for ease of access by, for example, cascading them. The third mouse button is used less in GNOME, but you can use it to click the title bar of the active window to bring the window underneath to the top.

Figure 7-7. *If your mouse has a scroll wheel, you can use it as a third mouse button in SUSE Linux.*

Tip Under KDE, middle-clicking has a number of other functions. Middle-click and hold one of the shortcut icons on the panel, for example, and you'll be able to move the icon, thereby repositioning it on the panel.

If your mouse doesn't have a scroll wheel, or if it has one that doesn't click, you might still be able to middle-click. Pressing the left and right mouse buttons at the same time emulates a middle-click, although it takes a little skill to get right. Generally speaking, you need to press one button a fraction of a second before you press the other button.

You can resize windows using the mouse in much the same way as in Windows. Just click and drag the edges and corner of the windows. There is one difference under GNOME, however. When a window is maximized, it can subsequently be moved by clicking and dragging the title bar. If you try this, you might also notice that the window you're dragging "snaps" back into place. Once a window nears the edge of the screen or, in some cases, another program window, it will jump the few pixels to fit flush against the edge. This makes lining up windows and organizing your desktop much easier.

Cutting and Pasting Text

SUSE Linux offers two separate methods of cutting and pasting text. The first method is identical to that under Windows. In a word processor or another application that deals with text, you can click and drag the mouse to highlight text, right-click anywhere on it, and then select to copy or cut the text. In many programs, you can also use the keyboard shortcuts of Ctrl+X to cut, Ctrl+C to copy, and Ctrl+V to paste.

However, there's a quicker method of copying and pasting. Simply click and drag to highlight some text, and then immediately click the middle mouse button where you want the text to appear. This will copy and paste the highlighted text automatically, as shown in Figure 7-8. This special method of cutting and pasting bypasses the usual clipboard, so you should find that any text you've copied or cut previously is still there. The downside is that it doesn't work across all applications within SUSE Linux, although it does work with the majority of them.

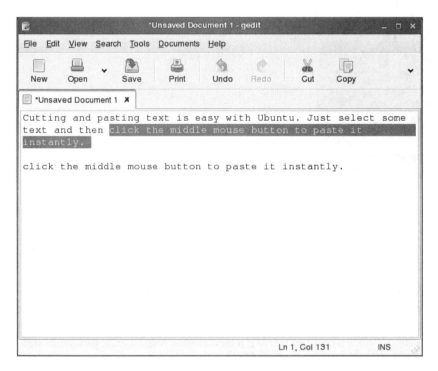

Figure 7-8. *Put the text cursor where you want the text to appear, highlight the text, and then middle-click to paste it instantly.*

Summary

This chapter covered booting into SUSE Linux for the first time and discovering the desktop. We've looked at starting programs, working with virtual desktops, using the mouse on the SUSE Linux desktop, and much more. You should have become confident in some basic SUSE Linux skills and ready to learn more!

In the next chapter, we'll look at getting your system up and running, focusing on items of hardware that experience day-to-day use.

CHAPTER 8

■■■

Getting Everything Up and Running

Like all modern Linux distributions, SUSE Linux is largely automated when it comes to setting up key hardware and software components. Key systems will work straight "out of the box," and most hardware will be automatically configured. However, you might need to tweak a few settings to make everything work correctly, and that's what this chapter is all about. You'll learn about hardware configuration, as well as a couple of vital software setups, including e-mail client configuration. By the end of this chapter, your system should be up and running efficiently, and ready for typical day-to-day tasks.

Before you start configuring hardware, you should understand a few fundamental facts about how SUSE Linux sees your computer hardware. Also, you need to know how to use the SUSE Linux configuration tools. After that, you can go directly to the section that covers the hardware or software device you wish to configure.

Hardware Support Under SUSE Linux

As with all modern versions of Linux, SUSE Linux is designed to work as well as possible as soon as it's installed. When Windows has been freshly installed, you might be used to installing drivers, but SUSE Linux has the majority of drivers built in. However, although drivers come installed for the majority of hardware, a little extra configuration might be necessary. Your printer will need basic setup before it can be used, for example. Also, in few cases, as for some wireless cards and 3D graphics cards, you may need to install a driver.

Other times in this chapter, I simply give advice on the best way of using particular hardware. For example, there are some notes you should bear in mind when using removable storage devices such as USB memory sticks. These work instantly, without configuration, but using them in the same way you might be used to under Windows could lead to data loss.

■**Note** In this chapter I don't explain how to configure the SUSE Linux multimedia system for playback of common audio and video file formats. Those configurations are covered in Chapters 18 and 19. However, I do spend a little time explaining how to configure the sound system so that you have complete control over its functions.

What Hardware Works?

The question of which hardware works under SUSE Linux is not one that's easily answered. However, Linux has a feather in its cap when it comes to hardware. Linux views hardware generically, rather than by make or model, and this makes hardware support easier. The people behind Linux work on providing drivers for the underlying hardware, rather than for actual makes and models. In fact, in many cases, the make and model information is ignored; SUSE Linux will probe the hardware to find out its technical details and provide a driver to match.

For all of this to make sense, you need to understand that, although many manufacturers produce their own branded hardware, there are usually only a handful of core technologies used throughout. In many cases, manufacturers reproduce "reference" hardware designs created by a couple of manufacturers. They simply apply their own branding and, often, their own exterior design to the hardware.

■**Note** This use of reference designs is especially true of 3D graphics cards. Open any computer hardware review magazine and take a look at photos of graphics cards from different manufacturers that utilize the same hardware. You'll see that they're practically clones of each other. The circuit boards use the same layout and the same components.

The result is that SUSE Linux hardware support is more comprehensive because it's less specific. Unlike with Windows, where a specific driver works for a certain piece of hardware, one driver under Linux can work with many hardware items.

■**Note** Sadly, Linux has not yet reached the stage of popularity where hardware vendors automatically offer drivers on the CD accompanying the product, as with Windows (and, to a lesser extent, Mac OS X).

Proprietary vs. Open Source

The people behind SUSE Linux are committed to using open source hardware drivers throughout. Other distributions of Linux often include proprietary drivers, for which the source code isn't shared, but this doesn't happen with SUSE Linux.

Unfortunately, this causes a handful of problems, Sometimes open source drivers are not available for esoteric items of hardware that have specialized goals and aren't commonly used. For example, open source drivers might not be available for business card printers, which are unique one-off devices produced by a specific manufacturer, or for barcode readers. In such cases, which are in the minority and probably won't affect the average user, you might need to download and install proprietary closed-source drivers. The good news is that very good installation instructions are often included within the driver file.

Sometimes you might find that an open source driver is available for a piece of hardware but is lacking vital functions that you need. An example is a 3D graphics card. Currently, most open source drivers for graphics cards don't fully utilize the 3D functions, although they do provide full 2D functionality, so are fine for general desktop use. The reason for this is that open source hardware drivers are normally produced by Linux kernel hackers, often independently of the manufacturers. The Linux kernel programmers would need to "reverse engineer" the graphics card to figure out how the 3D components work, and this is extremely difficult. The manufacturers of 3D cards are aware of this limitation and so make proprietary drivers available.

■**Note** The 3D graphics card manufacturers don't release their own open source drivers, because to do so would be to reveal trade secrets within their hardware to their competitors.

Later in this chapter, I'll explain how to install proprietary 3D graphics drivers, which you can use to replace the built-in open source drivers that SUSE Linux uses. You might wish to do this if you want to play 3D games under SUSE Linux. I'll also describe how to configure multiple-monitor support via dual-head graphics cards, which requires proprietary drivers because open source drivers don't currently support this function (with the exception of Matrox graphics cards).

Also, not all wireless card manufacturers release open source drivers for their cards, and you may need to install a wireless card driver. I'll explain how to do this in the "Using Wireless Networking Technology" section later in this chapter.

System Hardware Information

SUSE Linux offers an excellent tool to examine your system's hardware. The Hardware Information applet is contained within YaST, which is the core system tool that you'll use throughout most of this chapter to configure hardware and software. To access the tool, start YaST (in KDE, select K menu ➤ System ➤ YaST; in GNOME, select Desktop ➤ YaST), click the Hardware icon on the left, and then click the Hardware Information icon on the right.

The Hardware Information applet organizes the data according to hardware type, such as Disk, Keyboard, Network Card, and so on. Some hardware components are organized under the heading of the particular bus system they use, such as PCI or USB. This is especially true of some of the underlying system components, such as motherboard chipsets.

Click the small plus symbol next to each entry in the list on the left of the window to expand the tree view, and then look for your hardware, as shown in Figure 8-1. You will see a lot of information, all of it read straight from the hardware itself via Plug and Play probing. Within that, you should be able to find the name of the hardware device, which can be invaluable when trying to solve hardware problems (remember that the hardware will probably be identified by the hardware it contains, rather than by manufacturer model name).

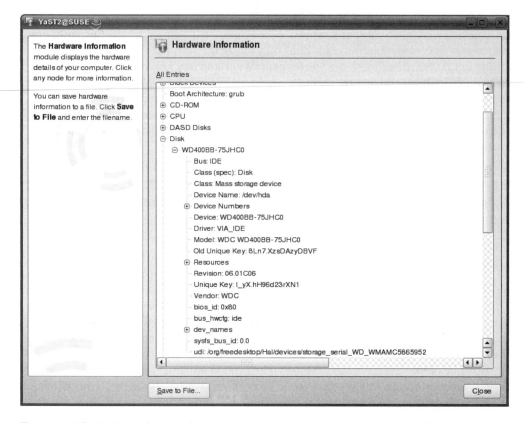

Figure 8-1. *The YaST Hardware Information tool reports details on every piece of hardware within your system.*

You might have noticed similarities with the Windows Device Manager applet, but there are some differences. As its name suggests, Device Manager is designed to let you tweak hardware settings (even if most people merely use it as an information tool). In contrast, Hardware Information simply shows details of your system. Most hardware configuration is handled by other modules within YaST, as described throughout the rest of this chapter.

Getting Started with the Configuration Tools

As noted in the previous section, YaST is the central SUSE Linux configuration tool. You can use it for the majority of tasks discussed in this chapter. However, for some tasks, you will need to issue commands directly within SUSE Linux by opening a terminal window and typing at a command-line prompt. Here, I'll explain the basics of using each of these tools.

Using YaST

YaST is SUSE Linux's unique and powerful system configuration software. It's similar to the Control Panel within Microsoft Windows, except much more powerful. It contains a variety of applet programs designed to let you configure hardware and software services.

To start YaST under the GNOME desktop, click Desktop ➤ YaST. Under KDE, click K menu ➤ System ➤ YaST. You'll need to enter the root password to use YaST, because it allows configuration of all hardware and software services.

The fundamentals of using YaST are easy to understand. On the left are several icons that represent general areas of your system that you're likely to want to configure, such as Hardware, Security and Users, and Software. Figure 8-2 shows an example. When you click a general icon on the left, a variety of additional icons appear on the right of the YaST window, offering fine-grained control over various aspects of your system. Simply click the icon to start that particular configuration applet.

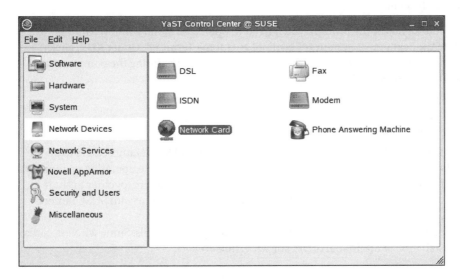

Figure 8-2. *The YaST categories are listed on the left side of the window, and the individual configuration applets are listed on the right.*

In the instructions in this chapter, I generally use the following format: Click Network Devices ➤ Network Card. By this, I mean to click the Network Devices icon on the left side of the program window, and then the Network Card icon in the list of icons that appears on the right.

Most configuration applets are wizard-based, so you should simply fill in the relevant details and click the Next button. Eventually, when all the necessary information has been gathered, click the Finish button. If you decide that you don't want to complete the wizard, click the Abort button.

Using the Command-Line Prompt

For some configuration steps discussed in this chapter, you will need to open a terminal window. This will give you access to the command-line prompt, where you can issue commands directly to SUSE Linux. The Linux command-line prompt is a little like MS-DOS, which you might have used in the early days of Windows, except it's a lot more powerful. As with DOS, you should hit Enter after typing each command.

I explain how to use the command-line prompt in detail in Part 4 of this book, beginning with Chapter 13. For this chapter's instructions, you should bear in mind the following:

- Type any commands exactly as they're written, including lowercase and uppercase letters.

- Check the command once you've typed it to be sure that it reads as is printed on the page. Even a stray space in the command could cause havoc.

- Don't be tempted to experiment at the prompt at this stage of your Linux learning curve. This is especially true when you switch to root user, which you'll be doing for nearly all the commands.

To enter commands at the prompt, you'll need to open a terminal window. Under GNOME, click Applications ➤ System ➤ Terminal ➤ Gnome Terminal. Under KDE, click K menu ➤ System ➤ Terminal ➤ Konsole. When you've finished entering the commands, simply close the terminal window.

Getting Online

Connecting your computer to the Internet is vital these days, and SUSE Linux caters to all the standard ways of doing so. Linux was built from the start to be an online operating system and is based on Unix, which pioneered the concept of networking computers together to share data back in the 1970s. However, none of this is to say that getting online with SUSE Linux is difficult! In fact, it's very easy.

In many cases, all you need to do is enter a few configuration details. Some wireless cards require the installation of additional driver software, however.

■**Caution** As soon as you successfully connect to the Internet, I advise you head straight to Chapter 9 and follow the instructions to update your system online. This will download many system bug fixes and security patches, some of which might make it easier to configure the rest of your hardware.

SUSE Linux offers two methods for connecting to networks: NetworkManager and ifup. Which you use depends on whether your computer is part of a wired or wireless network. The methods work as follows:

ifup: This is the component of SUSE Linux that traditionally controls networking. It is configured via a YaST module and is the standard method of connecting to Ethernet networks. It can also be used to join wireless networks, but it isn't as flexible as NetworkManager. If you use wired networks (Ethernet) exclusively, I recommend that you use ifup, and therefore configure your network via YaST.

NetworkManager: This is a new component within SUSE 10.1 that is designed to let you harness the flexibility offered by wireless networks. Once up and running, NetworkManager sits in the system tray and senses any wireless networks that are in range. NetworkManager settings persist across reboots, provided the network you last configured is in range. This means that NetworkManager is ideal for all kinds of wireless network card users, from those who frequently switch between different networks (mobile workers) to those who use a single wireless network card connection, such as that provided by a wireless network broadband router in a home/small office environment.

I'll explain how to use ifup to configure Ethernet connections, and then how to use NetworkManager to manage wireless connections, as well as how to install a wireless card driver, if necessary. If your Internet connection is through a dial-up modem, you can skip to the "Using Dial-Up Telephone Modems" section that follows the wireless technology discussion.

Using an Ethernet Card

Ethernet is one of the oldest and most established network technologies. When we talk about Ethernet, we're referring to wired networks—a configuration where all the computers on the network are connected by cabling to a central hub or router. This allows them to communicate and access shared resources, such as servers or printers. If an Internet gateway is available, this can also be shared among users.

■**Note** There are other wired network technologies in addition to Ethernet, such as Token Ring. However, these are old and have been largely superseded by Ethernet, which is by far the dominant form of wired network technology used today.

However, not all Ethernet setups are complex. If you have DSL or cable Internet broadband service, you might use a router, to which your computer might connect via Ethernet. In this case, you form a network of just one computer.

If you're running SUSE Linux on a desktop PC in an office environment, it's very likely that you will connect to the local area network using an Ethernet card.

Configuring via DHCP

Most computers that connect to a broadband router or an office network receive their configuration data via the Dynamic Host Control Protocol (DHCP), which is to say that your computer receives its IP, gateway, subnet mask, and Domain Name Service (DNS) addresses automatically, usually during bootup (or when the network cable is first attached if the computer is already up and running). The chances are that, if your computer is part of an Ethernet network via a wired connection, this is how it will work. The alternative is to use a static IP address, where the details are manually set on each computer, as described in the next section.

The good news is that, if your setup offers DHCP, no configuration is necessary. Provided the network cable is inserted, SUSE Linux will automatically use the connection, and you should be able to connect to the network or, if the service is available, go online.

If you find you can't get on the network, and you are sure DHCP is in use, you can take the following steps to confirm your network setup within SUSE Linux.

■**Note** It might sound patronizing, but if you run into problems, don't forget to make sure that the network cable is inserted! Check to make sure it's fully connected and that you hear the click that indicates it's locked into position. On the back of the Ethernet port, you should see LED lights start to flicker once this happens.

1. Start YaST and click Network Devices ➤ Network Card.

2. Select Traditional Method with ifup, and then click the Next button.

3. Select your network card in the list, as shown in Figure 8-3. Bear in mind that some modern computers have multiple network inputs, such as one for 10/100Mbit and another for 1Gbit, so be sure to click the entry that relates to the socket your network cable is plugged into. Then click Edit.

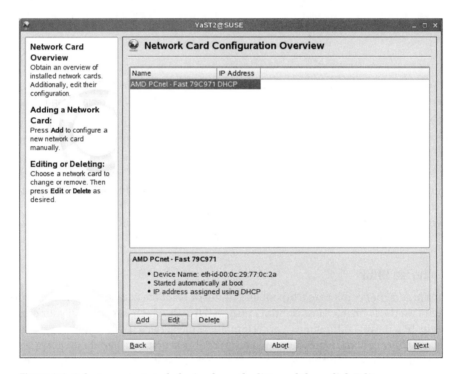

Figure 8-3. *Select your network device from the list, and then click Edit.*

4. In the window that appears, make sure that Automatic Address Setup via DHCP is selected. Then click Next.

5. This should return you to the original window. Click Next again. This will write the configuration changes to the system and reactivate the card.

Your network card should now be configured. You can test this by attempting to browse to a web site or use a network resource, if your computer is part of an office network without a shared Internet connection.

Configuring a Static IP Address

On some networks, you might be assigned an IP address, which you must enter manually, along with a few other networking addresses. This is normally referred to as a *static IP address*.

You should speak to your system administrator or technical support person to determine these settings. Ask the administrator for your *IP address*, *DNS server addresses* (there are usually two or three of these), your *subnet mask*, and the *router address* (sometimes referred to as the *gateway address*). The settings you will get from your system administrator will usually be in the form of a series of four numbers separated by dots, something like 192.168.1.233.

Once you know your settings, proceed as follows.

1. Start YaST and click Network Devices ➤ Network Card.

2. Select Traditional Method with ifup, and then click the Next button.

3. Select your network card in the list. Bear in mind that some modern computers have multiple network inputs, such as one for 10/100Mbit and another for 1Gbit, so be sure to click the entry that relates to the socket your network cable is plugged into. Then click Edit.

4. In the window that appears, click Static Address Setup, and then click Next.

5. In the Network Address Setup window, type the computer's designated static IP address in the IP Address box. In the Subnet Mask box, type the network's subnet mask. An example setup for my test network is shown in Figure 8-4.

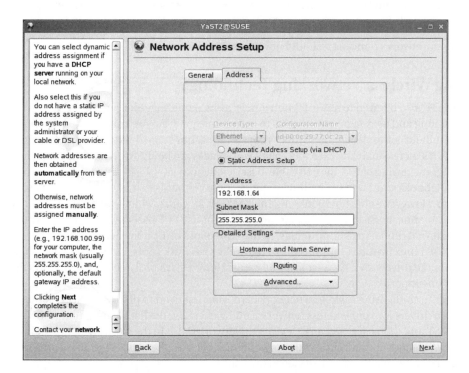

Figure 8-4. *Fill in the static IP address details in the relevant boxes, including the subnet mask.*

   6. Click the Hostname and Name Server button. At this stage, you may see a dialog box with a message stating that the resolver configuration file has been temporarily modified. Click the Modify button.

   7. In the window that appears, enter the DNS IP addresses into the Name Server boxes. You might first need to remove the check from the Update Name Servers and Search List via DHCP box. Usually, two DNS addresses are provided for a static IP setup, but you might find you need to use only one. Leave the other settings as they are, and then click the OK button.

   8. In the Network Address Setup window, click the Routing button.

   9. In the Default Gateway box, type the gateway address you were given (this is sometimes referred to as the *router address*). Then click the OK button.

■**Tip** In most small network setups, the gateway address is almost always identical to the IP address, except it will end with a 1. So if your IP address is 192.168.1.56, the gateway address will probably be 192.168.1.1.

---

   10. In the Network Address Setup window, click the Next button. Then click Next again in the following window. This will write your configuration changes and reactivate the network device.

   Your network connection should now work. If it doesn't, try rebooting.

Using Wireless Networking Technology

A wireless (also referred to as Wi-Fi) network is, as its name suggests, a network that does away with cabling and uses radio frequencies to communicate. It's more common for notebooks and handheld computers to use wireless connections, but some desktop computers also do. Indeed, it's increasingly the case that many workplaces are being switched to wireless networking, eschewing old-fashioned cable-based networking.

Notebooks and PDAs typically use wireless network cards that have an antenna built into the case. However, some notebooks might use PCMCIA cards, which will have an external square antenna, and some desktop computers might use PCI-based wireless cards, which have external rubber/plastic antennas, in the style of old cell-phone aerials.

SUSE Linux includes support for some wireless network cards, but not all. This is because open source drivers aren't available for all cards. However, it's possible to use Windows drivers for the unsupported cards.

Before configuring a wireless network card, you first need to discover if SUSE Linux has installed drivers for your wireless network card by checking the list of configurable devices. Start YaST and then click Network Devices ➤ Network Card. In the Network Setup Method window, select User Controlled with NetworkManager, and then click Next to see this list. Look for your wireless network device in the list.

■**Caution** Be sure that you aren't mistaken when trying to identify the wireless network card. Most computers with wireless network cards also have a wired Ethernet port, which will be included in the list of network devices. There's no hard-and-fast way of identifying the wireless network card, apart from the fact that *Wireless*, *Wifi*, or *wlan* might appear in its name within the list.

If your card isn't present in the list, then you'll need to install the Windows drivers using the ndiswrapper utility. Click the Abort button and then follow the instructions in the "Installing Windows Network Card Drivers" section later in this chapter.

If your wireless card does appear in the list of configurable devices, you do not need to install any drivers. You can proceed with managing your connections, as described next.

Managing Wireless Connections

I strongly recommend that you use NetworkManager to manage your wireless connections. Compared to using YaST for the same purpose, NetworkManager is more flexible, easier to use, and offers functionality that many wireless network users find useful, such as displaying the signal strength.

■**Note** In fact, only the GNOME desktop offers NetworkManager. The KDE desktop offers KNetworkManager, which looks a little different than the GNOME NetworkManager, but offers identical functionality and operates in almost exactly the same way. There are a handful of differences to do with password handling, which I'll mention in the instructions, but otherwise, the instructions for NetworkManager also work for KNetworkManager, and I don't differentiate between the two.

To activate NetworkManager, if it isn't already activated, start YaST and click Network Devices ➤ Network Card. In the window that appears, select User Controlled with NetworkManager. Click Next, and then click Next again. At this point, you should see a new system tray/notification area applet appear, as shown in Figure 8-5.

Figure 8-5. *The NetworkManager (bottom) or KNetworkManager (top) icon should appear in the system tray/notification area when you select to use NetworkManager within YaST.*

■**Note** On my KDE test system, the KNetworkManager icon didn't appear in the system tray until I logged out and logged back in again. To do this, click K menu ➤ Log Out, and then click the End Current Session button. Then log back in again using your username and password.

With NetworkManager activated, you can connect to a wireless network base station, whether or not it broadcasts its Service Set Identifier (SSID) name, and configure WiFi Protected Access (WPA) and Wired-Equivalent Privacy (WEP). The following sections explain how.

Connecting to a Wireless Network Base Station

If the wireless network base station you wish to connect to broadcasts its SSID name, it's easy to make the connection.

Click the NetworkManager applet to see a menu showing all wireless network base stations in your vicinity, along with a bar showing their signal strength, as shown in Figure 8-6. If any base station is protected with WEP or WPA, a shield icon will appear alongside the name (if you're using KNetworkManager under KDE, a padlock icon will appear). Select the base station you wish you connect to by clicking its entry in the list.

Figure 8-6. *Click the NetworkManager applet, and a list of the wireless networks in your locality will be displayed. In this case, the morse wireless network is available.*

After a few seconds, you will connect to the base station. If the base station has no WEP/WPA protection, a dialog box will appear on top of the NetworkManager applet explaining that you're connected. If the base station is protected with WEP or WPA, a dialog box will appear asking for the password/passphrase. In this case, see the upcoming "Configuring WPA/WEP Protection" section.

Connecting to a Wireless Network Base Station That Doesn't Broadcast Its SSID

Some wireless network base stations are set not to broadcast their SSID. This is a security measure to avoid any strangers in the vicinity stumbling across the wireless network station and connecting (sometimes by accident, if the computer is configured to connect to the nearest base station).

To connect to a base station that doesn't broadcast its SSID, follow these steps:

1. Click the NetworkManager applet and select Connect to Other Wireless Network.

2. In the dialog box, enter the SSID of the base station in the Network Name box, if you're using GNOME, or enter the SSID into the Name (ESSID) box if you're using KDE.

3. If the network has WEP/WPA protection, select it from the Wireless Security drop-down list if you're using GNOME. Under KDE, put a check in the Use Encryption box. Then refer to the next section.

Configuring WEP/WPA Protection

WEP and WPA are the two forms of encryption used to protect wireless network transmissions. They also protect the network against users joining without permission. Bearing in mind that some computers are configured to connect automatically to the nearest unprotected wireless network, this is a very good thing!

WPA is the more modern form of protection and is considered very secure. WEP is older and can be cracked by malicious interests in both its 40/64 and 128-bit forms.

■Note WPA2 has superseded WPA and fixes a number of security issues. However, it isn't as widely implemented as WPA.

SUSE Linux has excellent support for 40/64-bit and 128-bit WEP protection. It has moderate support for WPA Personal (also known as Pre-Shared Key, or PSK) and WPA Enterprise systems. In fact, support for WPA within SUSE Linux depends a lot on the wireless network hardware in use, including the wireless network device on the computer as well as the base station.

Although it is not as secure as WPA, I suggest that you use the older WEP protection in your wireless network setup, because this offers the highest chance of successful configuration under SUSE Linux. Indeed, in my tests, I could not configure my notebook or desktop computers to join a WPA network under SUSE Linux using Personal/PSK mode, the most common form of WPA. However, connecting to a wireless network protected with 40/64 and 128-bit WEP worked fine on both computers.

■Note Although WEP is often described as easy to crack, it still requires special skills that are beyond the range of most people. Consider your immediate environment. If your wireless network is within your home, is it likely that your neighbors will have the know-how to crack a wireless network connection? Do they even have a computer? What is the genuine likelihood that someone will attempt to crack your connection?

If you are worried about the security risks presented by WEP, consider why you need security. In most home and office environments, WEP and WPA are used simply to deter unauthorized users from connecting to the wireless network. WEP offers enough protection to prevent this. On the other hand, if you regularly transfer confidential data on the network—if you work in an office dealing with financial information, for example—then you should investigate the possibility of using WPA.

■**Caution** Some would argue that using any wireless network connection if you work with confidential data is foolish, even if you use WPA. If such data is being transmitted across the network, then a traditional wired network offers much greater security because the attacker must have physical access to the premises in order to connect a computer to the network. With wireless, an attacker can theoretically hack a network from outside the building, such as from a car, provided the signal reaches that far.

To configure WEP or WPA protection, follow these steps:

1. Assuming that the connection has already been established, as described in the previous sections, the NetworkManager applet should show a Wireless Security drop-down list offering a variety of WEP/WPA types (under KDE, you'll see a drop-down list under the Encryption heading). See Table 8-1 for a brief description of the protection types offered. Note that some types of protection listed in Table 8-1 might not be visible in the NetworkManager list. SUSE Linux is clever enough to detect if you're connecting to a WEP network, for example, and offer only WEP-related options.

2. Type your wireless network key, password, or passphrase into the Passphrase box or Key box. Figure 8-7 shows the dialog box in WEP mode, requesting a key. Unlike with some wireless network configuration utilities, there's no need to precede hex digits with 0x. Just type the password/passphrase directly into the box. If you're typing a passphrase and don't want it to be obscured by asterisks as you type, check the Show Passphrase box or Show Key box (under KDE, click the Show Credentials box).

Figure 8-7. *Once you've chosen the network you want to join, you'll be prompted to enter your password or passphrase. Type it into the Key box.*

3. If your network is protected with WPA Enterprise, you should consult your system administrator for the address of the RADIUS server, along with any login details you need (and possibly certificate files; your system administrator should be able to advise you further).

4. Once you click the Login to Network button, you'll be invited to store the WEP/WPA key, password, or passphrase in the GNOME Keyring or the KDE Wallet. If you don't wish to do this, click Cancel in the Keyring or Wallet setup screens. This will mean that you will need to enter the key, password, or passphrase each time you connect to the network. If you do wish to store the details, proceed as follows:

   - If you're running GNOME, NetworkManager will store your WEP/WPA password in an encrypted keyring file on the hard disk. Every time you connect to a new protected network, the WEP/WPA password for that network will be added to this keyring file. Upon first using the keyring (first connecting to a WEP/WPA network with NetworkManager), you'll be prompted to enter a password that will protect the keyring file. Following this, you'll need to enter the password whenever you connect to the wireless network, or whenever you set up a new wireless network connection, as shown in Figure 8-8.

Figure 8-8. *WPA and WEP passwords/passphrases are stored in a encrypted keyring file under GNOME.*

   - If you're running KDE, the WEP/WPA password for your connection will be stored in the KDE Wallet. If you haven't used this prior to setting up a WEP/WPA password, the Wallet Setup Wizard will automatically appear. Choose the Basic Setup, click Next, and then put a check alongside Yes, I Wish to Use the KDE Wallet to Store My Personal Information. Enter the password that you will use to protect the wallet, and then click Finish.

Provided you've entered the correct WEP/WPA key, you should now connect to the wireless network you selected earlier, although it might take a few seconds for a connection to be established.

Table 8-1. *WPA/WEP Modes Supported by NetworkManager*

Security Mode	Description
WEP 128-bit Passphrase	A sentence of up to 32 characters that can include characters and also spaces. Sometimes a long gibberish word is used. The passphrase system is designed to make it easier to remember passwords; in fact, the passphrase is converted to a hex key behind the scenes and this is used as the password.
WEP 64/128-bit Hex	A series of either 28 digits (14 hex pairs), in the case of a 128-bit hex key, or 10 digits (five hex pairs) in the case of a 64-bit hex key. Note that 64-bit hex is sometimes referred to as 40-bit hex. Here are some examples: `8f1c65aba8` (64-bit) and `7326d7f4c3f02376bf4544cc2c` (128-bit).
WEP 64/128-bit ASCII	A series of five characters, in the case of 64-bit ASCII, or 13 characters in the case of 128-bit ASCII.
WPA Enterprise	Also known as WPA-802.1x, a form of WPA used in corporate environments that involves the use of a Remote Authentication Dial In User Service (RADIUS) server. Users connect to the server via Extensible Authentication Protocol (EAP) for authentication purposes. Users might need a combination of passwords, usernames, and sometimes certificate files in order to connect, depending on the setup in use.
WPA Personal	Also known as Pre-Shared Key (PSK) mode, based on a passphrase that's between 8 and 63 characters long. It's the most common form of WPA protection and is frequently used in homes and offices. The passphrase can be a word or a series of words in a sentence, including spaces. Sometimes a long chain of gibberish characters is used.
WPA2 Enterprise	A revised and more secure implementation of WPA Enterprise.
WPA2 Personal	A revised and more secure implementation of WPA Personal.

SECURE CONNECTIONS ON THE NET

For home users, the use of online banking services involves the transfer of confidential data. So is this a good reason to use the strongest form of wireless network encryption with your broadband router? No, it isn't. In fact, it makes no difference.

This is because the transfer of confidential or financial data across the Web—to and from online banking sites, for example—is nearly always protected by Secure Socket Layer (SSL) HTTP. You can tell if this is the case with any site because the address will begin with `https://`. Additionally, most browsers display a padlock symbol at the bottom of the screen (the Firefox browser will also turn the background of the address bar yellow). Accessing such sites should be safe, even if your wireless network connection is "open," which is to say it isn't protected with either WEP or WPA.

Similarly, although online shopping sites don't use SSL while you're browsing, when it's time to pay, they always use SSL. This ensures your credit card details are encrypted. If the store doesn't adopt an `https://` address when you click to visit the virtual checkout, you shouldn't shop there!

So do you even need WEP or WPA protection if you simply use your wireless connection to browse the Internet? Yes. In addition to the risk of unauthorized users hopping onto your connection if it isn't protected, some web mail services transfer your username and password "in the clear," which is to say without using SSL. This means this information could be picked up by an eavesdropper. In the case of Hotmail and Yahoo Mail, you can select secure login, but it isn't activated by default. Google Mail appears to use SSL all the time for login, but after this, your e-mail messages are transmitted across the Internet in the clear and, in theory, can be eavesdropped by anyone, anywhere.

Installing Windows Network Card Drivers

Ndiswrapper is effectively an open source driver (technically described as a *kernel module*) that allows Linux to use standard Windows drivers for wireless network cards. You might think of ndiswrapper as a translation layer between the Linux kernel and the Windows drivers, which can be installed using ndiswrapper's configuration tools.

Using ndiswrapper is relatively simple; just a handful of commands are required. However, getting hold of the necessary Windows driver files is harder work because, unfortunately, ndiswrapper isn't designed to work with the usual method of driver distribution, which is through .exe files. Instead, ndiswrapper needs the specific .inf and .sys files—the Windows system files—that constitute the driver. These are contained within the .exe file and must be manually extracted.

■**Note** Of course, sometimes drivers are distributed as zip files. In that case, the relevant files are easy to get. Keep your fingers crossed that this will be the case for your particular hardware!

Not all cards have been proven to work with ndiswrapper, and it's not necessarily the case that, just because a driver is available for Windows, it will work under Linux. Sometimes trial and error is required. Annoyingly, drivers sometimes appear to work but then prove unreliable. Some might stop working. Some might even crash your system. The best plan is simply to give it a try.

■**Tip** Ndiswrapper gets better and better with every new release. This is why it's a good idea to update your system on a regular basis, as described in Chapter 9.

Ndiswrapper consists of two components: the kernel module and some configuration tools. Both are installed using the same software package, which is contained on the SUSE Linux installation DVD-ROM provided with this book. Follow these steps to install ndiswrapper:

1. Start YaST and click Software ➤ Software Management.

2. In the window that appears, type ndiswrapper into the Search box and click Search.

3. In the list of results on the right, put a check alongside the entry for ndiswrapper, as shown in Figure 8-9. (*Don't* click any of the entries beneath for ndiswrapper-kmp-bigsmp and so on, unless you're using the bigsmp kernel, which is likely only if your computer is a very high-end workstation or server.)

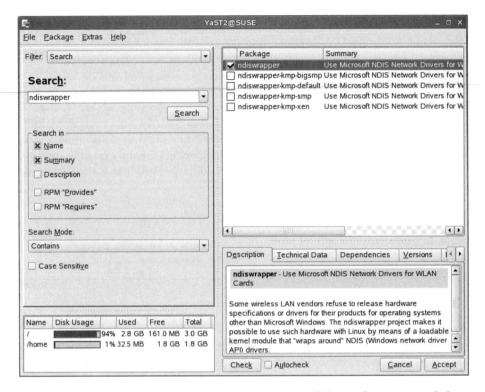

Figure 8-9. *Before using ndiswrapper, it's necessary to install the configuration tools from the SUSE Linux DVD.*

4. You'll be shown a warning about ndiswrapper being unsupported by SUSE, but it's safe to ignore this, so click OK to close the dialog box.

5. Click the Accept button at the bottom right of the software installation window. You'll need the SUSE Linux installation DVD-ROM, so insert it when prompted.

Once the ndiswrapper configuration software is installed, you can install the Windows XP wireless network card drivers. This is a three-part procedure:

- Identify the wireless network card hardware and then source the appropriate Windows driver.

- Extract the necessary .sys and .inf files from the driver archive (and possibly .bin files, although this is rare).

- Use the ndiswrapper configuration tools to install the Windows driver.

You will need another computer that's already online to download some files and check the ndiswrapper web site for information. If your computer dual-boots, you can use your Windows setup to do this.

In the following instructions for completing this procedure, I explain how to make an ASUS 802.11g wireless network card, built into an ASUS A6R notebook, work under SUSE Linux using ndiswrapper. The instructions remain essentially the same for all types of wireless network cards. Obviously, some specific details, such as download addresses, will differ.

Note that these steps make your wireless network card accessible under Linux. Once completed, you can use the NetworkManager applet to connect to wireless base stations and configure WEP/WPA protection, as described earlier.

Identifying Your Wireless Card and Sourcing Drivers

To identify the wireless network card for use with ndiswrapper, it's necessary to discover two sets of information: the make and model of the hardware, as reported by the SUSE Hardware Information tool, and the PCI ID number. The make and model of the hardware are as identified by SUSE Linux as a result of system probing, rather than what's quoted on the packaging for the wireless network card or in its documentation. These details will usually relate to the manufacturer of the underlying hardware, rather than the company that manufactured the wireless card. The PCI ID is two four-digit hexadecimal numbers used by your computer to identify the card internally. The same PCI ID numbering system is used by both Windows and SUSE Linux, which is why it's so useful in this instance.

You can find both the PCI ID and the make/model information using the YaST Hardware Information tool, as follows:

1. Start YaST and click Hardware ➤ Hardware Information.

2. In the hardware list that appears, look for the entry relating to your wireless network card. Even though it doesn't have a driver installed, it will still appear in this list, most likely under the Network Card heading. Click the small plus symbol alongside any menu entry to expand it. On my test notebook, containing an ASUS wireless network card, the card's model name and number were listed as BCM4318 [AirForce One 54g] 802.11g Wireless Lan Controller. As anticipated, the make and model don't relate to those listed in the wireless network card's documentation (the notebook's manual lists the card simply as an ASUS 802.11g card). This is because SUSE Linux is identifying the hardware generically, reading information from its component hardware.

3. Click the plus symbol next to the entry for the wireless network card to expand it in the list. Then look for the line that begins udi:. At the end of this line, you will see two sets of four letters and numbers that are separated by underscore characters. For example, on my test notebook these were 14e4 and 4318, as shown in Figure 8-10.

■Note These two clusters of letters and numbers are actually hexadecimal digits. For more details on the hexadecimal system, see http://en.wikipedia.org/wiki/Hexadecimal.

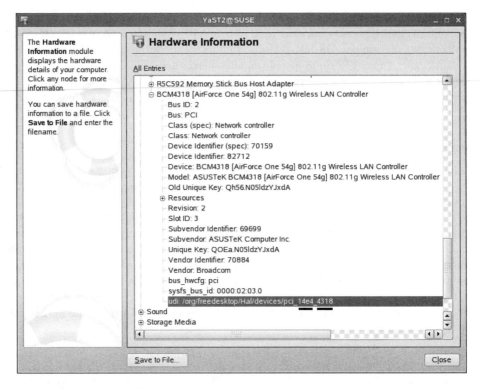

Figure 8-10. *Find the PCI ID of your wireless network card by looking at the two clusters of numbers and letters at the end of the* udi: *line. I've underlined them in this screenshot taken on my test system.*

4. Make a note of the four letters and numbers at the end of the udi: line. When written alongside each other, these become the PCI ID number. In written form, they're usually separated by a colon, so in my case, the PCI ID of the wireless network card is 14e4:4318. If either of the sets of letters or numbers is less than four characters, simply add preceding 0s to make four characters. For example, on my desktop PC, the end of the udi: line read 1814_201. I added a 0 before 201, making for the complete PCI ID of 1814:0201. On another of my test PCs, the end of the udi: line read 168c_13. I added two zeros before the 13 to make a PCI ID of 168c:0013.

5. Using another computer that's able to go online, visit http://ndiswrapper.sourceforge. net/mediawiki/index.php/List. This is a listing of the wireless network devices that have been proven to work with ndiswrapper.

■**Note** The URL in step 5 was correct as this book went to press. If you find it is no longer accurate, use a search engine to find the list, using "ndiswrapper list" as a search term.

---

6. Using the search function of your browser, look for the PCI ID number you noted earlier, in the format described in step 4. For example, with the PCI ID I discovered on my test notebook, I searched for 14e4:4318.

7. Many entries in the list may match your PCI ID. If that's the case, keep searching and try to find the one that best matches your hardware. Do this by matching not only the PCI ID, but also the manufacturer and model name of the hardware, which will be listed in the Card: part of the entry in the list (and/or within the Chipset: section, too). Remember that you should look for the make and model details reported by the YaST Hardware Information tool, rather than the make and model number quoted on the hardware itself or within its documentation. In my case, I found an entry in the list quoting the correct PCI ID, and also quoting the make and model number of Broadcom Corporation BCM4318 [AirForce One 54g] 802.11g Wireless LAN. A perfect match for my notebook! If you can't find an exact match for the make and model, select one that sounds likely. For example, if the PCI ID matches but the model number is slightly different, try it anyway.

■**Note** The rest of the description within the entry on the ndiswrapper web site might relate to a different computer than yours, or a different Linux distro. This can be ignored. The only thing to watch out for is any mention of x86_64, which indicates the entry in the list relates to 64-bit Linux. The version of SUSE Linux supplied with this book is 32-bit. If you encounter an entry relating to x86_64, keep searching.

---

8. Look within the entry in the list for a direct link to the driver file. Sometimes this isn't given and a manufacturer web site address will be mentioned, which you can visit and then navigate through to the driver download section (usually under the Support section within the web site). Download the Windows XP driver release.

Extracting the Driver Components

Once the drivers are downloaded, you'll need to extract the .sys and .inf files relevant to your wireless network card. These are all that ndiswrapper needs. However, extracting the files can be hard to do, because often they're contained within an .exe file. Most driver .exe files are actually self-extracting archive files. Additionally, the driver file will probably contain drivers for several different models of hardware, and it's necessary to identify the particular driver .inf file relevant to your wireless network card.

If the driver you've downloaded is a zip file, your task will probably be much easier. Simply double-click the downloaded zip file to look within it.

If the driver is an .exe file, you need to extract the files within it. With any luck, you might be able to do this using an archive tool like WinZip (www.winzip.com), assuming that you've downloaded the file using Windows. Open the archive using the File ➤ Open menu option within WinZip. You may need to select All Files from the File Type drop-down list in order for the .exe file to show up in the file list. As a better alternative, if you're using Windows, I recommend an open source and free-of-charge program called Universal Extractor, which can be downloaded from www.legroom.net/modules.php?op=modload&name=Open_Source&file= index&page=software&app=uniextract. This program can extract files from virtually every kind of archive, including most driver installation files. After you've installed Universal Extractor, right-click the installation .exe file and select UniExtract to Subdir. This will create a new folder in the same directory as the downloaded file, containing the contents of the installer file.

After you've opened your zip file or extracted your .exe file, look for the directory containing the actual driver files. Often, this directory is called driver; sometimes it's named after the operating system for which it contains files, such as Win_XP. If you've ever installed Windows drivers, this will sound familiar. Once you've found the relevant directory, click and drag the .inf, .sys, and .bin files (although you may not find any .bin files; they're only used in a handful of drivers) to a separate folder. You can ignore any other files, such as .cab and .cat files.

The task now is to find the .inf file for your hardware. If there's only one .inf file, that's the one you need. Otherwise, you'll need to search each .inf file until you find the correct one. Open the .inf file in a text editor (double-clicking will do this in Windows) and, using the search tool, search for the first part of the PCI ID, as discovered earlier. For example, I searched for 14e4. If this isn't found within the file, move on to the next .inf file and search again. When you get a search match, it will probably be in a long line of text but to the right of the text VEN_. Then look further along that line to see if the rest of the PCI ID is mentioned, probably to the right of text that reads DEV_. In my case, the entire line within the .inf file read as follows (I've highlighted the two PCI ID parts in bold):

%BCM430B_DeviceDesc% = BCM43XX, PCI\VEN_**14E4**&DEV_**4301**&SUBSYS_12F3103C

If you see both component parts of the PCI ID in the line, as in my example, you've found the .inf file you need.

You must now transfer the .inf file, along with the .sys and .bin files (if any .bin files were included with the driver) to the computer on which you want to install the drivers. Put them on some sort of removable media (a floppy disk, CD, or USB memory stick, for example). On the computer on which you wish to install the drivers, copy the files from the removable storage device into an empty folder on the desktop. Name the empty folder driver.

■**Note** If you've used a USB memory stick to transfer the files, the memory stick should appear automatically on the desktop as an icon as soon as it's inserted. When you've finished with it, right-click it and select Unmount Volume. You must do this before physically removing any kind of USB memory device, as explained later in this chapter.

Using Ndiswrapper to Install the Drivers

To install the driver using ndiswrapper, follow these instructions:

1. Open a terminal window. Under GNOME, click Applications ➤ System ➤ Terminal ➤ Gnome Terminal. Under KDE, click K menu ➤ System ➤ Terminal ➤ Konsole.

2. In the terminal window, type the following, entering your root password when prompted:

```
su -
[Enter root password]
```

3. Type the following to switch to the directory containing the driver files (replace *<username>* with your own username):

   cd /home/*<username>*/Desktop/driver

4. To install the driver, type the following (replace *filename.inf* with the name of the .inf file you discovered following the instructions in the previous section):

   ndiswrapper -i *filename.inf*

5. Type the following:

   ndiswrapper -m

   This will write the ndiswrapper configuration to the Linux kernel system files.

6. Close the terminal window.

7. Start YaST and click Network Devices ➤ Network Card.

8. In the Network Setup Method window, select User Controlled with NetworkManager.

9. In the Network Card Configuration Overview window, click the Add button.

10. In the Manual Network Card Configuration window, select Wireless from the Device Type drop-down list. In the Module Name box, type ndiswrapper. *Leave all the other fields containing their default contents,* even if that means they're left blank. When you've finished, the Manual Network Card Configuration window should appear as shown in Figure 8-11. Click Next to continue.

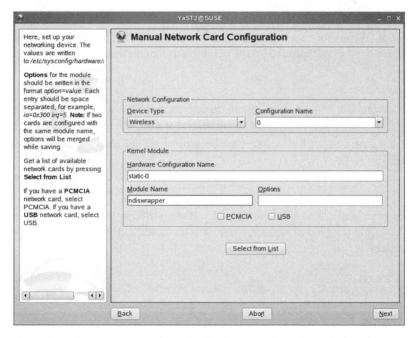

Figure 8-11. *Choose Wireless from the Device Type drop-down list, and type ndiswrapper into the Module Name box. But don't alter anything else!*

11. In the Network Address Setup window, click Next without changing anything.

12. In the Wireless Network Card Configuration window, click Next without changing anything. You'll see a warning dialog box about not using encryption, which you can ignore (you will be given the chance to configure encryption separately later on).

13. In the Network Card Configuration Overview window, click Next again. Then close YaST.

At this point, you can delete the desktop directory containing the driver files. The wireless network device should now be fully functional. You can connect to a wireless base station and configure WEP/WPA encryption, if applicable, as described earlier in the chapter.

■**Caution** On one of my test PCs, I found that the wireless network connection wouldn't work correctly until I rebooted. After that, it worked fine.

Using Dial-Up Telephone Modems

In our world of high-speed broadband connections, we sometimes forget that a sizable minority of people use telephone dial-up to connect to an ISP. For such people, SUSE Linux offers good and bad news. The good news is that SUSE Linux includes fuss-free software that can be used to configure connections and then dial up with the click of a mouse. The bad news is that, taken as a whole, SUSE Linux support for dial-up modems isn't very strong.

If your modem is external and connects to the serial port, there's a very good chance SUSE Linux will work fine with it. However, if the modem connects to the USB port, is built into your computer, or is provided on a PCMCIA card, then SUSE Linux support is less certain. This is because the drivers for many modems like this aren't released under an open source license. Therefore, they aren't included on the SUSE Linux installation DVD.

■**Note** Unlike with previous releases of SUSE Linux, the developers of SUSE 10.1 decided not to distribute modules that aren't licensed under the GNU Public License (GPL) or a GPL-compatible license. The practical upshot of this is that some modems that worked with older versions of SUSE Linux may no longer work under SUSE Linux 10.1.

There's no quick way to find out if your modem is supported, other than to follow the instructions for configuring it and attempt to use it. If the modem doesn't work, you can try using a winmodem.

WINMODEMS

Some years ago, hardware manufacturers realized that they could produce dial-up modems more cheaply if they shifted the hard work of decoding the signal onto the computer itself. With the work offloaded, the modem's circuitry could contain fewer and simpler components, thus saving money.

For this to work, a special hardware driver was needed that effectively works as a middleman, handing the decoding work to the computer's CPU. Unlike with other hardware drivers, it isn't simply a matter of making the hardware work with the operating system. Effectively, the drivers for such modems needed are a separate piece of software within themselves. Because of their need for this special driver software, which usually only ran on Windows, the modems became known as *winmodems*.

As you might anticipate, using the modems under Linux presents many problems, chief among them being that Windows and Linux are two separate operating systems and, generally speaking, are incompatible. Although solutions exist and the problems aren't insurmountable, setting up a winmodem under Linux often involves quite a lot of additional configuration. Additionally, the software required isn't released under a license compatible with SUSE Linux, and for this reason isn't included on the SUSE Linux DVD supplied with this book.

There are many types of winmodems, and each is configured in a different way. You can find step-by-step information and the necessary software at the linmodems.org web site. Using a computer that can get online, visit http://linmodems.org. Additionally, the user-friendly guide at http://linmodems.technion.ac.il/first.html might also be of help.

Configuring the Modem Hardware

Before installing and configuring the dial-up software, you need to set up the modem hardware using YaST. This involves creating a dial-up profile, so you'll need the dial-up ISP phone number as well as your username.

To configure a modem for dial-up access, follow these steps:

1. Make sure that NetworkManager is disabled (if you're using a notebook, it may have been activated by default).

2. Start YaST and click Network Devices ➤ Network Card.

3. In the window that appears, click Traditional Method with ifup, click Next, and then click Next again in the following window.

4. You should find that YaST is still running and the network configuration window is active. Click the Modem icon.

5. YaST will attempt to detect your modem, which might take a few seconds. If your modem is detected, it will appear in the list. Make sure it's selected, and then click the Edit button. If you are using an external modem connected to your serial port, it might not be detected. In that case, click the Add button. Both actions lead to the same configuration windows.

■**Caution** As mentioned earlier in this chapter, SUSE Linux sees your computer in terms of the actual hardware components it uses, rather than by make and model. Sometimes this means you need to keep your wits about you. On my test PC, my external USB modem was branded on the box and on its case as a Zoom V.90 USB Faxmodem. However, SUSE Linux identified it as a Conexant Systems (Rockwell) USB ACF Modem, because this is the name of the hardware inside the modem.

---

6. In the Modem Parameters window, set the parameters as follows:

  - If your modem wasn't detected by YaST and is connected to the serial port, you should select /dev/ttyS0 from the Modem Device drop-down list, as shown in Figure 8-12. This assumes that your modem is connected to the first serial port (if your computer has two serial ports). If later you find the modem doesn't work, return to this step and select /dev/ttyS1. If the modem *was* automatically detected, leave the contents of the Modem Device box unchanged.

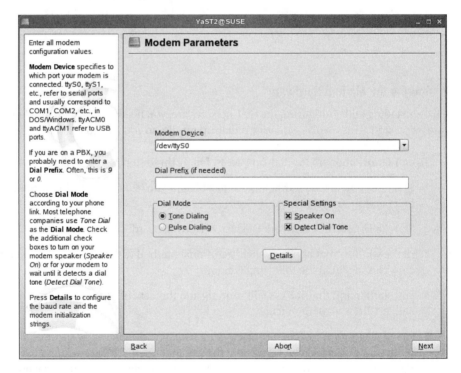

Figure 8-12. *If your modem was detected by SUSE Linux, don't change the entry in the Modem Device field.*

  - If you work in an office where a number must be dialed to get an outside line, enter it into the Dial Prefix box. Otherwise, leave this field blank.

- In the Dial Mode section, select either Tone Dialing or Pulse Dialing. Very nearly all modern telephone systems use tone dialing, but if you know your local phone system uses pulse dialing, select it here.

- In the Special Settings section, you can select whether to turn the modem speaker on when dialing. This is useful because it serves as confirmation that the modem is working. You can also configure the modem to dial only if it can detect the modem dial tone. It's sometimes useful to deactivate this feature if you have telephone services that notify you by changing the dial tone.

7. Once you've made your choices, click the Next button.

8. SUSE Linux uses a database containing details of many worldwide ISPs, including the dial-up numbers. You should certainly investigate this, but I recommend that you define your own entry by clicking the New button.

9. Fill in your ISP information, as follows:

- In the Provider Name box, enter a name that you can use for future reference. This can be anything you wish.

- In the Phone Number box, type the phone number as you would type it on a phone handset, including any area code.

- In the Authorization box, type your username into the relevant field. This should be the username for your ISP, not your SUSE Linux login username!

- If you would like SUSE Linux to remember the password for your dial-up account, remove the check from Always Ask for Password, and then type the password. Alternatively, if you don't want to store the password on your hard disk and would like to be prompted each time for the password, leave the box checked.

10. After you've entered the ISP details, click the Next button.

11. In the next window, configure your connection, as follows:

- Put a check alongside Dial on Demand if you would like you computer to dial up whenever you attempt to go online, such as when you open the browser and attempt to open a site. This can be useful, but you'll need to remember to manually go offline when you've finished, as explained in the following sections.

- The Modify DNS When Connected and Automatically Retrieve DNS boxes should both be left checked. These are technical settings related to how SUSE Linux looks up Internet addresses.

- The Stupid Mode check box should be left unchecked, unless you find that you can't connect later on. It ignores some prompts from the ISP's connection server that might be incompatible with the way SUSE Linux works. However, this option is rarely necessary.

- The Idle Time-Out Setting specifies the time after which, when there's been no activity (data sent or received), the connection should automatically disconnect. By default, this is set to 300 seconds (5 minutes). You might want to set it to less, but 5 minutes is a good average, bearing in mind it's easy to spend a couple of minutes reading a web page without requesting any further data from the ISP.

  - The IP Details box allows you to specify a static IP address. Very few ISPs make use of this feature, so it can be ignored.

12. Click Next, and then click the Finish button. You'll see a dialog box asking if you want to configure e-mail. This is designed to configure SUSE Linux's built-in mail system for use with dial-up connections, and most people don't use the mail system, so click the No button.

Installing KInternet

You must now install the KInternet application that's used to actually dial up on demand in KDE and GNOME. Follow these steps:

1. Start YaST and click Software ➤ Software Management.

2. In the window that appears, type kinternet in the Search box and click the Search button.

3. Put a check alongside the kinternet entry in the list. Then click Accept.

4. You'll need the SUSE Linux installation DVD. Once installation has finished, click No when asked if you want to install any other packages.

Your modem is now configured and ready for use. The next section explains how to connect and disconnect.

Dialing Up to Your ISP

Under KDE and GNOME, you can use KInternet to both connect and disconnect from your ISP.

■**Note** In theory, the Modem Lights applet could be used under the GNOME desktop to connect and disconnect from your ISP. However, this isn't set up for use with the modem profile you configured using YaST. Additionally, the KInternet application is arguably much more powerful than Modem Lights and a better choice.

Follow these steps to use KInternet:

1. Under GNOME, click Applications ➤ Internet ➤ Dial-up ➤ KInternet. Under KDE, click K menu ➤ Internet ➤ Dial-Up. After a few moments, the KInternet icon will appear in the notification area/system tray.

2. To connect, simply click the icon once. Alternatively, right-click the icon and select Dial-In. A lightning flash will appear above the icon, as shown in Figure 8-13.

Figure 8-13. *When KInternet is attempting to dial up, the icon will have a lightning flash above it.*

3. If during modem setup you selected to type the password each time you log in, at this stage, you will see the KDE Wallet Setup Wizard window, even if you're running the GNOME desktop. This can securely store the ISP password. If you want to store the password in the secure wallet file, choose Basic Setup, click Next, and then put a check alongside Yes, I Wish to Use the KDE Wallet to Store My Personal Information. Enter the password that you will use to protect the wallet, and then click Finish. You'll then be asked to input your ISP dial-up password, so do so. If you don't want to store the password on the hard disk, and type it each time, simply choose not to use the wallet.

4. If you don't connect the first time you try, as can happen sometimes with dial-up connections, click to try again. You'll be able to tell when the modem is connected because the system tray icon will change to be a plug and socket connected together. When data is transferred, the icon will also change to indicate the flow of data.

5. To disconnect from your ISP, click the KInternet icon again. Alternatively, right-click and select Hang-Up.

NOTEBOOK TOUCHPAD CONFIGURATION

Generally, a notebook computer will not need any configuration above and beyond what's outlined in this chapter. For example, if you have a PCMCIA wireless network card, you can simply follow the instructions for configuring a wireless card.

However, there is one major difference between a notebook and a desktop computer: many notebooks include a touchpad for controlling the mouse. Sadly, SUSE Linux doesn't offer a tool to configure the touchpad. You might already have noticed that the standard tools under GNOME and KDE don't affect the touchpad. They apply only to any standard mice that are attached, perhaps by the USB port.

Continues

This doesn't matter a great deal, unless you happen to dislike the tap-to-click function of touchpads, whereby a tap on the touchpad acts as a single left click. Often this can lead to misclicks. This function is activated by default under SUSE Linux. Deactivating it involves editing a configuration file. This may not be a common procedure for beginners, but if you follow these instructions, you shouldn't have any problems.

1. Open a terminal window. Under GNOME, click Applications ➤ System ➤ Terminal ➤ Gnome Terminal. Under KDE, click K menu ➤ System ➤ Terminal ➤ Konsole.

2. In the terminal window, type the following:

   ```
   su -
   [Enter your root password]
   ```

3. If you're running GNOME, type the following:

   ```
   gedit /etc/X11/xorg.conf
   ```

   If you're running KDE, type the following:

   ```
   kate /etc/X11/xorg.conf
   ```

   Don't worry about error output in the Gnome Terminal window. Eventually, an error Session Chooser dialog box will appear. Click New Session.

4. In the text editor, press Ctrl+F to bring up the search box. In the search field, type `synaptics`. Then click Find.

5. You should find the search function highlights the word within the file. Close the search box (if it hasn't already closed), and then scroll down to the end of the cluster of lines that the word `synaptic` is within. At the bottom will be a line that reads similar to the following, although the numbers might be different:

   ```
   Option    "ZAxisMapping" "4 5"
   ```

6. Press Enter at the end of that line to insert a new line, and then type the following:

   ```
   Option    "MaxTapTime" "0"
   ```

   The line mentioning `ZAxisMapping` will be followed by your new line, and then a line that reads `EndSection`.

7. Click File ➤ Save, and then quit the text editor.

8. Reboot your computer. When the desktop appears, you should find that the tap-to-click function no longer works.

Adding a Printer

SUSE Linux has extremely capable printer support, and you should find that most models work perfectly once they've been configured. In the rare instance of a printer driver not being available, as sometimes happens with models of printers new to the market, you can usually find a near match that works.

Printing under Linux is handled by the Common Unix Printing System (CUPS). As the name suggests, this is the printing system used under most versions of Linux and Unix, as well as Mac OS X. Although many CUPS printer drivers usually aren't created by the printer manufacturers, it's claimed that they offer equal, if not better, control over the printer.

In addition to working with a printer directly attached to your computer, SUSE Linux can also use network printers. If you work in an office environment, you may be expected to access a shared printer that might be connected directly to the network via a printer server or connected to a computer server/workstation. SUSE Linux is compatible with both.

Configuring a Local Printer

Although both GNOME and KDE offer their own tools to add and configure printers, I advise using YaST because it offers quick and pain-free configuration.

■**Note** The printer configuration tools under GNOME, KDE, and YaST all do the same thing: they act as an interface by which the CUPS system can be configured. Because of this, configuring a printer using YaST will mean it's available to both GNOME and KDE, because both use CUPS.

Follow these steps to configure a local printer:

1. Start YaST and click Hardware ➤ Printer.

2. YaST should automatically detect your printer, and it should appear in the list. Make sure it's selected and click the Edit button. If your printer is a very old parallel port model, it might not be detected. In that case, read the instructions for configuring an unrecognized printer in the next section.

3. Choose your make and then the model of your printer from the list, as shown in Figure 8-14, and then click Next. If you can't find an identical match, choose the nearest model. For example, the Epson Stylus CX-3600 printer attached to my test PC wasn't in the list, so I chose the Stylus CX-3200 instead.

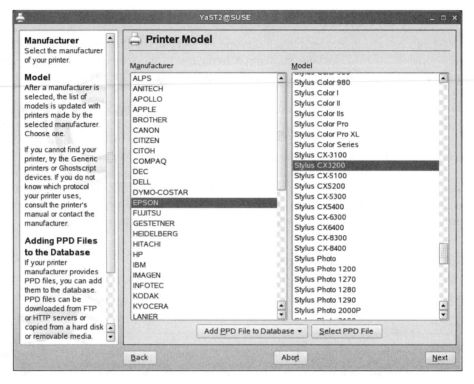

Figure 8-14. *Choose your make and model from the lists within YaST. If you can't find an exact match, choose the nearest similar model.*

4. You now have an opportunity to fine-tune some of the printer's settings. These settings will then be used as the default. The Restriction Settings option can be used to limit which users can use the printer. On a system with only one user, this can be ignored. The State and Banner Settings options let you add text to each printout, which can be useful in an office environment.

5. To tweak the printer's quality settings, double-click the Filter Settings entry in the list. This will open the Configuration Options window. The choices made here will become the default settings, used for all printouts. The options you'll see depend on the model of printer you're using. To change an option, select it in the Options list, and then make your choice in the Values box beneath. Clicking the Test button will send a test page to the printer. Once this is clicked, a dialog box will appear offering the type of test print you want. Usually, it's helpful to see how photos are printed, so select Test Graphical Printing with Photo.

> **Tip** One option I changed was Printout Mode, which I switched from Normal to High Quality. On my particular printer, an Epson Stylus Color CX-3600, this was more akin to the standard printing mode I was used to under Windows. The default printer mode that SUSE Linux selected was more like draft mode.

6. When you've finished making your choices in the Configuration Options window, click the Next button. This will return you to the main configuration window.

7. Click OK, and then click Finish to write the new printer configuration to file. The printer is now ready for use.

Before attempting to print, you should read the upcoming section about printing from popular SUSE Linux applications.

Configuring an Unrecognized Printer

If your printer attaches via USB, it should be automatically recognized, and you should be able to configure it as described in the previous section. If you find that it isn't recognized, start with common-sense problem-solving work: make sure that it's switched on (it might be necessary to power cycle the printer), and then make sure the USB cable is attached at both ends. If it still isn't recognized, try attaching the printer to a different USB port on your computer.

The following instructions are primarily included here for those configuring older printers that attach to your computer via the parallel port, or even via the serial port. However, they can also be used to attempt to add a USB printer that doesn't appear to be recognized.

1. Start YaST and click Hardware ➤ Printer.

2. In the Printer Configuration window, click the Add button.

3. In the Printer Type window, click the Directly Connected Printers button, and then click Next.

4. In the Directly Connected Printers list, select the method by which your printer is connected to your PC, and then configure it as follows:

   - If you selected USB, specify which USB printer you want to configure. Unless there is another already configured USB printer attached to your computer, the First USB Printer (/dev/usb/lp0) option should be used. At this point, you can test to see whether SUSE Linux can "see" the printer by clicking the Test Printer Connection button. If the printer responds in any way, then there's a connection. If it does nothing, there's clearly a fundamental hardware communication problem.

   - If you selected Parallel Printer, the next window will ask you to confirm the port you want to use. Most computers have only one parallel port, and this will be selected, so simply click the Next button.

5. You'll be asked to enter details about the printer. All that's needed is a name in the Name for Printing box. This can be anything, but it makes sense to enter the make and model of the printer, so it can be easily identified in future. See Figure 8-15 for example. Click Next to continue.

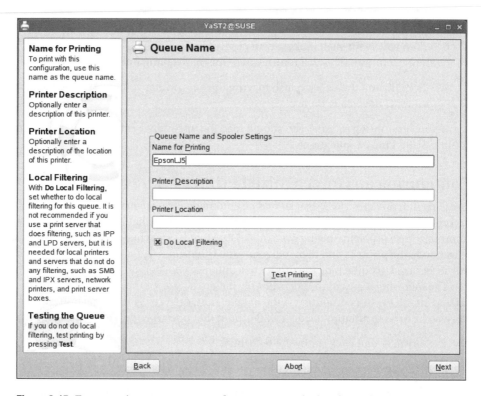

Figure 8-15. *Enter a printer queue name that represents the hardware being used.*

6. In the next window, select your make and then the model of your printer from the list. If you can't find an identical match, choose the nearest model. For example, the Epson Stylus CX-3600 printer attached to my test PC wasn't in the list, so I chose the Stylus CX-3200 instead. When you're finished, click Next.

Tip If the printer is a laser printer, and you can't find a make and model match, consider selecting HP LaserJet. Most laser printers produced in recent times offer LaserJet compatibility modes.

---

7. Set preferences for the printer and complete the setup, as described in steps 4 through 7 in the previous section.

Once the printer is configured, see the following notes about printing from popular applications.

Printing from Popular Applications

SUSE Linux doesn't offer a unified printer interface, as you might be used to under Windows. Instead, various applications offer different options when it comes to setting print quality, paper size, and so on. Some applications don't offer any options at all and rely on the default settings you created during printer configuration.

To give you an idea, the following sections describe printing under OpenOffice.org, The GIMP, and Mozilla Firefox.

Printing from OpenOffice.org

To change print settings within any OpenOffice.org application, click File ➤ Printer Setup, and then click the Properties button. You can select the paper size and scaling of the print in the dialog box that appears. Click the Device tab to access the same range of printer configuration options as displayed during printer configuration, as shown in Figure 8-16. You should be able to change the print quality settings, as well as various other options, depending on the make and model of printer in use.

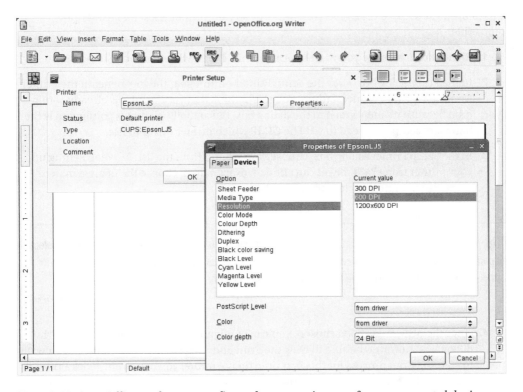

Figure 8-16. *OpenOffice.org lets you configure the same printer preferences presented during initial printer configuration.*

The changes you make last only as long as the OpenOffice.org application is open. Once the application is closed, the settings revert to their default settings.

Printing from The GIMP

The GIMP offers by far the most control over printing. However, perhaps ironically, The
GIMP needs extra configuration before it can print. This is because it assumes your printer
is PostScript-compatible, which is not true of most nonprofessional printers. If you're in
doubt about whether your model supports PostScript, check the documentation that came
with your printer, as well as the packaging, and look for the PostScript logo. However, unless
you specifically opted to purchase a PostScript-compatible model, it's unlikely the function
will be supported.

■**Note** Many of the printer drivers used by the CUPS software originated within the GIMP-Print project
(http://gimp-print.sourceforge.net), which was an attempt to bring high-quality printing to The GIMP
image editor. Gimp-Print is now known as Guttenprint and has expanded to bringing high-quality printer
drivers to all Unix/Linux systems.

Follow these steps to configure The GIMP to use your printer if it's not PostScript-
compatible.

1. Right-click the image you want to print within The GIMP and select File ➤ Print.

2. In the Print dialog box, click the Setup Printer button near the top, beneath the Printer
   Name and Printer Model settings. You might think that your printer is already configured because it's mentioned in the dialog box, but actually, all that is configured is the
   hardware setup. You need to tell The GIMP which printer driver to use.

3. In the Setup Printer dialog box, choose your printer from the list. As when setting up
   your printer using YaST, if you can't find an exact match, choose the nearest match.
   Click the OK button to close the dialog box.

■**Tip** The dialog box that appears at this stage was very small on my system, making it difficult to select
my printer model from the list. However, I was able to resize the dialog box by clicking and dragging the
bottom-right corner, thus making the list much easier to work with.

---

4. Once the printer has been chosen, you can configure the print output from the Print
   dialog box. However, be sure to click the Print and Save Settings button when you want
   to start the print process for this first time (in the future, you can simply click Print). If
   you don't do this, your choice of printer will be lost.

Following this, and each time you print, you can select the print quality settings in the
Print dialog box. Perhaps the most important control is the Size slider, at the bottom of the dialog box, which controls the size of the printed image relative to the size of the paper. The dialog
box includes two tabs at the top right. On the Printer Settings tab, you can select the paper type

from the Media Type drop-down list. The Image/Output Settings tab has printer quality settings. You can select the type of output you're printing and, by clicking the Adjust Output, you can alter the color balance, brightness, contrast, and other image properties, as shown in Figure 8-17. The changes will be previewed in the image window, but bear in mind that these won't necessarily precisely reflect the printed output, because printers have their own peculiarities when it comes to output.

■Note You might be used to using color profiles within Windows. By applying a color profile to every output device, including your monitor, these aim to match up what you see on screen with what is eventually printed out. Unfortunately, SUSE Linux currently doesn't support this functionality.

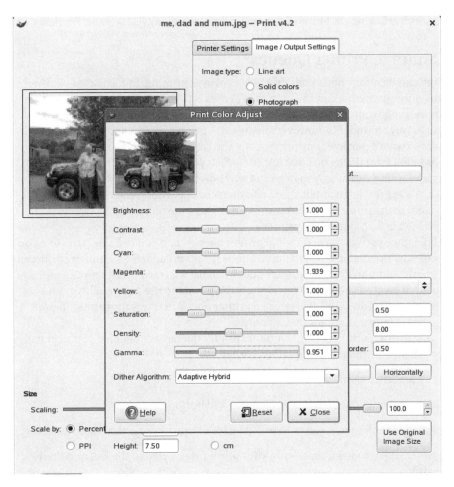

Figure 8-17. *You can alter color settings by clicking the Adjust Output button on the Image/Output Settings tab of The GIMP's Print dialog box.*

When you've finished making your changes, click the Print button at the bottom right. If you've created a particular set of configuration choices that you want to keep, click the Save Settings button. The choices you make (including color settings) will then be automatically selected each time you print.

Printing from Mozilla Firefox

Mozilla Firefox doesn't offer much control over print quality. It uses the default printer settings entered when the printer was initially configured. To print, simply click File ➤ Print. Clicking the Properties button in the Print dialog box offers a chance to set the paper size, alter the margins, and switch between color and grayscale printing.

To switch to landscape mode, click Print ➤ Page Setup. Here, you can also alter the scale of the web site print, which can be useful if the web site won't print correctly because it's simply too large. Removing the check from the Shrink to Fit Page Width option and then setting a value of less than 100% will shrink images and text by a corresponding percentage. You can preview the results by clicking OK in the dialog box and then clicking File ➤ Print Preview.

Creating Multiple Printer Queues

Many SUSE Linux applications don't offer much control over printing. Indeed, after clicking File ➤ Print, the only option that can be set in many cases is the paper size. You can't set special paper printing modes, alter the printing resolution, or make other adjustments.

There's a neat way around this, however: create extra printer queues and alter the default settings of each to create a particular printing setup. You can then select the queue with the desired settings in the Print dialog box that appears when you select File ➤ Print.

To understand what a queue is, you need to know how SUSE Linux handles printing. When you click File ➤ Print in an application, and then click OK within the Print dialog box, the print job is sent to the printer queue. Assuming that there are no other jobs waiting to be printed, the print job is then sent to the printer.

Under SUSE Linux, you can have multiple printer queues, and you can select the one you want to use from the Print dialog boxes of applications (printers can have a number of queues "attached" to them). Additionally, each printer queue can have its own printer profile settings. You might choose to create a printer queue that sets the printer to use high-quality photograph paper, for example. You could also create a printer queue that sets the printer in draft mode, where speed is more important than quality.

The following instructions to create additional printer queues assume that you've already configured the printer within YaST, as explained earlier.

1. Start YaST and click Hardware ➤ Printer.

2. In the Printer Configuration window, click the Add button.

3. In the Printer Type window, select New Queue for Existing Printer, and then click Next.

4. In the window that follows, make sure your printer is selected in the list, and then click Next.

5. As with setting up a printer, you can choose various options in the configuration window. Start by double-clicking the Name and Basic Settings entry and giving the printer queue a relevant name. If you're creating a printer queue for high-quality printing on photographic paper, a name like PhotoPrinting might be a good idea. Note that the printer queue name cannot contain any spaces.

6. To select paper types and resolution settings, double-click the Filter Settings entry, and then make your changes. The options offered here vary depending on the model of printer in use.

7. After specifying the settings, click Next, and then click Next again. Click Finish to save your changes.

After this, whenever you click File ➤ Print, you should be able to select from the list of printer queues in the Print dialog box. Sometimes these might be identified within the Print dialog box as actual printers, but, of course, you know better!

Managing Printing

The work of printing is handled not by the applications themselves, but by the *printer spooler*, a behind-the-scenes component of SUSE Linux. As explained in the previous section, like Windows, SUSE Linux uses *print queues* to handle printing. When you print from an application, the print job is actually sent to the spooler, and is then held in the print queue. If the queue is empty, the job is printed immediately. If there are other jobs waiting to be printed, or if a print job is already in progress, the new job is added to the queue.

GNOME and KDE offer tools to control the print queue. These allow printing to be stopped and started, and jobs can also be deleted before they're printed.

■Note Printing will probably pause automatically if there's a problem with the printer, such as a paper jam.

Access the print queue tools as follows:

- Under GNOME, select Desktop ➤ Control Center and click Printers. Then double-click the entry for your printer. In the window that appears, you should see the jobs waiting to be printed, if any. Right-clicking them will let you delete jobs.

- Under KDE, click the Printer icon on the desktop. If you've deleted this, click K menu ➤ Personal Settings ➤ Utilities ➤ Printing ➤ KJobViewer. Right-clicking should let you delete any queued print jobs.

■Note If you've set up any additional printer queues, as described in the "Creating Multiple Printer Queues" section, these will also be visible within the printer management tools.

There are rules when it comes to managing a printer. Users can delete print jobs that they created. However, a user can't cancel the print job of another user (if there are multiple users on the system). Additionally, printing can't be paused or resumed by anyone other than the root user. The root user also has the ability to cancel any print job created by any other user.

■**Note** Although I talk about pausing and resuming printing here, I'm referring only to SUSE Linux's handling of printer jobs. Pausing and resuming the print job has nothing to do with the printer being on- or offline (if, indeed, your printer has an offline mode; many modern printers do away with this function).

GNOME: Pausing/Resuming Printing

To fully administer the printer under GNOME, you need to start the GNOME printer manager application as the root user from a terminal window. Here are the steps:

1. Click Applications ➤ System ➤ Terminal ➤ Gnome Terminal.

2. In the terminal window, type the following:

```
su -
[Enter root password]
gnome-cups-manager
```

3. To pause or resume printing, click the relevant entry under the Printer menu.

4. Once you've finished, close both the printer queue window and the terminal window.

KDE: Pausing/Resuming Printing

Printer queue administration is handled by the KJobViewer application, which can be started as a separate application by clicking the Printer desktop icon. However, KJobViewer is actually a plug-in for the broader Printer component of the KDE Personal Settings application. The Printer component within Personal Settings is used to pause and resume printing, as follows:

1. Click K menu ➤ System ➤ Terminal ➤ Konsole.

2. In the Konsole window, type the following:

```
su -
[Enter root password]
kcmshell 'printers'
```

3. This will start the Printers component of KDE's Personal Settings program with the root privileges necessary to administer a printer. Select your printer in the list.

4. Click the Printer icon, near the top of the window, and then select Start/Stop Printer in the menu that appears, as shown in Figure 8-18. Pause or resume printing by clicking the relevant menu option.

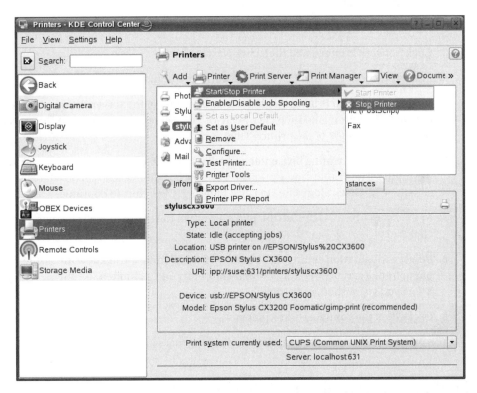

Figure 8-18. *You can start or stop a print job using KDE's Personal Settings program, but it must be run as the root user.*

5. When you've finished, close the program window, and then close the terminal window.

Configuring a Network Printer

If you use SUSE Linux in a work environment, you might be expected to use a printer that connects to the network through a print server. This means that the printer is directly accessible by all computers on the network.

This section describes how to connect to a print server running the Line Printing Daemon (LPD) service. This function is offered by virtually every print server in existence. In addition to LPD, SUSE Linux is compatible with CUPS/IPP, Raw format, and IPX. It is also compatible with SMB/Windows printer sharing, as explained in the next section.

To connect to the print server, you'll need to know the address of the print server and the name of the printer (also known as the queue name). These can be obtained from your system administrator. Once you have this information, follow these instructions:

1. Start YaST and click Hardware ➤ Printer.

2. In the Printer Configuration window, click the Add button.

3. Click Network Printers, and then click Next.

4. In the list, click Print via LPD-Style Network Server, and then click Next.

5. In the Hostname of Print Server box, enter the name of the server. Alternatively, click the Look Up button, and then click Scan for LPD Servers. In the Remote Queue Name box, enter the name of the printer. Then click Next.

6. In the Name for Printing box, enter a familiar name by which you would like to identify the printer. The Printer Description and Printer Location boxes can be left blank. Make sure there's a check alongside Do Local Filtering. Click Next to continue.

7. In the list of printers, choose the make and then the model of your printer. Then click Next.

8. Adjust configuration settings as necessary. For example, if you know the printer takes paper from a certain feed tray, double-click Filter Settings and make the selection. When you've finished, click Next.

9. Click OK in the configuration window.

The printer is now ready for use, just like a printer that's connected locally.

Configuring a Windows/SMB Shared Printer

Sharing a printer from a Windows computer is a cost-effective way of making the printer available to everyone on a network. As such, it's often done in a home environment, where a printer can be shared among computers used by family members, or in an office environment, where a printer might be connected to a particular workstation or server.

To connect to a shared printer from SUSE Linux, you'll need to know the following:

- The network address of the computer. This can be the IP address or fully qualified domain name (FQDN).

■**Caution** In my tests, the NetBIOS name of the computer, referred to within Windows as the *Full Computer Name*, wouldn't work when I used it when setting up the printer within SUSE Linux.

- The share name of the printer. To find this name, on the Windows computer, open the Printers and Faxes window, right-click the printer, and select Sharing. You'll see the name in the Share Name box.

- The username and password required to access the share, if required.

Here's how to add a Windows/SMB shared printer within SUSE Linux:

1. Start YaST and click Hardware ➤ Printer.

2. In the Printer Configuration window, click Add.

3. Click Network Printers, and then click the Next button.

4. In the list, select Print via SMB Network Server, and then click Next.

5. Enter connection information as follows:

   - The Workgroup box can be left blank, unless you work in a large office environment with multiple network workgroups—see your administrator if this is the case.

   - Enter the network address of the computer into the Hostname of Print Server box.

   - In the Remote Queue Name box, enter the share name of the printer.

Note You can try clicking the Look Up button, which is supposed to probe the remote computer to find out the printer share name, but it didn't work for me. Maybe you'll have better luck!

   - If the printer is attached to a Windows XP Professional, 2000, or NT computer, you may need to enter a valid Windows username and password in the Username and Password boxes to be able to access the printer, so do so. If you're running Windows XP Home, which doesn't normally require a username and password to access a shared resource, you still need to enter *something* in the Username box, even if it's gibberish. I suggest entering guest. Without an entry for the username, YaST will report an error. In the case of a Windows XP Home printer share, you can leave the Password box empty.

6. Click the Test Remote SMB Access button. If you've entered the correct details, you should see a dialog box saying the connection works correctly, as in Figure 8-19. If you get a message saying that SUSE Linux can't connect, check the details in the text boxes. Click Next when you're ready to continue.

Tip If you can't connect to the printer, you should also check the firewall settings on the Windows machine.

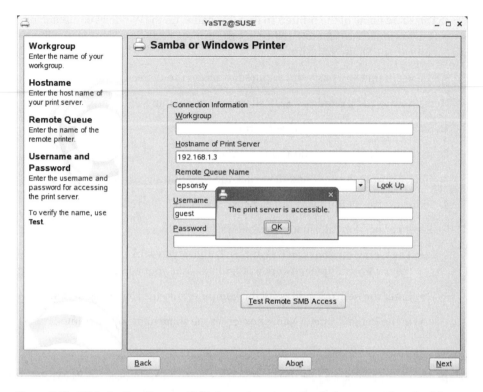

Figure 8-19. *Click the Test Remote SMB Access button to check the connection (in this case, I've connected to a printer on a Windows XP Home machine). If it works, you'll be told via a dialog box.*

7. In the Name for Printing box, enter a familiar name by which you can identify the printer in future. The Printer Description and Printer Location boxes can be left empty. Make sure there's a check in the Do Local Filtering box. Click Next.

8. Choose your make and model of printer from the list. If you can't find an exact match, choose the nearest model. Then click Next.

9. You now have an opportunity to fine-tune some of the printer's settings. These settings will then be used as the default. The Restriction Settings option can be used to limit which users can use the printer. The State and Banner Settings options let you add text to each printout.

10. To tweak the printer quality settings, double-click the Filter Settings entry in the list. This will open the Configuration Options window. The range of options you'll see depend on the model of printer you're using. To change an option, select it in the Options list, and then make your choice in the Values box beneath. When you've finished, click OK.

The printer will now be available within SUSE Linux applications.

Setting Up Digital Imaging Devices

One of the ironies of computers is that they're ruthlessly logical yet allow people to pursue their creative hobbies. Photography is just one example.

You may transfer your photos into your SUSE Linux system from your digital camera or by using a scanner. We'll look at both methods, starting with digital cameras.

Transferring Photos from a Digital Camera

Digital cameras have been around for a while now and offer a genuine alternative to traditional film photography. They store pictures on computer memory cards rather than on film, meaning their images can quickly and easily be downloaded to a PC.

You can transfer your pictures from your digital camera to your computer via a direct cable connection into your USB port or by using a card reader. The latter requires buying an extra piece of hardware into which you insert the memory card from the camera so you can download images from it.

■**Note** Very nearly all card readers are supported by SUSE Linux. If you find that your camera doesn't work via a direct cable connection, consider buying a card reader.

Regardless of whether you're using a digital camera or a card reader, simply attach the device to your computer using the USB cable. In the case of a card reader that's already attached, insert the memory card.

What happens next, and how you should proceed, varies depending on whether you're running the GNOME or KDE desktop.

GNOME: Using a Digital Camera or Card Reader

The default photo management software under GNOME is F-Spot. Like many picture management programs, it aims to catalog pictures according to the date the pictures were taken.

F-Spot's photo import wizard starts as soon as you attach the camera or insert a memory card into a card reader. If you click the Import Photos button in the dialog box, it will open a second dialog box by which you can actually import the pictures into F-Spot, as shown in Figure 8-20. Simply click the Import button to import all the photographs. To preview the photographs, click the thumbnails on the left side of the Import dialog box. Note that if you import pictures from a camera, you'll see a slightly different dialog box, without a preview window.

■**Note** The second Import dialog box seemed to have a bug when I used it. I had to select my memory card in the Import Source drop-down list before the pictures were actually detected by the F-Spot wizard. I also found that importing pictures from a digital camera was much slower than importing pictures from a card reader. Often, I had to wait a couple of minutes while nothing seemed to be happening.

Figure 8-20. *F-Spot manages digital photographs under GNOME, and its wizard will import them from your card reader or digital camera.*

F-Spot stores your photographs in the Photos directory within your /home directory, in subdirectories relating to the year, month, and day they were imported. Once they're imported, you can copy the pictures from the folder if you want to further manipulate them, burn them to CD, and so on.

If you're using a card reader, you might have noticed a new desktop shortcut appeared on the desktop when you inserted the card. This gives direct access to the memory card contents. This means that you can click the Ignore button in the initial F-Spot Import dialog box and copy the photos off the card yourself using either the Nautilus or Konqueror file browser, if you wish. Unfortunately, if you use a digital camera, it's likely you'll *have* to use F-Spot to download the images, although this depends on the camera. Some camera models are identified in a similar way to card readers by SUSE Linux, and you may find that a desktop icon appears.

■**Note** The desktop shortcut points to the *mount point* of the memory card. I explain more about mounting in Chapter 14.

Important! How to Safely Remove Devices Under GNOME

In the case of card readers, and cameras identified in a similar way to card readers (those for which a desktop icon appears), there's a very important caveat that applies to using them under SUSE Linux. With Windows, you might be used to inserting and removing cards at will. Even though Windows complains about the possibility of data loss, this rarely happens.

Under SUSE Linux, you should never simply remove a card or camera when you've finished with it! There is a genuine risk of data loss. Additionally, the card or camera might not be recognized properly when you next insert it.

You should always right-click the desktop shortcut and select Unmount Volume. This will make it safe to remove the card.

If your camera doesn't have a desktop icon, it's safe to simply unplug it when you've finished with it. However, you should wait a few seconds after any file transfers from the camera have finished before doing so.

KDE: Using a Digital Camera or Card Reader

Under KDE, you can use Digikam, the default image catalog program, to import your images, or you can simply browse the memory card/digital camera in a Konqueror window and copy the pictures manually. When the camera is attached, or a card inserted, you'll be presented with your choices, as shown in Figure 8-21. To use Digikam, select it from the list. To browse the contents of the camera or card in a Konqueror window, click Open in New Window. You could also select Browse with Gwenview, which just lets you view the images on the card, without importing them to your hard disk.

■**Note** Unlike with GNOME, you can view a digital camera's contents using Konqueror, KDE's built-in file manager.

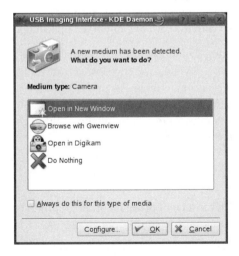

Figure 8-21. *Digikam is KDE's default image catalog program and can be selected when a camera/card reader is attached, or you can view the pictures in a new Konqueror window.*

To view the contents of the camera or card at any time within Konqueror, or from any Konqueror window, click Go ➤ Storage Media. Alternatively, type `system:/media` in the location bar.

▪Tip Why not create a shortcut location to the digital camera or card reader? Simply view it using Konqueror, and then click Bookmarks ➤ Add Bookmark.

If you choose to use Digikam, first-time use setup goes as follows:

1. You're invited to specify a directory within your `/home` directory where the Digikam library of photos will be stored. The default choice of `Pictures` is fine, so click OK.

2. If you're using a digital camera, you need to add your camera's hardware profile. Click Camera ➤ Add Camera. In the Configure dialog box, click the Auto-Detect button. This should automatically add your camera to the list of known cameras, so click the OK button.

3. To import photographs, select your camera from the Camera menu.

Following this initial setup, whenever you attach the camera and opt to import the photos into Digikam, the pictures should automatically appear in the Digikam preview window. You can select the pictures you want to import and click the Download button.

Important! How to Safely Remove Devices Under KDE

There's an important caveat to note when you've finished using the card reader or digital camera. With Windows, you might be used to inserting and removing cards at will. Even though Windows usually complains about the possibility of data loss, this rarely happens.

Under SUSE Linux, you should never simply remove a card! There is a genuine risk of data loss. Also, the card or camera might not be recognized properly when you next insert it.

Follow these steps to tell the system you've finished with the card or camera (if applicable):

1. Open a Konqueror file browser window by clicking K menu ➤ Home (Personal Files).

2. Click Go ➤ Storage Media.

3. Right-click the icon for your camera or card reader and select Safely Remove. Some cameras won't offer this option, in which case it's safe to simply unplug them, although you should wait a few seconds after any file transfers have finished.

Using a Photo or Film Scanner

Although scanners have fallen out of favor recently with the advent of digital photography, they're vital for getting nondigital photos and old documents onto your PC.

A lot of flatbed scanners can be made to work under SUSE Linux, but not all types are supported. You can check the list of currently supported scanners by visiting www.sane-project.org/sane-mfgs.html. Additional models are added to the list all the time, and this is another reason to make sure your system is completely up-to-date (see Chapter 9).

The best way to find out whether your scanner is supported under SUSE Linux is simply to test if it will work. Scanning within SUSE Linux is handled by the XSane utility. This is a stand-alone program that operates like the TWAIN drivers that you might have used under Windows, except it's a lot more powerful.

■**Note** XSane isn't installed by default under KDE. Instead, the Kooka program is offered. Although Kooka is very powerful, I advise you to use XSane because it most resembles the TWAIN drivers you might be used to under Windows.

Configuring the Scanner

Before the scanner can be used by XSane, it must be configured under YaST, as follows:

1. If you're using KDE, you must first install XSane (if you're using GNOME you can skip to step 2). Start YaST and click Software ➤ Software Management. In the Search box, type xsane, and then click Search. In the list of search results, put a check alongside the xsane entry, and then click the Accept button. When installation has finished, click No when asked if you want to install any other packages.

2. Start YaST, if it isn't already active, and click Hardware ➤ Scanner. You'll see a message about the scanner database being created. This might take a second or two, after which your scanner will be detected.

3. The Scanner Configuration window will appear. If it's blank, then your scanner hasn't been detected, which means that it's incompatible with SUSE Linux. If the scanner has been detected, it will appear in the list. Make sure it's selected, and then click the Edit button.

4. In the next window, choose your scanner from the list. This will associate a driver with the scanner. If you can't find a perfect match, choose a scanner within the same range. Click the Next button to continue.

5. The settings will be written to disk. When the various stages of configuration have completed, indicated by checks alongside the entries in the list, click the Next button.

6. Click the Finish button to close YaST. The scanner is now ready for use.

Scanning Pictures

Once the scanner has been set up in YaST, you can scan pictures using either the XSane program or The GIMP. If you use The GIMP, the scanned images will be imported for image editing. In both cases, the same XSane core components are used.

You can start XSane as follows:

- Under GNOME, start XSane by clicking Applications ➤ Graphics ➤ Scanning ➤ XSane.

- Under KDE, click K menu ➤ Graphics ➤ Scanning ➤ XSane.

- To start XSane from within The GIMP, start the program and click File ➤ Acquire ➤ XSane: Device Dialog.

When XSane first starts, you are asked to agree to a license, so click Accept to do so. The main XSane program window is similar in appearance to the TWAIN scanner drivers you might have used under Windows. The default setup consists of four windows:

- The main XSane window, with the commonly used program options

- The Standard Options window, which offers unique options for your scanner

- The Histogram window, which shows a graph of brightness/color levels in the scanned image

- The Preview window, which will show images once they've been scanned

Unless you require them, you can close the Histogram and Standard Options window, because the main XSane window is of most use. You can bring the other windows back later by clicking their entry on the Window menu in the main XSane window.

Here are the steps for using the XSane program to scan a picture:

1. At the top right of the main XSane window is the mode drop-down list. To scan a picture to save to disc, select the Save option.

2. From the Type drop-down list, select JPEG. This will save any files you create as .jpg files, which offer the best balance of file size and image quality.

3. In the drop-down list beneath Type, which is selected as Binary by default, select Color. This will switch XSane into color picture scanning mode, as opposed to two-color (Binary), and grayscale (Gray). Once Color is selected, the window options will change to offer functions relevant to color photo scanning.

4. Below the Color drop-down list is a drop-down list that sets the scanning type. You should select Full Color Range for scanning photographs or artwork, but you might also select slide (transparency) and negative scanning modes, if you have a compatible scanner.

5. Next is the dots per inch (DPI) setting. Generally, 300 DPI is acceptable for scanned photos; 150 DPI might work for artwork such as diagrams.

6. Beneath the DPI selection are the gamma, brightness, and contrast sliders, in that order. You can use these to adjust the quality of the scan later on, but leave them at their default settings for the moment. There are several other buttons beneath the sliders that offer more image-tweaking facilities, which you might like to explore later. These also can be left alone for now.

7. To scan a preview, click the Acquire Preview button in the Preview window. The scanned image should then appear in the Preview window, as shown in Figure 8-22.

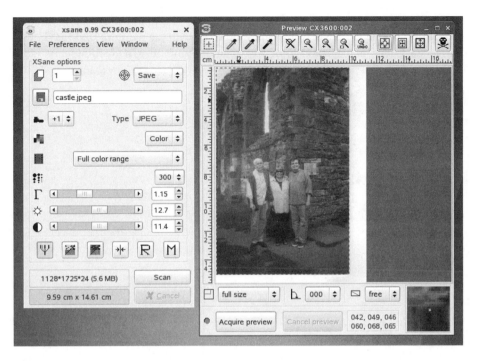

Figure 8-22. *XSane offers a multitude of options to scan photos, negatives, or transparencies.*

8. XSane will attempt to automatically crop the picture and delete any space around it. If you find it gets the cropping wrong, click and drag your own crop box around the image in the Preview window.

9. If you wish, you can adjust the brightness/contrast settings by clicking and dragging the sliders in the XSane window. The changes will be shown in the Preview window.

10. When you're satisfied with the image, enter a filename in the filename box near the top of the XSane window. The default filename is out.jpg, which you should replace with your own filename.

11. Click the Scan button. Files are saved to your /home directory, unless you specify a path in the filename box.

Using a USB Memory Stick

Although at one time the floppy disk drive ruled when it came to transferring small files between computers, nowadays, the USB memory stick has taken its place. These small devices, often incorporated into keyrings, contain nonvolatile memory and retain their contents even when no power is applied.

The good news is that SUSE Linux works with just about every make and model of memory stick. Simply insert the device, and then wait a few seconds while SUSE Linux recognizes it.

What happens next depends on which desktop environment you're using. Under KDE, a dialog box will appear, asking what you want to do with the memory stick, as shown in Figure 8-23. Click Open in New Window to open the contents in a file browser window.

Figure 8-23. *When you insert a memory card, under KDE, a dialog box will appear asking what you want to do with it.*

If you're running GNOME, a desktop shortcut icon will appear, providing quick access to the memory stick, and a file browser window will automatically open, showing the contents.

Under both desktop environments, the contents are "mounted" (made available) in the folder /media, which you can browse to using Nautilus or Konqueror. The name of the directory the contents appear in will depend on the volume name of the memory stick. Additionally, clicking Go ➤ Storage Media in a Konqueror window, or clicking the Places menu on the GNOME desktop, will provide quick access to the memory stick.

■**Note**   *Mounting* is the process of magically making the contents of an external storage device available within a directory of the SUSE Linux file system. The contents aren't actually in the folder—it's just a trick. I explain more about mounting in Chapter 14.

Important! As with memory card readers and certain digital cameras, when you're finished with the memory stick, you shouldn't simply unplug it. Instead, you need to unmount it first. Make sure you've saved and closed any files on the memory stick. You might also need to close any Nautilus file browser windows that are browsing the stick. Then, under GNOME, right-click its desktop icon and select Unmount Volume. Under KDE, open a Konqueror window, click Go ➤ Storage Media, right-click the memory stick's icon, and select Safely Remove.

Installing 3D Graphics Card Drivers

Virtually all graphics cards are automatically supported and configured within SUSE Linux. In most cases, you can stick with the default drivers installed by SUSE Linux. However, there are some instances where you might want to install the proprietary graphics drivers supplied by the manufacturers:

- You want to use your graphics card's advanced 3D functionality, usually to play 3D games or run 3D modeling software.

- You want to use more than one monitor at the same time (a *multiple monitor* setup) using recent Nvidia or ATI graphics cards that feature dual-head outputs.

- The built-in graphics drivers don't function correctly. Sometimes the built-in graphics drivers don't use the full resolution of the monitor. For example, this is sometimes true of computers with widescreen displays.

Installing proprietary graphics drivers requires that you download the driver software from the manufacturer's web site and then compile the driver module. This is largely automated but is nonetheless a complicated procedure. Therefore, you shouldn't install proprietary graphics drivers without good reason. In addition, unlike their open source counterparts installed by default under SUSE Linux, proprietary graphics drivers can be buggy.

Perhaps the most important reason not to use proprietary graphics card drivers is that every time the Linux kernel file is updated via an online update, the Xorg graphics subsystem will no longer function until the driver has been recompiled. This can prove annoying and, for a beginner to SUSE Linux, very confusing.

The instructions in this section cover installing ATI and Nvidia graphics cards which, between them, account for most of the 3D graphics card market. Then you'll learn how to configure multiple monitors.

■**Note** The instructions were correct as this book went to press. Unfortunately, both Nvidia and ATI have a habit of frequently changing the configuration method for their driver files. If you find the instructions are no longer current, visit http://opensuse.org and look under the documentation heading for instructions.

Preparing for Driver Installation

To install the graphics drivers, you'll need several software compilation tools, as well as the source code for the Linux kernel. Install these as follows:

1. Start YaST and click Software ➤ Software Management.

2. In the Search box, type make, and then click Search. In the list of results, put a check alongside the box, if it isn't already checked.

3. Search for gcc. Put a check in the box alongside gcc in the list of results.

4. Search for kernel-source. Put a check in the box alongside the entry in the list.

5. Click the Accept button. You may need to insert your SUSE Linux DVD, so do so. If you've updated online to a newer kernel file, the kernel-source package might need to be downloaded rather than installed from the DVD.

6. When the installation has finished, click No when asked if you want to install any other software packages, and then close the YaST window.

Installing ATI Graphics Drivers

Visit www.atitech.com and download the Linux graphics drivers for your card. At the time of writing, these could be found within the Drivers & Software section of the web site. Download the driver installation file to the desktop. Then follow these instructions:

1. Open a terminal window. In GNOME, click Applications ➤ System ➤ Terminal ➤ Gnome Terminal. In KDE, click K menu ➤ System ➤ Terminal ➤ Konsole.

2. Type the following in the terminal window (replace *filename.run* with the name of the file you downloaded):

```
chmod +x ~/Desktop/filename.run
```

■**Note**   Type the ~ (tilde) symbol by pressing Shift along with the key to the left of the 1 at the top of your keyboard. On UK keyboards, the symbol can be produced by pressing Shift+#.

---

3. Switch to the root user and run the installation file by typing the following (replace *<username>* with your username and *filename.run* with the name of the file you downloaded):

```
su -
[Enter root password]
/home/<username>/Desktop/filename.run
```

4. The graphical installer should appear. Make sure the Install Driver option is selected, and then click the Continue button.

5. The ATI license agreement will appear. To accept, click the I Agree button.

6. Select Automatic, and then click Continue.

7. The driver will now be compiled and installed. Once that's finished, click Exit to close the graphical installer.

8. Return to the terminal window and type the following:

```
cp /etc/X11/xorg.conf /etc/X11/xorg.conf.backup
aticonfig --initial
```

9. Close all open programs, and then restart your computer.

When the computer reboots, it should be using the ATI proprietary graphics driver.

You will need to repeat these steps whenever you update your kernel file via the system update feature, as described in Chapter 9. Note that you will need to repeat these steps before shutting down after the upgrade! If you reboot without performing these steps, then the graphical subsystem won't work and SUSE Linux will boot to a command prompt. If you find yourself in this situation, it should be possible to run the ATI installer from the command prompt. Log in as the root user and then run the installer. The questions asked should be the same as those in the graphical installer, except the installer will run in text mode.

Installing Nvidia Graphics Drivers

Visit www.nvidia.com to download graphics drivers for your card. At the time of writing, the drivers were found under the Download Drivers heading of the web site. Download the LinuxIA32 drivers to the desktop.

■**Note** You might see some instructions at the web site about configuring a special software repository to download the drivers. Unfortunately, this wouldn't work for me at the time of writing this book.

Then follow these instructions to install and compile the kernel module:

1. Open a terminal window. In GNOME, click Applications ➤ System ➤ Terminal ➤ Gnome Terminal. In KDE, click K menu ➤ System ➤ Terminal ➤ Konsole.

2. Type the following in the terminal window. This will back up a vital configuration file and then switch you to command-line mode (so first close any open applications and make sure your data is saved).

```
su -
[Enter root password]
cp /etc/X11/xorg.conf /etc/X11/xorg.conf.backup
init 3
```

3. Log in as the root at the command line, and then type the following (replace *<username>* with your username, and *filename.run* with the name of the file you downloaded):

```
cd /home/<username>/Desktop/
chmod +x filename.run
./filename.run
```

4. Agree to the license agreement. The cursor keys move the highlight from button to button, so press the left cursor key to highlight Accept, and then press Enter.

5. You'll be told that no precompiled kernel interface was found and asked if you want to download one. Highlight No and press Enter.

6. You'll be told that a new kernel interface must be compiled. Select OK.

7. You'll be asked if you would like to automatically run the nvidia-xconfig utility. Highlight Yes and press Enter.

8. Press Enter at the final confirmation message. This will end the installation program.

9. At the command prompt, type the following to reboot the computer:

   ```
   reboot
   ```

You will need to repeat these steps whenever you update your kernel file via the system update feature, as described in Chapter 9. After kernel update, you will find that the graphical subsystem won't start upon a reboot. Log in as root, and then run the installer, as described in step 3. You'll be asked if you want to delete the old kernel module, which is necessary, so highlight Yes and press Enter. Then work through the installer as described in the steps, and reboot at the end.

Reverting to a Safe Graphics Driver

If you find that the Nvidia or ATI graphics driver doesn't work correctly, or causes crashes or unexpected results, you can revert to your previous setup by following these instructions:

1. Restart your computer. At the boot menu, select SUSE Linux 10.1 (Failsafe), which is the bottom option on the boot menu.

2. Log in as the root user at the login prompt. Type root as the username, and then enter the root password when prompted.

3. At the command prompt, type the following:

   ```
   cp /etc/X11/xorg.conf.backup /etc/X11/xorg.conf
   reboot
   ```

Your system will now reboot and use the default graphics drivers.

Configuring Multiple Monitors

If you have a graphics card with two outputs, you can configure a dual-monitor setup. This is where the two monitors are attached to the two outputs and placed side by side. The desktop is "stretched" across both screens.

In the case of Nvidia and ATI graphics cards, you'll probably need to install the proprietary drivers, as described previously, to use multiple monitor output. If you have a Matrox graphics card with dual-head outputs, such as one in the G series, you should be able to use the default SUSE Linux drivers.

To configure multiple monitors, follow these steps:

1. Start YaST and click Hardware ➤ Graphics Card and Monitor.

2. In the Card and Monitor Properties window, put a check alongside Activate Dual Head Mode. Then click the Configure button.

3. In the configuration window, click Xinerama Multihead. In the Arrangement section, select the icon that best represents the placement of your monitors. In most cases, the 1-2 arrangement, as shown in Figure 8-24, will be the choice. Then click OK.

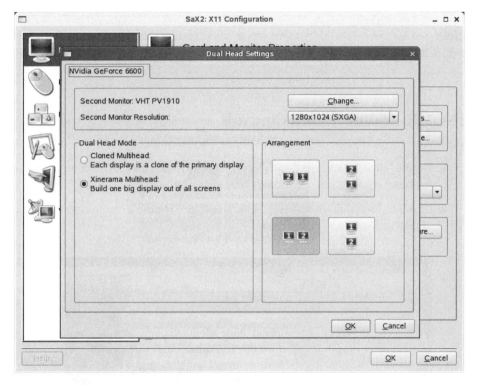

Figure 8-24. *Select Xinerama Multihead and the physical positioning of your monitors in the Dual Head Settings dialog box.*

4. Click OK in the configuration window.

5. A dialog box will appear offering the chance to test the new setup. It's a good idea to do so. When the test screen appears, make sure that your mouse can move freely "between" screens.

6. Assuming the setup works, click the Save button in the XFine2 dialog box.

7. A dialog box will appear asking if you want to exit Sax2. Click Yes, and the restart your computer in the usual way for the changes to take effect.

Configuring Sound Cards

In most cases, your sound card shouldn't require any additional configuration and should work immediately after you install SUSE Linux. The icon for the Volume Control applet is located at the bottom right of both the KDE and GNOME SUSE Linux desktops, and offers a quick way to control the master volume. However, if your sound card offers more than stereo output, such as multiple-speaker surround sound, then it's necessary to take some simple steps to allow full control of the hardware.

Note See Chapters 18 and 19 for instructions on how to configure the SUSE Linux multimedia system for playback of common audio and video file formats.

GNOME: Adding Sound Controls

Follow these steps to add controls to the Volume Control applet:

1. Double-click the Volume Control icon. This will open the master volume control dialog box.

2. Click Edit, and then click Preferences. The Volume Control Preferences dialog box appears, as shown in Figure 8-25.

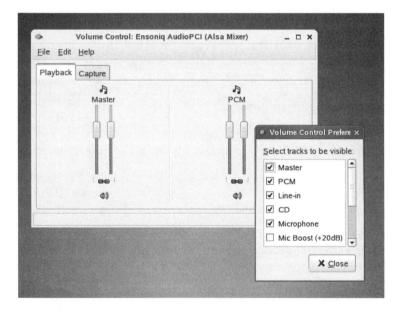

Figure 8-25. *The Volume Control Preferences dialog box under GNOME offers the chance to add controls to the applet.*

3. Select the sliders that you wish to be visible. For example, on my desktop computer that has 5.1 surround sound, I was able to add a slider for the center and back speakers. On my notebook that has a sound card featuring pseudo-surround sound, I was able to add a control to alter the intensity of the effect.

4. When you've finished, click the Close button.

KDE: Selecting Sound Functions

Follow these steps to set sound functions in KDE:

1. Right-click the Volume Control icon and select Show Mixer Window (KMix).

2. Click the Switches tab.

3. Select the functions you would like from the options. Clicking the "LED" light at the top of the dialog box selects the option.

4. Select any other options you wish to use from the drop-down lists alongside the switches. For example, on my notebook, I was able to alter the surround sound mode.

5. When you've finished, close the KMix dialog box. Your changes take effect instantly.

Setting Up E-Mail

Under GNOME, you can use the Evolution program to handle e-mail. Under KDE, KMail is the default e-mail application. The instructions in this section will get you up and running with these e-mail clients.

GNOME: Configuring E-Mail

The Evolution e-mail client can handle all of your e-mail needs and is the default e-mail client under the GNOME desktop. The version of Evolution used under SUSE Linux supports many different types of mail servers. Here, I'll cover setting up four of the most common: POP3, IMAP, Microsoft Exchange, and Novell GroupWare.

Before starting to configure Evolution, you'll need to find out the addresses of the mail servers you intend to use. In the case of POP3 and IMAP mail accounts, you'll need to know the incoming and outgoing server addresses (outgoing may be referred to as SMTP). In the case of Microsoft Exchange, you'll need to know the OWA URL and, optionally, the Active Directory/Global Address List server. With Novell GroupWare, you'll simply need to know the server name. You'll also need to know your username and password details for the incoming and possibly outgoing mail servers.

After gathering the necessary information, follow these steps to configure Evolution:

1. Start the Evolution e-mail client by clicking Applications ➤ Office ➤ Evolution.

2. When Evolution starts for the first time, you'll be invited to enter your configuration details via a wizard. Click the Forward button to begin.

3. The first window asks for your name and the e-mail address you wish to use within Evolution. These are what will appear in outgoing messages. Beneath this is a check box that you should leave checked if you want the account you're about to create to be the default account. In nearly all situations, this will be the correct choice. You can also fill in the Reply-To and Organization information if you wish, but these fields can be left blank. They're not normally displayed by most e-mail clients. Click the Forward button to continue.

4. The next window asks for details of the receiving (incoming) mail server that you want
to use, as shown in Figure 8-26. First, select the server type from the drop-down list. If
you don't know which option to use, select POP, which is currently the most common
type of incoming mail server. Enter the server address and username in the relevant
fields. It's very like you'll need to select Always from the Use Secure Connection drop-
down list, too. Most POP servers employ at least a password system, and some employ
more elaborate protection. You can find out what system your mail server uses by
clicking the Check for Supported Types button. Click Forward to continue.

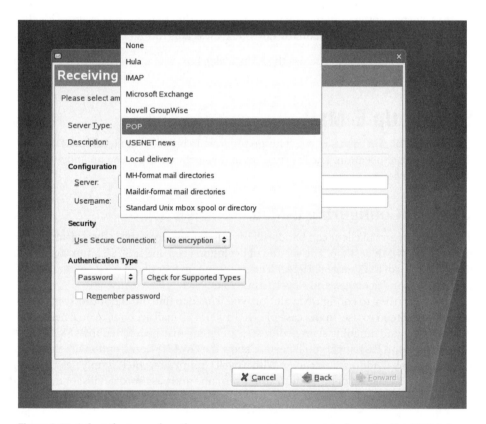

Figure 8-26. *Select the type of mail server you want to connect to from the list. POP is by
far the most common mail server in use today.*

5. You might need to enter your mail password, depending on which server type you
chose. In some cases, you'll need to type this later when you download your mail for
the first time. Click Forward to continue.

6. You're given the chance to choose between various additional options, such as how
often you want Evolution to check for new mail or if you want to delete mail from the
server after it has been downloaded. Unless you have been told otherwise or have special requirements, it should be okay to leave the default settings as they are. However, if
you use a Microsoft Exchange server, enter the Active Directory/Global Address List
server details here, if required. Click Forward to continue.

7. Depending on the server type you chose, you might now need to fill in the outgoing (SMTP) server address. Type this into the Server field. If your SMTP server requires authentication, put a check in the relevant box, and then enter your username. Click Check for Support Types to find out what, if any, authentication methods your SMTP server supports; select any of the entries that aren't scored through from the Type drop-down list when the check has finished. Click Forward to continue.

8. You're invited to enter a name for the account, by which it will be referred to while you use Evolution. The default is your e-mail address, but you can type something more memorable if you wish. Click Forward to continue.

9. Choose your location, which will have the effect of automatically defining the time zone you work under. Click any of the circles on the map closest to your location. This will ensure that e-mail messages are correctly time-stamped. Click Forward to continue

10. Click the Apply button in the confirmation window to finish the wizard.

Now that you have Evolution set up, you can begin using it. See Chapter 27 for an in-depth guide to Evolution.

KDE: Configuring E-Mail

E-mail under KDE is handled by KMail, which is part of the Kontact Personal Information Manager suite. KMail can work with POP or IMAP servers. If you need to use any other type e-mail server, such as Microsoft Exchange, I suggest that you use Evolution instead. Although Evolution was created for the GNOME desktop, there's no reason why it can't be used under KDE. To install it, use the Software Management tool of YaST, as described in Chapter 29.

■**Tip** There's a strong debate about which is better: Evolution or KMail. Personally, I think they're equal in terms of features. However, if you're used to Outlook or Outlook Express under Windows, you might prefer Evolution, which mirrors much of the look and feel of those Windows programs. KMail has an idiosyncratic way of working, which can take some getting used to. For example, it blocks HTML e-mail view by default.

Before starting your e-mail setup, you'll need your e-mail username and password, and the address of your sending and receiving e-mail server (a URL or an IP address). You can get these from your ISP or system administrator.

To set up your e-mail in KMail, follow these steps:

1. Start KMail by clicking K menu ➤ Internet ➤ E-Mail.

2. When KMail starts, click Settings ➤ Configure KMail.

3. The Configure - KMail window appears. Make sure the Identities icon is highlighted on the left side of the window. There's no need to set up a new account, because KMail attempts to do so automatically based on your login settings, so click Modify instead.

4. On the General tab, type your name in the Your Name field, as shown in Figure 8-27. This is what will appear on the e-mail you send to others. You can leave the Organization field blank, but you must fill in the Email Address field with the address from which you send and receive mail.

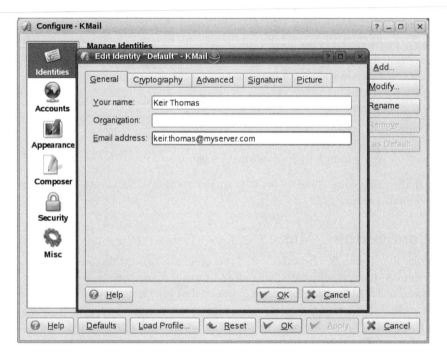

Figure 8-27. *Type your name and then your e-mail address into the relevant fields. The Organization field can be left blank.*

5. You can ignore the Cryptography, Advanced, Signature, and Picture tabs if you wish, but you might want to take a look at them. There's no need to fill in the Reply To Address field on the Advanced tab. However, you might want to change the Dictionary setting under the Advanced tab so that it reflects your locality (if you're in the UK, you might want to choose English [British], for example). The Signature tab lets you add an e-mail signature (or sig) to the bottom of each message automatically.

6. Click OK in the Edit Identity dialog box.

7. Click the Accounts icon on the left side of the Configure - KMail window.

8. Select the Sending tab, and then click Add. You'll be asked to choose a transport. If you're in an office or using an ISP, click SMTP.

■Note It's possible to choose Sendmail as your transport. This will send mail using the Mail Transport Agent (MTA) that is built into SUSE Linux. This has the advantage that you would still be able to send mail if your ISP or company's mail server stopped working temporarily. The problem is that many mail servers around the world refuse to accept mail from anything other than "genuine" mail servers (those registered via the DNS system). This is to prevent spam. All things considered, it's better to use the SMTP address supplied by your ISP or system administrator.

---

9. Select the General tab in the Add Transport dialog box that appears, and then enter a name for the server. This is just for your reference later, so it can be anything you wish. Beneath this, enter the address of the SMTP server in the Host field. (You'll need to contact your ISP or system administrator for this information.) Usually, it's something like smtp.example.com, or it may be an IP address in the format of four numbers separated by dots. You can leave the Precommand field empty, although if you know the SMTP server requires authentication, put a check in the box, and then enter your username and password.

10. Click the Security tab in the Add Transport dialog box. Here, you can set the type of authentication that your SMTP server supports. You can quickly check by clicking the Check What the Server Supports button. When you're finished, click OK.

11. In the Configure - KMail window, click the Receiving tab.

12. Click the Add button and select the type of mail account you want to add. This will very likely be POP3, especially if you go online using an ISP. Click OK.

13. Enter an Account Name for future reference. This can be anything you choose. The Login and Password fields are usually the same as your login username and password that you use to go online if you're using an ISP, although they might vary depending on the nature of your service package. In the Host field, type the address of the server, which will most likely take the format of mail.example.com. If you're unsure about any of this information, call the technical support line of your e-mail provider or ISP. If you're in an office, you should speak to your system administrator.

14. Put a check in the Store POP Password check box. This is insecure in that your e-mail password might be accessible to anyone who has access to the PC (although not to other users of your system, aside from the root user account, which has access to all files on the system). The benefit of storing the password in the configuration file is that you won't be asked for it each time you check your mail. If you consider storing the password on the hard disk to be a security risk, remove the check. However, you will be pestered for the password each time your mail is checked. The other fields can be left blank unless you have particular requirements.

15. Click the Extras tab to see a host of security settings. Clicking the Check What the Server Supports button will probe the e-mail server and change the settings automatically. Leave the Use Pipelining for Faster Mail Download box unchecked, unless you know that the mail server you want to connect to supports the function. Click OK to close the dialog box.

16. Click OK to close the Configure - KMail window. You should now be able to send and receive mail!

In most regards, KMail works like every Windows-based e-mail client. To create a new e-mail message, click the New icon on the KMail toolbar. To read new e-mail messages, select them in the list. An excellent beginner's guide to KMail can be found at the official web site: `http://docs.kde.org/development/en/kdepim/kmail/`.

Accessing Windows File Shares and Servers

If you work in an office environment, or your computer is connected to a home network along with other computers, you might want to access files on other computers. These files might be located on a dedicated server computer or simply on another workstation, where the user has opted to "share" a folder.

Accessing shared folders using SUSE Linux is easy, although the technique varies depending on whether you're running GNOME or KDE. Additionally, you'll need to reconfigure your firewall to allow the detection of other computers.

Configuring the Firewall to Allow File Sharing

In Chapter 9, I explain the SUSE Linux firewall fully but, for the moment, it's enough to know that in order for your SUSE Linux machine to detect other computers on the network, you need to ensure your network interface is in the Internal Zone of the SUSE Linux firewall.

■**Caution** The Internal Zone is a firewall mode created for computers on a trusted local area network that are protected by a third-party firewall device, such as a broadband router in a home environment. Do not configure your computer for the Internal Zone if it directly connects to the Internet. Examples of this type of setup include various modem configurations, including dial-up.

This step can be skipped if you wish. Accessing Windows file shares will still work if the network interface is in the External Zone of the firewall, which is the default setup under SUSE Linux. However, you won't have the ability to detect other computers with shares, and you won't be able to specify the user-friendly Network Name (also known as the NetBIOS name); instead, you will need to specify an IP address (or, if the facility exists, an FQDN).

Here's how to configure your firewall to allow file sharing:

1. Start YaST and click Security and Users ➤ Firewall.

2. In the Firewall Configuration window, click Interfaces in the menu on the left.

3. Select your network device, whether that's your Ethernet card or wireless network device, and then click the Change button.

4. In the dialog box that appears, select Internal Zone from the drop-down list, and then click OK.

5. Click Next, and then click Accept to both write the firewall configuration changes to disk and also restart the firewall.

GNOME: Accessing Windows Shares

GNOME includes an equivalent of the Network Neighborhood/My Network Places function under Windows that lets the user "search" the network for other computers. Click Places ➤ Network Servers to access it. You might then need to double-click the Windows Network icon to see the computers offering shares. Bear in mind that, as with Windows, network probing can take a few seconds to complete.

Also as with the Windows tool, computers aren't guaranteed to show up in the list and its reliability depends on how your network is configured. Therefore, it's often best to manually specify the computer to which you want to connect. To do this, open a Nautilus window (Places ➤ Home), and then click Go ➤ Location. In the location bar, type `smb://` followed by the IP address of the computer, its FQDN, or the NetBIOS name (known within Windows as the "Network Name"). For example, to access the computer located at IP address 192.168.1.3, type `smb://192.168.1.3`. Alternatively, you could try the computer's NetBIOS name, such as `smb://keir-office-pc`.

You can easily create a desktop shortcut to a Windows share, as follows:

1. Right-click a blank spot on the desktop and select Create Launcher.

2. In the Name field, type a familiar name for the shortcut. This is for your own future reference.

3. In the command field, type `nautilus smb://`, and then the address of the computer with the share, along with the name of the shared folder. For example, to access the `pictures` folder on 192.168.1.3, type the following:

   `nautilus smb://192.168.1.3/pictures`

4. All the other fields in the Create Launcher dialog box can be left empty, although you might like to click the No Icon button and choose an icon for the shortcut.

5. When you've finished, click the OK button.

KDE: Accessing Windows Shares

KDE also includes the equivalent of the Network Neighborhood/My Network Places function under Windows that lets the user "search" the network for other computers. Click K menu ➤ Home to open a Konqueror window, and then click Go ➤ Network Folders. Then click the SMB Shares link.

As with the Windows tool, computers aren't guaranteed to show up in the list. Therefore, it's often best to manually specify the computer to which you want to connect. To do this, open a Konqueror window. In the location bar, type `smb://` followed by the IP address of the computer, its FQDN, or the NetBIOS name (known within Windows as the "Network Name"). For example, to access the computer located at IP address 192.168.1.3, type `smb://192.168.1.3`. Alternatively, you could use the computer's NetBIOS name, as in `smb://keir-office-pc`.

You can easily create a desktop shortcut to a Windows share. Simply click and drag the shared folder onto the desktop. When you release the mouse button, a menu will appear. Select the Link Here option. To learn more about desktop shortcuts, see Chapter 10.

Summary

In this long chapter, I've explained how to configure commonly used hardware items for day-to-day use, regardless of whether they're inside your computer or attached to it. In addition, I've provided some guidance on how to use the hardware if there are certain caveats you should know about.

Near the end of the chapter, I explained how to configure e-mail systems under GNOME and KDE. Finally, you learned how you can access network file shares offered by other computers on your local area network.

In the next chapter, you'll learn all about security under SUSE Linux, and the steps you can take to make your computer watertight.

## CHAPTER 9

How to Secure Your Computer

Linux is widely considered to be one of the most secure operating systems around. On a basic level, Linux is built from the ground up to be fundamentally secure, and it forces users to work with security in mind. For instance, it enforces the system of ordinary users who are limited in what they can do, thus making it harder for virus infections to occur.

In addition, Linux contains a firewall that is hard-wired into the kernel. It's called iptables and is developed by the netfilter project (`www.netfilter.org`). It's considered among the best of all available solutions. Not only that, but it can protect your home PC just as well as it can protect the most powerful supercomputer.

In this chapter, you'll be introduced to typical security issues affecting desktop computer users. Then I'll describe the tools SUSE Linux offers to combat these threats, and explain how they're can be used effectively. I'll also cover some elementary steps that you can take to protect your system.

Security Threats

Security should always be a subject of ongoing concern for any computer user. However, the profile of security threats facing Linux is slightly different than that facing Windows users. For example, while most Windows systems feature an antivirus program, very few Linux users bother with such a thing because viruses aren't currently a significant threat to Linux.

Let's take a quick look at the threats typically facing computer systems and how important they are to Linux users.

Viruses

Viruses are small computer programs that usually have two main characteristics:

- They get onto your computer without your knowledge, typically by attaching themselves to an innocuous file in order to disguise their presence.

- Once onboard, they undertake some kind of malicious act, such as deleting data, although some viruses do little more than attempt to propagate themselves.

The world of Windows is plagued by viruses. For instance, Sophos (www.sophos.com) claims that approximately 1,000 new viruses are discovered every month, and its products help guard against just under 100,000 viruses.

In contrast, very few viruses affect Linux. One report from 2003 estimated the total number of Linux viruses at 40, and the number is unlikely to have risen much since then.

Working out why Linux is so blessed in this regard is difficult. Perhaps the simplest reason is that there are many more Windows users in the world, and virus writers seek fame and recognition. Linux may well be protected by its relative lack of popularity, although as Linux becomes more popular, this is almost certain to change.

Worms

A worm is a form of virus that typically spreads from one computer to the next using network connections. Worms differ from viruses in that they don't attach to other programs in order to disguise themselves. Instead, they are independent pieces of software that execute in memory, usually by means of a *buffer overflow*. A buffer overflow occurs when a computer program "leaks data" into surrounding memory areas. Worms use the buffer overflow to inject their code into memory on the machine they're trying to infect. This code is then executed, causing the worm to become active on the new machine.

The most famous worms of recent times are Blaster and Sasser, which caused misery for Windows XP users over 2003–2004. These exploited buffer overflow bugs in the Windows login and file-sharing systems.

Few worms affect Linux systems. Any in circulation tend to attack servers, rather than desktop systems. However, worms should be considered a real threat to any Linux system, so measures must be taken to defend against them.

Internet Attacks

Although it's a rare occurrence, all computer users should take measures to defend against a concerted attack by an individual to gain access to their computer. Additionally, users should be on guard for automated "bots." These are designed to turn the victim's computer into part of a "botnet," which can be used to attack larger computer systems (so-called distributed denial-of-service attacks).

Usually, these types of attacks occur within buffer overflow bugs found in Internet-facing software packages, as described in the previous section, and can be countered by the same protective measures.

ARE YOU A CRACKER OR A HACKER?

Linux users are often described as *hackers*. This doesn't mean they maliciously break into computers or write viruses. It's simply using the word *hacker* in its original sense from the 1970s, when it described a computer enthusiast who was interested in exploring the capabilities of computers. Many of the people behind multinational computing corporations started out as hackers. Examples are Steve Wozniak, a cofounder of Apple Computer, and Bill Joy, cofounder of Sun Microsystems.

The word *hacker* is believed to derive from model train enthusiasts who "hacked" train tracks together as part of their hobby. When computing became popular in the early 1970s, several of these enthusiasts also became interested in computing, and the term was carried across with them.

However, in recent years, the media has subverted the term *hacker* to apply to an individual who breaks into computer systems. This was based on ignorance, and many true hackers find the comparison extremely offensive. Because of this, the term *cracker* was invented to clearly define an individual who maliciously attacks computers.

Don't worry if an acquaintance describes himself as a Linux hacker, or tells you that he has spent the night "hacking." Many Linux types use the term as a badge of honor.

SUSE Linux Security

SUSE Linux includes a number of tools built into the kernel (the fundamental system file) that can be used to protect against security threats. I explain how to use these later in this chapter, but first it's important to understand what each does.

AppArmor

AppArmor is a Linux application security framework project steered by Novell that can be used to control exactly which resources a running program can access. It's a hugely powerful tool that's really designed to be used on large server systems. There's no reason why it can't be used to boost the security of desktop systems, although that could be described as using a sledgehammer to crack a nut.

AppArmor works on the basis of application profiling. The profile contains details of exactly which system resources an application can access. For example, if a video playback program is added to AppArmor's database, the profile will contain information about how the playback software attempts to access the sound hardware for audio playback.

Once the profile is created, the application won't be able to access any applications or system resources not listed within the profile. If a profiled video playback program suddenly wants to access the Firefox web browser, it will be denied.

The security benefits here are obvious. If the video playback program in our example has a bug that can lead to a buffer overflow situation, it will be a lot harder to exploit for nefarious ends. But the degree of security offered by the AppArmor system has some limitations:

- AppArmor guards only software for which a profile is created. All other software has full run of the system, as with any Linux system.

- Special attention should be given to each AppArmor profile to ensure that all contingencies of using the application are covered. If anything is missing from the profile, the program might not function correctly.

- Using AppArmor requires considerable knowledge of how Linux operates. Users need to know how Linux refers to the various resources on the system and what various low-level applications do.

Therefore, AppArmor is not ideal for beginners. Even intermediate-level users might find some aspects of it confusing.

Firewall

A *firewall* is a system component that protects your PC when it's online. It does this by watching what data attempts to enter your PC from the Internet and allowing in only what it is sure is secure (which usually is what you've asked for). It also attempts to close off various aspects of your Internet connection, so that intruders don't have a clear way in should they target your system.

SUSE Linux includes the iptables software, which provides its firewall component. Technically speaking, iptables is a network filter and has a variety of uses, but it is most commonly used for firewall purposes.

Iptables provides supreme security because it is built into the Linux kernel, so it works on a fundamental level. Most Linux distributions make use of it. However, SUSE Linux offers unique configuration software that's relatively easy to use, as described in the "Using the SUSE Linux Firewall" section later in this chapter.

NX Protection

As mentioned earlier, one of the biggest threats to a computer is buffer overflow. This is where a bug in a software package allows data to leak into surrounding memory. The bug can be exploited by intruders or computer viruses to get unwanted code onto your computer.

SUSE Linux includes nonexecute (NX) protection. This divides areas of the memory into executable and nonexecutable zones. In theory, any code that leaks into memory via a buffer overflow will be benign because it shouldn't be possible to execute it.

Recent computer processors include built-in NX support, and SUSE Linux will make use of the feature in that case, but SUSE Linux also includes NX emulation software that provides an equivalent function on all processors.

NX functionality is automatically activated on SUSE Linux, and the ordinary user doesn't have the ability to activate or deactivate it.

Common-Sense Security

Before we look at activating SUSE Linux's technical security functions, it's necessary to discuss some common-sense rules that apply to computer security.

Entering your password: Be very wary if you're asked to enter either your login password (outside of initial login, of course). In particular, you should be very wary when asked to provide the root password. You'll be asked to provide the root password when following many of the configuration steps within this book, for example, and this is acceptable and safe. But if you're asked to do so out of the blue, then you should be suspicious. If the root password prompt dialog box appears when you run a file that shouldn't really need root permissions, such as an MP3 or OpenOffice.org file, you should treat the situation with caution. See Figure 9-1 for an example of a root password box.

Figure 9-1. *Be wary if asked to supply your root password for a task that doesn't normally require it.*

Installing new software: Be careful when choosing programs to download and install. Because Linux works on the basis of open-source code, anyone can theoretically tamper with a program, and then offer it for download by the unwary. This very rarely happens in real life. Even so, it's wise to avoid downloading programs from unofficial sources, such as web sites you find online via a search engine and whose authenticity you cannot totally trust. Instead, obtain software from the web site of the people who made it in the first place or, ideally, from the official SUSE Linux software repositories (discussed in Chapter 8).

Updating your system: Always make sure your system software is completely up-to-date. As with Windows, or any operating system, many Linux programs have bugs that lead to security holes, and crackers will assuredly target such vulnerabilities. Downloading the latest versions of SUSE Linux software ensures that you not only get the latest features, but also that any critical security holes are patched. As with most versions of Linux, updating SUSE Linux is easy and, of course, it's also free of charge. You'll learn how to keep your system updated in the next section.

Locking up your PC: Limit who has physical access to your computer. Any SUSE Linux system can be compromised by a simple floppy boot disk, or even the SUSE Linux installation DVD. Booting a PC using such disks gives anyone complete root access to your system's files, with no limitations. This is for obvious reasons; the idea of a boot disk is to let you fix your PC should something go wrong, and you cannot do this if you're blocked from accessing certain files. When Linux is used on servers that hold confidential data, it's not uncommon for the floppy and CD-ROM drives to be removed, thus avoiding booting via a boot disk. Such computers are also usually locked away in a room, or even in a cupboard, denying physical access to the machine.

Updating the System

SUSE Linux includes a component that will check online software repositories for updates to your system and indicate when it is necessary to download updates. Most of these updates will fix potential security holes within your software, but you may also find that several general software updates are included.

> ■**Note** Although some updates may be described as "security updates," this doesn't necessarily mean that your system is in imminent danger. In most cases, it will merely indicate that someone has spotted the potential for a problem and fixed it. So there's no need to panic when you see that your system needs an update, although you should certainly retrieve it as soon as you can.

SUSE Linux offers updates free of charge, but to use this service, you first must register with the SUSE organization. This is easily done, and there's no need to send any personal data. Once registration has taken place, your system will automatically be configured to periodically connect to update servers and inform you when updates are available. However, before registering, you need to perform a one-time system update using YaST.

Updating Online for the First Time

Unfortunately, the software management system in the version of SUSE Linux 10.1 supplied with this book has a bug. This means that, before completing a system-wide update, special measures must be taken to update several system components. This needs to be done only once. Following this, after you've registered with SUSE, you can update your system using the instructions for updating online after you've registered.

> ■**Note** The Libzypp package management software that's new to SUSE Linux 10.1, discussed in Chapter 29, is broken. Because Libzypp is vital for updating, the system can't update until Libzypp is updated separately! This is something of a chicken-and-egg situation, but the work-around described here will fix the issue. If you use a different version of SUSE Linux than the one supplied with this book, these steps may not be necessary. In that case, you can skip to the next sections, describing how to register online and update online using the usual method. If you find that doesn't work, return to these steps.

To update your system for the first time if you're using the version of SUSE Linux supplied with this book, follow these instructions:

1. Start YaST. Under GNOME, click Desktop ➤ YaST. Under KDE, click K menu ➤ System ➤ YaST. Enter your root password when prompted.

2. Click the Software icon on the left side of the window, and then click the Installation Source icon on the right.

3. In the Media Containing the Software Catalog window, click the Add button, and then select HTTP from the list.

4. In the Server Name field, enter `ftp.gwgd.de`. In the Directory on Server field, enter `/pub/suse/update/10.1`. Be sure to type the address correctly, because it's easy to get wrong! Then click the OK button.

5. A dialog box should appear that reads "Adding catalog." This may stay on your screen for several minutes. When it's finished, a new entry will be added to the list in the window. Click the Finish button. Once again, this might take a few moments to complete (in my tests, it took even longer than the "Adding Catalog" step!).

■**Caution** You might notice that the Software Updater icon in the notification area/system tray has switched to an exclamation point icon. This indicates updates are available, but it's important that you don't download them. Just ignore this for now and continue following these steps.

---

6. Back in the main YaST window, select the Online Update icon.

7. A list of patches will appear on the left of the program window. However, if you scroll through the list, you'll find that only two entries are checked by default: `libzpp update` and `yast2-online-update`. This is correct. *Do not select any of the other updates or alter the default selection in any way, even if they're marked as urgent!* Simply click the Accept button.

8. The two updates will be downloaded and installed, along with several additional vital updates related to the YaST configuration tool. Click Finish when the updates have completed.

9. Return to the YaST window and click the Installation Source icon once again.

10. Select the new entry you created in the list. It should read `On  On  YUM  http://ftp.gwdg.de/pub/suse/update/10.1`. Click Delete, and then click Finish. As before, this may take some time to complete.

11. Restart your computer.

SUSE Linux has now been updated so that the software management system is able to automatically update. Now you can register for updates, which will allow you to update the rest of your system.

Registering for Updates

To register with SUSE so you can receive automatic updates, follow these steps:

1. Start YaST. Under GNOME, click Desktop ➤ YaST. Under KDE, click K menu ➤ System ➤ YaST. Enter your root password when prompted.

2. In the YaST window, select the Software icon on the left, and then click the Online Update Configuration icon on the right.

3. In the window that appears, make sure that the Configure Now (Recommended) radio button is selected, as shown in Figure 9-2. You can choose any of the Include for Convenience options you find acceptable. If you don't want to send any data to SUSE, clear all the boxes. The options work as follows:

   • The Hardware Profile option sends hardware information that will help SUSE better understand compatibility issues with SUSE Linux.

   • The Optional Information option merely sends additional hardware details, along with your computer's hostname (Chapter 5 describes how to set a personalized hostname). This is the only "personal" data that you'll be asked to send. No other data by which you can be identified will be sent.

- The Registration Code option is for those who have purchased SUSE Linux or are using SUSE Linux as part of a corporate registration scheme. You'll be prompted to enter the registration code when necessary. There's no need to provide a registration code if you're using the version of SUSE Linux provided with this book, so you can leave this check box empty.

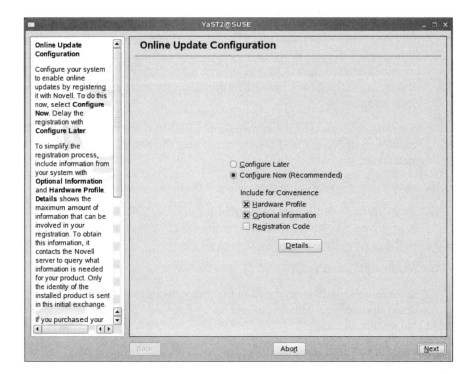

Figure 9-2. *You'll need to register before your system is configured for online updates.*

4. After you've made your choices, click the Next button. A window saying "Contacting server" will appear. At this point, your computer will contact the SUSE Linux server to receive an update server address.

■Note During my testing, the "Contacting server" step took quite some time, during which the process appeared to have frozen. It might be a good idea to get a cup of coffee while you're waiting!

---

5. Eventually, a dialog box should appear saying that configuration was successful, as shown in Figure 9-3. You can click the Details button to learn the address of the update server, or click OK to return to YaST, which can now be closed. If you are informed that

registration has failed, wait for a few hours, and then repeat the steps from the beginning. It's likely that the update server was too busy to deal with your inquiry, and it might succeed when you try again later.

■Note If you click the Details button, you might discover that you've been signed up with a mirror server. In other words, you might not have been connected to an official suse.com server. There's nothing to worry about here. The official suse.com server is simply unable to handle the high volume of SUSE users, so mirror servers are used to help spread the load.

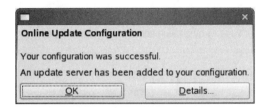

Figure 9-3. *You'll be informed if your update has been successful. If not, try again a little later.*

Updating Online

As soon as you registered your system, you should have noticed that the Software Updater icon in the system tray changed into an exclamation point (see Figure 9-4 for before and after views of the icon). This indicates that updates are available for your system.

■Tip If you find that an exclamation point icon doesn't appear, right-click the Software Updater icon and select Refresh. This will force Software Updater to download new software catalogs from the update server.

Figure 9-4. *The Software Updater icon will change to an exclamation point whenever updates are available.*

The following steps should be repeated each time Software Updater indicates that updates are available:

1. Click the Software Updater icon and wait while the software list is updated.

2. You can review the list of updates and, if necessary, deselect any that you don't want to apply to your system. This is something that only experts will be interested in, however, and generally you should apply all updates. At the very least, you should opt to update software indicated with a shield icon. This means that the software is a security update. All other updates are likely to be bug fixes, which might be important for the smooth running of your system but aren't as crucial as the security updates. If you want to know why an update is being offered, click Details at the bottom of the window to see a description of what the selected update will do, as shown in Figure 9-5.

Tip You might find it useful to resize the Software Updater window by clicking and dragging one of its edges.

Figure 9-5. *You can read about what each update fixes by clicking Details at the bottom of the Software Updater window.*

3. Once you've made your choices, click the Update button at the bottom of the window.

4. If this is the first time you're run Software Updater, you'll be asked to add `zmd` as a privileged user. This means that the background system component Software Updater relies on will be given permission to access system files. This is necessary for the updating process, so click the Add Privileged User button, and then enter your root password when prompted. Once that's completed, click the Update button again.

5. The updates will be downloaded and be applied to your system. If your system requires restarting to complete the installation of some software packages, a dialog box will appear offering the opportunity.

Sometimes you may find that Software Updater doesn't work, especially if you're using it for the first time. Keep in mind that it is new technology introduced with SUSE Linux 10.1 and is under development and being improved constantly.

In particular, you may find that Software Updater reports unresolved dependencies that mean it is unable to continue. In this case, you can revert to using the older and more established YaST Online Updater, as follows:

1. Start YaST. Click Desktop ➤ YaST under GNOME, or K menu ➤ System ➤ YaST under KDE. Enter your root password when prompted.

2. Click Software on the left side of the window, and then click Online Update on the right.

3. Available patches and updates will be listed on the left side of the window. Make sure that all are selected. A quick way of doing this is to right-click one and select All in This List ➤ Install.

4. Click the Accept button at the bottom right of the window. This will download and install the patches and updates.

5. When the downloads have finished, click the Finish button.

■**Caution** When I first updated my test systems, I found that Software Updater refused to work, so I switched to using YaST Online Updater. Although I selected all the available updates and patches, Software Updater downloaded only a few and then restarted YaST Online Update, automatically selecting all the patches again. Following this, I was able to update fully online.

WHERE'S THE ANTIVIRUS?

Viruses and worms are far rarer on Linux than they are on Windows. Very few antivirus products are aimed at the Linux desktop. However, AVG (www.grisoft.com) and Kaspersky (www.kaspersky.com) produce Linux workstation versions of their antivirus products.

The main issue with most Linux antivirus programs is that they're not open source, as with most of the Linux software included in SUSE Linux. If you absolutely must have your entire system running free software, consider ClamAV (www.clamav.net). This is a product designed to work on Linux servers but is flexible enough to run on desktop computers, too. ClamAV can be downloaded from ftp://ftp.suse.com/pub/projects/clamav, but must be installed manually. Installing software is explained in Chapter 29. Be aware that ClamAV is a command-line program. You'll need to read its man page to learn how it works. In addition, you might choose to read the online documentation at www.clamav.net/doc.

Configuring SUSE Linux's Security Features

As with all aspects of SUSE Linux, configuration of security settings is done via YaST. Three applets within YaST affect security: Local Security, Firewall, and AppArmor. Each of these is described in the following sections.

Setting Up Local Security

The Local Security applet lets you configure how files and users are handled on the system, as well as how passwords and user accounts are handled. Effectively, it lets you configure a security policy for users and their files. You can tighten security to quite a high level, which might be useful if SUSE Linux is installed on a computer in a public place with multiple users and you wish to provide every protection against user attack.

Follow these steps to configure Local Security:

1. Start YaST. Under GNOME, click Desktop ➤ YaST. Under KDE, click K menu ➤ System ➤ YaST. Enter your root password when prompted.

2. Click Security and Users on the left side of the YaST window, and then click the Local Security icon on the right.

3. You can choose from a series of predefined options, or customize your own settings. The latter offers the best range of options, so select that radio button and click Next.

4. The first window allows you to define password settings. This will set limits on what passwords can be set by users. (Setting passwords is described in detail in Chapter 30.) The options work as follows:

   - Check New Passwords performs a dictionary check against passwords entered by the user. The user will not be allowed to choose a new password that corresponds to words in the English dictionary. In theory, passwords that contain words in a dictionary are easier to crack.

- Test for Complicated Passwords prevents the user from defining a new password that's too simple. Simple passwords include those that are short and unsophisticated (they might involve just lowercase letters, for example). An ideal password has at least seven characters, with uppercase and lowercase letters, as well as numbers and punctuation symbols.

- Number of Passwords to Remember prevents the user from simply retyping her old password when prompted for a new one. You can set how many old passwords the system remembers.

- Password Encryption Method is the encryption method used to protect the passwords store file. The default, Blowfish, is the best option, as shown in Figure 9-6.

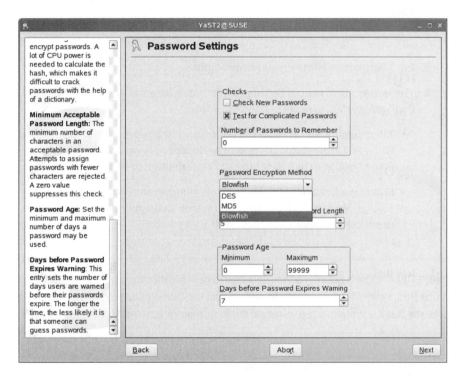

Figure 9-6. *You can change the method of password encryption, but the default of Blowfish is best for most users.*

- Minimum Acceptable Password Length defines how short passwords can be. This is similar to the previous option, Test for Complicated Passwords, but lets you set much longer default password lengths. In fact, the password length can be extended to 72 characters, although the actual length depends on the method of encryption. Bear in mind that a 72-character password is difficult to remember and also annoying to type at each login!

- The Password Age boxes let you set the minimum and maximum age of the passwords. The minimum applies to how long a password is used before the user can change it. The maximum applies to how long the password will remain in use before the user is prompted to change it. By setting a conservative maximum age, you can force users of the system to regularly change their passwords, adding extra security.

- Days Before Password Expires Warning determines how long before password expiration the user is warned that her password needs changing.

Caution At the date of password expiration, the user's login account will simply stop working if the password hasn't been changed.

---

5. Click Next after setting the password options.

6. The next window is Boot Settings. As its name suggests, the options in this window configure certain aspects of bootup, as follows:

   - Interpretation of Ctrl+Alt+Del controls what happens when someone presses Ctrl+Alt+Delete during bootup. The default of Reboot is useful, but you can also cause bootup to halt or set the key combination to be ignored.

   - Shutdown Behavior of KDM controls who can shut down the computer from the K Display Manager (KDM), the login screen that appears if KDE was chosen as the default desktop during installation.

Note The Shutdown Behavior setting appeared to have no influence on my test system. Even when set as Only Root, I was able to shut down the system from the KDM login screen without being logged in as root. I presume that this is due to a bug, or maybe this is an anachronistic setting that's no longer used.

---

7. Click Next after choosing Boot Settings options.

8. The Login Settings window appears. Here, you can set some miscellaneous settings relating to login:

   - Delay After Incorrect Login Attempt defines how long the system will pause after a bad username or password has been supplied. The default setting of 3 means the system will wait three seconds before asking again for a username. This is to prevent crackers from trying various username/password settings in quick combination, which could happen if the delay were set to 0.

- Record Successful Login Attempts writes an entry in the system log file upon successful login (bad logins are automatically recorded). This can be useful because, by checking the log file, you might spot that someone has logged in when you were away from your system, or perhaps from a remote machine. In that case, it would be clear that your computer's security has been compromised.

- Allow Remote Graphical Login lets the user log in using the graphical login screen across a network. For various reasons, it's best if this option is deactivated. If you're the only user of your system, there's no reason why it should be activated.

9. Click Next after choosing Login Settings options.

10. You're presented with the opportunity to set the minimum and maximum user and group ID figures. (Group and user ID, or GUID and UID, numbers are explained in Chapter 30.) The settings in this window are best left unchanged, so click Next.

■Tip If you're an experienced user, you might have realized that setting the User ID Limitations to a maximum and minimum of 1000 will make it impossible to add new users, because it will be impossible to assign them a new UID and GUI number. This can be a useful security measure in its own right, because it will mean that any intruder won't be able to create a new user account, something that is sometimes the first step toward taking control of a system. However, setting the UID and GUID numbers in this way is not a definitive block, because the intruder will probably be able to overcome it eventually.

---

11. The next window offers a handful of miscellaneous options:

- File Permissions relates to file permissions applied to system files. Choose from three settings: Easy, Secure, and Paranoid. Easy lets users access most system files. Secure locks certain sensitive system files from ordinary users, by setting the files as accessible only by root (`-rw-------` file permissions). For example, being able to read the system log files might present intruders with valuable information by which they can further their exploits, so in Secure mode, these files are readable only by root. In addition, it will no longer be possible to run the YaST software from an ordinary user account by typing the root password; only a user logged in as root will be able to run YaST. The Paranoid setting locks yet more system files and items of system software. With the Paranoid setting in effect, ordinary users will be blocked from attempting to undertake any kind of system configuration task or view any kind of system file. It will be impossible to type `su` and switch to root user from an ordinary user account, for example (see Figure 9-7 for an example of what will happen if users try to use `su`). The only way to configure the system will be to log in specifically as root user.

Note Secure and Paranoid modes provide a high degree of protection, but this comes at the expense of user convenience. For most ordinary users, the Easy option provides adequate protection. The curious might wish to try the Secure or Paranoid settings to see if their prohibitive policies affect their day-to-day use of SUSE Linux. However, bear in mind that once they're in operation, YaST will become inoperative to all but the root user. You won't be able to switch back to the Easy mode, unless you log in as root user and manually run YaST from the command line. To do this, hold down Ctrl+Alt and press F2. Type `root` at the login prompt, and then enter your password. Then type `yast2` and hit Enter. This will run YaST in text mode. You can navigate using the cursor keys. Pressing Tab will move you from field to field on the forms. Pressing the spacebar will select an option.

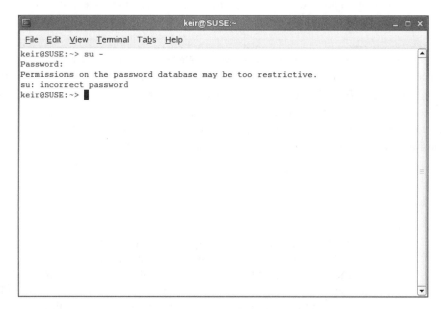

Figure 9-7. *When the Paranoid setting is chosen in the Miscellaneous window, you'll be locked out from switching users via the su command.*

- User Launching UpdateDB relates to the permissions with which the `updatedb` command is automatically run (see Chapter 14 for details on `updatedb` and `locate`). The `findutils-locate` package will need to be installed for this option to be relevant. When set to "nobody," the `updatedb` command will be run without root privileges, which means it will be able to catalog only files that are readable by nonroot users. This is good for security, bearing in mind that any user can use the `locate` command and therefore unearth the location of critical system files or personal files of other users. But it's bad for general use of `locate`, because fewer files will be cataloged. The "root" option will catalog all files.

- Current Directory in Path (of both root and regular users) relates to whether software can be run from the current directory without the user having to explicitly insert ./ before it. In other words, the current directory will be searched first when the user enters a command and, if matching software is found, it will be executed. For example, if the current directory contains an executable file called ls, and the user types ls from the command prompt, the executable file in the directory will be run. Ordinarily, the system will first look for ls in /usr/bin, and then look in other directories stated in the $PATH shell variable.

- Current Directory lets the user run software he has just downloaded by simply typing its filename. However, this option runs the risk of accidentally running software in the current directory, and virus writers could exploit the option by somehow dropping replacement software into the user's current directory. So, both this and the previous option are best left deactivated.

- Enable Magic SysRq Keys enables special key combinations that are hard-wired into the kernel. The kernel will respond to these key combinations no matter what else is happening. This option is mainly used by developers when debugging Linux and is best left deactivated.

12. When you've finished making your choices, click Finish. The changes will then be written to your system files.

Using the SUSE Linux Firewall

The SUSE Linux firewall component is activated by default. In its default state, it closes the computer to all outside connections that aren't direct responses to requests for data. For example, if your computer contacts a web site to request a particular web page, such a data connection will be allowed. But if a remote computer attempts to connect to your computer without being invited, the connection will be refused.

■**Note** There are many legitimate reasons why a computer would attempt to connect to your computer uninvited, so this isn't necessarily a bad thing. A good example is the SSH service, by which you can remotely connect to your computer, as explained in Chapter 34.

There is no need for the average user to change the default SUSE Linux firewall settings. The only reason to do so would be to enable some kind of server application, such as the popular BitTorrent file-sharing service. The following sections describe changes you may need to make to the default firewall settings for special requirements.

Changing Firewall Zones

The SUSE Linux firewall refers to three "zones." Your network device, regardless of whether it's an Ethernet card, wireless device, or even modem, is "placed" in one of these zones, which defines the degree of protection it is given. (In fact, if your computer has more than one network device, each can be placed in a different zone.)

Note The zones are actually three sets of firewall rules for iptables, the firewall component within SUSE Linux. This might help you understand how the SUSE Linux firewall works if you've used an alternative Linux distro.

The zones are as follows:

Internal Zone: Effectively, this is the "trusted" zone because it's assumed that all connections in the internal zone originate on a local area network (LAN) that uses private network addressing (sometimes known as *nonroutable* addresses), courtesy of some kind of Network Address Translation (NAT) device or software. In this zone, a wide variety of incoming connections are accepted by your computer.

External Zone: This zone is the opposite of the Internal Zone. If placed in this zone, your computer is "closed" to all incoming uninvited connections. This is the default zone that a network device is placed into, and it is the safest zone.

Demilitarized Zone: This zone is half and half of the other two zones. A network device placed in this zone can be accessed by computers on internal and external networks, but a piece of software utilizing a network device in this zone can't connect to other computers on the internal network. The Demilitarized Zone is used only in complicated firewall setups, where SUSE Linux itself is acting as the firewall computer for other computers, and isn't useful for home users.

By default, all network devices are placed in the External Zone, which is the most secure. There are very few situations when it's a good idea not to use the External Zone. Even if your computer is part of a LAN and is protected by a separate firewall device, using the External Zone is still a good idea, because it offers an additional layer of protection.

If your computer is part of a LAN on which resources are shared (such as shared folders and printers), it might be necessary to switch to the Internal Zone. In such a situation, it is assumed that all the computers on the network are protected by a separate firewall device, such as a broadband router. Switching to the Internal Zone is necessary to allow other computers to randomly connect to yours, and also to allow network file sharing to work correctly, such as Windows File Sharing/SMB.

Follow these steps to change the zone that your network device is placed within:

1. Start YaST (click Desktop ➤ YaST under GNOME; click K menu ➤ System ➤ YaST under KDE).

2. Click Security and Users on the left side of the window, and then click Firewall on the right.

3. In the Firewall Configuration window, click Interfaces on the menu on the left.

4. Select your network device from the list, and then click the Change button.

5. In the dialog box that appears, select the new zone, as shown in Figure 9-8. Then click OK.

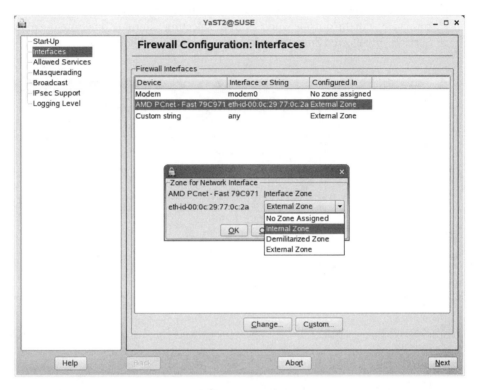

Figure 9-8. *Change the firewall zone by selecting it from the drop-down list.*

6. In the Firewall Configuration window, click the Next button, and then Accept. This will write the changes and restart the firewall using them.

Configuring the SUSE Linux Firewall

If your computer is in the External Zone, sometimes it might be necessary to open a "hole" in the firewall to allow through uninvited incoming connections. This is referred to as *opening a port* on the firewall. If you're running some kind of server on your computer, this will be necessary. For home users, one of the few situations where opening a port in the firewall is required is to allow uninvited SSH connections for remote administration of your computer. (For details on remote administration, see Chapter 34.)

Here's how to open a port in the firewall:

1. Start YaST (click Desktop ➤ YaST under GNOME; click K menu ➤ System ➤ YaST under KDE).

2. Click Security and Users on the left side of the window, and then click Firewall on the right.

3. Click the Allowed Services entry on the left side of the window.

4. In the Allowed Services window, you can opt to allow uninvited connections from external computers by adding *services*—effectively, items of software that need to communicate with the outside world. Start by selecting External Zone from the Allowed Services for Selected Zone drop-down list, as shown in Figure 9-9.

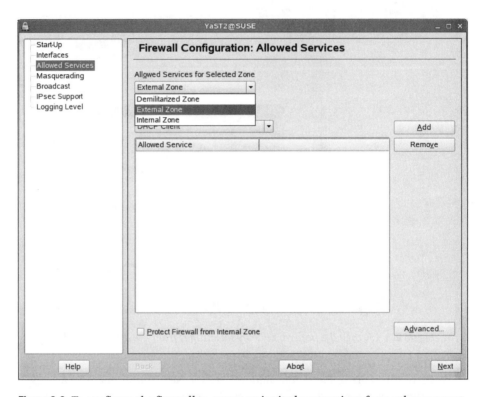

Figure 9-9. *To configure the firewall to accept uninvited connections from other computers, start by selecting External Zone from the Allowed Services drop-down list.*

5. To configure your computer to accept incoming Samba/Windows file sharing requests, select SSH from the Services to Allow drop-down list. Then click the Add button.

6. You can also manually define a service by clicking the Advanced button. In the window that appears, you can define the TCP port, the UDP port, the RPC port, or simply name the IP protocol you wish to allow through (according to the IANA list of protocol names, which you can find at www.iana.org/assignments/service-names). The service you define will not appear in the Allowed Service window, but the settings will be confirmed when you click the Next button.

7. When you've finished, click the Next button. You'll be shown a summary of the settings you've changed. To apply them, click the Accept button.

Using AppArmor

AppArmor is a hugely powerful piece of software. It finds its way into SUSE Linux via SUSE Linux's big brother, SUSE Linux Enterprise Server, where AppArmor forms part of an industrial-grade security system. Using AppArmor requires knowledge of the way Linux works and experience with Linux systems. It is a complex component to configure.

The goal of the software is to confine particular software applications to a definable set of resources within the system. This guards against bugs in the software that might lead to buffer overflow situations. By confining the application to a strict set of resources, any attempt to exploit a buffer overflow by injecting code should be impossible, because the additional code won't be authorized to access resources.

It's impractical to use AppArmor to protect every application on the system because that would take too long. Therefore, it's a better idea to use it to guard specific applications that an attacker might use to gain access to the system. That normally equates specifically to applications that access the network/Internet.

To this end, several profiles for common network-facing applications are included with AppArmor by default. Others can be defined but, again, it is impractically time-consuming to protect all network/Internet-facing applications using AppArmor.

If you want to use AppArmor, I suggest that you profile only proprietary applications. As I mentioned earlier in this chapter, any severe bugs in open-source software that might lead to buffer overflow situations are normally patched very quickly by system updates. However, proprietary software may not be upgraded as quickly. Additionally, the closed-source nature of proprietary software means that bugs are harder to spot because the source code isn't open to inspection.

As an example, the following steps outline how to create an AppArmor profile for the RealPlayer media playback software. The same techniques can be applied to virtually any application. (Note that this isn't an implication that the RealPlayer software contains any kind of bug that may lead to security threat.)

1. Before starting the AppArmor component of YaST, run the software in question to ensure that it works correctly. It is also necessary to step through any first-run setup wizards, because the goal is to profile the application as it normally runs. Therefore, you should start RealPlayer by clicking its menu entry (in GNOME, Applications ➤ Multimedia ➤ RealPlayer 10; in KDE, K menu ➤ Multimedia ➤ RealPlayer). Close the application when you've finished.

2. Start YaST (click Desktop ➤ YaST under GNOME; click K menu ➤ System ➤ YaST under KDE).

3. Click the Novell AppArmor icon on the left side of the window, and then click the Add Profile Wizard icon on the right.

4. You'll be prompted for the command-line name of the application. In the case of RealPlayer, this is `realplay`. You can find out the command-line name of the program by opening a terminal window and simply trying to guess it, or by examining the application's menu shortcut.

5. Click the Create button. Then run the application as usual from its Application/K menu entry. Fully exploit all the functionality of the application. In the case of RealPlayer, load movies and audio files, and play movie files in full screen, as shown in Figure 9-10. While you are doing this, the system is logging the resources the program accesses. This will be utilized to create the profile.

■**Caution** When I say use every function, I really mean it! If you don't do this, the AppArmor Profile Wizard might not pick up on that particular function, and so might not allow it. In the case of RealPlayer, you should open every type of file you're likely to play in it, connect to the Internet to play streaming media, and so on.

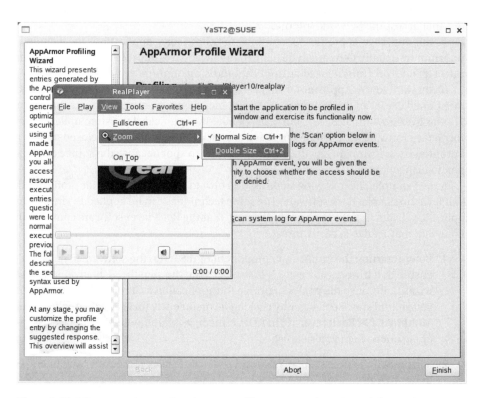

Figure 9-10. *When creating an AppArmor profile, use every function of the application.*

6. When you've finished, quit the program in question and return to the AppArmor Profile Wizard window.

7. Click the Scan System Log for AppArmor Events button.

8. The AppArmor wizard walks you through the various system resources and applications that RealPlayer used while it was running. There are usually two main options: Accept or Deny. However, if the application being profile accessed applications

previously profiled within AppArmor, it can inherit the profile of that application when using that application, and a button marked Inherit will appear.

9. The wizard shows each resource being accessed. Unless you're extremely knowledgeable about Linux, click Accept or Inherit for each option. This will create a profile that lets the application access the system components it needs. Work through the wizard, clicking Inherit or Accept for each option.

10. When you've finished, you'll be returned to the AppArmor wizard window that you saw previously. Click the Finish button to write the profile to disk. The application will now be profiled within AppArmor. You can test the application by running it from the Applications or K menu.

11. If you find the application isn't working correctly, and that AppArmor is stopping the application from performing a task, return to the AppArmor component of YaST and click Update Profile Wizard.

12. The Update Profile Wizard function will pick up any AppArmor deny messages in the log, and you'll be offered a chance to allow them, as shown in Figure 9-11. Be careful to only allow permissions for the applications you've profiled. The Update Profile Wizard will pick up deny messages for *all* applications profiled by AppArmor. You should click Deny for any application other than the one whose profile you're interested in amending.

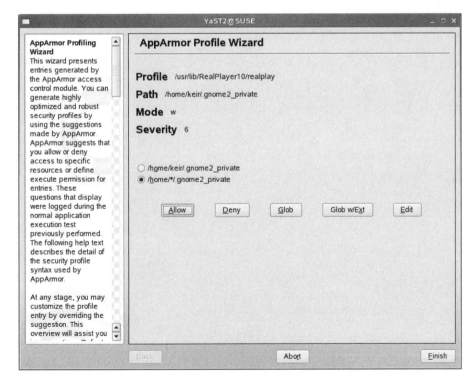

Figure 9-11. *If you find an application isn't working correctly after creating an AppArmor profile, run the Update Profile Wizard and amend the permissions list.*

> **Tip** AppArmor is a sophisticated application, and I've only scratched the surface of its capabilities. For more information, you can read Novell's AppArmor documentation. You'll find a QuickStart Guide at www.novell.com/documentation/apparmor/pdfdoc/apparmor_install/apparmor_install.pdf and an Administration Guide at www.novell.com/documentation/apparmor/pdfdoc/apparmor_user/apparmor_user.pdf.

Summary

In this chapter, we looked at what threats your system faces and how security holes can be exploited by malicious interests. You learned about measures you can take to protect your system: updating it online, setting up local security, configuring the system's firewall, and creating AppArmor profiles. We also discussed some common-sense rules you can follow to keep your system safe.

In the next chapter, we move on to looking at how your SUSE Linux system can be personalized and how to set up everything to suit your own preferences.

CHAPTER 10

▪▪▪

Personalizing SUSE Linux: Getting Everything Just Right

If you've read this book from Chapter 1, by now you've become comfortable with SUSE Linux. You've started to realize its advantages and are on the way to making it your operating system of choice.

But things still might not be quite right. For instance, you might find the color scheme is not to your tastes. Or perhaps you feel that the mouse cursor moves a little too fast (or too slowly). Maybe you simply want to stamp your own individuality on your system.

That's what this chapter is all about. You'll discover how to personalize SUSE Linux so that you're completely happy with your user experience. Under each main heading, you'll find instructions for the GNOME desktop, followed by the corresponding instructions for KDE.

Changing the Look and Feel

SUSE Linux is similar to Windows in many ways, but the developers behind it introduced improvements and tweaks that many claim make the software easier to use. For example, SUSE Linux offers multiple virtual desktops—long considered a very useful user-interface feature that seems to have passed Microsoft by. However, if you're not satisfied with SUSE Linux's out-of-the-box look and feel, you can change it.

You might be used to changing the desktop colors or wallpaper under Windows, but the GNOME and KDE desktops under SUSE Linux go to extremes and let you alter the look and feel of the entire desktop. Everything from the styling of the program windows to the desktop icons can be altered quickly and easily.

SUSE Linux refers to the look of the desktop as a *theme*. Because it's built on the GNOME and KDE desktops, SUSE Linux allows you to radically personalize your desktop theme. Several different themes come with the distribution, and you can download many others. Each lets you change the way the windows look, including the buttons and the icon set (although some themes come without additional icons).

Without further ado, let's get on with customizing the desktop!

SWITCHING BETWEEN KDE AND GNOME

When you installed SUSE Linux (covered in Chapter 5), you made a fundamental choice: which desktop environment to install and use. At that point, you selected either KDE or GNOME. Now that you've been using SUSE Linux for some time, you may have found that your initial choice fails to meet your needs and expectations.

The good news is that switching between GNOME and KDE is easy. This doesn't have to be a permanent change. You can try using KDE or GNOME to see if you like it, and if you find it's not for you, switch back to your previous choice with a few mouse clicks.

Start by ensuring that both KDE and GNOME are installed, as follows:

1. Start YaST. Under KDE, click K menu ➤ System ➤ YaST. Under GNOME, click Desktop ➤ YaST. You'll need to enter your root password, so do so.

2. Select the Software icon on the left side of the YaST window, and then click the Software Management icon on the right side of the window.

3. In the Filter drop-down list at the top left of the Software Management window, choose the Selections option. In the list on the left side, put a check in the KDE Desktop Environment or GNOME System box (of course, one of these boxes will already be checked, depending on which choice you made during installation).

4. Click the Accept button, and then insert your SUSE Linux DVD-ROM to install the software.

To choose between GNOME and KDE, log out so that you're returned to the login screen. To log out under KDE, click K menu ➤ Log Out, then End Current Session. Under GNOME, click Desktop ➤ Log Out. What to do next depends on which choice you made during installation, because this defined whether you use the KDE or GNOME display manager (known as KDM and GDM, respectively).

- If you chose GNOME as the default during installation, and now want to try KDE, click the Session button at the bottom left of the login screen and, in the dialog box that appears, select KDE in order to boot the KDE desktop. Then type your username and password in the relevant fields (hitting Enter when you've finished typing your password will log you on). Later on, you can repeat this step to switch back to GNOME.

- If you chose KDE during installation, and now want to try the GNOME desktop, click the Session Type button at the bottom left of the screen and select GNOME from the list. Then log in by entering your username and password.

GNOME: Altering the Theme

GNOME offers many tools to personalize the user experience, sometimes quite radically. However, unlike Windows themes, most GNOME themes normally don't change the fonts used on the desktop, and the wallpaper and color scheme will probably remain broadly the same. You can change these manually, as described in the "Setting Font Preferences" and "Changing the Wallpaper" sections, coming up after the discussion of themes and theme components.

Selecting a Theme

To select a new theme, click Desktop ➤ Control Center, and then double-click the Theme icon under the Look and Feel heading. In the Theme Preferences dialog box, you can choose a theme from the list, as shown in Figure 10-1. A useful hint is to open a Nautilus file browser window in the background (Places ➤ Desktop), so you can see how the changes will affect a typical window.

Figure 10-1. *SUSE Linux comes with several theme choices.*

My favorite themes are Clearlooks and Mist, largely because they're uncomplicated. Remember that you'll be working with the theme on a daily basis, so it should be practical and not too distracting. Those miniature close, minimize, and maximize buttons might look stylish, but they're useless if they're so small that you can't reliably click them with your mouse.

As well as changing the overall theme, you can also modify individual theme components, and even download more theme components.

Changing Individual Theme Components

You can alter the three aspects that constitute a GNOME theme: the controls (sometimes known as *widgets*), the window borders, and the icons. Controls are simply the elements you click within dialog boxes and windows: buttons, scroll bars, and so on. The window borders are, as seems obvious, the borders of program windows and dialog boxes, with particular attention paid to the top of the window, where the program name appears along with the minimize, maximize, and close buttons.

Note To make matters a little confusing, some window borders have their own selection of close, minimize, and maximize controls, which can't be overridden with individual selections for controls.

To make changes to a theme, click the Theme Details button in the Theme Preferences dialog box (Figure 10-1), and then click each tab to see your choices, as shown in Figure 10-2. Unfortunately, there are no thumbnail previews of each style, but as soon as you click each option, it will be automatically applied to the currently open windows. To preview the effects fully, the best policy is to keep a Nautilus window open (Places ➤ Desktop).

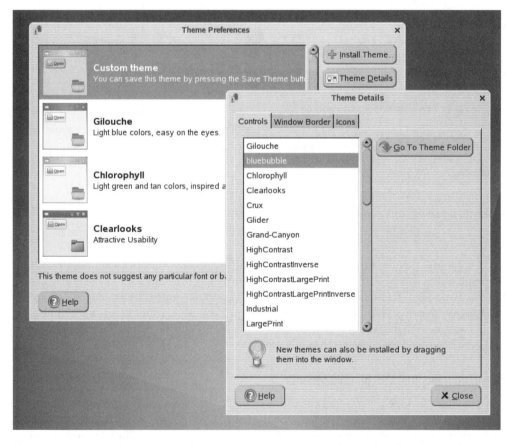

Figure 10-2. *You can create a theme by choosing your own controls, window borders, and icons.*

When you've made your choices, you can save the theme for further use by clicking the Save Theme button in the Theme Preferences dialog box. You'll need to give the theme a name and, if you wish, a short description for future reference. If you don't save the theme, as soon as you select another one, the changes you made will be lost.

Installing Additional Theme Components

If you get tired of the built-in possibilities, you can download additional theme components, such as window borders and controls, to enhance your desktop experience. These are best downloaded from the official GNOME Art web site (`http://art.gnome.org`), which will give you access to just about every theme ever created for GNOME. In fact, the site also offers wallpaper selections, icons, and much more. All of the offerings are free to use, and most of the packages are created by enthusiasts.

Installing new theme components is easy. If you wish to install a new window border, for example, click the link to browse the examples, and when you find one you like, click to download it. It will be contained in a `.tar.gz` archive, but you don't need to unpack it. Simply open the Theme applet (Desktop ➤ Control Center, and then double-click Theme), and click the Install Theme button in the Theme Preferences dialog box. Then browse to the downloaded theme and click Open. You can delete the downloaded file when you're finished.

After you've installed a theme component, to select it, click Theme Details, and then click the corresponding tab in the dialog box.

■**Note** The same principle of sharing that underlies the GPL software license is also usually applied to themes. This means that one person can take a theme created by someone else, tweak it, and then release it as a new theme. This ensures constant innovation and improvement.

Changing the Wallpaper

To choose a different wallpaper, right-click the desktop and click Change Desktop Background. If you want to use a picture of your own as wallpaper, click the Add Wallpaper button, and then browse to its location.

In the Style drop-down list, you can select from the following choices, which affect how the wallpaper is displayed:

Centered: This option places the wallpaper in the center of the screen. If the wallpaper is not big enough to fill the screen, a border appears around the edge. If it's bigger than the screen, the edges of the wallpaper are cropped off.

Fill Screen: This option forces the picture to fit the screen, including squashing or expanding it if necessary (known as altering its aspect ratio). If the wallpaper isn't in the same ratio as the screen, it will look distorted, as shown in Figure 10-3. Most digital camera shots should be okay, because they use the same 4:3 ratio as most monitors (although if you have a widescreen monitor, a digital camera picture will be stretched horizontally).

Figure 10-3. *Wallpaper can be stretched to fill the screen, but doing so may distort its proportions and make it look odd.*

Scaled: Like the Fill Screen option, this option enlarges the image if it's too small or shrinks it if it's too big, but it maintains the aspect ratio, thus avoiding distortion. However, if the picture is in a different aspect ratio than the monitor, it may have borders at the edges.

Tiled: If the picture is smaller than the desktop resolution, this option simply repeats the picture (starting from the top left) until the screen is filled. This option is primarily designed for patterned graphics.

Don't forget that the GNOME Art web site (http://art.gnome.org) offers many wallpaper packages for download.

Selecting a Screensaver

The GNOME desktop of SUSE Linux comes with a handful of screensavers. Although the days when screen burn-in was an issue are long gone, the GNOME screensaver provides something to look at during down moments and also automatically locks the screen so that no one can use the computer until the user's password is entered.

To choose a screensaver, click Desktop ➤ Control Center, and then double-click the Screensaver icon beneath the Look and Feel heading. You can click and drag the Set Session as Idle slider to set how quickly the screensaver kicks in after the computer hasn't been used for some time. To specify that your login password is needed to bring the computer out of the screensaver, put a check in the Lock Screen When Screensaver Is Active box.

Setting Font Preferences

SUSE Linux lets you change the fonts that are used throughout SUSE Linux (referred to as system fonts). You can also alter how they're displayed.

To change a system font, select Desktop ➤ Control Center and then double-click the Fonts icon under the Look and Feel heading.

In the Font Preferences dialog box, click the button next to the system font you want to change, and then choose from the list. You can also set the font point size so, for example, you can make the labels beneath icons easier to read.

The Font Rendering heading in the Font Preferences dialog box contains options to control how fonts look on your monitor, in terms of their antialiasing. Sadly, not all of these configuration settings work. On my test system I found that switching between Monochrome, Best Shapes, and Best Contrast made little difference. However, the Subpixel Smoothing (LCDs) option did appear to work correctly and improved the appearance of fonts on my TFT screen.

TURNING OFF FONT ANTIALIASING

The SUSE Linux font display system assumes that you want antialiasing activated at all times. Most people find antialiasing acceptable, but if you're among those who think it makes letters look blurry or "dirty," you'll be pleased to hear there's something you can do about it.

Although both the GNOME and KDE desktops claim to let you deactivate antialiasing using the font configuration tools, they really don't do a complete job of turning it off. This can leave fonts looking even worse than they did originally.

To fully deactivate antialiasing, at least for fonts below a certain size, it's necessary to edit a configuration file.

Start by opening a terminal window. In GNOME, click Applications ➤ System ➤ Terminal ➤ Gnome Terminal. In KDE, click K menu ➤ System ➤ Terminal ➤ Konsole. Then, in GNOME, type the following to switch to the root user and open the relevant file using the GNOME Gedit text editor:

```
su -
[Enter root password]
gedit /etc/sysconfig/fonts-config
```

Continues

Those using KDE should type the following to open the file using the Kate text editor:

```
su -
[Enter root password]
kate /etc/sysconfig/fonts-config
```

Scroll down to the line that begins BYTECODE_BW_MAX_PIXEL= and change the 0 to a 16. This number refers to the point size at which antialiasing kicks in. A setting of 16 points is good because larger fonts always look worse without antialiasing, since the jagged edges are much more apparent.

Save the file and then, in the terminal window, type the following:

```
SuSEconfig
```

Once this command has completed, which may take a few moments, log out and then back in to the current session, or simply reboot.

On one of my test systems, I noticed that the fonts looked awful after deactivating antialiasing, no matter what I did. I suspect this was due to a buggy monitor profile that had incorrect DPI settings. To reverse the effect, and thereby reactivate antialiasing, I repeated the procedure and restored the BYTECODE_BW_MAX_PIXEL= value to 0. Then I ran SuSEconfig again, logged out, and logged back in again.

KDE: Altering the Theme

As with GNOME, you can change the look and feel of the KDE desktop. In fact, KDE offers many more options for themes, window decorations, theme components, and so on, giving you a lot of control over your desktop's appearance and behavior.

Selecting an Overall Theme

Theme configuration within KDE is broadly similar to that in GNOME, although it has its own peculiarities. As with many KDE-specific components, you can choose theme settings using the KDE Control Center.

To change the theme, start by clicking K menu ➤ Personal Settings. In the window that appears, click the Appearance & Themes icon on the left, and then click Theme Manager in the new list of icons on the left. In the Theme Manager window, you can choose from the various complete themes, as shown in Figure 10-4. When you click a theme in the Theme list, you'll see a preview on the right side of the window. When you've happy with your choice, click the Apply button.

Figure 10-4. *A variety of complete themes are available under the KDE desktop, or you can choose to customize individual theme components.*

Changing Window Decorations

KDE lets you adjust the borders of windows and buttons in title bars. To make changes, click K menu ➤ Personal Settings. In the window that appears, click the Appearance & Themes icon on the left, and then click the Window Decorations icon on the left.

In the Window Decorations window, choose a window decoration you like from the drop-down list, and you'll see a preview at the bottom of the window. Some window decorations bring with them their own set of settings that can be tweaked. The best policy is to experiment with these. Clicking the Apply button will activate the settings so you can see the effect.

The Border Size drop-down list lets you set the thickness of the window border. This is a matter of personal preference, but I prefer to set it to Tiny, so that windows don't have over-whelming black outlines.

Click the Buttons tab to add and remove items from the window title bar. If you wish, you can remove the close, minimize, and maximize buttons, although that would be foolish! You can add a few buttons, such as Shade, which will "fold up" the window when it's clicked (clicking the button again will unfold the window). You can also alter the placement of buttons and insert spaces between them. To make these changes, click the Spacer button.

Changing Individual Theme Components

In the Theme Manager window (Figure 10-4), you may have noticed six buttons running along the bottom, labeled Background, Colors, Style, Icons, Fonts, and Screen Saver. Clicking each button opens a window where you can change the named component of a theme, as described in the following sections. After making changes, be sure to click the Apply button so that your changes take effect.

Background

Clicking the Background button lets you change the wallpaper. At the top of the window, you can select whether the choices you make apply to the current desktop or to all desktops, assuming you're using the virtual desktop feature (see Chapter 7). If the current desktop option is selected, you can later switch to each individual desktop and apply individual wallpaper settings.

Under the Background heading, you can choose what the background contains: No Picture, Picture, or Slide Show (for a changing series of pictures). If you select the Slide Show option, you will be present with a dialog box for choosing the pictures and also the time period before the picture is changed. If you choose the Picture option, you can select from a drop-down list of wallpapers. Many are supplied by default, offering a variety of interesting styles. Alternatively, by clicking the folder icon next to the list, you can choose a wallpaper from your own selection of pictures on the hard disk.

Under the Options heading, you can choose how the wallpaper is displayed. Alternatively, if you selected No Picture, you can change how the colored background is displayed. The Position drop-down list offers the following options:

Centered: The image will appear on the desktop at its full size, without being stretched. If it's too big for the screen, parts of it will be cropped off. If it's too small, the background color will show through.

Tiled: Starting from the left corner, the image will be repeated until it reaches the bottom right. Of course, if the image is the same size as the screen, or larger, this option won't have much effect. But if the picture is a small, patterned texture designed to be tiled, then this option is useful.

Center Tiled: Like the Tiled choice, this option tiles the picture. However, rather than start from the top left, the tiling starts from the center and works up to the left corner and down to the right corner.

Centered Maxpect: If the picture is too small, this option will enlarge it until the top and bottom of the image hit the top and bottom of the screen. However, the image won't be stretched horizontally, so the background color might show through.

Tile Maxpect: The picture is placed in the top-left corner and then stretched until it meets either the right side of the screen or the bottom of the screen. Once this happens, the image will then be tiled at the same size, so that any remaining space is also filled with the scaled image.

Scaled: The picture is stretched to fit the desktop. Each corner of the image is stretched to each corner of the screen. Note that this may distort the image if the aspect ratio isn't exactly the same as the screen.

Centered Auto Fit: This option is designed for images larger than the desktop resolution. The image is shrunk to fill the screen, although it isn't stretched, so the background colors may show through in parts.

Scale and Crop: This is like the Scaled option, in that the image is stretched to fill the desktop, but it isn't distorted. Instead, the image is centered and then stretched until it meets all the edges, even if this means that some edges are cropped off.

The Colors drop-down list offers a selection of color blends, such as gradients. Bear in mind that these probably won't be visible if you're using wallpaper. Beneath the drop-down list, select either the two colors that make up the blend or the single color that is shown if the Single Color option is selected in the Color drop-down list.

The Blending drop-down list lets you mix the wallpaper with the background color in a variety of ways. In Figure 10-5, you can see a Horizontal blend in effect. The Balance slider controls the quantity of wallpaper versus the quantity of background color used in the blend.

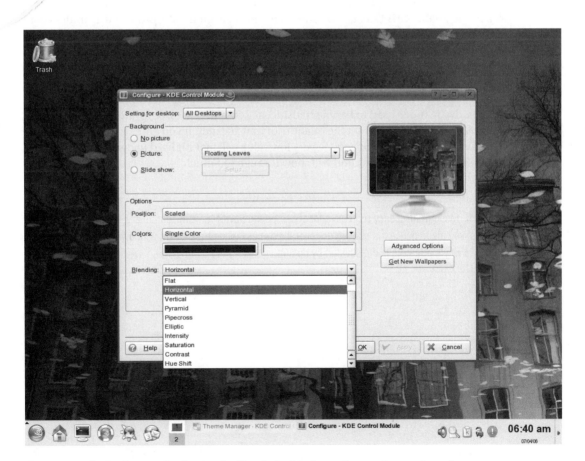

Figure 10-5. *The background color can be blended with the wallpaper in a variety of ways.*

Colors

The Colors window offers a variety of color schemes that are applied to the current window style and widget theme. (*Widgets* are elements within program windows and dialog boxes, such as buttons and scroll bars.) Simply select from the list under the Color Scheme heading. As the scheme is changed, the preview at the top of the window will show what it looks like (note that this is a preview using a generic theme, rather than the current theme).

Alternatively, you can define your own color scheme by clicking an item in the preview, and then clicking the color bar in the Widget Color box. Then select the color you want from the color wheel.

The Contrast slider lets you select the hardness of the 3D-effect edges on buttons, windows, and so on. A Low setting reduces the effect; a High setting emphasizes it. This effect isn't always noticeable and depends on the theme and color selections in operation.

Style

The Style button lets you alter the widget theme—the styling of the buttons, scroll bars, and other on-screen elements. A number of predefined themes are available in the Widget Style drop-down list. Selecting them instantly applies them to the preview.

Clicking the Effects tab lets you activate various visual effects. Make sure there's a check in the Enable GUI Effects box, and then choose from the drop-down lists under each heading.

The Menu Translucency Type settings are activated when the Make Translucent option is selected in the Menu Effect drop-down list. *Translucency* is what people sometimes refer to as "see-through." In this case, it will be possible to see through menus to whatever is behind, as shown in Figure 10-6. Under the Menu Translucency Type drop-down list, you can select the type of hardware mode used to handle translucency. In most cases, Software Tint is the best option. Beneath this, you can set the quantity of translucency. If you enter too high a value, the menu will be practically opaque. A very low value will make it hard to discern what's on the menu, because the background will show through too much.

■**Caution** Menu translucency requires a lot of computing power to work seamlessly. Even on the fastest computers, you might notice the odd lag or general slowness when translucent windows appear or disappear. This is why the feature is deactivated by default.

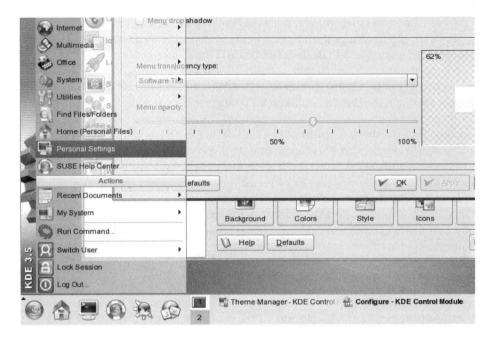

Figure 10-6. *The translucency effect makes menus "see-through," so that whatever is behind will show through.*

The Toolbar tab contains options for how toolbars are displayed within KDE, as well as other special effects for toolbars.

Icons

The Icons window offers choices for the icon theme used by KDE. By default, only two options appear, and they're practically identical. You can download third-party icon themes from web sites like `www.kde-look.org`. See the "Installing Additional Theme Components" section for instructions on installing them.

By clicking the Advanced tab, you can alter some of the details relating to icons, such as their default size. You can also change the look of various icon states. For example, when the mouse moves over an icon, it is said to be "active" and it is brightened accordingly. By clicking the Set Effect button beneath the Active icon, you can select what happens to the icon when the mouse moves over it. Alternatives include changing color or desaturating color. Or you can simply select No Effect, so that nothing happens.

Fonts

In the Fonts window, you can set the fonts that are used throughout the KDE desktop, such as the font for desktop icons, the font in window title bars, and so on. Simply click the Choose button alongside the entry, and then make a choice from the list.

Alternatively, you can click the Adjust All Fonts button to make global changes to all fonts. In the Font dialog box that appears, put a check alongside the attributes that you wish to change. For example, to change the font size, but leave the individual font choices for each element unchanged, put a check in the font size box and then make your selection.

The Fonts applet also lets you change antialiasing settings. *Antialiasing* softens the edges of each letter to make them appear less jagged. You can activate and deactivate antialiasing by checking the Use Anti-Aliasing for Fonts box. Be aware that fonts won't look good without antialiasing. Clicking the Configure button will give you a number of options relating to antialiasing settings. The first of these, Exclude Range, lets you turn off antialiasing for fonts under a certain size. This can be useful for very small fonts, which can turn into a blurry mess if antialiased. Use Sub-Pixel Hinting activates a feature that makes fonts appear better on thin film transistor (TFT) screens. You can also select the pixel order from the drop-down list, although the default of RGB is usually correct.

The Hinting Style options affect the spacing and shaping of the letters. Selecting Full here is generally a good idea, although some people prefer other settings such as Medium, Slight, or even None.

Screensaver

To change the screensaver properties, click the Screen Saver button in the Theme Manager window. Many screensavers are available under KDE, arranged in a tree list on the left side of the window.

To have the screensaver appear after a predefined amount of time, put a check in the Start Automatically box, and then set a time period. Choosing the Require Password to Stop option will cause the computer to require the user to enter a password before the screensaver is deactivated. Note that a separate time period can be set here, so that the requirement for a password can be set to kick in *after* the screensaver has started. This can be useful if you want the screensaver to start after a short period of inactivity, but since you're likely to still be at your desk (maybe during a phone call), you don't want to have to type in your password each time. However, if your computer is unused for a longer period, during which time it's likely you'll be away from the desk, the password protection will be enforced.

Setting Program Launch Feedback

KDE lets you control the mouse cursor animation effects that appear when a program is launched. To make changes, click K menu ➤ Personal Settings. In the window that appears, click the Appearance & Themes icon on the left, and then click the Launch Feedback icon on the left.

In the Busy Cursor drop-down list, you can select from a bouncing cursor, a blinking cursor, or a standard busy cursor. In the Taskbar Notification section, you can control if a "busy" taskbar button appears when new programs are launched. If this option is deactivated, the taskbar button won't appear until the application has launched.

Changing the Splash Screen

The splash screen appears when KDE first starts up, indicating when KDE subsystems have started. To select a splash screen, click K menu ➤ Personal Settings. In the window that appears, click the Appearance & Themes icon on the left, and then click the Splash Screen icon on the left.

A number of splash screen designs are available, including Redmond, which is a copy of the Windows XP boot screen, as shown in Figure 10-7. Just select one from the list. Previews are shown on the right side of the window.

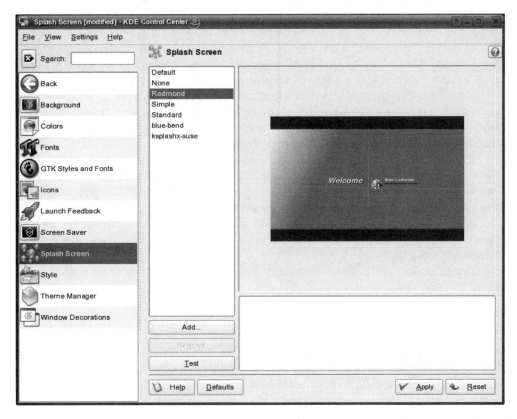

Figure 10-7. *You can change the splash screen that appears whenever KDE starts up. The Redmond option is good for those who love Microsoft products!*

Installing Additional Theme Components

A number of third-party theme components for KDE are available from web sites like www.kde-look.org. Themes are normally supplied in tar.gz packages. Once they're downloaded, it's necessary to decompress them before installation. To do this, right-click the package and click Extract ➤ Extract Here.

To install the new theme component, click K menu ➤ Personal Settings. In the Personal Settings window, click the Appearance & Themes icon on the left, and then click Theme Manager in the list on the left. In the Theme Manager window, click the Install New Theme button. Navigate to the location where you extracted the files and look for the .kth file. Select it and click the Open button. This will install the theme, and you should be able to select it from the list of themes.

You can delete the extracted files once the theme is installed.

ALTERNATIVE DESKTOPS

GNOME and KDE are by no means the only desktop environments available for SUSE Linux. There are many more available, although they're not supplied on the installation DVD-ROM and must be installed separately. For instructions on how to install software under SUSE, see Chapter 29.

Perhaps the third best choice for beginning Linux users, after GNOME and KDE, is Xfce (www.xfce.org). This is a little like a stripped-down version of the GNOME desktop. This stripping down is intentional, because one of the goals of Xfce is to run quickly on older, less-powerful hardware. However, this doesn't come at the sacrifice of usability or good looks, and Xfce contains all the functions you need for day-to-day use.

A choice of many experienced Linux users is Enlightenment (www.enlightenment.org). Technically speaking, Enlightenment is a window manager, which means it provides just the basics of the user interface. Users must therefore source "extras," such as a file manager, from third parties (although the Konqueror and Nautilus programs from GNOME and KDE can be used, of course).

Those who want the totally stripped-down experience will appreciate IceWM (www.icewm.org), where features are sacrificed for simplicity and, to paraphrase the official web site, simplicity is offered in order to stop the interface from getting in the user's way. Like Enlightenment, IceWM is a window manager, rather than a desktop environment, so it supplies just the basics of the user interface.

In terms of the user experience, both Enlightenment and IceWM introduce radical and innovative concepts to the Linux desktop, and so the learning curve can be a little steep. They're certainly not clones of Windows and/or Mac OS X!

To see a complete list of desktop environments and window managers, and to learn more about them, visit http://xwinman.org.

Configuring Input Devices

Mouse and key repeat speeds are personal to each user, and you may find the default SUSE Linux settings not to your taste, particularly if you have a high-resolution mouse such as a gaming model. Fortunately, changing each setting is easy.

GNOME: Changing Keyboard and Mouse Settings

As with most user-oriented customization options, you'll find the keyboard and mouse configuration applets within the GNOME Control Center. To access this, click Desktop ➤ Control Center.

Configuring Mouse Options

Double-click the Mouse icon, under the Hardware heading of the Control Center, to open the Mouse Preferences dialog box, which has three tabs:

Buttons: This tab lets you set whether the mouse is to be used by a left-handed or right-handed person. Effectively, it swaps the functions of the right and left buttons. Beneath this is the double-click timeout setting. This is ideal for people who are less physically dexterous because the double-click speed can be slowed down. On the other hand, if you find yourself accidentally double-clicking items, you can speed it up.

Cursors: On this tab, you can select from any mouse cursor themes that are installed. You can also activate the Locate Pointer option, which causes a box to appear around the mouse cursor when you press the Ctrl key. This can help you find the cursor on a busy desktop.

Motion: This tab, shown in Figure 10-8, lets you alter the speed of the mouse pointer, as well as the drag-and-drop threshold. Changes are made as each setting is adjusted, so to test the new settings, simply move your mouse. Here's what the settings do:

- The Acceleration setting controls how fast the mouse moves. Whenever you move the mouse, the pointer on screen moves a corresponding amount. However, the cursor actually increases in speed the more you move your hand (otherwise, you would need to drag your hand across the desk to get from one side of the screen to the other). This is referred to as *acceleration*. If you set the acceleration too high, the pointer will fly around the screen, seemingly unable to stop. If you set it too slow, you'll need to ramp the mouse several times to make it go anywhere.

- The Sensitivity setting controls how quickly the acceleration kicks in when you first move the mouse. Choosing a higher setting means that you can move the mouse relatively quickly before it starts to accelerate and cover more screen space. A low setting means that acceleration will begin almost as soon as you move the mouse. Higher-sensitivity settings give you more control over the mouse, which can be useful if you use image-editing programs, for example.

- The Threshold setting determines the amount of mouse movement allowed in a click-and-drag maneuver before the item under the cursor is moved. This setting is designed for people who have limited dexterity and who might be unable to keep the mouse perfectly still when clicking or double-clicking an icon. In such cases, a large threshold value may be preferred.

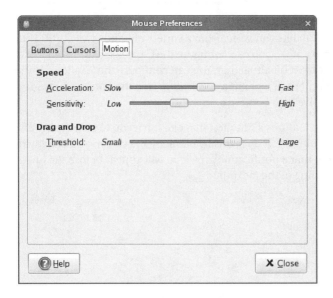

Figure 10-8. *The Mouse Preferences dialog box lets you tame that mouse.*

Changing Keyboard Settings

Double-click the Keyboard icon within the GNOME Control Center to open the Keyboard Preferences dialog box. This dialog box has four tabs:

Keyboard: Using the Keyboard tab, you can alter the rate of key repeat. This can be useful if you often find yourself holding down the Backspace key to delete a sentence; a shorter setting on the Delay slider and a faster setting on the Speed slider can help. However, if you get the settings wrong, you may find double characters creeping into your documents; typing *f* may result in *ff*, for example. Beneath the Repeat Keys setting is the Cursor Blinking slider. Altering this may help if you sometimes lose the cursor in a document; a faster speed will mean that the cursor spends less time being invisible between flashes.

Layouts: On the Layouts tab, you can choose to add an alternative keyboard layout, as shown in Figure 10-9. For example, if you write in two different languages on your keyboard, it may be helpful to be able to switch between them. Click the Add button and select the second language from the list. You'll need to add the Keyboard Indicator applet to choose between layouts. To do this, right-click a blank spot on the panel at the bottom of the screen and, in the dialog box that appears, select Keyboard Indicator and click the Add button. After this, switching the keyboard layout is simply a matter of clicking the new icon on the panel; this will cycle through the language options you've set.

■**Note** A preview will appear on the right of the window when you are selecting keyboard layouts. You might find it useful to click and drag the edge of the window to make it bigger so that the keyboard preview is readable.

Layout Options: This tab lets you select from a variety of handy tweaks that affect how the keyboard works. For example, you can configure the Caps Lock key to act like a simple Shift key, or you can turn it off altogether. You can configure the Windows key so that it performs a different function, too. Put a check alongside the option you want after reading through the extensive list of options.

Typing Break: This tab features a function that can force you to stop typing after a predetermined number of minutes. It does this by blanking the screen and displaying a "Take a break!" message. Note that a notification area icon will appear before the break time to give you advance warning of the lockout.

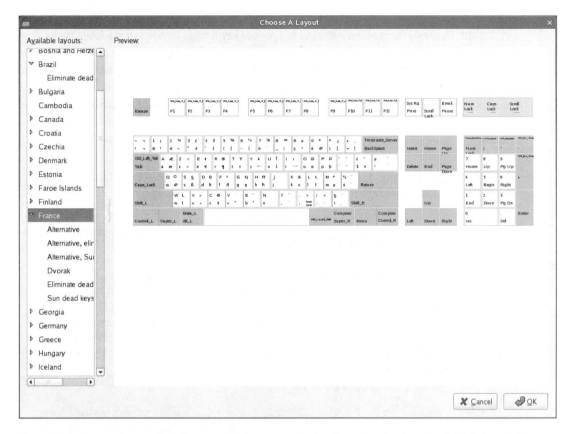

Figure 10-9. *You can have more than one language setting in place for a keyboard, which is handy if you need to type in a foreign language.*

Creating Keyboard Shortcuts

The GNOME desktop of SUSE Linux lets you define your own keyboard shortcuts for just about any action on the system. To create a shortcut, referred to within GNOME as an *accelerator,* double-click the Shortcuts icon under the Personal heading in the GNOME Control Center. In the dialog box, the actions are collected under three headings relating to the functionality they offer: Desktop, Sound, and Window Management. Search through the lists for the action you want to create a shortcut for, click it, and then press the key (or key combination) you want to use.

For example, you might locate the Volume Up and Volume Down entries in the list under the Sound heading, click each, and then press Ctrl+left arrow and Ctrl+right arrow. Then you will be able to turn the volume of your sound card up or down by holding down Ctrl and tapping the left or right arrow key, respectively.

■**Caution** Be careful not to assign a shortcut to a popular key. It might be nice to make Totem Media Player appear when you hit the spacebar, for example, but that will mean that it will start up several times whenever you type a sentence in a word processor! Also be aware that some key combinations are used by applications. Within OpenOffice.org's Writer, for example, the Ctrl+left/right arrow key combination moves you from word to word in a paragraph. If you define those combinations as shortcuts, you will no longer have this functionality.

I like to configure my /home folder to appear whenever I press the Home button on the keyboard. The Home Folder option is listed under the Desktop heading.

SETTING UP GNOME'S ASSISTIVE TECHNOLOGY SUPPORT

You might know about the Accessibility tools under Windows, which help people with special needs use the computer. It's possible to use an on-screen magnifier so that users can better see what they're typing or reading, for example.

Under the GNOME desktop, the Accessibility tools are referred to as Assistive Technology Support, and can be activated by clicking Desktop ➤ Control Center, double-clicking the Assistive Technology icon, and putting a check in the Enable Assistive Technology box. In addition, several accessibility tools can be activated by double-clicking the Accessibility icon within the Control Center window.

Among the many tools available are the following:

- **Sticky Keys:** Activate this tool in the Accessibility window. Put a check in the Enable Keyboard Accessibility Features box, and then click Enable Sticky Keys (or simply press Shift, Ctrl, or Alt five times in succession, as with Windows). Then click OK in the Sticky Keys dialog box. Thereafter, pressing Shift, Ctrl, or Alt once will "hold" the key until another key is pressed. For example, pressing Ctrl once and then S will be the equivalent of holding down Ctrl and pressing the S key.

- **Screenreader:** Activate this tool in the Assistive Technology dialog box. You'll need to restart GNOME for the Screenreader to be activated. It uses a speech synthesizer to announce whatever you click on, as well as whatever you type. To alter its settings, click the Preferences button in the Gnopernicus dialog box that appears after you've restarted GNOME, and then click the Speech button in the Preferences dialog box.

- **GNOME Onscreen Keyboard (GOK):** This tool can be used with a mouse, but it's most useful with an alternative input device, such as a touch screen. It can be activated within the Assistive Technology dialog box by putting a check in the On-Screen Keyboard box. As with the Screenreader, you'll need to restart GNOME after making this selection. As well as presenting a virtual keyboard, GOK shows the options on screen as a large and easy-to-activate series of buttons. For more information, click the Help button when GOK starts.

- **Magnifier:** This is the final component offered by the Assistive Technology dialog box. Once activated, it divides the screen into two halves. The right side displays a magnified version of the left side. To learn more, click the Help button in the Gnopernicus dialog box.

KDE: Changing Keyboard and Mouse Settings

To access the keyboard and mouse configuration components of KDE, click K menu ➤ Personal Settings, and then click the Peripherals icon on the left side of the window. Click the Keyboard or Mouse icon, depending on which device you would like to configure.

Configuring Mouse Options

Several options are available to configure the mouse, arranged on General, Cursor Theme, Advanced, and Mouse Navigation tabs.

General

The options under the General tab relate to use of the mouse.

Button Order: This option lets you configure the mouse for left- or right-handed use. This simply swaps the two buttons around—with the left-handed setting, the second mouse button becomes the left, and vice versa.

Reverse Scroll Direction: Checking this option will invert the scrolling that occurs when the mouse scroll wheel is turned. Some people find this allows for more intuitive scrolling.

Icons: The options under this heading control mouse interaction with icons. You can set whether a single-click is enough to activate icons, or whether a double-click is required, as with Windows. The Change Pointer Shape Over Icons option controls whether the mouse cursor turns into a pointing hand when it's moved over icons. This can be helpful for newcomers to identify what are icons and what are background graphics. The Automatically Select Icons option is useful for the physically less able. When the mouse is placed over an icon for a certain period, which can be set by dragging the slider, it is automatically selected. This doesn't mean it's activated. It is as if it has been single-clicked under Windows. The Visual Feedback on Activation option controls whether a small animated box appears at the cursor position whenever an icon is activated.

Cursor Theme

The Cursor Theme tab simply lets you choose a different mouse theme, as shown in Figure 10-10. Like the overall look and feel theme, the mouse cursor theme can be changed. Several options are available, and you can also download new themes from `http://kde-look.org` (at the time of writing, the themes were organized under the X11 Mouse Themes header). Simply download the theme and click the Install New Theme button. Then browse to the download location and select the file. It should appear in the list automatically.

■**Note** There's no need to unpack the downloaded cursor theme file before installing it, as with other KDE themes.

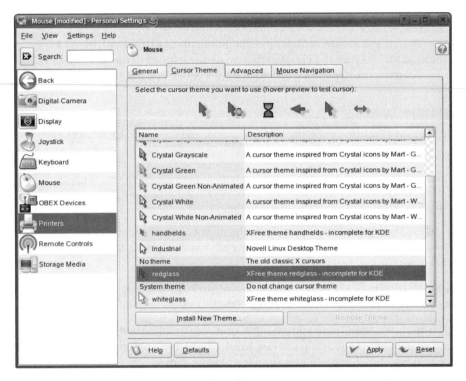

Figure 10-10. *Several alternative mouse cursor themes are available, some of which are more radical than others.*

After selecting a new cursor theme, click Apply, and then restart KDE for the theme to take effect.

Advanced

The Advanced tab contains settings for characteristics of the mouse, such as its speed. Several options are available, as follows:

Pointer Acceleration: This option effectively controls how fast the pointer moves. The acceleration referred to here is how fast the pointer moves on screen relative to the actual movement of the physical mouse. Higher values mean the mouse moves faster, which some users appreciate, but others find it hard to be accurate at higher settings.

Pointer Threshold: This option is related to the Pointer Acceleration setting and refers to the distance the mouse must move before acceleration takes effect. A higher setting here means that the mouse can be moved quite significantly before it starts to move quickly. This can be useful if you use photo-editing software, for example, where small movements of the mouse during editing procedures are common, and where accelerated mouse movement isn't desired.

Double Click Interval: This is the value that tells the system precisely when it should interpret two clicks of the mouse as a double-click, rather than as two separate clicks. Higher values mean that longer times between the two clicks are interpreted as a double-click.

This is useful for the physically less able who might find it difficult to rapidly double-click. For most users, however, shorter values are best.

Drag Start Time: This option controls the time interval that the system will wait before interpreting clicking an icon as a click-and-drag movement. This option is useful for less-physically–able individuals who may find that they accidentally click the mouse and drag icons. A higher value, measured in milliseconds, is therefore good for such people. A short value might sound better for average users, but be aware that nearly everyone misclicks. Therefore, it is necessary to find a good average for your personal needs. The default setting is good for most users.

Drag Start Distance: This option controls how much the mouse must move when a click-and-drag operation is taking place before the icon under the cursor is actually moved. This is another option useful for the less physically able, who may find themselves accidentally clicking the mouse. A higher value, which is measured in pixels, might be good for such individuals. A shorter value may result in accidental clicking and dragging, even for average users.

Mouse Wheel Scrolls By: This controls how many lines of text are scrolled when the mouse scroll wheel is turned by one "click" (assuming that your mouse wheel clicks; some turn freely). Note that this option affects only KDE-specific applications, such as the Konqueror browser.

Mouse Navigation

The Mouse Navigation tab allows users to move the mouse pointer using the numeric keypad. This is good for those who are less physically able and find using a mouse awkward. It can also be useful if the computer is in a cramped location where there simply isn't room to use a mouse. The following options are available:

Acceleration Delay: This setting affects how soon after a prolonged key press that the system interprets the additional key press data as requests for the mouse cursor to move. The feature is designed for those who find their fingers linger on a key longer than they would like. However, a high value here means that, when a key is pressed down, there will be a delay after the initial movement before the mouse cursor moves again.

Repeat Interval: This controls how many times per second the reading taken from the key is applied to mouse movement. A lower value means the mouse movement will be smoother. A higher value means the motion will be jerky (the mouse cursor will appear to "leap"). In general, the default setting is fine.

Acceleration Time: This controls how long before acceleration kicks in, which is to say speeding up of the cursor after a few seconds of movement. Acceleration is controlled by the Acceleration Profile slider on this tab.

Maximum Speed: This governs the maximum number of pixels the mouse cursor can move in response to a prolonged key press. It can be used with the Repeat Interval setting to avoid the mouse cursor leaping too much when a higher Repeat Interval value is set.

Acceleration Profile: This a technical setting related to the properties of the mouse acceleration. Higher or lower values, above and below 0, will apply a quicker acceleration to the cursor after it has started moving. Smaller increases or decreases are good here, although most users should find the default setting works fine.

Configuring Keyboard Options

Compared to the range of options available for mouse control under KDE, the keyboard settings are blissfully simple (see Figure 10-11 for an example). The options are as follows:

Keyboard Repeat: This controls how quickly keys repeat after they're held down. The Delay slider setting is the time period after a key is held down but before the repeat steps in. The Rate slider controls how quickly the keys repeat once the repeating starts. Setting the wrong values here can mean that the keyboard becomes too responsive—typing a single *f*, for example, may mean that *ff* appears because the repeat has stepped in too early.

NumLock on KDE Startup: Some people like to use the numeric keypad as a series of directional keys. If Num Lock is switched on, however, the keys are used to represent numbers. Num Lock is normally turned on and off using the top-left key on the numeric keypad. Using this option, you can set it to be automatically turned on when KDE starts. The Leave Unchanged option will inherit Num Lock settings from the computer's BIOS, if you're booting up, or from whatever software was running previously if you've manually started KDE.

Key Click Volume: It's possible within KDE to have a key click sound whenever keys are pressed. This can be useful for those using smaller keyboards, such as portable Bluetooth devices, where it might not be immediately clear if a key press has registered. Dragging the slider controls the volume of the key click that will be heard.

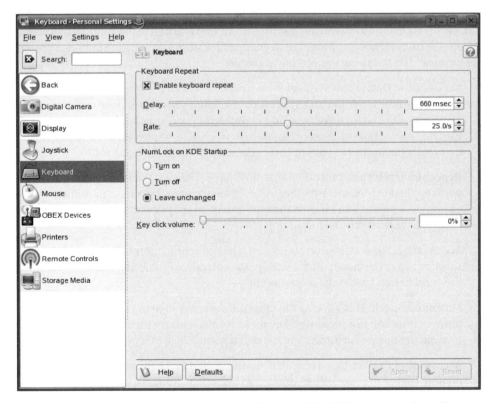

Figure 10-11. *The options for configuring the keyboard within KDE are simple but effective.*

Changing the Keyboard Language

If you work with multiple languages, you can change the keyboard layout via an applet in the system tray. This is done via the Keyboard Layout module of Personal Settings. To access it, click K menu ➤ Personal Settings, click the Regional and Accessibility icon, and then click the Keyboard Layout icon.

Start by putting a check in the Enable Keyboard Layouts option. Then click the Apply button. To add a wider selection of layouts, select them from the Available Layouts list, as shown in Figure 10-12, click the Add button, and then click Apply.

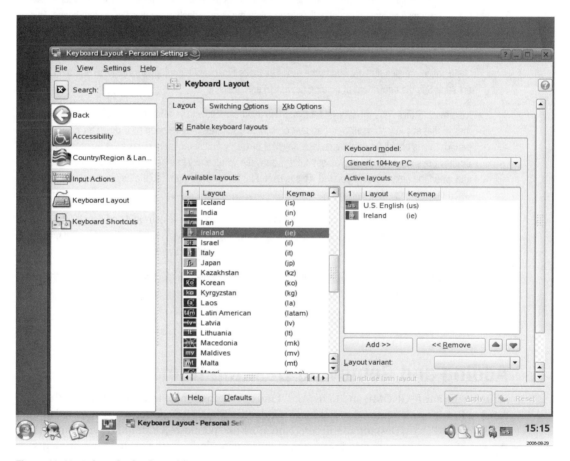

Figure 10-12. *Select the keyboard layouts you want to be able to use from the list on the left, and then click the Add button. Then click the flag icon in the system tray to switch between them.*

After you've applied your changes, your system tray should have an icon showing the current keyboard layout (the icon is a flag indicating the country in which the layout is normally used). To use the alternative layout, simply click the system tray icon. It will then change to the next keyboard layout in your list. Clicking the icon again will revert to the previous layout, if only two are in the list, or it will cycle through the layouts if you selected more than two.

KDE ACCESSIBILITY OPTIONS

KDE isn't as well stocked at GNOME when it comes to accessibility options to help those with physical disabilities, but it includes the core tools that most find useful, such as Sticky Keys.

To see the accessibility options, open the KDE Personal Settings window (K menu ➤ Personal Settings) and click the Region and Accessibility icon. Then click the Accessibility icon. Several tabs are available, offering a range of options, as follows:

- **Bell:** You can change the system warning beep, known as the *bell*, to a different sound, such as a WAV file. You can also activate a visual bell, which makes the screen flash whenever the system beeps. This is useful for the hard of hearing.

- **Modifier Keys:** You can activate the Sticky Keys function, whereby the Ctrl, Shift, and Alt keys are "held" once pressed and applied to the next key that's typed. For example, pressing Ctrl and then pressing S is the equivalent of holding down Ctrl and pressing S.

- **Keyboard Filters:** This tab lets you activate two functions: Slow Keys and Bounce Keys. Slow Keys means that any key presses won't appear on screen until after they've been held down for a short period. This is useful for those who lack physical dexterity and sometimes press keys unintentionally. Bounce Keys is similar. It lets you set a delay between when a key has been pressed and registered and when the next key is registered. This is useful for those who might tap the key two or more times when they mean to hit it only once.

- **Activation Gestures:** You can control how the accessibility options are activated and deactivated. For example, putting a check in the Use Gestures for Activating Sticky Keys and Slow Keys box will mean that hitting Shift, Ctrl, or Alt five times will be enough to activate Sticky Keys.

For more details about KDE's accessibility options, and how to use them, click the Help button at the bottom left of the Personal Settings window when the Accessibility window is visible.

Adding and Removing Desktop Items

Virtually the entire GNOME and KDE SUSE Linux desktops can be redesigned and restructured to fit with your personal preferences. Under the GNOME desktop, you can get rid of the Applications/Places/Desktop menu set, to be more like Windows. Under KDE, you can shrink the size of the taskbar so it dominates less of the screen. Under both desktop environments, you can add numerous desktop shortcuts to applications and/or files.

GNOME: Personalizing the Desktop

GNOME is extremely easy to personalize—usually the options are little more than a right-click away. Your options range from rearranging items on the screen to replacing them with the menus and shortcuts of your choice.

Rearranging Panel Items

All items on the panel can be moved, including icons and applets, by right-clicking them and selecting the Move option. The item will then move with the mouse. Click the mouse button when the item is in position to make the move permanent.

Even the main menus can be moved in this way, as can the clock. Some panel items, such as the Window List (known as the taskbar in Windows), and the notification area, have drag handles, located on their left side. To move these, click and drag the drag handles.

To prevent any item from being moved in the future, right-click the drag handle and select Lock to Panel.

■**Tip** If you find that you can't move an item, right-click it and remove the check next to Lock to Panel.

Adding a Shortcut

The GNOME desktop's nearest equivalent to a Windows-style desktop shortcut is a *launcher*. An important difference, however, is that launchers are designed to run a certain command. Therefore, they can point only to programs. Still, you could create a launcher that contained a command chain required to run a particular program and file. To use The GIMP to open a picture, you might create a launcher that read gimp picture.jpg, for example.

If you want to make a shortcut to a data file, such as a picture, you need to create a *link*. This is just as easy as creating a launcher and is described in the next section.

You can create a launcher two ways. One way is to simply click and drag an icon from one of the main menus to the desktop. This effectively copies the menu's launcher to the desktop, rather than creating a new launcher, but the effect is the same.

■**Caution** I noticed that sometimes the click and drag from the main menu would be curiously slow to react. Often, I had to keep my finger on the mouse button for an extra second or two before dropping the icon on the desktop, even though it appeared nothing was happening. This may be a deliberate feature implemented by the GNOME developers to prevent users from accidentally creating shortcuts by misclicking.

The other way to create a launcher is to right-click the desktop and select Create Launcher. In the Create Launcher dialog box, you need to fill in only the Name and Command fields; the other fields can be left blank. The Command field must contain an executable program, command, or script. If you want to use a command-line program or script, you must check the Run in Terminal box. This will open a terminal window automatically and run the command or script within it. The terminal window will disappear as soon as the command has finished.

To choose an icon for your launcher, click the Icon button in the Create Launcher dialog box. If you don't choose an icon, the stock GNOME one is used (the same icon as is used for unidentified and/or system files). You can select from several predefined icons or choose your own picture by clicking the Browse button, as shown in Figure 10-13.

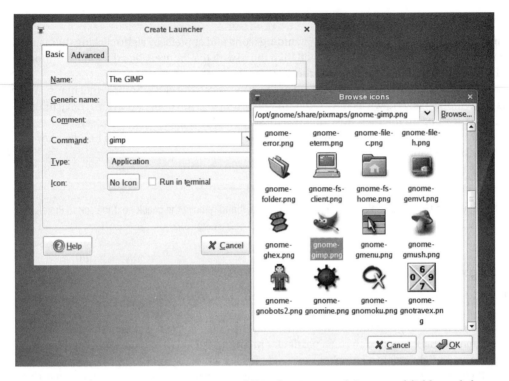

Figure 10-13. *Creating a launcher is easy. Just fill in the Name and Command fields, and choose an icon.*

Creating a Link

Although you can create a link to a program, which will then work the same as a launcher, links are usually used to create shortcuts to files. If you then double-click the shortcut, the application associated with that file type will open the file. If you create a shortcut to a picture, for example, when you double-click it, the Eye of GNOME previewer will start.

To create a link, locate the file you want to create the link to, right-click it, and select Make Link. Then copy the new link to wherever you want it to appear, such as the desktop. You don't need to choose an icon, because the link inherits the icon of the original file. For example, if it's a picture link, it will inherit the thumbnail preview icon.

Note If you find the Make Link option grayed out, it's likely that you don't have sufficient permissions to write the link to the directory in question.

Adding and Removing Menus

The Applications/Places/Desktop menu system at the bottom of the screen is an innovative addition to the desktop. These menus offer a lot of functionality, but it comes at the expense of space on the panel.

It's possible to add a single button to the panel that will offer all the functionality of the Applications, Places, and Desktop menus, via a Windows-like submenu system. You can then remove the Applications, Places, and Desktop menus.

Here are the necessary steps:

1. Right-click a blank spot on the bottom panel and select Add to Panel.

2. Scroll down the list of items until you get to Traditional Main Menu, which is located near the bottom.

3. Select the entry in the list and click the Add button at the bottom of the dialog box. You'll notice a new icon appear on the panel.

4. Right-click anywhere on the Applications, Places, and Desktop menus and select Remove from Panel.

5. Right-click the new menu icon you created earlier and select Move. Then drag it to the left panel, in the location where the Windows Start button is normally found.

When you're finished, the Applications menu should appear as shown in Figure 10-14. The Places and Desktop menus will now be submenus at the bottom of the main menu, and your programs will be located above. In addition, a Run Application entry is added to the list, whereby you can type an application's name to run it directly from the menu.

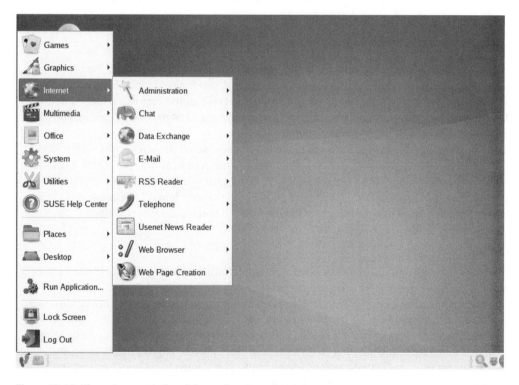

Figure 10-14. *If you just can't do without that Start button, you can re-create one on your SUSE Linux desktop.*

Tip You can have as many instances of the menus on the desktop as you wish, although this won't be a good use of desktop space! But if you use multiple monitors, you might want to have a menu button on the panel of each desktop.

To delete any menu, simply right-click anywhere on that menu and select Remove from Panel.

Personalizing the Panels

Panels are the long strips that appear at the top and bottom of the SUSE Linux screen and play host to a choice of applets and/or icons. You can add a new panel by simply right-clicking an existing one and selecting New Panel, or you can remove a panel by right-clicking it and selecting Delete This Panel.

If you want to move a panel, right-click a blank spot on it and select Allow Panel to Be Moved. Then click and drag the panel to its new location. To make a panel lock down once more, right-click a blank spot on the panel and select Lock Panel Position.

Caution If you delete a panel, the arrangement of applets it contains will be lost. Of course, you can always re-create the collection of applets on a different panel.

By right-clicking a panel and selecting Properties, you can change its size and dimensions. For example, by unchecking the Expand box, you can make the panel shrink to its smallest possible size. Then, when you add new applets (or, in the case of a panel containing the Window List, a new program is run), the panel will expand as necessary. This can be a neat effect and also creates more desktop space.

Selecting the Autohide feature will make the panel slide off the screen when there isn't a mouse over it. It will appear again when the mouse is hovered near the spot where it disappeared. Choosing Show Hide Buttons will make small arrows appear on either side of the panel so that you can click to slide it off the side of the screen when it's not in use. This will leave a small arrow at the point of exit; clicking this will make the panel reappear.

Working with Applets

Almost everything you see on the desktop is an applet, with the exception of shortcut icons and the panels. A menu is a form of applet, for example, as is the Workspace Switcher.

SUSE Linux provides many more applets that you can choose to add to the desktop to provide a host of useful or entertaining functionality. To add an applet, right-click the panel and select Add to Panel. As shown in Figure 10-15, you have a wide choice of applets. Many require configuration after they've been added, so you may need to right-click them and select Properties (or sometimes Preferences). For example, you'll need to set your location in the Weather Report applet's properties so it can provide accurate forecasting for your area.

Figure 10-15. *A wide variety of applets are available. Some are informative; others are just fun.*

See Table 10-1 for a list of applets along with brief descriptions of what they do and what must be done, if anything, to configure them for immediate use.

To remove an applet, right-click it and select Remove from Panel.

Table 10-1. *Applets Offered by the GNOME Desktop*

Applet	Description	Configuration[1]
Address Book Search	Lets you quickly retrieve contact information from your Evolution address book	None required
Battery Charge Monitor	Shows the battery level on notebooks, and whether outlet power is in use	None needed
Blog Entry Poster	Lets you quickly post blog entries to Blogger.com, Advogato, and LiveJournal, as well as WordPress, MovableType, and PyBlosxom systems	Configuration window will appear after selection; enter blog type and login details
Character Palette	Displays a palette of accented or unusual characters; click a character to insert it into the text	None needed
Clock	Displays the time and date (active by default)	None needed
Command Line	Displays a text box into which commands can be entered, primarily to run programs	None needed

Continues

Table 10-1. *Continued*

Applet	Description	Configuration[1]
Connect to Server	Lets you quickly connect to remote servers, such as FTP (equivalent of clicking Places ➤ Connect to Server)	None needed
CPU Frequency Scaling Monitor	Shows CPU frequency and, on compatible hardware, lets you change CPU frequency (active by default on notebook computers)	Right-click to change frequency on compatible hardware
Dictionary Lookup	Displays a text box that will look up words according to online dictionaries	None needed
Disk Mounter	Lets you quickly mount and unmount removable disks	None needed
Drawer	Displays a drawer icon that, when clicked, "slides out" to reveal yet more applets	Right-click icon and click Add to Drawer to add applets
Force Quit	Lets you quit a crashed program	None needed
Geyes	Displays two eyes whose pupils follow the mouse cursor	None needed
Keyboard Accessibility Status	Shows whether Sticky Keys or other accessibility functions are activated	None needed
Keyboard Indicator	Shows the current language settings of the keyboard	None needed
Linphone	Provides quick access to Linphone functions	Clicking applet will open the Linphone call dialog box
Lock Screen	Adds an icon that, when clicked, blanks the screen and displays password prompt	None needed
Log Out	Lets you log out or shut down	None needed
Menu Bar	Adds a new Applications, Places, and Desktop menu bar to the panel	None needed
Modem Lights	Displays virtual LEDs showing when modem data is sent/received, and also lets you quickly dial up with a single click	None needed
Network Monitor	Displays virtual LEDs showing data send/receive via networking devices	None needed
Notification Area	Adds a notification area to the panel (active by default)	None needed
Pilot Applet	Lets you quickly connect to Palm devices via gnome-pilot software	If gnome-pilot hasn't already been set up, a configuration dialog box will appear
Run Application	Adds an icon that, when clicked, makes the Run Application dialog box appear	None needed
Search for Files	Provides one-click access to Nautilus's search mode	None needed
Show Desktop	Minimizes all desktop windows (active by default)	None needed
Sticky Notes	Lets you create virtual "sticky notes"	None needed

Applet	Description	Configuration[1]
Stock Ticker	Adds a text-based scrolling stock ticker to the panel	Right-click and select Preferences to add individual stock symbols to the list
System Monitor	Adds a small graph that shows system resource usage	Right-click and select Preferences to choose system areas to be monitored
Take Screenshot	Captures current screen output	None needed
Tomboy Notes	Lets you add "sticky notes" to the desktop (active by default)	None needed
Traditional Main Menu	Lets you add a single icon Start-like system menu	None needed
Trash	Adds the Trash icon to the panel, where files can be dropped for removal to Trash	None needed
Volume Control	Adds volume controls (active by default)	None needed
Weather Report	Adds an icon that shows current weather conditions	Right-click, select Preferences, and then the Location tab to set your location
Window List	Adds a list of windows, which you can use to switch between currently running programs (active by default)	None needed
Window Selector	Adds an icon that, when clicked, switches between currently open windows (alternative to Window List)	None needed
Workspace Switcher	Shows virtual desktop selector	None needed

1. *Nearly all applets have configuration options that can be used to tweak them in various ways. This column only indicates if immediate configuration is needed*

KDE: Personalizing the Desktop

As with the GNOME desktop, KDE is easy to personalize. The options are normally little more than a right-click away. You can rearrange desktop items, add shortcuts, and customize the panel.

Rearranging Panel Items

Most items on the panel can be moved by right-clicking them and selecting the Move option. Some items, such as the shortcut icons next to the K menu, can be moved by simply clicking and dragging. However, be careful when releasing the mouse button, because if the icon is dropped over another icon, KDE will interpret this as an attempt to open that particular application using the icon file as input.

Some panel items, such as the taskbar, pager, and system tray, have grab handles that you can click and drag to reposition them. These are normally hidden and appear only when the mouse rolls over them. They're located to the left of the item in question.

All items can be moved, including the K menu itself.

Adding a Shortcut

Adding your own icons to either the desktop or panel is easy. Just select the program you want on the K menu, but rather than single-clicking it, click and hold. Then drag it to where you want the shortcut to appear.

When you release the mouse button, you'll be asked if you want to Copy Here or Link Here (when you're creating a panel shortcut, it will simply be copied across automatically without prompting). In the case of desktop links, you should select Copy Here because, effectively, you're copying the shortcut link on the menu. See Figure 10-16 for an example.

Figure 10-16. *To create a shortcut, simply click and drag from a menu, and then select Copy Here.*

Alternatively, you can manually create a shortcut by right-clicking anywhere on the desktop and clicking Create New ➤ Link to Application. On the General tab, enter the name you would like to assign to the shortcut, and then click the cog icon to select a specific icon that the shortcut will use. Click the Application tab and enter the command-line name of the application in the Command field. Then click OK to create the new shortcut.

Personalizing the Panel

Personalizing the panel is easy. Simply right-click a blank spot on an existing panel and select Preferences. This will open the Configure dialog box. You can change the following aspects of the panel:

Panel position: The entries under the Position heading let you align and center the panel. As with Windows, when the panel is aligned along the left or right sides of the screen, text on the taskbar buttons will no longer be visible. Instead, icons will represent the buttons.

Panel length: You can change the length of the panel by clicking and dragging the slider under the Length heading. The percentage figure refers to the width of the screen: 100% is the full width, 50% is half the width, and so on. If you want the panel to be a set size, be sure to remove the check from the Expand As Required to Fit Contents box. When this option is activated, the panel will expand if, for example, several programs are open.

Panel size: Below the length slider is an option to set the size of the panel. This effectively sets its thickness. The Normal setting (the default) allows for good-sized shortcut icons, and taskbar buttons are stacked two high. The Small setting is more like Windows, with relatively small icons and single-height taskbar buttons. Other sizes are available, and it's also possible to set your own size, measured in pixels, by selecting Custom and dragging the slider.

Working with Applets

Several applets are available that provide useful functions. All can be added to the panel for quick access by right-clicking the panel and selecting Add Applet to Panel. This will open the Add Applet dialog box. It's a good idea to resize this dialog box manually by clicking and dragging one of the edges so that more of the contents are displayed, as shown in Figure 10-17.

Figure 10-17. *The Add Applet dialog box lets you select from many handy applets that will then appear on the panel.*

Click the applet you want to add, and then click the Add to Panel button. The applet will then "fly" down to the location on the panel where it will live. To subsequently move it, right-click it and select Move.

Most applets can be removed by right-clicking them and selecting the relevant option. Some have grab handles that display a small up-pointing arrow when you hover the mouse over them. Clicking this arrow will reveal a context menu with an option to remove the applet. In some cases, this context menu will also have configuration options.

Some applets require additional configuration after they have been added to the panel. Table 10-2 lists the applets offered by KDE and notes any required configuration.

Table 10-2. *Applets Offered by KDE.*

Applet	Description	Configuration
Binary Clock	Displays the time as a series of binary virtual LEDs	None required
Bookmarks Menu	Shows the Konqueror Bookmarks menu	None required
Clock	Places a clock on the panel (active by default)	None required
Color Picker	Lets you click anywhere on the screen and immediately view the RGB decimal and hex values of the color under the cursor	None required
Desktop Preview & Pager	Lets you access KDE's virtual desktops feature (active by default)	None required
Find	Provides quick access to Konqueror's file and web search modes	None required
Klipper	Gives more control over your clipboard history, allowing you to recall items that were cut or copied some time ago (active by default)	None required
K menu	Adds a K menu to the panel (active by default)	None required
Konqueror Profiles	Lets you start Konqueror in one of its many modes, such as web browsing mode or file browsing mode	None required
Lock/Logout Buttons	Adds a button that brings up the End Session dialog box	None required
Math Expression Evaluator	Adds a text box into which you can type mathematical expressions; pressing Enter gives results	None required
Media Control	Provides tape-recorder-like icons to control the media player	Right-click the new applet, click Configure Media Control, and choose your media player from the list (for example, amaroK)
My System	Allows quick access to file system locations	None required
Network Folders	Provides shortcuts to predefined network locations	To add network places, click the icon and click Add Network Folder

Applet	Description	Configuration
News Ticker	Shows scrolling display of headlines based on an RDF feed	Open the grab bar menu and click Configure News Ticker to select feeds
Non-KDE Application Launcher	Lets you create panel shortcut icons to non-KDE applications	Dialog box will appear when the applet is selected; fill in details of the application
Print System	Provides quick access to printer configuration options	None required
Public File Server	Lets users quickly create HTTP-based file sharing	Adding the applet will open a configuration dialog box
Quick File Browser	Displays a menu of files within a particular directory	Selecting the applet will open a dialog box where the directory can be chosen
Quick Launcher	Adds an icon range to the panel that allows one-click start of popular applications (similar to Windows Quick Launch toolbar)	None required
Recent Documents	Displays a menu of recently accessed files	None required
Runaway Process Catcher	Detects processes that are consuming system resources unnecessarily (such as buggy software)	None required
Run Command	Adds a text field to the panel where you can enter commands	None required
Settings	Adds an icon to panel that provides access to icons within the KDE Control Center (also known as Personal Settings)	None required
Show Desktop	Instantly minimizes all open windows	None required
Sound Mixer	Adds a volume control icon (active by default)	None required
Storage Media	Provides quick access to removable storage devices	None required
System Guard	Adds a more complex version of System Monitor	None required
System Monitor	Adds a simple bar-graph–based system monitor	None required
Taskbar	Allows you to choose between currently running programs (active by default)	None required
Terminal Sessions	Allows the quick start of Konsole in various user modes	None required
Trash	Adds a Trash icon to the panel onto which files can be dropped	None required
Window List Menu	Adds an icon to the panel that, when clicked, shows a submenu that lets you select between all open windows	None required

Summary

In this chapter, you've learned how to completely personalize the KDE and GNOME desktops of SUSE Linux to your own tastes. We looked at changing the theme so that the desktop has a new appearance, and examined how to make the input devices behave exactly as you would like.

In addition, you've learned how to add and remove applets from the desktop in order to add functionality or simply make SUSE Linux work the way you would like.

In the next chapter, we will look at what programs are available under SUSE Linux to replace those Windows favorites you might miss.

■■■

SUSE Linux Replacements for Windows Programs

SUSE Linux is a thoroughly modern operating system and, as such, includes a comprehensive selection of software for just about every day-to-day task. Regardless of whether you want to write letters, edit images, or listen to music, SUSE Linux offers something for you.

This chapter introduces the software under SUSE Linux that performs the tasks you might be used to under Windows. It's not a detailed guide to each piece of software. Instead, this chapter aims to get you up and running with the SUSE Linux replacement as quickly as possible. The chapter will tell you the name of the software, where you can find it on SUSE Linux's menus, and a few basic facts about how to use it. In many cases, these applications are covered in far more depth later in this book.

Available Software

SUSE Linux includes a number of programs that are used under both GNOME and KDE, such as the OpenOffice.org office suite and The GIMP image editor, but the GNOME and KDE desktops also have their own software for some specific tasks, such as playing back multimedia. Table 11-1 lists various popular Windows programs alongside their SUSE Linux counterparts for the GNOME and KDE desktop environments. All of the programs mentioned in the table are located on SUSE Linux's applications menu. In the case of the GNOME desktop, this is the menu at the bottom of the screen marked Applications; in the case of the KDE desktop, this is the green gecko icon at the bottom left (referred to throughout this book as the *K menu*).

Tip Although KDE and GNOME include their own specific software packages, they'll run fine within alternative desktop environments. For example, there's no reason why you can't run the KDE K3b CD-burning application under the GNOME desktop, or the GNOME Nautilus file manager under the KDE desktop. Working this way gives you an excellent choice of software for your system.

In addition to listing SUSE Linux replacements for Windows favorites, Table 11-1 also includes a number of other alternatives, some of which are installed by default under SUSE Linux. You might want to try these later on. As you might expect, they're all free of charge, so you have nothing to lose. Many of them are available on the SUSE Linux DVD supplied with this book (see Chapter 29 to learn how to install new software). Others must be downloaded and installed from the web sites mentioned in the table.

Table 11-1 lists only a fraction of the programs available under Linux. There are quite literally thousands of others. The programs listed here are those that work like their Windows equivalents and therefore provide an easy transition.

The remainder of this chapter outlines a handful of the programs listed in Table 11-1. As I noted at the beginning of this chapter, my goal is to give you a head start in using each program. In many instances, the software introduced in this chapter is covered in far more detail later in this book. You'll find more information about The GIMP image editor, multimedia tools, and office applications in Parts 5 and 6.

LINUX HAS IT ALL

The SUSE Linux software archives contain thousands of programs to cover just about every task you might wish to do on your computer. Diversity is vitally important within the Linux world. For example, rather than offering just one e-mail program, you'll find many available. They compete with each other in a gentle way, and it's up to you which one you settle down with and use.

Part of the fun of using Linux is exploring what's available. Of course, the added bonus is that virtually all this software is free of charge, so you can simply download, install, and play around. If you don't like a program, just remove it from your system. However, don't forget to revisit the program's homepage after a few months; chances are the program will have been expanded and improved in that short period, and it might be better at meeting your needs.

Table 11-1. *SUSE Linux Alternatives to Windows Software*

Type of Program	Windows	GNOME	KDE	Alternatives
Word processor	Microsoft Word	OpenOffice.org Writer	OpenOffice.org Writer	AbiWord (www.abisource.com), KOffice KWord (www.koffice.org/kword)
Spreadsheet	Microsoft Excel	OpenOffice.org Calc	OpenOffice.org Calc	Gnumeric (www.gnome.org/projects/gnumeric/), KOffice KSpread (www.koffice.org/kspread)
Presentations	Microsoft PowerPoint	OpenOffice.org Impress	OpenOffice.org Impress	KOffice KPresenter (www.koffice.org/kpresenter)
Drawing (vector art)	Adobe Illustrator	OpenOffice.org Draw	OpenOffice.org Draw	Inkscape (www.inkscape.org), KOffice Karbon14 (www.koffice.org/karbon)
Database	Microsoft Access	OpenOffice.org Base	OpenOffice.org Base	Rekall (www.thekompany.com/products/rekall/)
Web page creation	Microsoft FrontPage	OpenOffice.org Writer	OpenOffice.org Writer	Mozilla Composer (www.mozilla.org), Amaya (www.w3.org/Amaya/)
E-mail	Microsoft Outlook	Evolution	KMail	Thunderbird (www.mozilla.com)
Contacts manager/ calendar	Microsoft Outlook	Evolution	Kontact	Chandler (www.osafoundation.org)
Web browser	Microsoft Internet Explorer	Mozilla Firefox	Konqueror (www.konqueror.org)	Opera (www.opera.com)[1]
CD/DVD burning	Nero	Nautilus[2]	K3b	X-CD-Roast (www.xcdroast.org)
MP3 player	Winamp	Banshee	amaroK	XMMS (www.xmms.org)
CD player	Windows Media Player	CD Player	KsCD	XMMS (www.xmms.org), AlsaPlayer (www.alsaplayer.org)
Movie/DVD player	Windows Media Player	Totem Media Player	Kaffeine	MPlayer (www.mplayerhq.hu/homepage/)
Image editor	Adobe Photoshop	The GIMP	The GIMP	KOffice Krita (www.koffice.org/krita)
Zip files	WinZip	File Roller	Ark	TkZip (www.woodsway.com/TkZip/)
MS-DOS prompt	cmd.exe/command.exe	GNOME Terminal	Konsole	Xterm (www.x.org)[3]
Calculator	Calc	Gcalctool	KCalc	Too many to mention!
Text editor/viewer	Notepad	Gedit	Kate	KWrite (www.kde-apps.org/content/show.php?content=9901)

1. *Opera is a proprietary project, rather than open source; however, it is free of charge.*
2. *Nautilus is the file manager under the GNOME desktop. To activate its CD/DVD burning mode, open a standard Nautilus file browsing window and click Go* ▶ *CD/DVD Creator.*
3. *Xterm is part of the X.org package, so it is installed by default under SUSE Linux. To use it, type xterm in a GNOME Terminal window. See Chapter 10 to learn how to create a permanent desktop shortcut for xterm.*

Quick Start: General Software

This section contains an overview of Linux software that isn't included specifically with either the GNOME or KDE desktop environment. Instead, it is included within SUSE Linux with the intention that both GNOME and KDE users will employ it.

■**Note** Keep in mind that Linux doesn't aim to be an exact clone of Windows. Some of the programs will work in a similar way to Windows software, but that's not true of all of them. Because of this, it's very easy to get frustrated early on when programs don't seem to work quite how you want or respond in strange ways. Some patience is required, but it will eventually pay off as you get used to Linux.

Word Processing: OpenOffice.org Writer

Start OpenOffice.org Writer as follows:

- In GNOME, click Applications ➤ Office ➤ Word Processor ➤ OpenOffice.org Writer

- In KDE, click K menu ➤ Office ➤ Word Processor

OpenOffice.org is an entire office suite for Linux that was built from the ground up to compete with Microsoft Office. Because of this, you'll find much of the functionality of Microsoft Office is replicated in OpenOffice.org, and the look and feel are also similar. The major difference is that OpenOffice.org is open source and therefore free of charge.

OpenOffice.org Writer, shown in Figure 11-1, is the word processor component. As with Microsoft Word, it's fully WYSIWYG (What You See Is What You Get), so you can quickly format text and paragraphs. This means the program can be used for elementary desktop publishing, and pictures can be easily inserted (using the Insert menu).

Writer's toolbars provide quick access to the formatting tools, as well as to other common functions. The vast majority of menu options match those found in Word. Right-clicking the text itself also offers quick access to text-formatting tools.

A number of higher-level functions are provided, such as mail merge and spell-checking, (found on the Tools menu). You can perform spell-checking on the fly, with incorrect words underlined in red as you type.

As with all OpenOffice.org packages, Writer is fully compatible with Microsoft Office files, so you can save and open .doc files. Just select the file type in the Save As dialog box. The only exceptions are password-protected Word files, which cannot be opened. You can also export documents as PDF files (using File ➤ Export As PDF), so they can be read on any computer that has Adobe Reader installed.

OpenOffice.org Writer is covered in more detail in Chapter 23.

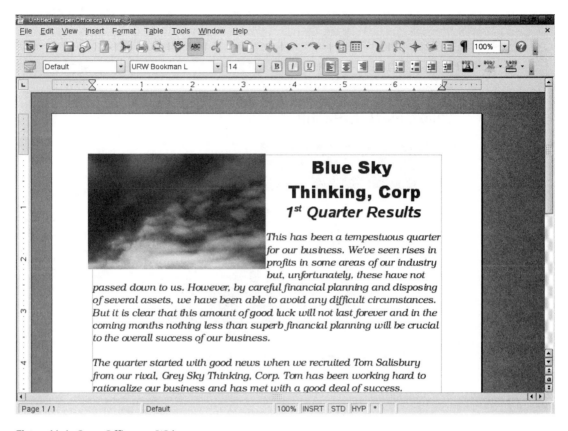

Figure 11-1. *OpenOffice.org Writer*

Spreadsheet: OpenOffice.org Calc

Start OpenOffice.org Calc as follows:

- In GNOME, click Applications ➤ Office ➤ Spreadsheet ➤ OpenOffice.org Calc

- In KDE, click K menu ➤ Office ➤ Spreadsheet ➤ OpenOffice.org Calc

As with most of the packages that form the OpenOffice.org suite, Calc does a good impersonation of its Windows counterpart, Microsoft Excel, both in terms of powerful features and also the look and feel, as you can see in Figure 11-2. However, it doesn't run Excel Visual Basic for Applications (VBA) macros. Instead, Calc (and all OpenOffice.org programs) uses its own macro language called OpenOffice.org Basic (for more information, see http://development.openoffice.org).

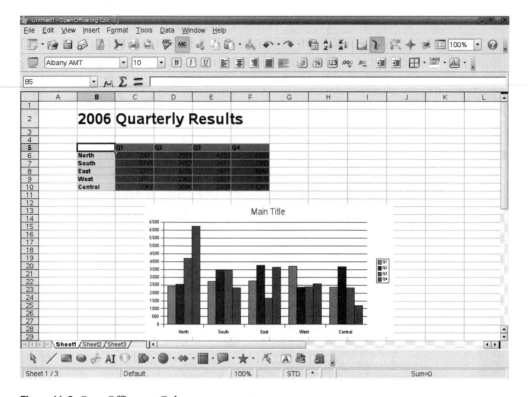

Figure 11-2. *OpenOffice.org Calc*

Calc has a vast number of mathematical functions. To see a list, choose Insert ➤ Function. The list includes a brief explanation of each function to help you get started. Just as with Excel, you can access the functions via the toolbar (by clicking the Function Wizard button), or you can enter them directly into cells by typing an equal sign and then the formula code. Calc is intelligent enough to realize when formula cells have been moved and to recalculate accordingly. It will even attempt to calculate formulas automatically and can work out what you mean if you type something like sales + expenses as a formula.

As you would expect, Calc also provides automated charting and graphing tools (under Insert ➤ Chart). In Figure 11-2, you can see an example of a simple chart created automatically by the charting tool.

You can format cells using the main toolbar buttons or automatically apply user-defined styles (choose Format ➤ Styles and Formatting).

Tip In all the OpenOffice.org applications, you can hover the mouse cursor over each button for one second to see a tooltip showing what it does.

If you're a business user, you'll be pleased to hear that you can import databases to perform serious number-crunching. Use Insert ➤ Link to External Data to get the data, and then employ the tools on the Data and Tools menus to manipulate it.

As with all OpenOffice.org programs, compatibility with its Microsoft counterpart—Excel files in this case—is guaranteed. You can also open other common data file formats, such as comma-separated values (CSV) and Lotus 1-2-3 files.

OpenOffice.org Calc is covered in more detail in Chapter 24.

Presentations: OpenOffice.org Impress

Start OpenOffice.org Impress as follows:

- In GNOME, click Applications ➤ Office ➤ Presentation ➤ OpenOffice.org Impress

- In KDE, click K menu ➤ Office ➤ Presentation

Anyone who has used PowerPoint will immediately feel at home with Impress, OpenOffice.org's presentation package, shown in Figure 11-3. Impress duplicates most of the common features found in PowerPoint, with a helping of OpenOffice.org-specific extras.

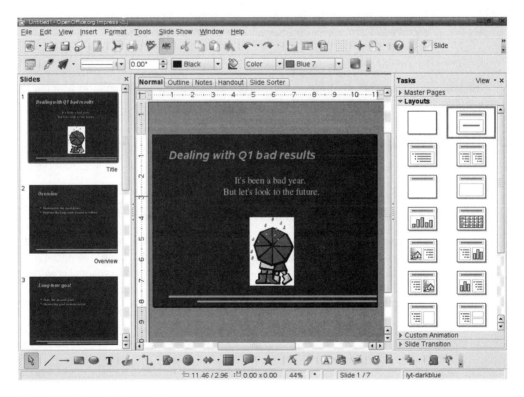

Figure 11-3. *OpenOffice.org Impress*

The program works via templates into which you enter you data. Starting the program causes the Presentation Wizard to appear. This wizard guides you through selecting a style of presentation fitting the job you have in mind. At this point, you can even select the type of transition effects you want between the various slides.

Once the wizard has finished, you can choose from the usual master and outline view modes (look under the View menu). Outline mode lets you enter your thoughts quickly, while master mode lets you type straight onto presentation slides.

You can format text by highlighting it and right-clicking it, by using the Text Formatting toolbar that appears whenever you click inside a text box, or by selecting an entry on the Format menu. Impress also features a healthy selection of drawing tools, on the Drawing toolbar along the bottom of the screen, so you can create even quite complex diagrams. You can also easily insert pictures, other graphics, and sound effects.

You can open and edit existing PowerPoint (PPT) files and, as with all OpenOffice.org packages, save your presentation as a PDF file. Unique to Impress is the ability to export your presentation as an Adobe Flash file (SWF). This means that anyone with a browser and Adobe's Flash plug-in can view the file, either after it's put online or via e-mail. Simply click File ➤ Export, and then choose Macromedia Flash from the File Type drop-down list.

■**Note** Although Adobe now owns and distributes Macromedia software, including Flash, OpenOffice.org still refers to it as Macromedia Flash. Presumably, this will be changed in a later version.

Along with slide presentations, Impress also lets you produce handouts to support your work. OpenOffice.org Impress is covered in more detail in Chapter 25.

Database: OpenOffice.org Base

Start OpenOffice.org Base as follows:

- In GNOME, click Applications ➤ Office ➤ Database ➤ OpenOffice.org Base

- In KDE, click K menu ➤ Office ➤ Database ➤ OpenOffice.org Base

Base, shown in Figure 11-4, is the newest component of OpenOffice.org, introduced with version 2. Base allows you to create relational databases using a built-in database engine, although it also can interface with external databases. It's very similar to Microsoft Access in look and feel, although it lacks some of Access's high-end functions. For most database uses, it should prove perfectly adequate.

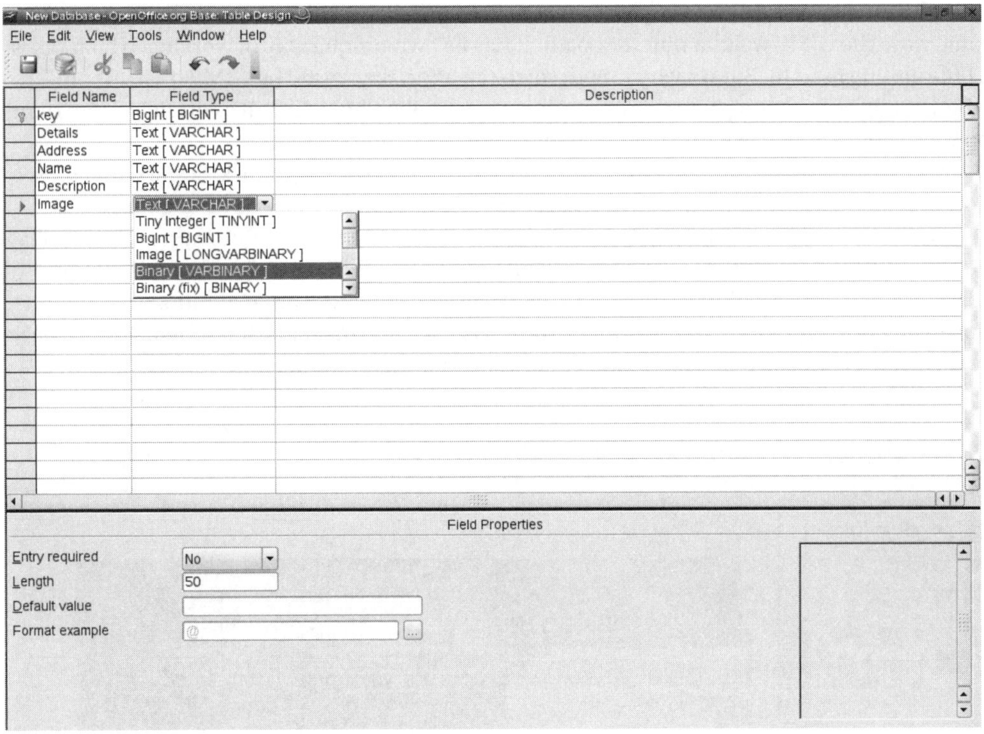

Figure 11-4. *OpenOffice.org Base*

If you know the fundamentals of database technology, you shouldn't have any trouble getting started with Base immediately. When the program starts, a wizard guides you through the creation of a simple database.

As with Access, Base is designed on the principles of tables of data, forms by which the data is input or accessed, and queries and reports by which the data can be examined and output. Once again, wizards are available to walk you through the creation of each of these, or you can dive straight in and edit each by hand by selecting the relevant option.

Each field in the table can be of various types, including several different integer and text types, as well as binary and Boolean values.

Forms can contain a variety of controls, ranging from simple text boxes to radio buttons and scrolling lists, all of which can make data entry easier. Reports can feature a variety of text formatting and can also rely on queries to manipulate the data. The queries themselves can feature a variety of functions and filters in order to sort data down to the finest detail.

You'll learn more about Base in Chapter 26.

Photo Editing: The GIMP

Start The GIMP as follows:

- In GNOME, click Applications ➤ Graphics ➤ Image Editing ➤ The GIMP

- In KDE, click K menu ➤ Graphics ➤ Image Editing

While many of the other programs introduced so far mirror the Windows look and feel in some way, The GIMP walks a different path. It has its own unique way of working, which takes a little getting used to. But it's very much worth the effort, because The GIMP offers photo-editing tools on par with professional products like Adobe Photoshop. It's certainly more than powerful enough for tweaking digital camera snapshots.

When you initially run The GIMP, it will install itself on your hard disk. Some of the questions it asks look complicated, but you can stick with the default choices throughout.

Once the program is running, you'll notice that it's actually little more than a large toolbar on the left side of the screen, as shown in Figure 11-5. Everything else that runs within The GIMP—whether it's a window containing the image you're editing or an additional configuration dialog box—uses its own program window. This also means that each program item that you activate gets its own button on the panel at the bottom of the screen.

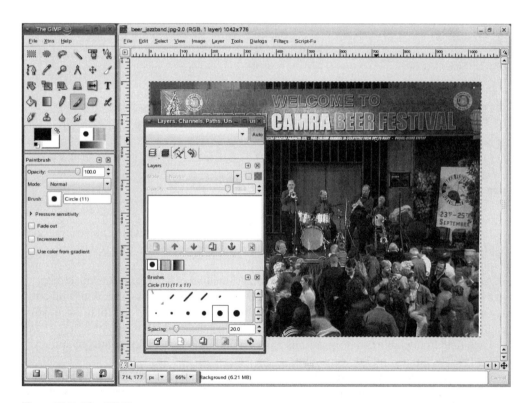

Figure 11-5. *The GIMP*

To open a picture, select File ➤ Open and select your image from the hard disk. Once an image file is opened, you can manipulate it using the tools on the toolbar (which are similar to those found in other image editors). On the bottom half of the main program window, you'll find the settings for each tool, which can be altered, usually via click-and-drag sliders.

To apply filters or other corrective changes, right-click anywhere on the image to bring up a context menu with a variety of options. Simple tools to improve brightness and contrast can be found on the Layer ➤ Colors submenu.

For an in-depth look at The GIMP package, see Chapter 20.

KDE VS. GNOME

KDE and GNOME are the two primary desktop environments offered by SUSE Linux. Which you use is entirely up to personal preference, and you will most likely have made this choice during installation.

Although similar in many ways, GNOME and KDE are developed by different organizations. This means that each has different goals and uses different technologies. Broadly speaking, the differences fall into the follow categories:

- **Tookits:** On a technical level, KDE is built using the QT toolkit, and GNOME is built using the GTK+ toolkit. What this means to those who aren't programmers is that software written for the KDE desktop looks different from software written for GNOME. Buttons, scroll bars, and other assorted "widgets" have a different appearance. This also means that themes applied to the GNOME desktop won't affect KDE applications, and vice versa.

- **Usability:** The two projects take a different approach to usability, meaning that the feel of the programs can vary quite radically. Generally speaking, KDE programs tend to be packed with more features than their GNOME equivalents, which sacrifice a comprehensive feature set for ease of use. Nowhere is this better demonstrated that with the right-click menu. Within KDE, a right-click menu will present a complex list of options. In contrast, a similar menu within GNOME will be short and simple— deliberately designed that way to meet a strict set of usability guidelines.

- **Users:** GNOME is found in more business-oriented Linux distributions, such as Red Hat, and is aimed at corporate users who may not be computer-literate. Arguably, KDE is favored by power users and experienced Linux users (although it includes ease-of-use features designed to appeal to a mass audience). The difference in user audience is reflected in the choice of software supplied with each desktop. GNOME's Evolution e-mail client can connect to corporate Microsoft Exchange and Novell GroupWare servers, for example, which KDE's KMail application cannot do.

Until recently, SUSE Linux was seen as a KDE-based distribution of Linux. Indeed, within the huge SUSE Linux community of established users, KDE is undoubtedly the desktop of choice. However, the tide turned with Novell's acquisition of SUSE in 2004. Through its acquisition of the Ximian organization a year earlier, Novell found itself employing several key GNOME developers, who were put to work on SUSE Linux.

This led to a strong push to improve the GNOME desktop under SUSE Linux. SUSE now flies the flag for the GNOME desktop, and it is arguably the first choice on SUSE Linux distributions, particularly those aimed at the corporate marketplace, including SUSE Linux Enterprise Desktop. KDE is officially supported only within the openSUSE community-driven project.

Novell is currently sponsoring a great deal of cutting-edge GNOME development, such as the Xgl composite desktop project (`www.freedesktop.org/wiki/Software/Xgl`), that brings 3D effects to the desktop. It already sponsors the development of the Evolution e-mail client and personal information manager.

Quick Start: GNOME Software

The software in this section is designed for use under the GNOME desktop environment and, as such, as allied to the look and feel of other GNOME applications. Of course, this software will function perfectly under the KDE desktop environment as well.

E-Mail/Personal Information Manager: Evolution

Start Evolution as follows:

- In GNOME, click Applications ➤ Internet ➤ Email ➤ Evolution Email

- In KDE, click K menu ➤ Internet ➤ Email ➤ Evolution Email

Evolution is a little like Microsoft Outlook in that, in addition to being an e-mail client, it can also keep track of your appointments and contacts.

Before using the program, you'll need to set it up with your incoming and (if applicable) outgoing mail server settings, as detailed in Chapter 8. Evolution is compatible with POP/SMTP, IMAP, Novell GroupWise, and Microsoft Exchange servers.

Once the program is up and running, you can create a new message by clicking the New button on the toolbar. To reply to any e-mail, simply select it in the list, and then click the Reply or Reply To All button, depending on whether you want to reply to the sender or to all the recipients of the message.

To switch to Contacts view, click the relevant button on the bottom left. If you reply to anyone via e-mail, that recipient is automatically added to this Contacts list. You can also add entries manually by either right-clicking someone's address in an open e-mail or right-clicking in a blank space in the Contacts view.

Clicking the Calendar view shows a day-and-month diary, as shown in Figure 11-6. To add an appointment, simply select the day, and then double-click the time you want the appointment to start. You can opt to set an alarm when creating the appointment, so that you're reminded of it when it's scheduled.

By clicking the Tasks button, you can create a to do list. To add a task, click the bar at the top of the list. Once an entry has been created, you can put a check in its box to mark it as completed. Completed tasks are marked with strike-through, so you can see at a glance what you still need to do.

In addition to the setup guide in Chapter 8, you'll find a full explanation of Evolution's features in Chapter 27.

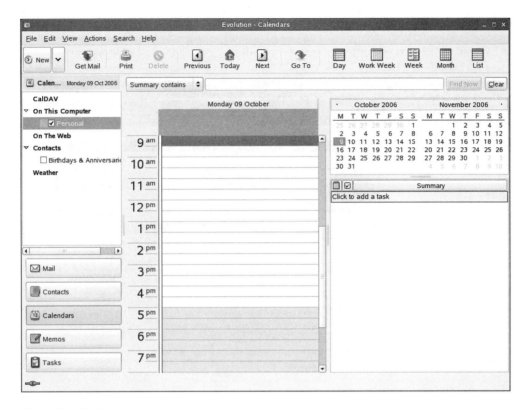

Figure 11-6. *Evolution*

Web Browser: Firefox

Start Firefox as follows:

- In GNOME, click Applications ➤ Internet ➤ Web Browser ➤ Firefox

- In KDE, click K menu ➤ Internet ➤ Web browser ➤ Firefox

You might already know of Mozilla Firefox under Windows, where it has firmly established itself as the alternative browser of choice. The good news is that the Linux version of Firefox is nearly identical to its Windows counterpart, as shown in Figure 11-7.

Figure 11-7. *Mozilla Firefox*

When the program starts, you can type an address into the URL bar to visit a web site. If you wish to add a site to your bookmarks list, click Bookmarks ➤ Bookmark This Page. Alternatively, you can press Ctrl+D.

Searching is very easy within Firefox, using its search bar at the top right of the window. By default, Firefox uses Google for searches. To choose from other search engines, click the small down arrow on the left side of the search box. You can even enter your own choice of site if your favorite isn't already in the list.

The main benefit of Firefox over Internet Explorer is the principle of tabbed browsing, which means you can have more than one site open at once. To open a new tab, type Ctrl+T. You can move between the tabs by clicking each one.

■**Tip** When Firefox starts, tabs aren't activated. If you would like to keep tabs in view all the time, click Edit ➤ Preferences, and then click the Advanced icon. In the Tabbed Browsing section of the window, remove the check from "Hide the tab bar when only one web site is open."

Firefox is compatible with the same range of extensions you might have used under the Windows version of the browser. You can download new extensions from `https://addons.mozilla.org/extensions`. In addition, Firefox under SUSE Linux can work with Flash animations, although you may need to download the Flash Player software first. See the instructions in Chapter 19 to learn more.

■**Note** Flash Player is automatically installed on the version of SUSE Linux provided with this book.

Audio Playback: Banshee and CD Player

Start Banshee as follows:

- In GNOME, click Applications ➤ Multimedia ➤ Audio Player ➤ Banshee

- In KDE, click K menu ➤ Multimedia ➤ Audio Player ➤ Banshee

Start CD Player as follows:

- In GNOME, click Applications ➤ Multimedia ➤ CD Player ➤ CD Player

- In KDE, click K menu ➤ Multimedia ➤ CD Player ➤ CD Player

The GNOME desktop's multimedia software is simple but effective. It can play back the majority of audio files, as long as it has been configured properly.

■**Note** The version of SUSE Linux supplied with this book has built-in support for MP3. However, if you're using a different version of SUSE Linux, such as that provided by the openSUSE project, you might need to add in support manually.

Banshee is the audio player under GNOME. It handles not only music file playback, but also CD music playback, as shown in Figure 11-8. Banshee will start automatically whenever a CD is inserted into your computer's CD/DVD-ROM drive (alternatively, you can double-click the Audio Disc icon to start playback).

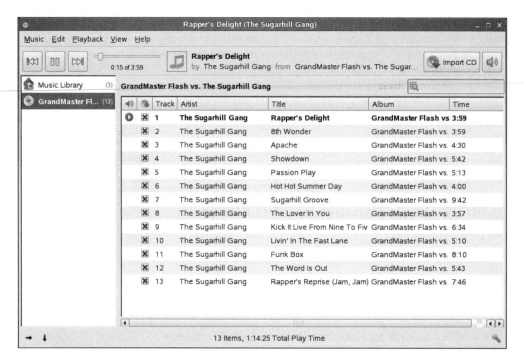

Figure 11-8. *Banshee (in CD playback mode)*

When Banshee is run for the first time in non-CD-playback mode (when you double-click an MP3 file, or start it from the Applications menu), it will offer to find and then catalog your music collection. Simply click the Import Music Source button. You might be used to this kind of functionality with Windows utilities like iTunes. After this initial file search, whenever Banshee runs, you will find your tracks listed by artist or name, provided that they have the relevant tag information embedded in them (such as ID3 tags in MP3 music).

■**Note** Unlike iTunes, Banshee can't play Digital Rights Management (DRM)–protected files.

To start playing a music track, double-click it in the list. You can adjust the volume of playback by clicking the speaker icon at the top right of the screen. Progress through the track is indicated by the slider at the top left; clicking and dragging this slider will alter the playback position.

The CD player functionality works in exactly the same way. The same tape-recorder-like controls are used to stop and pause playback, and you can click the skip ahead/back buttons to change tracks. Banshee is able to automatically look up the artist and track information about most CDs online, and then save the information for future reference. By clicking the Import CD button at the top right, you can "rip" the CD tracks to your hard disk. For more details, see Chapter 18.

Movie Playback: Totem Movie Player

Start Totem Movie Player as follows:

- In GNOME, click Applications ➤ Multimedia ➤ Video Player ➤ Totem

- In KDE, click K menu ➤ Multimedia ➤ Video Player ➤ Totem

As with Banshee and CD Player, Totem is a simple and uncomplicated application, as shown in Figure 11-9. The video file will play in the top left of the window. A playlist detailing movies you have queued appears in the top right. You can remove the playlist, to give the video window more room, by clicking the Sidebar button.

Figure 11-9. *Totem Movie Player*

You can control video playback using the tape-recorder-like controls at the bottom left. In addition, provided that a compatible video format is being played, you can use the Time bar to move backward and forward within the video file. You can switch to full-screen playback by clicking View ➤ Fullscreen. To switch back, simply press the Esc key. If you're watching a program that has been ripped from TV, you might want to use the Deinterlace feature on the View menu to remove any interference patterns.

■**Note** Although Totem is a very capable media player application, in Chapter 19 of this book, I explain how to install MPlayer, a much more established media playback application. In addition, I explain how you can install support for popular file formats, such as Windows Media Player and QuickTime.

CD/DVD Burning: Nautilus and Banshee

Start Nautilus in CD/DVD Creator mode as follows:

- In GNOME, click Applications ➤ CD/DVD Burning ➤ GNOME CD/DVD Creator

- In KDE, click K menu ➤ Multimedia ➤ CD/DVD Burning ➤ GNOME CD/DVD Creator

Start Banshee as follows:

- In GNOME, click Applications ➤ Multimedia ➤ Audio Player ➤ Banshee

- In KDE, click K menu ➤ Multimedia ➤ Audio Player ➤ Banshee

Under the GNOME desktop, you can burn data CD/DVDs using Nautilus in CD/DVD Creator mode. To create audio CDs, use Banshee.

Although the SUSE Linux menu refers to the GNOME CD/DVD Creator, this is actually the Nautilus file browser running in its built-in CD/DVD Creator mode, as shown in Figure 11-10. You can switch to CD/DVD Creator mode in any open Nautilus window by clicking Go ➤ CD/DVD Creator.

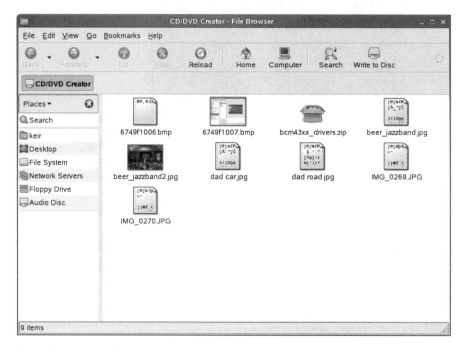

Figure 11-10. *Nautilus CD/DVD Creator*

To use the CD/DVD Creator, just drag-and-drop files onto the window. This will create shortcuts to the files, but Nautilus will actually burn the files from their original locations. When you've finished choosing files, click the Write to Disc button on the toolbar. Unfortunately, you won't see a warning if the disc's file size has been exceeded until you try to write to the disc. However, by right-clicking an empty space in the Nautilus window and selecting Properties, you can discover the total size of the files. Remember that most CDs hold 700MB, and most DVD+/-R discs hold around 4.3GB (some dual-layer discs hold twice this amount; see the DVD disc packaging for details).

To burn an audio CD, start Banshee and highlight the tracks you want to burn (you can hold down Ctrl to select multiple tracks, or Shift to select many contiguous tracks). Then click the Write CD button. Note that you might not be able to write certain audio files, like MP3s, to CDs unless you have the relevant codecs installed. See Chapter 18 to learn more.

■**Tip** Most modern CD/DVD recorders utilize burn-proof technology, which helps ensure error-free disc creation. To activate this under the GNOME desktop, click Applications ➤ System ➤ Configuration ➤ GNOME Configuration Editor. Click Edit ➤ Find, and type `burnproof`. Make sure there's a check in Search Also in Key Names. In the search results at the bottom of the window, click the first result (`/apps/nautilus-cd-burner/burnproof`) and make sure there's a check in `burnproof` at the top right of the window. Then close the Configuration Editor.

Quick Start: KDE Software

This section covers a selection of the most useful software supplied under the KDE desktop, and which duplicates the majority of functions found within Windows favorites. Just as you can easily run the GNOME software under KDE, you can add this KDE software to your GNOME setup.

■**Tip** In the case of K3b, the KDE CD/DVD burning software, running KDE software under GNOME is something of a necessity, because GNOME currently lacks a full-fledged CD/DVD burning application.

E-Mail/Contacts Manager: Kontact

Start Kontact as follows:

- In KDE, click K menu ➤ Office ➤ Kontact

- In GNOME, click Applications ➤ Office ➤ Kontact

If you're familiar with Microsoft Outlook, you'll feel immediately at home with Kontact, which mirrors Outlook's look and feel, as well as providing identical functionality.

As shown in Figure 11-11, on the left side of the screen are various icons that provide shortcuts to e-mail, contacts management, a calendar, and a to do list. In fact, the functions within Kontact are available separately. Its e-mail function is provided by KMail, for example, which has its own K menu entry under Internet ➤ Email ➤ KMail. However, running everything within Kontact is an ideal way of keeping yourself organized and sharing data among the applications.

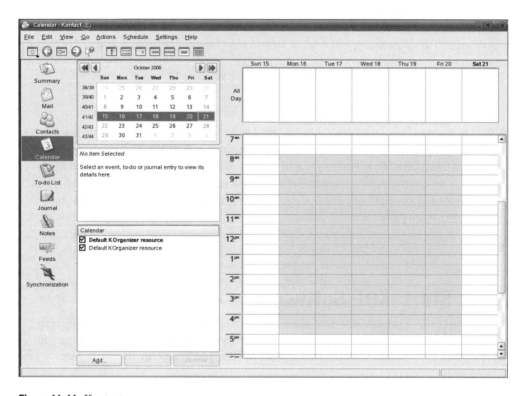

Figure 11-11. *Kontact*

When you click each icon on the left side of the screen, the toolbar and menu change accordingly, to offer features appropriate to whatever you're doing.

In the contact manager, you can either create new contacts from scratch or edit those that have been added by programs like KMail (contacts are generated automatically when you reply to e-mail).

The Todo List tool is fairly advanced. To create a new task, right-click in some empty space and select New Todo. As well as simply letting you create a list of tasks, it allows you to mark each as completed to a certain percentage.

The calendar ties into the Todo List tool, in that it will remind you when tasks are due. However, it also adds a variety of other organizational functions. Events can be added for every half hour of every day.

The e-mail program, provided by KMail, is extremely powerful in itself. The program can understand HTML e-mail and includes filtering tools for sorting new mail. You can also search e-mail messages—according to their message body, sender, or a variety of other options—by clicking the button on the toolbar.

Web Browsing and File Management: Konqueror

Start Konqueror as follows:

- In KDE, click K menu ➤ Internet ➤ Web Browser ➤ Konqueror

- In GNOME, click Applications ➤ Internet ➤ Web Browser ➤ Konqueror

Konqueror is KDE's built-in web browser. It uses the same browsing concept as Windows, in that the same program is used to manage local files as well as to browse the Internet. This means that you can quickly jump from seeing what's in a folder on your hard disk to browsing your favorite web site by simply entering an Internet URL rather than a file location in the address bar. FTP and SFTP sites are handled natively within Konqueror, too, providing a graphic way to upload and download files.

As shown in Figure 11-12, Konqueror features everything you might find in Internet Explorer, such as a bookmarks list and a packed toolbar that lets you navigate even the most complicated site. The toolbar offers the usual array of tools, such as the ability to move backward and forward in the browsing history. However, Konqueror's toolbar offers additional functionality. To the right of the left arrow, which provides the standard Back function, is an up arrow, which lets you move backward in the web server's file system (for example, clicking it will move you from `www.example.com/folder1/` to `www.example.com`).

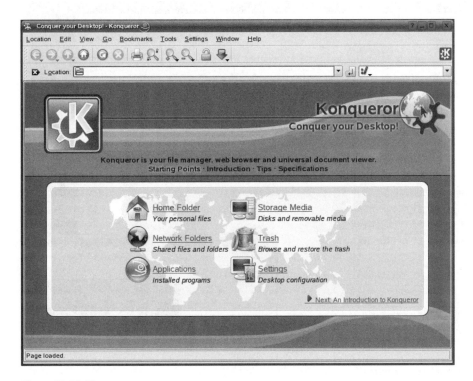

Figure 11-12. *Konqueror*

Konqueror is built using KHTML technology, which is also used in Apple's Safari web browser. KHTML is one of the most standards-compliant browsing engines available. However, not all sites work well with it, and you might find glitches on certain pages, or you might find yourself simply turned away with an error message. In such cases, you can simply use Firefox, the other browser installed under SUSE Linux.

Audio Playback: KsCD and amaroK

Start KsCD as follows:

- In KDE, click K menu ➤ Multimedia ➤ CD Player ➤ KsCD

- In GNOME, click Applications ➤ Multimedia ➤ CD Player ➤ KsCD

Start amaroK as follows:

- In KDE, click K menu ➤ Multimedia ➤ Audio Player ➤ amaroK

- In GNOME, click Applications ➤ Multimedia ➤ Audio Player ➤ amaroK

Audio playback under the KDE desktop is very strong, although the tasks of playing back music files and playing back CDs are handled by separate programs. amaroK is ordinarily used for playback of MP3 files (see Chapter 19 for more details), while KsCD is used for the playback of CDs. Figure 11-13 shows both programs.

Figure 11-13. *KsCD and amaroK*

When you insert an audio CD, a dialog box appears, asking if you want to play the CD. Choosing to do so starts KsCD, which keeps things very simple. It lets you move backward and forward through tracks, as well as click and drag a slider to skip through the song to your favorite section. Adjust the volume by clicking the icon just to the right of the slider.

Additionally, KsCD will attempt to download track and artist information in the background via the online CD Database (CDDB) service, so you no longer need to deal with just track numbers. You can even edit the track information if you find it wrong or unacceptable; just click the CDDB button to make changes.

When you first run amaroK, it will attempt to catalog your music collection by searching your hard disk. Once this is done, a track listing will appear on the left side of the screen. By double-clicking tracks, you can quickly build up a playlist, which will appear on the right side of the screen. To start playing your playlist, click the Play button at the bottom of the program window. See Chapter 18 for more information about using amaroK.

Movie Playback: Kaffeine Media Player

Start Kaffeine as follows:

- In KDE, click K menu ➤ Multimedia ➤ Video Player ➤ Kaffeine

- In, GNOME, click Applications ➤ Multimedia ➤ Video Player ➤ Kaffeine

Using Kaffeine is simple. Click the Open Files link to play a video file located on your hard disk, as shown in Figure 11-14. You can switch to full-screen mode by clicking View ➤ Full Screen Mode, or by pressing Ctrl+Shift+F.

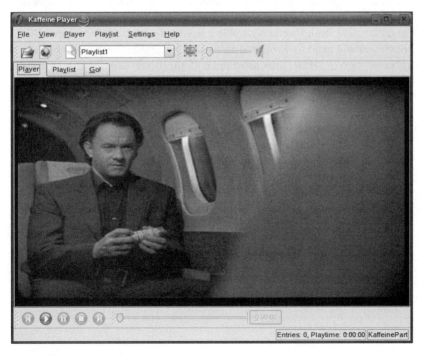

Figure 11-14. *Kaffeine*

Kaffeine integrates with the Konqueror web browser, and will immediately start up when you click any compatible video links on web sites (if you want to avoid this and save the video file to disk, right-click the link and select Save Link As). Kaffeine will also start automatically when you click video files on your hard disk.

You can attempt to improve the picture quality by adjusting the brightness, contrast, and other aspects; select Player ➤ Video ➤ Video Settings to access these options. You can also adjust the sound quality by clicking Player ➤ Audio ➤ Equalizer.

■**Note** Although Kaffeine is a very capable media player application, in Chapter 19 of this book, I explain how to install MPlayer, a much more established media playback software. In addition, I explain how you can install support for popular file formats, such as Windows Media Player and QuickTime.

CD/DVD Burning: K3b

Start K3b as follows:

- In KDE, click K menu ➤ Multimedia ➤ CD/DVD Burning ➤ K3b

- In GNOME, click Applications ➤ Multimedia ➤ CD/DVD Burning ➤ K3b

Users of popular Windows CD-burning programs will feel at home with K3b. In fact, K3b is a jewel in the crown of the KDE software base because it's one of the most popular burning programs available for Linux, regardless of whether you use GNOME, KDE, or any other desktop environment.

You can use it to create data, audio, and DVDs. K3b lets you create audio CDs from MP3s and copy CDs, although you will need to download and install additional software to burn MP3s if you're using the version of SUSE Linux provided with this book. See Chapter 18 for more information.

As shown in Figure 11-15, K3b provides a fully graphic interface that employs click and drag for most of its functions.

To create a disc, simply click the icon representing the project type at the bottom of the program window when K3b first starts. After this, compiling a disc is simply a matter of clicking and dragging files from the top of the window to the bottom. This applies to both data and music CDs. Watch the green line at the bottom to see how full your CD is.

When you're ready to create your disc, click the Burn button on the toolbar in the middle of the screen (alternatively, click Project ➤ Burn). In the dialog box that appears, you can choose the writing speed and also whether you want to do a test burn first.

■**Tip** To create a CD-ROM that can be read by Windows systems, click the Filesystem tab in the Burn dialog box and make sure there's a check in the Generate Joliet Extensions box.

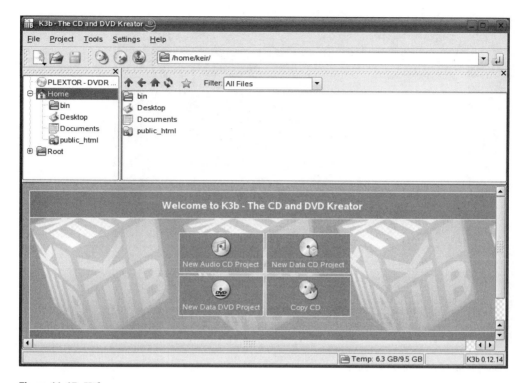

Figure 11-15. *K3b*

Other Handy Applications

Many additional applications might prove useful on a day-to-day basis. Here, I'll review some of the more common ones.

Calculator

Start the calculator application as follows:

- In GNOME, click Applications ➤ Utilities ➤ Calculator ➤ Gcalctool

- In KDE, click K menu ➤ Utilities ➤ Calculator ➤ KCalc

Both the KDE and GNOME desktops come with their own calculator applications. Figure 11-16 shows both calculators.

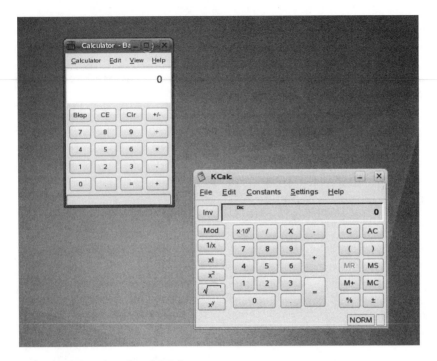

Figure 11-16. *Gcalctool and KCalc*

The GNOME Calculator (also known as Gcalctool) shouldn't present any challenges to anyone who has ever used a real-life calculator, although the Bksp key might be new. This simply deletes the last number you typed (handy if you press the wrong key during a calculation).

Both the KDE and GNOME calculators offer scientific modes, as well as statistical and financial modes. To access these modes, click the View menu within Gcalctool, and the Settings menu within KCalc.

Gcalctool also offers an Advanced mode, which is a more complicated version of the basic calculator. It can store numbers in several memory locations, for example, and carry out less-common calculations, such as square roots and reciprocals.

Floppy Disk Formatting

Start the floppy disk formatter as follows:

- In GNOME, click Applications ➤ System ➤ File System ➤ Floppy Formatter

- In KDE, click K menu ➤ System ➤ File System ➤ KFloppy

Within Linux, floppy disks are formatted using special programs, rather than right-clicking the floppy drive's icon and selecting Format, as with Windows. GNOME includes Floppy Formatter, and KDE offers KFloppy, as shown in Figure 11-17.

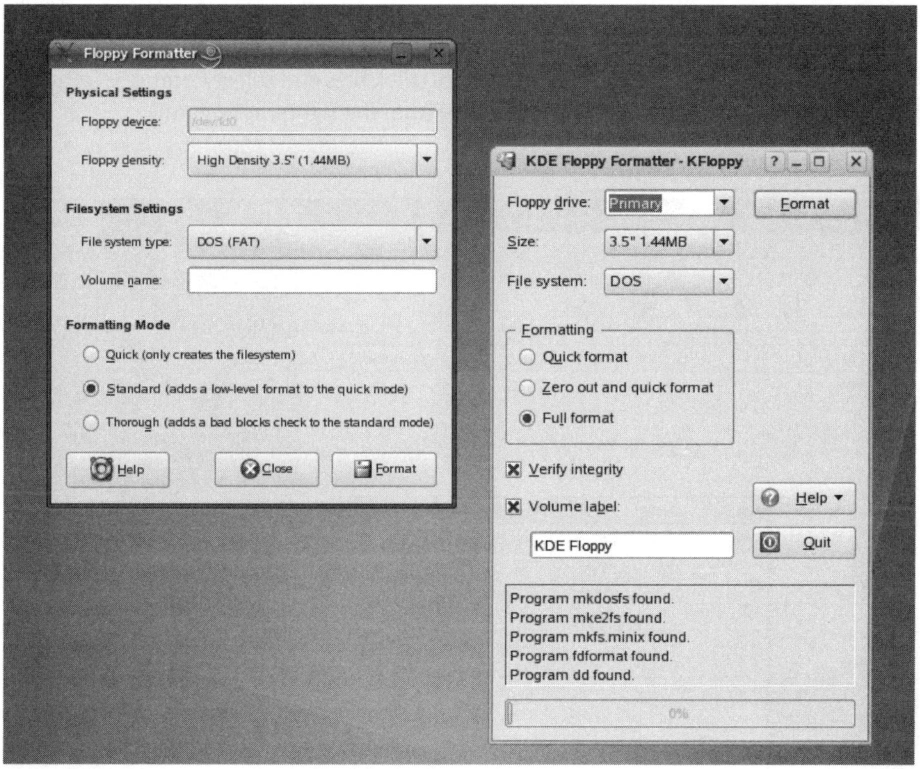

Figure 11-17. *Floppy Formatter and KFloppy*

Both are simple programs designed to format 3.5-inch floppy disks. The programs can format disks in Linux (ext2) or DOS format. The latter is the best option, bearing in mind you might be sharing disks with others who run Windows. There's also no harm in doing so, since DOS-formatted disks will work fine under SUSE Linux, too. In both programs, you can also choose the Quick format option, which will simply overwrite the disk's file listing rather than overwrite its actual data.

Compression/Archive Tools

Start the archiving application as follows:

- In GNOME, click Applications ➤ Utilities ➤ Archiving ➤ File Roller

- In KDE, click K menu ➤ Utilities ➤ Archiving ➤ Ark

The GNOME desktop offers Archive Manager (also known as File Roller) to take care of compressing and decompressing files. It's counterpart under the KDE desktop is Ark. Figure 11-18 shows both programs. Each program will open automatically whenever you double-click .zip files (or .tar, .gz, or .bzip2 files, which are the native archive file formats under Linux). Alternatively, you can start the program manually, if you wish to create archives from scratch (although within KDE you can also right-click files and select Compress from the menu; under GNOME, you can select Create Archive from the right-click menu).

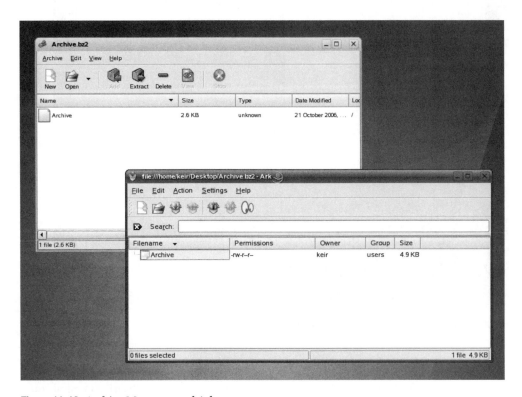

Figure 11-18. *Archive Manager and Ark*

To extract files from an archive, select the archive file (hold down the Ctrl key to select more than one file), and then click the Extract button on the toolbar.

To create an archive, start Ark or File Roller and click the New button on the toolbar. Give the archive a name, and then drag-and-drop files onto the program window. When you've finished, simply close the program window.

Dictionary

Start the Dictionary as follows:

- In GNOME, click Applications ➤ Office ➤ Dictionary ➤ Dictionary

- In KDE, click K menu ➤ Office ➤ Dictionary

The Dictionary tool is part of the GNOME desktop, but you can use it in KDE without any problems. It looks up the definition of words in an online dictionary, as shown in Figure 11-19.

Figure 11-19. *Dictionary*

The `http://dict.org` online dictionary is the default choice, but you can choose from a variety of others. Click Edit ➤ Preferences and then click the Web Sites tab. Choose another dictionary site by clicking the In Dictionary drop-down list next to the Look-up field.

Note Changing the default dictionary is a good idea, because `http://dict.org` relies on a 1913 edition of Webster's, so its word definitions are hardly current and don't take into account any recent vocabulary. But it does have the advantage of being out of copyright, so you can cut and paste the word definitions into your own documents without fear of legal reprisals.

Chat

Start the chat application as follows:

- In GNOME, click Applications ➤ Internet ➤ Chat ➤ Gaim

- In KDE, click K menu ➤ Internet ➤ Chat ➤ Kopete

Gaim is the instant messaging software provided with the GNOME desktop. Kopete is its counterpart under the KDE desktop. Both programs are shown in Figure 11-20.

Figure 11-20. *Gaim and Kopete*

Unlike most other messaging programs, Gaim and Kopete aren't exclusive to one chat protocol. In other words, you can use them to connect to MSN, AOL/ICQ, Yahoo!, and many other services.

Once they're up and running, you can chat with any of your buddies by double-clicking their icon. To set your status, click the icon at the bottom left (or right, in the case of Kopete) and select a status message. In both programs, you can manage many functions by right-clicking the notification area icon that appears when the program starts. For example, you can set your status or sign off from there.

Games

Start a game from the Games menu:

- In GNOME, click Applications ➤ Games

- In KDE, click K menu ➤ Games

A variety of games are available under SUSE Linux, provided by the GNOME and KDE projects, respectively. The Games menu categorizes games by types, such as Arcade (action), Board Games, Card Games, Puzzle, and Tactics and Strategy.

You'll find clones of popular Windows desktop games under these menus, such as Mines (under the Puzzle menu), which is a faithful reproduction of Minesweeper, or AisleRot Solitaire, which is a version of the popular Solitaire/Patience card game.

Also worthy of note are Frozen-Bubble, under the Arcade menu, which is a reproduction of Puzzle Bobble, and SuperTux, which is a clone of the Super Mario series of games. Tetris fans will appreciate Gnometris, under the Arcade menu, while Civilization fans will find Freeciv, under the Tactics and Strategy menu, a compelling alternative. Figure 11-21 shows two games in action.

Figure 11-21. *Frozen-Bubble and Klondike Solitaire*

Phone/Video Conferencing

Start GnomeMeeting as follows:

- In GNOME, click Applications ➤ Internet ➤ Telephone ➤ GnomeMeeting

- In KDE, click K menu ➤ Internet ➤ Telephone ➤ GnomeMeeting

Start Linphone as follows:

- In GNOME, click Applications ➤ Internet ➤ Telephone ➤ Linphone

- In KDE, click K menu ➤ Internet ➤ Telephone ➤ Linphone

If you want to conduct a video conference using SUSE Linux, then GnomeMeeting is for you. Linphone lets you make phone calls through your computer. Both applications are shown in Figure 11-22.

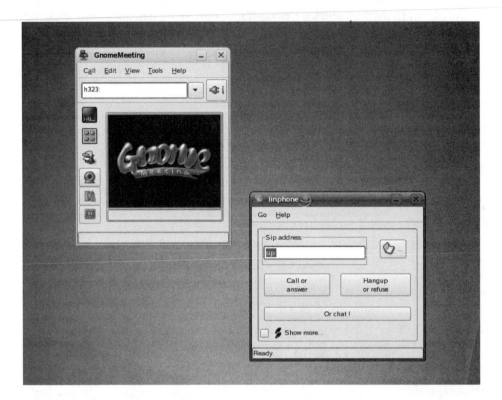

Figure 11-22. *GnomeMeeting and Linphone*

GnomeMeeting works fine under both KDE and GNOME desktops, and supports the commonly used H.323 protocol, as used by Microsoft's NetMeeting. It also lets you register to an Internet Locator Service (ILS) directory, as well as take part in multiple-user calls via a Multipoint Control Unit (MCU). In addition, by registering using the link provided, you can make PC telephone calls, although this requires paying a fee and setting up an account.

If you want to use Voice Over Internet Protocol (VoIP) and have registered for a Session Initiation Protocol (SIP) service, you can use Linphone. Simply enter the SIP address of the person you wish to call, and then click the Call or Answer button. When you've finished the call, click the Hangup or Refuse button. You can also text chat by clicking the Or Chat! button.

Summary

In this chapter, we've taken a look at some SUSE Linux programs that provide vital functions that you might have used daily under Windows. The aim was to get you started with this software as quickly as possible by pointing out key features. You've seen how some programs mirror the look and feel of their Windows counterparts almost to the letter, while others resolutely strike out on their own path. It takes just a little time to become familiar with SUSE Linux software, and then using these programs will become second nature.

In the next chapter, we'll move on to more fundamental SUSE Linux tasks: manipulating files. However, once again, this is not too dissimilar from the Windows experience, which makes getting used to the system very easy.

■■■

## CHAPTER 12

Managing Your Files

Files are what make the world of Linux go round. They're the currency of any kind of operating system, because every time you use your computer, you generate new files, even if they're only temporary.

How Linux views files, as well as the disks and partitions that contain them, varies somewhat from how Windows handles files. In many ways, the Linux system of file management is far simpler than that in Windows (which, ironically, was created as an attempt to make everything easy!). The Linux system is also much more established.

In this chapter, I will explain how you can manage your files under SUSE Linux. This isn't a definitive guide; you'll need to wait until Chapter 14 to learn the technical ins and outs of the file system. However, it provides enough information for you to understand how the system works, where and how you should store your data, and what software you should use to do so.

Essential File System Concepts

Just like Windows, SUSE Linux has a file system that is shared among software components and your own personal data, such as documents that you've generated within various applications or downloaded from the Internet. However, SUSE Linux differs from Windows in a couple of important ways.

Drive References

Perhaps the most important differences in Linux are that it doesn't use drive letters and it uses a forward slash (/) instead of a backslash (\) in filename paths. In other words, something like /home/john/myfile is typical under SUSE Linux, as opposed to C:\Documents and Settings\John\myfile under Windows. The root of the hard disk partition is usually referred to as C:\ under Windows. In SUSE Linux, it's referred to simply with a forward slash (/).

If you have more than one hard disk, the drives' partitions are usually combined together into the one file system under Linux. This is done by *mounting*, so that any additional drives appear as virtual folders under the file system. In other words, you browse the other hard disks by switching to various directories within the main file system. I explain mounting in more detail in Chapter 14.

Case Sensitivity

Another important difference between SUSE Linux and Windows is that filenames in SUSE Linux are case-sensitive. This means that MyFile is distinctly different from myfile. Uppercase letters are vitally important. In Windows, filenames might appear to have uppercase letters in them but, actually, these are ignored when you rename or otherwise manipulate files.

Because of this case sensitivity, you could have two separate files existing in the same place, one called MyFile and another called myfile. In fact, you could also have myFile, Myfile, MYFILE, and so on, as shown in Figure 12-1.

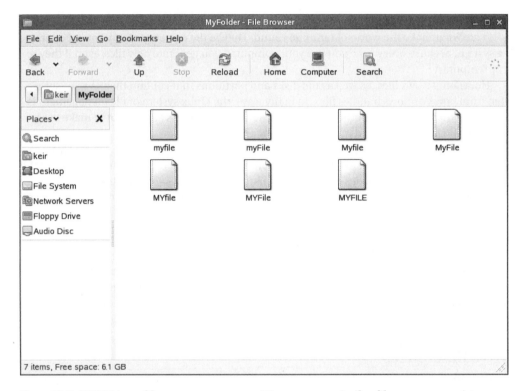

Figure 12-1. *SUSE Linux filenames are case-sensitive, so many similar filenames can exist, differing only in which letters are capitalized.*

File Access and Storage

Under Windows XP on a desktop computer, you have access to the entire hard disk. You can write, read, or delete files anywhere (unless the system has specifically been configured otherwise). You can save your personal files in C:\Windows, for example. Under SUSE Linux, ordinary users can browse most of the hard disk, but they aren't able to write files to the majority of folders (in some cases, they won't even be able to access files).

Although Chapter 14 covers the file system in much more depth, for the moment, it's enough to know that you've been given your own part of the hard disk in which to store your stuff. This is a directory located within the `/home` directory, and its name is taken from your username. If your login name is `louisesmith`, your place for storing files will be `/home/louisesmith`. Figure 12-2 shows an example of a user's `/home` directory.

■**Note** Linux generally uses the terms *directory* and *subdirectory* for the places you put files, whereas Windows XP refers to them as *folders*. It's merely a matter of semantics. However, within the Nautilus and Konqueror file browsers, directories are pictured as folders and are referred to as such in menus, thus furthering the confusion!

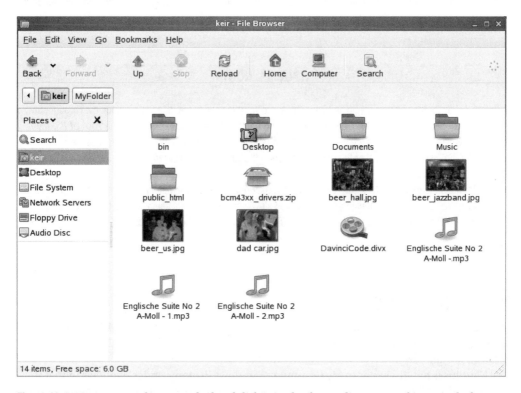

Figure 12-2. *Your personal area on the hard disk is in the /home directory and is named after your username; in this case, the username is keir.*

Some programs might create subdirectories in your `/home` directory in order to store and organize their output. For example, a digital camera program might create a `Pictures` directory within your `/home` directory. It's up to you whether you use these. The standard practice within the Linux community is to simply save everything into your /home subdirectory (for example, /home/keir) and sort it out later!

Files within SUSE Linux remember who owns them. If user johnsmith creates a file, he can make it so that only he can read or write that file (the default setting is that other users will be able to read the file but not write any new data to it). Directories, too, are owned by people, and the owner can set access permissions. By default, all users on a system can access each other's /home directories and read files, but they cannot change the files or write new files to any directory within /home that isn't theirs. One exception to this is the Documents directory within a user's /home directory, which is accessible by only the user who owns it. So if you wish to ensure a file's privacy, save it in your Documents directory.

▪**Note** Any user with superuser powers, such as the root user, has access to all of the system and can create, edit, and delete files in all directories. This is so that user can perform essential system maintenance.

ROOT VS. ROOT

Unfortunately for those who are new to Linux, the same word is used twice in Linux terminology. Throughout this book, I frequently refer to the *root user*, who is the administrator of the system, and the *root of the file system*, which is the bottom of the Linux directory structure (often indicated by a single forward slash, /).

The root user and the root of the tile system aren't the same thing and aren't directly connected. They are two separate concepts.

To make the matter a little more blurry, the root user has a personal directory in the root of the file system called root! Confused? Don't worry. All this will slowly but surely make sense as you use Linux. Just remember that the *root user* and the *root of the file system* are two different things.

Using Nautilus

The Nautilus file browser is the default file manager offered under the GNOME desktop. Although KDE users can use Nautilus if they wish, the KDE desktop provides its own file browser, Konqueror, which is covered in the next section.

Nautilus is not dissimilar to My Computer/Windows Explorer under Windows in that it presents a list of files on the right side of the window and a series of shortcuts to popular locations within the file system on the left side.

Starting Nautilus is simply a matter of clicking the Places menu and choosing a location, as shown in Figure 12-3. Alternatively, you can click Applications ➤ System ➤ File Manager ➤ Nautilus, which will open the default browsing location (your /home folder).

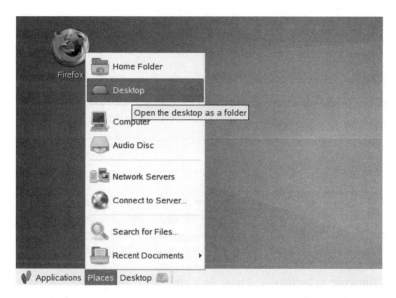

Figure 12-3. *You can open a file browser window by selecting a location under the Places menu.*

The Nautilus window (see Figures 12-1 and 12-2) consists of several elements:

Menu bar: The menus offer options for controlling the way files are displayed in the Nautilus window, as well as the look and feel of Nautilus itself. The Bookmarks menu lets you create web-browser-like shortcuts to certain locations in your file system so you can access them instantly.

Toolbar: As in a web browser, the toolbar allows you to quickly move backward and forward from place to place in your browsing history. In addition, you can reload the file listing, in order to reflect any changes that might have taken place since the Nautilus window opened, and quickly navigate to popular file system locations, such as your /home folder.

Location bar: This feature, located beneath the toolbar, is unique to Nautilus. It lets you see where you are in your file system, as well as quickly and easily move through your file-browsing history. For example, if you to start in /home/keir and then browse to /home/keir/pictures/holiday/disneyworld, clicking the pictures button will return you to /home/keir/pictures. The other folders listed on the location bar (holiday and disneyworld in this example) won't disappear, so you can return to those as well. It's best demonstrated by example, so give it a try!

Places pane: The Places pane on the left lists the most popular locations within the file system. Double-clicking each icon takes you to that location instantly. Clicking the File System entry takes you to the root of the file system (/). Clicking the X at the top right of the pane will hide the Places component of the window. To make it visible again, click View ➤ Side Pane.

As under Windows, you can right-click each file in the file browser window to see a context menu with options to rename the file, delete it, open it with particular applications, and so on. The Properties option on the context menu lets you view information about the file and alter certain aspects of it, such as its access permissions (discussed in Chapter 14). You can even add some text notes about the file if you wish!

■**Caution** You should never delete your /home folder. Doing so will most likely destroy your personal SUSE Linux setup and prevent you from logging in.

File Views

You can switch between list and icon view by clicking View ➤ View As Icons or View As List. When in list view, you can reorder the listing by clicking any of the headers. For example, to order the files by size, click the Size header. Clicking once will organize the files in ascending order of size (smallest to largest); clicking again will reverse this so that the files are listed in descending order.

To change the size of the icons in both list and icon view, click the Zoom In and Zoom Out entries on the View menu. This can be useful in folders containing digital images that have been thumbnailed in icon view, as shown in Figure 12-4.

Figure 12-4. *Whenever you view a folder full of pictures in icon view, they will be automatically thumbnailed.*

Each folder "remembers" the last view settings used, so you don't need to manually save the settings. However, you can set the default view settings by clicking Edit ➤ Preferences.

File and Folder Icons

You can change the icon for any file or folder to whatever you want. Right-click the file or folder, click Properties, and then click the Select Custom Icon option. You can choose from a wide range of supplied icons or click the Browse button and locate your own graphic. Virtually any image can be used, regardless of format or even size, so you can use digital camera snapshots if you wish.

Files and folders can also have *emblems* applied to them. These are smaller icons that are "tagged on" to the larger icons in both list view and icon view. Emblems are designed to give you quick clues about the nature of the file. To apply an emblem, right-click the file or folder, select Properties, and then click the Emblems tab. As shown in Figure 12-5, a range of icons is available; in fact, any file or folder can have several emblems applied at once. Simply put a check in the box beside the icons you wish to apply.

■Note Nautilus makes use of a handful of emblem icons for its own needs, too. For example, a file with a lock emblem attached to it indicates that you don't have the necessary file permissions to edit or delete that file. An X emblem means you don't have permissions to access that file or folder at all, not even to view it. In most cases, the emblems are self-explanatory.

Figure 12-5. *A variety of miniature emblems can be applied to an icon to aid recognition of the file.*

Special Nautilus Windows

As well as letting you view your files, Nautilus has a number of *object modes*. This is a complicated way of saying that Nautilus lets you view things other than files.

The most obvious example of this is the computer view of your file system, which presents an eagle's eye view of your storage devices. To access this view, click Places ➤ Computer. If you have a picture card reader attached, it will appear here, as will any Windows partitions that may be on your hard disk. Double-clicking each item opens a standard Nautilus file browser window (for this to work with Windows partitions, they must be set up correctly, as described in the "Accessing Windows Files" section later in this chapter).

Another Nautilus object mode is the fonts view, which lets you see at a glance any fonts installed on your computer. To access fonts view, click Go ➤ Location in any open Nautilus window, and then type `fonts://`.

Object mode comes into its own when viewing network locations. Clicking Places ➤ Network Servers brings up the network browser view, for example. You can also browse to FTP sites by clicking Go ➤ Location in a file browser window and entering an FTP address (prefacing it with `ftp://`; for example, to browse to `ftp.suse.com`, type `ftp://ftp.suse.com`).

■**Note** You might be used to dragging-and-dropping files onto program windows or taskbar buttons within Windows in order to open the file. This works with only some programs within SUSE Linux. Generally, the best policy is to try it and see what happens. If the program starts but your file isn't opened, it obviously didn't work.

HIDDEN FILES AND DIRECTORIES

When you view your `/home` directory via Nautilus or Konqueror, you're not seeing every file that's there. Several hidden files and directories relating to your system configuration also exist. You can take a look at them by clicking View ➤ Hidden Files in Nautilus, or View ➤ Show Hidden Files in Konqueror. Clicking this option again will hide the files and directories.

You might notice something curious about the hidden items: they all have a period before their filenames. In fact, this is all that's needed to hide any file or directory: simply place a period at the front of the filename. There's no magic involved above and beyond this.

For example, to hide the file `partypicture.jpg`, you could simply right-click it and rename it `.partypicture.jpg`. You'll need to click the Reload button on the toolbar for the file view to be updated and for the file to disappear. As you might expect, removing the period will unhide the file.

Files are usually hidden for a reason, and it's no coincidence that most of the hidden files are system files. In addition, every program that you install, or is installed by default, will usually create its own hidden folder for its system configuration data. Deleting such files by accident can be catastrophic.

Using Konqueror

Konqueror is the KDE desktop's combined file manager and web browser. It's a little like My Computer/Windows Explorer under Windows, except that it's a lot more powerful and packed with features.

Starting Konqueror is easy: just click the Home icon on the KDE toolbar next to the K menu, or click K menu ➤ Home (Personal Files).

In standard file browser mode, the left side of the Konqueror window shows the directory structure, represented in a familiar tree view. Click a directory in the left pane to see its contents displayed in the right pane, as shown in Figure 12-6. The top of the Konqueror window consists of the following elements:

Menu bar: The menu bar offers access to all of Konqueror's features, including those that alter the look and feel of Konqueror, as well as those that let you manipulate files. For example, the Edit menu has options for creating new folders, and copying and moving files. The View menu lets you switch between list and icon modes, and alter the size of the icons. The Bookmarks menu lets you define shortcuts to certain locations in the file system, just like a web browser lets you create shortcuts to certain web sites.

Toolbar: The same toolbar is shared between Konqueror's file browser and web browser modes, and works identically in both modes. The Back button, represented by a left arrow, will take you to the previous location you were browsing. The Up button, represented by an arrow pointing upward, will move you to the parent folder of the one you're currently browsing (so clicking this button while browsing /home/keir, will move you to /home). You can also click the Home button to return to your home directory instantly, and switch between various view modes.

Location bar: This is where the path of the current location you're browsing will appear. In addition, you can type a new path here and, after you press Enter, Konqueror will display the files and/or folders in that location. Clicking the down arrow on the right side of the location bar reveals Konqueror's browsing history—a list of locations that you've recently accessed.

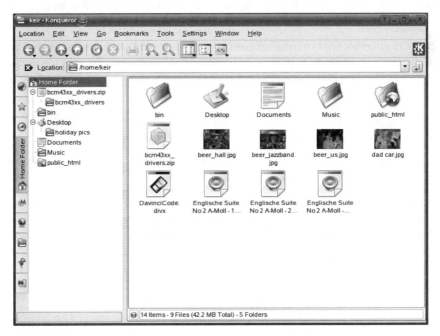

Figure 12-6. *On the left of a standard Konqueror window is the tree view, showing the directory structure, and on the right is the file list.*

■Tip Konqueror makes particularly good use of the context menu, and many useful features available on the menu or the toolbar also can be found there. Simply right-click any file or folder, or right-click in some blank space in a Konqueror window, to see this menu.

Shortcut Tabs

Located on the far left side of any Konqueror window are shortcut tabs that take you to various locations within the file system or switch Konqueror into various "modes" (described in the next section). In general, each tab will alter the context view in the left pane of the Konqueror window. In order, the shortcut tabs are as follows:

Amarok: This activates the amaroK music player's context mode, which will let you quickly choose and play audio tracks or playlists. Note that this shortcut tab might not appear until you have run amaroK for the first time (see Chapter 18).

Bookmarks: This tab presents a list of the bookmarks in the left pane of the Konqueror window. Clicking a bookmark in the list will display the files at that location in the right pane.

History: This tab presents a list of the file locations that you've recently browsed using Konqueror. It's a handy way of finding your way back to a particular location if you've forgotten the exact path. To make life easier, a search bar is provided into which you can type any snippets of the path that you might remember.

Home: This tab displays the directory structure and files of your /home directory. This is the default mode for Konqueror whenever it is opened.

Metabar: Clicking this tab turns the left pane of Konqueror into an information display, similar to what you see when you right-click a file and select Properties from the menu. Using the metabar, you can change the program that opens the file, discover its file permissions, and see a preview of the file (if applicable).

Network: This tab provides shortcuts to various network locations, including SMB (Windows) file shares on the local network, FTP sites, and even web sites.

Root folder: This tab displays the root directory structure in the left pane of the window. Clicking any directory will cause Konqueror to start browsing it.

Services: This tab shows a list of the various Konqueror modes in the left pane of the window (see the next section for a description of Konqueror's modes). For example, Konqueror includes a Bluetooth file browser mode and an Apple iPod browser mode. You can also access the system fonts here.

Konqueror's Browsing Modes

Konqueror is more than a file and web site browser. It has a number of additional browsing modes, referred to within the Konqueror documentation as *services*, which allow access to various types of files stored in special locations. Some modes even allow system configuration.

You can access some of these modes using the Services shortcut tab on the left side of the Konqueror window, but any Konqueror window can be switched to one of these modes by simply preceding an address with a certain URL. For example, to browse a local network for SMB-based file shares (sometimes known as *Windows shares*), type the following into the location bar:

```
smb://<IP address>
```

In a similar way, you can browse your iPod device by typing `ipod:/` in the location bar. To view and manage fonts, type `fonts:/`, as shown in Figure 12-7. Table 12-1 shows a list of some of the more useful Konqueror modes.

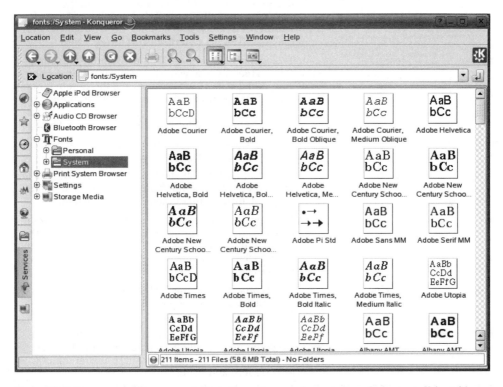

Figure 12-7. *You can use Konqueror's fonts browsing mode to view and also install font files.*

Table 12-1. *Some Konqueror Modes*

Mode	URL	Description
Web browsing	`http://<address>`	Effectively, switching to web browsing mode is the same as clicking the web browser icon on the main desktop toolbar and entering a web site address.
SMB/file sharing	`smb://<address>`	SMB browsing mode allows you to connect to shared files and folders contained on other PCs within the local network.[1]
FTP	`ftp://<address>`	By entering a valid URL, you can browse remote FTP sites. Konqueror will present the site's contents as if it were a directory on your local hard disk, letting you copy, write, and delete files (provided that you have the correct permissions on the remote computer).
SFTP	`sftp://<address>`	This browsing mode allows you to access SFTP (SSH) locations (see Chapter 34).
Apple iPod	`ipod:/`	This mode will let you access any Apple iPod device that's connected to the computer, provided the iPod device is compatible with SUSE Linux (at the time of writing, most are; if your iPod has been formatted with the Mac HFS+ file system, it won't be readable).
Fonts	`fonts:/`	Typing this URL switches Konqueror into a font configuration tool. You can view your own fonts (those only your user account has access to) and the system fonts (available to all users). By dragging-and-dropping, you can also add new fonts, although you'll need root powers to be able to add fonts to the system font folder.[1]
Print system	`print:/`	This mode lets you view any printers attached to the computer and manage print jobs.[2]
Bluetooth	`bluetooth:/`	If your computer is Bluetooth-enabled, this URL will let you browse for other Bluetooth-connected computers in the vicinity, in order to send and receive files.
Audio CD	`audiocd:/`	If an audio CD is inserted in the drive, this lets you start playing any tracks by double-clicking their entry in the Konqueror window. This mode ties in with amaroK, and any CDDB information and converted MP3/Ogg files will also be available here.
Settings	`settings:/`	This is broadly the same as clicking Personal Settings on the K menu. It allows you to fine-tune elements of the KDE interface and the way it works.
Storage media	`media:/`	This presents a list of any storage devices attached to the computer, including the hard disk and CD/DVD player, as well as USB memory sticks, digital cameras, MP3 players, and so on.

1.   *This also works in GNOME's Nautilus: click Go ➤ Location.*
2.   *The printer must be set up via YaST for it to appear here.*

Tip You can change the icon of any folder by right-clicking it, selecting Properties, and clicking the icon in the Properties window. Simply select a new icon from the list.

Launching Files and Running Programs

As with Windows, most of the programs on your SUSE Linux system are automatically associated with various file types that they understand. For example, double-clicking a picture under the GNOME desktop will automatically open the Eye of GNOME viewer application, and double-clicking a .doc file will start OpenOffice.org Writer under both KDE and GNOME.

Although KDE and GNOME under SUSE Linux are automatically set up to view common file types, you might find Table 12-2 useful. It shows which programs are required for viewing certain types of documents.

Note Whenever you install new software from the installation CD or the official software repositories, it should add an entry to the K menu/Applications menu. If for some reason this doesn't happen, you can create a shortcut using the techniques explained in Chapter 10.

Table 12-2. *Common File Types*

File Type	File Extension	Viewer (KDE)	Viewer (GNOME)
Word processor document	.doc, .rtf	OpenOffice.org Writer	OpenOffice.org Writer
Spreadsheet	.xls	OpenOffice.org Calc	OpenOffice.org Calc
Presentation	.ppt	OpenOffice.org	Impress OpenOffice.org Impress
PDF file	.pdf	Adobe Acrobat	Adobe Acrobat
Compressed file	.zip, .tar, .gz, .bz2, and others	File Roller	Ark
Image file	.jpg, .gif, .tif, .bmp, and others	Eye of GNOME	Konqueror
HTML file	.htm, .html	Firefox	Konqueror
Text file	.txt, .log	Gedit	Kate
Audio file	.wav, .mp3	Banshee	amaroK
Video file	.mpg, .mpeg, .avi	Totem	Kaffeine

If you want a file type to open in a different program, you can change the program associated with it, as follows:

- In GNOME, right-click any file of the type whose association you want to change, select Open with Other Application, and choose the other program, as shown in Figure 12-8. From that point on, every time you right-click, you'll be offered the choice of the program to open the file.

- In KDE, right-click any file of the type whose association you want to change, and then click Open With ➤ Other. Select the application from the list and make sure that there's a check alongside Remember Application Association for This Type of File.

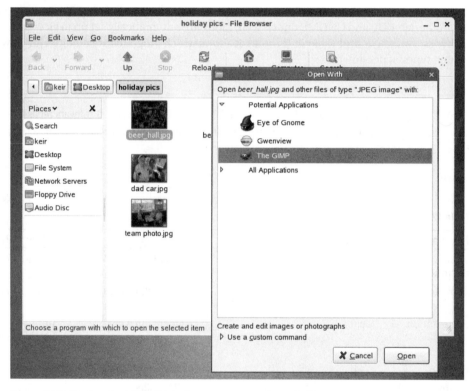

Figure 12-8. *Under the GNOME desktop, you can select which program to use to open a file by right-clicking and selecting Open with Other Application.*

■**Note** Under Windows, you can use Windows Explorer to launch program executables by just browsing to their location within `Program Files` and double-clicking their `.exe` file. It's technically possible to run programs by browsing to their location using Nautilus/Konqueror, but this is discouraged. One reason is that SUSE Linux doesn't store all of its programs in one central folder, as does Windows. However, most programs that are used on a daily basis can be found in `/usr/bin`. If the program itself isn't stored in `/usr/bin`, it will contain a symbolic link (effectively, a shortcut) to the program's actual location on the hard disk.

Accessing Windows Files

Running SUSE Linux on your PC makes you a relative stranger in a world of Windows users. It's likely that you'll need to access Windows files on a regular basis. If you've chosen to dual-boot with Windows, you might want to grab files from the Windows partition on your own hard disk. If your PC is part of a network, you might need to access files on a Windows-based server or workstation on which a shared folder has been created.

Working with Files in Windows Partitions

SUSE Linux should have detected your Windows partition during setup and automatically made it available. As mentioned at the beginning of this chapter, all hard disks and partitions are made available as "virtual" directories within the SUSE Linux file system. In the case of Windows partitions, simply browse to the /windows directory and look for a directory named C. Accessing this directory will then show the contents of your Windows partition, as shown in Figure 12-9.

■**Note** If your hard disk has more than one FAT32 or NTFS partition, the partitions will appear as directories named C, D, E, and so on.

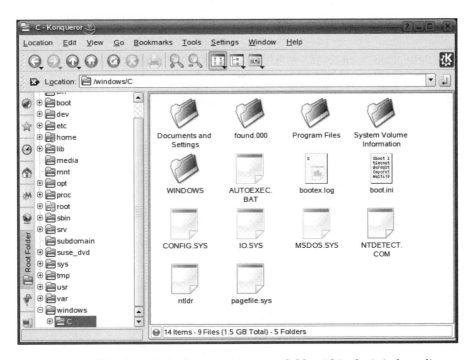

Figure 12-9. *You'll find your Windows partitions available within the /windows directory.*

There are certain rules to bear in mind when accessing Windows partitions. The chief one is that you can read and write to FAT32 partitions, but you cannot write to or edit files in NTFS partitions. Windows NT, 2000, and XP default to NTFS partitions. Windows 95, 98, and Me default to FAT32.

■**Note** It's possible for an installation of Windows 2000 or XP to use FAT32 instead of NTFS, but this requires the user to make a deliberate choice during the initial installation of Windows. Unless you know your Windows 2000 or XP system has been formatted with FAT32, it's very likely that it is NTFS.

Although it is technically possible for SUSE Linux to write to NTFS partitions, it's not advisable because of various technical limitations. Therefore, SUSE Linux makes the NTFS partition read-only. If you have a desperate need to write files to your Windows NTFS partition from within SUSE Linux, you might consider converting it to FAT32. This can be done using a variety of commercial partitioning programs, such as PartitionMagic (www.symantec.com).

Manually Mounting a Windows Partition

If you find your Windows partitions are not made available by SUSE Linux automatically, you can manually mount them. Mounting is the process of making the external file system available as part of SUSE Linux's root file system. I discuss mounting in detail in Chapter 14.

To mount the Windows partition so that it appears automatically each time you boot, you must do two things:

- Create a permanent *mount point*, which is a directory through which the contents of the Windows partition will be made accessible.

- Edit the /etc/fstab file. The fstab file contains details of all your regular mounts (this file is discussed in Chapter 14).

Here are the steps:

1. Open a terminal window. Under GNOME, click Applications ➤ System ➤ Terminal ➤ Gnome Terminal. Under KDE, click K menu ➤ System ➤ Terminal ➤ Konsole.

2. In the terminal window, type the following, entering your root password when prompted:

```
su -
[Enter root password]
mkdir -p /windows/C
chmod -R +x /windows/C
```

3. To open the fstab file in the Pico text editor, type the following in the terminal window:

```
pico /etc/fstab
```

4. If the partition is NTFS (Windows NT, 2000, or XP), scroll to the bottom of the file and add the following line on a completely new line of its own:

```
/dev/hda1  /windows/C  ntfs  ro,users,gid=users,umask=0002,nls=utf8  0  0
```

If the partition is FAT32, scroll down to the bottom of the file and add the following line on a completely new line of its own:

```
/dev/hda1  /windows/C  vfat  users,gid=users,umask=0002,utf8=true  0  0
```

Type either line exactly as it is shown here. You should put two spaces between each element on the line. This step assumes that the Windows partition is the first on your hard disk, which will be the case in the majority of instances. If you know it is the second partition, change /dev/hda1 to read /dev/hda2. Additionally, if you're using SATA hard disks, replace hda with sda (/dev/sda1, for example).

5. To save the file and close the Pico text editor, press Ctrl+X. Type **Y** to save the file, and then press Enter to save it with the /etc/fstab filename.

To immediately mount the Windows partition, type the following command in a terminal window:

```
mount /windows/C
```

The Windows partition will now be available within the /windows/C directory, as described in the previous section.

■**Tip** Any files you copy from the NTFS partition will be read-only. To change this, after you've copied the file across, under GNOME, right-click the file, select Properties, click the Permissions tab, and put a check in the Write box on the Owner line. In KDE, right-click the file, select Properties, click the Permissions tab, and select Can Read and Write from the Owner drop-down list.

Accessing Removable Storage Devices

SUSE Linux automatically makes available any form of removable storage you insert into your computer, whether that is a CD, DVD, floppy disk, or USB storage device (such as a memory stick, digital camera, or MP3 player).

If you're running the GNOME desktop, the storage device should appear automatically on the desktop as an icon, and a Nautilus window will appear showing the drive's contents. If you're running KDE, a dialog box will appear informing you that a removable storage device has been inserted and asking what you want to do (such as open a file browser window).

Alternatively, you can access storage devices by opening the computer browsing view of Nautilus or Konqueror. To do this under the GNOME desktop, click Places ➤ Computer. Under KDE, just click the My Computer icon on the desktop. In the computer browsing view, you'll find icons for all of the storage devices attached to your computer, as shown in Figure 12-10 (which shows the Nautilus computer view). However, because of the way floppy drives work, SUSE Linux isn't able to automatically detect if a floppy has been inserted. Instead, the floppy drive is always present in the list and, after inserting a disk, you'll need to double-click the icon to access its contents, as with Windows.

Note In days of old, special tools were used to access MS-DOS floppies under Linux, and you might hear some Linux old hands talking about them. Nowadays, you can simply use Nautilus or Konqueror without needing to take any special steps.

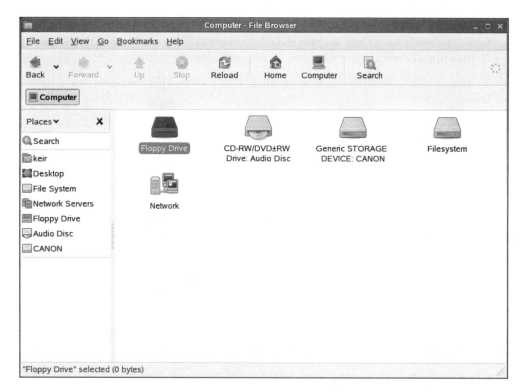

Figure 12-10. *Under the GNOME desktop, click Places ➤ Computer to access your removable storage drives.*

Whenever you double-click any entry in the Computer window, it will open a file browser window. You can copy files by clicking and dragging. Right-click a file to see a context menu offering related options.

Ejecting Media from Drives

SUSE Linux isn't quite like Windows when it comes to ejecting or unplugging removable storage devices. In many cases, devices must be *unmounted*, which is to say that you need to tell SUSE Linux that you're finished with the device in question and that you're about to unplug it. If you don't do this, you run the risk of file corruption.

Table 12-3 explains how you should unmount each type of storage. Note that in each case, you will not be able to unmount the device unless you have stopped browsing it. This means closing any open file browser windows that are accessing its contents, and closing any files on the removable storage device that you might have open.

■**Note** If the device refuses to unmount, you might even have to quit any software that was accessing files on the device. For example, if OpenOffice.org's Writer had been accessing a Word document on the device, you may need to quit Writer before being able to unmount. It's rare that this might happen, but it's worth bearing in mind.

Table 12-3. *Unmounting Removable Storage*

Device	Notes
CD/DVD-ROM	Press the eject button on the drive. If this doesn't work, right-click the drive's icon on the desktop or in the Computer/My Computer browsing view and click Eject. Under KDE, you might need to select Unmount and then Eject.
Floppy disk	Right-click the floppy disk's icon on the desktop or in the Computer/My Computer browsing view and select Unmount or Eject. Then press the eject button on the drive itself to remove the disk.
USB memory stick	Right-click the memory stick's icon on the desktop or in the Computer/My Computer browsing view and select Unmount (GNOME) or Safely Remove (KDE). Then physically unplug the device.
Digital camera/MP3 player	Right-click the camera's or player's icon on the desktop or in the Computer/My Computer browsing view and select Unmount (GNOME) or Safely Remove (KDE). Then physically unplug the device.

Formatting Floppies

Formatting floppy disks isn't done in Nautilus or Konqueror. Instead, you must use a special program:

- In GNOME, use Floppy Formatter (click Applications ➤ System ➤ File System ➤ Floppy Formatter).

- In KDE, use KFloppy (click K Menu ➤ System ➤ File System ➤ KFloppy).

Floppy Formatter and KFloppy are similar to the disk-formatting tool in Windows, and most of the options are self-explanatory. If you intend to share the disk with Windows users, make sure DOS (FAT) is selected in the File System (KDE) or File System Type (GNOME) box, as shown in Figure 12-11. You can format a floppy using ext2 file system format, used by many Linux distros, or even using Minix disk format, but there's little to be gained by doing so.

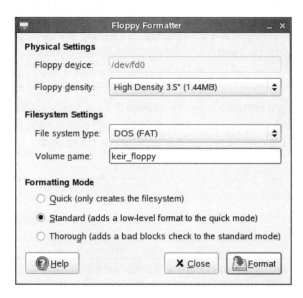

Figure 12-11. *Under the GNOME desktop, formatting floppy disks is done using the Floppy Formatter tool.*

Summary

This chapter has led you on your first steps in exploring the Linux file system. The file system is vitally important to how Linux works, and we'll go into it in much depth in upcoming chapters.

Here, you were introduced to elementary concepts, such as where personal files are stored and the basic rules that govern what you can and cannot do with files. We also looked at the principle method of accessing files via the GUI: the Nautilus or Konqueror file manager. Additionally, you learned how to run programs manually, as well as how to access any Windows partition or files that may exist on your hard disk.

In Part 4 of this book, starting in the next chapter, we will look at some of the underlying technology that makes SUSE Linux work and how you can gain more control over your computer. Chapter 13 introduces the BASH shell—perhaps the most powerful piece of software offered by SUSE Linux to control your system.

PART IV

■■■

The Shell and Beyond

CHAPTER 13

■ ■ ■

Introducing the BASH Shell

As you learned in Chapter 1, strictly speaking, the word *Linux* refers to just the kernel, which is the fundamental, invisible program that runs your PC and lets everything happen. On its own, the kernel is completely useless. It needs programs to let users interact with the PC and do cool stuff, and it needs a lot of system files (also referred to as *libraries*) to provide vital functions.

The GNU Project provides many of these low-level pieces of code and programs. This is why many people refer to the Linux operating system as GNU/Linux, giving credit to the fact that, without the GNU components, Linux wouldn't have gotten off the starting blocks.

The GNU Project provides various shell programs, too. Some of these offer graphical functionality, but most are text only. These text shell programs are also known as *terminal programs*, and they're often colloquially referred to as *command-line prompts*, in reference to the most important component they provide. This kind of shell lets you take control of your system in a quick and efficient way. Like a GUI, it's another way of interfacing with your computer, except that you type commands, rather than use a mouse.

By learning the shell, you'll become the true master of your own system. In this part of the book, you'll learn all you need to know about using the shell. This chapter introduces the BASH shell, which is the default under SUSE Linux.

What Is the BASH Shell?

The best way of explaining the BASH shell to a Windows user is to compare it to the DOS command prompt. It lets you issue commands directly to the operating system via the keyboard without needing to mess around with the mouse and windows (although it is sometimes possible to use the mouse within a BASH shell to copy and paste text, and sometimes to control simple text-based menus). The big difference is that the BASH shell has commands for just about everything you might do on your system, whereas the DOS command prompt merely offers tools to manipulate files or, on Windows 2000/XP machines, configure certain system settings.

In the old days, the DOS command prompt was also the visible layer of an entire operating system in which DOS programs were designed to be run. In Linux, the shell is merely one of the many ways of accessing the kernel and subsystems. It's true that there are many programs designed to run via the BASH shell, but technically speaking, most actually run on the Linux operating system, and simply take input and show their output via the BASH shell.

■Note Linux purists will point out another reason why the shell isn't exactly the same as a DOS command prompt within Windows: it doesn't run in *virtual machine mode*, a CPU trick by which part of the memory is subdivided to let programs run as if they had the PC all to themselves.

Linux finds itself with the BASH shell largely because Linux is a clone of Unix. In the early days of Unix, the text-based shell was all that was offered as a way of letting users control the computer. Typing commands in directly is one of the most fundamental ways of controlling any type of computer and, in the evolutionary scale, comes straight after needing to set switches and watch blinking lights in order to run programs.

That the BASH shell can trace its history back to the early days of Unix might sound like a tacit indication that the BASH shell is somehow primitive, but that's far from true. It's one of the most efficient and immediate ways of working with your computer. Many people consider the command-line shell to be a way of using a computer that has yet to be superseded by a better method.

■Note When you run a shell on a Linux system, the system refers to it as a *tty device*. This stands for teletypewriter, a direct reference to the old system of inputting data on what were effectively electronic typewriters connected to mainframe computers. These, in turn, took their names from the devices used to automate the sending and receiving of telegrams in the early part of the twentieth century.

Most Linux distributions come with a choice of different kinds of shell programs. However, the default shell is BASH, as is the case in SUSE Linux. BASH stands for Bourne Again SHell. This is based on the Bourne shell, a tried-and-tested program that originated in the early days of Unix.

The other shells available include PDKSH (Public Domain Korn SHell, based on Korn Shell, another early Unix shell), and ZSH (Z SHell), a more recent addition. These are usually used by people who want to program Linux in various ways, or by those who simply aren't happy with BASH.

The BASH shell is considered by many to be the best of all worlds in that it's easy enough for beginners to learn, yet is able to grow with them and offer more power as necessary. BASH is capable of scripting, for example, which means you can even create your own simple programs.

■Note Technically speaking, a *shell* refers to any type of user interface. The windowing system offered by Windows and Macintosh operating systems is a type of shell. However, many people in the Linux and Unix worlds use the word *shell* as shorthand for a shell that offers a command line.

Why Bother with the Shell?

You might have followed the instructions in Part 2 of this book and consider yourself an expert in Linux. But the real measure of a Linux user comes from his or her abilities at the shell.

In our modern age, the GUI is mistakenly considered "progress." We've been led to believe by companies like Microsoft and Apple that using a mouse and clicking on icons is always the most efficient way of using a computer. While it's invaluable in certain situations—it would be difficult to imagine browsing the Web or editing images without a mouse, for example—in many other situations, such as when manipulating files, directly typing commands is considered far more efficient by many people.

Most modern Linux distributions prefer you to use the GUI to do nearly everything. This is because they acknowledge the dominance of Windows and realize they need to cater to mouse-oriented users who might not even know the shell exists. To this end, they provide GUI tools for just about every task you might wish to undertake. SUSE Linux is particularly strong in this regard, and you can configure virtually everything using the YaST2 program.

However, it's well worth developing at least some command-line shell skills, for a number of reasons:

It's simple and fast. The shell is the simplest and fastest way of working with SUSE Linux. As just one example, consider the task of changing the IP address of your network card. If you're running the GNOME desktop, you could click the Desktop menu, and then on YaST2, and then on Network Devices, and then on Network Card, and then follow the wizard interface through several screens where you can change settings. That will take at least a minute or two if you know what you're doing, and perhaps longer if it's new to you. Alternatively, you could simply open a shell and type `ifconfig eth0 192.168.0.15 up`.

It's versatile. Everything can be done via the shell—from deleting files, to configuring hardware, to creating MP3s. A lot of GUI programs actually make use of programs you can access via the shell.

It's consistent among distributions. All Linux systems have shells and understand the same commands (broadly speaking). However, not all Linux systems will have YaST2. Ubuntu Linux uses its own GUI configuration tools, as does Mandriva Linux. Therefore, if you ever need to use another system, or decide to switch distributions, a reliance on GUI tools will mean learning everything from scratch. Knowing a few shell commands will let you get started instantly.

It's crucial for troubleshooting. The shell offers a vital way of fixing your system should it go wrong. Your Linux installation might be damaged to the extent that it cannot boot to the GUI, but you'll almost certainly be able to boot into a shell. A shell doesn't require much of the system other than the ability to display characters on the screen and take input from the keyboard, which most PCs can do, even when they're in a sorry state. This is why most rescue floppies offer shells to let you fix your system.

It's useful for remote access. One handy thing about the shell is that you don't need to be in front of your PC to use it. Programs like Secure Shell (SSH) let you log in to your PC across the Internet and use the shell to control your PC (as described in Chapter 34). This is invaluable in accessing data on a remote machine, or even fixing it when you're unable to attend the machine's location. This is why Linux is preferred on many server systems when the system administrator isn't always present on the site.

It's respected in the community. Using a shell earns you enormous brownie points when speaking to other Linux users. It separates the wheat from the chaff and the men from the boys (or women from the girls). If you intend to use Linux professionally, you will most certainly need to be a master at the shell.

Seen in this light, learning at least a handful of shell commands is vital to truly mastering your PC.

The drawback when using a command-line shell is that it's not entirely intuitive. Consider the following command for changing the network card's IP address:

```
ifconfig eth0 192.168.0.15 up
```

If you've never used the shell before, it might as well be Sanskrit. What on earth does `ifconfig` mean? And why is there the word up at the end?

▌Note If you're curious, the command tells the network card, referred to by Linux as `eth0`, to adopt the specified IP address. The word `up` at the end merely tells it to activate—to start working now. If the word `down` were there instead, it would deactivate! Don't worry about understanding all of this right now; later in this chapter, I'll explain how you can learn more about every Linux command.

Learning to use the shell involves learning terms like these. There are hundreds of commands available, but you really need to learn only around 10 or 20 for everyday use. The comparison with a new language is apt because, although you might think it daunting to learn new terminology, with a bit of practice, it will all become second nature. Once you've used a command a few times, you'll know how to use it in the future.

The main thing to realize is that the shell is your friend. It's there to help you get stuff done as quickly as possible. When you become familiar with it, you'll see that it is a beautiful concept. The shell is simple, elegant, and powerful.

When Should You Use the Shell?

The amount of use the Linux shell sees is highly dependent on the user. Some Linux buffs couldn't manage without it. They use it to read and compose e-mail, and even to browse the Web.

> ■**Tip** Mutt is a popular command-line e-mail program, and Lynx is a handy command-line web browser. Both these programs can be installed via YaST2 if you would like to try them out.

However, most people simply use it to manage files, view text files (like program documentation), and run programs. You can start all kinds of programs—including GUI and command-line applications—from the shell. As you'll learn in Chapter 29, unlike with Windows, installing a program on SUSE Linux doesn't necessarily mean the program will automatically appear on the Applications menu (or K menu if you're running the KDE desktop). In fact, unless the installation routine is specifically made for the version of Linux you're running, this is unlikely. Therefore, using the shell is a necessity for most people.

> ■**Note** Unlike with DOS programs, Linux programs that describe themselves as "command-line" are rarely designed to run solely via the command-line shell. All programs are like machines that take input at one end and output objects at the other. Where the input comes from and where the output goes to is by no means limited to the command line. Usually, with a command-line program, the input and output are provided via the shell. However, a GUI program designed to, for example, burn CDs, will also require the installation of a command-line program that will actually do the hard work on its behalf.

There's another reason why the shell is used to run programs: you can specify how a particular program runs before starting it. For example, to launch the Totem Movie Player in full-screen mode playing the `myvideofile.mpg` file, you could type this:

```
totem --fullscreen myvideofile.mpg
```

This saves the bother of starting the program, loading a clip, and then selecting the full-screen option. Once you've typed the command once or twice, you'll be able to remember it for the next time. No matter how much you love the mouse, you'll have to admit that this method of running programs is simply more efficient.

When you get used to using the shell, it's likely you'll have it open most of the time behind your other program windows.

Getting Started with the Shell

You can start the shell in a number of ways. The most common is to use a terminal emulator program. As its name suggests, this runs a shell inside a program window on your desktop.

If you're running the GNOME desktop, you can start the GNOME Terminal program by clicking Applications ➤ System ➤ Terminal ➤ Gnome Terminal, as shown in Figure 13-1. If you're running the KDE desktop, you can start Konsole, the built-in KDE shell emulator, by opening the K menu (click the green gecko icon at the bottom left of the screen), and then clicking System ➤ Terminal ➤ Konsole (Terminal Program).

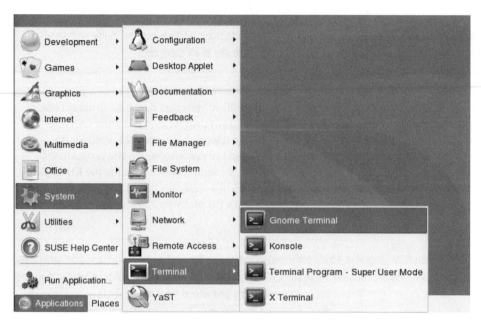

Figure 13-1. *You can start the GNOME from the Applications menu.*

You should see the terminal window—a blank, white window that looks similar to a simple word processor window. It will show what's referred to as a *command prompt*: a few words followed by the > symbol. On my test system, this is what I see:

```
keir@suse:~>
```

The first part is my username—the user account I created during installation and use to log in to the PC. After the @ sign is the name of the PC, which you had the chance to set when you installed SUSE Linux.

■Note Your PC might be called `localhost`. This is simply the default name for a computer that Linux uses when it hasn't been told to use anything else.

The name of the PC isn't important on most desktop PCs; it's a legacy from the days of Unix. After the colon is indicated the current directory you're browsing. In this example, the tilde symbol (~) appears instead of an actual path or directory name. This is merely SUSE Linux shorthand for the user's home directory. In other words, wherever I see a ~ on my test PC, I read it as /home/keir. After this is a cursor, and this is where you can start typing commands!

■Note If you were to log in as root, a hash symbol (#) would appear instead of the > symbol. This is important to remember because often in magazines and some computer manuals, the use of the hash symbol before a command indicates that it should be run as root. In addition, if you use the rescue function of the SUSE DVD, you'll be running as root, and a hash symbol will appear at the prompt. See Chapter 14 for more information about the root user.

Running Programs

When we refer to *commands* at the shell, we're actually talking about small programs. When you type a command to list a directory, for example, you're actually starting a small program that will do that job. Seen in this light, the shell's main function is to simply let you run programs—either those that are built into the shell, such as ones that let you manipulate files, or other, more complicated programs that you've installed yourself.

The shell is clever enough to know where your programs are stored. This information was given to it when you first installed SUSE Linux and is stored in a system variable.

■Note A *variable* is the method SUSE Linux uses to remember things like names, directory paths, or other data. There are many system variables that are vital for the running of SUSE Linux.

The information about where your programs are stored, and therefore where SUSE Linux should look for commands you type in, as well as any programs you might want to run, is stored in the PATH variable. You can take a look at what's currently stored there by typing the following:

```
echo $PATH
```

Don't forget that the difference between uppercase and lowercase letters matters to SUSE Linux, unlike with Windows and DOS.

The echo command merely tells the shell to print something on screen. In this case, you're telling it to "echo" the PATH variable onto your screen. On my test PC, this returned the following information:

```
/home/keir/bin:/usr/local/bin:/usr/bin:/usr/X11R6/bin:/bin:/usr/games:/opt/gnome
/bin:/opt/kde3/bin:/usr/lib/mit/bin:/usr/lib/mit/sbin
```

There are actually several directories in that list, and each is separated by a colon.

Don't worry too much about the details right now. The important thing to know is that whenever you type a program name, the shell looks in each of the listed directories in sequence. In other words, when you type ls, the command that will give you a directory listing, the shell will look in each of the directories, starting with the first in the list, to see if the ls program can be found. The first instance it finds is the one it will run.

But what if you want to run a program that is not contained in a directory listed in your PATH? In this case, you must tell the shell exactly where the program is. Here's an example:

```
/home/keir/myprogram
```

This will run a program called `myprogram` in the `/home/keir` directory. It will do this regardless of the directory you're currently browsing, and regardless of whether there is anything else on your system called `myprogram`.

If you're already in the directory where the program in question is located, you can type the following:

```
./myprogram
```

So, just enter a dot and a forward slash, followed by the program name. The dot tells BASH that what you're referring to is "right here." Like the tilde symbol mentioned earlier, this dot is BASH shorthand.

Getting Help

You can use a variety of methods to get help at the shell. Each command usually has help built in, which you can query (a little like typing `/?` after a command when using DOS). This will explain what the command does and how it should be used. For example, you can get some instant help on the `ifconfig` command by typing this:

```
ifconfig --help
```

You'll see the help screen shown in Figure 13-2.

The `--help` option is fairly universal, and most programs will respond to it, although sometimes you might need to use a single dash. Just type the command along with `--help` to see what happens. You'll be told if you're doing anything wrong.

Nearly always when you use the `help` command option, you'll be shown an example of the command in use, along with the range of command options that can be used with it.

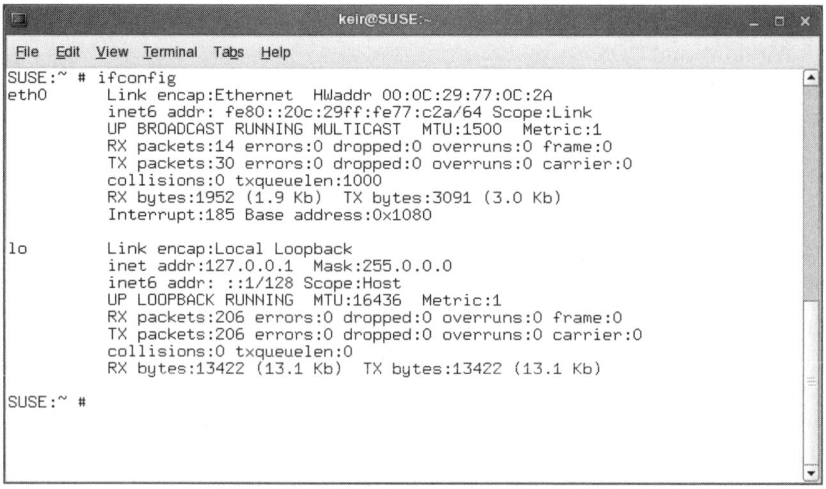

Figure 13-2. *Most commands contain built-in help to give you a clue as to how they're used.*

In addition, most commands have manuals that you can read to gain a fairly complete understanding of how they work. Virtually every SUSE Linux setup has a set of these man pages, which can be accessed by typing this:

```
man <command>
```

However, man pages are often technical and designed for experienced SUSE Linux users who understand the terminology.

There are also info pages, which offer slightly more down-to-earth guides. You can read these by typing this:

```
info <command>
```

Some commands aren't covered by the info system, however. In that case, you'll be shown the default screen explaining basic facts about how the info command works.

Note that both man and info have their own man and info pages, explaining how they work. Just type man man or info info. (Appendix C explains how to read and understand man and info pages.)

Running the Shell via a Virtual Console

As noted earlier, there are a number of ways to start a shell. The most common way among Linux diehards is via a virtual console. To access a virtual console, press Ctrl+Alt, and then press one of the function keys from F1 through F6 (the keys at the top of your keyboard).

Using a virtual console is a little like switching desks to a completely different PC. Pressing Ctrl+Alt+F1 will cause your GUI to disappear, and the screen to be taken over by a command-line prompt (don't worry; your GUI is still there and running in the background). You'll be asked to enter your username and your password.

Any programs you run in a virtual console won't affect the rest of the system, unless they're system commands and you're logged in as the root user. (As discussed in Chapter 16, one way to rescue a crashed GUI program is to switch to a virtual console, become root user, and attempt to terminate the program from there.)

You can switch back to the GUI by pressing Ctrl+Alt+F7. Don't forget to quit your virtual console when you're finished with it, by typing exit.

BOOTING INTO THE SHELL

If you're really in love with the shell, you can choose to boot into it, avoiding the GUI completely. You can later start the GUI by typing startx at the command line.

You can set up for booting into the shell by altering the current *run level*. A run level is how the operating mode that SUSE Linux is currently running in is described. Run level 5 is most widely used on desktop PCs and means that SUSE Linux is running with a graphical interface. Run level 3 will put the system in text-only mode, although it's still possible to start a GUI manually. Run level 1 is the single-user mode. When this mode is in force, the networking aspect of SUSE Linux is deactivated, and several other system processes are stopped, too. This lets you fix things. It's a bit like Safe Mode under Windows.

Continues

You can change the run level on the fly by typing the following commands:

```
su -
[enter your root password]
init <run level number>
```

The first command, su, makes you temporarily the root user (and ensures you adopt the root user's PATH, so you can run root-only commands). You should be careful what you type after you've switched to the root user, because an error can cause serious damage.

The init command is used to switch to a different run level. Typing init 3 will switch you to run level 3, for example, and also instantly closes your GUI, and SUSE Linux won't ask if you want to save your files first!

Working with Files

So let's start actually using the shell. If you've ever used DOS, then you have a head start over most shell beginners, although you'll still need to learn some new commands. Table 13-1 shows various DOS commands alongside their SUSE Linux equivalents. This table also serves as a handy guide to some BASH commands, even if you've never used DOS. (In Appendix B, you'll find a comprehensive list of useful shell commands, together with explanations of what they do and examples of typical usage.)

Table 13-1. *DOS Commands and Their Shell Equivalents*

Command	DOS Command	Linux Shell Command	Usage
Copy files	COPY	cp	cp <filename> <new location>
Move files	MOVE	mv	mv <filename> <new location>
Rename files	RENAME	mv	mv <old filename> <new filename>[1]
Delete files	DEL	rm	rm <filename>[2]
Create directories	MKDIR	mkdir	mkdir <directory name>
Delete directories	DELTREE/RMDIR	rm	rm –rf <directory name>
Change directory	CD	cd	cd <directory name>
View directories graphically	TREE	tree	tree
Edit text files	EDIT	vi	vi <filename>
View text files	TYPE	less	less <filename>[3]
Print text files	PRINT	lpr	lpr <filename>
Compare files	FC	diff	diff <file1> <file2>
Find files	FIND	find	find –name <name of file>
Check disk integrity	SCANDISK	fsck	fsck[4]

Command	DOS Command	Linux Shell Command	Usage
View network settings	IPCONFIG	ifconfig	ifconfig[5]
Check a network connection	PING	ping	ping *<address>*
View a network route	TRACERT	traceroute	traceroute *<address>*[5]
Clear screen	CLS	clear	clear
Get help	HELP	man	man *<command>*[6]
Quit	EXIT	exit	exit

1. *The SUSE Linux shell offers a rename command, but this is chiefly used to rename many files at once.*
2. *To avoid being asked to confirm each file deletion, you can add the* -f *option. Be aware that the* rm *command deletes data instantly, without the safety net of the Trash/Recycle Bin, as with the GNOME/KDE desktop environments.*
3. *Use the cursor keys to move up and down in the document. Type* Q *to quit.*
4. *This is a system command and can be run only on a disk that isn't currently in use. To scan the main partition, you'll need to use a rescue floppy (see Chapter 13).*
5. *This is a system command that can be run only by users with root privileges.*
6. *The info command can also be used.*

CREATING ALIASES

If you've ever used DOS, you might find yourself inadvertently typing DOS commands at the shell prompt. Some of these will actually work, because most Linux distribution companies create command aliases to ease the transition of newcomers to Linux.

Aliases mean that whenever you type certain words, they will be interpreted as meaning something else. However, an alias won't work with any of the command-line switches used in DOS. In the long term, you should try to learn the BASH equivalents.

You can create your own command aliases quickly and simply. Just start a BASH shell and type the following:

```
alias <DOS command>='<Linux shell command>'
```

For example, to create an alias that lets you type copy instead of cp, type this:

```
alias copy='cp'
```

Note that the SUSE Linux command must appear in single quotation marks.

Listing Files

Possibly the most fundamentally useful BASH command is ls. This will list the files in the current directory, as shown (with a few other typical commands) in Figure 13-3. If there are a lot of files, they might scroll off the screen. If you're running GNOME Terminal or Konsole, you can use the scroll bar on the right side of the window to view the list.

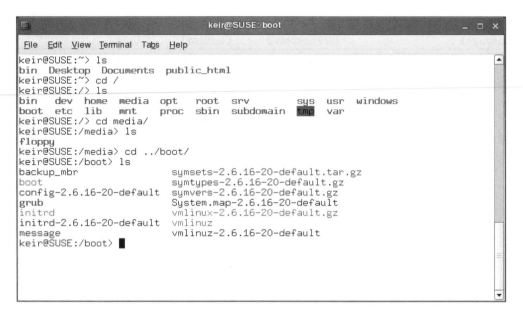

Figure 13-3. *The ls command lists the files in the current directory.*

Having the files scroll off the screen can be annoying, so you can cram as many as possible onto each line by typing the following:

```
ls -m
```

The dash after the command indicates that you're using a *command option*. These are also referred to as command-line *flags* or *switches*. Nearly all shell commands have options like this. In fact, some commands won't do anything unless you specify various options. In the case of the ls command, only one dash is necessary, but some commands need two dashes to indicate an option.

You can see a list of all the command options for ls by typing the following (ironically, itself a command option):

```
ls --help
```

Once again, the output will scroll off the screen, and you can use the window's scroll bars to examine it. (In Chapter 17, you'll learn a trick you can use to be able to read this output without needing to fiddle around with the scroll bars, even if there's screen after screen of it.)

With most commands, you can use many command options at once, as long as they don't contradict each other. For example, you could type the following:

```
ls -lh
```

This tells the ls command to produce "long" output and also to produce "human-readable" output. The long option (-l) lists file sizes and ownership permissions, among other details (permissions describe what users can do with a file and who can access it, and are covered in the next chapter). The human-readable option (-h) means that rather than listing files in terms of bytes (such as 1029725 bytes), it will list them in kilobytes and megabytes. In other words, you can simply list the options after the dash; you don't need to give each option its own dash.

■**Caution** I've said it before, and I'll say it again: don't forget that case sensitivity is vitally important in SUSE Linux! Typing ls -L is not the same as typing ls -l. It will produce different results.

Copying Files

So what other useful commands are there for dealing with files? Well, you can copy files with cp. You can use the cp command in the following way:

```
cp myfile /home/keir/
```

This will copy the file to the location specified.

One important command-line option for cp is -r. This stands for *recursive* and tells BASH that you want to copy a directory and its contents (as well as any directories within this directory). Most commands that deal with files have a recursive option.

■**Note** Only a handful of BASH commands default to recursive copying. Even though it's extremely common to copy folders, you still need to specify the -r command option most of the time. In some cases, the recursive command option is -R (with a capital *R*); check the command's man page for details.

One curious trick is that you can copy a file from one place to another but, by specifying a filename in the destination part of the command, change its name. Here's an example:

```
cp myfile /home/keir/myfile2
```

This will copy myfile to /home/keir, but rename it as myfile2. Be careful not to add a final slash to the command when you do this. In the example here, doing so would cause BASH to think that myfile2 is a directory.

This way of copying files is a handy way of duplicating files. By not specifying a new location in the destination part of the command, but still specifying a different filename, you effectively duplicate the file within the same directory:

```
cp myfile myfile2
```

This will result in two identical files: one called myfile and one called myfile2.

Moving Files

The mv command can be used in a similar way to cp, except that rather than copying the file, the old one is removed. You can move files from one directory to another, for example, like this:

```
mv myfile /home/keir/
```

You can also use the mv command to quickly rename files:

```
mv myfile myfile2
```

Figure 13-4 shows the results of using mv to rename a file.

■**Note** Getting technical for a moment, moving a file in Linux isn't the same as in Windows, where a file is copied and then the original deleted. Under SUSE Linux, the file's absolute path is rewritten, causing it to simply appear in a different place in the file structure. However, the end result is the same.

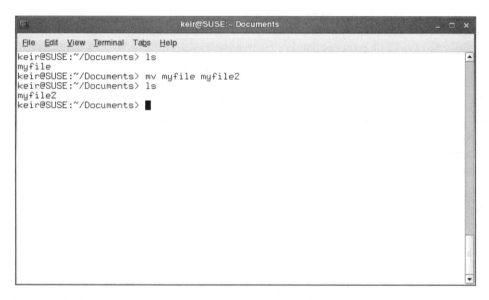

Figure 13-4. *You can also use the mv command to rename files.*

Deleting Files

But how do you get rid of files? Again, this is relatively easy, but first a word of caution: the shell doesn't operate any kind of Recycle Bin. Once a file is deleted, it's gone forever. (There are utilities you can use to recover files, but these are specialized tools and aren't to be relied on for day-to-day use.)

Removing a file is achieved by typing something like this:

```
rm myfile
```

It's as simple as that.

You'll be asked to confirm the deletion after you issue the command. If you want to delete a file without being asked to confirm it, type the following:

```
rm -f myfile
```

The f stands for force (that is, force the deletion).

If you try to use the rm command to remove a directory, you'll see an error message. This is because the command needs an additional option:

```
rm -rf mydirectory
```

As noted in the previous section, the -r stands for recursive and indicates that any folder specified afterward should be deleted, in addition to any files it contains.

Tip You might have used wildcards within Windows and DOS. They can be used within SUSE Linux, too. For example, the asterisk (*) can be used to mean any file. So, you can type rm -f * to delete all files within a directory, or type rm -f myfile* to delete all files that start with the word myfile. But remember to be careful with the rm command. Keep in mind that you cannot salvage files easily if you delete them!

Changing and Creating Directories

Another handy directory command is cd, for change directory. This lets you move around the file system, from directory to directory. Say you're in a directory that has another directory in it, named mydirectory2. Switching to it is easy:

```
cd mydirectory2
```

But how do you get out of this directory once you're in it? Try the following command:

```
cd ..
```

The .. refers to the "parent" directory, which is the one containing the directory you're currently browsing. Using two dots to indicate this may seem odd, but it's just the way that SUSE Linux (and Unix before it) does things. It's one of the many conventions that Linux relies on and that you'll pick up as you go along.

You can create directories with the mkdir command:

```
mkdir mydirectory
```

Summary

This chapter introduced the command-line shell, considered by many to be the heart of Linux. We've discussed its similarities to the DOS command prompt, and shown that these are only cursory; knowledge of DOS doesn't equate to skill within BASH. In the long run, you should work to polish your BASH skills.

This chapter also introduced some elementary commands used within BASH, such as those used to provide directory listings and to copy files. We looked at how to use command-line options to control BASH tools. In many cases, these are mandatory, so you learned how the BASH shell itself can be used to investigate a command and find out vital information about how it works.

At this point, your newfound knowledge will have no doubt caused you to venture into the SUSE Linux file system itself, which can be a confusing, if not terrifying, place for the inexperienced. But don't worry. The next chapter explains everything you need to know about the file system and what you'll find in it.

■■■■

## CHAPTER 14

Understanding Linux Files and Users

Most of us are used to dealing with files—the things that live on our hard disks, floppies, and CD-ROMs, and contain data and program code. It should come as no surprise that Linux has its own file structure, which is different from Windows, in terms of where data is stored and also the underlying technology.

Taking a page from Unix, SUSE Linux takes the concept and use of the file system to extremes when compared to Windows. To SUSE Linux, almost everything is treated as a file: your PC's hardware, network computers connected to your PC, information about the current state of your computer . . . almost everything finds a home within the Linux file system.

In the world of Linux, users are equally important. They "own" the various files and can therefore decide who can and cannot access various files they create or that are transferred to their ownership.

In this chapter, we'll delve into users, files, and permissions. You'll be introduced to how SUSE Linux handles files and how files are tied into the system of user accounts.

Real Files and Virtual Files

Linux sees virtually everything as a series of files. This might sound absurd and therefore requires further explanation.

Let's start with the example of plugging in a piece of hardware. Whenever you attach something to a USB socket, the Linux kernel finds it, sees if it can make the hardware work, and, if everything checks out okay, it will usually make the hardware available as a file under the /dev directory on your hard disk (dev is short for devices). Figure 14-1 shows an example of a /dev directory.

The file created in the /dev directory is not a real file, of course. It's a file system shortcut plumbed through to the input and output components of the hardware you've just attached.

■**Note** As a user, you're not expected to delve into the /dev directory and deal with this hardware directly. Most of the time, you'll use various software packages that will access the hardware for you, or use special BASH commands or GUI programs to make the hardware available in a more accessible way for day-to-day use.

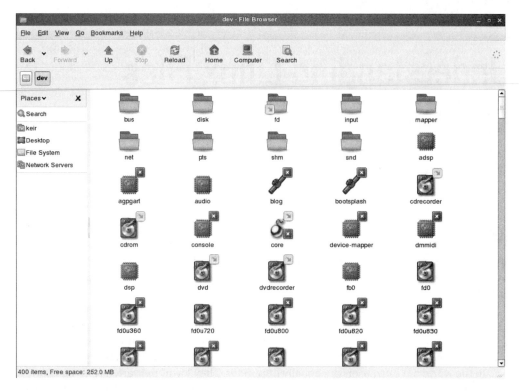

Figure 14-1. *Hardware devices under Linux are accessed as if they were files and can be found in the /dev folder.*

Here's another example. Say you're working in an office and you want to connect to a central file server. To do this under Linux, you must *mount* the files that the server offers, making it a part of the SUSE Linux file system. Doing this involves creating an empty directory (or using one that already exists) and using the mount command at the BASH shell to make the server's contents magically appear whenever that directory is accessed. We'll discuss how this is done later in this chapter, in the "Mounting" section (but remember that SUSE Linux may do this automatically, as discussed in Chapter 12).

Once the network server is mounted, it is treated exactly like a directory on your hard disk. You can copy files to and from it, just as you would normally, using the same tools as you use for dealing with any other files. In fact, less-knowledgeable users won't even be aware that they're accessing something that isn't located on their PC's hard disk (or, technically speaking, within their SUSE Linux partition and file system).

By treating everything as a file, Linux makes system administration easier. To probe and test your hardware, for example, you can use the same tools you use to manipulate files.

So how do you know which files are real and which are virtual? One method is to use the following command, which was introduced in the previous chapter:

```
ls -l
```

The -l option tells the ls command to list nearly all the details about the files. If you do this using the GNOME Terminal or Konsole program, you'll see that the listing is color-coded. Table 14-1 shows what each color indicates. The command returns a lot of additional information, including who owns which file and what you and others can do with it. This requires an understanding of users and file permissions, which we'll discuss next.

■**Tip** The command ls -la will give you even more information—perhaps too much for general use. In most instances, ls -l should show enough information.

Table 14-1. *Color-Coding Within Terminal Programs*

Color	Type of File
Black text	Standard file
Light-blue text	Directory
Black outline with yellow text	Virtual device[1]
Green text	Program or script[2]
Cyan text	Symbolic link to another file[3]
Pink text	Image file
Red text	Archive[4]

1. *This is found only in the* /dev *directory.*
2. *Technically speaking, green text indicates a program or script that has merely been marked as being executable.*
3. *A symbolic link is similar to a Windows desktop shortcut.*
4. *Installation files are also marked red because they're usually contained in archives.*

Users and File Permissions

The concept of users and permissions is as important to SUSE Linux as the idea of a central and all-encompassing file system.

When initially installing Linux, you should have created at least one user account. By now, this will have formed the day-to-day login that you use to access Linux and run programs. (Remember that you should use the root account only for essential maintenance work; if you're using it for day-to-day work, stop doing so immediately!)

Although you might not realize it, as a user, you also belong to a group. In fact, every user on the system belongs to a group. Under SUSE Linux, all ordinary users belong to a group called users by default (under other versions of Linux, you might find that you belong to a group based on your username).

■**Note** Groups are yet another reminder of SUSE Linux's Unix origins. Unix is often used on huge computer systems with hundreds or thousands of users. By putting each user into a group, the system administrator's job is a lot easier. When controlling system resources, the administrator can control groups of users rather than hundreds of individual users. On most home user PCs, the concept of groups is a little redundant, because there's normally a single user, or at most, two or three. However, the concept of groups is central to the way that Linux handles files.

A standard user account under SUSE Linux is normally limited in what it can do. This is set when the account is first set up. As a standard user, you can save files to your own private area of the disk, located in the /home directory, as shown in Figure 14-2, but usually nowhere else. You can move around the file system, but some directories are strictly out of bounds. In a similar way, some files can be opened as read-only, so you cannot save changes to them. All of this is achieved using file permissions.

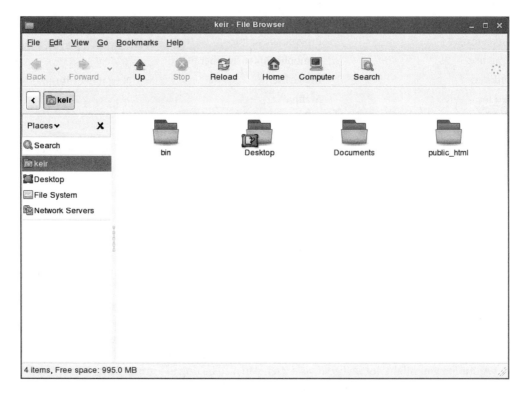

Figure 14-2. *Your personal directory within home is your area on the hard disk. This is enforced via file permissions.*

Every file and directory is owned by a user. In addition, files and directories have three separate settings that indicate who within the Linux system can read them, who can write to them, and, if the file in question is "runnable" (usually a program or a script), who can run it ("execute" it). In the case of directories, it's also possible to set who can browse them, as well as who can write files to them. If you try to access a file or directory for which you don't have permission, you'll be turned away with an "access denied" error message.

Viewing Permissions

When you issue the `ls -l` command, each file is listed on an individual line. Here's an example of one line of a file listing from my test PC:

```
-rw-r--r--    2 keir users 673985982 2004-07-07 17:19 myfile
```

The r, w, and - symbols on the very left of the listing indicate the file permissions. The permission list usually consists of the characters r (for read), w (for write), x (for execute), or - (meaning none are applicable).

They're followed by a number indicating the link count, which you can ignore. Next is the owner of the file (keir in the example) and the group that he belongs to (users). This is followed by the file size (in bytes), then the date and time the file was last accessed, and finally the filename itself.

The file permissions part of the listing might look confusing, but it's actually quite simple. To understand what's going on, you need to split it into groups of four, as illustrated in Figure 14-3.

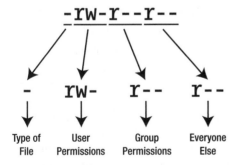

Figure 14-3. *The file permissions part of a file listing can be broken down into four separate parts.*

The four groups are as follows:

Type of file: This character represents the file type. A standard data file is indicated with a dash (-). Most files on your system fall into this category. A d shows that the entry is not a file, but a directory. Table 14-2 lists the file type codes.

User permissions: Next come the permissions of the person who owns the file. The three characters indicate what the person who owns the file can do with it. The owner of a file is usually the user who created it, although it's also possible to change the owner later on. In this example, you see rw-. This means that the owner of the file can read (r) and write (w) the file. In other words, he can look at it and also save changes to it. However, there's a dash afterward, and this indicates that the user cannot execute the file. If this were possible, there would be an x in this spot instead.

Group permissions: After the owner's permissions are the permissions given to members of that user's group. This is indicated by another three characters in the same style as those for user permissions. In our example, the group's permission is r--, which means that the group members can read the file but don't have permission to write to it or to execute it, since there are dashes where the w and x would appear. In other words, as far as they're concerned, the file is read-only.

Everyone else's permissions: The last set of permissions indicates the permissions of everyone else on the system (other users in other groups). In our example, they can only read the file (r). The two dashes afterward indicate that they cannot write to the file or execute it.

Table 14-2. *File Type Codes*

Code	File Type
-	Standard file
d	Standard directory
l	Symbolic link (a shortcut to another file)
p	Named pipe (a file that acts as a conduit for data between two programs)
s	Socket (a file designed to send and receive data over a network)
c	Character device (a hardware device driver, usually found in /dev)
b	Block device (a hardware device driver, usually found in /dev)

As you might remember from Windows, programs are stored as files on your hard disk, just like standard data files. On Linux, program files need to be explicitly marked as being executable. This is indicated in the permission listing by an x. Therefore, if there's no x in a file's permissions, it's a good bet that the file in question isn't a program or script (although this isn't always true for various technical reasons).

To make matters a little more confusing, if the entry in the list of files is a directory (indicated by a d), then the rules are different. In this case, an x indicates that the user can access that directory. If there's no x, then the user's attempts to browse to that directory will be met with an "access denied" message.

File permissions can be difficult to understand, so let's look at a few real-world examples. These examples assume that you're logged in to Linux as the user keir throughout.

LESS-COMMON FILE TYPES

Instead of the x in the list of permissions for a directory, you might sometimes see a t. This means that the only people who can delete or alter a file in that directory are the users who created the file in the first place. This is a useful option to have in some circumstances.

You might sometimes see a set of permissions like rws. The s stands for setuid. Like x, it indicates that the file is executable, except, in this case, it means that the file will be run with the permissions of the person who owns it, rather than the user who is executing it. In other words, if user frank tries to run a program owned by keir that has the execute permission set as s, that program will be run as if keir were running it. This can be useful, because the root user can use this trick to make programs that require root access usable by ordinary users. This trick can also be used to make some items of hardware usable by all users. However, both of these uses of the setuid permission introduce security risks.

Typical Data File Permissions

Let's take a look at the first of our examples, which is taken from my SUSE Linux test system:

```
-rw-rw----   2 keir users 1450 2004-07-07 09:19 myfile2
```

You see immediately that this file is owned by user keir because that username appears directly after the permissions. You also see that this user is a member of the group users.

Reading the file permissions from left to right, you see that the initial character is a dash. That indicates that this is an ordinary file and has no special characteristics. It's also not a directory.

After that is the first part of the permissions, rw-. These are the permissions for owner of the file, keir. You're logged in as that user, so this file belongs to you, and these permissions apply to you. You can read and write the file, but not execute it. Because you cannot execute the file, you can infer that this is a data file rather than a program (there are certain exceptions to this rule, but we'll ignore them for the sake of simplicity).

Following this is the next part of the file permissions, rw-. This tells you what other members of your group can do with the file. It's fairly useless information if you're the only user of your PC but, for the record, you're told that anyone else belonging to the group called users can also read and write the file, but not execute it.

■**Note** If more than one user uses your computer, then the group permissions are clearly important. SUSE Linux adds all new users to the group users by default. In this example, any user on the PC can read and write to this file, which is not always desirable. The next section describes how to change file permissions to prevent this from happening.

Finally, the last three characters tell you the permissions of everyone else on the system. The three dashes (---) mean that they have no permissions at all regarding the file. There's a dash where the r normally appears, so they cannot even read it. The dashes afterward tell you they cannot write to the file or execute it. If they try to do anything with the file, they'll get a "permission denied" error.

Permissions on a User's Directory

Here's example number two:

```
drwxr-xr-x   7 keir users 824 2004-07-07 10:01 mydirectory
```

The list of permissions starts with d, which tells you that this isn't a file but a directory. After this is the list of permissions for the owner of the directory (keir), who can read files in the directory and also create new ones there. The x indicates that you can access this directory, as opposed to being turned away with an "access denied" message. You might think being able to access the directory is taken for granted if the user can read and write to it, but that's not the case.

Next are the permissions for the group members. They can read files in the directory but not write any new ones there (although they can modify files already in there, provided the permissions of the individual files allow this). Once again, there's an x at the end of their particular permission listing, which indicates that the group members can access the directory.

Following the group's permissions are those of everyone else. They can read the directory and browse it, but not write new files to it, as with the group users' permissions.

Permissions on a Directory Owned by Root

Here's the last example:

```
drwx------   25 root root 1000 2004-08-06 15:44 root
```

You can see that the file is owned by root. Remember that in this example, you're logged in as keir and your group is users.

The list of permissions starts with a d, so you can tell that this is actually a directory. After this, you see that the owner of the directory, root, has permission to read, write, and access the directory.

Next are the permissions for the group: three dashes. In other words, members of the group called root have no permission to access this directory in any way. They cannot browse it, create new files in it, or even access it.

Following this are the permissions for the rest of the users. This includes you, because you're not the user root and don't belong to its group. The three dashes means you don't have permission to read, write, or access this directory.

SWITCHING USERS

It's possible to switch users on the fly while you're working at the shell by using the `su` command, which stands for substitute user. On my test PC, I have an additional user account called `frank`. While logged in as any user, I can temporarily switch to this user by typing the following command:

```
su frank
```

I'll then be asked for user `frank`'s password. Once this is typed, I will effectively have logged in as user `frank`. Any files I create will be saved with `frank`'s ownership.

When the `su` command is used on its own, the shell will assume I want to become root user. This is a handy way of quickly switching to root in order to undertake system administration tasks. If a dash is added, `su -`, then I also take on the root user's `$PATH`, meaning I can access certain essential system tools.

In both cases, I can log out of the user I've temporarily switched into by typing `exit`. Remember to keep an eye on the command prompt. This will tell you which user you're currently logged in as.

Altering Permissions

You can easily change permissions of files and directories by using the `chmod` command. For example, if you want to change a file so that everyone on the system can read and write to it, type the following:

```
chmod a+rw myfile
```

In other words, you're adding add read and write (`rw`) permissions for all users (a).

Here's another example:

```
chmod a-w myfile
```

This tells Linux that you want to take away (`-`) the ability of all users (a) to write (`w`) to the file. However, you want to leave the other permissions as they are. You can replace the a with a g to change group permissions instead.

The most useful use of `chmod` is in making a program file that you've downloaded executable. Due to the way the Internet works, if you download a program to install on your computer, it can lose its executable status while in transit. In this case, issue the following command:

```
chmod +x myprogram
```

Because nothing is specified before the `+x`, the shell assumes that the changes to be applied to the file are for the current user only.

To change the owner of a file, use the `chown` command. Only users with root powers are allowed to change file ownerships, so you'll first need to switch to the root user by typing `su`.

To set the owner of `myfile` as `frank`, type this command:

```
chown frank myfile
```

■**Tip** The `chown` command is handy if you create or download a file as root and want to make it accessible by your standard user login.

The File System Explained

Now that you understand the principles of files and users, we can take a bird's-eye view of the Linux file system and start to make sense of it.

You might already have ventured beyond the /home directory and wandered through the file system. You no doubt found it thoroughly confusing, largely because it's not like anything you're used to. The good news it that it's not actually very hard to understand. If nothing else, you should be aware that nearly everything can be ignored during everyday use.

■**Note** The SUSE Linux file system is referred to as a *hierarchical* file system. This means that it consists of a lot of directories that contain files. Windows also uses a hierarchical file system. SUSE Linux refers to the very bottom level of the file system as the *root*. This has no connection with the root user.

You can switch to the root of the file system by typing the following shell command:

```
cd /
```

When used on its own, the forward slash is interpreted as a shortcut for the root of the file system.

If I do this on my PC and then ask for a long file listing (`ls -l`), I see the following:

```
keir@linux:~> cd /
keir@linux:/> ls -l
total 21
drwxr-xr-x   2 root root 2928 2006-01-22 07:07 bin
drwxr-xr-x   3 root root  624 2006-01-22 07:14 boot
drwxr-xr-x  11 root root 7900 2006-01-23 02:17 dev
drwxr-xr-x  80 root root 6720 2006-01-23 02:18 etc
drwxr-xr-x   3 root root   72 2006-01-22 07:19 home
drwxr-xr-x  10 root root 3824 2006-01-22 07:07 lib
drwxr-xr-x   5 root root  128 2006-01-23 02:18 media
drwxr-xr-x   2 root root   48 2006-01-19 10:29 mnt
drwxr-xr-x   5 root root  120 2006-01-22 07:04 opt
dr-xr-xr-x 100 root root    0 2006-01-22 21:18 proc
drwx------  16 root root  624 2006-01-23 02:17 root
drwxr-xr-x   3 root root 6992 2006-01-22 17:30 sbin
```

```
drwxr-xr-x    4 root root     96 2006-01-22 07:00 srv
drwxr-xr-x    2 root root     48 2006-01-17 04:47 subdomain
drwxr-xr-x   10 root root      0 2006-01-22 21:18 sys
drwxrwxrwt   13 root root    624 2006-01-23 04:15 tmp
drwxr-xr-x   12 root root    344 2006-01-22 07:05 usr
drwxr-xr-x   14 root root    360 2006-01-22 07:02 var
```

The first thing you'll notice from this is that the root of the file system contains nothing but directories and that they're all owned by root.

Only the root user can write files to the root of the file system. This is to prevent damage from ordinary users, since most of the directories in the root of the file system are vital to the correct running of Linux and contain essential programs or data.

■**Caution** It's incredibly easy to slip up when using the command-line shell and thereby cause a lot of damage. For example, simply mistyping a forward slash in a command can mean the difference between deleting the files in a directory and deleting the directory itself. This is just another reason why you should always work as a standard user and log in as root only when it's absolutely necessary. It also explains why, by default, all the system directories are owned by the root user and protected against ordinary users making changes to them.

As you can see from the file permissions of each directory in the root of the file system, most directories allow all users to browse them and access the files within (the last three characters of the permissions read r-x). You just won't be able to create new files there or delete the directories themselves. You might be able to modify or execute programs contained within the directory, but this will depend on the permissions of each individual file.

Table 14-3 provides a brief description of what each directory in the SUSE Linux root file system contains. This is for reference only; there's no need for you to learn this information.

■**Note** The SUSE Linux file system broadly follows the principles laid down in the Filesystem Hierarchy Standard, as with most versions of Linux, but it does have its own subtleties. The Filesystem Hierarchy Standard is simply a document that describes where files should live on Unix and Linux operating systems. Its purpose is to ensure that using one version of Linux is like using an alternative. Most Linux distros and versions of Unix stick to it closely, although most deviate in subtle ways. You can find more details about the Filesystem Hierarchy Standard at www.pathname.com/fhs/.

Table 14-3. *Directories in the SUSE Linux Root File System*

Directory	Contents
bin	Vital tools necessary to get the system running or for use when repairing the system and diagnosing problems
boot	Boot loader programs and configuration files (the boot loader is the menu that appears when you first boot Linux)
dev	Virtual files representing hardware installed on your system
etc	Central repository of configuration files for your system
home	Where each user's personal directory is stored
lib	Shared system files used by Linux as well as the software that runs on it
media	Where the directories representing various mounted removable storage devices are made available
mnt	Directory in which external file systems can be temporarily mounted
opt	Software that is theoretically optional and not vital to the running of the system (many software packages you use daily can be found here)
proc	Virtual directory containing data about your system and its current status
root	The root user's personal directory
sbin	Programs essential to administration of the system
subdomain	Component of the SUSE Linux security system.
srv	Configuration files for any network servers you might have running on your system
sys	Mount point of the sysfs file system, which is used by the kernel to administer your system's hardware
tmp	Temporary files stored by the system
usr	Programs and data that might be shared with other systems (such as in a large networking setup with many users)[1]
var	Used by the system to store data that is constantly updated, such as printer spooling output

1. *The* usr *directory contains its own set of directories that are full of programs and data. Many system programs, such as X11, are located within the* /usr *directory. Note that the* /usr *directory is used even if your system will never act as a server to other systems.*

TYPES OF FILE SYSTEMS

Linux is all about choice, and this extends to the technology that makes the file system work. Unlike with Windows, where you can choose between just NTFS and FAT32 (with the emphasis being on NTFS), Linux offers many different types of file system technologies. Each is designed for varying tasks. Most are scalable, however, which means that they will work just as happily on a desktop PC as on a massive cluster of computers.

SUSE Linux uses the reiserfs file system. The Red Hat distribution normally offers the ext3 system. People are constantly arguing about which file system is best. The principal measuring stick is performance. Your computer spends a lot of time writing and reading files, so the faster a file system is, the faster your PC will be overall (although, in reality, the hardware is of equal importance).

It's worth noting that we're talking here about the underlying and invisible technology of the file system. In day-to-day use, the end user won't be aware of any difference between ext3, reiserfs, or another file system technology (although when things go wrong, different tools are used to attempt repairs; their selection is automated within SUSE Linux).

Here are the various types along with notes about what they offer:

- **ext2:** Fast, stable, and well established, ext2 was once the most popular type of file system technology used on Linux. It's now been eclipsed by ext3.

- **ext3:** An extension of ext2, ext3 allows journaling, a way of recording what's been written to disk so that a recovery can be attempted when things go wrong.

- **reiserfs:** This is another journaling file system, which claims to be faster than others and also offers better security features.

- **jfs:** This is a journaling file system created by IBM. It's used on industrial implementations of Unix.

- **xfs:** This is a 64-bit journaling file system created by Silicon Graphics, Inc. (SGI) and used on its own version of Unix, as well as Linux.

Mounting

Described in technical terms, *mounting* is the practice of making a file system available under Linux. This can take the form of a partition on your hard disk, a CD-ROM, a network server, or many other things.

Mounting drives might seem a strange concept, but it actually makes everything much simpler than it might be otherwise. For example, once a drive is mounted, there's no need to use any special commands or software to access its contents. You can use the same programs and tools that you use to access all of your other files. Mounting creates a level playing field on which everything is equal and can therefore be accessed quickly and efficiently.

Using the mount Command

Mounting is usually done via the mount command. Under SUSE Linux, you must be the root user to do this.

With most modern versions of Linux, mount can be used in two ways: by specifying all the settings immediately after the command, or by making reference to an entry within the fstab file. This is a configuration file stored in the /etc directory that contains details of all file systems of the PC that can be mounted.

■Note The root file system is itself mounted automatically during bootup, shortly after the kernel has started and has all your hardware up and running. Every file system that Linux uses must be mounted at some point.

Let's say that I insert a floppy into my computer's floppy disk drive. To mount it and make it available to Linux (something that is actually done automatically as soon as you put a disc in the drive, so this example is for demonstration purposes only), I would type:

```
mount /media/floppy
```

The `mount` command first looks in my `fstab` file in the `/etc` directory to find what I'm referring to. Figure 14-4 shows an example of the contents of that file. (The example in the figure uses the `cat` command, which is discussed in Chapter 15.) Using this information, the `mount` command attempts to make the contents of the floppy disk drive available in the `/media/floppy` directory. Note that this is done in a virtual way; the files are not literally copied into the directory. The directory is merely a magical conduit that allows you to read the floppy's contents.

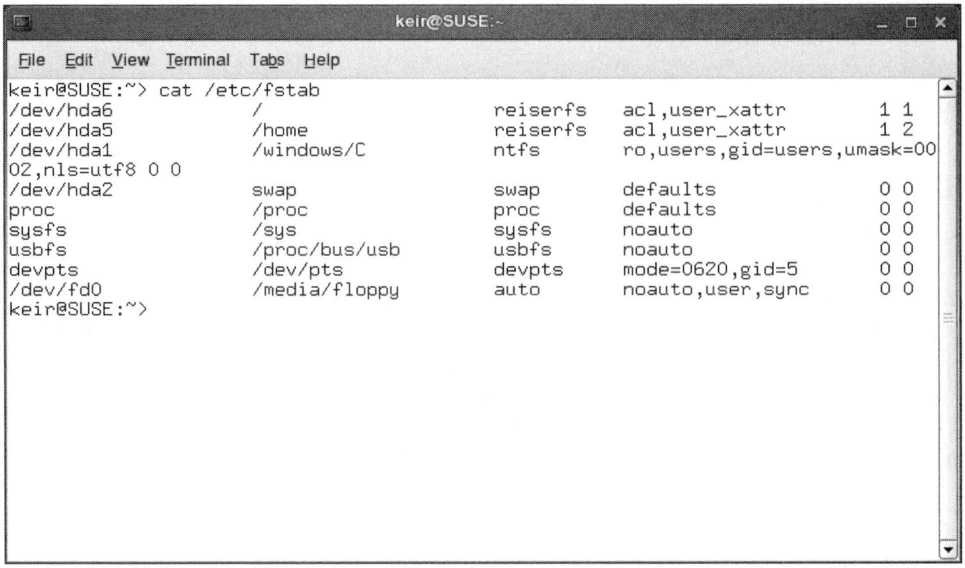
keir@SUSE:~
File Edit View Terminal Tabs Help
keir@SUSE:~> cat /etc/fstab
/dev/hda6 / reiserfs acl,user_xattr 1 1
/dev/hda5 /home reiserfs acl,user_xattr 1 2
/dev/hda1 /windows/C ntfs ro,users,gid=users,umask=00
02,nls=utf8 0 0
/dev/hda2 swap swap defaults 0 0
proc /proc proc defaults 0 0
sysfs /sys sysfs noauto 0 0
usbfs /proc/bus/usb usbfs noauto 0 0
devpts /dev/pts devpts mode=0620,gid=5 0 0
/dev/fd0 /media/floppy auto noauto,user,sync 0 0
keir@SUSE:~>

Figure 14-4. *Details of all frequently mounted file systems are held in the /etc/fstab file.*

There aren't any special commands used to work with mounted drives. The shell commands discussed in Chapter 13 should do everything you need.

The mount command doesn't see widespread usage by most users nowadays, because most removable storage devices like CDs, DVDs, and even photographic memory card readers are mounted automatically under SUSE Linux. However, there will be occasions when you need to mount a drive manually.

Mounting a Drive Manually

Let's look at an example of when you might need to mount a drive manually. Suppose that you've just added a second hard disk to your PC that has previously been used on a Windows system. This has been added as the primary slave.

The first thing to do is create a mount point, which is an empty directory that will act as a location where you can tell mount to make the disk accessible. You can create this directory anywhere, but under SUSE Linux, the convention is to create it in the /mnt directory. Therefore, the following command should do the trick (assuming you've switched to root user):

```
mkdir /mnt/windows
```

You now need to know what kind of partition type is used on the disk, because you need to specify this when mounting. To discover this, use the fdisk command (you'll have to switch to root first—type su -). Type the following exactly as it appears:

```
fdisk -l /dev/hdb
```

This will list the partitions on the second disk drive (assuming an average PC system). With most hard disks used under Windows, you should find a single partition that will be either NTFS or FAT32.

■**Caution** Be aware that fdisk is a dangerous system command that can damage your system. The program is designed to partition disks and can wipe your data if you're not careful!

With this information in hand, you're now ready to mount the disk. For a FAT32 disk, type the following:

```
mount -t vfat /dev/hdb1 /mnt/windows
```

For an NTFS disk, type the following:

```
mount -t ntfs /dev/hdb1 /mnt/windows
```

The -t command option is used to specify the file system type. After this, you specify the relevant file in the /dev directory (this file is only virtual, of course, and merely represents the hardware), and then specify the directory that is acting as your mount point.

■Note You can only read from NTFS drives under Linux because writing to them is considered too risky and might result in data loss. However, you can both read and write to FAT32 partitions because of the much simpler technology used.

Now when you browse to the /mnt/windows directory, by typing cd /mnt/windows, you should find the contents of the hard disk accessible.

For more information about the mount command, read its man page (type man mount).

Removing a Mounted System

What if you want to get rid of a mounted system?

There's a special command designed for the purposes of unmounting: umount (notice there's no n after the first u). It's used in the following simple way:

umount /media/floppy

This will unmount the floppy disk drive.

Note that if you're currently browsing the mounted directory, you'll need to leave it before you can unmount it. The same is true of all kinds of access to the mounted directory. If you're browsing the mounted drive with Nautilus or Konqueror, or if a piece of software is accessing it, you won't be able to unmount it until you've quit the program and closed the file browsing window (or browsed to a different part of the file system).

File Searches

Files frequently get lost. Well, technically speaking, they don't actually get lost. We just forget where we've put them. But because of this, the shell includes some handy commands to search for files.

Using the find Command

The find command is installed on SUSE Linux by default. Like the Search option on the Windows XP Start menu, this command manually searches through all the files on the hard disk in order to find what you're seeking. It's not a particularly fast way of finding a file, but it is reliable.

Here's an example:

find /home/keir -name "myfile"

This will search for myfile using /home/keir as a starting point (which is to say that it will search all directories within /home/keir, and any directories within those directories, and so on, because it's recursive).

You can search the entire file system by leaving out the initial path. In this case, find will assume you want the search to start from /, the root of the file system.

If the file is found, you'll see it appear in the output of the command. The path will be shown next to the filename.

Period punctuation symbols have interesting meanings within file listings and therefore within the output of the find command. As you learned in Chapter 13, .. refers to the parent directory of the one you're currently browsing. In a similar way, a single . refers to the directory you're in at the moment; it's shorthand for "right here." So, if find returns a result like ./myfile, it means that myfile is right here in the current directory.

However, when a single period is used at the *beginning of a filename*, such as in .bashrc, it has the effect of hiding the file. In other words, that file won't appear when you type ls (although you can type ls -a to see all files, even those that are hidden).

If you give find a try, you'll see that it's not a particularly good way of searching. Apart from being slow, it will also return a lot of error messages about directories it cannot search. This is because, when you run the find command, it takes on your user permissions. Whenever find comes across a directory it cannot access, it will report it to you, as shown in the example in Figure 14-5. There are frequently so many of these warnings that the output can hide the instances where find actually locates the file in question!

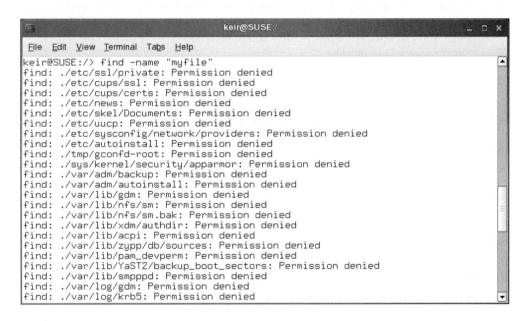

Figure 14-5. *The find command is useful for finding files but isn't problem-free.*

You can avoid these error messages in various ways, but perhaps the quickest solution is to use the su command to switch to the root user before using the find command. Because the root user has access to every file on the hard disk, the find command will be unrestricted in where it can search, so it won't run into any directories it doesn't have permission to enter.

> ■**Caution** Using the `find` command with root powers may represent an invasion of privacy if you have more than one user on your system. The `find` command will search other users' /home directories and report any instances of files found there, too.

However, an even better solution for finding files is to use the `locate` command.

Using the locate Command

Although `locate` comes as standard on most versions of Linux, it's not installed on SUSE Linux by default. You can easily install it using YaST (Chapter 29 examines installing software using YaST). Simply search for the `findutils-locate` package.

However, before using the `locate` command, you must first build its search database. To create this database, type the following command at the shell prompt as the root user:

```
updatedb
```

This will probably take a minute or two to complete. You probably won't need to use this command again, because when the `locate` package was installed, the `updatedb` command was automatically added to the scheduled task list that SUSE Linux carries out on a daily basis.

After this, you can use the following command to search for a file (you don't need to be logged in as the root user to do so):

```
locate myfile
```

The benefit of using the `locate` command is that it's instantaneous. Instead of searching the file system, `locate` searches the database built by `updatedb`.

The downside of using the `locate` command is that it relies on the database being up-to-date. If you save a file, and then an hour later use `locate` to find it, the chances are the database won't have been updated during that period. In such a case, the `find` command is a better bet. Alternatively, you could simply run `updatedb` again, although you may have to wait for a few minutes while the database is updated.

Using the whereis Command

One other command worth mentioning in the context of searching is `whereis`. This command locates where programs are stored and is an excellent way of exploring your system. Using it is simply a matter of typing something like this:

```
whereis cp
```

This will tell you where the `cp` program is located on your hard disk. It will also tell you where its source code and `man` page are located (if applicable). However, the first path returned by the search will be the location of the program itself.

> ## USING BEAGLE DESKTOP SEARCH
>
> Both the KDE and GNOME desktops offer a search facility similar to Google Desktop Search under Windows or Spotlight under Macintosh OS X. Under the GNOME desktop, this is referred to as Beagle Desktop Search; under the KDE desktop, it is called Kerry Beagle Desktop Search. Both use the same technology, although Kerry Beagle is tweaked so that it works better with the KDE desktop. Both are accessed by clicking the magnifying glass icon in the notification area, next to the software update icon.
>
> Beagle Desktop Search relies on a stored database of information, so it doesn't manually search the disk each time a query is entered. However, it's radically different from most search tools because, as its name suggests, it's limited to your desktop data (in fact, its database is limited to items within your /home folder). In addition, along with files, chat conversations, e-mail, web history, and many other items are cataloged. Alongside the filenames in the list of results will be all the data about the files. For example, if you search for an image file, Beagle Desktop Search lists the resolution, file size, and much more.
>
> There's little doubt that making good use of Beagle Desktop Search can make life easier for the user. However, for full file system searches, it's still best to use system commands such as locate and find.

File Size and Free Space

Often, it's necessary to understand how large files are and to know how much space they're taking up on the hard disk. In addition, it's often handy to know how much free space is left on a disk.

Viewing File Sizes

Using the ls -l command option will tell you how large each file is in terms of bytes. Adding the -h option converts these file sizes to kilobytes, megabytes, and even gigabytes, depending on their size.

In order to get an idea of which are the largest files and which are the smallest, you can add the -S command option. This will order the files in the list in terms of the largest and smallest files.

The following will return a list of all the files in the current directory, in order of size (largest first), detailing the sizes in kilobytes, megabytes, or gigabytes:

```
ls -Slh
```

Another, more powerful way of presenting this information is by using the du command, which stands for disk usage. When used on its own without command switches, du simply presents the size of directories alongside their names (starting in the current directory). It will show any hidden directories (directories whose names start with a period), and will also present a total at the end of the list. This will probably be quite a long list. Once again, you can add the -h command option to force the du command to produce human-readable measurements.

If you specify a file or directory when using the du command and use the -s command option, you can find out its total file size:

```
du -sh mydirectoryname
```

This will show the size taken up on the disk by mydirectoryname, adding to the total any files or subdirectories it contains.

However, du is limited by the same file permission problems as the find tool, as shown in Figure 14-6. If you run du as an ordinary user, it won't be able to calculate the total for any directories you don't have permission to access. Therefore, you might consider running the command as the root user.

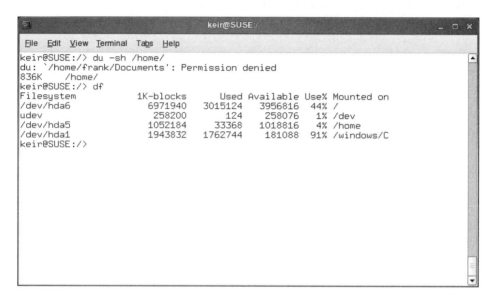

Figure 14-6. *The du command shows the size of a file, and the df command can be used to gauge the amount of free space on the disk.*

Discovering the Amount of Free Space

What if you want to find out how much free space is left on the disk? In this case, you can use the df command. This command is also demonstrated in Figure 14-6.

The df command works on a partition-by-partition basis. Typing it at the command prompt will show you how much space is free on the entire disk. Once again, you can add the -h option to the df command to have the file sizes returned in megabytes and gigabytes (and even terabytes if your hard disk is big enough!).

■**Note** There's as much space free in any directory as there is space on the disk, which is why df displays data about the entire partition. If you're using a system managed by a system administrator within a business environment, you might find that quotas have been used to limit how much disk space you can use. However, if you're using a desktop PC and are the only user, this won't be activated.

Summary

In this chapter, we examined how the SUSE Linux file system lies at the heart of an understanding of how the operating system works. We also discussed how the file system and user accounts go hand-in-hand and are inextricably linked. This involved discussing the concept of file ownership and usage permissions, plus how these can be manipulated using command-line shell tools.

We also discussed the overall structure of the SUSE Linux file system and how external file systems can be mounted and made available within SUSE Linux. Finally, we looked at how to find files and how to gauge how much free space there is within the file system.

In the next chapter, we'll look at how the BASH shell can be used to view and otherwise manipulate text files, which are also important to the way SUSE Linux works.

CHAPTER 15

■ ■ ■

Working with Text Files

Windows views text files as just another file type, but to SUSE Linux, they can be essential components that make the system work. Configuration files are stored as plain text, and program documentation is also stored as text. This is clearly different from Windows, where it's very likely any information you're supposed to read will be contained in a Windows Help file, a rich text format (RTF) file, or even a Microsoft Word document.

Because of the reliance on text files, the shell includes several commands that let you display, edit, and otherwise manipulate text files in various ways. Learning to use the shell, and therefore learning how to administer your SUSE Linux system, involves having a good understanding of these text tools. You'll use text tools for editing configuration files and viewing log files, as just two examples.

Viewing Text Files

You can easily view files using command-line tools, including `cat`, `less`, `head`, and `tail`. The simplest command for dealing with text files is `cat`.

Using the cat Command

When followed with a filename, the `cat` command will display the text file on screen:

```
cat mytextfile
```

`cat` is short for concatenate, and it isn't designed just to display text files. That it can do so is simply a side effect of its real purpose in life, which is to join two or more files together. However, when used with a single file, it simply displays its contents on screen.

If you try to use `cat`, you'll realize that it's good for only short text files; large files scroll off the screen.

Using the less Command

Because `cat` works well only with short files, and to give you more control when viewing text files, the `less` and `more` commands were created. The `more` command came first but was considered too primitive, so someone came up with less, which is preferred by many Linux users. However, both are usually available on the average Linux installation.

Let's look at using less to read the The GIMP's README file, which contains information about the current release of the image editor (discussed in Chapter 20). The file is located at /usr/share/doc/packages/gimp, so to use less to read it, type the following:

```
less /usr/share/doc/packages/gimp
```

You can scroll up and down within the less display by using the cursor keys. If you want to scroll by bigger amounts of text, you can use the Page Up and Page Down keys. Alternatively, you can use the spacebar and B key, both of which are commonly used by old-hand Linux/Unix users for the same function. In addition, the Home and End keys will take you to the start and end of the document, respectively.

When using less, keep an eye on the bottom part of the screen, where you'll see a brief status bar. Alongside the filename, you'll see how many lines the document has and which line you're currently up to. In addition, you'll see as a percentage the amount of document you've already read through, so you'll know how much is left to go.

less lets you search forward through the file by typing a slash (/), and then entering your search term. Any words that are matched will be highlighted on screen. To repeat the search, type n. To search backward in a file from your current point, type a question mark (?). To quit less, simply type q.

Although it's supposedly a simple program, less is packed with features. You can see what options are available by reading its man page or by typing less −help.

Using the head and tail Commands

A couple of other handy commands that you can use to view text files are head and tail. As their names suggest, these let you quickly view the beginning (head) of a file or the end (tail) of it.

Using the commands is simple:

```
tail mytextfile
head mytextfile
```

By default, both commands will display ten lines of the file. You can override this by using the -n command option followed by the number of lines you want to see. For example, the following will show the last five lines of mytextfile:

```
tail -n5 mytextfile
```

These two commands are very useful when viewing log files that might contain hundreds of lines of text. The most recent information is always at the end, so you can use tail to see what's happened last on your system, as shown in the example in Figure 15-1.

Although they're powerful, all of these shell commands don't let you do much more than view text files. If you want to edit files, you'll need to use a text editor such as vi.

Figure 15-1. *The tail command can be very useful for viewing the last few lines of a log file.*

STANDARD INPUT AND OUTPUT

If you've read any of the SUSE Linux man pages, you might have seen references to *standard input* and *standard output*. Like many things in SUSE Linux, this sounds complicated but is merely a long-winded way of referring to something that is relatively simple.

Standard input is simply the device that SUSE Linux normally takes input from. In other words, on the majority of desktop PCs when you're using the command-line shell, standard input refers to the keyboard. However, it's important to note that it could also feasibly refer to the mouse or any other device on your system capable of providing input; even some software can take the role of providing standard input.

Standard output is similar. It refers to the device to which output from a command is usually sent. In the majority of cases at the command line, this refers to the monitor screen, although it could feasibly be any kind of output device, such as your PC's sound card and speakers.

For example, the man page for the cat command says that it will "concatenate files and print on the standard output." In other words, for the majority of desktop SUSE Linux installations, it will combine (concatenate) any number of files together and print the results on screen. If you specify just one file, it will display that single file on your screen.

In addition to hardware devices, input can also come from a file containing commands, and output can also be sent to a file instead of the screen, or even sent directly to another command. This is just one reason why the command-line shell is so flexible and powerful.

Using a Command-Line Text Editor

A variety of text editors can be used within the shell, but three stand out as being ubiquitous: ed, vi, and Emacs. The first in that list, ed, is by far the simplest. That doesn't necessarily mean that it's simple to use or lacks powerful features, but it just doesn't match the astonishing power of both vi and Emacs. To call vi and Emacs simple text editors is to do them a disservice, because both are extremely powerful interactive environments. There are entire books written solely about Emacs and vi. Both text editors are normally available on virtually every installation of Linux or Unix.

■**Tip** A fourth shell-based text editor found on many Linux systems is nano. This editor offers many word processor–like features that can be helpful if you've come to Linux from a Windows background.

The downside of all the power within Emacs and vi is that both packages can be difficult to learn to use. They're considered idiosyncratic by even their most ardent fans. Both involve the user learning certain unfamiliar concepts, as well as keyboard shortcuts and commands.

Although there are debates about which text editor is better and which is best, it's generally agreed that vi offers substantial text-editing power but isn't too all-encompassing. Emacs is considered practically an operating system in itself, and some users of Linux treat it as their shell, executing commands and performing everyday tasks, such as reading and sending e-mail from within it.

On SUSE Linux, vi is installed by default and Emacs must be installed as an optional extra. We'll concentrate on using vi here.

It's important to understand that there isn't just one program called vi. There are many versions. The original vi program, supplied with Unix, is rarely used nowadays. The most common version of vi is a clone called vim, for vi improved, and this is the version supplied with SUSE Linux. However, there are other versions, such as Elvis. Most work in a virtually identical way.

■**Note** There's always been a constant flame war between advocates of vi and Emacs, as to which is better. This could be quite a vicious and desperate debate, and the text editor you used was often taken as a measure of your character! Nowadays, the battle between the two camps has softened, and the Emacs versus vi debate is considered an entertaining cliché of Linux and Unix use. Declaring online which text editor a user prefers is often followed by a smiley symbol to acknowledge the once-fevered emotions. For a detailed analysis of this situation, visit http://en.wikipedia.org/wiki/Editor_wars.

Understanding vi Modes

The key to understanding how vi works is to learn the difference between the various modes. Three modes are important: Command mode, Insert mode, and Command-Line mode.

Command Mode

Command mode is vi's central mode. When the editor starts up, it's in Command mode, as shown in Figure 15-2. This lets you move around the text and delete words or lines of text. vi returns to Command mode after most operations. In this mode, the status bar at the bottom of the screen shows information such as the percentage progress through the document.

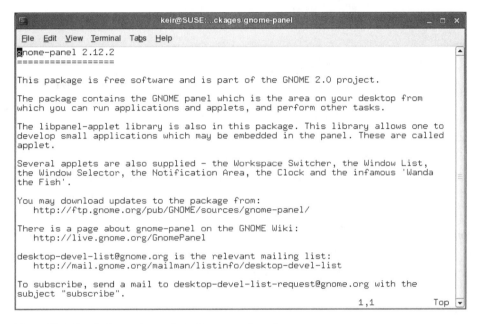

Figure 15-2. *In vi, the main mode is Command mode.*

Although you cannot insert text in this mode, you can delete and otherwise manipulate words and lines within the file. You can also move through the text using the cursor keys and the Page Up and Page Down keys.

Table 15-1 shows a list of the commands you can use in Command mode (consider photocopying it and sticking it to the side of your monitor as a handy reference).

Table 15-1. *vi Command Mode Commands*

Command	Description
Delete Text	
dd	Delete current line
*n*dd	Delete *n* number of lines (for example, 5dd will delete five lines)[1]
dw	Delete the current word under the cursor[2]
db	Delete the word before the cursor[2]
D	Delete everything from the cursor to the end of the line[1]

Continued

Table 15-1. *Continued*

Command	Description
Search	
/	Search forward (type the search text directly after the slash)
?	Search backward
n	Repeat search in a forward direction
N	Repeat search in a backward direction
Cut and Paste	
yy	Copy the current line[3]
*n*yy	Copy *n* number of lines into the buffer from the cursor downward (for example, 5yy copies five lines of text)
p	Paste the contents of the clipboard[3]
Insert Text	
i	Switch to Insert mode at the cursor
o	Switch to Insert mode, placing the cursor below the current line
O	Switch to Insert mode, placing the cursor above the current line
A	Append text to the end of the line
Navigation[4]	
$	Move the cursor to the end of the current line
w	Move the cursor to the next word
b	Move the cursor to the previous word
Miscellaneous	
.	Repeat the last command
u	Undo the last command

1. *A line ends where a line-break control character occurs in the file. Because of this, a line of text may actually take up several lines of the on-screen display.*
2. *This will delete the remainder of the current word before/after the cursor if the cursor is in the middle of a word.*
3. *The standard documentation refers to copying as "yanking" and the clipboard as the "buffer."*
4. *You can also use the cursor keys to move around the file and the Page Up and Page Down keys to move up and down a page at a time. Additionally, press 0 (zero) on the main keyboard, not the numeric keypad, to move the cursor to the start of the current line, or Shift+0 to move forward one sentence (until the next full stop).*

Insert Mode

To type your own text or edit text, you need to switch to Insert mode. This is normally done by typing i, but you can also type O or o to change to Insert mode, which is indicated by the word INSERT appearing at the bottom of the screen, as shown in Figure 15-3. The difference between the commands required to switch into Insert mode is that some let you insert before or after the cursor. Generally, i is most useful, because what you type will appear before the character under the cursor, as with most word processors. The commands that activate Insert mode are listed in Table 15-1, under "Insert Text."

Tip By typing A (Shift+A), you can add text to the end of the line on which the cursor currently resides.

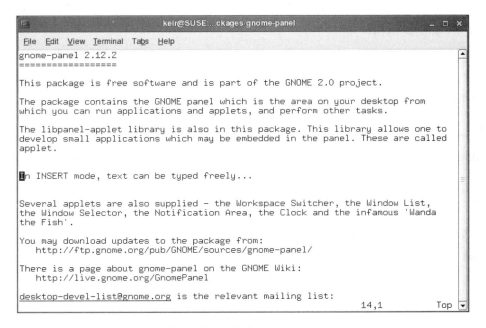

Figure 15-3. *Use vi's Insert mode to add and edit text.*

In Insert mode, you can still move around the text using the cursor keys. Anything you type will appear the point of the cursor. To quit this mode, press the Esc key. This will return you to Command mode.

Command-Line Mode

The third mode you should be aware of is Command-Line mode (note that, irritatingly, this is not the same as the Command mode). As its name suggests, this is the mode in which you can enter commands to save and load files, as well as perform other fundamental tasks to control vi or to quit the program.

You can enter Command-Line mode by typing a colon (:), although if you're in Insert mode, you'll first need to leave it by pressing the Esc key. You can identify when vi is in this mode because the cursor will be at the bottom of the screen next to a colon symbol, as shown in Figure 15-4. To quit Command-Line mode, press the Esc key. You'll be returned to Command mode. Note that you'll automatically leave Command-Line mode after each command you issue has completed.

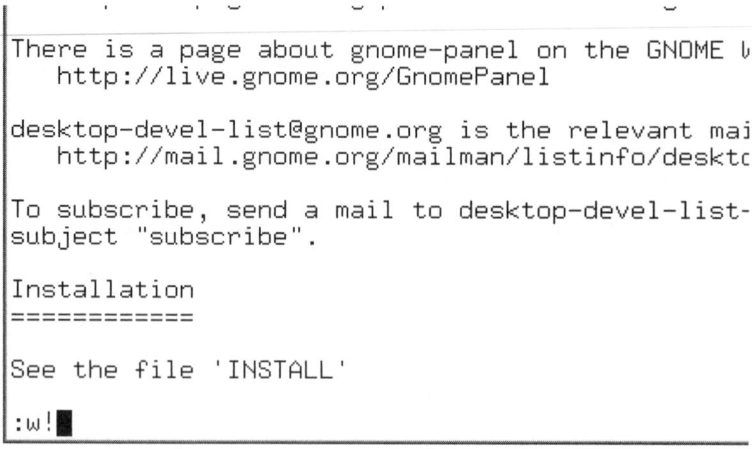

```
There is a page about gnome-panel on the GNOME L
    http://live.gnome.org/GnomePanel

desktop-devel-list@gnome.org is the relevant mai
    http://mail.gnome.org/mailman/listinfo/desktc

To subscribe, send a mail to desktop-devel-list-
subject "subscribe".

Installation
============

See the file 'INSTALL'

:w!█
```

Figure 15-4. *Use vi's Command-Line mode to issue commands.*

For a list of basic Command-Line mode commands, see Table 15-2.

Table 15-2. *Some vi Command-Line Mode Commands*

Command	Description
:w	Save the file
:w!	Save the file and ignore errors such as an existing file with the same filename
:q	Quit vi
:q!	Quit vi and ignore errors such as an unsaved file
:s/*word*/*replacement*/	Search from the cursor downward and replace any instances of the word with the replacement[1]
:help	View help documentation

1. *The search tool is very powerful and uses a number of command options for additional flexibility. Read the* vi *help file to learn more.*

Using vi to Edit a File

As an example, let's use vi to edit the The GIMP's README file. You don't want to actually alter this file, so start by making a copy of it in your home directory:

```
cp /usr/share/doc/packages/gimp/README ~
```

This will copy the file README to your /home directory, which you indicate using the ~ symbol. Then fire up vi with the file, like this:

```
vi README
```

■**Note** Windows makes a lot of use of file extensions in order to recognize files and therefore know what program to use to run them. By default, a file with a .doc extension tells Windows that it should use Microsoft Word to open the file, for example. Linux uses a different system based on the first few bytes of each file. Because of this, file extensions are used within Linux simply to let the users know what type of file they're dealing with. Often, they're not used at all. If a file is called README, you can be fairly certain that it's a text file, for example.

Once the file is opened, you'll find yourself automatically in Command mode and will be able to move around the file using the cursor keys. Altering the text is achieved using various commands (see Table 15-1). For example, typing dd will delete the line of text that the cursor is currently within. Typing x will delete the letter under the cursor. Typing dw will delete the current word under the cursor. Try some of these to see how they work.

To actually edit a file and type text, you'll need to switch to Insert mode. Type i to do this. Insert mode is fairly easy to understand. You can move around the text using the cursor keys, and then simply start typing wherever you want. The Delete key will delete text in front of the cursor.

■**Note** In vi, the Backspace key will delete any text you've just typed, but *won't* delete any existing text in the document. To do that, you must use the Delete key.

When you're finished, press the Esc key to return to Command mode. Once back in Command mode, you can page through the text. The Page Up and Page Down keys will move a screenful of text at a time. Pressing the up and down cursor keys will cause the screen to scroll when the cursor reaches the top or bottom.

After you're finished editing, you'll need to save the file. This is done in Command-Line mode. You can enter this mode by typing a colon (:). You'll see a colon appear at the bottom of the screen, and this is where you type the commands. Note that after you type a command, you'll immediately exit Command-Line mode, so if you want to issue another command, you'll need to type a colon again.

To save a file, in Command-Line mode, type :w (which stands for "write"). If you want to save the current file with a different name, you'll need to enter a filename after the w command, like this:

```
:w mytextfile
```

To quit `vi`, type `:q`. However, if you've edited a file, you won't be able to quit until the file has been saved. If you want to save the file and then quit, you can type `:wq`. If you don't want to save the file, type `:q!`. The exclamation point tells `vi` to override any objections it might have. You can also use it with the save command—`:w!`—to force the overwriting of a file that already exists.

■Note If you don't have the correct permissions to write to a file, `vi` might tell you that you can use `:w!` to override. In this case, it's wrong. The only way to write to a file for which you don't have permissions is to change its permissions using the `chmod` command, as described in Chapter 14.

Creating a New Text File Using vi

Creating and editing a new file with `vi` is easy. From any command-line shell, simply type this:

```
vi myfile
```

This will start `vi` and give your new file a name. However, the file won't be saved until you manually issue the save command (`:w`) in `vi`. This means that if your computer crashes before you save, the file will be lost!

■Note The version of `vi` provided with SUSE Linux, `vim`, includes some elementary file-save protection. If, for any reason, `vim` is not shut down properly, there's a chance you'll be able to recover a version of the file the next time `vim` starts. However, as with all such protection in any kind of program, you shouldn't rely on this. You should use the `:w` command to save your file periodically.

As always with `vi`, you start out in the default Command mode. To start typing immediately, enter Insert mode by typing `i`. You'll notice when typing that although the text is wrapped on each line, words are not carried over, and they often break across lines in an ugly way. This is because `vi` is primarily a text editor, not a word processor. For people who create text files, like programmers, having line breaks shown in this way can be useful.

When you're finished typing a sentence or paragraph, you can press the Enter key as usual to start a new line. You should then be able to move between lines using the up and down cursor keys. You'll notice an odd thing when you try to do this, however: unlike with a word processor, moving up a line of text that spreads across more than one line on screen will take the cursor to the start of the line, rather than into the middle of it. This again relates to `vi`'s text editor focus, where such a feature is useful when editing documents such as program configuration files.

When you're finished, press the Esc key to switch to Command mode. Then type a colon to enter Command-Line mode. Type `:w` to save the file using the filename you gave it earlier. If you started `vi` without specifying a filename, you'll need to specify a filename with the save command, such as `:w myfile`.

USING GUI TEXT EDITORS

If all this talk of vi sounds like too much hard work, don't forget that the GNOME desktop includes an excellent text editor in the form of Gedit. The KDE equivalent is Kate. Both of these programs include many handy word processor-like features.

You can call Gedit and open a file in it from the command-line prompt as follows:

```
gedit <filename>
```

Do the same to open a file in Kate:

```
kate <filename>
```

You'll find both programs fairly straightforward to use. If you need to edit a file that requires root powers, simply switch to the root user first, and then issue the command.

Searching Through Files

You can search for particular words or phrases in text files by loading the file into less or vi; you'll find the search commands for vi listed in Table 15-1. The maneuverability offered by both programs lets you leap from point to point in the text, and their use is generally user-friendly.

However, using vi or less can take precious seconds. There's a quicker command-line option that will search through a file in double-quick speed: grep.

Using grep to Find Text

grep stands for Global Regular Expression Print. grep is an extremely powerful tool that can use pattern-based searching techniques to find text in files. *Pattern-based searching* means that grep offers various options to loosen the search so that more results are returned.

The simplest way of using grep is to specify some brief text, followed by the name of the file you want to search. Here's an example:

```
grep 'helloworld' myfile
```

This will search for the phrase helloworld within myfile. If it's found, the entire line that helloworld is on will be displayed on screen.

If you specify the * wildcard instead of a filename, grep will search every file in the directory for the text. Adding the -r command option will cause grep to search all the files, and also search through any directories that are present:

```
grep -r 'helloworld' *
```

Another handy command option is -i, which tells grep to ignore uppercase and lowercase letters when it's searching. Figure 15-5 shows an example of using grep.

Figure 15-5. *grep is a powerful tool that can search for text within files.*

■Tip You might never choose to use grep for searching for text within files, but it can prove very handy when used to search through the output of other commands. This is done by "piping" the output from one command to another, as explained in Chapter 17.

Using Regular Expressions

The true power of grep is achieved by the use of search patterns known as *regular expressions*, or regexes for short. Put simply, regexes allow you to be vague rather than specific when searching, meaning that grep (and many similar tools that use the system of regexes, such as the find command discussed in Chapter 14) will return more results.

For example, you can specify a selection or series of characters (called a *string* in regex terminology) that might appear in a word or phrase you're searching for. This can be useful if you're looking for a word that might be spelled differently from how you anticipate, for example.

The most basic form of regex is the bracket expansion. This is where additional search terms are enclosed in square brackets within a search string. For example, suppose you want to find a file that refers to several drafts of a document you've been working on. The files are called myfile_1draft.doc, myfile_2draft.doc, and so on. To find any document that mentions these files, you could type this:

```
grep 'myfile_[1-9]draft\.doc' *
```

The use of square brackets tells grep to fill in details within the search string based on what's inside the square brackets. In this case, 1-9 means that all the numbers from one to nine should be applied to the search string. It's as if you've told grep to search for myfile_1draft.doc, and then told it to search for myfile_2draft.doc, and so on. Notice that the example has a backslash before the period separating the file extension from the filename. This indicates to grep that it should interpret the period as an element of the string to be searched for, rather than as a wildcard character, which is how grep usually interprets periods.

You don't need to specify a range of characters in this way. You can simply enter whatever selection of characters you want to substitute into the search string. Here's an example:

```
grep 'myfile[12345]\.doc' *
```

This will attempt to find any mention of myfile1.doc, myfile2.doc, myfile3.doc, and so on, in any file within the directory.

Here's another example:

```
grep '[GgNn]ome' *
```

This will let you search for the word Gnome within files, taking into account possible misspelling of the word by people who forget to use the silent *G*, as well as any use of uppercase or lowercase.

This is only scratching the surface of what regexes can do. For example, many regexes can be combined together into one long search string, which can provide astonishing accuracy when searching. Table 15-3 contains some simple examples that should give you an idea of the power and flexibility of regexes.

Table 15-3. *Some Examples of Regular Expressions*

Search String	Description
'document[a-z]'	Returns any lines containing the string "document" followed by any single letter from the range a through z.
'document[A-Za-z]'	Returns any lines containing the string "document" followed by the letters A through Z or a through z. Note that no comma or other character is needed to separate possibilities within square brackets.
'document.'	Returns any lines containing the string "document" followed by any other character. The period is used as a wildcard signifying any single character.
'document[[:digit:]]'	Returns any lines containing the string "document" followed by any number.
'document[[:alpha:]]'	Returns any lines containing the string "document" followed by any character.
'^document'	Returns any lines that have the string "document" at the beginning. The caret symbol (^) tells grep to look only at the beginning of each line.
'document$'	Returns any line that has the string "document" at the end of the line. The dollar sign symbol ($) tells grep to look for the string only at the end of lines.
'document[^1-6]'	Returns lines that have the string "document" in them but not if it's followed by the numbers 1 through 6. When used in square brackets, the caret character (^) produces a nonmatching list—a list of results that don't contain the string.

grep is very powerful. It can be complicated to master, but coupled with good use of regexes, it offers a lot of scope for performing extremely precise searches that ensure you find only what you're seeking. It's well worth reading through its man pages. You can also refer to books on the subject of regexes, of which there are many. A good example is *Regular Expression Recipes: A Problem-Solution Approach*, by Nathan A. Good (1-59059-441-X; Apress, 2004).

Comparing Text Files

If you want to compare the differences between two text files, one way to do this is to use the diff command. This is designed primarily to uncover small changes in otherwise identical documents, such as revisions made by another person. Of course, it can also be used to prove that two files are identical. If you run the files through diff, and it shows no output, it has been unable to spot any differences.

diff is ordinarily used like this:

```
diff mytextfile1 mytextfile2
```

If diff spots any differences between the files, the results are a little more complicated than you might expect. Any lines that are different within the files will appear on screen. Those lines that are identical won't be displayed. Lines preceded with a left angle bracket (<) are from the first file, while those with a right angle bracket (>) are from the second file.

For a different display, you could type something like this:

```
diff -y mytextfile1 mytextfile2
```

This places the two lists side by side and highlights lines that are different with a pipe symbol (|). However, it requires a lot more screen space than using diff without the -y option.

■**Note** When you use the -y command option with diff, it will struggle to fit the output in a standard GNOME Terminal/Konsole window. If it is maximized on a 17-inch screen (1024×768 resolution), it should be just large enough to fit the information in, depending on the complexity of the files being compared.

By specifying the -a command option, you can make diff process binary files, too. This is a handy way of comparing virtually any kind of files, including program files, to see if they're identical. If there's no output from diff, then the two files are identical. If your screen fills with gibberish, then the files are clearly different.

Incidentally, if you want to compare three documents, you can use a very similar command: diff3. Check the command's man page to learn more about how it works.

Summary

In this chapter, we examined how text files can be manipulated. In many ways, the BASH shell is built around manipulating text, and we explored various tools created with this goal in mind. We started with the commands that can display text files (or part of them).

We then looked at how the vi text editor can be used to both edit and create documents. Next, we explored how regexes can be used with the grep command to create sophisticated search strings, which can uncover any text within documents. Finally, you saw how to compare text files.

In the next chapter, we'll look at how you can use various command-line tools to take control of your system.

■■■

## CHAPTER 16

Taking Control of the System

By now, you should be starting to realize that the shell offers an enormous amount of power when it comes to administering your PC. The BASH shell commands give you quick and efficient control over most aspects of your Linux setup. However, the shell truly excels in one area: controlling the processes on your system.

Controlling processes is essential for administration of your system. You can tidy up crashed programs, for example, or even alter the priority of a program so that it runs with a little more consideration for other programs. Unlike with Windows, this degree of control is not considered out of bounds. This is just one more example of how Linux provides complete access to its inner workings and puts you in control.

Without further ado, let's take a look at what can be done.

Viewing Processes

A *process* is something that exists entirely behind the scenes. When the user runs a program, one or many processes might be started, but they're usually invisible unless the user specifically chooses to manipulate them. You might say that programs exist in the world of the user, but processes belong in the world of the system.

Processes can be started not only by the user, but also by the system itself to undertake tasks such as system maintenance, or even to provide basic functionality, such as the GUI system. Many processes are started when the computer boots up, and then they sit in the background, waiting until they're needed (such as programs that send mail). Other processes are designed to work periodically to accomplish certain tasks, such as ensuring system files are up-to-date.

You can see what processes are currently running on your computer by running the top program. Running top is simply a matter of typing the command at the shell prompt.

As you can see in Figure 16-1, top provides very comprehensive information and can be a bit overwhelming at first sight. However, the main area of interest is the list of processes (which top refers to as *tasks*).

```
                                 keir@SUSE:~                          _ □ ×

File  Edit  View  Terminal  Tabs  Help
top - 20:55:08 up 50 min,   3 users,   load average: 0.00, 0.04, 0.08
Tasks:  80 total,   1 running,  79 sleeping,   0 stopped,   0 zombie
Cpu(s):  1.0% us,   1.3% sy,   0.0% ni, 97.3% id,   0.0% wa,   0.3% hi,   0.0% si
Mem:    516400k total,     482732k used,    33668k free,    86012k buffers
Swap:   514072k total,          0k used,   514072k free,   250548k cached

  PID USER      PR  NI  VIRT  RES  SHR S %CPU %MEM   TIME+   COMMAND
 4696 root      15   0 38548  13m 6444 S  1.7  2.7  0:35.47 X
 4790 keir      15   0  184m  24m  18m S  0.3  4.9  0:06.64 nautilus
 4792 keir      15   0  238m 8624 6780 S  0.3  1.7  0:00.20 resapplet
 5252 keir      15   0 35264  15m  10m S  0.3  3.1  0:02.27 gnome-terminal
 5554 keir      16   0  2184 1000  760 R  0.3  0.2  0:00.02 top
    1 root      16   0   716  292  244 S  0.0  0.1  0:00.65 init
    2 root      34  19     0    0    0 S  0.0  0.0  0:00.00 ksoftirqd/0
    3 root      10  -5     0    0    0 S  0.0  0.0  0:00.18 events/0
    4 root      10  -5     0    0    0 S  0.0  0.0  0:00.00 khelper
    5 root      11  -5     0    0    0 S  0.0  0.0  0:00.00 kthread
    7 root      10  -5     0    0    0 S  0.0  0.0  0:00.06 kblockd/0
    8 root      20  -5     0    0    0 S  0.0  0.0  0:00.00 kacpid
   96 root      20   0     0    0    0 S  0.0  0.0  0:00.00 pdflush
   97 root      15   0     0    0    0 S  0.0  0.0  0:00.86 pdflush
   99 root      20  -5     0    0    0 S  0.0  0.0  0:00.00 aio/0
   98 root      15   0     0    0    0 S  0.0  0.0  0:00.11 kswapd0
  305 root      11  -5     0    0    0 S  0.0  0.0  0:00.00 cqueue/0
  306 root      10  -5     0    0    0 S  0.0  0.0  0:00.00 kseriod
  346 root      11  -5     0    0    0 S  0.0  0.0  0:00.00 kpsmoused
  730 root      11  -5     0    0    0 S  0.0  0.0  0:00.00 scsi_eh_0
  762 root      10  -5     0    0    0 S  0.0  0.0  0:00.02 reiserfs/0
```

Figure 16-1. *The top program gives you an eagle-eye view of the processes running on your system.*

Here's an example of a line taken from top's output on my test PC, shown with the column headings from the process list:

```
PID   USER  PR  NI  VIRT   RES  SHR  S  %CPU  %MEM TIME+     COMMAND
5499  root  15  0   78052  25m  60m  S  2.3   5.0  6:11.72   X
```

A lot of information is presented here, as described in Table 16-1.

Table 16-1. *The top Program Process Information*

Column	Description
PID	The first number is the process ID (PID). This is the unique number that the system uses to track the process. The PID comes in handy if you want to kill (terminate) the process (as explained in the next section of this chapter).
USER	This column lists the owner of the particular process. As with files, all processes must have an owner. A lot of processes will appear to be owned by the root user. Some of them are system processes that need to access the system hardware, which is something only the root user is normally allowed to do. Other processes are owned by root for protection; root ownership means that ordinary users cannot tamper with these processes.
PR	This column shows the priority of the process. This is a dynamic number, showing where the particular process is in the CPU queue at the present time.

Column	Description
NI	This column shows the "nice" value of the process. This refers to how charitable a process is in its desire for CPU time. A high figure here (up to 19) indicates that the process is willing to be interrupted for the sake of other processes. A negative value means the opposite: the process is more aggressive than others in its desire for CPU time. Some programs need to operate in this way, and this is not necessarily a bad thing.
VIRT	This column shows the amount of virtual memory used by the process.[1]
RES	This column shows the total amount of physical memory used.[1]
SHR	This column shows the amount of shared memory used. This refers to memory that contains code that is relied on by other processes and programs.
S	This column shows the current status of the task. Generally, the status will either be sleeping, in which case an S will appear, or running, in which case an R will appear. Most processes will be sleeping, even ones that appear to be active. Don't worry about this; it just reflects the way the Linux kernel works. A Z in this column indicates a zombie process (a child of a process that has been terminated).
%CPU	This column shows the CPU use, expressed as a percentage.[2]
%MEM	This column shows the memory use, again expressed as a percentage.[2]
TIME+	This column shows a measure of how long the process has been up and running.
COMMAND	This shows the actual name of the process itself.

1. *Both VIRT and RES are measured in kilobytes unless an m appears alongside the number; in which case, you should read the figure as megabytes.*
2. *The %CPU and %MEM entries tell you in easy-to-understand terms how much of the system resources a process is taking up.*

This list will probably be longer than the screen has space to display, so top orders the list of processes by the amount of CPU time the processes are using. Every few seconds, it updates the list. You can test this quite easily. Let your PC rest for a few seconds, without touching the mouse or typing. Then move the mouse around for a few seconds. You'll see that the process called X leaps to the top of the list (or appears very near the top). X is the program that provides the graphical subsystem for Linux, and making the mouse cursor appear to move around the screen requires CPU time. When nothing else is going on, moving the mouse causes X to appear as the number one user of CPU time on your system.

■**Tip** Typing d while top is running lets you alter the update interval, which is the time between screen updates. The default is three seconds, but you can reduce that to one second or even less if you wish. However, a constantly updating top program starts to consume system resources and can therefore skew the diagnostic results you're investigating. Because of this, a longer, rather than shorter, interval is preferable.

It's possible to alter the ordering of the process list according to other criteria. For example, you can list the processes by the percentage of memory they're using, by typing M while top is up and running. You can switch back to CPU ordering by typing P.

RENICING A PROCESS

You can set how much CPU time a process receives while it's actually running. This is done by *renicing* the process. This isn't something you should do on a regular basis, but it can prove very handy if you start a program that then uses a lot of system resources and makes the system unbearably slow.

The first thing to do is to use top to spot the process that needs to be restrained and find out its PID number. This will be listed on the left of the program's entry on the list. Once you know this, type r, and then type in the PID number. You'll then be asked to specify a renice value. The scale goes from –20, which is considered the highest priority, to 19, which is considered the lowest. Therefore, you should type 19. After this, you should find some responsiveness has returned to the system, although how much (if any) depends on the nature of the programs you're running.

You might be tempted to bump up the priority of a process to make it run faster, but this may not work because of complexities in the Linux kernel. In fact, it might cause serious problems. Therefore, you should renice with care and only when you must.

Controlling Processes

Despite the fact that processes running on your computer are usually hidden away, Linux offers complete, unrestricted, and unapologetic control over them. You can terminate processes, change their properties, and learn every item of information there is to know about them.

This provides ample scope for damaging the currently running system but, in spite of this, even standard users have complete control over processes that they personally started (one exception is *zombie* processes, described a bit later in this section). As you might expect, the root user (or any user who adopts superuser powers) has control over all processes that were created by ordinary users, as well as those processes started by the system itself.

The user is given this degree of control over processes in order to enact repairs when something goes wrong, such as when a program crashes and won't terminate cleanly. It's impossible for standard users to damage the currently running system by undertaking such work, although they can cause themselves a number of problems.

■**Note** This control over processes is what makes Linux so reliable. Because any user can delve into the workings of the kernel and terminate individual processes, crashed programs can be cleaned up with negligible impact on the rest of the system.

Killing Processes

Whenever you quit a program or, in some cases, when it completes the task you've asked of it, it will terminate itself. This means ending its own process and also that of any other processes it created in order to run. The main process is called the *parent*, and the ones it creates are referred to as *child processes*.

■**Tip** You can see a nice graphical display of which parent owns which child process by typing `pstree` at the command-line shell.

While this should mean your system runs smoothly, badly behaved programs sometimes don't go away. They stick around in the process list. Alternatively, you might find that a program crashes and so isn't able to terminate itself. In very rare cases, some programs that appear otherwise healthy might get carried away and start consuming a lot of system resources. You can tell when this happens because your system will start slowing down for no reason, as less and less memory and/or CPU time is available to run actual programs.

In all of these cases, the user usually must kill the process in order to terminate it manually. You can do this easily by using `top`.

The first task is to track down the crashed or otherwise problematic process. In `top`, look for a process that matches the name of the program, as shown in Figure 16-2. For example, the Firefox web browser generally runs as a process called `firefox-bin`.

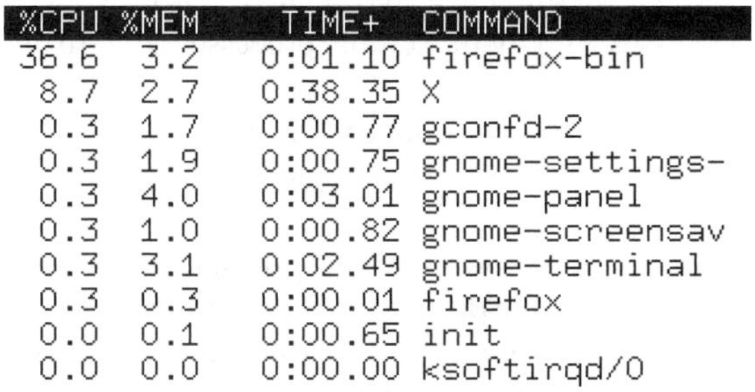

```
%CPU %MEM    TIME+   COMMAND
36.6   3.2   0:01.10 firefox-bin
 8.7   2.7   0:38.35 X
 0.3   1.7   0:00.77 gconfd-2
 0.3   1.9   0:00.75 gnome-settings-
 0.3   4.0   0:03.01 gnome-panel
 0.3   1.0   0:00.82 gnome-screensav
 0.3   3.1   0:02.49 gnome-terminal
 0.3   0.3   0:00.01 firefox
 0.0   0.1   0:00.65 init
 0.0   0.0   0:00.00 ksoftirqd/0
```

Figure 16-2. *You can normally identify a program by its name in the process list.*

■**Caution** You should be absolutely sure that you know the correct process before killing it. If you get it wrong, you could cause other programs to stop running.

Because `top` doesn't show every single process on its screen, tracking down the trouble-causing process can be difficult. A handy tip is to make `top` show only the processes created by the user you're logged in under. This will remove the background processes started by root. You can do this within `top` by typing u, and then entering your username.

Once you've spotted the crashed process, make a note of its PID number, which will be at the very left of its entry in the list. Then type k. You'll be asked to enter the PID number. Enter that number, and then press Enter once again (this will accept the default signal value of 15, which will tell the program to terminate).

With any luck, the process (and the program in question) will disappear. If it doesn't, the process you've killed might be the child of another process that also must be killed. To track down the parent process, you need to configure top to add the PPID field, for the parent process ID, to its display. To add this field, type f, and then b. Press Enter to return to the process list. The PPID column will appear next to the process name on the right of the window. It simply shows the PID of the parent process. You can use this information to look for the parent process within the main list of processes.

The trick here is to make sure that the parent process isn't something that's vital to the running of the system. If it isn't, you can safely kill it. This should have the result of killing the child process you uncovered prior to this.

■**Caution** If the PPID field in top displays a value of 1, that means the process doesn't have a parent process. In both the PPID and PID fields, you should always watch out for low numbers, particularly one-, two-, and three-digit numbers. These are usually processes that started early on when Linux booted and that are essential to the system.

Controlling Zombie Processes

Zombie processes are those that are children of processes that have terminated. However, for some reason, they failed to take their child processes with them. Zombie processes are rare on most Linux systems.

Despite their name, zombie processes are harmless. They're not actually running and don't take up system resources. However, if you want your system to be spick-and-span, you can attempt to kill them.

In the top-right area of top, you can see a display that shows how many zombie processes are running on your system, as shown in Figure 16-3. Zombie processes are easily identified because they have a Z in the status (S) column within top's process list. To kill a zombie process, type k, and then type its PID. Then type 9, rather than accept the default signal of 15.

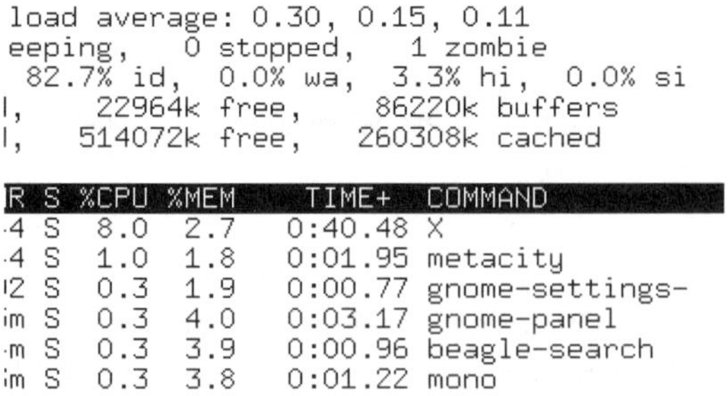

```
load average: 0.30, 0.15, 0.11
eeping,    0 stopped,    1 zombie
 82.7% id,   0.0% wa,   3.3% hi,   0.0% si
|,     22964k free,    86220k buffers
|,    514072k free,   260308k cached

R  S  %CPU  %MEM     TIME+   COMMAND
4  S   8.0   2.7   0:40.48 X
4  S   1.0   1.8   0:01.95 metacity
2  S   0.3   1.9   0:00.77 gnome-settings-
im S   0.3   4.0   0:03.17 gnome-panel
m  S   0.3   3.9   0:00.96 beagle-search
im S   0.3   3.8   0:01.22 mono
```

Figure 16-3. *You can see at a glance how many zombie processes are on your system by looking at the top right of top's display.*

> **■Note** No magic is involved in killing processes. All that happens is that `top` sends them a "terminate" signal. In other words, it contacts them and asks them to terminate. By default, all processes are designed to listen for commands such as this; it's part and parcel of how programs work under Linux. When a program is described as crashed, it means that the user is unable to use the program itself to issue the terminate command (such as `Quit`). A crashed program might not be taking input, but its processes will probably still be running.

In many cases, zombie processes simply won't go away. When this happens, you have two options. The first is to restart the program that is likely to be the zombie's owner, in the hope that it will reattach with the zombie, and then quit the program. With any luck, it will take the zombie child with it this time. Alternatively, you can simply reboot your PC. But it's important to note that zombie processes are harmless and can be left in peace on your system!

Using Other Commands to Control Processes

You don't always need to use `top` to control processes. A range of quick and cheerful shell commands can diagnose and treat process problems.

The first of these is the `ps` command. This stands for Process Status and will report a list of currently running processes on your system. This command is normally used with the `-aux` options:

```
ps -aux
```

These limit the results to your user account, returning a list something like what you see when you run `top`.

If you can spot the problematic process, look for its PID and issue the following command:

```
kill <PID number>
```

For example, to kill a process with a PID of 5122, you would type this:

```
kill 5122
```

If, after this, you find the process isn't killed, then you should use the `top` program, as described in the previous sections, because it allows for a more in-depth investigation.

Another handy process-killing command lets you use the actual process name. The `killall` command is handy if you already know from past experience what a program's process is called. For example, to kill the process called `firefox-bin`, which is the chief process of the Firefox web browser, you would use the following command:

```
killall firefox-bin
```

> **■Caution** Make sure you're as specific as possible when using the `killall` command. Issuing a command like `killall bin` will kill all processes that might have the word `bin` in them!

CLEARING UP CRASHES

Sometimes, a crashed process can cause all kinds of problems. The shell you're working at may stop working, or the GUI itself might stop working properly.

In cases like this, it's important to remember that you can have more that one instance of the command-line shell up and running at any one time. For example, if a process crashes and locks up GNOME Terminal or Konsole, simply start a new instance of GNOME Terminal/Konsole. Then use `top` within the new window to kill the process that is causing trouble for the other terminal window.

If the crashed program affects the entire GUI, you can switch to a virtual console by pressing Ctrl+Alt+F1. Although the GUI disappears, you will not have killed it, and no programs will stop running. Instead, you've simply moved the GUI to the background while a shell console takes over the screen. Then you can use the virtual console to run `top` and attempt to kill the process that is causing all the problems. When you're ready, you can switch back to the GUI by pressing Ctrl+Alt+F7.

Controlling Jobs

Whenever you start a program at the shell, it's assigned a job number. Jobs are quite separate from processes and are designed primarily for users to understand what programs are running on the system.

You can see which jobs are running at any one time by typing the following at the shell prompt:

```
jobs
```

When you run a program, it usually takes over the shell in some way and stops you from doing anything until it's finished what it's doing. However, it doesn't have to be this way. Adding an ampersand symbol (&) after the command will cause it to run in the background. This is not much use for commands that require user input, such as `vi` or `top`, but it can be very handy for commands that churn away until they're completed.

For example, suppose that you want to decompress a large zip file. For this, you can use the `unzip` command. As with Windows, decompressing large zip files can take a lot of time, during which time the shell would effectively be unusable. However, you can type the following to retain use of the shell:

```
unzip myfile.zip &
```

When you do this, you'll see something similar to the following, although the four-digit number will be different:

```
[1] 7483
```

This tells you that `unzip` is running in the background and has been given job number 1. It also has been given process number 7483 (although bear in mind that when some programs start, they instantly kick off other processes and terminate the one they're currently running, so this won't necessarily be accurate).

Tip If you've ever tried to run a GUI program from the shell, you might have realized that the shell is inaccessible while it's running. Once you quit the GUI program, the control of the shell will be returned to you. By specifying that the program should run in the background with the & (ampersand symbol), you can run the GUI program and still be able to type away and run other commands.

You can send several jobs to the background, and each one will be given a different job number. In this case, when you wish to switch into a running job, you can type its number. For example, the following command will switch you to the background job assigned the number 3:

%3

You can exit a job that is currently running by pressing Ctrl+Z. It will still be there in the background, but it won't be running (it's said to be *sleeping*). To restart it, you can switch back to it, as just described. Alternatively, you can restart it but still keep it in the background. For example, to restart job 2 in the background, leaving the shell prompt free for you to enter other commands, type the following:

%2 &

You can bring the command in the background into the foreground by typing the following:

fg

When a background job has finished, something like the following will appear at the shell:

```
[1]+ Done unzip myfile.zip
```

Using jobs within the shell can be a good way of managing your workload. For example, you can move programs into the background temporarily while you get on with something else. If you're editing a file in vi, you can press Ctrl+Z to stop the program. It will remain in the background, and you'll be returned to the shell, where you can type other commands. You can then resume vi later on by typing fg or by typing % followed by its job number.

Summary

This chapter has covered taking complete control of your system. We've looked at what processes are, how they're separate from programs, and how they can be controlled or viewed using programs such as top and ps. In addition, we explored job management under BASH. You saw that you can stop, start, and pause programs at your convenience.

In the next chapter, we'll take a look at several tricks and techniques that you can use with the BASH shell to finely hone your command-line skills.

■ ■ ■

## CHAPTER 17

Cool Shell Tricks

The BASH shell is the product of many years of development work by a lot of people. It comes from the old days of Unix and was an important step in the evolution of computer software. It's a program that retains complete simplicity, yet packs in more features than most users could ever hope to use.

One of the best things about the shell is its sheer power. If you ever wonder if you can do a task differently (and more efficiently), you'll probably find that one of the many BASH developers has implemented a method to do so. Once you learn these techniques, you'll find you can whiz around the shell at blinding speed. It's just a matter of exploring the far reaches of the shell, and that's what you'll do in this chapter. Hold onto your hats, because it's an exciting ride!

Using Autocompletion

The Tab key is your best friend when using the shell, because it will cause BASH to automatically complete whatever you type. For example, if you want to run the Firefox web browser, you can enter firefox at the command line. However, to save yourself some time, you can type fir, and then press Tab. You'll then find that BASH fills in the rest for you. It does this by caching the names of the programs you might run according to the directories listed in your $PATH variable (see Chapter 13).

Of course, autocompletion has some limitations. On my SUSE Linux test system, typing loc didn't autocomplete locate, the search command discussed in Chapter 14. Instead, it caused BASH to beep. This is because on a default SUSE Linux installation, there is more than one possible match. Pressing Tab again shows those matches. Depending on how much you type (how much of an initial clue you give BASH), you might find there are many possible matches.

In this case, the experienced BASH user simply types another letter, which will be enough to distinguish the almost-typed word from the rest, and presses Tab again. With any luck, this should be enough for BASH to fill in the rest.

Autocompletion with Files and Paths

Tab autocompletion also works with files and paths. If you type the first few letters of a directory name, BASH will try to fill in the rest. This also obviously has limitations. There's no point in typing cd myfol and pressing Tab if there's nothing in the current directory that starts with the letters myfol. This particular autocomplete function works by looking at your current directory and seeing what's available.

Alternatively, you can specify an initial path for BASH to use in order to autocomplete. Typing cd /ho and pressing Tab will cause BASH to autocomplete the path by looking in the root directory (/). In other words, it will autocomplete the command with the directory home. In a similar way, typing cd myfolder/myfo will cause BASH to attempt to autocomplete by looking for a match in myfolder.

If you want to run a program that resides in the current directory, such as one you've just downloaded for example, typing ./, followed by the first part of the program name, and then pressing Tab should be enough to have BASH autocomplete the rest. In this case, the dot and slash tell BASH to look in the current directory for any executable programs or scripts (programs with x as part of their permissions) and use them as possible autocomplete options.

BASH is clever enough to spot whether the command you're using is likely to require a file, directory, or executable, and it will autocomplete with only relevant file or directory names.

Viewing Available Options

The autocomplete function has a neat side effect. As I mentioned earlier, if BASH cannot find a match, pressing Tab again causes BASH to show all the available options. For example, typing ba at the shell, and then pressing Tab twice will cause BASH to show all the possible commands starting with the letters ba. On my test PC, this produces the following list of commands:

banshee basename bash bashbug batch

This can be a nice way of exploring what commands are available on your system. You can then use each command with the –help command option to find out what it does, or browse the command's man page.

When you apply this trick to directory and filename autocompletion, it's even more useful. For example, typing cd in a directory and then pressing the Tab key twice will cause BASH to show the available directories, providing a handy way of retrieving a brief directory listing. Alternatively, if you've forgotten how a directory name is spelled, you can use this technique to find out prior to switching into it.

Figure 17-1 shows a few examples of using this technique with BASH.

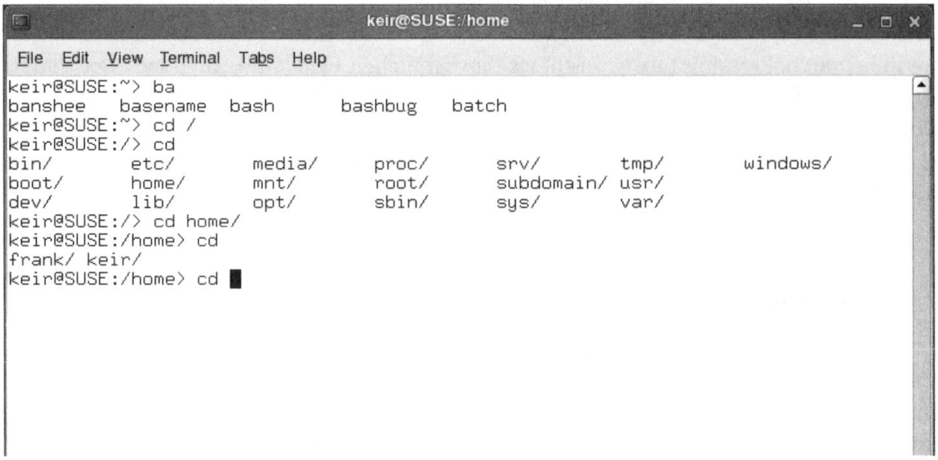

Figure 17-1. *Autocompletion makes using BASH much easier.*

Using Keyboard Shortcuts

Your other good friends when using BASH are the Ctrl and Alt keys. These keys provide shortcuts to vital command-line shell functions. They also let you work more efficiently when typing by providing what most programs call keyboard shortcuts.

Shortcuts for Working in BASH

Table 17-1 lists the most common keyboard shortcuts in BASH (there are many more; see BASH's man page for details). If you've explored the Emacs text editor, you might find these shortcuts familiar. Such keyboard shortcuts are largely the same across many of the software packages that originate from the GNU Project. Often, you'll find an option within many SUSE Linux software packages that lets you use Emacs-style navigation, in which case these keyboard shortcuts will most likely work equally well.

Table 17-1. *Keyboard Shortcuts in BASH*

Shortcut	Description
Navigation	
Left/right cursor key	Move left/right in text
Ctrl+A	Move to beginning of line
Ctrl+E	Move to end of line
Ctrl+right arrow	Move forward one word
Ctrl+left arrow	Move left one word
Editing	
Ctrl+U	Delete everything behind cursor to start of line
Ctrl+K	Delete from cursor to end of line
Ctrl+W	Delete from cursor to beginning of word
Alt+D	Delete from cursor to end of word
Ctrl+T	Transpose characters on left and right of cursor
Alt+T	Transpose words on left and right of cursor
Miscellaneous	
Ctrl+L	Clear screen (everything above current line)
Ctrl+U	Undo everything since last command[1]
Alt+R	Undo changes made to the line[2]
Ctrl+Y	Undo deletion of word or line caused by using Ctrl+K, Ctrl+W, and so on[3]
Alt+L	Lowercase current word (from the cursor to end of word)

1. *In most cases, this has the effect of clearing the line.*
2. *This is different from Ctrl+U, because it will leave intact any command already on the line, such as one pulled from your command history.*
3. *This allows primitive cutting and pasting. Delete the text and then immediately undo, after which the text will remain in the buffer and can be pasted with Ctrl+Y.*

Shortcuts for System Control

In terms of the control over your system offered by keyboard commands, as mentioned in Chapter 16, pressing Ctrl+Z has the effect of stopping the current program. It suspends the program until you switch back into it or tell it to resume in another way, or manually kill it.

In the same style, pressing Ctrl+C while a program is running will quit it. This sends the program's process a termination signal, a little like killing it using the top program. Ctrl+C can prove handy if you start a program by accident and quickly want to end it, or if a command takes longer than you expected to work and you cannot wait for it to complete. It's also a handy way of attempting to end crashed programs. Some more complex programs don't take too kindly to being quit in this way, particularly those that need to save data before they terminate. However, most should be okay.

Ctrl+D is another handy keyboard shortcut. This sends the program an end-of-file (EOF) message. In effect, this tells the program that you've finished your input. This can have a variety of effects, depending on the program you're running. For example, pressing Ctrl+D on its own at the shell prompt when no program is running will cause you to log out (if you're using a GUI terminal emulator like GNOME Terminal or Konsole, the program will quit). This happens because pressing Ctrl+D informs the BASH shell program that you've finished your input. BASH then interprets this as the cue that it should log you out. After all, what else can it do if told there will be no more input?

While it might not seem very useful for day-to-day work, Ctrl+D is vital for programs that expect you to enter data at the command line. You might run into these as you explore BASH. If you ever read in a man page that a program requires an EOF message during input, you'll know what to press.

Using the Command History

The original hackers who invented the tools used under Unix hated waiting around for things to happen. After all, being a hacker is all about finding the most efficient way of doing any particular task.

Because of this, the BASH shell includes many features designed to optimize the user experience. The most important of these is the *command history*. BASH remembers every command you enter (even the ones that don't work!) and stores them as a list on your hard disk.

During any BASH session, you can cycle through this history using the up and down arrow keys. Pressing the up arrow key takes you back into the command history, and pressing the down arrow key takes you forward.

The potential of the command history is enormous. For example, rather than retype that long command that runs a program with command options, you can simply use the cursor keys to locate it in the history and press Enter.

■**Tip** Typing !-3 will cause BASH to move three paces back in the history file and run that command. In other words, it will run what you entered three commands ago.

On my SUSE Linux test system, BASH remembers 1,000 commands. You can view all of the remembered commands by typing `history` at the command prompt. The history list will scroll off the screen because it's so large, but you can use the scroll bars of the GNOME Terminal/Konsole window to read it.

Each command in the history list is assigned a number. You can run any of the history commands by preceding their number with an exclamation mark (!), referred to as a *bang*, or sometimes a *shriek*. For example, you might type `!923`. On my test system, command number 923 in the BASH history is `cd ..`, so this has the effect of switching me into the parent directory.

Command numbering remains in place until you log out (close the GNOME Terminal/Konsole window or end a virtual console session). After this, the numbering is reordered. There will still be 1,000 commands, but the last command you entered before logging out will be at the end of the list, and the numbering will work back 1,000 places until the first command in the history list.

■**Tip** One neat trick is to type two bangs: `!!`. This tells BASH to repeat the last command you entered.

Rather than specifying a command number, you can type something like `!cd`. This will cause BASH to look in the history file, find the last instance of a command line that started with `cd`, and then run it.

Pressing Ctrl+R lets you search the command history from the command prompt. This particular tool can be tricky to get used to, however. As soon as you start typing, BASH will autocomplete the command based on matches found in the history file, starting with the last command in the history. What you type appears before the colon, while the autocompletion appears afterward.

Because BASH autocompletes as you type, things can get a little confusing when you're working with the command history, particularly if it initially gets the match wrong. For example, typing `cd` will show the last instance of the use of `cd`, as in the example in Figure 17-2. This might not be what you're looking for, so you must keep typing the command you do want until it autocompletes correctly.

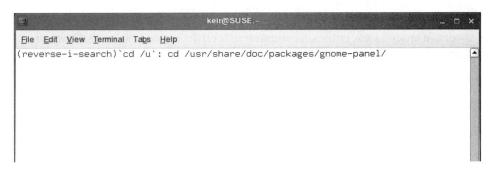

Figure 17-2. *BASH history completion is very useful but can also be confusing.*

Piping and Redirecting Output

It's not uncommon for a directory listing or output from another command to scroll off the screen. When using a GUI program like GNOME Terminal or Konsole, you can use the scroll bars to view the output, but what if you are working at the bare command-line prompt?

By pressing Shift+Page Up and Shift+Page Down, you can "scroll" the window up to take a look at some of the old output, but very little is cached in this way, and you won't see more than a few screens. A far better solution is to *pipe* the output of the directory listing into a text viewer. Another useful technique is to *redirect* output to a file.

Piping the Output of Commands

Piping was one of the original innovations provided by Unix. It simply means that you can pass the output of one command to another, which is to say the output of one command can be used as input for another.

This is possible because shell commands work like machines. They usually take input from the keyboard (referred to technically as *standard input*) and, when they've done their job, usually show their output on the screen (known as *standard output*).

The commands don't need to take input from the keyboard, and they don't need to output to the screen. Piping is the process of diverting the output before it reaches the screen and passing it to another command for further processing.

Let's assume that you have a directory that is packed full of files. You want to do a long directory listing (ls -l) to see what permissions various files have. But doing this produces reams of output that fly off the screen. Typing something like the following provides a solution:

```
ls -l | less
```

The | symbol between the two commands is the pipe. It can be found on most US keyboards next to the square bracket keys (above the Enter key; you'll need to hold down the Shift key to get it).

What happens in the example is that ls -l is run by the shell, but rather than sending the output to the screen, the pipe symbol (|) tells BASH to send it to the command that follows—to less. In other words, the listing is displayed within less, where you can read it at your leisure. You can use Page Up and Page Down or the arrow keys to scroll through it. Once you quit less, the listing evaporates into thin air; the piped output is never actually stored as a file.

In the previous section, you saw how you can use the history command to view the command history. At around 1,000 entries, its output scrolls off the screen in seconds. However, you can pipe it to less, like so:

```
history | less
```

Figure 17-3 shows the result on my test PC.

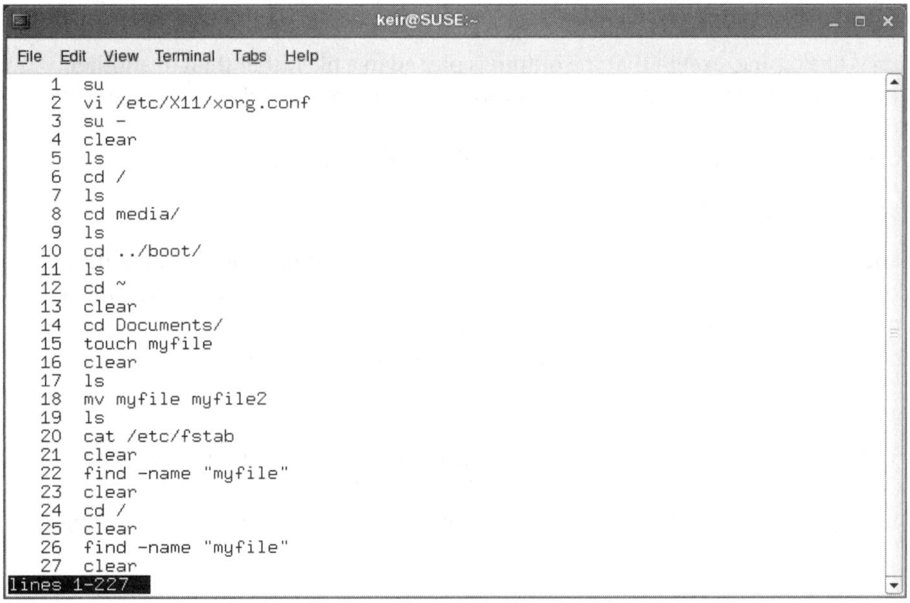

```
                          keir@SUSE:~                    _ □ x
File  Edit  View  Terminal  Tabs  Help
    1   su
    2   vi /etc/X11/xorg.conf
    3   su -
    4   clear
    5   ls
    6   cd /
    7   ls
    8   cd media/
    9   ls
   10   cd ../boot/
   11   ls
   12   cd ~
   13   clear
   14   cd Documents/
   15   touch myfile
   16   clear
   17   ls
   18   mv myfile myfile2
   19   ls
   20   cat /etc/fstab
   21   clear
   22   find -name "myfile"
   23   clear
   24   cd /
   25   clear
   26   find -name "myfile"
   27   clear
lines 1-227
```

Figure 17-3. *Piping the output of the history command into the less command lets you read the output fully.*

You can pipe the output of any command. One of the most common uses is when searching for a particular string in the output of a command. For example, let's say you know that, within a crowded directory, there's a file with a picture of some flowers. You know that the word *flower* is in the filename, but can't recall any other details. One solution is to perform a directory listing, and then pipe the results to grep, which is able to search through text for a user-defined string (see Chapter 15):

```
ls -l | grep -i 'flower'
```

In this example, the shell runs the ls -l command and then passes the output to grep. The grep command then searches the output for the word *flower* (the -i option tells it to ignore uppercase and lowercase). If grep finds any results, it will show them on your screen.

The key point to remember is that grep is used here as it normally is at the command prompt. The only difference is that it's being passed input from a previous command, rather than being used on its own.

You can pipe more than once on a command line. Suppose you know that the filename of the picture you want includes the words *flower* and *daffodil*, yet you're unsure of where they might fall in the filename. In this case, you could type the following:

```
ls -l | grep -i flower | grep -i daffodil
```

This will pass the result of the directory listing to the first grep, which will search the output for the word *flower*. The second pipe causes the output from grep to be passed to the second grep command, where it's then searched for the word *daffodil*. Any results are then displayed on your screen.

Redirecting Output

Redirecting is like piping, except that the output is passed to a file rather than to another command. Redirecting can also work the other way: the contents of a file can be passed to a command.

If you wanted to create a file that contained a directory listing, you could type this:

```
ls -l > directorylisting.txt
```

The angle bracket (>) between the commands tells BASH to direct the output of the `ls -l` command into a file called `directorylisting.txt`. If a file with this name exists, it's overwritten with new data. If it doesn't exist, it's created from scratch.

You can add data to an already existing file using two angle brackets:

```
ls -l >> directorylisting.txt
```

This will append the result of the directory listing to the end of the file `directorylisting.txt`, although, once again, if the file doesn't exist, it will be created from scratch.

Redirecting output can get very sophisticated and useful. Take a look at the following:

```
cat myfile1.txt myfile2.txt > myfile3.txt
```

As you learned in Chapter 15, the `cat` command joins two or more files together. If the command were used on its own without the redirection, it would cause BASH to print `myfile1.txt` on the screen, immediately followed by `myfile2.txt`. As far as BASH is concerned, it has joined `myfile1.txt` to `myfile2.txt`, and then sent them to standard output (the screen). By specifying a redirection, you have BASH send the output to a third file. Using `cat` with redirection is a handy way of combining two files.

It's also possible to direct the contents of a file back into a command. Take a look at the following:

```
sort < textfile.txt > sortedtext.txt
```

The `sort` command simply sorts words into alphanumeric order (it actually sorts them according to the ASCII table of characters, which places symbols and numbers before alphabetic characters). Directly after the `sort` command is a left angle bracket, which directs the contents of the file specified immediately after the bracket into the `sort` command. This is followed by a right angle bracket, which directs the output of the command into another file.

■**Tip** To see a table of the ASCII characters, type `man ascii` at the command-line prompt.

There aren't many instances where you'll want to use the left angle bracket. It's mostly used with the text-based `mail` program (which lets you send e-mail from the shell), and in shell scripting, in which a lot of commands are combined together to form a simple program.

REDIRECTING STANDARD ERROR OUTPUT

Standard input and *standard output* are what BASH calls your keyboard and screen, respectively. These are the default input and output methods that programs use unless you specify something else, such as redirecting or piping output and input.

When a program goes wrong, its error message doesn't usually form part of standard output. Instead, it is output via standard error. Like standard output, this usually appears on the screen.

Sometimes, it's very beneficial to capture an error message in a text file. This can be done by redirecting the *standard error* output. The technique is very similar to redirecting standard output:

```
cdrecord –scanbus 2> errormessage.txt
```

The `cdrecord` command is used to burn CDs, and with the `–scanbus` command option, you tell it to search for CD-R/RW drives on the system, something which frequently results in an error message if your system is not properly configured.

After the initial command, you see the redirection. To redirect standard error, all you need to do is type `2>`, rather than simply `>`. This effectively tells BASH to use the second type of output: standard error.

You can direct both standard output and standard error to the same file. This is done in the following way:

```
cdrecord –scanbus > error.txt 2>&1
```

This is a little more complicated. The standard output from `cdrecord –scanbus` is sent to the file `error.txt`. The second redirect tells BASH to include standard error in the standard output. In other words, it's not a case of standard output being written to a file, and then standard error being added to it. Instead, the standard error is added to standard output by BASH, and then this is written to a file.

Summary

In this chapter, we've looked at some tricks and tips to help you use the BASH shell more effectively. You've seen how BASH can help by autocompleting commands, filenames, and directories. You also learned about keyboard shortcuts that can be used to speed up operations within the shell.

This chapter also covered the command history function and how it can be used to reuse old commands, saving valuable typing time. Finally, we looked at two key functions provided by BASH: redirection and piping. This involved the explanation of standard input, output, and error.

In Part 5 of the book, starting with the next chapter, we move on to discuss the multimedia functionality within SUSE Linux.

PART V

Multimedia

## CHAPTER 18

Digital Music

Today's PC is a multimedia powerhouse, and it's hard to come across a home computer that doesn't have at least a set of speakers attached. Some people take this to extremes, adding surround-sound and even large monitors for crystal-clear video playback. In an effort to meet the growing demand for using Linux as a multimedia station, the people behind SUSE Linux include audio and video players with the distribution.

In this chapter, you'll learn how to listen to audio files on your SUSE Linux system, as well as rip and burn CDs. In the next chapter, you'll learn how to manage video playback.

Issues Surrounding Multimedia on Linux

As you might have read in the press, multimedia playback on computer devices, and Linux in particular, is hindered by a number of issues, including software patents and Digital Rights Management (DRM).

Audio and video playback technologies such as MPEG (including MP3) are patented in countries that allow software to be patented, such as the United States. A *patent* protects the implementation of an idea, as opposed to a *copyright*, which protects the actual software. Patents are designed to restrict the use of a particular technological concept unless permission is granted, usually via a payment to the license holder.

■Note The United States and Japan both have laws allowing software to be patented. Most other countries, including those within the European Union, do not currently allow software patents.

Because Linux is based on the sharing of computing technology and knowledge, organizations like SUSE are fundamentally and philosophically opposed to any kind of software patenting. This means that some patented multimedia technologies aren't supported under SUSE Linux out of the box. This doesn't make playback of popular music and video files impossible under SUSE Linux, but it does mean that, in some cases, extra software must be downloaded and installed.

Much more concerning than patenting is DRM, a technology tied into audio and video playback software. It's designed to control how, where, when, and on what device you can play certain media. For example, Apple's iTunes DRM scheme intends for you to play back MP3s bought from iTunes only on its iPod range of devices (including the Motorola Rokr phone) or using the iTunes software. DVD movie players include a form of DRM called Content Scrambling System (CSS), which prevents users from playing DVDs on computers unless special software is purchased.

Perhaps it goes without saying that the Linux community, including the SUSE Linux project, is fundamentally opposed to DRM. Because of this, practically no DRM software has been officially ported to Linux, so you can't, for example, play music purchased via the iTunes or Napster online stores.

Linux and other open source programmers are very resourceful and are often able to reverse-engineer technology formats in order to get around DRM or patent issues. But the laws in many countries—with the United States as a particularly strident example—prohibit reverse-engineering in this way. In addition, the laws in some countries seek to prohibit use of software resulting from this process.

■**Note** You may be wondering why music and movie corporations are so intent on enforcing DRM and patenting if these schemes give their customers such a hard time. To learn more, and to find out what you can do to help halt the progress of such technology, visit the Electronic Frontier Foundation's web site at www.eff.org.

Programmers have also come up with Free Software alternatives to proprietary formats. Examples include the Ogg Vorbis media format, which is every bit as good as MP3 and unencumbered by patent issues. But at the moment, there's no ideal open source video format in widespread use.

The version of SUSE Linux supplied with this book comes with built-in support for MP3, courtesy of RealPlayer. However, if you're using a version of SUSE Linux 10.1 sourced from the http://opensuse.org web site, you'll need to manually add in MP3 support. And if you want to be able to play popular video file formats, such as Windows Media and QuickTime, you'll need to add support for those.

Throughout this and the next chapter, you'll learn how to install the necessary software, some of which may have issues surrounding patenting. In one case, the software is designed to bypass the DRM scheme that protects DVD movie discs.

How SUSE Linux Handles Multimedia

In simple terms, you need the following three software components for multimedia playback under SUSE Linux:

Player application: This is the software that's actually used to listen to music or watch videos. Under the GNOME desktop of SUSE Linux, Totem Movie Player is used to play back video and Banshee Music Player is used to handle audio. Under the KDE desktop, Kaffeine is used to play back movies and armaroK is used to handle audio playback.

Multimedia framework: This is like the behind-the-scenes middleman who puts the player application in touch with the *codecs*, which are described next. The multimedia framework is a background component of your system, and you won't come into direct contact with it, except when you're initially configuring your system for media playback.

However, the multimedia framework can be switched for another, and this is sometimes necessary to use certain codecs. The multimedia framework preferred by the GNOME desktop is called GStreamer. The KDE desktop's multimedia framework is called Xine.

Codecs: Short for *coder-decoder*, codecs are the small pieces of software that handle multimedia file decoding. Codecs do all the hard work. Most multimedia file formats are compressed, and the codec's job is to expand the files again so that they can be played back on your computer. (Some codecs also work the other way around to shrink files.) Several codecs are installed on SUSE Linux by default, including those to play back MP3 and Ogg Vorbis (Ogg, for short) files.

Under SUSE Linux, the player applications and multimedia frameworks are installed by default. However, to play back common video formats, such as Windows Media and Quick-Time, you need to install additional codecs. These are normally downloaded from third-party web sites.

Adding MP3 Support to SUSE Linux

The version of SUSE Linux supplied with this book includes MP3 support out of the box, courtesy of RealPlayer. MP3 playback isn't limited to the RealPlayer application, though. A RealPlayer plug-in called Helix Engine is used to extend MP3 playback to Banshee, provided with the GNOME desktop, and amaroK, provided with KDE. Therefore, you can skip this section if you're using the version of SUSE Linux supplied with this book. However, if you've downloaded SUSE Linux 10.1 from the http://opensuse.org web site, you can add MP3 support as described here.

Downloading the Fluendo Codec

Fluendo, a software development company, has released a version of the MP3 codec for use with GStreamer. The GStreamer multimedia framework is used by default under GNOME, but it can also be used with the KDE desktop's multimedia applications.

Although there are other versions of the MP3 codec available for Linux, Fluendo has paid licensing fees to the patent holders of MP3, meaning all Linux users can enjoy listening to MP3s without any potential misgivings about using unlicensed software.

■**Note** Of course, using a licensed MP3 codec doesn't do away with the issues surrounding patenting that makes many Free Software users dislike the MP3 format. However, it does leave you, as a user, in the best possible ethical position if you wish to play back MP3 music on your computer.

To download the codec, visit www.fluendo.com. Currently, the steps to download the codec are as follows (it's possible that the web site will have changed since this book was written):

1. Click the Downloads link, and then click the link for the Fluendo Webshop.

2. Click the link to purchase the i386 without IPP MP3 codec (there is no charge for the codec, but you must still go through the motions of buying it), as shown in Figure 18-1.

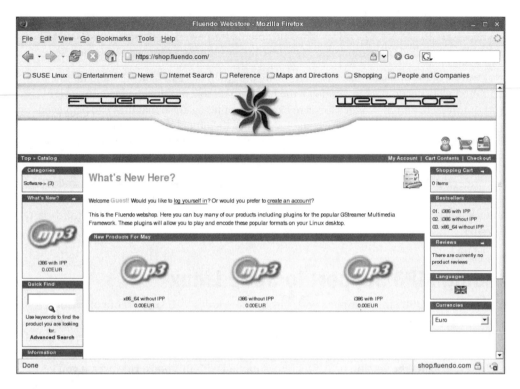

Figure 18-1. *Fluendo offers a free and legally licensed MP3 codec for use under all versions of Linux.*

■**Note** IPP stands for Intel Performance Primitives. Put simply, IPP-enabled software should run faster on certain processors. I advise that you download the non-IPP version of the MP3 codec to ensure full compatibility. The non-IPP version will appear to be as quick as the IPP version on nearly all computers.

---

3. In the distribution drop-down list on the following page, select Generic, and then click the Add to Cart button.

4. Click Checkout on the next web page.

5. Choose to create an account.

6. After you've created an account, continue to the checkout page and place the order.

7. You should receive an e-mail message that includes a link to an invoice address. Follow this link, and you should find the download link for the codec at the bottom of the page.

GNOME: Installing the MP3 Codec Under Banshee

After you've downloaded the Fluendo MP3 codec file, you just need to enter a few commands to install it.

■**Note** The instructions here are necessary (and will work) only if you're using a version of SUSE Linux 10.1 downloaded from http://opensuse.org, in which Banshee is configured to use GStreamer. The version of Banshee provided with this book is configured to use the Helix Engine framework and already includes MP3 support.

Open a terminal window (Applications ➤ System ➤ Terminal ➤ Gnome Terminal) and type the following commands (assuming that the file has been downloaded to the desktop):

```
tar zxf Desktop/gst-fluendo-mp3-0.10.0.i386.tar.gz
mkdir -p ~/.gstreamer-0.10/plugins
cp ~/gst-fluendo-mp3-0.10.0.i386/libgstflump3dec.so ~/.gstreamer-0.10/plugins
```

In these commands, you may need to replace the name shown here with the name of the file you downloaded, as well as replace the name of the folder created from the archive file. If Banshee was already running when you installed the MP3 codec, you will need to restart it.

Once this is done, you will find that MP3 files play perfectly in Banshee, GNOME's MP3 player. For instructions on how to use Banshee, see the "Playing Music Files" section later in this chapter.

KDE: Installing the MP3 Codec Under amaroK

In the openSUSE version of SUSE Linux 10.1, amaroK is configured to use the Xine multimedia framework. However, it can be made to work with GStreamer, which means that you can use the Fluendo MP3 codec.

■**Note** The instructions here are necessary only if you're using a version of SUSE Linux 10.1 downloaded from http://opensuse.org, in which amaroK is configured to use the Xine multimedia framework. The version of amaroK provided with this book is configured to use the Helix Engine framework and already includes MP3 support.

After you've downloaded the Fluendo codec, follow these steps to switch to GStreamer, install the codec, and configure amaroK:

1. Open a browser window and visit the following address:

    ```
    http://download.opensuse.org/distribution/SL-10.1/inst-source/suse ➥
    /i586/amarok-gstreamer-1.3.8-34.i586.rpm
    ```

2. This will prompt you to download a file. Save it to your desktop.

3. Open a Konsole terminal window (K menu ➤ System ➤ Terminal ➤ Konsole) and type the following:

```
su
[Enter root password]
rug install gstreamer010
rpm -Uvh Desktop/amarok-gstreamer-1.3.8-34.i586.rpm
rug install gstreamer010-plugins-base gstreamer010-plugins-good gs ➥
treamer010-plugins-base-oil gstreamer010-plugins-base-visual
exit
```

4. Insert the SUSE Linux DVD to install the software, as prompted.

5. In a terminal window, type the following commands (assuming that the file has been downloaded to the desktop):

```
tar zxf Desktop/gst-fluendo-mp3-0.10.0.i386.tar.gz
mkdir -p ~/.gstreamer-0.10/plugins
cp ~/gst-fluendo-mp3-0.10.0.i386/libgstflump3dec.so ~/.gstreamer-0.10/plugins
```

In these commands, you may need to replace the name shown here with the name of the file you downloaded, as well as replace the name of the folder created from the archive file.

6. Start amaroK (K menu ➤ Multimedia ➤ Audio Player) and cancel the startup wizard.

7. Select Settings ➤ Configure amaroK.

8. Click the Engine icon on the left side of the dialog box. In the Sound System drop-down list, select GStreamer 0.10 Engine. Click OK to close the dialog box.

amaroK should now be able to play MP3 files. The following section provides instructions on how to use amaroK.

Playing Music Files

As noted earlier, the GNOME and KDE desktops use different audio player applications. GNOME offers Banshee; KDE offers amaroK. Both are loosely similar to Apple's iTunes, which you might have used under Windows, in that they not only play MP3s, but also include tools to help manage your MP3 collection.

■**Tip** Don't forget that there's no reason why KDE's amaroK application can't be used under GNOME, or Banshee under KDE. Just search for and install the software using YaST2's Software Manager applet, and then run it from either the K or Applications menu.

GNOME: Using Banshee

You'll find Banshee on the Applications ➤ Multimedia ➤ Audio Player menu. It's a relatively unsophisticated application that's very easy to use.

The first time you run the program, the Import Music to Library dialog box will appear. By selecting the location of your MP3 collection in the Choose an Import Source drop-down list, you can catalog the music within Banshee, which makes playing any of your MP3 tunes a matter of selecting them within Banshee's main listing.

■**Note** Unlike Apple iTunes, Banshee won't automatically copy any music it imports into its own library. If you wish this to happen, click Edit ➤ Preferences within the program, and then check the option to Copy Files to Banshee Music Folder When Importing to Library. Banshee's music collection is stored in the `Music` directory within your `/home` folder.

When the program starts, your music files will be listed on the right side of the program window. Any playlists you might have created are listed on the left side on the program window. Selecting the Music Library icon will show all the files in your MP3 collection, as shown in Figure 18-2.

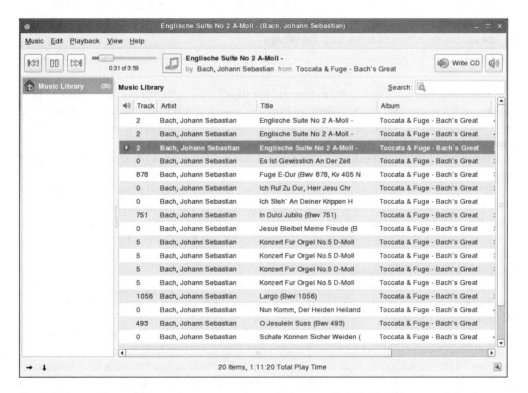

Figure 18-2. *Banshee will organize your music tracks into an alphabetical list, sorted first by artist name and then by track name.*

At the top left of the program window are simple transport controls that allow you to play or pause music, or move backward and forward in the track listing. Whenever an MP3 track is playing, or paused, a time bar will appear here, indicating the progress through the current track. Beneath this will be a display of the progress in seconds and minutes.

Playing a track is simply a matter of double-clicking it in the list. Once the track is finished, Banshee will play the next track in the MP3 file list.

To create a playlist, select Music ➤ New Playlist. Click the new entry twice and enter a name for your playlist. To add tracks to the playlist, click the Music Library icon to reveal your entire file listing, and then drag and drop files onto your new playlist entry. To start the playlist, click the first track in its list. You can rearrange the tracks within any playlist by clicking and dragging them.

KDE: Using amaroK

amaroK is available from the K menu, under Multimedia ➤ Audio Player. It's a sophisticated and innovative program that can work in two ways: using either a single iTunes-like program window, which catalogs your music collection and includes playback functions, or like Winamp, with a small player application and a separate playlist window. When you first start the program, a wizard will start and, after clicking Next, you'll be asked to choose between these two modes.

■**Note** If the wizard doesn't appear when you first run amaroK, click Tools ➤ First-Run Wizard in the amaroK program window. If you find that amaroK doesn't seem to start at all, look in the system tray for its icon (a wolf). Click this icon to maximize the window.

Following this, you'll be invited to import your music collection. Simply put a check in the box alongside where your music collection lives. For most users, it should be sufficient to check the Home box. If you wish to be more accurate, you can click the small plus next to the Home check box to choose from folders within the /home directory.

If you later want to import any MP3s into amaroK, you can simply drag-and-drop them from any Konqueror file browser window onto the main amaroK window.

The right side of the amaroK window shows the currently selected playlist. The left side shows tabbed panes that provide access to key features of amaroK. The main one of these is the Collection tab, which lists all the tracks in your MP3 collection. You can also access your playlists from the Playlist tab. The Media Device tab lets you access any compatible mobile MP3 players, such as iPods, and the Context pane displays relevant information about the track that's currently playing, as shown in Figure 18-3.

At the bottom of the program window are transport controls for playing music and altering the volume. Alternatively, to play any track, simply double-click its entry on the right side of the program window.

To create a new playlist, select the Collection tab. In the left pane, double-click each track that you want to add to the playlist, and it will appear in the list in the right pane. After you've selected all the tracks you want in your playlist, click the Playlists tab. Click the Save button and give the playlist a name. It will now appear in the list of playlists on the left side of the amaroK program window, and you can select it from there.

Figure 18-3. *Whenever amaroK plays a track, it will show an on-screen display giving details.*

■**Note** When you click the close button in the amaroK window, it won't actually close but will minimize to the system tray area. You can then maximize it later on. If you want to exit the program, right-click the system tray icon and select Quit.

Listening to Audio CDs

Listening to audio CDs under SUSE Linux is simple. Under KDE, simply insert the CD, and then wait a few seconds until a dialog box appears asking what you would like to do. Selecting Play from the list will start playing the CD's first track in the KsCD application. If you always want audio CDs to play in future, put a check in the box marked Always Do This for This Type of Media.

If you're running GNOME, an icon will appear on the desktop once the CD is inserted. Double-clicking this will then open the CD in Banshee, the same application that is used to handle MP3 file playback.

GNOME: Playing CDs Using Banshee

Playing an audio CD using Banshee is very similar to listening to MP3 tracks. A track listing appears on the right side of the program window; double-clicking any entry will initiate playback of that track. The transport controls at the top of the screen let you move backward and forward in the track listing.

Banshee will automatically look up artists, track listings, and even sleeve art details using an online CDDB database for most CDs.

■**Note** CDDB databases are online stores of information about CDs. They're created by ordinary users as a service to other users. Unfortunately, Banshee doesn't allow you to contribute to the CDDB database it uses, but KDE's KsCD application does, as explained in the next section.

To view the cover artwork in detail, click View ➤ Show Cover Art. It will then appear at the bottom left of Banshee's program window. You can make the image larger by clicking and dragging the divider between the left and right sides of the program window.

To seek forward or backward in a track, hold down the Ctrl key and press the left or right arrow key, to move backward or forward, respectively. Each key press will move backward or forward in ten-second increments. Alternatively, you can click the track progress slider at the top left of the program window.

■**Tip** To turn on random play in Banshee, click Playback ➤ Shuffle.

To alter playback volume, click the speaker icon in the top right of the program window and drag the slider.

You can eject the CD by pressing the button on the CD drive.

KDE: Playing CDs using KsCD

If you've ever used a CD-playing application under Windows, then you'll know what to expect with KsCD, because it looks similar and offers similar functions.

As shown in Figure 18-4, all KsCD's main buttons are clearly labeled, and are like those of any CD player. To jump to another track, click the drop-down list at the top of the program window and select the track you would like to play. To move backward and forward in a track, click and drag the track progress slider at the top of the program window.

Figure 18-4. *The KsCD application is simple but effective and can retrieve artist and track information online.*

Like Banshee, KsCD is capable of looking up track listing and artist details using an online database, but this functionality isn't configured by default. To configure it, click the Extras button and select Configure KsCD. Click the CDDB icon on the left, select Cache and Remote under the Mode heading on the right side of the dialog box, and then click OK. You'll need to eject and reinsert the CD for its details to be read from the online database.

In the rare instance of the CD not being listed in the CDDB database, you can type in your own track listing by clicking the CDDB button. Just fill in the relevant fields and, when you've finished, click the Upload button. This information will then be made available to others around the world.

Tip As with all applications, you can hover the mouse cursor over each button in KsCD to display a tooltip that describes what it does.

As with amaroK, the CD player application will minimize to the system tray when you close it. To actually end the program, right-click its icon (a CD with a musical note inset against it) and select Quit.

Ripping Music from CDs

Ripping is the process of converting audio CD tracks into compressed music files for playback and storage on your computer. These files don't necessarily have to be encoded as MP3 tracks, although this will give you the most compatibility with mobile music players.

Under the GNOME desktop of SUSE Linux, the capable Banshee music player can be used to rip CD tracks. Under KDE, you use the KAudioCreator application to rip CDs.

AUDIO FORMATS

There are four basic choices for audio file formats under SUSE Linux: Ogg Vorbis, FLAC, MP3, and Wave/PCM. Each has advantages and disadvantages. Let's look at what each has to offer.

- **Ogg Vorbis:** This is the Free Software alternative to MP3. Unless you have a trained ear, you won't be able to tell the difference between an Ogg and MP3 file (if you do have a trained ear, then you'll find Ogg better!). The two technologies generate files of around the same size, an average of 4MB to 5MB per song. The downside of Ogg is that not many portable audio players support it (although this situation is slowly changing), and other operating systems like Windows won't be able to play back Ogg files unless some additional software is installed (see www.vorbis.com/setup/). However, by using Ogg, you'll be supporting the Free Software community and lessening the stronghold that the patent-encumbered MP3 has over music playback on computers. For this reason alone, you should consider Ogg your first choice.

- **FLAC:** This stands for Free Lossless Audio Codec, and it's the choice of the audiophile. Ogg and MP3 are lossy formats, which means that some of the audio data is lost in order to significantly shrink the file. FLAC doesn't lose any audio data but still manages to compress files to a certain degree (although they're still much larger than an equivalent MP3 or Ogg file). FLAC scores points because it's Free Software, like Ogg, but you'll face the same lack of support in portable audio players and other operating systems (unless additional software is installed; see http://flac.sourceforge.net/download.html).

- **MP3:** This is by far the most ubiquitous music file format and practically everyone who owns a computer has at least a handful of MP3 tracks. This means software support for MP3 playback is strong and, of course, portable audio players are built around the MP3 format. The only problem for you, as a Linux user, is the issue of surrounding patents, as explained at the beginning of this chapter. Using the MP3 format is to go against a lot of what the Free Software movement stands for. But in the end, the choice is up to you.

- **Wave/PCM:** Wave files, sometimes referred to as PCM (Pulse Code Modulation) files, are the simplest type of audio file. They're effectively straight audio data, uncompressed in any way. This means that the file sizes are very large, but the files are sonically identical to the original CD tracks. With hard drives getting larger and larger, encoding files as Wave/PCM is certainly an option. You can expect a typical track to be between 40MB and 60MB in size.

GNOME: Using Banshee to Rip CD Tracks

As with all operations within Banshee, ripping CD tracks is extremely simple. Just insert a CD and double-click the desktop icon that appears for the CD. This will start Banshee and load the CD's details.

To choose which output file format you want (MP3, Ogg, FLAC, or Wave), click Edit ➤ Preferences and then click the Encoding tab. Look in the Encoding Profile drop-down list, where you should find that Xing MP3 is selected by default, which will cause Banshee to output MP3 files. Clicking the list will let you select other formats, as shown in Figure 18-5. To the right, you can select the bitrate (the quality) of the encoding. The default setting of 160Kbps should produce reasonable quality files, but many people prefer 192Kbps, which results in slightly better audio quality. This will increase the file size, but not by too much. Once you're happy with the settings, click OK.

Figure 18-5. *You can choose between MP3, Ogg, FlAC, or Wave encoding within Banshee.*

To rip the tracks from CD, simply click the Import CD button at the top right of the program window. This will import all the tracks (there isn't any way of encoding only selected tracks).

The files will be output to a directory within the Music directory of your /home directory that is named after the artist. Within that directory will be a directory named after the album title, where you'll find the audio tracks.

KDE: Using KAudioCreator to Rip CD Tracks

Although KAudioCreator can be used to rip CD tracks to FLAC, Ogg, or Wave format, the LAME MP3 software must be installed to rip to MP3 format.

To install the LAME MP3 software, open a web browser and visit http://packman. links2linux.org/. In the search box, type lame and press Enter. Click the link for LAME, and then select the download link next to the Package heading, beneath the Download heading near the bottom of the page. Choose to download the file to your /home directory.

■Note In terms of licensing, the LAME software lives in a legally gray area. Unlike the Fluendo codec discussed earlier, it isn't licensed with the patent holder of MP3 technology. However, the developers claim this isn't necessary for a variety of reasons. For more details, see point 6 in the LAME technical FAQ at `http://lame.sourceforge.net/tech-FAQ.txt`.

Once the file has downloaded, open a Konsole terminal window (K menu ➤ System ➤ Terminal ➤ Konsole), and type the following, which will install the software:

```
su
[Enter root password]
rpm -Uvh packagename.rpm
```

Replace *packagename.rpm* with the name of the file you downloaded. On my test system, the file was called `lame-3.96.1-2.i586.rpm`.

When installation has finished, you can close the terminal window.

To rip tracks, simply insert an audio CD and, instead of selecting Play in the dialog box that appears, select Extract and Encode Audio Tracks. Alternatively, if you find that the audio CD starts playing automatically, close the CD player application and click K menu ➤ Multimedia ➤ CD/DVD Tools.

To choose the audio format that you would like to use, click Settings ➤ Configure KAudioCreator. Then click the Encoder icon on the left side of the dialog box. Under the Encoder Configuration heading, select the format as follows:

- To encode as MP3 files, click Lame.

- To encode as Ogg, select OggEnc.

- To encode as FLAC, select FLAC.

- To encode as Wave files, select Leave As Wav File.

You don't need to alter any of the other settings, so click OK after making your format selection.

■Note Unfortunately, there's no easy way to alter the bitrate when using KAudioCreator. However, Ogg and MP3 files output by KAudioCreator are encoded at variable bitrates, which should give you high audio quality.

Back in the main program window, click each track to select it for subsequent ripping. The tracks will then have a check alongside them. To deselect a track, simply remove the check. Once you're happy with the track selections, click the Rip Selection icon on the toolbar (third from the left). You can then watch the progress of the encoding by clicking the Jobs tab.

MAKING MUSIC AND RECORDING AUDIO

Most PCs come with sound cards that are capable of making music. You can use many open source programs, designed for both amateurs and professionals alike, to create music or record and edit audio.

In terms of musical sequencers, Muse (www.muse-sequencer.org), Rosegarden (www.rosegardenmusic.com), and JAZZ++ (www.jazzware.com/zope) are well worth investigating. Like all modern MIDI sequencers, all three programs let you record audio tracks, effectively turning your PC into a recording studio.

It's also possible to run virtual synthesizers on your PC, which effectively turn even the most basic sound card into a powerful musical instrument. Examples include Bristol (www.slabexchange.org) and FluidSynth (www.fluidsynth.org). If you're interested in only audio recording and processing, Sweep (www.metadecks.org/software/sweep/) and Audacity (http://audacity.sourceforge.net) are worth a look. In addition to audio recording and playback, both feature graphical waveform editing and powerful filters.

Several of the packages mentioned here are available from the SUSE Linux software repositories, while others can be downloaded from the Packman software repository (http://packman.links2linux.org).

Creating Your Own CDs

The ripping process can be reversed, and any audio files you have on your hard disk can be burned to CDs. This will produce audio CDs that can then be played on practically any domestic sound system, car stereo, or computer via its CD player application.

Under GNOME, the process is once again handled by Banshee. Under KDE, the process is handled by K3b, although additional software must be installed before you can burn CDs.

GNOME: Burning Audio CDs

As with most audio file operations under GNOME, burning audio CDs is handled by the capable but simple Banshee program.

Here are the steps for burning a CD using Banshee:

1. Start Banshee and either create a new playlist of the tracks you would like to burn or select an existing playlist. Creating a new playlist is a good idea because, at the bottom of the program window, Banshee will tell you how long the playlist is, in minutes. This allows you to make sure that the tracks you select remain beneath the 80-minute limit of most audio CDs.

2. On the right of the program window, select the tracks you would like to burn, as in the example in Figure 18-6. You can select more than one track by holding down the Ctrl key.

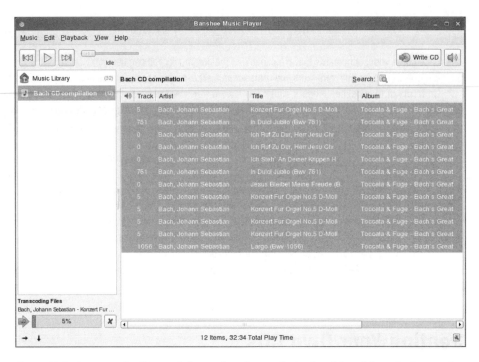

Figure 18-6. *Create a playlist, and then select the tracks in the right of the window, and click the Write CD button.*

3. Insert a blank CD and click the Write CD button at the top right of the program window. Before burning, the tracks are converted to pure digital audio files, and you can monitor the progress of this in the bottom right of the window.

■**Tip** By clicking Edit ➤ Preferences before burning, and then clicking the Burning tab in the dialog box that appears, you can set various options, such as the write speed and whether or not "burnproof" protection is activated.

KDE: Burning Audio CDs

KDE uses the K3b application to burn both audio and data CDs and DVDs. If your audio files are in Ogg, FLAC, or Wave format, you don't need any other software to create audio CDs. However, because of the contentious patenting and licensing issue, it lacks support for MP3 files.

The solution is radical but works well: you can download an entirely new version of K3b, which features MP3 support, from the third-party Packman site (http://packman.links2linux.org). Packman is a site run by enthusiasts that packages nonstandard software for free use by SUSE Linux users. In this case, they've recompiled the same version of K3b that is offered ordinarily by SUSE Linux, but activated MP3 support.

■**Caution** In addition to downloading and installing a new version of K3b, you'll need to install several MP3 codec packages and, as with the LAME software discussed earlier, these are unlicensed implementations of MP3 technology. The download of the additional packages is handled automatically if you follow the instructions in this section.

The easiest way to install software from the Packman site, such as the new version of K3b, is to set up a new software repository. This is explained in detail in Chapter 29, but for the moment, it should be sufficient to follow these instructions:

1. Open a Konsole terminal window by clicking K menu ➤ System ➤ Terminal ➤ Konsole.

2. Type the following:

```
su -
[Enter root password]
rug service-add http://packman.mirrors.skynet.be/pub/packman/suse/ ➥
10.1/ packman
rug subscribe packman
```

   This will add the Packman repository to your system. Note the space before the final packman in the `rug service-add` line.

■**Tip** In the command for adding the Packman repository, I've used a Belgian mirror (copy) of the Packman repository. If you find this doesn't work, visit `ftp://packman.links2linux.de/pub/packman/MIRRORS` in your web browser. This page lists other Packman mirror sites around the world. Choose a different site closer to your location. Simply substitute the address you discover with the one in the command in step 2.

---

3. Type the following to update your system with the new repository listing and then install the updated version of K3b.

```
rug refresh
rug install k3b
```

4. At this point, you'll be informed that several additional packages must be installed, so agree to this.

5. After the installation has finished, it's necessary to unsubscribe from the new Packman repository. If you don't, it will attempt to update your system with several new components (you might have noticed the System Updater system tray change to indicate that updates are available after you set up the Packman repository). To unsubscribe, type the following:

```
rug unsubscribe packman
```

6. Right-click the Software Updater tray icon and click Refresh. After a few moments, it should return to its previous state, prior to setting up the Packman repositories. At this stage, you can close the terminal window.

Tip The Packman repository can be reactivated at any time by typing `rug subscribe packman`. For more information about the use of software repositories, see Chapter 29.

To start K3b, click K menu ➤ Multimedia ➤ CD/DVD Burning. In the main program window, click New Audio CD Project. Use the file listing in the top left of the window to navigate to the location of your MP3 (or other format) tracks. Once you click the folder that contains them, a file listing will appear on the right side of the K3b program window. To select tracks for your CD, drag-and-drop the files onto the bottom of the K3b window. Keep an eye on the time bar at the bottom of the program window. As shown in Figure 18-7, this will indicate how full the CD is becoming, based on the average 80-minute CD.

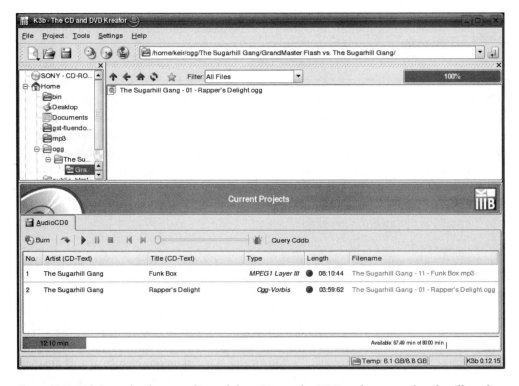

Figure 18-7. *K3b is used to burn audio and data CDs under KDE and, once updated, will work with MP3 files.*

Once you've finished the compilation, click the Burn button (located just above the compilation listing, in the middle left of the program window). In the dialog box that appears, you can set the write speed but, generally, the default settings work fine.

To actually burn the CD, simply insert a blank CD, and then click the Burn button.

Tip There's no reason why you can't mix and match MP3, FLAC, Wave, and MP3 tracks when compiling an audio CD.

TUNING IN TO ONLINE RADIO STATIONS

There are fundamentally two types of digital audio you can listen to on your computer: audio files and streaming audio. The latter is where the audio data isn't downloaded to your computer in one large chunk. Instead, your computer downloads a constant trickle of data, which is decoded and played back live. It's the computer equivalent of listening to a traditional radio station and, indeed, that's its primary use: to tune into online radio stations.

Once your computer is set up for MP3 playback, you should be able to listen to radio stations on sites like www.live365.com or www.shoutcast.com. After you've selected a station to listen to, these sites will offer to save a .pls file to your computer. When double-clicked, this file will open in Totem Movie Player under GNOME or amaroK under KDE, and the radio station will start streaming automatically.

Some radio stations broadcast in RealPlayer or Windows Media format. In the next chapter, I explain how to install codecs that will allow you to not only play back RealPlayer and Windows Media video files, but also tune into streaming audio in those formats. Once the codecs are installed, playback should happen within the pop-up windows that appear when you select to "listen live" on the radio station's web page.

Summary

This chapter covered the audio functions built into SUSE Linux. You learned how you can listen to audio, convert CDs into music files, and create CDs using audio files.

In the next chapter, we'll look at how you can play back movies and online animations using SUSE Linux.

## CHAPTER 19

Movies and Multimedia

Movie playback is becoming increasingly popular on computers. Modern PCs come equipped with DVD-ROM drives and, coupled with the right software, these can play DVD movie discs. In addition, many web sites feature streaming movie clips or offer them for download.

SUSE Linux provides support for movie playback, but you'll need to install additional codecs in order to enjoy the broadest range of playback options. This chapter explains how to set up SUSE Linux for watching videos and DVDs on your computer.

Movie Playback Issues

Just as with audio (discussed in Chapter 18), various technologies are used in the computing world for video playback. Key among these are RealPlayer, Apple QuickTime, Windows Media Player, and DivX. Currently, only DivX and RealPlayer are supported natively under Linux, which is to say DivX and Real provide playback software along with the associated codecs. (As explained in Chapter 18, *codecs* are small pieces of software that handle multimedia file decoding.) Neither Apple's QuickTime nor Windows Media Player is supported.

■**Note** Just as this book was going to press, SUSE announced that it had partnered with Real to distribute a version of RealPlayer that features licensed Windows Media playback technology. This is to be included with its SUSE Linux Enterprise Desktop product. It's not clear whether this version of RealPlayer will be offered for other SUSE products.

Nonetheless, adding support for all these formats, plus additional lesser-used formats, is very simple: just copy across the system files used for video playback under Windows. What actually happens is that people within the wider Linux community copy the system files from Windows and package them for easy installation under Linux. They're normally referred to as the *Win32 codecs*, or just *w32codecs*. You'll learn how to use these codecs in this chapter.

In terms of legalities, usage of these codecs resides in a gray area. Some argue that if you have the relevant playback software installed under Windows (on a computer that dual-boots), then using these system files is legally acceptable because you're simply utilizing Windows components in a different way. One thing is certain: the w32codec package has been distributed for several years, and no attempt has been made by any of the companies that created the codecs to stop distribution.

■**Note** The world of video playback is fiercely competitive and companies like Apple, Microsoft, and DivX are fighting tooth and nail to have their codec become the de facto form of video playback. This may be why they are prepared to turn a blind eye to codec distribution under Linux: it simply provides a wider user base for their codec technology and therefore allows them to achieve further market dominance.

For DVD playback, the issue is Digital Rights Management (DRM). As explained in Chapter 18, DVD movie discs are protected by a form of DRM called Content Scrambling System (CSS). This forces anyone who would like to create DVD playback software or hardware to pay a fee to the DVD Copy Control Association, an industry organization set up to protect DVD movie technology. Nearly all Linux advocates are scornful of any kind of DRM system. It isn't possible for end users to buy licensed DVD playback software for Linux but, even if it were, few would be willing to support what they see as prohibitive software technology.

Some open source advocates reverse-engineered CSS, creating the DeCSS software. This allows the playback of DVD movies under practically any operating system. Sadly, DeCSS is caught in a legal quagmire. The Motion Picture Association of America (MPAA) has attempted to stop its distribution within the United States but has failed. Some experts suggest that distributing DeCSS breaks copyright laws, but there has yet to be a case anywhere in the world that categorically proves this. Nor has there been a case proving or even suggesting that using DeCSS is in any way illegal.

SUSE Linux doesn't come with DeCSS installed by default, but you can download and install the software, as described in this chapter.

ETHICAL ISSUES

Installing the w32codec package raises important ethical issues for you as a Linux user. Most current video playback codecs—including QuickTime, Windows Media Player, and DivX—are based on video playback technology known as MPEG-4. This is covered by a number of restrictive software patents. As mentioned in the previous chapter, patents aim to restrict the *implementation* of an idea or concept, unless a license is granted (usually by the paying of a fee). It is not connected to the issue of copyright. Software patents are designed to restrict the implementation of certain ideas or concepts in computer programs, which many find morally indefensible.

Most of the people who develop and use Linux are opposed to patents being applied to software because it severely restricts the freedom to develop and distribute software, which is the core of the Free Software system. Therefore, it's argued that using restrictively patented video codecs under Linux is simply furthering the damaging and corrupt system of software patenting. However, it is the purpose of this book to provide a pragmatic and practical guide to using Linux on your computer. Playing back the majority of video file formats in use today is part of that. So, I'll describe how to use the codecs, and you'll need to decide for yourself whether this is a path you want to take.

Watching Movies

For movie playback, SUSE Linux provides the Totem Movie Player under the GNOME desktop and Kaffeine under the KDE desktop. Both are nice, but are lacking in features compared to what you might be used to under Windows or Mac OS X. In addition, I've found them to be buggy in some circumstances, and Totem can be difficult to configure for video playback using w32codecs. Because of these issues, I advise that you install MPlayer for movie playback.

MPlayer, shown in Figure 19-1, is a mature piece of open source software that's popular with many in the Linux community. It works seamlessly with the w32codec and DeCSS packages. It also has the smooth look and feel of professional DVD-player software that you might have used under Windows or Mac OS.

■**Note** Technically speaking, the playback application used by most Linux users is gmplayer. MPlayer is actually a command-line program, and the `gmplayer` package simply adds a GUI front-end. However, most people still refer to the program as MPlayer, and this is how it will appear on your Applications/K menu.

Figure 19-1. *MPlayer is a feature-packed, stable, and good-looking media player that, once configured, will handle all forms of media files.*

In addition, MPlayer is packed with features. For example, it features an on-screen display system to show volume levels or progress through the video file, and it allows you to view subtitles within discs or movie files that contain them.

■**Note** One limitation with MPlayer is that it doesn't display DVD menus—the (usually) animated systems put in place by the manufacturers to let you easily view various chapters or "extras" in the movie. This is because MPlayer's main purpose in life is to play video files, such as those contained on DVD movie discs.

MPlayer is both a playback application and multimedia framework in one self-contained package (see Chapter 18 for definitions of both these terms). Once installed, it shouldn't affect the multimedia framework already installed, so you should find that MP3 music files still play back correctly within Banshee/Totem under GNOME or amaroK under KDE. In fact, once the w32codec package is installed, MP3 files can also be played back in MPlayer, which can function as an audio player. And if you want to listen to streaming online audio via your web browser, MPlayer will automatically handle it, once it's set up correctly.

Installing MPlayer and Other Playback Software

The instructions for installing MPlayer are identical on both GNOME and KDE, and the same software is installed in both cases.

MPlayer isn't supplied on the SUSE Linux DVD-ROM. However, it can be found within the Packman software repository (http://packman.links2linux.de). As explained in the previous chapter, Packman is a site run by enthusiasts who package third-party software for use under SUSE Linux. Once access to Packman is configured on your system, you can download not only MPlayer, but also the w32codec package, which will allow the playback of all common video file formats.

■**Note** If you followed the instructions in the previous chapter describing how to install a new version of K3b under KDE, you can simply reactivate the Packman repository and skip the following instructions for adding the Packman repository. To reactivate the Packman repository, open a Konsole window (K menu ➤ System ➤ Terminal ➤ Konsole), switch to root user (type su, press Enter, and type your root password), and then type rug subscribe packman. Don't forget to unsubscribe when you've installed the software: rug unsubscribe packman.

Adding the Packman Repository

To install software via Packman, it's necessary to add a software repository to SUSE Linux. I explain how to install software and manage repositories in Chapter 29, but for the moment it should be sufficient to follow these instructions:

1. Right-click the System Updater system tray icon and select Configure. You'll probably need to wait a moment or two while the software system is "woken up," during which time the notice "Refreshing Services" will appear in the program window.

2. Click the Add Service button.

3. Although you can connect to the central Packman repository in Germany, it's a far better idea to connect to *mirrors*. These are essentially copies of the Packman repository located around the world, and you should choose one closest to your location. To review a list of mirrors, visit `ftp://packman.links2linux.de/pub/packman/MIRRORS` in your web browser.

4. In the Add Service dialog box, type the URL you chose from the Packman mirror list into the Service URI text box. In the Service Name text box, type a memorable name for the new repository—something like `Packman` should do the trick. You can leave the Registration Key text box blank. Your dialog box should look something like Figure 19-2. Click Add to continue.

■**Caution** I found that typing the addresses as they appeared on the mirror site list produced an error on my test system. I had to add `/suse/10.1/` to the end of the address. For example, I chose a Belgian mirror, `http://packman.mirrors.skynet.be/pub/packman/`, but for the Add Service dialog box to accept the address, I had to type `http://packman.mirrors.skynet.be/pub/packman/suse/10.1/`.

Figure 19-2. *By adding the Packman software repository, you can install MPlayer and the necessary codecs for file playback.*

5. Click the Catalogs tab and make sure there is a check alongside your new entry. This will subscribe you to the service, so you can use it to install software.

6. Click the Close button.

When you've finished installing MPlayer and the Win32 codecs, as described below, you should return to the Catalogs tab of the System Updater Configuration window and remove the check next to the Packman service you added in these steps. This will unsubscribe you. If you don't unsubscribe, System Updater will attempt to upgrade components of your system with software from the Packman repository.

■**Caution** As soon as you add the Packman repository, the System Updater icon will change to an exclamation mark, to indicate system updates are available. However, this isn't the case! All that has happened is that System Updater has detected different package versions of installed software in the Packman repository and is suggesting that you install them. You can ignore this. When you unsubscribe from the repository, the System Updater icon will return to the state it was in previously.

Installing MPlayer and Win32 Codecs

Installing the MPlayer and associated software is now a simple matter of starting the Software Installer applet as root user and then installing the required packages. Here's how:

1. Open a terminal window. In GNOME, select Applications ➤ System ➤ Terminal ➤ Gnome Terminal. In KDE, select K menu ➤ System ➤ Terminal ➤ Konsole). In the window, type the following:

   ```
   su
   [Enter root password]
   zen-installer
   ```

2. In the Software Installer window, search for mplayer. You should find two pieces of software in the results: mplayer and mplayer-plugin. Click the check box alongside both, and then click the Install button.

3. Once installation of mplayer has finished, use Software Installer to search for w32codec-all. Then click the check box next to it and click the Install button again.

4. When installation has finished, close the Software Installer window.

5. Right-click the System Updater system tray icon and select Configure. Click the Catalogs tab and remove the check next to the Packman service.

6. Don't forget to unsubscribe from the Packman repository, as described above.

Installing DeCSS for DVD Playback

As explained earlier in this chapter, DeCSS resides in a legally gray area because it overcomes the DRM scheme that protects DVD movie discs, but there is yet to be any proof that using the software is illegal. However, the laws in many countries prohibit *distribution* of DeCSS because it is classified as a device to overcome copy protection. This can make it difficult to get the software. If sites like Packman offer it for download, they will be breaking the law, so they no longer do so.

At the time of writing, it was possible to download a package file for the DeCSS software from the VideoLAN site (www.videolan.org). Here's how to do so:

1. Visit http://download.videolan.org/pub/libdvdcss/.

2. From the list of versions of the DeCSS software, choose the latest version of package (at the time of writing, this was 1.2.9) and click the link.

3. Click the link marked rpm/.

4. Download the latest version of the RPM file that doesn't contain the word devel in its title, or doesn't end with .src.rpm. At the time of writing, this was libdvdcss2-1.2.9-1.i386.rpm. You can look at your browser's status bar to see the full filename of the package.

5. Once the file has downloaded, open a terminal window. In GNOME, select Applications ➤ System ➤ Terminal ➤ Gnome Terminal. In KDE, select K menu ➤ System ➤ Terminal ➤ Konsole. Type the following (replace *packagename.rpm* with the name of the package you downloaded, and if you didn't download to the desktop, replace Desktop with directory location of the package):

```
su
[Type root password]
rpm -Uvh Desktop/packagename.rpm
```

Figure 19-3 shows an example of installing the DeCSS package.

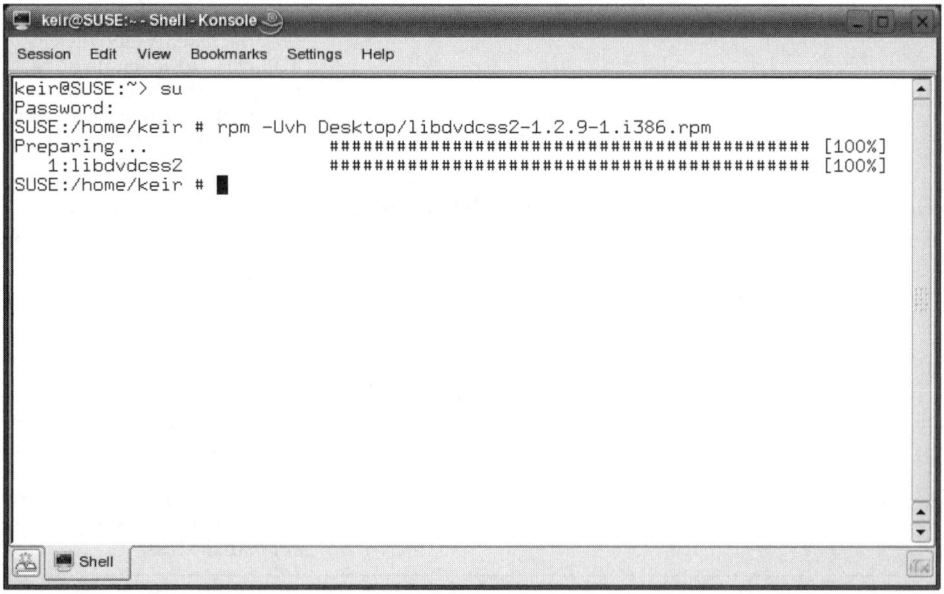

Figure 19-3. *The DeCSS software must be manually installed, although it isn't difficult to do so.*

Playing Movies

Once MPlayer is installed, you can use it to play movies by right-clicking the movie file and selecting Open With ➤ MPlayer.

To set up SUSE Linux so that it automatically plays back video files and DVDs within MPlayer, you'll need to do some configuration. The procedure depends on whether you are using the GNOME or KDE desktop, but for both, the steps should be performed for every file extension you want to play back: .avi, .mov, .wmv, .divx, and so on. See Table 19-1 for a list of typical movie file formats and their extensions.

Tip MPlayer can also play back most types of audio files. You can repeat the configuration steps to make MP3 files and RealAudio .rm files, for example, play in MPlayer.

Table 19-1. *Popular Movie File Formats*

Format	Typical File Extensions	Web Site	Notes
Windows Media Player 9	.wmv, .wma, .asx, .asf	www.microsoft.com/ windows/windowsmedia	Default format for Windows Media Player and, therefore, for most Windows users. Although it's possible to play Windows Media Player files under SUSE Linux, you won't be able to play DRM-restricted files (those that rely on the download and installation of a certificate).
RealVideo	.rm, .ram	www.real.com	By downloading the w32codec package, you can play back RealVideo files in MPlayer. However, if you're using the version of SUSE Linux 10.1 supplied with this book, RealPlayer comes installed by default.
QuickTime	.mov, .qt	www.quicktime.com	QuickTime is Apple's default media format and has gained ground on both Windows and Macintosh computers. As with Windows Media Player, you won't be able to play DRM-restricted files.
DivX	.avi, .divx	www.divx.com	The DivX format is one of the most popular formats for those in the Internet community who like to encode their own movies. It's renowned for its ability to shrink movies to very small sizes.

OPEN SOURCE MOVIE FILE FORMATS

A number of promising open source movie file formats are in development. Some are more mature than others, but few see widespread use at the moment. All promise much for the future. Many consider the following three formats as the chief contenders.

- XviD (www.xvid.org) is a reworking of the popular DivX MPEG-4-based file format. As such, it is able to encode movies to relatively small files sizes (a 90-minute movie can fit on a CD). Despite small file sizes, it can maintain good image and sound quality. In theory, it should also be possible to play XviD movies using any MPEG-4 codec, such as DivX or QuickTime. Unfortunately, XviD uses technology covered by patents in some parts of the world, so the project exists in a legally gray area. If you follow the instructions at the beginning of this chapter, you will be able to download the ported Windows version of the codec so you can play XviD files under SUSE Linux.

- Ogg Theora (www.theora.org) is being developed by the Xiph.Org Foundation, the people behind the Ogg Vorbis audio codec project that's a favorite among Linux users. As such, it promises to be a completely open source project. Although the technology is covered by patents, Xiph.Org has promised never to enforce them, meaning that anyone in the world can use Theora without charge. At the time of writing, Theora is still in the alpha development phase, but it will almost certainly become the open source video codec of choice in the future.

- The British Broadcasting Corporation (www.bbc.co.uk), the UK's largest public service broadcaster, is sponsoring development of the Dirac codec (see http://dirac.sourceforge.net). Dirac is less mature than both Theora and XviD at present, and it is aimed more at the broadcast/enthusiast market. For example, it is designed to support high-definition TV. However, it's certainly one to watch.

GNOME: Configuring MPlayer for Automatic Playback

Follow these steps to configure video files to play automatically in MPlayer:

1. Right-click the file and select Properties.

2. Click the Open With tab. If MPlayer isn't in the list of applications, click the Add button and select it from the list that appears. Then click the Add button.

3. In the Properties window, make sure the radio button next to MPlayer is selected. Then click the Close button.

■Caution It isn't enough just to click MPlayer's entry in the list. You must also make sure the radio button is activated by actually clicking it.

---

4. Click the Close button.

5. Repeat steps 1 through 4 for all relevant movie file extensions.

To make DVD movie discs play automatically when inserted, follow these steps:

1. Select Desktop ➤ Control Center.

2. In the dialog box that appears, click the Multimedia tab and put a check alongside "Play video DVD disks when inserted."

3. In the Command field, erase `totem` and replace it with `gmplayer`, so that the line reads `gmplayer %d`, as shown in Figure 19-4.

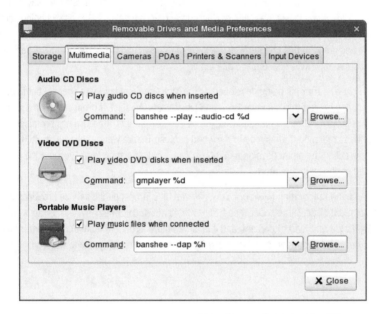

Figure 19-4. *SUSE Linux can be configured to play DVD movie discs as soon as they're inserted.*

4. Click the Close button.

KDE: Configuring MPlayer for Automatic Playback

Follow these steps to configure video files to play automatically in MPlayer:

1. Right-click the file and select Open With ➤ Other.

2. Select MPlayer from the list of applications.

3. Put a check next to Remember Association for This Type of File.

4. Click OK.

5. Repeat steps 1 through 4 for all relevant movie file extensions.

To make DVD movie discs play automatically when inserted, follow these steps:

1. Click K menu ➤ Personal Settings.

2. Click the Peripherals icon on the left side of the window that appears. Then click the Storage Media icon on the left.

3. In the Medium Types drop-down list, select DVD Video Disk.

4. Click the Add button.

5. In the dialog box, click DVD Video Disk in the list on the left.

6. In the Command field, replace `konqueror` with `gmplayer`, so that the line now reads `gmplayer %u`.

7. Click the right-facing arrow in the middle of the dialog box.

8. In the field at the top of the dialog box, which reads Unknown, type something more memorable, such as **DVD playback via MPlayer**.

9. Click the OK button.

10. Back in the Storage Media window, select your new entry, and then click the Toggle As Auto Action button.

11. Click the Apply button at the bottom left.

■**Note** If you find that DVD playback won't work, try starting MPlayer manually (Applications/K menu ➤ Multimedia ➤ Video Player ➤ MPlayer), and then right-click the video window and select DVD ➤ Open Disc. If you see an error message along the lines of "Couldn't open DVD device," some additional configuration may be necessary. Right-click the video window and click Preferences. Click the Misc tab and, in the DVD Device field, replace `/dev/dvd` with `/dev/hdc`. Note that this assumes your DVD drive is the first device on the secondary IDE channel. If it is a slave on the secondary channel (another hard disk or CD/DVD drive on the same channel as master), you should replace `/dev/hdc` with `/dev/hdd`.

Using MPlayer

MPlayer is a sophisticated application. When it starts, it will open two separate program windows: a video playback window and a control console. You can resize the video window by clicking and dragging its edges. If you've selected an audio file for playback, only the console component will appear.

■**Note** The version of MPlayer downloaded from Packman comes with an attractive interface. Interfaces are known as *skins*, and they can be swapped in and out for alternatives, as described in the "Changing MPlayer's Skin" section later in this chapter. Not all versions of MPlayer use the skin provided by Packman. You will find that if you download and install MPlayer for, say, Ubuntu Linux, it comes with a different skin.

For basic playback functions, use the console's standard array of controls, including play, pause, and stop. For a greater range of controls, right-click the video window to open a context menu of options. The following sections describe the console features and the options on the context menu.

■**Note** When attempting to play a video file, you may see the message "Error opening/initializing the selected video_out (-vo) device." To fix this, try the following. Right-click the video window, select Preferences, and in the dialog box that appears, click the Video tab. In the list, select X11 X11 (XImage/Shm). Then click OK and restart MPlayer. Note that this will mean the video window can't be resized.

The MPlayer Console

The MPlayer control console features a number of buttons and sliders, as well as informational displays, as shown in Figure 19-5.

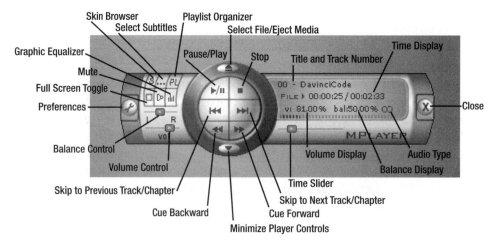

Figure 19-5. *The MPlayer console*

The console elements work as follows:

Skin Browser: Opens the Skin Browser dialog box. Once you've downloaded and installed additional skins for MPlayer (as described in the "Changing MPlayer's Skin" section later in this chapter), you'll be able to choose them here.

Select Subtitles: Activates subtitles, if the DVD-disc has subtitles available. Alternatively, if it is clicked when a video file is playing, any subtitles it contains will be displayed. If the video file doesn't contain subtitles, you will be prompted to load a subtitles file from disk.

Playlist Organizer: Opens a playlist dialog box, where you can select multiple tracks or video files, which will then be played in sequence. Unfortunately, the playlist organizer is a little primitive. It's necessary to browse to the relevant folder, such as your /home folder, on the left, and then select the track(s) you want in the top right, before clicking the Add button.

Pause/Play: Starts or pauses playback of the current file. When you click Pause, you can resume playback from the precise point playback ceased. This in contrast to clicking Stop, which returns playback to the beginning of the file.

Select File/Eject Media: Ejects the disc, if you're playing a DVD movie. Alternatively, if you're playing a video file, clicking here opens a File Open dialog box, from which you can select a different file.

Stop: Stops playback and returns the timeline to the beginning of the file.

Title and Track Number: Displays the current track number, if a playlist is in operation, and the name of the file/DVD currently being played.

Time Display: Shows the progress through the file in minutes and seconds. To the left is the current progress; to the right is the total length of the track.

Close: Terminates MPlayer.

Audio Type: Shows the audio type of the track. Two circles indicate stereo.

Balance Display: Shows, as a percentage, the balance between left and right audio tracks. A value of 50% indicates equal balance.

Volume Display: Shows the volume of MPlayer's output as a percentage.

Time Slider: Moves backward and forward through audio and video tracks, as you click and drag. Note that some video files are incompatible with this function, meaning that it will not be possible to click and drag the slider.

Skip to Next Track: Skips to the next track, if a playlist is in operation.

Cue Forward: Cues you forward in the audio or video track.

Minimize Player Controls: Minimizes the MPlayer controls to the panel, leaving the video window.

Cue Backward: Cues backward in the audio or video track.

Skip to Previous Track: Skips to the previous file in the playlist.

Volume Control: Adjusts the audio volume.

Balance Control: Alters the audio balance.

Preferences: Opens the MPlayer Preferences dialog box, where you can configure technical settings.

Full-Screen Toggle: Causes video playback to fill the screen, leaving just the console application and the desktop panel in view. Click it again to make the video fit within an on-screen window.

Mute: Silences the audio. Click it again to resume audio.

Graphic Equalizer: Opens the graphic equalizer dialog box, where you can alter the acoustic properties of the audio.

MPlayer Menu Options

Right-click the video window (see Figure 19-5) to open the context menu, as shown in Figure 19-6.

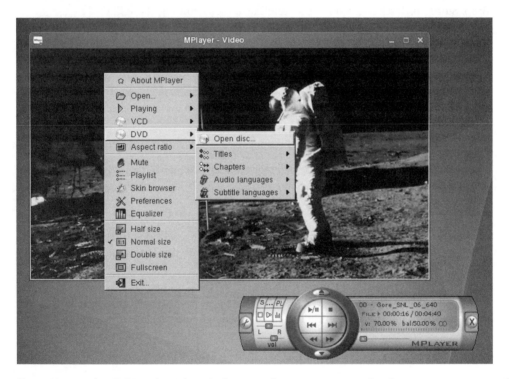

Figure 19-6. *Right-clicking the video window reveals a context menu that lets you access many of MPlayer's higher-level functions.*

The menu options work as follows:

Open: Allows you to load a new media file or start playback of DVD and VCD (Video CD) discs. It's also possible to stream a file straight from the Internet by clicking Play a URL. You can load subtitle files by clicking Load Subtitle, or get rid of any loaded subtitles by clicking Drop Subtitle.

Playing: Lets you play, pause, stop, or advance backward/forward in the playlist/DVD disc.

VCD: Lets you load a VCD, if one is inserted in the drive, and choose from the available titles (movies contained on the disc).

DVD: Similar to the VCD menu, except that it includes options to let you open a DVD movie disc and select chapters within individual movies. You can also activate any additional audio languages, by clicking the relevant submenu entry, and choose between subtitle languages (if applicable), as shown in Figure 19-7.

Figure 19-7. *You can switch between titles and chapters of a DVD movie disc by right-clicking the video window and selecting DVD.*

Aspect ratio: Lets you select an aspect ratio. If you select a nonnative aspect ratio, the video will be stretched accordingly.

■**Note** The *aspect ratio* refers to the width of the video file's image compared to its horizontal edge. For example, widescreen TV is 16:9 ratio, meaning that the horizontal edge is 16 units against 9 units for the vertical. Traditional TV images are 4:3. Normally, MPlayer plays back the video in the correct ratio, but you can alter it to a different ratio if desired.

Mute: Mutes the sound. Clicking again will reactive it.

Playlist: Opens the playlist dialog box.

Skin browser: Opens a dialog box from which you can select a new skin (visual appearance) for MPlayer, as described shortly.

Preferences: Opens MPlayer's Preferences dialog box, where you can manipulate various technical settings. Normally, the default settings are fine and there is no need to delve into this aspect of MPlayer.

Equalizer: Opens MPlayer's graphic equalizer dialog box, where you can adjust the properties of the audio.

Half size/Normal size/Double size/Full screen: Let you adjust the size of the video playback window, from half the size of the native resolution of the video file, to full-screen, where the video file will be stretched to the size of the desktop.

■**Note**   The context menu offers a different kind of full-screen playback than that available by clicking the button on the MPlayer console because the video will quite literally fill the screen and hide all desktop furniture and the MPlayer console. In full-screeen mode, you can control playback using keyboard shortcuts (see Table 19-2). Pressing Esc will return the desktop to view.

Exit: Quits MPlayer.

MPlayer Keyboard Shortcuts

You can use a number of keyboard shortcuts within MPlayer, as listed in Table 19-2. These are handy when you're viewing your movie in full-screen playback mode (when the console disappears), although they can be used at any time.

Table 19-2. *MPlayer Keyboard Shortcuts*

Key	Description
Esc	In regular playback modes, quits MPlayer. If pressed during full-screen playback, returns to the standard video window/MPlayer console.
Spacebar	Pauses/resumes playback.
Page Up	Moves forward 10 minutes.
Page Down	Moves backward 10 minutes.
<	Advances to the next item in the playlist.
>	Advances forward in the playlist.
End	Quits MPlayer.
Left arrow	Cues backward within the file.
Right arrow	Cues forward within the file.
O	Activates on-screen status display.
F	Toggles full-screen mode.

Changing MPlayer's Skin

A variety of replacement skins are available for MPlayer. These alter its look and feel to varying degrees. Some are more radical than others, but if you find the default MPlayer interface hard to work with, or just boring, skins are worth investigating.

The skins must be manually downloaded as `tar` archives and then unpacked into the `/usr/share/mplayer/Skin` directory. Here's how to get skins:

1. Visit the MPlayer homepage (`www.mplayerhq.hu`) and click the Download link on the left side of the screen.

2. Scroll down to the Skins heading and browse through the choices. When you've found one you want, choose to download it by clicking any of the links under the HTTP or FTP heading.

3. After downloading the skin package, open a terminal window. In GNOME, select Applications ➤ System ➤ Terminal ➤ Gnome Terminal. In KDE, select K menu ➤ System ➤ Terminal ➤ Konsole. In the window, type the following to copy the package to the MPlayer `Skin` directory and unpack it (replace *<username>* with your username, and *skin_package.tar.bz2* with the name of the file you downloaded; also, if you've downloaded to a directory other than your desktop, replace `Desktop` with that directory's name):

```
su
[Enter root password]
cd /usr/share/mplayer/Skin
tar jxf /home/<username>/Desktop/skin_package.tar.bz2
```

4. To activate the new skin, right-click the video window and select Skin Browser. In the dialog box, select your new skin from the list. See Figure 19-8 to see an alternative skin in action.

Figure 19-8. *A variety of attractive replacement MPlayer skins are available. This one is called Abyss.*

Editing Movies

The field of Linux movie-editing software is still young, and only a handful of programs are available for the nonprofessional user. One of the best is Kino (www.kinodv.org), which is installed by default under SUSE Linux on both the GNOME and KDE desktops. Although far from being a professional-level program, Kino allows competent users to import and edit videos, apply effects, and then output in either MPEG-1 or MPEG-2 format.

If you're looking for something more powerful, but also more complicated, then Cinelerra is well worth a look (http://heroinewarrior.com/cinelerra.php3). To quote the web site, Cinelerra is "the same kind of compositing and editing suite that the big boys use," except it's made for Linux! You can download Cinelerra from the download section of its web site (http://heroinewarrior.com/download.php3), where there are also instructions on how to install it.

MainActor (www.mainconcept.com) is the Linux version of a commercial Windows project. Although it's not free, most people agree that it's one of the most comprehensive video editors available for Linux at the moment, and possibly the easiest to use, too. You can download an evaluation version of the software at www.mainconcept.com/site/?id=399/.

Incidentally, professional moviemakers use Linux all the time, particularly when it comes to adding special effects to movies. Movies like Shrek 2, Stuart Little, and the Harry Potter series all benefited from the CinePaint software running under Linux! For more details, see www.cinepaint.org.

Summary

This chapter explained how you can watch movies on your PC. You've seen how you can update SUSE Linux to work with the most popular digital video technologies, such as Windows Media Player and QuickTime. In addition, we looked at how you can view online multimedia such as Flash animations on your computer and discussed video-editing possibilities.

In the next chapter, we will take a look at image editing under SUSE Linux. You'll learn about one of the crown jewels of the Linux software scene: The GIMP.

■■■

## CHAPTER 20

Image Editing

The PC has become an increasingly useful tool in the field of photography. In fact, these days it's hard to imagine a professional photographer who doesn't use a computer in some way, either to download digital camera images or to scan in images taken using traditional film-based cameras.

SUSE Linux includes a sophisticated and professional-level image-editing program called The GIMP. The title stands for GNU Image Manipulation Program. This chapter introduces this jewel in the crown of Linux software.

Getting Pictures onto Your PC

Before you can undertake any image editing, you need to transfer your images to your PC. Depending on the source of the pictures, there are a variety of ways of doing this. We have already looked at transferring images to your PC in Chapter 8, but let's briefly recap the procedure here.

Most modern cameras use memory cards to store the pictures. If you have such a model, when you plug the camera into your PC's USB port, you should find that SUSE Linux instantly recognizes it. Under GNOME, an icon should appear on the desktop and within the Computer Nautilus window, and double-clicking it should display the memory card contents. Under KDE, a dialog box should open asking what you want to do with the contents of the camera memory card.

Note Technically speaking, the memory card has been *mounted*. See Chapter 14 for an explanation of mounting.

If your camera doesn't appear to be recognized by SUSE Linux, you should consider buying a USB card reader. These devices are typically inexpensive and can read a wide variety of card types, making them a useful investment for the future. Some new PCs even come packaged with card readers. Most generic card readers should work fine under Linux, as will most new digital cameras.

If you're working with print photos, negative film, or transparencies, you can use a scanner to scan them in using the XSane image-scanning program, covered in Chapter 8. This works in a virtually identical way to the TWAIN modules supplied with Windows scanners, in that you need to set the dots per inch (DPI) figures, as well as the color depth. Generally speaking, 300 DPI and 24-bit color should lead to a true-to-life representation of most photos (although because of their smaller size, transparencies or negative film will require higher resolutions, on the order of 1,200 or 2,400 DPI).

Introducing The GIMP

The GIMP (www.gimp.org) is an extremely powerful image editor that offers the kind of functions usually associated with top-end software like Adobe Photoshop. Although it's not aimed at beginners, those new to image editing can get the most out of it, provided they put in a little work.

■**Tip** This chapter should give you enough information to become competent with The Gimp. However, if you're looking for a totally comprehensive reference guide, check out *Beginning GIMP: From Novice to Professional*, by Akkana Peck (1-59059-587-4; Apress, 2006).

The program relies on a few unusual concepts within its interface, which can catch many people off guard. The first of these is that each of the windows within the program, such as floating dialog boxes or palettes, gets its own Panel entry. In other words, The GIMP's icon bar, image window, settings window, and so on have their own buttons on the Panel alongside your other programs, as if they were separate programs.

■**Note** The GIMP's way of working is referred to as a *Single Document Interface*, or SDI. It's favored by a handful of programs that run under Linux and seems to be especially popular among programs that let you create things.

Because of the way that The Gimp runs, before you start up the program, it's a wise idea to switch to a different virtual desktop (virtual desktops are discussed in Chapter 7), which you can then dedicate entirely to The GIMP.

Click Applications ➤ Graphics ➤ Image Editing ➤ The GIMP to run the program. When The GIMP starts for the first time, it will run through its setup routine. Usually, you can use the default answers to the various questions asked by the wizard.

After the setup routine, you'll be greeted by what appears to be a complex assortment of program windows. Now you need to be aware of a second unusual aspect of the program: its reliance on right-clicking. Whereas right-clicking usually brings up a context menu offering a handful of options, within The GIMP, it's the principal way of accessing the program's functions. Right-clicking an image brings up a menu offering access to virtually everything you'll need while editing. SUSE Linux includes the latest version of The GIMP, 2.2 at the time of this writing, and this features a menu bar in the main image-editing window. This is considered sacrilege by many traditional The GIMP users, although it's undoubtedly useful for beginners. However, the right-click menu remains the most efficient way of accessing The GIMP's tools.

The main toolbar window, shown in Figure 20-1, is on the left. This can be considered the heart of The GIMP because, when you close it, all the other program windows are also closed. The menu bar on the toolbar window offers most of the options you're likely to use to start out with The GIMP. For example, File ➤ Open will open a browser dialog box in which you can select files to open in The GIMP. It's even possible to create new artwork from scratch by choosing File ➤ New, although you should be aware that The GIMP is primarily a photo editor. To create original artwork, a better choice is a program like Inkscape (on the Applications ➤ Graphics menu).

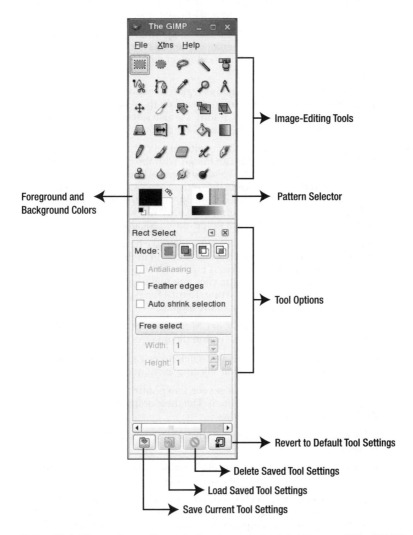

Figure 20-1. *The main toolbar window is a way to access most of The GIMP's options.*

Beneath the menu bar in the main toolbar window are the tools for working with images. Their functions are described in Table 20-1, which lists the tools in order from left to right, starting at the top left.

Table 20-1. *The GIMP Image-Editing Tools*

Tool	Description of Use
Rectangular selection tool	Click and drag to select a rectangular area within the image. This selected area can then be copied and pasted into a different part of the image or turned into a new layer.
Elliptical selection tool	Create an oval or circular selection area within the image, which you can then copy and paste.
Hand-drawn selection tool	Click and draw with the mouse to create a hand-drawn selection area. Your selection should end where it started. If not, The GIMP will draw a straight line between the start and end of the selection.
Contiguous regions selection tool	Known as the "magic wand" in other image editors, this tool creates a selection area based on the color of the pixels where you click. For example, clicking a red car hood will select most, if not all of the hood, because it is mostly red.
Color region selection tool	This tool works like the contiguous region selection tool, but will create a selection across the entire image based on the color you select. In other words, selecting a black T-shirt will also select a black signpost elsewhere in the picture if the shades are similar.
Shape selection tool	Another "magical" tool, the shape selector lets you create a selection by clicking various points within an image, with the program joining the points together based on the color differences between the two points. This means that you can select the outline of a car by clicking a few points around the edge of the car and, provided the color of the car is different from the background, The GIMP will work out the color differences and select the car's shape automatically.
Path creation tool	This tool draws Bezier curves in order to create paths. Paths are akin to selections and can be saved for use later on in the image-editing process. Creating a Bezier curve is not too hard to do: just click and drag to draw a curve. Each extra click you make will define a new curve, which will be joined to the last one. To turn the path into a selection, click the button at the bottom of the toolbar.
Color picker	This lets you see the RGB, HSV, or CMYK values of any color within the image. Simply click the mouse within the image.
Zoom tool	Click to zoom into the image, right-click to see various zoom options, and hold down the Alt key while clicking to zoom out.
Measurer	This tool measures distances between two points (in pixels) and also angles. Just click and drag to use it. The measurements will appear at the bottom of the image window.
Move tool	Click and drag to move any selection areas within the image, as well as rearrange the positioning of various layers.
Crop tool	Click and drag to define an area of the image to be cropped. Anything outside the selection area you create will be discarded.
Rotate tool	This tool rotates any selections you make and can also rotate entire layers. It opens a dialog box in which you can set the rotation manually. Alternatively, you can simply click and drag the handles behind the dialog box to rotate by hand.

Tool	Description of Use
Scale tool	Known in some other image editors as "transform," this tool lets you resize the selection area or layer. It presents a dialog box where you can enter numeric values, or you can click and drag the handles to resize by hand.
Shear tool	This tool lets you transform the image by shearing it. Slant a selection by clicking and dragging the corners of the selection area. (If the selection area isn't square, a rectangular grid will be applied to it for the purposes of transformation.)
Perspective tool	This tool lets you transform a selection by clicking and dragging its four corners and independently moving them without affecting the other corners. In this way, a sense of perspective can be emulated.
Flip tool	This tool flips a selection or image so that it is reversed on itself, either horizontally (click) or vertically (hold down Ctrl and click).
Text tool	Click the image to add text.
Fill tool	Fill a particular area with solid color, according to the color selected in the color box below.
Gradient fill	This tool will create a gradient fill based on the foreground and background colors by clicking and dragging.
Pencil tool	This tool lets you draw individual pixels when zoomed in, or hard-edge lines when zoomed out. Simply click and drag to draw freehand, and hold down Shift to draw lines between two points.
Brush tool	This tool lets you draw on the picture in a variety of brush styles to create artistic effects. A brush can also be created from an image, allowing for greater versatility.
Erase tool	Rather like the Brush tool in reverse, this tool deletes whatever is underneath the cursor. If layers are being used, the contents of the layer beneath will become visible.
Airbrush tool	This tool is also rather like the Brush tool, in that it draws on the picture in a variety of styles. However, the density of the color depends on the length of time you press the mouse button. Tap the mouse button, and only a light color will appear. Press and hold the mouse button, and the color will become more saturated.
Ink tool	This tool is like the Brush tool except that, rather like an ink pen, the faster you draw, the thinner the brush stroke is.
Pattern stamp	Commonly known as the Clone tool, this is a popular image-editing tool. It is able to copy one part of an image to another via drawing with a brushlike tool. The origin point is defined by holding down Ctrl and clicking.
Blur/sharpen tool	Clicking and drawing on the image will spot blur or sharpen the image, depending on the settings in the tool options area in the lower half of the toolbar.
Smudge tool	As its name suggests, clicking and drawing with this tool will smudge the image, rather like rubbing a still-wet painting with your finger (except slightly more precise).
Burn and dodge tool	This tool lets you spot lighten and darken an image by clicking and drawing on the image. The results depend on the settings in the tool options part of the window.

Directly beneath the image-editing tool icons, on the right, is an icon that shows the foreground and background colors that will be used when drawing with tools such as the Brush. To define a new color, double-click either the foreground (top) or background (bottom) color box. To the left is the pattern selector, which lets you choose which patterns are used with tools such as the Brush.

Beneath these icons, you'll see the various options for the selected tool. By using the buttons at the bottom of the window, you can save the current tool options, load tool options, and delete a previously saved set of tool options. Clicking the button on the bottom right lets you revert to the default settings for the tool currently being used (useful if you tweak too many settings!).

Editing Images with The GIMP

After you've started The GIMP (and assigned it a virtual desktop, as explained in Chapter 7), you can load an image by selecting File ➤ Open. The browser dialog box offers a preview facility on the right of the window.

You will probably need to resize the image window so that it fits within the remainder of the screen. You can then use the Zoom tool (refer to Table 20-1) to ensure that the image fills the editing window, which will make working with it much easier.

You can save any changes you make to an image by right-clicking it and selecting File ➤ Save As. You can also print the image from the same menu.

Before you begin editing with The GIMP, you need to be aware of some essential concepts that are vital to understand in order to get the most from the program:

Copy, cut, and paste buffers: The GIMP lets you cut or copy many selections from the image and store them for use later. It refers to these saved selections as *buffers*, and each must be given a name for future reference. A new buffer is created by selecting an area using any of the selection tools, then right-clicking within the selection area and selecting Edit ➤ Buffer ➤ Copy Named (or Cut Named). Pasting a buffer back is a matter of right-clicking the image and selecting Edit ➤ Buffer ➤ Paste Named.

Paths: The GIMP paths are not necessarily the same as selection areas, although it's nearly always possible to convert a selection into a path and vice versa (right-click within the selection or path and look for the relevant option on the Edit menu). In general, the tools used to create a path allow the creation of complex shapes rather than simple geometric shapes, as with the selection tools. You can also be more intricate in your selections, as shown in the example in Figure 20-2. You can save paths for later use. To view the Paths dialog box, right-click the image and select Dialogs ➤ Paths.

■**Tip** Getting rid of a selection or path you've drawn is easy. In the case of a path, simply click any other tool. This will cause the path to disappear. To get rid of a selection, select any selection tool and quickly click once on the image, being careful not to drag the mouse while doing so.

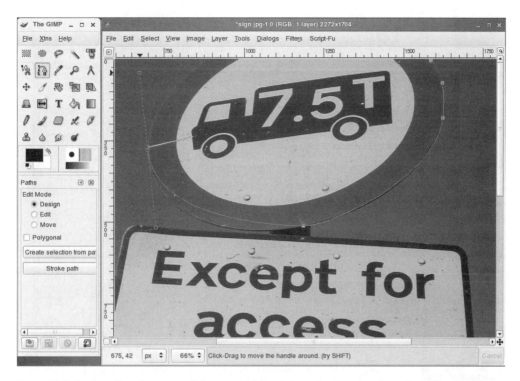

Figure 20-2. *Paths allow for more elaborate and intricate selections, such as those that involve curves.*

Layers: In The GIMP (along with most other image-editing programs), *layers* are like transparent sheets of plastic that are placed on top of the image. Anything can be drawn on each individual transparent sheet, and many layers can be overlaid in order to create a complicated image. Layers also let you cut and paste parts of the image between them. It's also possible to apply effects and transformations to a single layer, rather than to the entire image. To open the Layers dialog box, shown in Figure 20-3, right-click the image and select Dialogs ➤ Layers. You can reorder the layers by clicking and dragging them in the dialog box. In addition, you can alter the blending mode of each layer. A layer's blending mode determines how it interacts with the layer below it. For example, its opacity can be changed so that it appears semitransparent, thereby showing the contents of the layer beneath.

Figure 20-3. *Set the opacity of various layers by clicking and dragging the relevant slider in the Layers dialog box.*

Making Color Corrections

The first step when editing most images is to correct the brightness, contrast, and color saturation. This helps overcome some of the deficiencies that are inherent in digital photographs or scanned-in images. To do this, right-click the image and select Layers ➤ Colors. You'll find a variety of options to let you tweak the image, allowing you a lot of control over the process.

For trivial brightness and contrast changes, select the Brightness/Contrast menu option. This opens a dialog box with sliders that you can click and drag to alter the image. The changes you make will be previewed on the image itself, so you should be able to get things just right.

Similarly, the Hue/Saturation option will let you alter the color balance and also the strength of the colors (the saturation) by clicking and dragging sliders. By selecting the color bar options at the top of the window, you can choose individual colors to boost. Clicking the Master button will let you once again alter all colors at the same time.

The trouble with clicking and dragging sliders is that it relies on human intuition. This can easily be clouded by a badly calibrated monitor, which might be set too dark or too light. Because of this, The GIMP offers another handy option: Levels.

To access the Levels feature, right-click the image and select Layer ➤ Colors ➤ Levels. This presents a chart of the brightness levels in the photo and lets you set the dark, shadows, and highlight points, as shown in Figure 20-4. Three sliders beneath the chart represent, from left to right, the darkest point, the midtones (shadows), and the highlights within the picture. The first step is to set the dark and light sliders at the left and right of the edges of the chart. This will make sure that the range of brightness from the lightest point to the darkest point is set correctly. The next step is to adjust the middle slider so that it's roughly in the middle of the highest peak within the chart. This will accurately set the midtone point, ensuring an even spread of brightness across the image.

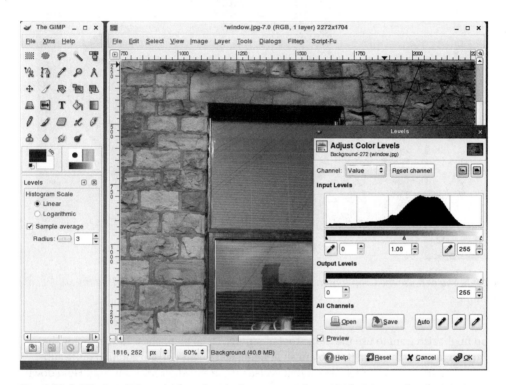

Figure 20-4. *The Levels function can be used to accurately set the brightness levels across an image.*

A little artistic license is usually allowed at this stage and, depending on the effect on the photo, moving the midtone slider a little to the left and/or right of the highest peak might produce more acceptable results. However, be aware that the monitor might be showing incorrect brightness/color values.

Cropping and Cloning

After you've adjusted the colors, you might want to use the Crop tool (refer to Table 20-1) to remove any extraneous details outside the focus of the image. For example, in a portrait of someone taken from a distance away, you might choose to crop the photo to show only the person's head and shoulders, or you might separate a group of people from their surroundings, as shown in Figure 20-5.

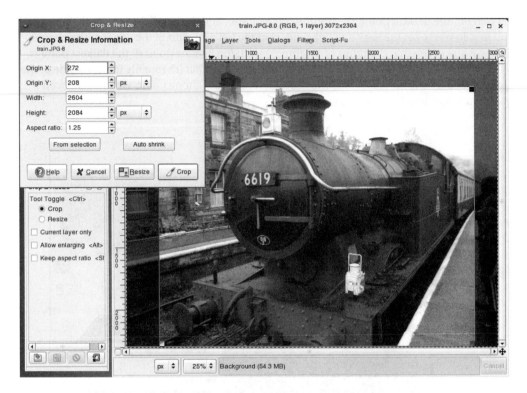

Figure 20-5. *You can use the Crop tool to remove any irrelevant details surrounding the subject of your photo.*

You might also want to use the Clone tool to remove facial blemishes. Start by using the Zoom tool to magnify the area. If the blemish is small, you might need to zoom in quite substantially. Then try to find an area of skin that is clear and from which you can copy. Hold down Ctrl and click in that area. Then click and draw over the blemish. The crosshair indicates the area from which you're copying.

Sharpening

One final handy trick employed by professional image editors to give their photos a shot in the arm is to use the Sharpen filter. This has the effect of adding definition to the image and negating any slight blur caused by things such as camera shake or poor focusing. To apply the Sharpen filter, right-click the image and select Filters ➤ Enhance ➤ Sharpen.

As shown in Figure 20-6, a small preview window will show the effect of the sharpening on the image (you might need to use the scroll bars to move to an appropriate part of the image). Clicking and dragging the slider at the bottom of the dialog box will alter the severity of the sharpening effect. Too much sharpening can ruin a picture, so be careful. Try to use the effect subtly.

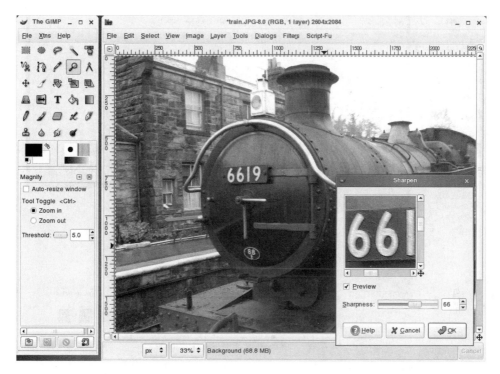

Figure 20-6. *Sharpening an image can give it a professional finish by adding definition.*

The Sharpen filter is just one of many filters you can apply in The GIMP, as explained in the next section.

Applying Filters

Like other image-editing programs, The GIMP includes many filters to add dramatic effects to your images with little, if any, user input. Filters are applied either to the currently selected layer or to a selection within the layer. To apply a filter, right-click the image and choose the relevant menu option. If you don't like an effect you've applied, you can reverse it by selecting Edit ➤ Undo, or by pressing Ctrl+Z.

The submenus offer filters grouped by categories, as follows:

Blur: These filters add various kinds of blur to the image or selection. For example, Motion Blur can imitate the effect of photographing an object moving at speed with a slow shutter. Perhaps the most popular blur option is Gaussian Blur, which has the effect of applying a soft and subtle blur.

Colors: This option includes many technical filters, mostly of interest to image technicians or those who want to uncover and otherwise manipulate the color breakdown within an image. However, Filter Pack might appeal to the general user. This filter can quickly adjust the hue, saturation, and other values within the image. Also of interest is Colorify, which can tint the image to any user-defined color. Figure 20-7 shows an example of using the Colorify filter.

Figure 20-7. *The Colorify filter can be used to add a sepia-like effect to a picture.*

Noise: This collection of filters is designed to add speckles or other types of usually unwanted artifacts to an image. These filters are offered within The GIMP for their potential artistic effects, but they can also be used to create a grainy film effect—simply click Scatter RGB.

Edge Detect: This set of filters can be used to automatically detect and delineate the edges of objects within an image. Although this type of filter can result in some interesting results that might fall into the category of special effects, it's primarily used in conjunction with other tools and effects.

Enhance: The Enhance effects are designed to remove various artifacts from an image or otherwise improve it. For example, the Despeckle effect will attempt to remove unwanted noise within an image (such as flecks of dust in a scanned image). The Sharpen filter discussed in the previous section is located here, as is the Unsharp Mask, which offers a high degree of control over the image-sharpening process.

Generic: In this category, you can find a handful of filters that don't seem to fall into any other category. Of particular interest is the Convolution Matrix option, which lets you create your own filters by inputting numeric values. According to The GIMP's programmers, this is designed primarily for mathematicians, but it can also be used by others to create random special effects. Simply input values and then preview the effect.

Glass Effects: As the name suggests, these filters can apply effects to the image to imitate the effects that come about when glass is used to produce an image. For example, the Apply Lens filter will apply the same kind of distortion caused by various wide-angle lenses used on cameras, as shown in Figure 20-8.

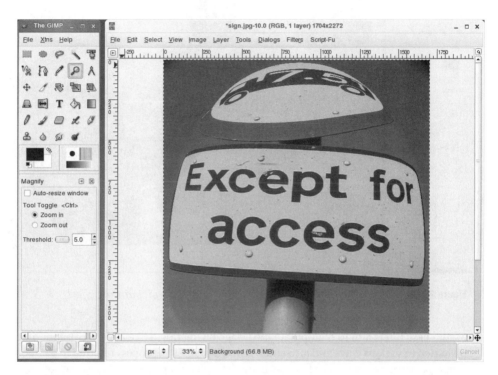

Figure 20-8. *The Glass Effects ➤ Apply Lens filter can be used to imitate a fish-eye lens.*

Light Effects: Here, you will find filters that imitate the effects that light can have on a picture, such as adding sparkle effects to highlights or imitating lens flare caused by a camera's lens.

Distorts: As the name of this category of filters suggests, the effects here distort the image in various ways. For example, Whirl and Pinch allow you to tug and push the image to distort it (to understand what is meant here, imagine the image is printed on rubber and then pinching or pushing the surface). This category also contains other special effects, such as Pagecurl, which imitates the curl of a page at the bottom of the picture.

Artistic: These filters allow you to add painterly effects to the image, such as making it appear as if the photo has been painted in impressionistic brushstrokes, or as if it were painted on canvas by overlaying the texture of canvas onto the picture. Figure 20-9 shows an example of applying a filter for an oil painting effect.

Figure 20-9. *The Artistic effects can be used to give images an oil painting effect.*

Map: These filters aim to manipulate the image by treating it like a piece of paper that can be folded in various ways and also stuck onto 3D shapes (a process referred to as mapping). Because the image is treated as if it were a piece of paper, it can also be copied, and the copies placed on top of each other to create various effects.

Render: Here, you'll find filters designed to create new images from scratch, such as clouds or flame effects. They obliterate anything that was previously underneath on that particular layer or within selection, and the original image has no bearing on what is generated by the filter.

Web: Here, you can create an image map for use in a web page. An *image map* is a single image broken up into separate hyperlinked areas, typically used on a web page as a sophisticated menu. For example, an image map is frequently used for a geographical map on which you can click to get more information about different regions.

Animation: These filters aim to manipulate and optimize GIF images, which are commonly used to create simple animated images for use on web sites.

Combine: Here, you'll find filters that combine two or more images into one.

Toys: These are so-called "Easter Eggs," which aren't designed to manipulate the image, but are present in the program as harmless animations for the user to enjoy. They're created by the programmers of The GIMP as a way of thanking you for using their program.

Tip The GIMP also includes Script-Fu and Python-Fu, scripting languages that can be used to daisy-chain several commands together to produce a particular effect or to automate a particular image-editing process. For more information, search for "script-fu" or "python-fu" using your favorite web search engine.

Summary

In this chapter, we took a look at image editing under SUSE Linux. This has involved an examination of one of the best programs available for the task under any operating system: The GIMP.

You learned how to start The GIMP and about some of the basic principles behind it. Next, we discussed some of the functions contained within The GIMP, including the image filters provided with the program.

In the next part of the book, we move on from multimedia to look at another core component of SUSE Linux: the OpenOffice.org suite, which provides word processing, spreadsheet, presentation, and other functions.

PART VI

Office Tasks

■■■

## CHAPTER 21

Making the Move to OpenOffice.org

You might be willing to believe that you can get a complete operating system for no cost. You might even be able to accept that this offers everything Windows does and much more. But one stumbling block many people have is in believing a Microsoft Office–compatible office suite comes as part of the zero-cost bundle. It's a step too far. Office costs hundreds of dollars—are they expecting us to believe that there's a rival product that is free?

Well, there is, and it's called OpenOffice.org. It comes preinstalled with SUSE Linux, as well as most other Linux distributions, making it the Linux office suite of choice. It's compatible with most Microsoft Office files, too, and even looks similar and works in a comparable way, making it easy to learn. What more could you want?

Office Similarities

OpenOffice.org started life as a proprietary product called Star Office. Sun Microsystems bought the company behind the product and released its source code in order to encourage community development. This led to the creation of the OpenOffice.org project, a collaboration between open source developers and Sun. This project has released several new versions of OpenOffice.org. At the time of writing, version 2 is the latest, and this is the version supplied with SUSE Linux.

■Note For what it's worth, Sun still sells Star Office. This is based on the OpenOffice.org code, so it's effectively the same program. However, in addition to the office suite itself, Sun includes several useful extras such as fonts, templates, and the all-important technical support, which you can contact if you get stuck trying to undertake a particular task. To learn more, visit `www.sun.com/software/star/staroffice/`.

OpenOffice.org features a word processor, spreadsheet program, presentation package, drawing tool (vector graphics), web site creation tool, database program, and several extras. As such, it matches Microsoft Office almost blow-for-blow in terms of core functionality. See Table 21-1 for a comparison of core packages.

Table 21-1. *How the Office and OpenOffice.org Suites Compare*

Microsoft Office	OpenOffice.org	Function
Word	Writer	Word processor
Excel	Calc	Spreadsheet
PowerPoint	Impress	Presentations
Visio	Draw[1]	Technical drawing/charting
FrontPage	Writer[2]	Web site creation
Access	Base[3]	Database

1. *Draw is a vector graphics creation tool akin to Adobe Illustrator. Creating flow charts or organizational diagrams is one of many things it can do.*
2. *Writer is used for word processing and HTML creation; when switched to Web mode, its functionality is altered appropriately.*
3. *Writer and Calc can be coupled to a third-party database application such as MySQL or Firebird; however, OpenOffice.org also comes with the Base relational database.*

You should find the functionality within the packages is duplicated, too, although some of the very specific features of Microsoft Office are not in OpenOffice.org. But OpenOffice.org also has its own range of such tools not yet found in Microsoft Office!

OpenOffice.org does have a couple of notable omissions. Perhaps the main one is that it doesn't offer a directly comparable Outlook replacement. However, as discussed in Chapter 27, the Evolution application offers an accurate reproduction of Outlook, presenting e-mail, contacts management, and calendar functions all in one location. In SUSE Linux, you'll find Evolution on the Applications ➤ Office menu. Evolution isn't directly linked to OpenOffice.org, but it retains the overall SUSE Linux look, feel, and way of operating.

OpenOffice.org Key Features

Key features of OpenOffice.org, apart from the duplication of much of what you find in Microsoft Office, include the ability to export documents in Portable Document Format (PDF) format across the entire suite of programs. PDF files can then be read on any computer equipped with PDF display software, such as Adobe Acrobat Reader.

OpenOffice.org features powerful accessibility features that can, for example, help those with vision disabilities use the programs more effectively. For those who are technically minded, OpenOffice.org can be extended very easily with a variety of plug-ins, which allow the easy creation of add-ons using many different programming languages.

■**Note** Technically minded users can write and run macros in OpenOffice.org Basic, Python, Java, BeanShell, and JavaScript. To learn more, visit `http://framework.openoffice.org/scripting/`.

Although OpenOffice.org largely mirrors the look and feel of Microsoft Office, it adds its own flourishes here and there. This can mean that some functions are located on different menus, for example. However, none of this poses a challenge for most users, and OpenOffice.org is generally regarded as very easy to learn.

File Compatibility

OpenOffice.org is able to read files from Microsoft Office versions up to and including Office 2003, the latest version of Office at the time of writing. When a new version of Office comes out with a new file format, future versions of OpenOffice.org will support it. This is just one more reason why you should regularly update SUSE Linux online in order to make sure you're running the very latest versions of each program.

■**Note** It's fair to say that many people still use the older Office file formats, even if they're using the latest version of Office. This is done to retain compatibility with other users who may not yet have upgraded.

Although file compatibility problems are rare, two issues occasionally crop up when opening Microsoft Office files in OpenOffice.org:

VBA compatibility: OpenOffice.org isn't compatible with Microsoft Office Visual Basic for Applications (VBA). It uses a similar but incompatible internal programming language. This means that Microsoft macros within a document probably won't work when the file is imported to OpenOffice.org. Such macros are typically used in Excel spreadsheets designed to calculate timesheets, for example. In general, however, only high-end users use VBA.

Document protection: OpenOffice.org is unable to open any Office files that have a password, either to protect the document from changes or to protect it from being viewed. Theoretically, it would be easy for OpenOffice.org's programmers to include such functionality, but the laws of many countries make creating such a program feature illegal (it would be seen as a device to overcome copy protection). The easiest solution is to ask whoever sent you the file to remove the password protection. For what it's worth, OpenOffice.org has its own form of password protection.

If you find that OpenOffice.org isn't able to open an Office file saved by your colleagues, you can always suggest that they, too, make the switch to OpenOffice.org. They don't need to be running SUSE Linux to do so. Versions are available to run on all Windows platforms, as well as on the Apple Macintosh. As with the SUSE Linux version, they're entirely free of charge. Indeed, for many people who are running versions of Office they've installed from "borrowed" CDs, OpenOffice.org offers a way to come clean and avoid pirating software. For more details and to download OpenOffice.org, visit www.openoffice.org.

Once your colleagues have made the switch, you can exchange files using OpenOffice.org's native format, or opt to save files in the Office file format. Figure 21-1 shows the file type options available in OpenOffice.org's word processor component's Save dialog box (to access the file type list, click the small arrow to the left of the File Type heading).

■Note OpenOffice.org also supports Rich Text Format (RTF) text documents and comma-separated value (CSV) data files, which are supported by practically every office suite program ever made.

Figure 21-1. *All the OpenOffice.org components are fully compatible with Microsoft Office file formats.*

When it comes to sharing files, there's another option: save your files in a non-Office format such as PDF or HTML. OpenOffice.org is able to export documents in both formats, and most modern PCs equipped with Adobe Acrobat or a simple web browser will be able to read them. However, while OpenOffice.org can open and edit HTML files, it can export documents only as PDF files, so this format is best reserved for files not intended for further editing.

OPEN DOCUMENT FORMAT

One of the principles behind all open source software is the idea of open file formats. This means that if someone creates a new open source word processor, he also makes sure that the technology behind the file format is explained, so that other people can adapt their programs to read and/or save in that file format.

Compare this to Microsoft's approach. It recently published details of its new Office 2007 file formats, but only after questions were raised in national governments about whether rival software developers could compete with Microsoft without such knowledge. In the past, the only way for Office competitors like OpenOffice.org to understand earlier Office file formats was to reverse-engineer them—to try to figure out how they work by taking them apart. This is a time-consuming process and, increasingly, resides in a legal gray area in many countries.

> To meet the goals of open source software, the OpenDocument Format (ODF) was created. This is a completely open and free-to-use file format that all software suites can adopt. The idea is that ODF will make it easy to swap files between all office suites.
>
> Sadly, Microsoft has decided not to support ODF and is sticking with its own proprietary file formats. However, several other local governments in countries all around the world have recently adopted ODF. There's little doubt that it won't be long before ODF will become one of the main ways of disseminating and sharing documents online.
>
> Perhaps it goes without saying that OpenOffice.org version 2, as supplied with SUSE Linux, fully supports ODF. In fact, ODF was originally based on earlier OpenOffice.org file formats.

The Right Fonts

One key to compatibility with the majority of Microsoft Office files is ensuring you have the correct fonts. This is an issue even when using Windows. It's very common to open an Office document to find the formatting incorrect because you don't have the fonts used in the construction of the document.

Although most Windows systems have many fonts, people tend to rely on a handful of core fonts, which are included on most Windows installations. These core fonts include Arial and Times New Roman.

You can obtain these fonts and install them on your SUSE Linux system in several ways. Here, we'll cover two methods: copying your fonts from Windows and installing Microsoft's TrueType Core Fonts.

Copying Windows Fonts

If you dual-boot SUSE Linux with Windows, you can delve into your Windows partition's font folder and copy across every font you have available under Windows. This method is useful if you wish to copy all the fonts installed by third-party applications. If you wish to get just Arial and Times New Roman, you might want to skip ahead to the next section.

■**Caution** Installing Windows fonts under SUSE Linux is a legally gray area. Technically speaking, there's no reason why you shouldn't be able to use the fonts under SUSE Linux. Purchasing Windows as well as any software running on it should also have meant you purchased a license to use the fonts. But the license document for Windows XP makes no mention of font licensing, so the matter is far from clear-cut.

Copying Fonts to the GNOME Desktop

Here's how to copy across your Windows fonts if you're running the GNOME desktop:

1. Click Applications ➤ System ➤ GNOME Terminal. In the window that appears, type the following:

```
nautilus /windows/C/;nautilus fonts://
```

2. Two Nautilus file browsing windows appear. One displays the directories in your Windows partition, and the other shows the SUSE Linux collection of fonts. In the Nautilus window displaying the Windows directories, navigate to your Windows font folder. The location of this folder varies depending on which version of Windows you're using. On my Windows XP test machine, it was located in the `WINDOWS/Fonts/` directory.

3. Click View ➤ View As List. In the list, click the Type column header so that the list is sorted according to file extensions. Scroll down to the list of TrueType fonts and select them all (click the first one, hold down the Shift key, and then click the last one).

4. Click and drag all the TrueType fonts to the Nautilus window displaying your SUSE Linux font collection. The fonts will be copied across.

5. Close all the windows. Log out of SUSE Linux, and then log back in again. You should find your Windows fonts are now available, as shown in Figure 21-2.

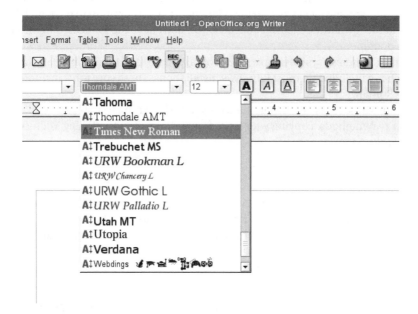

Figure 21-2. *Installing vital Windows fonts means that any documents you create will be more compatible with Microsoft Office documents.*

Copying Fonts to the KDE Desktop

Here's how to copy across your Windows fonts if you're running the KDE desktop:

1. Click K menu ➤ System ➤ Terminal ➤ Konsole. In the window that appears, type the following:

```
konqueror /windows/C/;konqueror fonts:/
```

2. Two Konqueror file browsing windows appear. One displays the directories in your Windows partition, and the other shows the SUSE Linux collection of fonts, split into two folders: `Personal` and `System`. In the Konqueror window displaying the Windows directories, navigate to your Windows font folder. The location of this folder varies depending on which version of Windows you're using. On my Windows XP test machine, it was located in the `WINDOWS/Fonts/` directory.

3. Click View ➤ View Mode ➤ Detailed List View. In the list, click the File Type column header so that the list is sorted according to file extensions. Locate the list of TrueType fonts and select them all (click the first one, hold down the Shift key, and then click the last one).

4. Click and drag all the TrueType fonts to the Konqueror window displaying your SUSE Linux font collection and drop the fonts over the `Personal` folder. The fonts will be copied across.

5. Close all the windows. Log out of SUSE Linux, and then log back in again. You should find your Windows fonts are now available.

Installing the Microsoft TrueType Core Fonts Package

Back in 1996 Microsoft made many of its standard Windows fonts available for free download. The intention was to allow broad website font compatibility, but there are no restrictions on downloading and installing the fonts for other uses, such as office document compatibility.

■**Tip** Wikipedia has an interesting article outlining the history of the Core Fonts and why Microsoft made them available: `http://en.wikipedia.org/wiki/Core_fonts_for_the_Web`.

As you might expect, Microsoft doesn't make a SUSE Linux compatible package available, so it's necessary to download the fonts from a third party website and then install them manually. This isn't too difficult.

Here's how to install the Microsoft TrueType Core Fonts package:

1. Open a web browser and visit the following website:

    `ftp://ftp.gwdg.de/pub/linux/misc/suser-jengelh/UNSPEC/noarch/`

2. Click to download the `MicrosoftFonts-0-8.noarch.rpm` file to your desktop.

■**Note** The file might have been updated since this book was written, and the filename changed correspondingly, but it should be obvious which file to download. If the filename has changed you'll need to substitute the filename in the `rpm` command in Step 3 below.

---

3. Once the file has downloaded, open a terminal window and type the following (to open a terminal window in GNOME, click Applications ➤ System ➤ Terminal ➤ Gnome Terminal; in KDE click K menu ➤ System ➤ Terminal ➤ Konsole):

```
su -
[Enter root password]
rpm -Uvh /home/<username>/Desktop/MicrosoftFonts-0-8.noarch.rpm
```

Replace *<username>* above with your username.

4. Once this has completed, log out and then back in again.

Following this the Microsoft fonts will be available within your applications.

OTHER LINUX OFFICE SUITES

OpenOffice.org is widely regarded as one of the best Linux office suites, but it's not the only one. Its main open source competitor is KOffice. KOffice tightly integrates into the KDE desktop and mirrors much of its look and feel. It includes a word processor, spreadsheet, presentation package, flow-charting tool, database-access tool, and much more. As with OpenOffice.org, in most cases, you can load and save Microsoft Office files. For more details, see its home page at `www.koffice.org`. It's available with SUSE Linux, too, and can be found on the SUSE Linux installation DVD. Just use the Software Management component of YaST2 to search for and install it.

In addition, there are several open source office applications that aren't complete office suites. For example, AbiWord is considered an excellent word processor, which packs in a lot of features but keeps the user interface very simple. It's partnered by Gnumeric, a spreadsheet application that is developed separately (although both aim to be integrated into the GNOME desktop environment). For more details, see `www.abisource.com` and `www.gnome.org/projects/gnumeric/`, respectively. You can also find both of these programs on the SUSE Linux installation DVD (use the Software Management component of YaST2 to search for them).

If you don't mind paying for proprietary software, Hancom Office is extremely popular in Asian countries, and an English language version is also available. It offers a word processor, spreadsheet, presentations package, and more. A 30-day trial version and more details are available from `http://en.hancom.com`.

Summary

This chapter was a general introduction to OpenOffice.org, providing an overview of what you can expect from the programs within the suite. In particular, we focused on the extent of the suite's similarities with Microsoft Office and discussed issues surrounding file compatibility with Microsoft Office. We also looked at how Windows fonts can be brought into SUSE Linux, which aids in successfully importing and creating compatible documents.

In the next chapter, you'll learn about the configuration options globally applicable to the suite, as well as common functions provided across all the programs.

## CHAPTER 22

OpenOffice.org Overview

All the programs in the OpenOffice.org suite rely on a common interface, and therefore look and operate in a similar way. They are also configured in an identical way, and all rely on central concepts such as wizards, which guide you through the creation of particular types of documents. In addition, many components within the suite are shared across the various programs. For example, the automatic chart creation tool within Calc can also be used within Writer.

In this chapter, we'll look at the OpenOffice.org suite as a whole, and explain how it's used and configured. In the following chapters, we'll examine some specific programs in the suite.

Introducing the Interface

If you've ever used an office suite, such as Microsoft Office, you shouldn't find it too hard to become familiar with OpenOffice.org. As with Microsoft Office, OpenOffice.org relies primarily on toolbars, a main menu, and separate context-sensitive menus that appear when you right-click. In addition, OpenOffice.org provides floating palettes that offer quick access to useful functions, such as paragraph styles within Writer.

Figure 22-1 provides a quick guide to the OpenOffice.org interface, showing the following components:

Menu bar: The menus provide access to most of the OpenOffice.org functions.

Standard toolbar: This toolbar provides quick access to global operations, such as saving, opening, and printing files, as well as key functions within the program being used. The Standard toolbar appears in all OpenOffice.org programs and also provides a way to activate the various floating palettes, such as the Navigator, which lets you easily move around various elements within the document.

Formatting toolbar: As its name suggests, this toolbar offers quick access to text-formatting functions, similar to the type of toolbar used in Microsoft Office applications. Clicking the B icon will boldface any selected text, for example. This toolbar appears in Calc, Writer, and Impress.

Ruler: The ruler lets you set tabs and alter margins and indents (within programs that use rulers).

Status bar: The status bar shows various aspects of the configuration, such as whether Insert or Overtype mode is in use.

Document area: This is the main editing area.

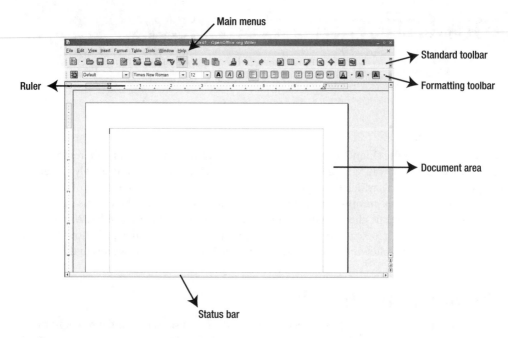

Figure 22-1. *The OpenOffice.org interface has several components.*

Most of the programs rely on the Standard and Formatting toolbars to provide access to their functions, and some programs have additional toolbars. For example, applications such as Impress (a presentation program) and Draw (for drawing vector graphics) have the Drawing toolbar, which provides quick access to tools for drawing shapes, adding lines, and creating fills (the blocks of color within shapes).

Customizing the Interface

You can select which toolbars are visible on your screen, as well as customize those that are already there. You can also add new toolbars and customize the OpenOffice.org menus.

Adding Functions to Toolbars

The quickest way to add icons and functions to any toolbar is to click the two small arrows at the right of a toolbar and select the Visible Buttons entry on the menu that appears. This will present a list of currently visible icons and functions, along with those that might prove useful on that toolbar but are currently hidden. Any option already visible will have a check next to it.

Additionally, you can add practically any function to a toolbar, including the options from the main menus and many more than those that are ordinarily visible. Here are the steps:

1. Click the two small arrows to the right of a toolbar and select the Customize Toolbar option.

2. In the Customize dialog box, click the Add button in the Toolbar Content section to open the Add Commands dialog box, as shown in Figure 22-2.

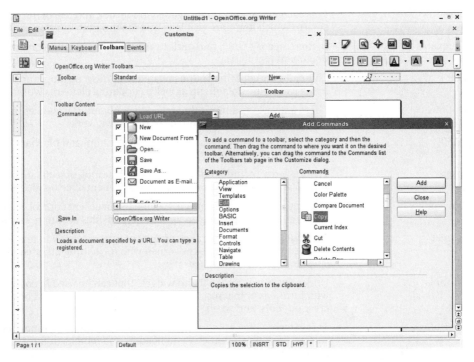

Figure 22-2. *Adding a new function to the toolbar is very easy within OpenOffice.org.*

3. Choose a category from the list on the left to see the available commands in the list on the right. The categories of functions are extremely comprehensive. For example, under the Format category, you'll find entries related to specific functions, such as shrinking font sizes or setting a shadow effect behind text. Table 22-1 provides brief descriptions of each of the categories listed in the Add Commands dialog box.

4. Select the function you want to add on the right side of the Add Commands dialog box, and then click the Add button.

5. Click the Close button. You'll then see your new function in the list of icons in the Customize dialog box.

6. Click and drag to move the new function left or right on the toolbar itself (you'll see the toolbar itself update when you release the mouse button). Alternatively, you can highlight the icon and click the up or down arrow next to the list.

Table 22-1. *OpenOffice.org Toolbar Customization Categories*

Category	Description
Application	These options relate to the specific OpenOffice.org application you're using. For example, if you select to customize a toolbar within Writer, the Application category menu will offer functions to start AutoPilots (effectively wizards) that will build word processor documents.
View	This category offers options related to the look and feel of the suite, such as which items are visible within the program interface.
Templates	In this category, you'll find options related to the creation and use of document templates.
Edit	This category contains options related to cutting, pasting, and copying items within the document, as well as updating elements within it.
Options	These are various options that relate to configuration choices in OpenOffice.org, allowing you to control how it works.
BASIC	Options under this category relate to the creation and playback of OpenOffice.org macros.
Insert	This category includes options related to inserting objects, such as sound, graphics, and elements from other OpenOffice.org documents.
Documents	This category provides options specific to document control, such as those related to exporting documents as PDF files or simply saving files.
Format	This category includes a range of options related largely to text formatting, but also some concerned with formatting other elements, such as drawings and images.
Controls	Under this heading, you'll find widgets that can be used in conjunction with formulas or macros, such as check boxes, buttons, text box creation tools, and so on.
Navigate	This category offers tools that let you move around a document quickly, such as the ability to quickly edit headers and footers, or move from the top of the page to the end very quickly.
Table	This category provides options related to the creation of tables.
Drawing	The tools in this category allow you to draw objects, such as shapes and lines, and also to create floating text boxes.
Graphic	This category presents a handful of options related to manipulating bitmap graphics that are inserted into the document.
Data	This category offers a couple of options related to working with information sources, such as databases.
Frame	These options relate to any frames inserted into the document, such as how elements within the frame are aligned and how text is wrapped around the frame.
Numbering	These are various options related to creating automatic numbered or bulleted lists.
Modify	These options relate to the drawing components within OpenOffice.org and let you manipulate images or drawings in various ways by applying filters.
OpenOffice.org BASIC Macros	Here, you can select from various ready-made macros, which provide some of OpenOffice.org's functions.

Many functions that can be added are automatically given a relevant toolbar icon, but you can choose another icon for a function by selecting the icon in the list in the Customize dialog box, clicking Modify, and then selecting Change Icon. You can also use this method to change an icon that already appears on a toolbar.

■ **Note** To delete an icon from a toolbar, click the two small arrows to the right of a toolbar and select the Customize Toolbar option. Select the icon you want to remove, click the Modify button, and choose to delete it.

Adding a New Toolbar

If you want to add your own new toolbar to offer particular functions, you'll find it easy to do. Here are the steps:

1. Click the two small arrows to the right of any toolbar and select Customize Toolbar from the list of options. Don't worry—you're not actually going to customize that particular toolbar!

2. In the Customize dialog box, click the New button at the top right.

3. Give the toolbar a name. The default entry for the Save In field is correct, so you don't need to alter it.

4. Populate the new toolbar, following the instructions in the previous section.

5. Once you've finished, click the OK button.

You should see your new toolbar beneath the main toolbars. If you want to hide it, click View ➤ Toolbars, and then remove the check alongside the name of your toolbar.

Customizing Menus

You can also customize the OpenOffice.org menus. Here are the steps:

1. Select Tools ➤ Customize from the menu bar.

2. In the Customize dialog box, select the Menus tab.

3. Choose which menu you wish to customize from the Menu drop-down list.

4. Select the position where you wish the new function to appear on the menu, by selecting an entry on the menu function list, and then click the Add button.

5. Add commands to the menu, as described earlier in the "Adding Functions to Toolbars" section.

The up and down arrows in the Customize dialog box allow you to alter the position of entries on the menu. You could move those items you use frequently to the top of the menu, for example.

You can remove an existing menu item by highlighting it in the Customize dialog box, clicking the Modify button, and then clicking Delete.

If you make a mistake, simply click the Reset button at the bottom right of the Customize dialog box to return the menus to their default state.

Configuring OpenOffice.org Options

In addition to the wealth of customization options, OpenOffice.org offers a range of configuration options that allow you to make it work exactly how you wish. Within an OpenOffice.org program, select Tools ➤ Options from the menu to open the Options dialog box, as shown in Figure 22-3.

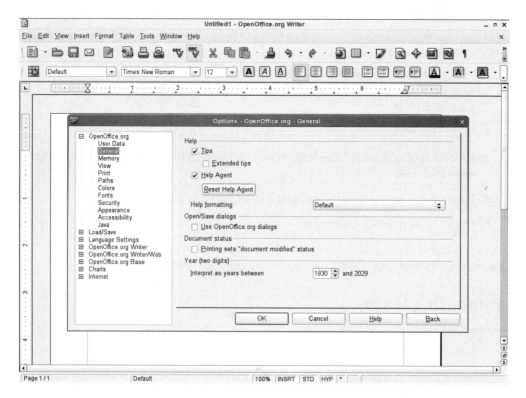

Figure 22-3. *OpenOffice.org's main configuration options are accessed by selecting Tools ➤ Options.*

Most of the configuration options offered within each program apply across the suite, but those under the heading of the program's name apply only to the program in use. In other words, to set the options for Writer, you need to use the Writer Options dialog box. But to set global options for the entire suite, you can use any program's Options dialog box.

A variety of options are offered, allowing you to tweak everything from the default file format to the colors used by default within the software. Table 22-2 briefly describes each of the OpenOffice.org configuration options.

Table 22-2. *OpenOffice.org Configuration Options*

Option	Description
OpenOffice.org	
User Data	This is the personal data that will be added to the documents you create. You can leave this area blank if you wish.
General	This offers a handful of miscellaneous options, such as how to handle two-digit dates, when the help system should step in to offer tips, how the help system should be formatted (such as in high resolution for people with vision problems), and whether printing a document is interpreted by OpenOffice.org as modifying it.
Memory	This entry relates to how much system memory OpenOffice.org can use. You can limit the number of undo steps, for example, and alter the cache memory used for holding graphical objects.
View	This option allows you to alter the look, feel, and operation of OpenOffice.org. You can define whether the middle mouse button performs a paste operation (which is consistent with how SUSE Linux works), or whether it should perform a scrolling function, as with Windows. You can also alter elements such as whether icons appear in menus and if fonts are previewed in the toolbar menu.
Print	This option lets you adjust how printing is handled within OpenOffice.org. The functions relate to those that can stop documents from printing incorrectly, such as reducing any transparency effects within the documents so on-page elements don't appear faint or completely disappear in the final output. (Note that specific print functions are handled within the Print dialog box when you actually print a document.)
Paths	This is where the file paths for user-configured and vital system tools are handled. Generally, there's little reason to edit this list, although you might choose to alter the default location where your documents are saved (simply double-click the My Documents entry to do this).
Colors	This option lets you define the default color palette that appears in the various programs in the suite.
Fonts	By creating entries here, you can automatically substitute fonts within documents you open for others on your system. If you don't have the Microsoft core fonts installed, this might prove useful. For example, you might choose to substitute Arial, commonly used in Microsoft Office documents, for Sans, one of the sans serif fonts used under SUSE Linux.
Security	This option controls which types of functions can be run within OpenOffice.org. For example, you can choose whether macros created by third parties should be run when you open a new document.
Appearance	This option lets you alter the color scheme used within OpenOffice.org, in a similar way to how you can alter the default SUSE Linux desktop color scheme. Individual elements within documents and pages can be modified, too.
Accessibility	This option relates to features that might help people with vision disabilities to use OpenOffice.org. For example, you can define whether animated graphics are shown on the screen.
Java	This option lets you control whether you use the Java Runtime Environment, which may be necessary to use some of OpenOffice.org's features.

Continued

Table 22-2. *Continued*

Option	Description
Load/Save	
General	This option includes settings that relate to how files are saved. You can select whether the default is to save in OpenOffice.org or Microsoft Office format. Choosing the latter is useful if you share a lot of documents with colleagues who are not running OpenOffice.org.
VBA Properties	This option relates to how Visual Basic for Applications (VBA) code is handled when Microsoft Office documents are opened. Specifically, it ensures that the code isn't lost when the file is saved again.
Microsoft Office	This option provides functions specifically needed to convert or open Microsoft Office files within OpenOffice.org.
HTML Compatibility	This option includes settings that affect the compatibility of HTML files saved within OpenOffice.org.
Language Settings	
Languages	This option lets you set your local language so that documents are spell-checked correctly. In addition, you can activate Asian language support, which allows for more-complex document layout options.
Writing Aids	Under this option, you can activate or deactivate various plug-ins designed to help format documents, such as the hyphenator or the spell-checking component. In addition, you can alter how the spell-checker works, such as whether it ignores capitalized words.
OpenOffice.org Writer	
General	This option allows you to alter various settings related to the editing of word processor documents, such as which measurements are used on the ruler (centimeter, inches, picas, and so on).
View	Under this option, you can configure the look and feel of the Writer program, such as which scroll bars are visible by default. You can also turn off the display of various page elements, such as tables and graphics.
Formatting Aids	This option lets you choose which symbols appear for "invisible" elements (such as the carriage return symbol or a dot symbol to indicate where spaces have been inserted) in Writer.
Grid	This controls whether page elements will snap to an invisible grid. You can also define the dimensions and spacing of the grid cells here.
Basic Fonts (Western)	This controls which fonts are used by default in the various text styles, such as for the default text and within lists.
Print	This option offers control over printing options specific to Writer, such as which page elements are printed (you might choose to turn off the printing of graphics, for example).
Tables	This option lets you control how tables are created and how you interact with them within Writer. For example, you can control what happens when a table is resized, such as whether the entire table responds to the changes or merely the cell you're resizing.
Changes	This option lets you define how changes are displayed when the track changes function is activated.
Compatibility	This option lets you set specifics of how Writer handles the import and export of Microsoft Word documents.

Option	Description
AutoCaption	This option offers settings for the AutoCaption feature within Writer.
Mail Merge E-Mail	This option lets you control the sending of e-mail mail merge messages.

OpenOffice.org Writer/Web

View	This option lets you control the HTML editor component of OpenOffice.org (effectively an extension of Writer). You can control the look and feel of the HTML editor, including which elements are displayed on the screen.
Formatting Aids	As with the similar entry for Writer under Text Document, this option lets you view symbols in place of usually hidden text elements.
Grid	This lets you define a grid that on-screen elements are able to "snap to" in order to aid accurate positioning.
Print	This option allows you to define how HTML documents created within OpenOffice.org are printed.
Table	Similar to the Tables entry under Text Document, this option controls how tables are created and handled within HTML documents.
Background	This option lets you set the default background color for HTML documents.

OpenOffice.org Calc

General	This option lets you modify miscellaneous settings related to Calc, such as which measurement units are used within the program and how the formatting of cells is changed when new data is input.
View	This option relates to the look and feel of Calc, such as the color of the grid lines between cells and which elements are displayed on the screen. For example, you can configure whether zero values are displayed, and whether overflow text within cells is shown or simply truncated at the cell boundary.
Calculate	This option relates to how numbers are handled during certain types of formula calculations, such as those involving dates.
Sort Lists	This option lets you create lists that are applied to relevant cells when the user chooses to sort them. Several lists are predefined to correctly sort days of the week or months of the year.
Changes	This option relates to the on-screen formatting for changes when the track changes function is activated.
Grid	This option lets you configure an invisible grid that stretches across the sheet, and also which page objects can be set to snap to the grid for correct alignment.
Print	This option relates to printing specifically from Calc, such as whether Calc should avoid printing empty pages that might occur within documents.

OpenOffice.org Impress

General	This option refers to miscellaneous settings within the Impress program, such as whether the program should always start with a wizard and which units of measurement should be used.
View	This option relates to the look and feel of Impress, and, in particular, whether certain on-screen elements are displayed.

Continued

Table 22-2. *Continued*

Option	Description
Grid	This controls whether an invisible grid is applied to the page and whether objects should snap to it.
Print	This option controls how printing is handled within Impress and, in particular, how items in the document will appear on the printed page.
OpenOffice.org Draw	
General	This option relates to miscellaneous settings within Draw (the vector graphics component of OpenOffice.org).
View	This option allows you to set specific preferences with regard to which objects are visible on the screen while you're editing with Draw.
Grid	This option relates to the invisible grid that can be applied to the page.
Print	This option lets you define which on-screen elements are printed and which are not printed.
OpenOffice.org Base	
Connections	This option lets you control how any data sources you attach to are handled.
Databases	You can use this option to configure which databases are registered for use within Base.
Chart	
Default Colors	You can use this option to set the default color palette that should be used when creating charts, usually within the Calc program.
Internet	
Proxy	Using this option, you can configure network proxy settings specifically for OpenOffice.org, if necessary.
Search	Certain functions within various OpenOffice.org programs let you search the Internet. Here, you can configure how these search functions work.
E-mail	This option lets you specify which program you wish OpenOffice.org to use for e-mail.
Mozilla Plug-in	This option allows integration of OpenOffice.org into the Mozilla and/or Netscape browsers, so you can view OpenOffice.org documents within the browser window.

Using OpenOffice.org Core Functions

Although the various programs within OpenOffice.org are designed for very specific tasks, they all share several core functions that work in broadly similar ways. In addition, each program is able to borrow components from other programs in the suite.

Using Wizards

One of the core functions you'll find most useful when creating new documents is the wizard system, which you can access from the File menu. A wizard guides you through creating a new document by answering questions and following a wizard-based interface. This replaces the template-based approach within Microsoft Office, although it's worth noting that OpenOffice.org is still able to use templates.

A wizard will usually offer a variety of document styles. Some wizards will even prompt you to fill in salient details, which they will then insert into your document in the relevant areas.

Getting Help

OpenOffice.org employs a comprehensive help system, complete with automatic context-sensitive help, called the Help Agent, which will appear if the program detects you're performing a particular task. Usually, the Help Agent takes the form of a light bulb graphic, which will appear at the bottom-right corner of the screen. If you ignore the Help Agent, it will disappear within a few seconds. Clicking it causes a help window to open. Alternatively, you can access the main searchable help file by clicking the relevant menu entry.

Inserting Objects with Object Linking and Embedding

All the OpenOffice.org programs are able to make use of Object Linking and Embedding (OLE). This effectively means that one OpenOffice.org document can be inserted into another. For example, you might choose to insert a Calc spreadsheet into a Writer document.

The main benefit of using OLE over simply copying and pasting the data is that the OLE item (referred to as an *object*) will be updated whenever the original document is revised. In this way, you can prepare a report featuring a spreadsheet full of figures, for example, and not need to worry about updating the report when the figures change. Figure 22-4 shows an example of a spreadsheet from Calc inserted into a Writer document.

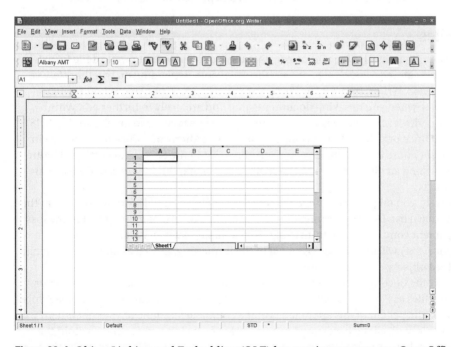

Figure 22-4. *Object Linking and Embedding (OLE) lets you incorporate one OpenOffice.org document into another.*

Whenever you click inside the OLE object, the user interface will change so that you can access functions specific to that object. For example, if you had inserted an Impress object into a Calc document, clicking within the object would cause the Calc interface to temporarily turn into that of Impress. Clicking outside the OLE object would restore the interface back to Calc.

You can explore OLE objects by selecting Insert ➤ Object ➤ OLE Object. This option lets you create and insert a new OLE object, as well as add one based on an existing file.

Creating Macros

OpenOffice.org employs a powerful BASIC-like programming language, which you can use to create your own functions. Although this language is called BASIC, it is several generations beyond the BASIC you might have used in the past. OpenOffice.org's BASIC is a high-level, object-oriented environment designed to appeal to programmers who wish to quickly add their own functions to the suite.

However, it's possible for any user to record a series of actions as a macro, which is then automatically turned into a simple BASIC program. This can be very useful if you wish to automate a simple, repetitive task, such as the insertion of a paragraph of text, or even something more complicated, such as searching and replacing text within a document.

To record a macro, select Tools ➤ Macro ➤ Record Macro. After you've selected this option, any subsequent actions will be recorded. All keyboard strokes and clicks of the mouse will be captured and turned automatically into BASIC commands. To stop the recording, simply click the button on the floating toolbar. After this, you'll be invited to give the macro a name (look to the top left of the dialog box). Once you've done so, click Save. You can then run your macro in the future by choosing Tools ➤ Macro ➤ Run Macro. Simply expand the My Macros and Standard entries at the top left of the dialog box, select your macro in the list, and then click Run.

Saving Files

As mentioned in Chapter 21, OpenOffice.org uses the OpenDocument range of file formats. The files end with an .ods, .odt, .odp, or .odb file extension, depending on whether they've been saved by Calc, Writer, Impress, or Base, respectively. The OpenDocument format is the best choice when you're saving documents that you are likely to further edit within OpenOffice.org. However, if you wish to share files with colleagues who aren't running SUSE Linux or OpenOffice.org, the solution is to save the files as Microsoft Office files. To save in this format, just choose it from the Save As drop-down list in the Save As dialog box. If your colleague is running an older version of OpenOffice.org or StarOffice, you can also save in those file formats.

Alternatively, you might wish to save the file in one of the other file formats offered in the Save As drop-down list. However, saving files in an alternative format might result in the loss of some document components or formatting. For example, saving a Writer document as a simple text file (.txt) will lead to the loss of all of the formatting, as well as any of the original file's embedded objects, such as pictures.

To avoid losing document components or formatting, you might choose to output your OpenOffice.org files as Portable Document Format (PDF) files, which can be read by the Adobe Acrobat viewer. The benefit of this approach is that a complete facsimile of your document will be made available, with all the necessary fonts and on-screen elements included within the PDF file. The drawback is that PDF files cannot be loaded into OpenOffice.org for further editing, so you should always save an additional copy of the file in the native OpenOffice.org format. To save any file as a PDF throughout the suite, select File ➤ Export As PDF. Then choose PDF in the File Format drop-down box, as shown in Figure 22-5.

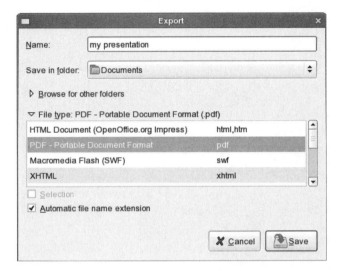

Figure 22-5. *All the programs in the suite can export files in Adobe PDF format.*

Summary

In this chapter, we looked at the configuration options provided with OpenOffice.org. You were introduced to the user interface, which is shared across all the programs within the suite, and learned how it can be customized. We also examined some common tools provided across the suite of programs, such as macro generation.

Over the following chapters, we will look at each major component of the suite, starting with Writer.

■■■

## CHAPTER 23

In Depth: Writer

The word processor is arguably the most popular element within any office suite. That said, you'll be happy to know that OpenOffice.org's Writer component doesn't skimp on features. It offers full text-editing and formatting functionality, along with powerful higher-level features such as mail merge. You'll find it on the Applications ➤ Office ➤ Word Processor menu within GNOME. Within KDE, click K menu ➤ Office ➤ Word Processor.

In this chapter, we'll take a look at some of Writer's most useful features. As with all of the components in the OpenOffice.org suite, describing the features within Writer could easily fill an entire book. You should do some exploring on your own by clicking around to discover new features, as well as make judicious use of the help system.

Formatting Text

You can format text within Writer using several methods. Here, we'll look at using the Formatting toolbar, the context menu, and the Style and Formatting palette.

The Formatting Toolbar

Formatting text is easy to do via the Formatting toolbar, which is just above the ruler and main document area. Using the toolbar buttons, you can select the type of font you wish to use, its point size, and its style (normal, bold, italics, and so on). The range of fonts is previewed in the Font drop-down list, making it easy to select the right typeface.

In addition, the Formatting toolbar lets you justify text so that it's aligned to the left or right margin, centered, or fully justified. You can also indent text using the relevant icons. As with elsewhere in SUSE Linux, a tooltip will appear over each icon when you hover the mouse cursor over it, as shown in Figure 23-1. To the right of the indentation buttons are tools to change the text background and foreground colors, and also a tool to create highlighter pen-style effects.

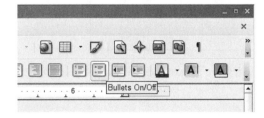

Figure 23-1. *When you hover your mouse over an icon, a tooltip appears to explain what it does.*

Context Menu

Rather than use the Formatting toolbar, you can format text using the context menu. Right-click the text you want to format, and a context menu will present options for the font, size, style, alignment, and line spacing. The context menu also allows you to change the case of the highlighted characters—from uppercase to lowercase, and vice versa.

By selecting the Character option from the context menu, you obtain ultimate control over the font formatting. This will present a dialog box that includes every possible option, such as rotating the text and altering the individual character spacing.

■**Tip** The Character dialog box lets you create interesting typographical effects. The Paragraph dialog box has many options for formatting paragraphs. These tools open up the possibility of using Writer for simple desktop publishing work.

Selecting Paragraph from the context menu displays the Paragraph dialog box, as shown in Figure 23-2. This gives you control over paragraph elements, such as line spacing, indentation, and automatic numbering. Here, you will also find an option to automatically create drop caps, so you can start a piece of writing in style!

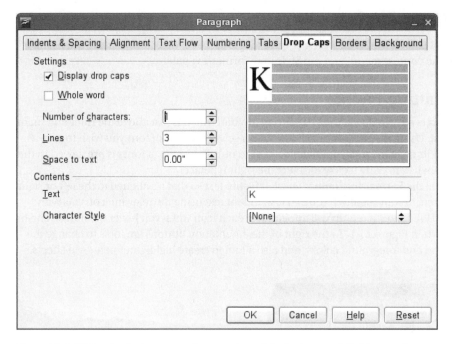

Figure 23-2. *Writer includes many elements found in desktop publishing packages, such as the ability to create drop caps.*

The Style and Formatting Palette

The Style and Formatting palette offers a variety of predefined formatting styles that you can apply to selected text or enable before you begin adding text. To make it appear, click Formatting ➤ Styles and Formatting, or press F11. You can click the palette's close button to hide it.

You can easily add your own text styles to the Style and Formatting palette. Simply select some text that has the desired formatting applied, click the top-right button (denoted by a paragraph symbol next to a block of text), and then select New Style from Selection in the list. You'll be invited to give the style a name, and when you click OK, it will appear in the list.

Spell-Checking

Writer is able to automatically spell-check as you type. Any words it considers misspelled will be underlined in red. You can choose from a list of possible corrections by right-clicking the word and selecting from the context menu. If you're sure the word is spelled correctly but it doesn't appear to be in the dictionary, you can select Add ➤ Standard.dic from the context menu, as shown in Figure 23-3. This will add the word to your own personal dictionary extension (other users won't have access to your dictionary and will need to create their own list of approved words).

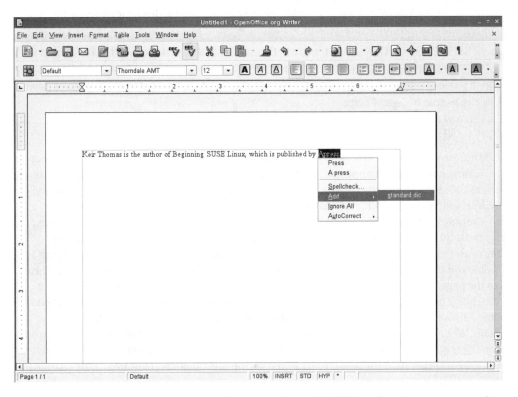

Figure 23-3. *Any words you're going to use frequently, but which Writer doesn't recognize, can be added to your personal dictionary.*

Tip You might find that the spell-checker is set for US English. If you live outside the United States, or need to create documents for readers in other countries, you can choose a dictionary tailored to your locality or needs. To change the language, select Tools ➤ Options. In the list on the left, select Language Settings, and then Languages. In the Default Languages for Documents list, select your local variation. This will then become the default for all new documents.

If you find live spell-checking invasive or distracting, you can deactivate it by selecting Tools ➤ Spellcheck, clicking the Options button, and removing the check next to Check Spelling As You Type.

You can manually spell-check the document at any time by clicking Tools ➤ Spellcheck. This will scan through the document and prompt you for corrections for words the program considers misspelled.

Inserting Pictures

Writer includes quite substantial desktop publishing-like functions, such as the ability to insert pictures into text documents and to have text flow around pictures.

Inserting any kind of graphic—a graph, digital camera photo, drawing, or any other type of image—is easy. Simply choose Insert ➤ Picture ➤ From File.

Tip If you have a scanner, you can also scan pictures directly into Writer documents. Simply click Insert ➤ Picture ➤ Scan ➤ Select Source.

After you've inserted a picture, you can place it anywhere on the page. When you select the picture, a new toolbar appears. This toolbar contains various simple image-tweaking tools, such as those for altering the brightness, contrast, and color balance of the image. Additionally, by clicking and dragging the blue handles surrounding the image, you can resize it.

Graphics that are imported into Writer must be anchored in some way. In other words, they must be linked to a page element so that they don't move unexpectedly. By default, they're anchored to the nearest paragraph, which means that if that paragraph moves, the graphic will move, too. Alternatively, by right-clicking the graphic, you can choose to anchor it to the page, paragraph, or character it is on or next to, as shown in Figure 23-4. Selecting to anchor it to the page will fix it firmly in place, regardless of what happens to the contents of the surrounding text. The As Character option is slightly different from the To Character option. When you choose As Character, the image will be anchored to the character it is next to, and it is actually inserted in the same line as that character, as if it were a character itself. If the image is bigger than the line it is anchored in, the line height will automatically change to accommodate it.

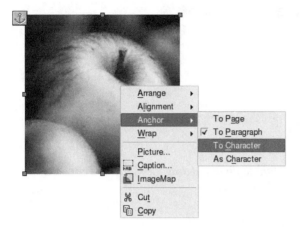

Figure 23-4. *A picture can be "anchored" to the page, paragraph, or a character. This affects how it responds to the paragraphs surrounding it.*

As you can see in Figure 23-4, the context menu also includes a Wrap option, which lets you set the type of text wrap you want to use. By default, Optimal Page Wrap is selected. This causes the text to wrap down just one side of the picture—the side on which the picture is farthest from the edge of the page. Alternatives include No Wrap, which causes the graphic to occupy the entire space on the page; no text is allowed on either side of it. However, Page Wrap is the best option if you're looking for a desktop publishing-style effect, because the text will wrap around both sides of the picture. Alternatively, if you wish the image to appear in the background of the page with text flowing across it, you can select the relevant option from the context menu.

As always within OpenOffice.org, ultimate control is achieved by opening the relevant dialog box. You can set up how graphics are treated on the page by right-clicking the image and selecting Picture. In the dialog box that appears, you can select the wrap effect, specify the invisible border around the wrap (which governs how close the text is to the image), and give the image a border frame.

Working with Tables

Often, it's useful to present columns of numbers or text within a word processor document. To make it easy to align the columns, OpenOffice.org offers the Table tool. With it, you can quickly and easily create a grid in which to enter numbers or other information. You can even turn tables into simple spreadsheets, and tally rows or columns via simple formulas.

To insert a table, click and hold the Table icon on the Standard toolbar (which runs across the top of the screen beneath the menu). Then simply drag the mouse in the table diagram that appears until you have the desired number of rows and columns, and release the mouse button to create the table, as shown in Figure 23-5.

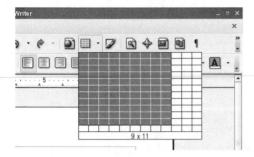

Figure 23-5. *Just select the Table icon on the Main toolbar and drag the mouse to define the size of the table. Release the mouse button when you're finished.*

Whenever your cursor is inside the table, a new toolbar will appear, offering handy options. Once again, simply hover your mouse over each button to find out what it does via a tooltip.

As with spreadsheets, tables consist of cells arranged into rows (running horizontally) and columns (running vertically). Altering the size of a column is easy. Just hover the mouse over the edge of a cell until it changes to a resizing cursor, and then click and drag. You can do the same on a horizontal bar to alter a cell's height, but a far better method is to right-click within the cell, select Row ➤ Height, and enter a value. This will ensure that subsequent cells are shifted down to make space for the newly enlarged cell, which doesn't happen when you click and drag the cell's border.

■**Tip** An alternative way of resizing cells is to click in a cell and press the Enter key, which inserts a carriage return. Cells expand to fit their contents.

Once the cursor is within a table, you can move from cell to cell using the Tab key. Alternatively, you can move backward through the cells by pressing Shift+Tab.

To add more rows or columns, click the relevant icon on the Table toolbar (the fourth and fifth buttons on the bottom row). To split an existing cell, ensure your cursor is inside it, right-click, select Cell from the menu, and then click Split.

If you want to total figures within a table, click in an empty cell, and then click the Sum icon on the Table toolbar (the Greek sigma symbol on the right side of the bottom row). This is similar to inserting a function in a spreadsheet. The cell holds the formula for the sum, and clicking additional cells, or a range of cells, adds them to the sum.

■**Note** Only correctly formatted cells can be summed using the Sum icon on the Table toolbar. Cells with spaces or text within them cannot be added to the formula.

You can alter the styling of any cell using various icons on the Table toolbar, as well as the standard text-formatting tools on the Formatting toolbar. The Table toolbar allows you to add borders to the cells and change the background colors. Alternatively, you can choose to remove all borders from the cells by clicking the Borders icon and then selecting the No Borders option (note that gray borders will remain in place, but these are only for your convenience and won't appear in printouts).

Mail Merging

Mail merging refers to automatically applying a database of details, such as names and addresses, to a document, so that many personalized copies are produced. It's ordinarily used to create form letters for mailings.

OpenOffice.org makes the procedure very easy, but it requires source data that will be merged into the document. As with Microsoft Word, you can either enter this data within Writer itself or choose to import data from a separate document. Unless you have enough knowledge of databases to connect one to OpenOffice.org (the program works with dBase and MySQL files, among others), you may want to input existing data in the form of a comma-separated value (CSV) text file. This is the simplest form of data file that is understood by the majority of office programs and databases.

Here, we're going to look at entering the data within Writer, which is the best policy for smaller mail merge operations. You can then output the data as a CSV file, so you can use it again later. Here are the steps for using mail merge:

1. Select Tools ➤ Mail Merge Wizard to start the wizard, as shown in Figure 23-6.

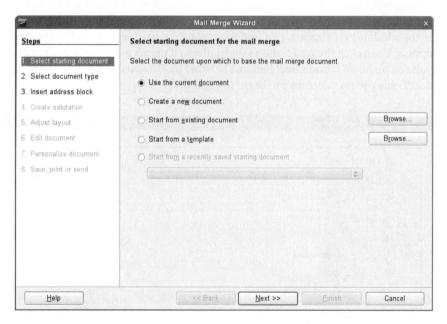

Figure 23-6. *The Mail Merge Wizard makes creating multiple documents from a data source incredibly easy.*

2. Specify your starting document, which is the document in which the merged data will appear. You can opt to use the current document, create a new document, open a document from file, or use a template as the basis for your file.

3. Choose the mail merge type. You can choose to create a merged e-mail (for sending to multiple recipients) or a merged letter.

4. You're asked to tell Writer about your data. Writer needs to know where to find the addresses that will be merged into the document. Click the Select Address List button.

5. In the window that appears, you have a number of options. You can raid your Evolution e-mail address book for the data, click Add to select an already existing data source (such as a database or CSV file), or create a data source from scratch. For this example, choose to create a data source to enter the data in Writer.

Note The fourth option for choosing a mail merge data source, Filter, allows you to filter the database source you select after clicking Add, so that you can import only specific data. To learn more about this technique, browse the OpenOffice.org help file (click Help ➤ OpenOffice.org Help) and search for Filtering ➤ Data in Databases.

---

6. You're presented with a form for entering the data for each individual you want to receive the mail-merged letter, as shown in Figure 23-7. You don't need to fill in each field; you'll be able to choose which data fields to use in the document later on. If you wish to enter your own specific data types in addition to address details, you can click the Customize button to add your own field to the list. Using the up and down arrows in the window that appears, position the highlight where you would like the data to appear. Then click the Add button (alternatively, if there's a data field you're not using, you can highlight it and select Rename to reuse it). Obviously, you should add any new data fields you want before you begin to enter data!

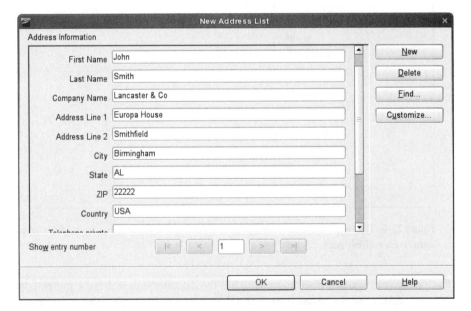

Figure 23-7. *Enter the data for each person you want to receive the letter.*

7. Type in the data and press Enter at the end of each line. When you get to the last field, click the New button at the top right. When you've finished entering all the data, click OK. Then accept Writer's offer to save the data as a CSV file.

8. You're returned to the data-selection screen, and your just-saved file will be at the top of the list. Click OK.

9. You're returned to the main Mail Merge Wizard window, where you can select whether or not to include an address block. All this means is that Writer will automatically add the merge fields to your document in what it considers the correct format (for example, title, followed by first and last name, with each line of the address underneath, and so on). You can insert the merge fields manually later on if you wish; in that case, remove the check from the "This document shall contain an address block" check box. Click Next.

10. You're invited to create the salutation that will head the letter. This will contain the merge data as well, so that you can personalize the letter. Again, you can accept the default, tweak it slightly, or choose not to have an automated salutation (so that you can create your own later).

11. Depending on your previous choices, and whether you accepted the automatic address block and salutation, you are now given the choice to adjust the layout of the document in a rough way or to actually edit it (note that even if you accepted the address block and/or salutation, you'll get a chance to edit the document in the next step anyway).

12. If you opt to edit the document, you can insert your choice of merge fields by clicking Insert ➤ Fields ➤ Other. Select the Database tab in the window that appears, and then select Mail Merge Fields on the left side of the window. Click the small plus symbol next to the data file you created earlier, which should be listed on the right, and you can then select and insert the merge fields. Once you've finished, click the Return to Mail Merge Wizard button.

13. Click Next to perform the merge. You're then given a chance to edit the actual mail-merged documents (which, depending on the quantity of data entries you created earlier, could number in the tens, hundreds, or even thousands!).

14. You can save or print the *merged* document containing the data. To save the document creating the merge fields, click Save Starting Document.

Adding Headers and Footers

You may want to add headers and footers to long documents to aid navigation. They appear at the top and bottom of each page, respectively, and can include the document title, page number, and other information. Headers and footers are created and edited independently of the main document.

As you might expect, inserting both headers and footers takes just a couple of clicks. Select Insert ➤ Header or Insert ➤ Footer, depending on which you wish to insert (documents can have both, of course). Writer will then display an editing area where you can type text to appear in the header or footer.

■Tip If you can't see the boundaries of the editing area, click View ➤ Text Boundaries.

For more options, right-click in the header or footer area, select Page, and then click the Header or Footer tab. Here, you can control the formatting and nature of the header or footer. Clicking the More button will let you apply borders or background colors.

You might wish to insert page numbers that will be updated automatically as the document progresses. OpenOffice.org refers to data that automatically updates as a *field*. You can insert a wide variety of fields by selecting Insert ➤ Fields, as shown in Figure 23-8. For example, along with the page number, you can insert the document title and author name (which is read from the details entered into the Options dialog box, accessed from the Tools menu). In addition, you can enter mail merge fields by clicking Other (see the previous section for a description of how to associate mail merge data with a document).

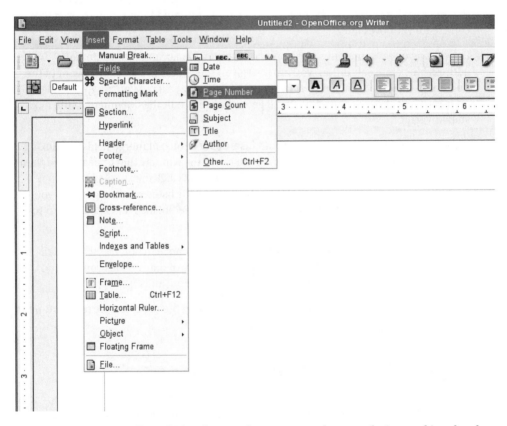

Figure 23-8. *Automatically updating data, such as page numbers, can be inserted into headers and footers.*

Summary

In this chapter, we've examined Writer, one of the core components of OpenOffice.org. We've looked at the some of the key tools, which enable quick and easy document creation. In particular, you've learned how to format text, use the spell-checking component, insert pictures, create and edit tables, mail merge, and add headers and footers.

In the next chapter, we move on to another vital part of OpenOffice.org: Calc, the spreadsheet component.

■ ■ ■

## CHAPTER 24

In Depth: Calc

Calc is the spreadsheet component of OpenOffice.org. Like most modern spreadsheet programs, it contains hundreds of features, many of which few users will ever use. However, it doesn't abandon its user-friendliness in the process and remains very simple for those who want to work on modest calculations, such as home finances or mortgage interest payments. In many regards, Calc is practically a clone of Excel, and anyone who has used Microsoft's spreadsheet program will be able to get started with it immediately.

In this chapter, you'll learn about some of the best features of Calc, as well as the basics of spreadsheet creation.

Entering and Formatting Data

Start Calc by clicking Applications ➤ Office ➤ Spreadsheet ➤ OpenOffice.org Calc under GNOME, or click K menu ➤ Office ➤ Spreadsheet ➤ OpenOffice.org Calc under KDE.

As with all spreadsheets, entering data into a Calc document is simply a matter of selecting a cell and starting to type. You can enter practically anything into a cell, but a handful of symbols are not allowed. For example, you cannot enter an equal sign (=) followed by a number and have it appear in a cell, because Calc will assume that this is part of a formula.

■**Tip** To enter any character into a cell, including an equal sign followed by a digit, precede it with an apostrophe ('). The apostrophe itself won't be visible within the spreadsheet, and whatever you type won't be interpreted in any special way; it will be seen as plain text.

Entering a sequence of data across a range of cells can be automated. Start typing the sequence of numbers, highlight them, and then click and drag the small handle to the bottom right of the last cell. This will continue the sequence. You'll see a tooltip window, indicating what the content of each cell will be. Figure 24-1 illustrates this process.

Cells can be formatted in a variety of ways. For trivial formatting changes, such as selecting a different font or changing the number format, you can use the Formatting toolbar. For example, to turn the cell into one that displays currency, click the Currency icon (remember that hovering the mouse cursor over each icon will reveal a tooltip). You can also increase or decrease the number of visible decimal places by clicking the relevant Formatting toolbar icon.

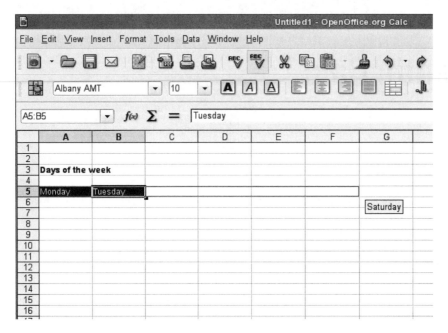

Figure 24-1. *You can automate the entering of data sequences by clicking and dragging.*

For more formatting options, right-click the individual cell and select Format Cells from the menu. This displays the Format Cell dialog box, where you can change the style of the typeface, rotate text, place text at various angles, and so on. The Border tab of the Format Cell dialog box includes options for cell gridlines of varying thicknesses, which will appear when the document is eventually printed out.

Deleting and Inserting Data and Cells

Deleting data is also easy. Just highlight the cell or cells with the data you want to delete, and then press the Delete key. If you want to totally eradicate the cell along with its contents, right-click it and select Delete. This will cause the data to the sides of the cell to move in. You'll be given a choice on where you want the cells to shift from to fill the space: left, right, above, or below.

To insert a new cell, right-click where you would like to it to appear and select Insert. Again, you'll be prompted about where you want to shift the surrounding cells in order to make space for the new cell.

Working with Formulas

Calc includes a large number of formulas. In addition to simple and complex math functions, Calc offers a range of logical functions, as well as statistical and database tools. Certain formulas can also be used to manipulate text strings, such as dates.

You can get an idea of the available functions by clicking the Function Wizard button on the Formula bar (which is just below the Formatting toolbar). This will bring up a categorized list of formulas, along with brief outlines of what function the formula performs. If you would like more details, use the help system, which contains comprehensive descriptions of most of the formulas, complete with examples of the correct syntax.

■Note The Function Wizard is actually a continuation of the wizard system you've seen in other OpenOffice.org programs, and some of the functions are also available elsewhere in the suite.

You can reuse formulas by cutting and pasting them. Calc is intelligent enough to work out which cells the transplanted formula should refer to, but it's always a good idea to check to make sure the correct cells are referenced.

Using the Function Wizard

To use the Function Wizard to add a function, click the relevant button on the Formula bar, select the desired type of formula from the Category drop-down list, and then double-click an entry in the function list to select it. Following this, you'll be prompted to input the relevant values or define the appropriate data sources. Next to each text-entry box is a "shrink" button, which temporarily hides the wizard window, so you can select cells to be used within the formula.

Let's look at a quick example of using the wizard to work out an average value of a number of cells.

1. Select the cell in which you want the result of the formula to appear.

2. Start the Function Wizard by clicking the button on the Formula bar. In the left-hand list of functions, double-click AVERAGE. The wizard will then present a list of fields on the right side of the dialog box, where you can enter the values to be averaged. You could type numeric values directly into these fields, but it's more likely that you'll want to reference individual cells from the spreadsheet.

3. Click and drag the top of the dialog box to move it so that the spreadsheet underneath is at least partially visible.

4. Click the cursor in the first field of the dialog box, and then click the first cell you want to include in the calculation. This will automatically enter that cell reference into the field.

5. Click the next field in the dialog box, and then click the next cell you wish to include.

6. Repeat step 5 until all the cells you wish to include have been added to the fields in the dialog box (up to 30 can be selected; use the scroll bar on the right side of the wizard dialog box to reveal more fields).

7. Once you've finished, click the OK button. Calc will insert the formula into the cell you selected at the start, showing the result of the formula.

After you've added a formula with the wizard, you can edit it manually by clicking it and overtyping its contents in the Formula bar editing area. Alternatively, you can use the Function Wizard once again, by clicking the button on the Formula bar.

Summing Figures

To add the values of a number of cells, you could use the Function Wizard and select the SUM function, as shown in Figure 24-2. The procedure for choosing the cells is the same as described in the previous section.

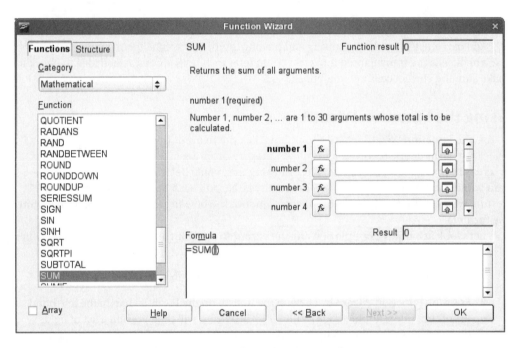

Figure 24-2. *Creating formulas is easy using the Function Wizard.*

However, Calc provides a far easier method of creating the sum formula. After positioning the cursor in an empty cell, simply click the Sum icon (the Greek sigma character) on the Formula bar, and then select the cells you wish to include in the sum. Then press Enter to see the results. If you place the cursor in a cell directly beneath a column of numbers, Calc may be clever enough to guess which cells you want to sum and automatically select them. If it's incorrect, simply highlight the correct range of cells.

■**Tip** You can select more than one cell by holding down the Ctrl key. You can select a range of cells in succession by clicking and dragging the mouse.

Sorting Data

Within a spreadsheet, you may want to sort data according to any number of criteria. For example, you might want to show a list of numbers from highest to lowest, or rearrange a list of names so that they're in alphabetical order. This is easy to do within Calc.

Start by highlighting the range of data you wish to sort. Alternatively, you can simply select one cell within it, because Calc is usually able to figure out the range of cells you want to use. Then select Data ➤ Sort from the main menu. Calc will automatically select a sort key, which will appear in the Sort By drop-down list, as shown in Figure 24-3. However, you can also choose your own sort key from the drop-down menu if you wish, and you can choose to further refine your selection by choosing up to two more sort subkeys from the other drop-down menus.

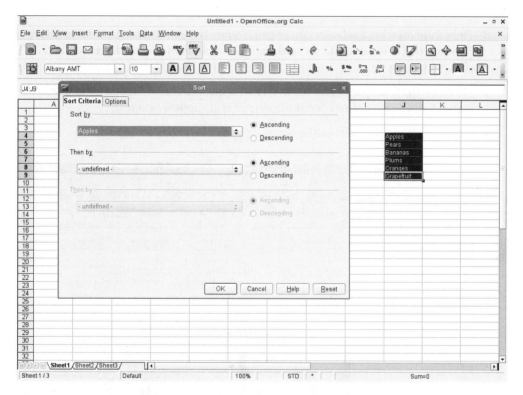

Figure 24-3. *Data can be sorted so that it's in alphabetical or numerical order.*

Creating Charts

Charts are useful because they present a quick visual summary of data. Calc produces charts through a step-by-step wizard, so it becomes very easy indeed. Here are the steps:

1. Highlight the data you want to graph. Be careful to include only the data itself and not any surrounding cells, or even the cell that contains the title for the array of data.

2. Select the Insert ➤ Chart menu option, or click the Insert Chart button on the Standard toolbar.

3. The cursor turns into a target with a small graph next to it. Click and drag on the spreadsheet itself to define the area of the graph. This can be any size. Also, you can resize it later.

4. The wizard starts. The first step is to define the range of cells to be used for the chart. By highlighting the cells before you started, you've already done this, so you can click the Next button. However, first make sure that the First Row As Label option is selected.

5. Choose the type of chart you wish to use. For most simple data selections, a bar graph is usually best. However, you might also choose to select a horizontal bar graph. Then click Next.

6. The wizard presents a subselection of graph types. You can also select whether grid-lines are used to separate the various areas of the graph. Make your selections and click Next.

7. The last step allows you to give the chart a title and also choose whether you want a legend (a key that explains what the axes refer to) to appear next to it.

8. Click Create, and the chart will be created. Figure 24-4 shows an example.

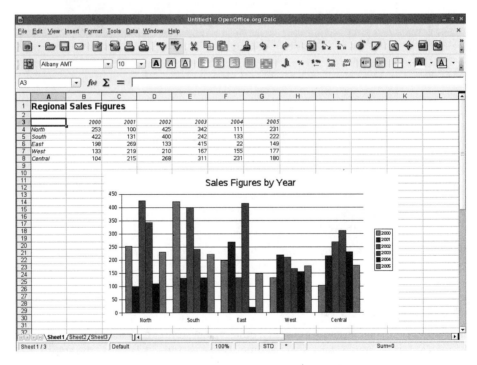

Figure 24-4. *Creating a chart is easy within Calc and adds a professional flourish to your spreadsheet.*

You can alter a chart's size by clicking and dragging the handles. You can also change various graphical aspects by double-clicking them. However, keep in mind that the graph is actually a picture, so the properties you edit are limited to changing the color and size of various elements.

The chart is linked to your data. Whenever your data changes, so will your chart. This is done automatically and doesn't require any user input.

Using Filters

The Filter function in Calc lets you selectively hide rows of data. The spreadsheet user then selects which of the rows of data to view from a drop-down list that appears in the cell at the top of the rows, as shown in the example in Figure 24-5.

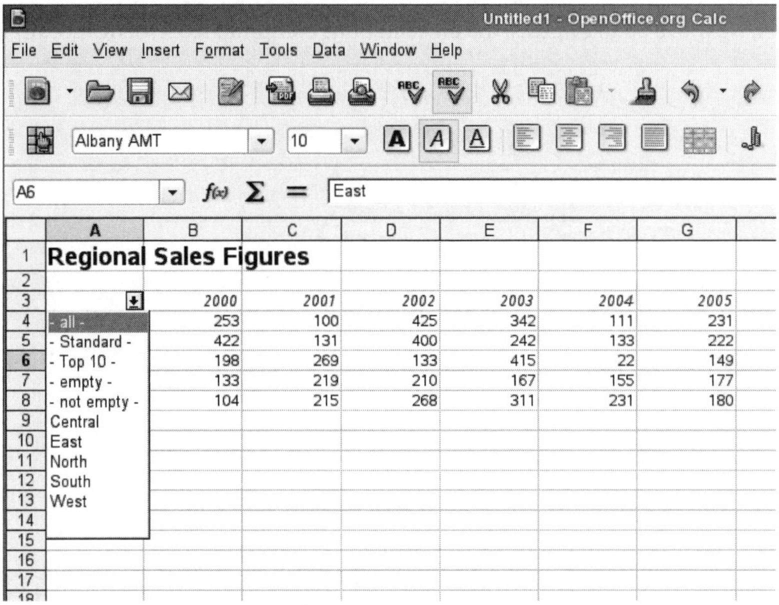

Figure 24-5. *Filters allow you to selectively hide or show rows of data in a spreadsheet.*

■**Note** A Calc filter is a little like an Excel pivot chart, especially when it's combined with an automatically generated chart.

Using filters in this way can be useful when you're dealing with a very large table of data. It helps isolate figures so you can compare them side by side in an easy-to-follow format. For example, you could filter a table of sales figures by year.

To use the Filter function, start by highlighting the data you wish to see in the drop-down list. Make sure the column header for the data is included, too. If you're using the Filter feature on a table of data, this selection can be any column within the table, although it obviously makes sense to use a column that is pertinent to the filtering that will take place. After you've selected the data to filter, select Data ➤ Filter ➤ Autofilter. You should find that, in place of the column header, a drop-down list appears. When a user selects an entry in the list, Calc will display only the corresponding row of the spreadsheet beneath.

To remove a filter, select Data ➤ Filter ➤ Hide Autofilter.

Summary

In this chapter, we examined OpenOffice.org Calc. We looked at the basics of how data can be entered into a cell and how it can be formatted. Then you learned how to create formulas. This is easy to do with the Function Wizard function, which automates the task.

Next, you saw how to sort data in a spreadsheet. We also went through the steps for creating charts using a Calc wizard. Finally, we looked at creating data filters, which work similarly to pivot charts in Microsoft Excel.

In the next chapter, we move on to Impress, the presentations component of OpenOffice.org.

■ ■ ■

## CHAPTER 25

In Depth: Impress

Impress is the presentation package within OpenOffice.org. At first glance, it appears to be the simplest of the key OpenOffice.org components, and also the one that borrows most the look and feel from Microsoft Office. However, delving into its feature set reveals more than a few surprises, including sophisticated animation effects and drawing tools. Impress can also export presentations as Macromedia Flash–compatible files, which means that many Internet-enabled desktop computers around the world will be able to view the files, even if they don't have Impress or PowerPoint installed on their computers.

In this chapter, you'll learn about the main features of Impress, as well as the basics of working with presentations.

Creating a Quick Presentation

Start Impress by clicking Applications ➤ Office ➤ Presentations ➤ OpenOffice.org Impress under GNOME, or clicking K menu ➤ Office ➤ Presentation under KDE. As soon as the program starts, it will offer to guide you through the creation of a presentation using a wizard. This makes designing your document a matter of following a few steps.

You'll initially be offered three choices: Empty Presentation, From Template, or Open Existing Presentation. When Impress refers to *templates*, it means presentations that are both predesigned and also contain sample content. Only two templates are supplied with Impress, so this option is somewhat redundant. However, you might want to take a look at them, if only to get an idea of what a presentation consists of and how it's made.

■**Tip** When you become experienced in working with Impress, you can create your own templates or download some from the Internet. To create your own template, simply select to save your document as a template in the File Type drop-down list in the Save As dialog box. Make sure you place any templates you download or create in the `/usr/lib/ooo-2.0/share/template/en-US/presnt/` directory (you will need to have superuser powers to do this and should make sure the file permissions are readable for all users).

The standard way of getting started is to create an empty presentation. This sounds more daunting than it actually is, because the Presentation Wizard will start, asking you to choose from a couple of ready-made basic designs, as shown in Figure 25-1. You'll also be given a chance to choose which format you want the presentation to take: whether it's designed primarily to be viewed on the screen or printed out.

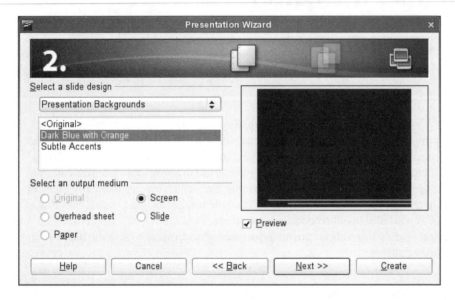

Figure 25-1. *The Impress Presentation Wizard guides you through the creation of a new presentation.*

After this, you'll be invited to choose the presentation effects, including the transition effect that will separate each slide when the presentation is viewed and the speed of the transition. If you wish, you can set the pause between slides, too, as well as the length of time each slide stays on the screen.

After clicking the Create button in the wizard, Impress will start, and you'll be invited to choose a layout for your initial slide. These are previewed on the right side of the program window. You can choose from a variety of design templates, ranging from those that contain mostly text to those that feature pictures and/or graphs.

Depending on which template you choose, you should end up with a handful of text boxes on your screen. Editing the text in these is simply a matter of clicking within them. The formatting of the text will be set automatically.

Tip   You can move and shrink each text box by clicking the handles surrounding the box. To draw a new text box, select the relevant tool on the Drawing toolbar, which runs along the bottom of the screen. Simply click and drag to draw a box of whatever size you want.

Working in Impress

When the Presentation Wizard has finished and Impress has started, you'll notice three main elements in the program window, from left to right, as shown in Figure 25-2. You work in these panes as follows:

Slides pane: This pane shows the slides in your presentation in order, one beneath the other. Simply click to select whichever slide you want to work on, or click and drag to reorder the slides. To create a new slide, right-click in a blank area in the Slides pane. Right-clicking any existing slide will present a range of options, including one to delete the slide.

Main work area: This is in the middle of the program window and lets you edit the various slides, as well as any other elements attached to the presentation, such as notes or handout documents. Simply click the relevant tab.

Tasks pane: Here, you can access the elements that will make up your presentation, such as slide templates, animations, and transition effects. Select the slide you wish to apply the elements to in the Slides pane, and then click the effect or template you wish to apply in the Tasks pane. In the case of animations or transitions, you can change various detailed settings relating to the selected element.

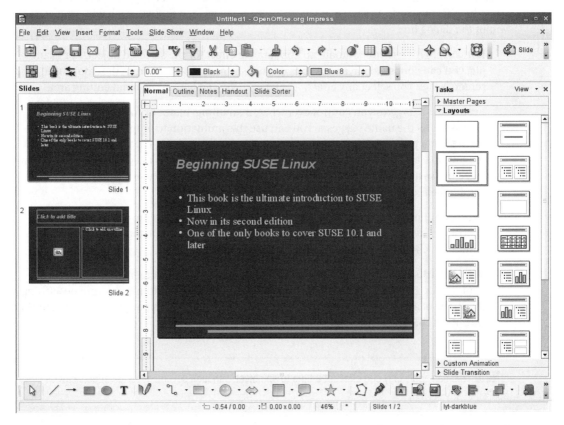

Figure 25-2. *The main Impress window is split into three elements: the Slides pane, the main work area, and the Tasks pane.*

In addition, Impress has a Drawing toolbar, which appears at the bottom of the screen. This lets you draw various items on screen, such as lines, circles, and rectangles, and also contains a handful of special-effect tools, which I'll discuss later in this chapter, in the "Applying Fontwork" and "Using 3D Effects" sections.

You can hide each on-screen item by clicking the View menu and then removing the check next to it. Alternatively, by clicking the vertical borders between each pane, you can resize the pane and make it either more or less prominent on screen. This is handy if you wish to temporarily gain more work space but don't want to lose sight of the previews in the Slides pane, for example.

Animating Slides

All elements within Impress can be animated in a variety of ways. For example, you might choose to have the contents of a particular text box fly in from the edge of the screen during the presentation. This can help add variety to your presentation, and perhaps even wake up your audience!

Setting an animation effect is simply a matter of clicking the border of the object you wish to animate in the main editing area so that it is selected, selecting Custom Animation in the Tasks pane, and then clicking the Add button. In the dialog box that appears, select how you want the effect to work. As shown in Figure 25-3, you have four choices, each with its own tab within the dialog box:

Entrance: This lets you animate an appearance effect for the selected object. For example, you can choose to have a text box dissolve into view or fly in from the side of the screen. When you select any effect, it will be previewed within the main editing area.

Emphasis: This gives you control over what, if anything, happens to the object while it's on screen. As the name suggests, you can use this animation to emphasize various elements while you're giving the presentation. Some emphasis effects are more dramatic than others, and this lets you control the impact. If you want to make an important point, you can use a dramatic effect. For more moderate information, you may choose to apply a subdued effect.

Exit: As you might expect, this lets you add an exit animation to the object. You might choose to have it fly off the side of the screen or spin away off the top of the screen. The animation choices here are identical to the Entrance choices.

Motion paths: This makes the selected element fly around on screen according to a particular path. For example, selecting Heart will cause the element to fly around describing the shape of a heart, eventually returning to its origin. A motion path is effectively another way of emphasizing a particular object.

■**Note** You can apply only one effect at a time to an object, although several separate effects can be applied to any object.

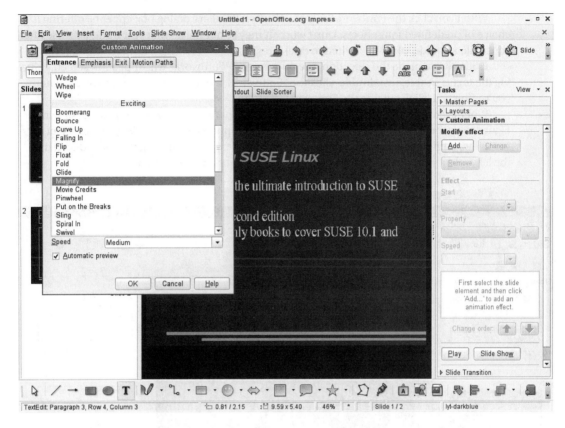

Figure 25-3. *You can choose from a wide variety of animation effects for on-screen elements.*

For each animation, you can select the playback speed, ranging from Very Slow to Fast. Simply make the selection at the bottom of the dialog box.

Once the animation has been defined and you've clicked OK, it will appear in a list at the bottom of the Custom Animation dialog box. You can choose to add more than one animation to an object by clicking the Add button again (ensuring the object is still selected in the main editing area). The animations will play in the order they're listed. You can click the Change Order up and down arrows to alter the order.

To fine-tune an effect, double-click it in the list to open its Effect Options dialog box (you can even add sound effects here). Under the Timing tab, you can control what cues the effect, such as a click of a mouse, or whether it will appear in sequence with other effects before or after in the list.

Applying Fontwork

The Fontwork tool lets you manipulate text in various playful ways, such as making it follow specific curved paths. You can find this tool on the Drawing toolbar, located at the bottom of the program window.

When you click the Fontwork icon, the Fontwork Gallery dialog box appears, offering a choice of predefined font effects. Don't worry if they're not quite what you want, because after you make a choice, you'll be invited to fine-tune it.

Once you've made the selection, the dummy text "Fontwork" will appear on screen. Editing the text is simple: just double-click the "Fontwork" text and type your own words. When you've finished, click outside the Fontwork selection.

Whenever the new Fontwork item is selected, a floating toolbar will appear, as shown in Figure 25-4. You can use this toolbar to alter various options. For example, you can select a completely different Fontwork selection from the gallery or, by clicking the second icon on the left, select your own path that you want the Fontwork item to follow.

Figure 25-4. *The Fontwork tool can add some special effects to your presentations.*

You'll also see that the Formatting toolbar changes to allow you to alter the formatting of the Fontwork element. You can alter the thickness of the letter outlines, for example, or the color of the letters. Once again, the best way to learn how the tool works is to play around with the options and see what you can achieve.

To remove a Fontwork item, just select its border and press the Delete key on your keyboard.

Using 3D Effects

In addition to Fontwork effects, Impress includes a powerful 3D tool, which can give just about any on-screen element a 3D flourish (this tool is also available in some other OpenOffice.org applications). To use it, create a text box or shape using the Drawing toolbar at the bottom of the screen. Then right-click the text box or shape and select Convert ➤ 3D.

▌Note The 3D Object option is designed simply to give your object depth. If you want to create a genuine 3D object that you can rotate in 3D space, select the 3D Rotation Object option.

You can gain much more control over the 3D effect by right-clicking it and selecting 3D Effects. This will open a floating palette window with five configuration panels, as shown in Figure 25-5. Click the icons at the top of the palette to adjust the type of 3D effect and its lighting, as follows:

Geometry: This defines how the 3D effect will look when it's applied to on-screen selections. For example, you can increase or decrease the rounded-edges value, and this will make any sharp objects on the screen appear softer when the 3D effect is applied.

Shading: This affects not the actual texture of the 3D object, but instead alters its color gradient. This is best demonstrated in action, so select the various shading modes from the drop-down list to see the effect. In addition, you can choose whether a shadow is applied to the effect, as well as the position of the virtual camera (the position of the hypothetical viewer looking at the 3D object).

Illumination: This lets you set the lighting effect. All 3D graphics usually need a light source because this helps illustrate the 3D effect; without a light source, the object will appear flat. Various predefined light sources are available. You can click and drag the light source in the preview window.

Textures: This affects how the textures will be applied to the 3D object. A texture is effectively a picture that is "wrapped around" the 3D object. Clever use of textures can add realism to a 3D object. A map of the world applied to a sphere can make it look like a globe, for example, or you could add wood or brickwork textures to make objects appear as tabletops or walls.

Material: This lets you apply various color overlays on the texture. This can radically alter the texture's look and feel, so it is quite a powerful option. To change the texture itself, right-click the object and select Area. This will present a list of predefined textures. Alternatively, you can select to use a color or pattern.

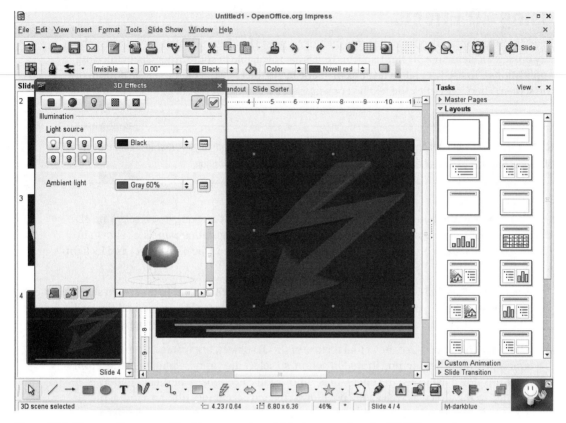

Figure 25-5. *You can fine-tune 3D objects to quite a high degree using the 3D Effects palette.*

To apply any changes you make, click the check mark button at the top right of the palette. As with the other presentation effects, the best policy is simply to experiment until you're happy with the results.

Exporting a Presentation As a Flash File

If you plan to put your presentation online, or you want to send it to a colleague who doesn't have Impress or PowerPoint installed, outputting your presentation as a Flash animation could be a good idea. The process is simple. Just select File ➤ Export, and then select Macromedia Flash (SWF) in the File Format drop-down list. (SWF is the Flash file type, which stands for Shockwave Flash.) No further configuration is necessary.

In order to play the file, it needs to be opened within a web browser that has the Flash Player installed. This can be done by selecting File ➤ Open on most browsers, although you can also drag and drop the SWF file onto the browser window under Microsoft Windows. There shouldn't be much of a problem with compatibility, since the Flash Player is ubiquitous these days. If the web browser doesn't already have Flash installed, it's easy to download and install it (see www.macromedia.com/go/getflashplayer).

When you open the Flash file in a web browser, the presentation starts, as shown in Figure 25-6. You can progress through it by clicking anywhere on the screen.

Figure 25-6. *You can save any presentation as a Flash animation, which can be played back in a suitably equipped web browser.*

Summary

In this chapter, we examined Impress, which is the presentations component within OpenOffice.org. We started by looking at how you can use the Presentation Wizard function to automate production of a basic Impress document. Then you saw how various effects can be added to the presentation, including 3D effects. Finally, we looked at how the presentation can be exported as a Shockwave Flash file for playback on virtually any web browser.

In the next chapter, we will explore the database component within OpenOffice.org: Base.

■ ■ ■

In Depth: Base

OpenOffice.org includes a number of tools to both interface with database servers and perform tasks such as enter and edit data. However, for most users, creating such a setup is rather complicated. It requires some knowledge of how databases work on a technical level. For this reason, a new component was added to OpenOffice.org 2.0: Base.

Base is a relational database along the lines of Microsoft Access and is perfect for database applications of all sizes, including more modest efforts. For example, you could use it to create an inventory database to produce a report showing all products added for a certain geographical region on a certain date, or you could use it to catalog items in your personal stamp collection.

Relational databases such as those created by Base are ideal for quickly creating catalogs of information, such as inventory lists. In addition to making database creation simple and quick, relational databases let you easily query data to produce reports tailored to individual needs.

Base works on a number of levels depending on the knowledge of the user, but in its most basic form, it offers a design-based approach to the creation of tables and forms. Anyone who has previously created a database under Access will feel right at home.

In this chapter, we'll work through an example of using Base to create a simple database cataloging a collection of music. You can use the same techniques to create any kind of relational database.

Getting Started with Base

Start Base by clicking Applications ➤ Office ➤ Database ➤ OpenOffice.org Base within GNOME, or K menu ➤ Office ➤ Database ➤ OpenOffice.org Base within KDE. When the program first starts, the Database Wizard guides you through either creating a new database or opening an existing one, as shown in Figure 26-1.

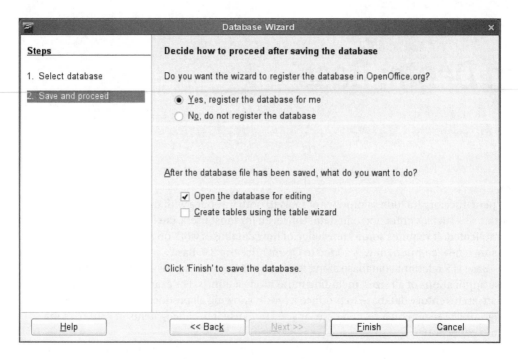

Figure 26-1. *Base starts with the Database Wizard to facilitate the quick and easy creation of new databases.*

The first step in creating a new database is to register it within OpenOffice.org. This means that it will be made available in other OpenOffice.org programs, such as Calc and Writer. Although the knowledge needed to use a database in this way is quite advanced, there's no harm in agreeing to this option. It might prove useful in the future as you learn more about OpenOffice.org.

Following this, you can choose to open the database for editing and/or start the Table Wizard. Once you click the Finish button, you'll be invited to give the database a name and save it immediately.

■Note Databases aren't like other office files in that they automatically save and update themselves. When using the finished database, you can simply enter data and then quit the program, without needing to deliberately opt to save the file.

Assuming that you did not opt to go directly to the Table Wizard, you'll now see the main Base program window. On the right side of the Base program window are the Tasks and Data panes. The Tasks pane allows you to create new database elements, depending on what's selected in the Database pane on the left side of the program window. The Data pane shows any elements you've already created. The Database pane contains the four elements of the database that you can create and manipulate:

Tables: A table is what holds the actual data you'll eventually input. Therefore, a table is the first thing that needs to be created within a new database. Creating a table involves defining the types of data that you want to store and giving the individual data fields easy-to-understand names.

Forms: Although it's possible to enter data directly into a table, it isn't particularly intuitive or easy. Because of this, forms are used to make the data fields presentable. As the name suggests, in terms of layout these are not unlike the paper forms that you fill in to facilitate the collection of data by businesses. As with tables, forms must be created from scratch in a new database. Forms have controls, which are used to facilitate data entry, or to allow users to navigate the database or otherwise manipulate it. The most common type of control is a text-entry field, which is then tied to a data field within the table, but you can also have controls that perform certain functions, such as deleting a record in the database.

Queries: A query is a way of filtering the database so that you see only a subset of it. For example, in a database detailing sales figures from across the country, you might create a query to show only the data from a particular state.

Reports: A report is a way of presenting data for human consumption, usually in a printed format. For example, you could create a report that details sales figures in the form of a letter, or you might make a report to produce address labels using addresses stored in the database.

■**Note** Both queries and reports can be saved and used over and over again. This means that you could use the same query each month to examine just a small section of the data. Base offers wizards to automate the creation of both queries and reports.

Double-clicking an item in the Database pane displays or activates that item. Right-clicking a Database pane item displays a variety of options related to editing the file.

Now, let's work through an example of using Base. First, you'll create a table, and then you'll create a form.

Creating a Database

As an example of using Base, you'll build a database, ready for data entry. The first step in the creation of a database is to make a table. This will hold the data that you will eventually enter using a form.

Adding a Table

As with all components within Base, you can use a wizard to create the table. The Table Wizard offers a number of predefined data fields corresponding to typical databases. It is fine for general use, but if you have a specific and unusual database in mind, you will need to create the table manually.

Here, you'll create a database to catalog CDs. This is easily accomplished with the Table Wizard, as follows:

1. Click the Tables icon in the Database pane, and then click the Use Wizard to Create Table icon. The Table Wizard starts.

2. You're given a choice between creating a business or personal database. As you would expect, business databases are likely to contain fields relating to business matters, such as accounting, and the fields in the personal section relate more to domestic matters. Choose Personal for this example.

3. Choose an entry from the Sample Tables drop-down list. For this example, select CD Collection.

4. In the Available Fields box, you now see a number of data fields that would prove handy for a CD collection. You don't need to use all of these. Instead, select only those you want in your table, and then click the single right-facing arrow button to transfer them to the Selected Fields box. For this example, select AlbumTitle, Artist, ReleaseYear, and Review, as shown in Figure 26-2. Then click the Next button. (Don't worry if you find the fields lacking or if you want to add your own—you'll see how to do just that in step 6).

Figure 26-2. *The Table Wizard contains ready-made data fields for a wide variety of uses.*

5. Check to make sure the fields you selected are of the correct type. Click each to see the information in the right area of the dialog box. Fields can take various forms depending on what kind of data they're supposed to hold. For example, one field might be designed to contain text, while another might need to contain numbers. Yet another might need to contain dates, and some can even contain pictures. As you might expect, the wizard has automatically selected the correct data types for the pre-defined fields.

6. For this example, you want to add a check box that shows whether the CD is scratched. If the CD in question is scratched, the user can click in a check box. If the CD isn't scratched, the box can be left blank. To create a check box, you need a special kind of data field called a Boolean. This means that the data field can be either true or false or, to put it a simpler way, it can hold either yes or no. To create a yes/no data field, click the plus button at the bottom of the Selected Fields box. This allows you to add another field. In the Field Name box, type **Scratched**. For the Field Type, click the drop-down list and locate the entry marked Yes/No [BOOLEAN]. The other options can remain as they are. Click Next to continue.

7. You're asked if you want to create a primary key. This is the unique numeric field that the database uses to keep track of each entry in the database. It's a must in a database like this one. The default choices are correct, so you can click Next again.

8. You've completed the Table Wizard. The next step is to create a form, so select Create a Form Based on This Table, and then click the Finish button.

Creating a Form

Database forms facilitate data entry. They present data fields that you've just created within the table in an easy-to-understand format.

Base is able to walk you through the creation of forms via the Form Wizard. If you didn't select to run the Form Wizard previously, you can start it by clicking Forms in the Database pane, and then clicking Use Wizard to Create Form. Then follow these steps:

1. In the Form Wizard's first step, select which fields you want to appear on the form. As with the Table Wizard, this is simply a matter of selecting the fields, and then clicking the right-arrow button so that they appear under the Fields on the Form heading. Alternatively, by clicking the double-arrow button, you can select all of them in one fell swoop, which is what you want for this example. Click Next.

2. You're asked if you want to create a subform. As its name suggests, this is effectively a form within your main form. A subform is useful with more complicated databases, where it might be necessary to view other data while filling in the form. For this simple example, leave the Add Subform box unchecked and click Next.

3. Choose a general layout for the data fields. The default is the table view, which many find ugly, so you might choose one of the first two options (in my database, I chose the second option, as you can see in Figures 26-3 and 26-4). These arrange the data fields in a spacious manner and make the form much more usable. If you look behind the wizard dialog box, you'll see a preview of how the form will look. When you're happy with the results, click Next.

4. You're asked whether or not you want existing data to be displayed on the form. You can choose to treat the form as one created only for entering new data, so that you can't use it to navigate through the database and see existing data you've already entered. This might be useful in applications where you don't want users to see the other data in the database. However, for a database for your own personal use, being able to see the existing data is very handy, which is why The Form Is to Display All Data option is selected by default. For this example, simply click the Next button to accept the default.

5. Choose a look and feel for your form from the variety of color schemes available, as shown in Figure 26-3. Again, you can see them previewed behind the wizard dialog box. Feel free to experiment with the options under the Field Border heading. I prefer the 3D Look option, which gives the form elements a slight interior shadow, a common feature on most modern user interfaces. The Flat option simply adds a black border to the boxes, and the No Border option removes the border completely.

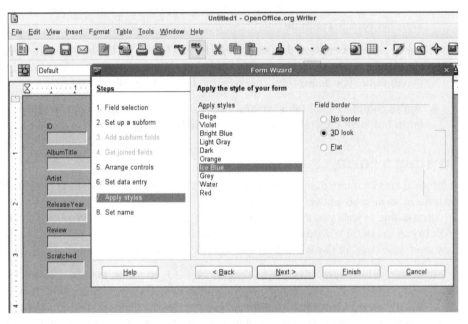

Figure 26-3. *You can choose from a variety of look and feel options for your form, and each will be previewed behind the wizard dialog box.*

6. You're invited to give the form a name. Enter a suitable name, such as **CD-Collection**. You are also given the option of entering data directly into the form or modifying it manually. You might have noticed that the field you created, the Scratched yes/no check box, isn't present on the form. Therefore, you need to add it to the form, so select to modify it manually. You'll do that in the next section.

Note There are no rules governing form names, and you can use virtually any symbols and also insert spaces into the name. However, it's a good idea to keep the form name simple and concise.

Adding Controls to the Form Manually

When the Form Wizard finishes, you should find yourself editing the form directly. A floating palette—the Form Control toolbar—will appear, offering various form-specific functions. Follow these steps to add the check box field to your form:

Note If the Form Controls toolbar doesn't appear, click View ➤ Toolbars ➤ Form Controls.

---

1. On the Form Control toolbar, click the icon that looks like a check box (on my computer, it was the third down on the left), and then click and drag to draw a check box on the form. You need to make it big enough so that the label can be seen. If you release the mouse button too early, simply click and drag the handles at the edges to resize the control.

2. Once the check box has been drawn, double-click it. This will open Properties dialog box. Click the General tab, and in the Label box, delete what's there already, and type **Scratched?** (or anything else that will help you to identify the check box on the completed form).

3. Click the Data tab and, in the Data Field box, select Scratched from the drop-down list, as shown in Figure 26-4.

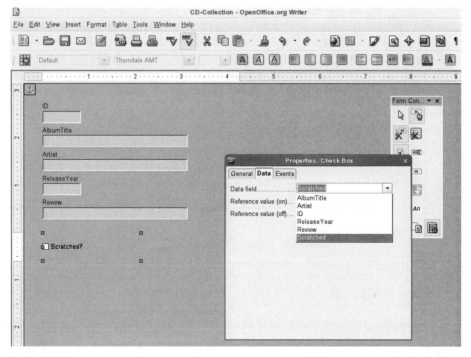

Figure 26-4. *Creating a custom control is simply a matter of drawing it on the form, and then matching it with a data field.*

4. Close and save the form.

You can add more custom controls following the same basic approach you used here. Simply draw the controls on the form, and then match them up with an entry in the table using the Data tab.

The database is almost ready for use. You just need to take one more step to modify the table, which you'll do next.

Editing the Database Table

Before you can use the database, you need to make a small change to the table you created earlier. Although the Table Wizard created a primary key, it didn't make it into an automatically updating number. Without this option activated, the user will need to manually number each entry in the database as it's created.

Follow these steps to edit the table and activate automatic numbering for the ID field:

1. Click the Tables icon in the Database pane of the main program window, right-click the table you created earlier, and select Edit.

2. Look for the entry in the table list labeled ID. It should be first in the list. Make sure that the cursor is on the ID line, and click the Autovalue drop-down list at the bottom of the window. Make sure that it reads Yes, as shown in Figure 26-5.

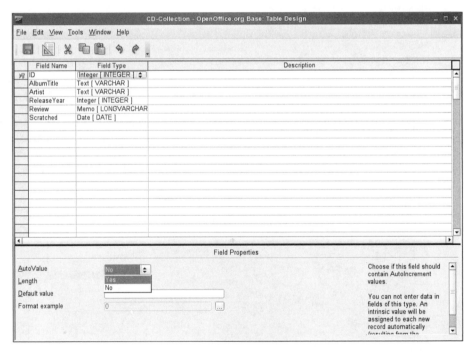

Figure 26-5. *Set the primary key to automatically update by editing its value in the table.*

3. Close the window and opt to save the table.

That's it! Your database is now ready to use.

Using the Database

Entering data into the finished database is easy. Click the Forms icon in the Database pane, and then double-click the form you created earlier.

The Form Control toolbar will still be visible. To hide it, click its close button at the top-right corner of the toolbar. After this, you can start to enter data into the form, as shown in the example in Figure 26-6. Note that you do not need to enter data in the ID field, because this will automatically be filled with the primary key number.

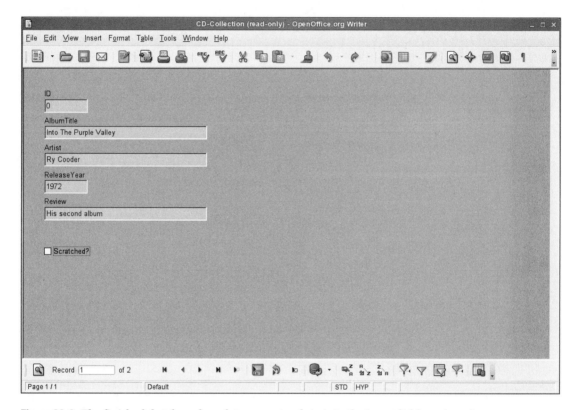

Figure 26-6. *The finished database form lets you enter data into the input fields and navigate using the toolbar at the bottom.*

Once you've filled in the form, you can click the Next Record button in the Form Navigation toolbar running along the bottom of the window (don't forget that hovering the mouse cursor over each button reveals a tooltip explaining what the button does). This will move you to the next blank form, where you can enter more data. Repeat this as many times as necessary.

The Form Navigation toolbar contains other handy tools. For example, the first button—a magnifying glass—lets you search the database for a particular entry. It's well worth investigating these toolbar functions.

Summary

In this chapter, we looked at the Base database component of OpenOffice.org and how to use it to easily create and edit simple databases. We stepped through an example of setting up a database table and creating a database form that users can employ to enter and edit data.

In the next chapter, we'll look at Evolution, an e-mail program commonly used with the GNOME desktop.

■■■■

## CHAPTER 27

In Depth: Evolution

Evolution isn't part of the OpenOffice.org suite. It was originally created by Ximian, an organization founded by the creators of the GNOME Desktop Project and acquired by Novell in August 2003. Even long after the acquisition, Evolution is still developed by many of the key GNOME desktop developers.

Although it's not explicitly described as such by its developers, Evolution is considered the "official" GNOME desktop e-mail program. Nearly every Linux distribution that uses the GNOME desktop system also uses Evolution. Evolution even retains the same look and feel as many elements of the SUSE Linux GNOME desktop.

In terms of functionality, Evolution is similar to Microsoft Outlook, in that as well as being a powerful e-mail client, it incorporates contacts management, a calendar, and a to-do list. Evolution is even able to connect to Microsoft Exchange (2000 and above) groupware servers and synchronize with contact and calendar data, in addition to fetching e-mail. Of course, it can also connect to standard POP3/SMTP e-mail servers, as well as IMAP and also Novell GroupMail servers. This means it is compatible with practically every e-mail system in use today.

Although Evolution offers many of the functions of Microsoft Outlook, it differs in some key ways. This chapter describes how to use its main features.

Evolution Modes

To start Evolution, click Applications ➤ Internet ➤ Email ➤ Evolution.

Evolution consists of five components: Mail, Contacts, Calendars, Memos, and Tasks. These are interconnected but operate as separate modes within the program. Each mode can be selected using the switcher located at the bottom-left side of the program window. Simply click the button for the mode you wish to use. The program window, toolbar, and menu system will change to accommodate whichever mode is selected. Figure 27-1 shows the program in Mail mode.

■**Tip** You can shrink the switcher component to small icons by clicking View ➤ Switcher Appearance ➤ Icons Only.

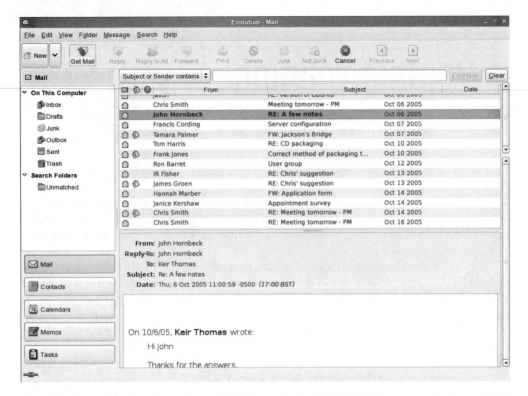

Figure 27-1. *You can switch between Evolution's modes by clicking the buttons at the bottom left of the program window.*

The four Evolution modes work as follows:

Mail: At the top left of the program window are the mail folders. Here, you'll find the Inbox and Sent folders, along with any other mail folders you create. On the right is the list of e-mail messages, and beneath this is the message preview pane, where the body of any message you select will be displayed. Above the message list is the search box, which works like most e-mail search routines: type the relevant word(s) and then click Find Now. Notable icons running along the top of the window include the New button, which will let you compose an e-mail message, and the Send/Receive button, which will download new messages and also send any messages in the Outbox folder.

Contacts: The contact folders appear on the left side of the program window. For most users, there will be just one, named Personal, but if you specified a groupware server during setup, you will also be able to connect to this by clicking its entry. At the top right is the list of contacts. Clicking any contact displays that individual's information at the bottom of the window, in the contact information area. The search bar at the top of the window beneath the toolbar lets you quickly search for contacts using their name. The New button on the toolbar lets you create a new contact.

Calendars: On the left side of the program window are the various calendars you can access. For most users, the Personal calendar will be the principal one, but you can also access shared calendars here. To the right is the monthly calendar and, in the middle of the program window, the appointment list. By default, the current day is shown. To select a different day, simply double-click the day in the month view. You can switch between day, week, and month appointment views by clicking the Day, Work Week, and Month buttons on the toolbar.

Memos: In this mode you can create very simple notes, perhaps as impromptu minutes during a telephone meeting. The window layout is almost identical to the Tasks view, described below. Once a memo has been created it will appear on the right-hand side of the program window in a list. To create a new memo, click File ➤ New ➤ Memo. Then type into the Memo Content box. To delete a memo, simply right-click its entry in the list and select Delete.

Tasks: Your task lists are listed on the left side of the program window. Once again, most users will use just the Personal task list. The task list itself appears in the main program window.

Basic E-Mail Tasks

Evolution's e-mail functionality is arguably the heart of the program. Although it offers a lot of features, it is quite simple to use. If you've ever used any other e-mail client, such as Microsoft Outlook, you have a head start.

When you start Evolution, the e-mail mode is selected automatically. However, if it isn't, or if you've switched to a different mode within the program, simply click the Mail button at the bottom left of the program window.

Sending and Receiving E-Mail

Once Evolution has been set up correctly to work with your e-mail servers, as outlined in Chapter 8, you can simply click the Send/Receive button on the toolbar to connect to the server(s) and both send and receive e-mail.

You may need to enter your password if you didn't enter it during setup. You can check the Remember Password box to avoid having to type it again, but this will mean the password is then stored on your hard disk, possibly posing a security risk (although it's stored in an encrypted format).

■**Note** Although e-mail is normally sent as soon as you click the Send button when composing e-mail, if the sending has been delayed for any reason (such as because you were offline at the time), it will be sent as soon as you click the Send/Receive button. Until that point, it will be held in the Outbox folder on the left side of the program window.

Any outstanding mail is sent first, and then the receiving procedure is started. As shown in Figure 27-2, a status dialog box will tell you how many messages there are and the progress of the download. Clicking the Cancel button will stop the procedure (although some messages may already have been downloaded).

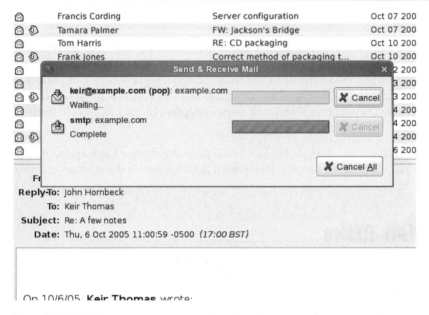

Figure 27-2. *You'll see a progress report showing the connection status whenever you click the Send/Receive button.*

Reading E-Mail

Simply click an e-mail message to view it in the preview pane at the bottom of the screen. Alternatively, you can double-click a message to open it in its own program window (selecting a message and pressing Enter will have the same effect).

As with most e-mail clients, any unread messages in the list appear in bold, and messages that have been read appear in ordinary type. By default, each message is marked as read after 1.5 seconds, but you can alter this value. To change it, click Edit ➤ Preferences, click the Mail Preferences icon in the Preferences dialog box, and then change the value under the Message Display heading. A value of 0 will cause the mail to switch to read status as soon as it's clicked, which can be useful if you want to quickly clear a lot of messages.

You can also mark many messages as read by highlighting them all, right-clicking an individual one, and selecting Mark As Read from the menu that appears. You can select multiple messages in the usual way: Shift-click to select a consecutive list or Ctrl-click for nonconsecutive selections.

Deleting Messages

You can delete messages by highlighting them and pressing the Delete key. Alternatively, right-click any message (or a selection of them) and select Delete. The message will then be moved to the Trash folder. To empty the Trash folder, simply right-click the folder and select Empty Trash.

If you move any messages from folder to folder, as described later in the "Sorting and Filtering Messages" section, a copy of the mail will end up in the Trash folder. This is because Evolution doesn't literally move messages. Instead, it copies them from the old to the new location and deletes the original. This can be a little disconcerting at first, but there's nothing to worry about. The mail message will remain wherever you moved it, and it won't disappear when you expunge any folders.

Figure 27-3. *To permanently delete messages, right-click the Trash folder and select Empty Trash.*

Flagging Messages

You can flag messages in a variety of ways to help remind you of their status or purpose. The simplest form of flagging is to mark a message as important: right-click the message and select Mark As Important, or click in the space beneath the Important column (this is located to the left of the From column).

Alternatively, you can add several different flags by right-clicking a message and selecting Mark for Follow Up. In the dialog box that appears, select from the Flag drop-down list; choices include Do Not Forward, No Response Necessary, and Review. This heading will then appear in the message preview at the bottom of the window whenever the mail is selected.

IMPORTING E-MAIL FROM OUTLOOK VIA THUNDERBIRD

Back in Chapter 4, I discussed a method of exporting e-mail from various Microsoft e-mail programs, which use proprietary formats, so that it can be imported under SUSE Linux. To recap, you can install the Mozilla Thunderbird e-mail client under Windows, import your e-mail into it from Outlook or Outlook Express, and then export Thunderbird's mailbox (.mbox) files for use within Evolution.

If you followed these instructions and now have the .mbox files ready for use with Evolution, it's easy to import them. Click File ➤ Import. In the Import dialog box, select to import a single file, click the Browse button, locate the .mbox file, and click Open. If you have more than one .mbox file, you'll need to import each one manually.

Composing a Message

Creating a new e-mail is as simple as clicking the New button at the top left of Evolution's program window. Fill in the To and Subject details as usual, and then type in the main body of the message.

To add a CC or BCC, click the To: button and select addresses from your contacts list in the dialog box that appears (selecting the CC or BCC button as appropriate). Alternatively, if you would like to have the CC and BCC fields visible and available at all times, click their entries under the View menu of the Compose a Message window.

As with most Microsoft mail programs, Evolution can send new e-mail either as plain text or as HTML. Plain text mode is the default. To switch to HTML, click the entry on the Format menu. The advantage of HTML mail is that you can vary the style, size, and coloring of text, so you can emphasize various words or paragraphs, as illustrated in Figure 27-4. In addition, if you click Insert ➤ Image, you can insert pictures from the hard disk. Other options on the Insert menu let you insert tables, dividing lines (click the Rule menu entry), and hyperlinks. The disadvantage of HTML e-mail is that the person receiving the message will need an HTML-compatible e-mail program to be able to read it.

■**Tip** Many people in the Linux community frown on HTML-formatted e-mail and prefer plain text messages.

Words are automatically spell-checked in the new e-mail and are underlined in red if the spell checker thinks they are misspelled. To correct the word, right-click it, select your dictionary language from the list (such as English), and then select the correctly spelled word from the list.

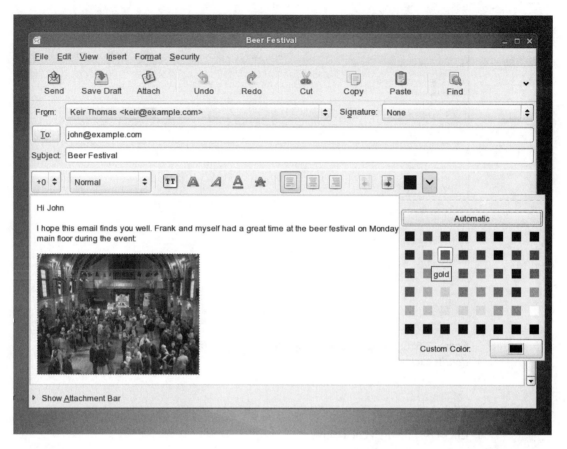

Figure 27-4. *New messages can be formatted in HTML, allowing you to change the color of text, as well as its size.*

Creating an E-Mail Signature

E-mail signatures are the blocks of text that appear automatically at the end of new e-mail messages you compose. They save you the bother of typing your name and contact details each time. To create an e-mail signature, follow these steps:

1. Click Edit ➤ Preferences. In the Preferences dialog box, click the Composer Preferences icon on the left.

2. Select the Signatures tab and then click the Add button at the top right of the window.

3. In the Edit Signature dialog box, type what you wish to appear as your signature. The signature can either be in plain text or HTML (click Format ➤ HTML). Don't forget that in HTML mode you can insert lines (Insert ➤ Rule), which can act as a natural divider at the top of your signature to separate it from the body of the e-mail, as shown in the example in Figure 27-5.

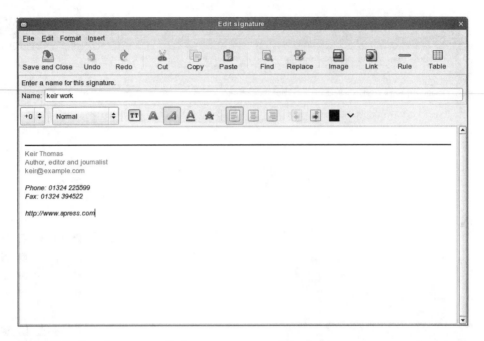

Figure 27-5. *Creating an e-mail signature saves you from having to type your contact details each time.*

4. Click the Save and Close icon at the top left.

5. Click OK, and then click Close.

■**Tip** Enter a few carriage returns at the top of your signature so that, when you create a new e-mail, you have enough space to click and type, without accidentally clicking within the signature.

Advanced E-Mail Tasks

Evolution offers several features that can help keep you to organize your e-mail. You can create new folders, as well as filter, sort, and search through your messages.

Creating New Folders

If you want to better organize your e-mail, you can create your own folders, which will then appear in the list on the left side of the program window.

To create a new top-level folder, which will appear in the list alongside the standard folders (Inbox, Junk, Outbox, and so on), right-click On This Computer and select New Folder. Then make sure that On This Computer is selected in the folder view of the dialog box that appears. Type a name and click Create.

You can also create second-level folders, which will effectively be "inside" other folders and will appear indented below their parent folder within the list. For example, you might want to create a series of folders within the main Inbox folder to sort your mail from various individuals or organizations. To do this, right-click Inbox, select New Folder, and give the folder a name in the dialog box that appears, as shown in Figure 27-6.

Figure 27-6. *You can create your own folders to better organize your mail.*

You can then drag and drop messages into the new folders, or simply right-click them and select Move to Folder. This can be useful if you wish to select a handful of messages by holding down the Ctrl key. All you need to do then is right-click one of them and select Move to Folder.

You can also copy messages from one location to another, thus producing two copies of the same message. Simply right-click the message and select Copy to Folder. Then select the folder from the list. Alternatively, you can hold down the Ctrl key while you drag the message to the new location.

Dealing with Junk E-Mail

Evolution includes intelligent junk mail filtering. Any mail that Evolution thinks is spam or junk mail will end up in the Junk folder. When you first start using Evolution, you should check the folder regularly, because there's a chance Evolution might have made a mistake. However, this is a good thing, because by right-clicking the message and selecting Mark As Not Junk, the Evolution junk mail filter will be able to better understand what to consider as junk in your particular Inbox.

In a similar way, if you find that Evolution misses a junk e-mail and it ends up in your Inbox, you can right-click it and select Mark As Junk.

To empty the Junk folder, select all the messages (Ctrl+A), right-click, select Delete, and then click Folder ➤ Expunge on the main menu. Bear in mind that, as when you delete messages from any folder, they will appear in the Trash view, from which they can be restored, if necessary.

Sorting and Filtering Messages

You can filter incoming messages according to practically any criteria, including who sent the message, its subject line, words within the body of the mail, its size, or even if it has attachments. Coupled with the ability to create folders, this allows you to automatically sort messages as soon as they're received.

To set up filters, click Edit ➤ Message Filters. Click the Add button and, in the Search Name box, start by giving the new rule a descriptive name by which you'll be able to recognize it in future. You might think this isn't important, but you may create tens, if not hundreds, of filters, so being able to identify filters will be very helpful.

As shown in Figure 27-7, the Add Rule dialog box is split into two halves: Find Items That Meet The Following Criteria and Then. This is rather like a sentence: *Find items that meet the criteria* and *then* carry out the described actions.

Figure 27-7. *Creating message filters lets you automatically organize your e-mail as soon as it's received.*

The Find Items part is used to identify the mail. You can select to filter based on almost any criteria, such as who appears in the Sender field of the message, words that appear in the Subject line, the date sent, and so on. Simply select what you require from the drop-down list directly beneath the Add button. In most cases, you'll then need to specify details for the filter. For example, if you select to filter by the address of the individual sending the e-mail, you'll need to provide that e-mail address.

■**Tip** Several rules can be created. For example, you could create a rule to filter by the address of the sender, and then click the Add button to create another rule to filter by text in the Subject line. By clicking If All Criteria Are Met in the Find Items drop-down list, the mail will be filtered only if both conditions are met. By selecting If Any Criteria Are Met from the drop-down list, the mail will be filtered if either condition is met.

Once you've set the Find Items conditions, you need to select from the Then section of the dialog box. This tells Evolution what to do with the filtered mail. The obvious course of action is to move the e-mail to a particular folder, which is the default choice, but you can also delete the e-mail, set a particular flag, beep, or even run a particular program! As with the Find Items rules, you can set more than one condition here, so you can have Evolution beep and then delete the message, for example.

TIPS FOR USING EVOLUTION E-MAIL

In many ways, Evolution is similar to e-mail programs you might have used in the past, but it also has a few of its own quirks and idiosyncratic ways of working. Here are a handful of preferences you might want to set to have Evolution behave in a more familiar way:

- **Forward e-mail inline:** If you attempt to forward a message, Evolution will attach it to a new message as a file. The person receiving the e-mail will then need to double-click the file to view the forwarded e-mail, which can be confusing. The solution is to make Evolution forward the message inline, which is to say that Evolution will quote it beneath the new mail message, as Microsoft e-mail programs do. To do this, click Edit ➤ Preferences, click Composer Preferences on the left side of the dialog box, click the Forward Style drop-down list, and select Inline.

- **Change the plain text font:** Any messages sent to you in plain text format, rather than HTML, will appear in the message preview pane in a Courier-style font. To have messages display in a more attractive and readable typeface, click Edit ➤ Preferences, select Mail Preferences on the left side of the dialog box, and then remove the check from Use the Same Fonts As Other Applications. In the Fixed Width Font drop-down list, select an alternative font. The standard SUSE Linux font is called Sans and is a good choice.

- **Always create HTML e-mail:** Evolution defaults to plain text e-mail for any new messages you create. If you want to always create HTML messages, click Edit ➤ Preferences, click Composer Preferences on the left side of the dialog box, and then put a check alongside Format Messages in HTML.

- **Empty Trash on exit:** To automatically remove deleted messages each time you quit Evolution, click Edit ➤ Preferences, click Mail Preferences on the left side of the program window, and put a check alongside Empty Trash Folders on Exit.

Creating Search Folders

Evolution's search folder feature is a more powerful alternative to message filters. Using search folders, you can filter mail based on a similar set of criteria, but you can choose to include messages in the results that might be *associated* with the filtered messages. For example, if you choose to filter by a specific individual's e-mail address, you can select to have any replies you sent to that person included in the results, rather than simply messages received from her. In addition, you can apply search folders to specific e-mail folders on an ongoing basis, rather than all incoming e-mail.

You can create a new search folder by clicking Edit ➤ Search Folders. As with creating message filters, clicking the drop-down box beneath the Add button will let you select criteria by which you can filter. The choices are broadly similar to those for message filters, in that you can filter by e-mail address, size of e-mail, message body, and so on.

In the Include Threads drop-down box, you can select what kind of results you would like the search filter to return:

- None simply returns e-mail messages matching the criteria.

- All Related returns every single message that is associated with the criteria.

- Replies returns results that include replies to the messages returned via the filter.

- Replies with Parents returns results that include replies and also any initial message that you or others might have sent that inspired the message included in the filter results.

Under the Search Folder Sources heading, select With All Local Folders from the drop-down list to search only local folders (those on your hard disk). This is best for POP3 mail users. If you read e-mail held on a remote email server, such as with IMAP or Microsoft Exchange servers, then select either With All Active Remote Folders, to apply the search filter to remote folders; or With All Local and Active Remove Folders, to apply the search to both local and remote folders. Search folder results are listed under the relevant folders on the left side of the Mail mode window.

The search folder feature is very powerful and worth spending some time investigating.

Contacts

Evolution includes a powerful contacts manager component that can catalog information about individuals. At its most basic, the contact manager stores e-mail addresses for use within the e-mail component of Evolution, but you can enter significant additional data about each individual, including addresses, phone numbers, fax numbers, and even a photograph for easy identification. This should allow Evolution to become your sole personal information manager.

To switch to Contacts mode, click the button at the bottom-left side of the program window. Once in Contacts mode, you can view information in several ways. Click View ➤ Current View to choose from the following views:

Address Cards: This is the default view and shows the contacts as virtual index cards arranged alongside each other at the top of the program window. Click the scroll bar beneath the cards to move through them.

Phone List: This shows the contact information as a simple list, arranged vertically, with various elements of the contact's personal information listed alongside, such as phone numbers and e-mail addresses.

By Company: This organizes the data in a similar way to Phone List view but sorted by the company the contacts work for (if such data has been entered into the contact entries).

Adding or Editing Contact Information

By far, the best way of initially building up your contacts list is to right-click e-mail addresses at the head of messages and select Add to Addressbook. This will add a simple contact record consisting of the individual's name and e-mail address.

When using some Microsoft mail applications, simply replying to an e-mail from an individual is enough to add that contact to your address book. Evolution is capable of this behavior, too, but the feature isn't activated by default. To set this up, click Edit ➤ Preferences, click Mail Preferences on the left side of the dialog box, click the Automatic Contacts heading, and then put a check in the box marked Automatically Create Entries in the Addressbook When Responding to Mail.

You can then edit the contact details by double-clicking the entry in Contacts mode. This will let you enter a variety of information, as shown in Figure 27-8. To import a photo for this contact, click the top-left icon. You can use any picture here, and you don't need to worry about its size, because it will be resized automatically by Evolution (although its aspect ratio will be preserved). The imported photo will appear on the contact's virtual card.

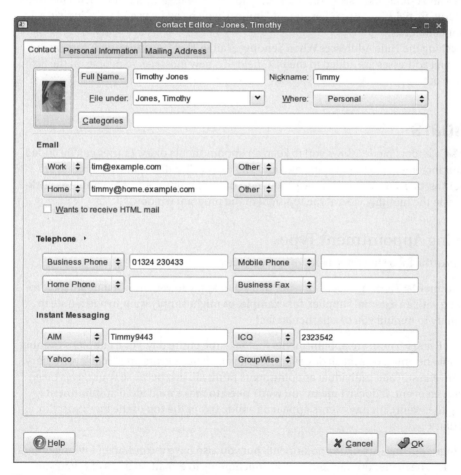

Figure 27-8. *A lot of information can be entered for each contact and, by clicking the button at the top left, you can also add a photograph.*

Creating a Contact List

Contact lists are simply lists of e-mail addresses. Once a list is created, you can right-click its entry in the contacts list, and then choose to send a message to the list or forward it to some-one else as a vCard. The obvious use of contact lists is for sending group e-mail messages.

■**Note** A vCard is a virtual business card. Effectively, it's a small file that contains personal information. As well as personal data, vCards can contain pictures and audio clips. They're understood by practically all business-level e-mail programs, including Microsoft Outlook and Apple Mail.

To create a contact list, click the small down arrow next to the New button in Contacts mode, and select the option from the list. Then simply click and drag contacts from the main program pane onto the bottom of the Contact List Editor pane. This will automatically add their names and e-mail addresses. Alternatively, you can type their e-mail addresses manually into the Members field, and then click the Add button, which can be useful if the individual isn't in your contact list.

By checking the Hide Addresses When Sending Mail to This List option, you can ensure that the e-mail addresses are added to the BCC field of a new message, so people on the list don't see the others on the list.

Calendars

Evolution's Calendars mode allows you to keep an appointments diary. Entries can be added in half-hour increments to the working day, and you can easily add events to days that are weeks, months, or even years in advance. Viewing a day's appointments is as simple as click-ing its entry in the monthly view at the top right of the program window.

Specifying Appointment Types

You can make the following three types of diary entries:

Appointments: These are events in your diary that apply to you only. You might have a meeting with an external supplier, for example, or might simply want to add a note to your diary to remind you of a particular fact.

All Day Events: These are appointments that take the entire day. For example, a training day could be entered as an all day event. However, all day events don't block your diary, and you can still add individual appointments (after all, just because your day is taken up with an event, it doesn't mean you won't need to make individual appointments during the event). All day events appear as a blue bar at the top of the day's entry in your diary.

Meetings: Meetings are like appointments but you also have the option of inviting others to attend. The invitations are sent as iCal attachments to e-mail, so users of Microsoft Outlook should be able to reply to them (provided Outlook is properly configured; see the program's documentation for details, and note that iCal is sometimes referred to as RFC

2446/2447). Once an individual receives a meeting invitation, he can click to accept or decline. Once Evolution receives this response, the individual's acceptance or declination will be automatically added to the diary entry.

Adding or Editing a Diary Entry

To add a new diary entry, simply select the day in the monthly view at the top right, and then select the time the appointment is to start. Then right-click and choose an appointment, an all day event, or a meeting. To edit an already existing diary entry, double-click its entry in the list.

At its most basic, all an appointment needs in order to be entered into your diary is some text in the Summary field, as shown in Figure 27-9. By default, appointments and meetings are assumed to last for half an hour, but you can change this by clicking the up and down buttons alongside the Hours and Minutes entries in the dialog box. For what it's worth, appointments can go on for days—just select a sufficiently long time period, in hours!

Figure 27-9. *When creating a new appointment you can add all the details you need, but don't forget to set the end time!*

By clicking the Recurrence icon, you can set the appointment to be booked into your diary according to certain intervals. Start by putting a check in the This Appointment Recurs box, and then select a time interval. For example, selecting 1 week will mean that the appointment is booked into your diary automatically on a weekly basis. After this, select a day of the week for the recurring appointment. Following this, you must either specify the number of recurrences or simply select Forever from the drop-down list. Then click the Add button to add the details of the recurring event to the appointment.

In the case of meeting appointments, you can click the Attendees button to invite others to the meeting, via iCal invitations which will be sent out by e-mail as soon as you've finished creating the appointment. type the name of the person you want to invite in the Search field. If the person is already in your contacts list, the name will be automatically completed, but you can also type individual e-mail addresses.

Clicking the Free/Busy button in the Meeting dialog box will show you who can and can't attend, according to replies to the invitations sent out (obviously, this is a feature you'll be using after you initially created the appointment). On the left side of the dialog box, you'll see the list of attendees, and the diagram on the right will show their status: whether they've accepted or not, or whether they've sent a busy/tentative reply (in which case, you might choose to reschedule the meeting).

Tasks

Tasks mode is the simplest component within Evolution and allows you to create a to-do list. After you've made an entry, clicking the check box alongside it will mark it as completed. Completed items appear with strike-through, as shown in Figure 27-10.

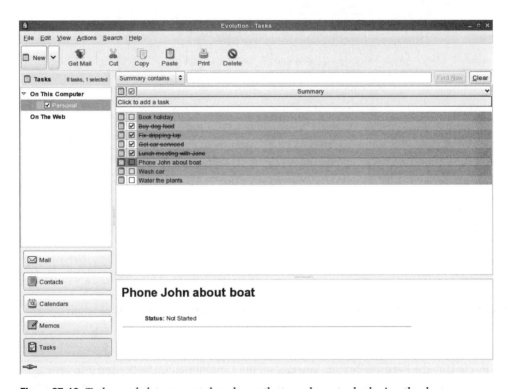

Figure 27-10. *Tasks mode lets you catalog chores that you have to do during the day.*

Switch to Tasks mode by clicking its button on the bottom-left side of the program window. To add a new task, click the bar that reads Click to Add a New Task. Type a description of the task, and then press Enter. You will then be able to enter further tasks in the same field.

Double-clicking a task allows you to fine-tune its details. For example, you can add a due date, so you'll know when the task must be completed. You can also add a description for future reference.

By clicking the Status Details button, you can also set a percentage figure for completion of the task, as well as its priority, ranging from Low to High.

Summary

This chapter has been a whistle-stop tour of Evolution's main features. We've looked at creating and organizing e-mail, managing contacts, working with the appointments calendar, and editing the task list.

Evolution is a powerful program. Be sure to take a look at its help documentation (Help ➤ Contents) to learn more about it.

In the next chapter, we'll look at running Microsoft Office under SUSE Linux. Yes, you read that right. It's entirely possible to run certain Windows applications under Linux.

■■■

## CHAPTER 28

Running Microsoft Office Under SUSE Linux

The title of this chapter might sound somewhat strange. How can a Windows program be run under Linux? The answer comes courtesy of the Wine project and the set of add-on programs it offers for Linux. Wine is an acronym for Wine Is Not an Emulator, which is a way of saying that the Wine software doesn't emulate Windows but instead re-creates certain parts of Windows known as the application programming interface (API).

In theory, the vast majority of Windows program can be run using Wine. The reality is that some work easily, some require a little configuration to run, and others don't work at all.

Getting a Windows program to run under Wine is rarely difficult, but essentially it's a "hack"—a way of making something work when it's not intended to do so. Such hacks are the lifeblood of Linux, but this should serve as a warning to the less-experienced SUSE Linux user: don't expect to be able to simply insert the Microsoft Office CD, click a few times, and have a working Office installation! A handful of preparatory steps are necessary.

In this chapter, you'll learn how to install both Wine and Microsoft Office. Because the presence of Internet Explorer is critical to many pieces of Windows software nowadays, we also cover the installation of this web browser.

Installing and Configuring Wine

Wine isn't installed by default under SUSE Linux. Normally, I would recommend download-ing Wine from the SUSE Linux online software repositories, or installing from the DVD. However, Wine is constantly being revised, and even a small point release by the developers can bring new features and compatibility with Windows programs. It's therefore a better idea to download Wine direct from the Wine Project web site. You'll find the latest version at the SourceForge.net site, where the project is hosted, as described next.

Downloading Wine

Open a web browser and head to the following web site:

```
http://sourceforge.net/project/showfiles.php?group_id=6241&package_id=79444
```

This should list the RPM packages of Wine available for various versions of SUSE Linux. Look for the version matching SUSE 10.1. The end of the filename should indicate for which version of SUSE the package is designed (for example, `wine...SuSELinux101.i586.rpm`). If that isn't available, download the package version matching SUSE 10.0. You want to download the `i586` package. Make sure that you save the file to disk, rather than choosing to open it with the software installer application.

Once the file has downloaded, open either GNOME Terminal or Konsole, depending on whether you're running GNOME or KDE desktop. Then switch to the directory containing the RPM file and install it. The file was downloaded to the desktop of my test system, so I typed the following:

```
cd ~/Desktop
sudo rpm -Uvh <filename of wine package>
```

You'll need to enter your root password for the last command in that list. Following this, Wine is installed, and you can delete the RPM file you downloaded. However, Wine is not yet ready to use; some further configuration is necessary.

CROSSOVER OFFICE

The developers behind Wine also produce a proprietary version of Wine called CrossOver Office. Technically speaking, this is actually no different from any other version of Wine, except that a GUI-based front end is added to make installation of programs simpler. It also includes several scripts to overcome various incompatibilities between Windows programs and Wine. This makes it possible to install the very latest version of Office, for example. In addition, CrossOver Office also lets you use Internet Explorer–based plug-ins within Linux-based browsers.

You can learn more about CrossOver Office by visiting its official web site at `www.codeweavers.com`. CrossOver Office is available for a fee from CodeWeavers, but considering they are one of the major sponsors of the Wine project, this is an excellent way of investing in the community.

Configuring Wine

One of the first things to do before using Wine is to install the standard Microsoft fonts, such as Arial, Times New Roman, and so on. I detail how to do this in Chapter 21 but, to summarize, you can either download the Microsoft TrueType Core Fonts package using SUSE Linux's online update facility, or copy the fonts across from your Windows partition if you dual-boot. The fonts ensure that any Windows applications you install, as well as the actual installation programs, display as they would on a native Windows system.

Following this, you should install the Sidenet Wine Configuration Utility. This is a series of scripts by a third-party programmer (who isn't related to the Wine project) that automatically configures Wine so that it's much more compatible with current software. Sidenet automates the installation of Internet Explorer 6 and Windows Media Player 6.4 (you might find the versions numbers differ). It also tweaks the Wine configuration in a handful of ways to make it work with a lot of software.

■**Note** A *script* is a series of commands within a text file. By running the script, you work through the series of commands automatically.

The Sidenet script can create several different types of Wine configuration. The first is a completely Microsoft-free Wine installation, which means that it won't install any Windows-based system files or Internet Explorer. The other options let you install Internet Explorer and Windows Media Player. This is strongly advisable, because many Windows programs demand the presence of these two programs (particularly Internet Explorer). Additionally, it's very useful to download several additional components that can then be installed using Sidenet.

■**Caution** According to the wording of Microsoft's End User License Agreements, you can download and install the Windows components only if you have a valid Windows license. That's to say you can download Internet Explorer and Windows Media Player only if you own Windows XP, 2000, Me, 98, or 95. If you don't own these operating systems, then you'll be violating copyright laws. Also, you can install DCOM98, an additional component, only if you have a Windows 98 license; to do otherwise is to break copyright laws.

Here are the steps for installation:

1. Open a web browser and go to `http://sidenet.ddo.jp/winetips/config.html`. From there, download the latest version of the Sidenet binary release. Save it to disk, rather than selecting the option to open it in an archive manager.

2. When the download of Sidenet has finished, open a GNOME Terminal or Konsole window and type the following at the prompt (change the filename listed on the `tar` line to match the name of the file you downloaded; this step assumes the file was downloaded to the desktop):

```
cd ~/Desktop
tar zxf wine-config-sidenet-1.9.0.tgz
```

This will switch to where the download has been saved and unpack the downloaded archive into its own directory.

3. Download the following manually and place the downloaded files in the Sidenet directory you created earlier (on my system, this was `wine-config-sidenet`):

   • DCOM for Windows 98 (`DCOM98.EXE`), from `www.microsoft.com/com/default.mspx`.

   • Windows Installer 2.0, from `www.microsoft.com/downloads/`. Visit this web page and search for `instmsia.exe`. In the list of results, look for the link marked "Windows Installer 2.0 Redistributable for Windows 95, 98 and Me."

- MFC 4.0 Runtime (`mfc40.zip`), from www.softlookup.com/download.asp?ID=10315. A variety of download sites are offered for this file. Choose the one closest to your location. The MFC 4.0 Runtime is supplied in a zip file. Extract all the contents of the zip to the Sidenet directory. Ensure that the `.dll` files are placed in the Sidenet directory and not in their own directory.

■**Note** The URLs for the additional Windows components were correct as this book went to press but it's possible that they may change. If that happens, searching the Web for the files in question should return ample download sites.

---

4. Once all the files are downloaded, click the GNOME Terminal/Konsole window and type the following (this again assumes that you created the Sidenet directory in your desktop directory):

```
cd ~/Desktop/wine-config-sidenet
./setup
```

5. Answer the prompts until you are offered the choice of the kind of Wine setup you want. Choose to manually install (this was option 3 on the version of Sidenet that I installed, but might be different for you).

6. You need to answer more questions about which programs you want to install. Answer Yes to each, including the option of linking your `~/.font` directory to the Wine installation. Agree to create the `C:\` folder in your `/home` directory. Agree to the installation of the MPlayer codecs.

■**Note** During installation of Sidenet, the Windows components you install might ask you to reboot. It isn't necessary for you to actually reboot Linux. Instead, a Windows reboot is faked within the Wine software (this is done automatically by Sidenet). You can do this yourself at any time from the GNOME Terminal/Konsole window by typing `wineboot`.

---

7. Eventually, the DCOM98 installation window will appear. As you would within Windows, work through the options, agreeing to install the software.

8. Following this, the Internet Explorer installation program will download and then start. Again, work through the installer. Choose the Install Now – Typical Set of Components option, as shown in Figure 28-1.

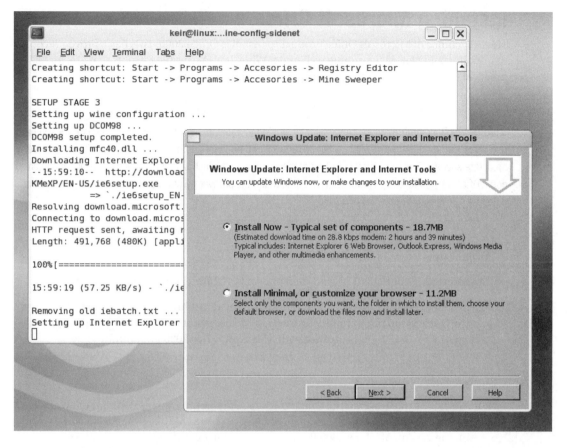

Figure 28-1. *The Sidenet script will download and install Internet Explorer and also configure vital Wine settings.*

9. At the end of installation, Internet Explorer icons will be created on the desktop. Internet Explorer will also start, although it might take a minute or two after the installation of Internet Explorer has finished for this to happen.

10. Once the Sidenet installation utility reports it has finished, close the terminal window. You can delete the `wine-config-sidenet` folder, as well as any other files you downloaded.

■**Note** I saw an error dialog box about `ieinfo5.ocx` when installing Internet Explorer. Don't worry if you see the same thing, or even a handful of other errors. Chances are everything will still run smoothly.

Installing Microsoft Office

The best choice of Microsoft Office product to install is Office 2000. This has a proven record of installing and generally running well under Wine. It also uses file formats that are, for all practical purposes, universally recognized in the business world.

■**Note** The Wine programmers are constantly striving to make Wine compatible with all Windows software packages, but at the time of writing, Office XP and 2003 didn't work, although some people have reported moderate success. The Wine project has a database explaining which software packages work and which don't. Often, any tricks or tips others have used to make the software work are also detailed. You'll find the database at `http://appdb.winehq.org`.

Follow these steps to install Office 2000:

1. Insert the Office 2000 CD, and then open a GNOME Terminal/Konsole window.

2. Switch to the directory the CD has been mounted in within /media, and use Wine to run the Office setup program (the instructions below assume the CD has been mounted at /media/O9PRMCD01, as is the case with Microsoft Office 2000 Premium):

   ```
   cd /media/O9PRMCD01
   wine SETUP.EXE
   ```

3. Work your way through the Office 2000 installation program as you would if you were running Windows. Select the default installation option (this is the Install Now option on the version of Office 2000 Premium I used during testing).

Installation didn't run perfectly smoothly on my test PC, although it may work fine for you. I received several errors messages, which I simply clicked through. At one point, the Office installer told me it was about to quit because of an error, but it didn't.

At the end, the Office installation program seemed to be locked into a cycle of configuring itself. Eventually, it finished and presented the Office installer maintenance dialog box. I clicked to cancel this, and was then told that installation had failed. However, I found that Office 2000 had, in fact, installed perfectly.

Another test I undertook resulted in error messages about Internet Explorer being split from the Windows Update process. In addition, the installation window was very small and the text within it largely illegible. However, I was able to work through the installation wizard by pressing Enter a few times.

As I mentioned at the beginning of this chapter, Wine is something of a hack, so you may encounter some challenges. However, with a little common sense, you should be able to get Office 2000 onto your computer.

Running Office Components

In order to install programs, Wine creates an entire pseudo file system that mirrors a typical Windows hard disk. This is normally located in the hidden .wine directory in your system folder, but the Sidenet script you used to configure Wine will have placed it in your /home directory. Therefore, you should be able to browse to /home/<username>/c/Program Files to see a listing of all installed Windows software (replacing <username> with your username).

Running the Office programs is a matter of navigating to the /home/<username>/c/Program Files/Microsoft Office/Office folder and running the executables via Wine. For example, to run Microsoft Word on my system, I typed (because of the spaces in the path, I enclosed the entire thing in quote marks):

```
wine "/home/keir/c/Program Files/Microsoft Office/Office/WINWORD.EXE"
```

To run Excel, you can type EXCEL.EXE. PowerPoint is POWERPNT.EXE, Access is MSACCESS.EXE, and Outlook is OUTLOOK.EXE. Don't forget that these must be typed in uppercase, because uppercase and lowercase matter in Linux. Figure 28-2 shows an example of running Word under SUSE Linux.

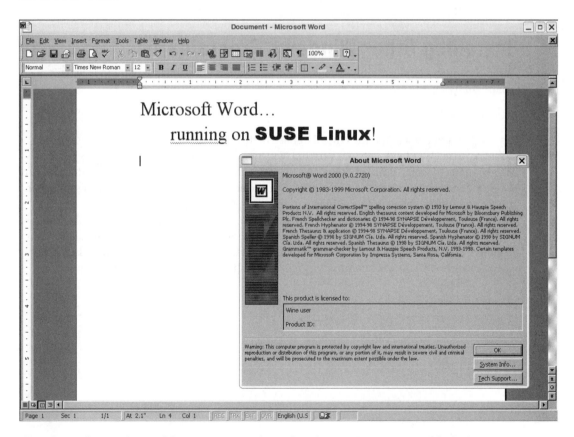

Figure 28-2. *It's entirely possible to run Microsoft Word under SUSE Linux. Just add a little Wine!*

Alternatively, you can easily create desktop shortcuts for your Office programs. See Chapter 10 for details on creating shortcuts.

Aside from being a subdirectory within it, the dummy C:\ drive is entirely separate from your main file system, which is to say that no Windows programs will ever be installed outside this subdirectory. This should give you some peace of mind when it comes to threats from viruses and worms. In theory at least, only the files in this directory will be affected should you pick up an infection. (The Wine developers have theorized that a Windows virus running under Wine could infect your main system, but it would have to be created with knowledge that it might be running under Wine, and no such viruses have yet been found.)

■**Note** I experienced a few weird bugs when running some Office programs. For example, the text in the Office Assistant dialog boxes didn't appear. I also found that the clipboard didn't work correctly when two or more Office applications were running (it seemed fine with just one application). You might encounter similar problems, but you should find that the key functions work.

Installing Other Windows Programs

A lot of Windows applications will install and work under Wine. Installing them is usually a matter of typing this:

```
wine <installer.exe>
```

As I mentioned earlier, the Wine database (http://appdb.winehq.org) often details the best way to get Windows software working. Very nearly every mainstream Windows program can be made to work, although it may take a little extra effort. If there's a program that doesn't work, you can suggest it to the developers. The site contains a list of the top 25 programs that don't work, but which people would like to see up and running under Wine.

In my tests, I managed to use Wine to install the popular WinZip archiving application as well as the Winamp Lite audio software. Once again, getting each to run after installation was a matter of navigating to their directories within the fake C:\ drive and preceding their executable name with the wine command. Figure 28-3 shows both up and running.

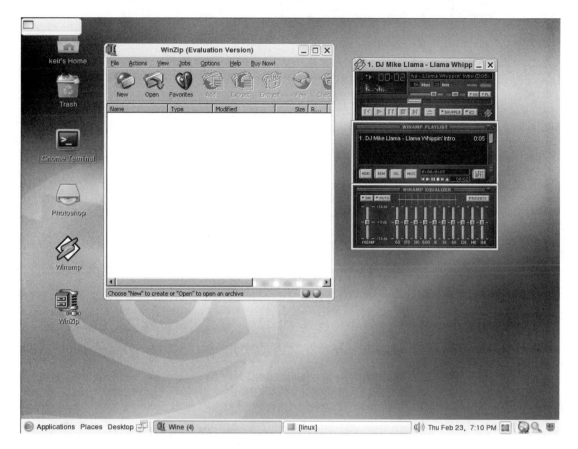

Figure 28-3. *Although it sometimes takes a bit of effort, virtually any Windows application can be made to run under SUSE Linux.*

Summary

In this chapter, we looked at how you can use the Wine project to install and run various Windows programs under SUSE Linux, including Microsoft Office. Because using Wine is not without problems, we looked at how it should be configured, and then walked through the steps needed to install Microsoft Office 2000. Then you saw how to install other Windows programs.

In Part 7 of the book, starting with the next chapter, we look at the techniques you need to know to keep your SUSE Linux system running smoothly. Chapter 29 explains how to install Linux software.

## PART VII

Keeping Your System Running

CHAPTER 29

■■■

Installing and Removing Software

One of the fun things about running any operating system is the ability to expand it—to add in new software over time to improve your workflow or just for entertainment value.

Linux is blessed in this regard, because tens of thousands of software titles are available to meet just about every need. However, even if you've tracked down the ideal software title, there's just one barrier to overcome: actually installing it on your system.

Installing software under SUSE Linux isn't the same as with Windows. Users are afforded a lot more power over what happens to their system, but this comes at the expense of needing to take a little time to understand the terminology and techniques.

In this chapter, you'll learn how to use SUSE Linux's various tools for managing software, but first we'll start with some basics of software installation.

Software Installation Basics

Installing programs on Windows is relatively easy. If you wish to use the Winamp media player, for example, you can browse to the appropriate web site, download the installer .exe file, and install the software.

Although you might not realize it, a lot of work goes into making this seemingly simple task possible. Once the original software has been created by the programmers, it must be made into a form that you, the end user, can run on your computer.

The first thing to happen is that the software is *compiled*. This is the process of turning the source code created by programmers into an actual file (or set of files) that can be used on a daily basis. On most systems, compiling source code involves a lot of number crunching. This takes time—whole days, in some cases— and this is why it isn't normal practice to compile the source code every time you want to run the program.

Once the program files have been compiled, there needs to be a way they can be installed on various systems and easily transported across the Internet. This is where *packaging* comes into the equation. Programs usually consist of many files. To make each program file individually available would mean that some are sure to get lost or corrupted, and the program wouldn't work. Therefore, the files are usually combined into a single archive file. In addition, third-party system files are added to ensure compatibility on all computers and an extra program, called an installer, is added so that users can quickly get the files onto their system.

All of this means that, to be able to install a program like Winamp on Windows, you just need to download the installer .exe file and run it once. No more work is necessary.

Linux is a little more involved, largely because it never assumes that users want their environment to be simplistic and with limited options. However, most Linux distributions still embrace the paradigm of packaging software into a single, easily transported file.

Formats of Linux Installation Files

If you visit the web site of a particular Linux application, you may find that it's available to download in a number of different formats. The program will almost certainly be available as *source code*—the original listing that the developer created. But it might also be available as a binary or as a package file.

■**Tip** Linux isn't the only operating system for which open source programs are created and used. There are open source projects for both Windows and Apple Macintosh, many of which are hosted at the `http://sourceforge.net` web site. Many other less-widely-used operating systems also rely on open source software to a greater or lesser extent.

Here are the formats by which Linux software is normally distributed:

Source code: Programmers write their software in various programming languages, such as C and C++, and the code that results is known as *source code*. To make source code usable, it must be *compiled* into a *binary file*. Because the cornerstone of the Linux philosophy is the sharing of source code, you'll almost always find the source code of a program available at the developer's web site. You can then download and compile this on your own system (or, if you're so inclined, study the source code to further your understanding). Although compiling source code isn't very hard to do, it's more convenient to download either a binary version of the program or a package.

Binary files: You might find binary files are available at the developer's web site. In other words, the programmer has taken his own source code and, as a service to users of the program, compiled it so that it's ready for use as soon as it's downloaded. For example, this is how Linux versions of the Mozilla Foundation software, like Thunderbird and Firefox, are currently distributed if you download them directly from `www.mozilla.com`. Sometimes binary files come with scripts to help you install them. However, in most cases, you simply place the files in a convenient location on your hard disk, and then run them from there.

■**Note** In both the case of source code and binary files, the files usually come in a *tarball*, which is a single archive file containing other files. A tarball isn't by definition compressed, but usually either the `bzip2` or `gzip` tools are used to shrink the file to ease transportation across the Internet.

Self-installing binaries: Some larger programs are made available as a self-installing binary file. This comes very close to the way Windows works because, when the file is executed, a GUI-based installation wizard takes you through installation. If you download

OpenOffice.org from the official web site (www.openoffice.org), for example, you'll end up with a single 80MB+ file, which you then simply run from the command line to install the program.

Package files: In many cases, you'll find that a package file of the program is available. In this case, someone has compiled the software files and put them altogether in a single easily transportable file. SUSE Linux package files end with .rpm file extensions, but other Linux distributions use other package formats, such as .deb (Debian-based distributions like Ubuntu).

■**Note** As a blanket rule, an installation package created for one distribution won't be compatible with another. It's possible to use a program called alien under SUSE Linux, which aims to convert packages between distributions and different package formats, but this should be seen as a last resort. The first resort it to simply obtain a package specifically designed for your Linux distribution.

Package Management

Of all the formats for Linux software distribution, packages are by far the most common and popular. SUSE Linux uses packages, as do nearly all other Linux distributions. In fact, the SUSE Linux DVD-ROM contains thousands of packages, as shown in Figure 29-1.

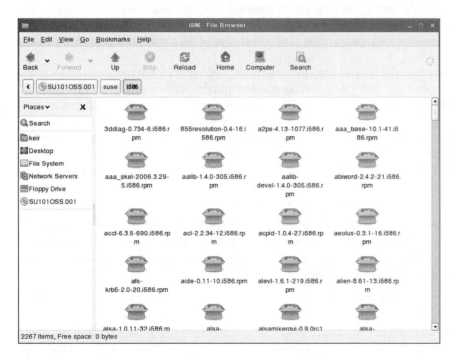

Figure 29-1. *Every part of the SUSE Linux system is contained within, and installed from, package files. The DVD-ROM contains thousands of them.*

It's important to understand what a package file actually is and what it contains. With Windows, an installation .exe file is effectively a piece of software combined with an archive of files. When you run the executable, it triggers a small program contained within it that then unpacks the contents of the file and installs them to the hard disk.

In contrast, package files used by SUSE Linux merely contain the program files, along with a handful of configuration files to ensure the software is set up correctly. Package files are useless without the various pieces of software that are used to manipulate them and do the hard work of installing, removing, and querying them. This software is known as the *package management system*.

A well-implemented package management system is able to install programs, upgrade them, and uninstall them, all with just a few keystrokes or clicks of the mouse on the user's part. Package systems vastly reduce the amount of work required to get new software onto your system, and make maintenance tasks easy, too.

The package management system builds its own database so that it knows exactly what programs are installed at any one time, so you can simply query the database rather than search the applications menu or hard disk. The package management system also keeps track of version numbers. This gives you much more control over the software on your system and makes updating easy. Additionally, if a program starts to act strangely, its configuration files can simply be refreshed using the package manager. There's no need to uninstall and then reinstall the software, as is so often the case with Windows programs.

Dependency Management

One of the key features offered by any package management system is *dependency management*. Put simply, the package manager must ensure that if you install a piece of software, any additional software it relies on to work properly is already present on the system. If the software isn't present, the package manager must either resolve the situation automatically or ask you what to do.

Sometimes the software you want to install might depend on other programs on your system, but more often, the dependencies take the form of system libraries. Library files contain pieces of code that are equivalent to .dll files under Windows—not software that you, as a user, will use directly. The key library on a SUSE Linux system is the GNU C Library, without which the Linux kernel couldn't function. But practically every program has its own needs when it comes to library files, and these requirements must be handled by the package management software.

■**Note** One reason Windows installation files are often so large is that they typically come with all the system files they need in case those files are not already present on the system. In other words, dependency isn't an issue under Windows because everything comes supplied. Windows isn't alone in this regard; installation files for the Apple Macintosh are similar.

Dependency management doesn't just mean adding in packages that a piece of software needs. It might also mean *removing* packages already present on your system. This might happen if certain packages are incompatible with new software you want to install, something that's referred to as *package conflict*. In addition, sometimes you might want to remove a package that other packages rely on, a situation known as *reverse dependency*. In such a case, the package manager either must stop you from removing that software, to avoid breaking the software that depends on it, or remove the reverse-dependency packages as well. In most cases, it will ask you what you wish to do.

DEPENDENCY HELL

If you try to install certain software packages, you will very likely find that they depend on other packages, such as software libraries. These other packages must either be already present on the system or installed at the same time for the software to work correctly. SUSE Linux will attempt to take care of the latter automatically. In a similar way, removing software also means that other packages that rely on that particular software must also be removed, because of reverse dependency.

Dependency hell is what happens when you have chains of dependencies. For example, let's say you install a program called Oscar. You're then told that this depends on another program called BigBird, which isn't installed. Fine, you think, I'll just add BigBird to the same installation command. But it then transpires that BigBird has its own dependency of Snuffleupagus. You add that, too. Alas! Snuffleupagus has its own dependency of MrHooper.

This can carry on for some time. It's less of a problem when installing software, because the sourcing of dependencies is usually automated, although it can be a problem when you're installing packages at the command line.

Dependencies can be a nightmare when you uninstall software, however. Here's a real-life example. The cdrecord software package is the low-level program that SUSE Linux uses to burn CDs and DVDs. Many programs use it, so attempting to remove cdrecord will produce a long list of reverse dependencies. For example, the Nautilus CD-burning component uses it. Therefore, attempting to remove cdrecord will cause SUSE Linux's software management tools to suggest the removal of Nautilus's CD-burning component, too. You might be prepared to accept this. However, Nautilus' CD-burning component has a dependency on a package called python-gnome-extras, because that package happens to contain a system component that the CD-burning component can't do without. So this will be marked for deletion as well. Unfortunately, this is a very popular piece of software that several other packages rely on, including the GNOME Blog Poster desktop applet.

In other words, attempting to remove cdrecord will mean that GNOME Blog Poster software must be removed, something which is completely unrelated to cdrecord and doesn't rely on it. You can see why this situation is referred to as a form of hell!

Dependency chains as deep as this are rare but a by-product of any package management system. The solution is often simple: don't remove the software package. After all, hard disks are extremely large nowadays and space is rarely an issue, so you don't need to get rid of software packages that have a lot of reverse dependencies.

Package Management System Components

SUSE's package management system has two components: RPM and Libzypp.

RPM is the most basic part of the system. It's used to install and uninstall software, and it can also be used to query any software that's currently installed. It's like the manager in a warehouse who is tasked with knowing exactly which boxes have been stored where. The manager doesn't know where the boxes come from, and he doesn't know anything about packages outside his warehouse. He just manages the boxes that are delivered to him and that are stored in his warehouse.

■**Note** RPM stands for Red Hat Package Manager, and is a technology that was created by Red Hat some years ago. It's still used on Red Hat–based versions of Linux, such as Fedora Core, as well as a number of other distros such as SUSE and Mandriva. You might think it strange that software created for use in one distro is used in rival versions of Linux, but one of the cornerstones of the world of Linux is the philosophy of sharing.

RPM is aware of dependency issues and will stop you if you don't have the necessary software needed for a specified package to work correctly. But it does not have the means to fix the situation automatically. Continuing with our analogy, this is like a warehouse manager who doesn't order more boxes. That's not his job. He will just tell you if boxes delivered to him are missing some of their components.

To address dependency issues, an additional layer of background software, called Libzypp, sits on top of RPM. Although it has an unglamorous name, Libzypp is very sophisticated. When you install software using Libzypp, any dependency issues will be worked out for you behind the scenes. In other words, the dependencies are automatically installed, too.

■**Note** Libzypp is a completely new component of SUSE Linux 10.1 and above. It isn't found in earlier versions of SUSE Linux. Those who are technically minded might like to know that it's a combination of YaST's package management system and Novell's Red Carpet package management service.

Libzypp can manage dependencies because it's designed to work with *software repositories*. These are collections of software from which the user can search and install packages. More often than not, these software repositories are online, but that's not always the case. The SUSE Linux DVD supplied with this book is one large software repository, for example.

Libzypp relies on the RPM system to take care of the actual installation. Effectively, RPM and Libzypp are two halves of the same coin.

■**Note** When I talk about RPM and Libzypp, I'm referring to behind-the-scenes system components within SUSE Linux that are normally used by other pieces of software. The Libzypp system is used by YaST's Software Management applet and the Software Installer/Remover tools, discussed in the "Managing Software via the GUI" section later in this chapter. In addition, the rug command-line tool uses the Libzypp system. It's also possible to use the RPM system from the command line, as described in the "Managing Software from the Shell" section later in this chapter.

As you might have realized, the package management system means that software installation (and removal) is a fundamentally different proposition under Linux compared to how it's handled with Windows or Mac OS X. If you want to install new software, the first place to look is the SUSE Linux software repositories, such as the repository contained on the installation DVD-ROM. In fact, the DVD-ROM contains more than 3,000 packages, which represent most of the popular software currently available for Linux.

It's comparatively rare under Linux to visit a web site and download a package file for installation, as is often the case for Windows users. The only time this normally happens is if you can't find what you're looking for in the official repositories.

Tip Software repositories don't have to be "official," or sanctioned by SUSE, to be used under SUSE Linux. Sometimes, you might opt to add repositories that contain particular software. For example, you might recall that in Chapters 18 and 19, I described how to add the Packman repositories so you could access multimedia playback software. This was necessary because the playback software is licensed under terms that SUSE doesn't agree with, and therefore declines to offer from its official repositories.

The tools used to manage software are detailed in this chapter. First, we'll look at graphical software that can be used to manage software, and then we'll look at the command-line tools you can use.

SOFTWARE VERSIONS

Because most Linux software is open source, a curious thing happens when it comes to software versions. Rather than there being just one "official" version of a program, such as with most Windows software (where you must download the official version of the file), many individuals and organizations take the source code, compile it, and make their own package files available for others to use.

For example, virtually all the software installed with SUSE Linux has been compiled by SUSE Linux developers. This means it can be quite different from what's "officially" available at the programmer's web site. In some cases, the source code is tweaked, so that notorious bugs are fixed or a different look and feel applied to the software so it integrates with the distribution. Often, the configuration files are changed so that the software works properly under SUSE Linux, such as integrating with other software packages.

The programmer behind the software doesn't mind when such things happen, because this way of working is part and parcel of open source software. In fact, the programmer is likely to encourage such tweaking.

Because of this, the first place to look if you want any additional software is not the developer's web site, but the SUSE Linux DVD. This way, you'll get an officially sanctioned SUSE Linux release that will fit in with the rest of your system and won't require much, if any, additional work to get up and running.

Managing Software via the GUI

To install and remove software via SUSE Linux's GUI, you can use either the Software Installer and Software Remover tools or YaST. Of the two options, YaST is the better choice because it provides much more information about the software packages and is generally more thorough. However, the Software Installer and Software Remover tools are quick and effective if you need to install or remove just one software package, and we'll look at those tools first.

Using the Software Installer and Software Remover Tools

You can start the Software Installer and Software Remover tools from the System ➤ Configuration menu. The System submenu is under the Applications menu within GNOME or under the K menu within KDE. The menu options for the tools are Install Software and Remove Software, as shown in Figure 29-2.

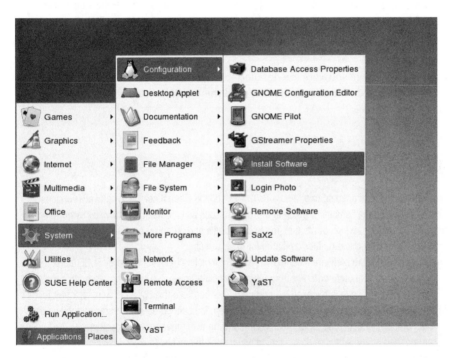

Figure 29-2. *The Install Software and Remove Software options are on the System ➤ Configuration menu.*

Software Installer and Software Remover work in a fundamentally similar way and look identical. Both present lists of software that you can search or simply scroll through. Typing in the Search box filters the list according to the search term. Putting a check in the box alongside the selection marks it for action (installation or removal).

Software Installer presents a list of software in all the repositories that the system has been configured to use (primarily the SUSE Linux installation DVD-ROM, but you can configure more, as explained in the "Adding Installation Sources" section later in this chapter). Software Remover displays a list of the software installed on the system. Once you've made a choice, the tools will work out solutions to any dependency issues.

If you're attempting to remove software, you will be presented with a summary of the actions that will be taken. For example, attempting to remove the Firefox web browser will result in a dialog box stating that the packages MozillaFirefox-translations and beagle-firefox will also need to be removed because of reverse-dependency issues, as shown in Figure 29-3. You can agree to this, or you can click Cancel if removing the other software will cause problems.

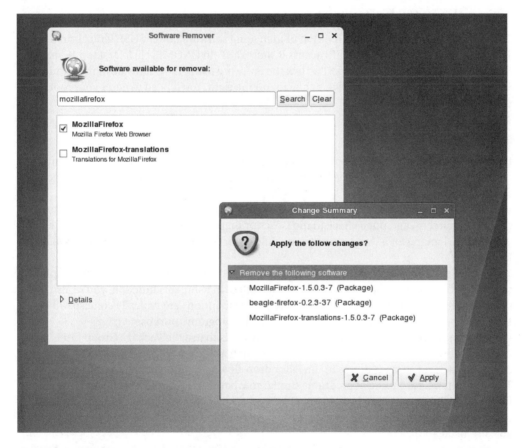

Figure 29-3. *Software Remover will calculate reverse dependencies and suggest removal of all offending packages. Make sure you check the list!*

Installing software is slightly different because any dependencies will automatically be added to the list of packages to be installed. This will be done in the background, and you won't be shown the list of additional packages.

■**Note** As this book went to press, the Software Installer and Software Remover tools appeared to have a bug whereby they ran with ordinary user privileges when, in fact, they need root powers to function (system installation and removal can be carried out only by the root user, for obvious security reasons). It's very likely this will have been fixed by a software update by the time you read this, so you should update online, if you haven't already (see Chapter 9). In the meantime, you can run Software Installer and Software Remover with root powers by opening a terminal window, switching to root user (type `su` at the command prompt), and then typing either `zen-installer` for Software Installer or `zen-remover` for Software Remover.

Using the YaST Software Management Tool

The oldest and most established method of managing software under SUSE Linux is to use the YaST Software Management tool. To access it, start YaST (in GNOME, click Desktop ➤ YaST; in KDE, click K menu ➤ System ➤ YaST), click the Software icon on the left side of the window, and then click the Software Management icon on the right. You'll need to enter your root password to use YaST.

Installing Software Using YaST

Installing software using YaST's Software Management tool is easy. You can search for any program by typing its name in the Search box. This will query your software repositories, such as the SUSE Linux DVD.

If you're looking for a program to fulfill a particular need but don't know its name, you can enter a search term and put a check in the Description box beneath the Search box. For example, if you're looking for a web browser, you could enter "browser" as a search term, as shown in Figure 29-4.

Search results are displayed on the right side of the screen. If the box next to the application has a check in it, that program is already installed. In using this function, you're also searching the description of each application. The descriptions are typically concise rather than verbose, but they usually give a good idea of the program's purpose.

An alternative way to look for and install software is to use the Package Group filter. This lists the software according to certain categories, such as Games, Office, Multimedia, and so on. Simply select Package Groups in the Filter drop-down list at the top of the YaST window. This filter shows a grouping of programs similar to what you might have seen when you first installed SUSE Linux, if you chose to install any additional components. It's a more friendly way to get acquainted with the programs you have installed on your system or that are available for installation.

When you're happy with your choice of packages to install, click the Accept button. You'll then see a brief summary of the actions that will be undertaken, including the number of packages as well as their location (such as on the DVD or an online repository). However, most of the details, such as the package names, will be hidden.

When installing software using the Software Management tool, any dependencies will automatically and invisibly be added to the list and installed automatically.

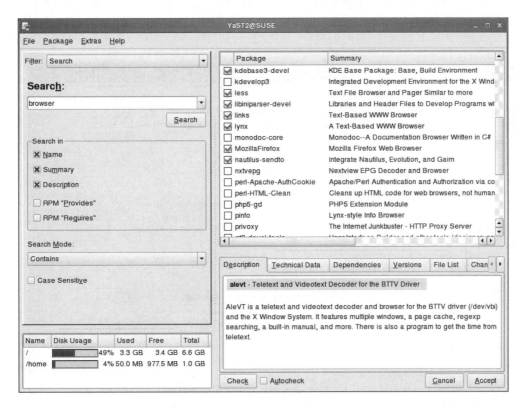

Figure 29-4. *To find software using YaST, you can use generic search terms, but it's a good idea to search Description text, too.*

Removing Software Using YaST

Removing programs using YaST is almost as simple as adding them. Once again, you will need to search for the program (if you're not already using the default Search mode of the Software Management tool, click Search in the Filter drop-down list), but this time, you're looking for software that has a check in the box alongside it. This indicates that the package in question is installed.

To mark the software for deletion, uncheck its box until a trash can icon appears. You need to click twice for this to happen. Clicking once only selects the program for an update, which reinstalls the program (this is useful for attempting to fix programs that have gone wrong).

Once you've marked any software package for deletion, click the Accept button at the bottom right. If YaST's Software Management tool encounters any reverse-dependency issues, it will ask what you want to do. The choices are to keep the software in question, remove it, or to ignore the issue, as shown in Figure 29-5. It won't let you actually remove *any* software until the reverse-dependency issues are resolved in some fashion.

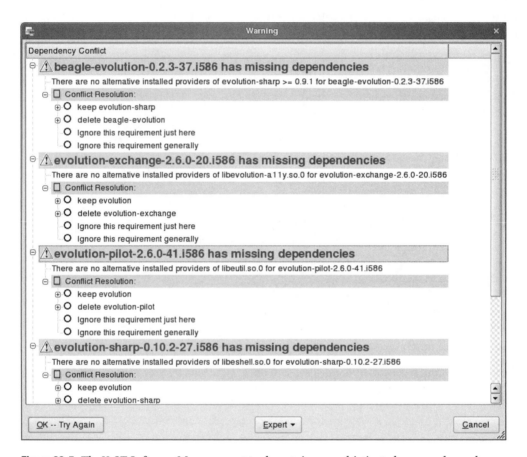

Figure 29-5. *The YaST Software Management tool contains a sophisticated reverse-dependency resolution tool that will ask what you wish to do.*

When there are reverse-dependency issues, keeping the software is the simplest solution and also the one most likely to work. Selecting to delete the package will attempt to remove the reverse-dependency package, but can cause additional reverse-dependency issues because other packages may rely on that particular package.

Choosing to ignore the reverse dependency is very foolish. This will cause the Software Management tool to proceed despite the problem. The result will be that certain software packages may refuse to work in the future. For example, if you remove cdrecord but then don't remove Banshee, which uses cdrecord for its CD-writing function and is therefore listed as a reverse dependency, Banshee simply won't work correctly from then on. Some software packages with missing reverse dependencies might not work at all.

You will need to work through the entire list of reverse-dependency issues, choosing solutions. Then click the OK – Try Again button. This causes the Software Management tool to once again calculate any dependency issues. At this point, any dependencies of dependencies will be highlighted, and must be resolved. This will keep going until all reverse-dependency issues have been solved.

Managing Software from the Shell

There may be times when command-line installation is necessary or just useful. Maybe your computer has gone wrong and you can't boot to a GUI, or maybe you're simply working at the shell and it's more convenient to type a few commands to install some software than it is to start up a GUI tool.

Two commands are available for software installation under SUSE Linux:

rpm: This command is fundamentally simple. It is designed to remove software already installed or to install packages that you've manually downloaded to your hard disk. rpm is aware of dependencies and will inform you when problems arise, but it relies on you to solve them. This can sometimes be difficult because, when installing software, rpm will only inform you about the actual system components that are missing and *not* the packages that contain them.

rug: This is the command-line interface for the Libzypp system, introduced earlier in this chapter. It contains a sophisticated dependency resolver and lets you access online repositories to install software. Unlike rpm, rug is fully aware of which packages contains which files, so is much better able to handle dependency issues. In fact, software dependencies are automatically taken care of when installing software using rug. When removing software, you'll find solutions are automatically calculated so that all you need to do is agree or disagree. rug isn't just about installing or removing software—it can be used to manage the whole Libzypp system. For example, you can use it to add new repositories, as discussed in the "Adding a Software Repository Using rug" section later in this chapter.

■**Note** It's also possible to use the yast2 command to install software, and you might still see this mentioned in some older tutorials online. However, with the release of SUSE Linux 10.1, rug and rpm are the preferred methods.

Before working with rug, it's necessary to know the basics of rpm, so we'll start with that command.

DECODING PACKAGE FILENAMES

SUSE Linux uses RPM package files for software installation. These are the files you'll sometimes have to deal with at the command line, and their filenames usually tell you everything you need to know about them. Here's one example:

```
mozilla-1.6-72.i586.rpm
```

At the beginning of the filename is the name of the program: the popular Mozilla web browser in this instance. Following this are the version numbers: `1.6-72`. These aren't guaranteed to follow the version number conventions used by the developer of the software, although they're very similar in most cases. However, the numbers after the dash in a version number tend to refer to the build of the RPM, which indicates the specific version of the RPM file. Many different RPMs might be created from the same version of the original software, so it's necessary to have a way of telling the different RPMs apart. This number is sometimes referred to as the *build number*.

After the name and version number is the platform on which the RPM file will work. `i586` indicates that this program will work on all Intel 80586–compatible processors—anything including a Pentium chip and above. `i586` refers to the numbering system used within CPU manufacturing.

In some instances, you might find packages stipulating `i686`, indicating that they're designed for a Pentium II processor and above. Also, many RPM files simply indicate `i386`, which means they'll work on any processor from the 80386 upward, including the 486, Pentium, Pentium II, and all subsequent Intel, AMD, IBM, and other improvements. Many packages are listed as `noarch`, which means they'll work on any processor and system.

SUSE produces a version of SUSE Linux that is optimized for the new 64-bit range of chips, such as the AMD Athlon 64. Unfortunately, RPM files compiled for use on these chips won't work on 32-bit systems, which include the majority of computers in use today. Such files are usually marked with an `x86_64` extension.

Using rpm to Install and Remove Software

Using the `rpm` command, you can perform nearly all SUSE Linux software installation and removal tasks. All the `rpm` commands discussed here must be run as the root user.

Installing Software Using rpm

The `rpm` command is never used on its own; it is controlled by various command-line options. Consider the following example:

```
rpm -i mozilla-1.6-72.i586.rpm
```

The `-i` command option tells the `rpm` command to install the specified file. If you're updating software with a newer version, you can use the `-U` option instead. In fact, using `-U` all the time is a good idea because, if the program isn't installed, `rpm` is clever enough to realize that and will install the program instead.

Let's try this out. `fortune` is a fun command-line program that displays a pithy and/or witty saying whenever you run it. It can be found on the SUSE Linux DVD. Insert the DVD and open a shell window. Then switch to the root user before using rpm to install the program:

```
su
[Enter root password]
rpm -U /media/SU1010_001/suse/i586/fortune-1.0-870.i586.rpm
```

You can then run your new software by typing fortune at the command-line prompt.

The trouble with running this command is that it will go through the process of installing the file, but give little, if any, feedback or indication of progress. Because of this, many people add the -v and -h command options. The -v specifies verbose output, meaning that more information is fed back to the user. The -h option simply causes rpm to indicate its progress with a progress bar consisting of hash symbols.

Putting all this together forms what many consider the standard command that should be issued to install a package you've manually downloaded:

```
rpm -Uvh fortune-1.0-870.i586.rpm
```

After each installation, under SUSE Linux, you should run the following command:

```
SuSEconfig
```

This will register the new program with any necessary background services and also update any necessary configuration files. Note that this is specific to SUSE Linux and isn't necessary on other distributions.

You can specify more than one file for installation at the same time, simply by listing the package names after each other, separated by a space:

```
rpm -Uvh package1.rpm package2.rpm package3.rpm
```

QUERYING WITH RPM

It's well worth reading the rpm man page because rpm is packed with features, all of which are accessed by command-line options. Perhaps the most useful, other than software installation and removal, is the query option: -q. The query option is unusual because it has it own set of command options. Anything that appears *after* -q is considered a query option.

By default, using -q without any query options queries installs RPM files (the main database). This is handy if you want to explore the list of installed programs. For example, typing rpm -q nautilus will show if the package Nautilus is installed. The -qa option, used without specifying a package, will list all of the installed programs.

To query an RPM file that's not installed, you need to add the -p option and then specify the package filename. Used together, the -qp options will tell you what program is contained within the specified RPM file—nothing more. If you want a listing of the files inside the package, add -l. Using -i will return some additional information about the program. Using all these command options together will reveal all the useful data the specified package has to offer:

```
rpm -qpli packagename |less
```

Notice that this example pipes the output into less, because the command can sometimes return quite a lot of information, which can scroll off the screen.

Removing Software Using rpm

Uninstalling an installed RPM file is just as easy as installing one. Simply specify the -e command option, like so:

```
rpm -e mozilla
```

In most cases, this is quick and simple. Note that there's no need to specify anything other than the main program name, unless you have a number of programs on your system with similar filenames. If this is the case, rpm will prompt you for more information.

Resolving Dependency Issues with rpm

If you try to use the rpm command to install or remove software, you'll come up against its limitations pretty quickly in the form of dependency issues. As an example, let's try to install the ClanBomber game, which is on the SUSE Linux DVD:

```
rpm -Uvh /media/SU1010_001/suse/i586/clanbomber-1.05-19.i586.rpm
```

Here's the output I saw on my test system:

```
libclanApp.so.2 is needed by clanbomber-1.05-19.i586
libclanCore.so.2 is needed by clanbomber-1.05-19.i586
libclanDisplay.so.2 is needed by clanbomber-1.05-19.i586
libclanMikMod.so.2 is needed by clanbomber-1.05-19.i586
libclanSound.so.2 is needed by clanbomber-1.05-19.i586
```

A quick search of the SUSE Linux DVD-ROM will reveal that there aren't any package files called libclanApp.so.2, or libclanCore.so.2. In fact, the missing components that rpm reports are most likely contained in one or more package files. rpm hasn't a clue what they are. It simply doesn't offer that level of functionality.

If you wish to install ClanBomber, you must somehow find out what the additional package files are called. You can do this using some rpm commands that query packages, but this is both difficult and time-consuming, to say the least!

rpm is just as useless if you try to remove a vital package. Here's what I see when I try to remove Nautilus, the file manager under GNOME:

```
# rpm -e nautilus
error: Failed dependencies:
        libnautilus-extension.so.1 is needed by (installed) control-center2-2.12 .2- ➥
56.i586
        libnautilus-extension.so.1 is needed by (installed) file-roller-2.12.2-2 2.i ➥
586
        libnautilus-extension.so.1 is needed by (installed) nautilus-cd-burner-2 .12 ➥
.3-20.i586
        libnautilus-extension.so.1 is needed by (installed) nautilus-open-termin al- ➥
0.6-16.i586
        libnautilus-extension.so.1 is needed by (installed) nautilus-sendto-0.4- 27. ➥
i586
```

```
        libnautilus-extension.so.1 is needed by (installed) nautilus-share-0.6.4 -29 ➥
.i586

        libnautilus-extension.so.1 is needed by (installed) totem-1.4.0-11.i586
        nautilus is needed by (installed) control-center2-2.12.2-56.i586
        nautilus is needed by (installed) nautilus-cd-burner-2.12.3-20.i586
        nautilus is needed by (installed) nautilus-sendto-0.4-27.i586
        nautilus = 2.12.2 is needed by (installed) nautilus-devel-2.12.2-61.i586
```

rpm simply won't let me uninstall Nautilus until the reverse dependencies are resolved, indicated by the list of "needed by" packages. I could try to resolve these manually, but it's very likely that each of the packages listed will have its own reverse dependencies, and so on.

Resolving any kind of dependency issue when using rpm is hard work. It's possible to do so, but it's far simpler to use the rug command to manage software, as described next.

RPM SECURITY

When installing programs, it's vital that some mechanism exists to prove that the RPM files used are genuine. By its very nature, open source software is open to abuse. A nefarious individual could alter the source code of a program, implanting something such as a trojan routine that could steal data. After inserting the code, he could then compile and package the file as if it were the genuine article provided by SUSE or the original developer.

The simplest defense is to make sure that you download only from web sites you can trust, such as that of SUSE itself. However, you can also use the RPM GNU Privacy Guard (GPG) key system.

Every officially released RPM file from SUSE is signed with a GPG hashcode. This hashcode is unique to each file and is generated based on the contents of the RPM using a so-called *secret key*, which only SUSE knows. All secret keys have public key counterparts, and the SUSE RPM public key is added by default to all SUSE Linux installations. The public key can be used to confirm that the hashcode is correct, based on the contents of the file. This allows for a high degree of security.

RPM files also contain checksums that can be used to confirm that the file is complete and not missing files, or that it doesn't contain altered files. Checksums are the results of mathematical formulas applied to the file. If the file changes in any way, no matter how small, then the checksum will change, too.

To check any kind of RPM file for both checksums and GPG hashcodes, type the following:

```
rpm --checksig -v filename.rpm
```

The results should read OK for each category. Of course, this depends on whether the GPG public key from the organization that created the RPM file is known to your system. If it's not, then you will see an error.

You can import public keys from third-party package sources using the following command:

```
rpm --import ftp://mysite.com/publickey
```

Ordinarily, the key is imported directly from an online source, such as an FTP server. You'll probably find the address listed somewhere on the web site, such as in the FAQ section. However, it could just as easily be imported from a text file on your own hard disk that you've downloaded, or that someone has given you. But, once again, this file must be from a trusted source. If you intend to use a new online RPM file archive, for example, you should make sure you use the key offered on its server. You certainly cannot assume that a site you stumble across using a search engine will contain an authentic public key for another download source.

Using rug to Install and Remove Software

The rug command handles all dependency issues and should be considered the de facto software administration command-line tool. rug should be run as root user for software installation or removal, although some tasks, such as searching through the software repositories, can be carried out as a normal user.

■**Note** Like Libzypp, rug is completely new to SUSE Linux 10.1 and isn't found in previous versions.

Refreshing Software Repository Lists

rug is used to install and remove software from software repositories, such as the SUSE Linux DVD or other repositories (see the "Adding Installation Sources" section later in this chapter). Before using rug, you should refresh its catalogs. This will read in any changes to the software repositories, such as the addition of new packages to online repositories. This is the equivalent of right-clicking the Software Updater icon and selecting Refresh.

To use rug to refresh the software repository lists, type the following command at the command line:

```
rug refresh
```

Depending on how many software repositories you have defined, and the speed and availability of online sources, this may take a minute or two to complete.

Installing Software Using rug

Installing software via rug is easy. Just specify its name along with the install command option.

■**Note** rug command options don't need dashes before them.

For example, to install the ClanBomber game mentioned earlier, enter the following command:

```
rug install clanbomber
```

First, rug searches the database of packages contained in the software repositories to find out whether the software you're specifying is available. Assuming that it is, rug then attempts to work out if it needs any dependencies, and also if the dependencies themselves have dependencies (and so on).

When I run this command on my system, I'm told that I also need to install clanlib-0.6.50364.i586, which is a dependency package. I'm told of its location, which in this case is the SUSE Linux DVD, along with some other details, such as the version number (most of which can be ignored). I'm then asked if I want to proceed. Tapping Y installs all the packages specified; a red bar indicates the installation's progress. Following this, I can run ClanBomber by typing `clanbomber` at the command line or by clicking its entry on the menu (Applications ➤ Games ➤ Arcade ➤ ClanBomber).

■**Caution** ClanBomber is a fun game in the mold of the classic BomberMan, but it contains some adult humor and cartoon-style violence, so perhaps isn't ideal for younger players.

Removing Software Using rug

Uninstalling software is as simple as installation. Just specify `remove` as a command option:

`rug remove clanbomber`

You'll see a brief message informing you that `rug` is working out any dependency issues, before the software is uninstalled.

When removing software, `rug` will work out any reverse-dependency issues and simply mark all reverse dependencies for removal (including dependencies or dependencies, and so on).

For example, if you try to remove the Nautilus file manager, you'll find that `rug` will also mark for removal a large chunk of the GNOME desktop system, including the Evolution mail client, the Beagle search system, the File Roller compression tool, and others. All of these depend on Nautilus, or the system files it provides, in some way.

Therefore, you should scrutinize any list of removal candidates very thoroughly. If you don't know what the packages in the list are, or what they do, then you shouldn't continue with the removal. As I've already mentioned, sometimes the best policy is simply to not remove the piece of software and leave it on the system.

If a particular package must be removed but you don't know what it does, you can use `rug`'s `info` command to learn more, as discussed in the upcoming "Querying Packages Using rug" section.

■**Note** Sometimes when using `rug`, you might see the message, `Waking up ZMD....` This simply means that the background service that `rug` relies on, ZMD, is being reactivated. It's nothing to worry about, although it might take a minute or two for reactivation to complete.

Searching Using rug

You can use `rug` to search through the software repository lists for particular software packages. This will search all of the repositories available to `rug`.

As you might expect, searching is easy: just use the `search` command option:

`rug search` *packagename*

Only the names of the packages are searched, and not the descriptions.

The results of the search are presented in a table with the following headings:

S: This indicates the status of the software. If the field is empty, the software package isn't installed. If an i appears in this field, the software is already installed.

Catalog: This heading indicates which software repository contains the package in question. Most commonly, you'll read the following:

SUSE-Linux-10.1-PromoDVD-i386-10.1-0-20060807-112808

This indicates the SUSE Linux installation DVD-ROM, as supplied with this book. If you read SUSE-Linux-10.1-Update, the package in question is most likely a patch, which is a small piece of software designed to provide a fix to software already installed. Installing a patch will *not* install the software.

Bundle: This heading indicates if the software is part of a grouping of software, known as a *bundle*, although this function doesn't appear to be used under SUSE Linux 10.1. However, if you use other SUSE Linux products, particularly the Enterprise distros, then you might find this feature is used.

Name: This heading indicates the name of the package, and this should be used for all rug commands, such as install and remove.

Version: This heading indicates both the software version number and also the package version.

Arch: This indicates the computer architecture with which the package is designed to work. In most cases, this will read i586, although it might also read noarch, which indicates that the package will work on all versions of SUSE Linux, regardless of the CPU system in use. Generally, you won't be subscribed to software repositories containing software for architectures different from your own, so this heading can be ignored.

Querying Packages Using rug

You can see a description of any package by using the info command option:

rug info *packagename*

This will also tell you if the package is installed and which repository it's contained in if it isn't. You'll also learn whether the package is up-to-date (whether a newer version of the package or a patch is available) and the size of the software (in bytes), along with a handful of other details.

By specifying the file-list command option, instead of info, you can list the files that any package contains. Far more useful is the info-requirements option, which can be used like this:

rug info-requirements *packagename*

This will provide a list of dependency packages for the specified package. However, this is only one level deep, which is to say that dependencies of dependencies won't be calculated.

The only way to see the entire "deep" list of dependencies for any package is to attempt to install the software. However, a neat trick is to specify the "dry-run" command option: -N. This will ask rug to pretend to install the software package, and therefore calculate dependencies, without actually writing any files to your hard disk. The following command will do a dry-run installation of ClanBomber:

```
rug install -N clanbomber
```

Installation will appear to have taken place but, crucially, it won't actually happen.

Updating Software Using rug

The rug command can also update your entire system. By now, you're no doubt getting the hang of using rug and its preference for plain-English commands, so you might already have guessed the necessary command option:

```
rug update
```

Of course, there's no need to specify a package name.

■**Tip** Refreshing the software repository database, using rug refresh, is a good idea before attempting an update.

Adding Installation Sources

For the package management system to work correctly, it needs to have access to at least one software repository. As you might expect, the DVD-ROM is added as the first of these, and this is set up automatically during initial installation of SUSE Linux. In addition, when you registered SUSE Linux and configured system updates (in Chapter 9), an additional online repository was added. This contains updates to the system (pieces of software known as *patches*) and is periodically checked by the Software Updater applet to ensure that your system is up-to-date.

■**Note** Patches are a neat idea. They're small pieces of code designed to be added into software already installed. There's no need to download the entire software package again if the program has a bug that needs to be fixed.

For most users, these two repositories are all that will be needed, but it's easy to add others. You may recall that during Chapters 18 and 19, we did just that to add an online repository containing third-party multimedia codecs. In fact, this is the main reason to set up additional repositories: to access software not offered in the main SUSE Linux repositories. The additional advantage of setting up third-party repositories is that any software you download and install from them will also be updated automatically when new versions are made available, as part of the update function offered by the Software Updater applet.

■**Tip** SUSE Linux is able to work with several different types of software repositories, including YUM, YaST sources, Zenworks Server, OpenCarpet Server, and Red Carpet Enterprise Server.

Using a software repository requires two main steps:

- Add the software repository to your computer's list of repositories.

- Subscribe to the new repository.

Subscription is a handy way of activating and deactivating particular repositories, without needing to remove them from the list (and therefore go through the trouble of adding them each time you wish to use them in future). The installation DVD-ROM repository and the online updates repository are subscribed to automatically. However, when you add other repositories, you must subscribe to them manually. Once you subscribe to a repository, you'll be able to install software from it. Additionally, Software Updater will read from any subscribed repository and, if necessary, suggest the download of updated packages. If you unsubscribe, any software in the repository won't appear in the search results and therefore can't be installed.

■**Note** After you've unsubscribed to a repository, it will be ignored if you use GUI applications like Software Installer to install applications. If you use the command-line `rug` tool, software in unsubscribed repositories *will* appear in search results, but you'll receive an error message when you try to install it.

SUSE Linux provides three methods for adding an installation source: using the Software Updater applet, using YaST, and using `rug` at the command line. The following sections describe how to use each of these methods to add a software repository and subscribe to it.

Adding a Software Repository Using Software Updater

To add a new installation source using the Software Updater applet, follow these steps:

1. Right-click the Software Updater applet in the system tray/notification area and select Configure.

2. Click Add Service, and then click the Add Service button.

3. In the Add Service dialog box, enter the address of the server in the Service URI text box. Type an easy-to-remember name into the Service Name text box, as shown in Figure 29-6. You can leave the Registration Key text box blank, unless you've been specifically instructed to type something there. This might be necessary if you're using SUSE Linux in a corporate environment and wish to connect to an update server that is offered as part of a support contract. Click Add to add the new repository.

■**Note** I noticed that when adding software repositories, I had to add the `suse/` directory to the end of the URI. For example, the nearest non-open source repository to my location is `http://suse.mirrors.tds.net/` `pub/opensuse/distribution/SL-10.1/non-oss-inst-source/` (non-open source repositories are official repositories that contain proprietary software like RealPlayer or Adobe Acrobat; there's no need for you to use this repository, because the packages are included on the DVD-ROM that comes with this book). For Software Updater to accept this address, it was necessary to add the `/suse/` suffix: `http://suse.mirrors.tds.net/` `pub/opensuse/distribution/SL-10.1/non-oss-inst-source/`**suse/**.

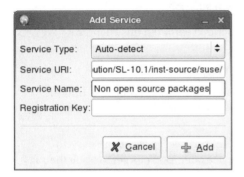

Figure 29-6. *Adding a new software repository is easy using the Software Updater applet.*

4. You'll be invited to enter the root password, so do so.

5. When the software has finished updating, click the Catalogs tab and make sure there's a check alongside the entry you just added. This will subscribe you to the repository. If you later wish to temporarily stop using the repository, you can return to this dialog box and remove the check in the box. This will unsubscribe you.

6. Click the Close button to close the Configuration dialog box.

7. Right-click the Software Updater applet and select Refresh. (This process will take a while.)

After the software repository has been added, you can install software from it using the methods described earlier in this chapter.

Adding a Software Repository Using YaST

To add a software repository using YaST, follow these steps:

1. Start YaST. In GNOME, click Desktop ➤ YaST. In KDE, click K menu ➤ System ➤ YaST.

2. Select the Software icon on the left side of the window, click Installation Source, and then click Add.

3. Select an option appropriate to the repository you're adding. In most cases, the FTP and HTTP options should be fine, depending on whether the repository is an HTTP or FTP address (whether it starts with http:// or ftp://).

4. Enter just the server address in the Server Name text box. This should be the first part of the address, *without* the directories afterward, and *without* the preceding http:// or ftp://. For example, with the address http://packman.inode.at/suse/10.1/, you would enter simply packman.inode.at.

5. In the Directory on Server text box, enter the *rest* of the address but don't include the first slash. So with the address in step 4, you would type suse/10.1/.

6. Click OK to add the repository, and then click Finish.

You can then add software using the methods described earlier in this chapter.

Adding a Software Repository Using rug

Adding a service using rug is simply a matter of using the service-add command option:

```
rug service-add service_URI service_name
```

Replace *service_URI* with the link to the service, and *service_name* with an easy-to-remember reference by which you can identify the service later. Don't forget to issue the rug refresh command to read from the new database.

Following this step, it is necessary to subscribe to the new repository:

```
rug subscribe service_name
```

Again, you should replace *service_name* with the name you assigned the repository when you added it.

If you later wish to stop using the repository for any length of time, you can unsubscribe using the following command:

```
rug unsubscribe service_name
```

Unlike with the GUI tools that are used to install and remove software, when searching with rug, you'll find that the results include software from unsubscribed repositories (don't forget that you can look under the Catalog heading of the search results to see in which repository the software mentioned is located). However, attempting to install the software will result in an error message.

You should issue the rug refresh command to read the list of the new repository once you've subscribed to it. There's no need to refresh after unsubscribing.

■Tip It is actually possible to install software from unsubscribed repositories. Simply use the -u command option with rug install. For example, the following would install *packagename* from an unsubscribed repository: rug install -u *packagename*.

Compiling from Source

Back in the old days of Unix, the only way to install software was from source code, a process known as *compiling*. This was because most people edited the source code themselves, or at least liked to have the option of doing so. Nowadays, innovations such as package management systems make compiling all but redundant for the average user. But knowing how to compile a program from source is still a good Linux skill to have. In some cases, it's your only option for installing certain programs because you may not be able to find a packaged binary.

It goes without saying that program compilation is usually handled at the command-line prompt. It's not the kind of thing you would do via a GUI program.

Installing the Compiler Tools

Before you can compile from source, you need to install several items of software: the make program, which oversees the process of creating a new program, and the GNU Compiler Collection (GCC), which does the hard work of turning the source code into a binary. In addition, if the software relies on certain library files, you'll need to install developer (devel) versions of them, as well as the libraries themselves if they're not already installed.

Under SUSE Linux, it's possible to install all the program-compilation tools you need by selecting the C/C++ Compiler and Tools selection within the YaST Software Management tool, as follows:

1. Start YaST. In GNOME, click Desktop ➤ YaST. In KDE, click K menu ➤ System ➤ YaST.

2. Click the Software icon on the left, and then click the Software Management icon on the right.

3. In the Filter drop-down list, make sure Selections is highlighted. In the list on the left side of the window, select C/C++ Compiler and Tools. Then click the Accept button.

Let's take a look at installing a program from source. Dillo is a stripped-down web browser that's designed for speed and small file size. It's a fun little program that's good to have around in the event of your main browser developing a glitch that you can't fix—at least you'll then be able to get online to fix it!

The Dillo homepage is www.dillo.org, so head over there and choose to download the latest version of the source code.

Unpacking the Tarball and Resolving Dependencies

The first thing to do is to unpack and uncompress the tarball (to learn more about the tar command, see Chapter 32):

```
tar jxf dillo-0.8.6.tar.bz2
```

Of course, you should replace the filename with that of the version you downloaded.

Next, you'll need to switch into the source code directory and take a look at the README file:

```
cd dillo-0.8.6
less README
```

This will tell you the dependencies Dillo has and also any caveats you may need to take into account in order to compile Dillo on a Linux system.

■Note Unlike binary files, source code is rarely designed with one specific computer platform in mind. For example, Dillo is able to compile on all types of Unix, including Linux, Solaris, BSD, and others. With a little work, it might even be possible to compile it under Windows!

Typically, the README file will be quite technical, but the trick is to let your eyes skip over anything confusing and look for the important headings. My eyes were drawn straight to the heading that read, "Dillo needs the following packages." Here, I could see that Dillo needs several library files, the first one of which is the glib libraries. This is a given on nearly all Linux systems that use the GNOME desktop, but you should check to make sure it's present. Additionally, in order to compile, Dillo will need the devel version of glib, which is unlikely to be part of the default SUSE Linux installation.

Next, I read that Dillo also needs the GTK+ 1.2 library. You must check to make sure that this is installed, and then make sure the devel version is installed.

Beneath that in Dillo's list of requirements is support for JPEG and PNG image formats, which is definitely installed on the average Linux system, and the WGET download tool, which is also included with most versions of Linux (although it's a good idea to use YaST or rug to check whether it's installed).

After finding out about dependencies, you should scroll down the README file to look for any notes about compiling under Linux. It turns out there might be some issues with older 2.4 versions of the Linux kernel, but SUSE Linux uses 2.6, so this isn't a problem.

In summary, before you can compile Dillo, you need to check to see if glib is installed, and also install the devel version of it. In addition, you must make sure the GTK+ 1.2 library is installed, and also install the devel version of it. Use rug with the info command option to check if these libraries are installed:

```
rug info gtk glib
```

Notice that you can specify both library names in the same command. rug is clever enough to realize this and process each separately. Additionally, as with all kinds of searches, it pays to simplify the search terms, so rather than searching for GTK+ 1.2, you can simply search for gtk.

In the results on my test system, I saw that both are installed. But now I need to install the devel versions of each library.

There are two paths you can take at this point. The first is to try to manually track down the devel package files. The major problem with this approach is that it's not always obvious which package contains which devel library file, so it can sometimes be like searching for a needle in a haystack.

A better method is to use the YaST Software Manager tool to automatically add in devel versions of all currently installed libraries. This will also mean that any future program compilation you undertake will be made easier because it's likely all the relevant devel library files will be installed, too.

To automatically add the devel libraries, start YaST, click the Software icon on the left, and then click the Software Manager icon. Then click Extras ➤ Install All Matching -devel Packages. You'll then be presented with a list of all newly selected packages, so simply click OK to close the dialog box, and then click Accept to install them.

■**Caution** The downside of installing all the devel libraries is that you'll end up installing many additional packages, and this will increase the burden when you perform online system updates. In other words, if any new versions of the devel libraries have been released, these will also be updated. You may find you need to update around 30% more files during an update procedure.

Compiling the Program

Now comes the exciting process of compiling the program! This is done via three commands, issued in sequence:

```
./configure
make
make install
```

The first command starts the configure script, created by the Dillo programmer, which checks your system to make sure that it meets Dillo's requirements. In other words, it checks to make sure the glib and GTK+ libraries are present. It also checks to make sure you have the correct software required to actually compile a program, such as GCC and make.

It's when the configure script is running that something is most likely to go wrong. In that case, more often than not, the error message will tell you that you're missing a dependency, which you must then resolve.

■**Note** Some configure scripts are very thorough and check for components that the program you're trying to install might not even need. Because of this, you shouldn't worry if, as the text scrolls past, you see that various components are missing. Unless configure complains about it, it's not a problem.

The next command, make, takes care of the actual program compilation. When it's run, the screen will fill with what might look like gibberish (see Figure 29-7), but this is merely the output of the GNU compiler. It provides a lot of valuable information to those who know about such things, but you can largely ignore it. However, you should keep your eyes peeled for any error messages. It's possible that the configure script might not have checked your system thoroughly enough, and you might be missing an important system component; in which case, make will halt.

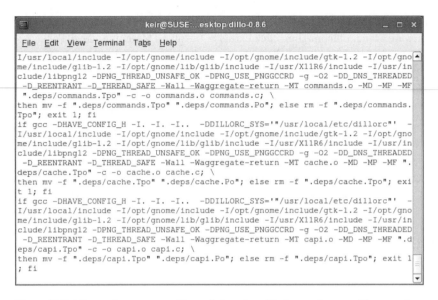

Figure 29-7. *The make process will result in a lot of information scrolling up the screen, but you can ignore most of it.*

Alternatively, the program simply might not be able to compile on your system without some tweaking to the makefile (the file that make uses). If such a situation arises, the best plan is to visit the web site of the developer of the software and see if there's a forum you can post to. Alternatively, check if the developer has an e-mail address you can contact to ask for help.

■**Note** I saw an error message at the end of the make session when compiling Dillo. I was able to follow up with the make install command, which also reported error messages. However, I found that Dillo worked fine! The moral of the story is that software compilation is something of a black art, with error messages designed for programmers, and not all error messages are fatal.

Eventually, the compilation will stop with a number of "exit" messages. Then you must run the final command: make install. This needs to be run as the root user, because its job is to copy the binary files you've just created to the relevant system directories, and only root can write to these directories.

Any documentation that comes with the program is also copied to the relevant location on your system.

Once the three commands have completed, you should be able to run the program by typing its name at the command prompt. If you've been playing along at home and have compiled Dillo, you can run it by typing dillo. Figure 29-8 shows an example of Dillo in action.

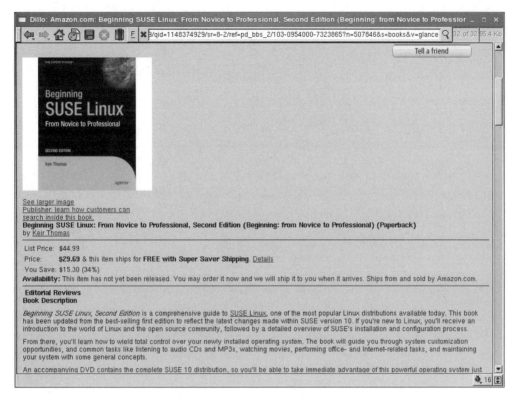

Figure 29-8. *Dillo in action—a certain satisfaction comes from compiling a program from source code.*

■**Tip** Perhaps it goes without saying that you'll need to add your own icon to the desktop or Applications menu. Source packages are usually designed to be installed on any version of Unix running a variety of desktop managers. So, it's not possible for the developer to know where to create desktop shortcuts.

Summary

This chapter described how to install software under SUSE Linux. We've looked at how this differs from Windows software installation, and how the package management system is designed to make life easier for Linux users.

You learned how to use the Software Installer and Software Remover tools, the YaST Software Management tool, the rpm command-line tool, and the rug command-line tool to manage software. You also learn how to add installation sources. Finally, we looked at how programs can be compiled from their source code, which is a fundamental process of all versions of Linux.

In the next chapter, we'll look at how the system of users under SUSE Linux can be administered.

■ ■ ■

## CHAPTER 30

Managing Users

SUSE Linux was designed from the ground up to be a multiuser system. When it is deployed on huge mainframe computers, it is capable of serving hundreds, if not thousands, of users at the same time, provided there are enough terminal computers for them to log in. In a more domestic setting, such as when SUSE Linux is installed on a desktop PC, it usually means that more than one family member can have their very own account on the PC. Any files users create will be private, and users will also get their own desktop environment that is separate from that of the other users.

And even if you're the only person using your PC, you can still take advantage of SUSE Linux's multiuser capabilities. Consider creating user accounts for various aspects of your life—perhaps one for work and one for time spent browsing the Web. Each user account can be tailored toward each specific need.

In this chapter, you'll learn how to administer multiple user accounts.

Understanding User and Group Accounts

The concepts of users and file ownership were explained in Chapter 14, but let's take a few minutes to recap and elaborate on some important points.

Each person who wishes to use SUSE Linux must have a user account. This will define what that user can do on the system, with specific reference to files. Because SUSE Linux is effectively one large file system, with even hardware devices seen as individual files (see Chapter 14), this means that user permissions lie at the heart of controlling the entire system. They can limit which user has access to which hardware and software, and therefore control access to various PC functions.

Each user also belongs to a group. Groups have the same style of permissions as individual users. Accessing a file can be denied to a user, depending on that person's group membership.

■**Note** As in real life, a group can have many members and can be based around various interests. In a business environment, this might mean that groups are created for members of the accounting department and members of the human resources department, for example. By changing the permissions on files created by the group members, each group can have files that only the group's members can access (although, as always, the root user can access all files).

On a default SUSE Linux system with just a handful of users, the group concept might seem somewhat redundant. However, the concept of groups is fundamental to the way SUSE Linux works and cannot be avoided. Even if you don't make use of groups, SUSE Linux still requires your user account to be part of one.

In addition to actual human users, the SUSE Linux system has its own set of user and group accounts. Various programs that access hardware resources or particular sets of files normally use these. Setting up system users and groups in this way makes the system more secure and easier to administer. However, the creation and use of these groups take place "behind the scenes," so it isn't something that you should worry about.

The root user has power over the entire system. Root can examine any file and configure any piece of hardware. Root also belongs to its own unique group, also called root.

Because of its power, the root user can cause a lot of accidental damage, so it's rare for anyone to log in as root. Instead, you can switch to root user temporarily from an ordinary user account using the su command.

Although we talk of user and group names, these are used only for the end user's benefit. SUSE Linux uses a numerical system to identify users and groups. These are referred to as user IDs (UIDs) and group IDs (GIDs), respectively.

For various reasons, under SUSE Linux, all the GID and UID numbers under 1000 are reserved for the system to use. This means that the first non-root user created on a system during installation will probably be given a UID of 1000. In addition, any new groups created after installation are numbered from 1000 upward, although the default group that standard users are added to by default has a GID of 100.

■**Note** UID and GID information isn't important during everyday use, and most commands used to administer users and file permissions understand the human-readable usernames. However, knowing UIDs and GUIDs can prove useful when you're undertaking more complicated system administration.

Creating New Users and Groups

The easiest and quickest way of adding new users and groups, or deleting existing ones, is to use YaST. Of course, you can also perform these tasks through the command line. Let's look at both techniques.

Adding and Deleting Users and Groups with YaST

Here are the basic steps for using YaST to add a new user:

1. Start YaST. If you're running the KDE desktop, click K menu ➤ System ➤ YaST. Under GNOME, click Desktop ➤ YaST. This requires root privileges, so enter your root password when prompted.

2. Click Security and Users on the left side of the YaST window, and then click User Management on the right side of the window.

3. You see a list of current ordinary (nonroot or system) users. To add a new user, click the Add button at the bottom-left side of the window.

4. You see a window virtually identical to that presented during initial installation, as shown in Figure 30-1. Enter the full name of the new user (for your own reference), the new username, and the password.

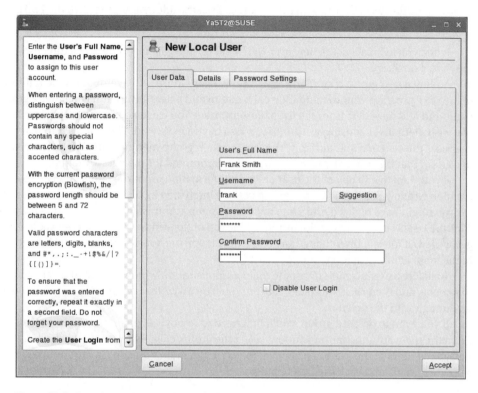

Figure 30-1. *Creating new users is easily done via the central YaST configuration program.*

5. If you want to set a password expiration time, click the Password Settings tab. This can be useful if you want to create a user account that is valid for a limited period because, when the password expires, the user account will be locked. This will happen even if the user changes the password. The simplest policy is to enter an expiration date, which should be in the form of year-month-day (such as 2006-10-23).

■**Note** Unlike under Windows NT, when a user account's password expires in SUSE Linux, the user won't then be prompted to enter a new password. The account will simply be disabled, at least until the root user steps in to reset the password. Also, the user won't be able to overcome the expiration by changing her password manually in advance. The expiration date applies to any password on the account.

---

6. If you want to manually enter a UID number, or adjust the groups to which the user belongs, click the Details tab. As discussed earlier, by default, the user will belong to a handful of system groups that will give that user access to particular hardware resources. You can see a list of these here. However, it's not advisable to change any default group memberships, because the user account could be seriously crippled when it comes to running programs on the system.

7. Click the Accept button on the New Local User window, and then click the Finish button in the main administration window to create the new user(s).

When you're finished, the new user will be set up and will have a personal directory within the /home/ directory.

Adding a new group is similarly easy. Simply click Group Management on the right side of the YaST program window, and then click Add to add a new group. You can enter a group name and add members from the list of current users. You can also manually specify a GID if you wish. Perhaps surprisingly, a group can also have a password. This comes into play when a user uses the newgrp command to temporarily switch group membership. If he tries to switch to a group that is password-protected, he will be prompted for the password first.

If you want to edit any of the user or group information, from the Users and Group Administration window, select the user or group you are interested in, and then click the Edit button. (As you might have realized, the same window lets you administer both users and groups; just click the Users and Groups radio buttons at the top of the window to switch between user and group views.) You can then change any of the details you previously entered. Click Next to return to the main administration window.

To delete a user account, from the main administration window, select the user you want to remove, and then click the Delete button. You'll be asked to confirm that you really want to go through with the deletion.

If you want to delete a group, you'll first need to remove all the members from the group. From the main administration window, select the group, click Edit, and uncheck all the boxes next to the users in the list. Then you can return to the main Edit and Create Groups window, select the group, and click the Delete button.

Adding and Deleting Users and Groups at the Command Line

Creating new users at the command-line shell is easily done using the useradd command. This command can be run only by root. When switching to the root user, use the following command in order to adopt the root user's $PATH details and thereby access root-only commands:

```
su -
```

The command to add a user is normally used in the following way:

```
useradd -m <username>
```

The -m command option tells the command to create a home directory for the user (this is created from a template, so it comes ready-made with SUSE-specific folders, configuration files, and so on). Used on its own, useradd merely updates system files with the new user's details and nothing else. There are several other useful command options, which can be discovered by a quick browse of the command's man page.

Creating a new user this way will automatically add the user to the users group—the default group that most ordinary users are added to under SUSE Linux. In addition, the command uses a range of skeleton settings that are applied to the account. In this way, the user will be added to the standard system groups necessary to access various pieces of hardware, and vital hidden system files for various pieces of software will be installed in his home directory, ready for use.

■**Caution** Creating a new user won't automatically apply a password to the account. Effectively, the new account will be locked until a password is applied, so the first thing you should do is to use the `passwd` command to assign a password to the new account, as I describe in the next section.

Perhaps unsurprisingly, deleting a user can be achieved with the userdel command. Used on its own, this sweeps the SUSE Linux system files, removing any mention of the user. However, the command is normally used with the -rf command options. These cause the user's home directory to be removed, too, along with any files it might contain. The -f option means that the command won't stop with an error if it comes across any files in the home directory that are not owned by the user. Because of this, userdel is a powerful command and should be used with care!

Groups can be added using the groupadd command in much the same way as using the useradd command. The -p option can be added to set a password for the new group (see the earlier instructions describing how to add a new group using YaST to learn why this is important). The groupdel command removes the group.

Changing Passwords

On a default SUSE Linux installation, ordinary users are able to change their passwords at the shell. In fact, under SUSE Linux 10.1, as supplied with this book, using shell commands is the only way users can change their password, because there's no GUI tool that will do this job.

The command to change the user's password is simple:

```
passwd
```

The user will be asked to confirm his current password, and then to enter the new password twice, to confirm that it has been typed correctly.

There are some rules imposed on the creation of new passwords. First, passwords under eight characters won't be accepted. Second, the user can't simply reuse the old password.

■**Note** The `passwd` command also won't allow any passwords that are *palindromes*—words that read backward exactly the same as they read forward. Examples include *racecar* and *madam*. This is probably because palindromic passwords are easier to crack by brute force than more secure passwords.

If the user breaks any of these rules, she will be told at the command prompt and allowed to try again, as shown in Figure 30-2. Up to three attempts can be made before the program will quit.

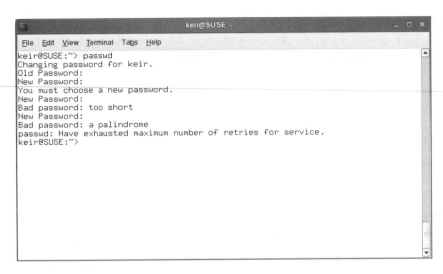

Figure 30-2. *Ordinary users can change their own passwords, but there are rules on size and style.*

The root user can use the passwd command to change anyone's password, as well as modify various other aspects relating to the user's login. All that's needed is to specify the user whose password is to be changed:

passwd frank

In this case, you won't be asked to enter the old password, because the user himself might have changed it. Instead, you'll simply be asked to enter the new password.

Just as when a regular user changes a password, the root user will see warnings if a password is too short or violates any of the other rules. However, the root user can override these warnings by simply retyping the password and thereby forcing it through.

A number of command options can be specified along with the passwd command when it is run as root user. For example, the -l option will lock the account so that it can't be accessed (the -u option will unlock it). The -e option will force the specified user to change his password the next time he logs in. He will be prompted to enter his old password and then told to choose a new one.

Sharing Root Powers via sudo

You may be wondering if it's always necessary to switch to root user in order to perform system maintenance. Although it's easy to type su to temporarily switch to root, it's also sometimes easy to forget that you're running as root user. Because of this, it can become very easy to make devastating mistakes. For this reason, the sudo command was invented.

■**Tip** Don't forget that the hash symbol (#) appears at the command prompt if you're running as root, whereas the right-facing angle bracket (>) appears if you're running as an ordinary user. These let you see at a glance what privileges you have.

Inserted before a command, `sudo` gives the user one-time root powers for that command only. When the command has finished running, the user returns to being an ordinary user. Technically speaking, the `sudo` command lets one user run a command as any other user. However, in most cases, it is used to temporarily gain root powers. (For more information, see the `sudo` man page.)

By default, under SUSE Linux, the `sudo` command works by asking for the root password. For example, typing the following will cause a password prompt to appear:

```
sudo vi /etc/fstab
```

Once the root password has been entered, `vi` will run as if it were started by root. This means any files it saves will be owned by the root user.

On some other Linux systems, `sudo` is used in a different way, which trades system security for convenience. In such a case, `sudo` can be used to adopt root powers without the user needing to know the root password. Instead, the user's password is entered. This might seem like casting security concerns to the wind, and it's certainly something that should be adopted only on a system you know is secure, such as one that only you access or for which you know and trust the other users.

If you want to allow an ordinary user to use the `sudo` command without entering the root password, you must edit the `/etc/sudoers` file (as the root user). A special command has been created for this purpose: `visudo`. This loads the `sudoers` file into `vi` and checks that anything added to the file is correct. After the `sudoers` file is open, move the cursor down to the section headed `# User alias specification`, and enter something similar to the following (substituting the name of the user for ⟨*username*⟩):

```
<username> ALL=(ALL) ALL
```

Then move down to the lines underneath that read `Defaults targetpw` and `ALL ALL=(ALL) ALL`, and put a hash symbol before them. Your file should look similar to Figure 30-3. Then save the file and exit `vi`.

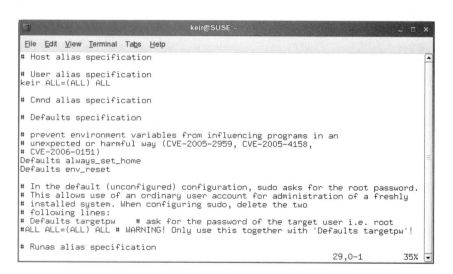

Figure 30-3. *The sudo command can give ordinary users root powers, but it must first be set up correctly.*

Following this, simply precede any command with sudo to run it with root powers. You'll then be prompted to enter your own login password. The instructions that appear on the screen should make it clear what is happening, and give a brief warning that you should use sudo responsibly.

Summary

In this chapter, we looked at the principles behind user and group accounts under SUSE Linux. We've examined how user and group accounts can be created, edited, and deleted using both the GUI and command line. We also looked at how passwords can be manipulated both by the root user and by the individual users themselves.

Finally, you learned how the sudo command can be used to run root-only programs, allowing users to avoid needing to switch to root user frequently.

In the next chapter, we'll look at how the system can be optimized. You'll also learn about several interesting and important system tools.

CHAPTER 31

■■■■

Optimizing Your System

One slight problem with SUSE Linux (and all Linux distributions) is that they take a "one-size-fits-all" approach—the default installation attempts to provide services for every kind of user. While this offers the widest range of compatibility, it doesn't always ensure an optimized system.

You may never attach a printer to SUSE Linux, for example, so what's the point of keeping the printing subsystem in memory? You can remove it from your Linux setup and not only free memory, but also speed up boot times, because you no longer need to wait for the printer service to start. While this might save only a couple of seconds, or just a couple of hundred kilobytes of memory, repeating the process and paring SUSE Linux down to the bone can produce an ultra-efficient system.

In this chapter, you'll learn how to target the various subsystems of your Linux system in order to optimize and speed up your computer. We'll look at everything from bootup, to hard disks, to streamlining the kernel itself.

Speeding Up Booting

Let's take a look at what happens when a SUSE Linux-equipped PC boots. Then we'll explore some ways to speed up the process.

Understanding Bootup

When you start your computer, and after the computer's power-on self-tests (POST), the computer's BIOS searches for a boot program on the hard disk. If SUSE Linux is installed on the computer, the boot program then runs the GRUB boot loader program. The job of the GRUB boot loader is twofold. First, it displays a menu from which you can choose which operating system to load. If you've installed SUSE Linux alongside Windows, you'll be able to choose between the two operating systems at this stage. Second, GRUB loads the Linux kernel, if a Linux operating system is chosen from the boot menu.

Once loaded, the kernel then starts the very first program that's run on any SUSE Linux system: init. The principal job of init is to run a variety of run-level scripts, which load the hardware and software necessary for the full and correct functioning of the system. All of these are located in /etc/init.d or its subdirectories.

■**Note** In this context, *scripts* can be defined as long chains of commands stored in a single file.

The first of these scripts is /etc/init.d/boot. This starts and configures the essential system hardware that will be used across all run levels. It also runs some additional startup scripts contained in the /etc/init.d/boot.d directory.

Following this, /etc/init.d/boot.local is run. This can contain additional hardware-oriented scripts placed there by the user, which are designed to be activated before the run level is entered. If you are running a nonstandard piece of hardware, you might need to use boot.local, but this is rare. On my test system, the boot.local file was empty, aside from a few comments at the top stating how the file is used.

■**Note** Comments within scripts are usually preceded by a hash (#) or sometimes a semicolon (;), which tells the computer not to interpret what follows on that line as an actual command. Comments are inserted to help you, as a user, understand what the script is supposed to do.

Following this, the run-level scripts are activated. These are located within the /etc/init.d directory but are referenced from symbolic links within the /etc/init.d/rcX.d directory, where X refers to the run level in use. Figure 31-1 shows the scripts at run level 5.

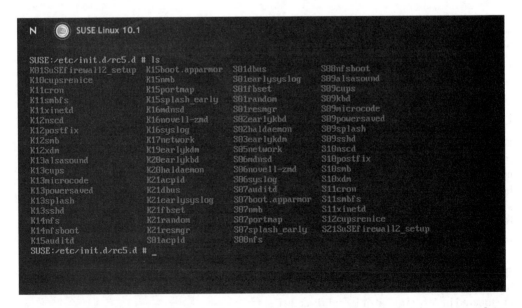

Figure 31-1. *The scripts for each run level are contained in the /etc/init.d/rcX.d directories, where X is the run-level number.*

Run-level scripts do two things: They start and configure any hardware that's specific to that particular run level. and they start any necessary system software (known as *services*) that is particular to that run level.

■**Note** Because the run level defines what software and hardware are in use on the computer, the run level could accurately be referred to as the *operating mode* of the computer.

For example, if run level 5 is activated, the X Display Manager (xdm) script will be run to start the GUI. xdm is missing from run level 3's scripts, because run levels 1 and 3 are usually configured to boot to a command-line prompt.

■**Note** In other parts of this book, I've referred to the GNOME and KDE Display Manager programs (gdm and kdm, respectively), rather than xdm. As far as run levels are concerned, xdm is the script responsible for starting gdm and kdm, depending on which desktop environment is installed (technically speaking, xdm merely starts whichever display manager is listed within /etc/sysconfig/displaymanager).

In terms of operating system components, it's during the run-level script stage that things like the printing services are started and network file sharing subsystems are made to run in the background. If the system is configured as a web server, software like Apache will be run at this stage, too.

On SUSE Linux, run levels 2 through 5 are defined as *multiuser*. Technically speaking, this means that they allow more than one user to log on, but for most desktop users, they're better defined as the day-to-day running modes of the computer. Run level 5 is the default run level under SUSE Linux. See Table 31-1 for a list of run levels and what they normally do.

■**Note** There's no reason why run levels 7, 8, and 9 can't be used under SUSE Linux. However, only run levels 0 through 6 are normally configured.

Table 31-1. *SUSE Linux Run Levels*

Run Level	Description
0	Halt; the computer will be shut down.
1	Single-user mode (root login); very few hardware and software services are activated. Normally used for troubleshooting.
2	Non-GUI; network interface deactivated. Multiple user logins allowed, unlike with run level 1.
3	Non-GUI; standard set of hardware and system services started, including network services.

Continues

Table 31-1. *Continued*

Run Level	Description
4	Unused.
5	GUI; default run level for SUSE Linux. Standard set of hardware and system services started.
6	Reboot; the computer will be shut down and then restarted.
S	Single-user mode; used when booting directly into single-user mode, rather than switching to single-user mode (run level 1).

The job of the run-level scripts is to define the user experience. When they've finished, the computer will be configured and ready for use in some fashion. However, that's not quite the end of things.

Although you'll be able to log on, the KDE or GNOME desktops have yet to start, and these, too, have their own set of initialization processes. They need to start their own set of programs, such as system tray/notification area applets, which provide handy functions like on-screen volume control. Once all that has finished, you can use the computer!

Because so much must take place for your system to come to life, booting SUSE Linux can take some time. On my test system, it averaged between one and two minutes. Certainly, you can shave some time from this.

Note Run levels don't just contain startup scripts. They also contain "kill" scripts, designed to shut down services should you change into a particular run level from another. For example, run level 3 contains a kill script designed to terminate xdm, so that the GUI is no longer active. However, there's no need to worry about kill scripts when considering how to optimize the SUSE Linux boot process.

Reducing the Boot Menu Delay

Getting rid of the GRUB boot menu delay can save some waiting around in the early stages of the boot process. The delay can be reduced to a few seconds, or even eradicated completely. Of course, in such a case, you won't be able to choose which operating system you want to load if you're dual-booting with Windows. Even if SUSE Linux is the only operating system on your computer, without the boot delay, you won't have the chance to boot into recovery mode, as offered on the GRUB menu. So you need to consider whether this is a worthwhile time-saving measure.

YaST offers a way of controlling the GRUB menu delay. Here's the procedure:

1. To start YaST, click Desktop ➤ YaST under GNOME; under KDE, click K menu ➤ System ➤ YaST. Enter your root password when prompted.

2. Click the System icon on the left, and then click the Boot Loader icon on the right.

3. In the Boot Loader Configuration window, click the Boot Loader Installation tab, and then click the Boot Loader Options button.

4. In the Boot Loader Options window, select a setting, in seconds, in the Boot Menu Time-Out box, as shown in Figure 31-2. To prevent the boot menu from appearing, either enter a value of 0 for the time-out or remove the check from the box marked Show Boot Menu.

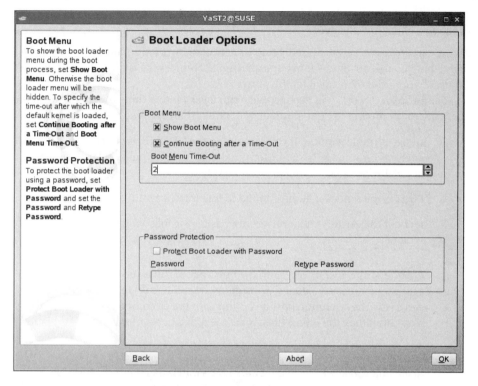

Figure 31-2. *You can stop the GRUB menu hanging around for so long by changing the time-out value in its configuration file.*

5. Click the OK button, and then click Finish to write the changes to disk.

Optimizing Run-Level Services

Perhaps it goes without saying that the majority of bootup time is spent starting the boot and run-level scripts. This is when the entire system comes to life—hardware and essential software services are activated. But this isn't to say that all run-level scripts are essential.

■**Note** A *service* is a piece of background software that provides something that you, the user, need on a day-to-day basis. Some services manage hardware, such as the graphical interface, printing services, and networking. Some services provide software services, such as logging files or checking the system clock against a time server.

The one-size-fits-all approach of SUSE Linux means that some services that are started up aren't always necessary. Approximately 60 run-level scripts start on a typical boot. By selective pruning, you can easily remove around a quarter of these, but caution is advised. You're altering a fundamental aspect of your system configuration, and one simple mistake can make the difference between a system that works and one that is no longer able to boot.

Creating a Custom Run Level

Because of the risk of seriously damaging your system by pruning run-level scripts, I recommend that you use run level 4 for your experiments. Run level 4 is officially designated as "unused" and is therefore ideal for the purpose.

For this plan to work, you need to make run level 4 into a clone of run level 5, and then configure the computer to boot to run level 4, rather than 5. Here's how to proceed:

1. Open a terminal window. If you're running the GNOME desktop, click Applications ➤ System ➤ Terminal ➤ GNOME Terminal. KDE users should click K menu ➤ System ➤ Terminal ➤ Konsole.

2. Switch to the root user at the command line by typing su -.

3. Clear out the existing run level 4 scripts using the following command:

   ```
   rm /etc/init.d/rc4.d/*
   ```

4. Copy the scripts for run level 5 to the directory of run level 4, thereby creating a clone. Because the run level 5 directory contains symbolic links to files in /etc/init.d, you need to use the -P command-line option with the cp command. That way, it copies the links, rather than the linked files. Issue the following command:

   ```
   cp -P /etc/init.d/rc5.d/* /etc/init.d/rc4.d/
   ```

5. The default run level that SUSE Linux boots into is listed in /etc/inittab. You need to edit this file to switch the default to run level 4 and also to enable run level 4 as a usable run level within the file, because ordinarily it is disabled.

   - Under the GNOME desktop, type the following to load /etc/inittab into the Gedit text editor:

     ```
     gedit /etc/inittab
     ```

   - Under KDE, type the following to load the file into the Kate text editor:

     ```
     kate /etc/inittab
     ```

6. In the text editor, look for the line that reads id:5:initdefault:. Change the 5 to a 4, so that the line now reads as follows:

   ```
   id:4:initdefault:
   ```

7. Scroll down the file to the line that reads as follows:

   ```
   #l4:4:wait:/etc/init.d/rc 4
   ```

8. Remove the hash at the beginning of the line, so that it reads like this:

```
l4:4:wait:/etc/init.d/rc 4
```

9. Save the file and quit the text editor.

10. Reboot your computer.

Tip While rebooting, pressing the Esc key will clear the boot graphic and show the status messages of the various run-level scripts. You can verify that you're entering the newly defined run level 4 by watching for a message along the lines of "Entering run level 4." This will appear around halfway through the boot procedure. When up and running, typing `runlevel` as the root user will display the current run level (two numbers will be quoted—the second indicates the current run level).

Pruning Run-Level Services

YaST includes a tool that allows you to control which run-level services start during bootup. To access it, start YaST (click Desktop ➤ YaST under GNOME, or K menu ➤ System ➤ YaST under KDE), click the System icon on the left, and then click the System Services (Runlevel) icon on the right. When the System Services (Runlevel) window appears, click the Expert Mode button. You should see a window similar to that shown in Figure 31-3.

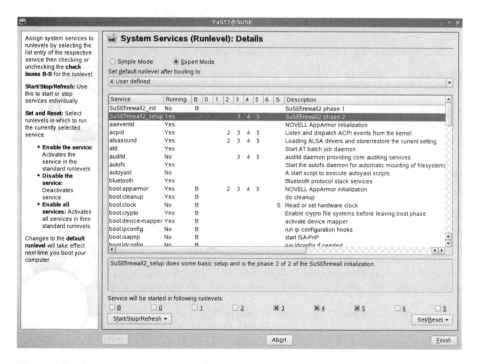

Figure 31-3. *The System Services (Runlevel): Details window shows each available service, whether the service is running, the run levels the service is normally active within, and a description.*

The Expert Mode listing might look confusing at first glance, but it is quite easy to understand. The columns contain the following information:

Services: On the left are listed the various services on the system. This list includes all available services, even if they're not active under any run level and are not used during boot (effectively, these are the services contained in the /etc/init.d/ directory).

Running: This column lists whether the service is running at the present time. This will be indicated by Yes or No in the list. It's important to note that not all services keep running after they're started. Some start during boot and terminate almost immediately, or after a short while. Therefore Yes or No in this column isn't a good indicator of whether the service is set to run in the current run level.

■Note You may wonder why some services are listed as currently running when they're not enabled in any run level. This is probably because they were started as a subprocess by another service that *is* activated within the current run level. Don't worry too much about these services.

B, 0, 1, 2, 3, 4, 5, 6, and S: These columns indicate within which run levels the services are activated. (See Table 31-1, shown earlier in the chapter, for a description of the purpose of each run level.) The B entry refers to services started by the boot script, which precedes the run-level scripts, as mentioned previously. You are interested solely in services that start in run level 4, which is the run level you have created especially to be pruned of unnecessary services.

Description: This column shows brief descriptions of what various run-level services do.

Beneath the list is a text box in which a longer description may appear when a run level is selected.

Take a look through the list and see what the various services do. This should give you an idea of which you might consider removing. In Table 31-2, I've listed some run-level services that I consider it safe to disable. Some of these may not be present on GNOME systems because they are KDE-specific. By removing these services, I managed to trim 10 seconds from the total boot time of my test PC.

You should follow some common-sense rules when removing entries:

- Don't remove a service whose purpose you don't understand. If in doubt, leave it be! Bear in mind that several services might look innocuous but may be essential because they support other, more essential system components.

- Disable services only for run level 4. Don't disable the service for any other run level, especially run level 5, which you will want to use later if your changes prove problematic.

- Avoid disabling any B run-level services. These configure and start various hardware items.

Table 31-2. *Services That You May Want to Disable*

Service	Description	Notes
cups	cups printing service component	Can be disabled if you do not have a printer attached to your computer and do not intend to print from the computer in the future.
cupsrenice	See cups	See cups.
fbset	Component of the graphic boot-time display	Can be disabled.[1]
nfs	Configures Network File Sharing (NFS)	Can be disabled if you don't access NFS shares (only corporate/advanced users are likely to do so).
nfsboot	See nfs	See nfs.
nfsserver	See nfs	See nfs.
nmb	Part of the SMB file sharing system	Can be disabled if you don't intend to share files or access shared files on other computers (including Windows computers).
postfix	Mail Transfer Agent (MTA)	Can be disabled if you use an external SMTP server, as most people do.
smb	See nmb	See nmb.
smbfs	See nmb	See nmb.
splash	Component of the graphic boot-time display	Can be disabled.[1]
splash_early	See splash	See splash.
sshd	SSH service	Can be disabled if you don't intend to remotely connect to your computer (see Chapter 34).

[1] *To fully disable the boot-time graphic, start YaST, click the System icon on the left, and then click the Boot Loader icon on the right. In the window that appears, select the SUSE Linux entry in the list and click the Edit button. Change the Other Kernel Parameters box entry from* splash=silent *to* splash=0. *Click OK, and then click Finish.*

Deactivating a service is easy. At the bottom of the YaST window you will see several check boxes corresponding to the various run levels. Simply remove the check in the box marked 4 to stop the service from starting in your custom run level.

When you've finished, click the Finish button. This will write the changes to disk. You should then reboot to test your new settings.

Restoring Run Level 5

If you are too aggressive when pruning run-level services, you may find that you've left your system in an unusable state. If this happens, you can simply switch the default run level back to 5, and then attempt to make repairs to your custom run level.

The following instructions assume a worst-case scenario, which is to say that you're unable to boot to a GUI, but they work under other circumstances as well.

1. Reboot the computer. At the GRUB boot menu, select Failsafe – SUSE Linux 10.1.

2. At the login prompt, log in as the root user.

3. Type the following to open the /etc/inittab file in the `pico` text editor:

   pico /etc/inittab

4. Scroll down to the line that reads `id:4:initdefault:`. Change the 4 to a 5, so the line now reads `id:5:initdefault:`.

5. Save the file by pressing Ctrl+O (the letter *O*). Press Enter to confirm the filename.

6. Press Ctrl+X to exit the `pico` text editor.

7. Type reboot at the command line to restart your computer.

STOP SEARCHING FOR AN ADDRESS

If you use an Ethernet or Wi-Fi connection to access the network, you'll find that SUSE Linux spends a few seconds each boot acquiring an Internet address. Therefore, one way to provide an instant speed boost is to give your computer a static IP address. (See Chapter 8 for details on how to configure your network interface.)

To assign a static address, you'll need to find out what IP address range your router uses. You can discover this address by looking at the router's configuration software (sometimes this is accessed via a web browser). Look for the configuration section with a heading like DHCP Configuration.

Normally, the addresses are in the 192.168.*x.x* range, where *x.x* can be any series of numbers from 1.1 to 255.255. For instance, the router within my test setup uses the 192.168.1.2-255 range.

In my case, choosing a static IP address that will work with the router is simply a matter of selecting an IP address in this range. However, I know that the router hands out addresses sequentially from 2 upward, so it's best if I choose an address it's unlikely to reach, even if I happen to have many computers connected to the network. Starting at 50 is a good idea, so I assign my test PC the address 192.168.1.50.

Don't forget that, when defining static IP addresses, you'll need to manually supply the gateway, subnet, and DNS addresses. In most cases, the subnet address will be 255.255.255.0. The DNS address will be the same as the gateway address.

Optimizing Hard Disk Settings

The hard disk is one of the key elements in the modern PC. Because most of your PC's data must travel to and from it, speeding up your hard disk means that your entire PC will be faster.

SUSE Linux provides a powerful command-line tool that you can use to control every aspect of your hard disk: hdparm. This is a power-user's tool. Not only must it be run as the root user, but you also must be careful not to mistype the commands. All changes are made instantly, so if you make a mistake, your system may crash, or at least suffer from serious problems. There's even the risk of data loss, although this is minimized by making sure that you have no other programs running at the same time you run hdparm.

Tip When switching to the root user to carry out the steps in this chapter, be sure to use the su - command, rather than simply su. Adding the dash will switch you to root user and also inherit root's path, so that you can use system configuration commands like hdparm that are normally contained in /sbin.

The good news is that changes made via hdparm will last for only the current session, so there's no risk of permanent damage. Any changes that are beneficial can be made permanent later.

In the context of optimization, hdparm lets you both benchmark the disk and change various technical settings, such as the sector multcount value. These adjustments can bring speed boosts.

Benchmarking Your Hard Disk

Because experimenting with hdparm can cause crashes, and because its benchmarking feature needs almost exclusive access to the hard disk, hdparm is best run with as few as possible additional programs up and running. Therefore, switching to run level 3 is a good idea. To do this, close all open programs, then open a terminal window (in GNOME, click Applications ➤ System ➤ Terminal ➤ GNOME Terminal; in KDE, click K menu ➤ System ➤ Terminal ➤ Konsole).

At the prompt, type the following to switch to run level 3:

```
su -
[Enter root password]
init 3
```

Note Technically speaking, switching to run level 1 is an even better idea, because this will deactivate all unnecessary services. Run level 1 is akin to the Windows Safe Mode, except without the GUI. However, you want realistic benchmark results to test the changes you make via hdparm, and it's debatable whether the restricted confines of run level 1 will provide such results.

Let's start by benchmarking your hard disk to see its performance based on the current settings. Type the following (assuming SUSE Linux is installed on the first hard disk in your system; if it's on the second hard disk, change /dev/hda to /dev/hdb):

```
hdparm -tT /dev/hda
```

This will benchmark your disk in two ways. The first tests the PC's memory throughput, measuring the data rate of the memory, CPU, and cache. The second actually tests the disk's data rate. The second test affects the outcome of the first, which is why the two are used together. Between them, these two methods of benchmarking present the standard way your disk is used on a day-to-day basis. Figure 31-4 shows the results on my system.

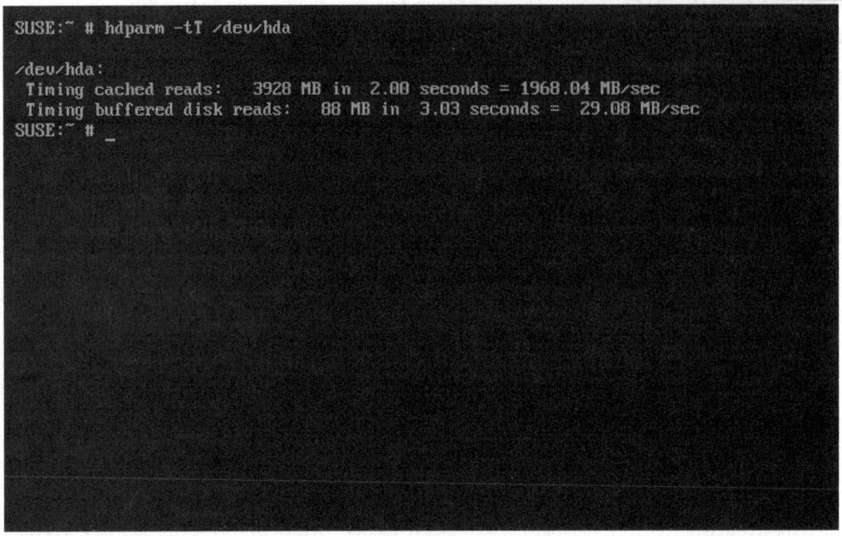

Figure 31-4. *The hdparm program can be used to both benchmark and optimize your hard disk.*

Make a note of the figures so that you can compare them to the results of these tests after you change hard disk settings.

Changing Hard Disk Settings

You can use hdparm to view your current hard disk settings by entering the following at the command prompt:

hdparm /dev/hda

On my test PC, these are the results I got:

```
/dev/hda:
 multcount    = 16 (on)
 IO_support   =  1 (32-bit)
 unmaskirq    =  1 (on)
 using_dma    =  1 (on)
 keepsettings =  0 (off)
 readonly     =  0 (off)
 readahead    = 1024 (on)
 geometry     = 65535/16/63, sectors = 78125000, start = 0
```

Let's take a look at what these settings mean.

The multcount Setting

The first setting, multcount, refers to how many sectors can be read from the hard disk at any one time. On many drives, a higher setting here is best, but on other drives, a lower setting is best. You can find out what your drive's maximum multcount setting is by issuing the following command:

```
hdparm -i /dev/hda
```

Look for MaxMultSect in the results. On my test PC, this read MaxMultSect=16.

You can experiment with the multcount setting on your hard disk by using the -m hdparm command option:

```
hdparm -m8 /dev/hda
```

Here, I've chosen a lower value than my drive's original setting (16).

You can then follow this by another benchmark to see if there is an improvement:

```
hdparm -tT /dev/hda
```

The IO_Support Setting

The IO_support setting refers to the input/output (I/O) mode used by the hard disk controller. This has three possible settings: 0 to disable 32-bit support, 1 to enable 32-bit support, and 3 to enable 32-bit support with a special sync signal.

You can change the IO_support setting with the -c hdparm command option, and the 32-bit support with sync option (3) is generally considered the best choice:

```
hdparm -c3 /dev/hda
```

The unmaskirq Setting

The third setting, unmaskirq, allows SUSE Linux to attend to other tasks while waiting for your hard disk to return data. This won't affect hard disk performance very much, and generally it's a good idea for the health of your system to activate it if isn't already switched on. This command activates unmaskirq:

```
hdparm -u1 /dev/hda
```

The using_dma Setting

The fourth setting refers to whether Direct Memory Access (DMA) is in use. Hard disks are sold on the basis of their DMA modes, such as UltraDMA Burst 2 and the like. DMA is considered an indicator of the speed of a hard disk, but the truth is that, like any specification, it is only a guide.

DMA is activated by default under SUSE Linux, but you can alter the DMA mode using the -X command option. However, on most modern PCs, this isn't necessary because the computer's BIOS defaults to the fastest DMA mode.

Other Settings

The last three settings, above the summary of the geometry and sector information of the disk, are those you shouldn't change:

- keepsettings refers to the ability of the drive to remember hdparm settings over a reboot (although not if the drive loses power).

- readonly sets whether or not the hard disk is read-only (so that no data can be written to it). Changing this setting is not advisable!

- readahead controls how many hard disk blocks are loaded in advance. It doesn't affect the performance of modern IDE-based hard disks, because the drive electronics contain buffers that perform this task themselves.

Making Disk Optimizations Permanent

When the PC is switched off, any changes you've made with hdparm are lost. To make the command run during bootup, you can create a custom service and add it to the current run level. This sounds more complicated than it actually is. Here are the steps:

1. Switch to the root user, using the su - command.

2. Enter the hdparm settings into a text file, using vi, for example. Simply type the command (for example, hdparm -d1 -m8 /dev/hda) in the editor window, and then save the file with a name along the lines of disk_optimize. (Make sure you add a carriage return after the line when entering it in vi.)

3. Make the text file an executable file, with the following command, which effectively turns the file into a run-level script:

   chmod +x disk_optimize

4. Save the file with all the other run-level scripts in the /etc/init.d/ folder:

   cp disk_optimize /etc/init.d/

5. Symbolically link the script to the current run level, using the following command, which assumes the default run level is 5:

   ln -s /etc/init.d/disk_optimize /etc/init.d/rc5.d/S99disk_optimize

The last step also changes the filename of the symbolically linked file to tell SUSE Linux when it should be run during bootup. A value of S99 means it will be run at the very end of the boot procedure. Any hard disk performance tweaking must take place as near as possible to the end of booting, because the changes it makes can negatively affect the startup of other services.

Prelinking

As discussed in Chapter 29, a lot of SUSE Linux software relies on other pieces of code to work. These are sometimes referred to as *libraries*, a term that is a good indicator of their purpose: to provide functions that programs can check in and out whenever they need them, as if they were borrowing books from a library.

Whenever a program starts, it must look for these other libraries and load them into memory so they're ready for use. This can take some time, particularly on larger and more-complicated programs. Because of this, the concept of *prelinking* was invented. By a series of complicated tricks, the prelink program makes each bit of software you might run aware of the libraries it needs, so that memory can be better allocated.

Prelinking claims to boost program startup times by up to 50% or more, but the problem is that it's a hack—a programming trick designed to make your system work in a nonstandard way. Because of this, some programs are incompatible with prelinking. In fact, some might simply refuse to work unless prelinking is deactivated. At the time of writing, such programs are in the minority. However, keep in mind that prelinking can be easily reversed if necessary. Alternatively, you might want to weigh whether it's actually worth setting up prelinking in the first place.

■Note Many of the GNOME programs under SUSE Linux aren't compiled in a way that's compatible with prelinking. Therefore, you might not see much of a speed boost using prelinking with the GNOME desktop.

Using Prelinking

If you decide to go ahead with prelinking, you'll need to download and install the relevant software because it isn't supplied on the installation DVD.

Installing the Prelink Software

You can download the `prelink` package from the "factory installation source," an online repository of all official SUSE Linux packages. Here's the procedure:

1. Using your web browser, head over to `http://download.opensuse.org/` and click the link for the Internet Installation Repository. This should then bring up what appears to be a file system view of files and folders.

2. Click the `suse` folder, which should be near the bottom of the list. Then click the `i586` link.

3. Give the file list a minute or two to load, and then search for a file that begins with `prelink`. During my testing, the file `prelink-0.3.6-7.i586.rpm` was the one I needed. While you're there, also download the file whose name begins with `libelf`, which is a dependency of `prelink`. During my testing, this file was `libelf-0.8.5-45.i586.rpm`.

4. Right-click each of the files and select Save Link As. Then save the files to the desktop.

5. Open a terminal window (in GNOME, click Applications ➤ System ➤ Terminal ➤ GNOME Terminal; in KDE, click K menu ➤ System ➤ Terminal ➤ Konsole) and switch to the root user (type su -).

6. Switch to the directory where you downloaded the files, and then type the following (assuming the directory does not contain any other installation RPM files):

```
rpm -Uvh *.rpm
```

Configuring and Running Prelink

Prelink will run automatically in the background periodically, but first you must activate it as a service. Then it's a good idea to run prelink manually for the first time. Follow these steps:

1. Open a terminal window and switch to the root user (type su -).

2. Navigate to the /etc/sysconfig/ directory and open the prelink file in a text editor.

3. Change the line that reads:

```
USE_PRELINK="no"
```

to

```
USE_PRELINK="yes"
```

4. Run the SuSEconfig program by typing SuSEconfig in the terminal window. This ensures that system configuration files are up-to-date, including those related to prelinking that have been added.

5. To run a prelink scan of your system whenever you want, issue this command (as the root user; type su -):

```
prelink -a
```

The prelink -a command will prelink practically all the binary files on your system and may take some time to complete. You may also see some error output, but you don't need to pay attention to it.

Deactivating Prelinking

Should you find prelinking makes a particular application malfunction or simply stop working, you can try undoing prelinking. To do this, find out where the main binary for the program resides, and then issue the prelink command with the --undo command option. For example, to remove prelinking from the Gedit text editor program, you could type the following (as the root user; type su -):

```
whereis gedit
prelink --undo /usr/bin/gedit
```

However, this may not work because some programs might rely on additional binaries on the system. Therefore, the solution might be to undo prelinking for the entire system, which you can do by typing the following (as the root user):

```
prelink -ua
```

After this, you should remove the `prelink` package to prevent it from running again in future. To do this, type the following as the root user:

```
rpm –e prelink
```

OPTIMIZING THE KERNEL

Using the Linux kernel source code, you can compile and install your own version of the program at the heart of Linux. This gives you total control over the kernel configuration, so you can leave out parts you don't want in order to free memory. You can also set certain optimization settings, such as creating a version of the kernel specifically built for your model of CPU.

Although compiling a kernel is a simple procedure, there are many complex questions that you'll need to answer, and an in-depth knowledge of the way Linux works is necessary.

In addition, compiling your own kernel brings up several issues. The first is that it may not work with any binary modules that you have installed, such as graphics cards or wireless drivers (including `ndiswrapper`, as discussed in Chapter 8). You can opt to install these yourself from scratch, but this adds to the complexity.

The second problem is that SUSE Linux is built around precompiled kernels. Several software packages expect to work with the precompiled kernel and, in addition, SUSE Linux may occasionally download an updated prepackaged kernel automatically as part of the system update feature and override the one you've created.

If there are any security problems with the kernel version you compiled, you'll need to recompile a new kernel from scratch (or patch the one you have). This means you'll need to keep an eye on the security news sites and take action when necessary.

That said, compiling a kernel is an excellent way of learning how Linux works, and the sense of achievement if it all goes well is enormous.

Some people choose to download the kernel source code from the official Linux kernel site, `www.kernel.org`. However, it makes more sense to download the official SUSE Linux release, because this will be tailored for the way your system works. Using the Software Management tool of YaST (see Chapter 29 for details), simply search for and install `kernel-source`.

You can find several guides to compiling your own kernel online. I recommend `www.digitalhermit.com/linux/Kernel-Build-HOWTO.html`.

Freeing Disk Space

After using SUSE Linux for some time, you might find that the disk begins to get full. You can keep an eye on disk usage by using the following command in a terminal window (in GNOME, click Applications ➤ System ➤ Terminal ➤ GNOME Terminal; in KDE, click K menu ➤ System ➤ Terminal ➤ Konsole):

```
df -h
```

This will show the free space in terms of megabytes or gigabytes, and also expressed as a percentage.

If the disk does start to get full, you can take some steps to make more space available.

Emptying the /tmp Folder

An easy way to regain disk space is to empty the /tmp folder. As with the Windows operating system, this is the folder in which temporary data is stored. Some applications clean up after themselves, but others don't, leaving behind many megabytes of detritus.

Because the /tmp folder is accessed practically every second the system is up and running, to empty it safely, it's necessary to switch to run level 1. This ensures few other programs are running and avoids the risk of deleting data that is in use. The following series of commands will switch to run level 1, empty the /tmp folder, and then reboot afterwards (this will stop the GUI, so make sure you close all running programs beforehand):

```
su -
[Enter root password]
init 1
[Enter root password again]
rm -rf /tmp/*
rm -rf /tmp/.*
reboot
```

■Tip On a similar theme, don't forget to empty the desktop Trash. This can hold many megabytes of old data. If you find permission errors are reported when emptying this folder, open a command-line prompt and type the following: sudo rm -rf .Trash/*. You'll need to type your root password.

Removing Unused Software

If you still need disk space, consider removing unused programs. As you learned in Chapter 29, you can manage software through YaST's Software Management tool (start YaST, click the Software icon, and then click the Software Management icon).

The best way of managing software is to switch to the Selection or Package Group view, by selecting the corresponding filter from the Filter drop-down list. The Selection filter lets you see which groups of programs you have installed, rather than viewing individual titles (removing individual programs might not free up too much space). The Package Group filter categorizes titles by what they do, as shown in Figure 31-5. For example, you might choose to remove software under the Games heading. Alternatively, if you don't use any office programs on your system, you might choose to deselect titles under the Productivity group heading.

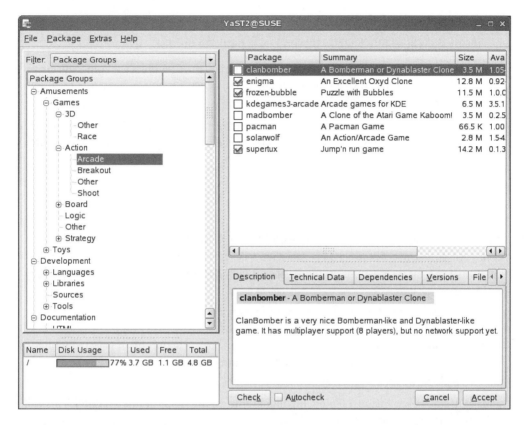

Figure 31-5. *Using the Package Group filter helps identify classes of programs that you might want to remove to free space, such as games.*

■**Caution** As always, removing software can create dependency problems, so you might find yourself limited in what software you can actually remove.

Adding Another Disk Drive

Another solution to the problem of running out of disk space is to add another hard disk drive, perhaps as a slave on the primary IDE channel. Using a new disk within SUSE Linux is very easy and can be done from the command-line shell.

Partitioning the Disk

Once the disk has been fitted, follow these steps to partition the disk:

1. Boot into SUSE Linux and open a terminal window (in GNOME, click Applications ➤ System ➤ Terminal ➤ GNOME Terminal; in KDE, click K menu ➤ System ➤ Terminal ➤ Konsole).

2. Use the cfdisk command to initially partition the disk. Assuming that you've added the new disk as a slave on the primary channel, issue the following command as the root user (type su -):

   ```
   cfdisk /dev/hdb
   ```

▪**Tip** Working out how SUSE Linux refers to the hard disks installed on the system isn't hard. Usually, they're given letters from a through to d. So, /dev/hda is the primary master, /dev/hdb is the primary slave, /dev/hdc is the secondary master (usually the CD/DVD-ROM drive), and /dev/hdd is the secondary slave. If your system uses SCSI drives, you'll find they're named /dev/sda, /dev/sdb, and so on.

---

3. To create a new partition, within the cfdisk program, use the cursor keys to highlight New, and then press Enter. The default partition size should automatically be all of the disk space, so press Enter again to confirm this.

4. With the new partition created, highlight Write on the menu and press Enter. This will write the new partition information.

5. Highlight Quit and press Enter.

6. Reboot the system to ensure the new partition is made available.

7. To make your partition accessible, when SUSE Linux is back up and running, open a terminal window and issue the following command as root user (again assuming that the new hard disk is /dev/hdb):

   ```
   mkfs -t reiserfs /dev/hdb1
   ```

   Note that you need to specify the partition number in this instance. Because there's only one partition on the disk, this is number 1. If you create two or more partitions, each will be numbered consecutively (1, 2, 3, and so on).

You've created a reiserfs-formatted partition, because this is the preferred standard used within SUSE Linux. Other versions of Linux might use different file systems, such as ext3.

Configuring SUSE Linux to Use the Drive

Now the new drive is ready for use, but you need a way of making it available within the SUSE Linux file system. Therefore, you need to create a mount point and also configure the system so that the disk is mounted automatically at boot.

As discussed in Chapter 14, creating a mount point is simply a matter of creating an empty folder. Therefore, you can create a directory in the root of the hard disk (or anywhere else) and call it something like second_disk. This directory must then be made writable, as follows (all commands should be entered as the root user):

```
mkdir /second_disk
chmod a+w /second_disk
```

Then you must edit the /etc/fstab file in order to make the new disk mount automatically. All you need to do is add a line at the end of the file, such as this:

```
/dev/hdb1 /second_disk reiserfs default 0 2
```

Note that it's important that you add a carriage return (press Enter) after the line.

You can test your new hard disk by rebooting. When SUSE Linux returns, you should find that the new disk is available by accessing the /second_disk directory. You can check its capacity by typing df -h.

Summary

In this chapter, we looked at streamlining your installation of SUSE Linux. This involved speeding up the boot procedure by decreasing the boot menu delay and deactivating various unnecessary run-level scripts that get loaded at boot time. We also looked at optimizing your hard disk settings to allow for greater efficiency in loading and saving files.

Additionally, we investigated prelinking programs so that they load faster, recompiling the kernel so that it's optimized for your system, freeing disk space by various means, and adding a second hard disk.

In the next chapter, you'll learn how to perform backups to safeguard your data.

CHAPTER 32

■■■

Backing Up Data

Every computer user knows that backing up data is vital. This is usually because every computer user has lost data at some point, perhaps because of a corrupted file or accidental deletion.

Some of the people behind Unix were well aware of such occurrences, and developed several advanced and useful backup tools. These have been mirrored within Linux, with the result that creating and maintaining backups is easy. Additionally, distributions like SUSE Linux include their own easy-to-use graphical backup programs.

In this chapter, we'll first look at what data should be backed up, and then explore two ways to make backups: using the YaST utility and from the command line.

What Data Should You Back Up?

Data on your system can be classified into three broad types: program data, configuration data, and personal data. It's traditionally reasoned that backing up all types of data is inefficient and difficult in most circumstances, largely because it would mean backing up practically the entire hard disk. Because of this, you usually want to back up the latter two types of data: configuration and personal. The theory is that if your PC is hit by a hard-disk–wrecking disaster, you can easily reinstall the operating system from the CD/DVD. Restoring your system from backup is then simply a matter of ensuring the configuration files are back in place, so your applications work as you would like them to, and making sure that your personal data is once again made accessible.

Practically all the personal configuration data for programs you use every day, as well as your personal data, is stored in your /home folder (although the configuration files for software used system-wide are stored in the /etc folder). If you take a look in your /home directory, you might think that previous sentence is incorrect. On a freshly installed system, the directory appears largely empty. However, most, if not all, of the configuration files are hidden; their directory and filenames are preceded with a period (.), which means that Linux doesn't display them during a standard directory listing.

To view hidden files and folders in both the Nautilus and Konqueror file managers, select View ➤ Show Hidden Files. This can be quite an eye-opener when you see the masses of data you didn't even realize were there, as shown in the example in Figure 32-1. To view hidden files at the shell prompt, simply use the -a command option with the ls command:

```
ls -a
```

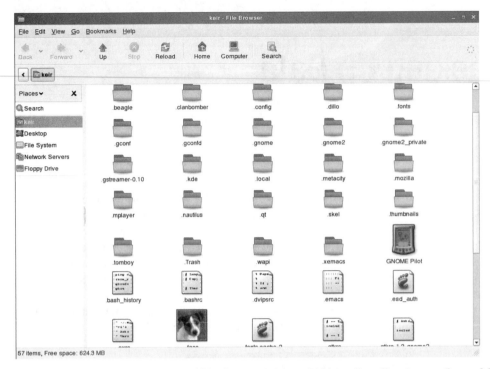

Figure 32-1. *Most of the configuration files for programs are hidden—literally—in your /home folder.*

The configuration files held in your /home folder relate solely to your user account. Any other users will have their own configuration files, entirely independent of yours. In this way, all users can have their own configuration settings for various applications.

Under SUSE Linux, you can back up both configuration data and personal files using the System Backup component of YaST. This is relatively primitive compared to many backup tools, but it performs the task adequately.

Keep in mind that there's little point in making backups if you leave the resultant archive files on your hard disk. For full backup protection, the archives should be stored elsewhere, such as on an external hard disk, a network mount, or a CD or DVD. Under GNOME, consider using the GNOME CD/DVD Creator (Applications ➤ Multimedia ➤ Gnome CD/DVD Creator). Under KDE, consider using K3b (K menu ➤ Multimedia ➤ CD/DVD Burning). I'll describe the procedure for using both of these tools in the "Burning the Backup File to CD/DVD" section later in this chapter.

Backing Up Using YaST

YaST includes a simple but effective backup tool, referred to simply as System Backup. It creates a single archive file which, unless you alter the default settings, will contain both system data and personal files. It is partnered with the System Restoration tool, which simply aims to restore files within the backup file to their original locations.

It's important to note that both programs are relatively unsophisticated. For example, although there are facilities for restoring individual files within an archive (useful if, for example, you find a word processing document has become corrupted), System Restoration isn't really built for that kind of use. Its main purpose is to restore the entire system to a previous state.

The first step is to configure System Backup to tell it which files to back up. Then you can create your backups, either manually or automatically according to a schedule you define. Then, if the worst happens and you lose data, you can restore a backup using System Restoration.

Defining a Backup Job

Computer administrators usually use the term *jobs* to refer to repetitive but essential tasks such as backup, which can be defined once and then run over and over again. Therefore, the first step when it comes to backing up your data is to define an initial backup job, which will detail which files are to be backed up.

Follow these steps to define a backup job:

1. Start YaST. Under GNOME, click Desktop ➤ YaST. Under KDE, click K menu ➤ System ➤ YaST. Enter your root password when prompted.

2. Click the System icon on the left, and then the System Backup icon on the right.

3. In the Profile Management drop-down list, select Add.

4. Give a name to the new backup job, as shown in Figure 32-2. This is purely for your future reference, so something like the date you created it will be fine. However, it is vital that no spaces appear in the name. If you wish to separate words, use an under-score character (_) instead. Click OK to continue.

■**Caution** System Backup won't stop you from inserting spaces into the name. But you shouldn't do so because this will cause the automatic backup feature to fail.

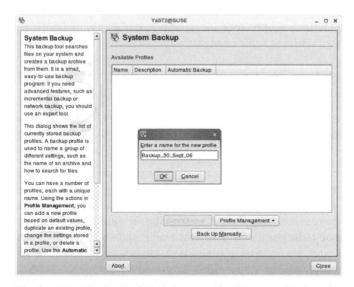

Figure 32-2. *Give the backup job a memorable name for future reference, but be careful not to use spaces in the name.*

5. In the Archive Settings window, specify backup settings as follows, and then click Next to continue.

- Give the archive a filename. Like the backup job name, this can be anything, although the standard rules of filenames apply (for example, you can't use some symbols such as slashes). Also, the filename must include the full path. On my test system, I could type something like /home/keir/backup_job. There's an option of saving it on a remote Network File System (NFS) mount, and if you work in a corporate environment, this option might be open to you. If you're creating a backup on a stand-alone workstation, the best option is to save the file to your home directory. Then you might put the file on a CD/DVD for permanent storage, as described in the "Burning the Backup File to CD/DVD" section later in this chapter.

- You can set the type of compression applied to the backup job. The default is gzip compression, which isn't particularly efficient. Click in the Archive Type drop-down list at the bottom of the window and select Tar with Tar-bzip2 Subarchives. (See the "Making Backups from the Command Line" section later in this chapter for more information about tar and compression types.)

- By clicking the Options button, you can select to create a multivolume archive. This simply splits the resulting backup file into small chunks that can be saved onto smaller removable storage media. By checking the Create a Multivolume Archive option and selecting CD-R/RW 700MB, you can create a series of files that can comfortably be saved on the majority of CDs sold today. If the backup file is 2GB, you'll need about three CDs to store it, which should prove both feasible and inexpensive.

6. In the Backup Options window, specify backup options as follows, and then click Next to continue.

- Choose whether to back up files that weren't created by installed packages. You certainly want to do this; otherwise, only system files will be backed up. Your /home directory would be ignored, and therefore your personal data would not be included. In the next step, you'll have a chance to prune the backup list to exclude certain files and directories. In effect, activating this option switches System Backup between creating a purely system backup and creating a full backup of the system plus your personal data.

- You can choose to display the list of files before the archive is created. This can be useful for problem-solving (or just to check that the backup job is working as you intended), but there's no need to activate this option.

- Select whether to check the MD5 sum instead of the time and size during backup. This refers to how SUSE Linux evaluates if a file has changed since it last performed the backup job. Obviously, it won't be much use during the initial backup, but it's vital during subsequent backups. Checking the date and time stamp of each file is a good indicator that the file hasn't been updated because, if it had, the date and time would be updated, too. However, for various reasons, this approach is considered unreliable, so there's also the option of checking the MD5 sum of each file. The MD5 sum is a unique number that is generated by applying a calculation to each file. If the number has changed, that's a good indication that the file has changed. The problem is checking the MD5 sum isn't particularly quick, because of the calculations involved. I recommend using the MD5 sum approach, unless you need the backups to occur quickly.

7. In the Search Constraints window, you'll be invited to choose any files or directories that are not to be included in the backup sweep, as shown in Figure 32-3. For example, backing up your MP3 file collection may result in a backup file that's many gigabytes, because MP3 files average around 4MB to 5MB each. Therefore, you might consider it more sensible to exclude them. In addition, certain directories are not viable for backup, because they include temporary data that would be pointless to back up. Also, it's vital to ensure that any mounts, such as the mount for your Windows directory, aren't included in the backup, because that can swell the backup file size.

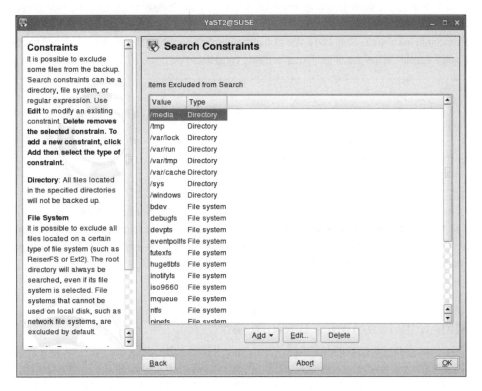

Figure 32-3. *You can select files or directories to be excluded from the backup. This is useful if you don't want to bloat the backup with large music or video files.*

■**Note** You might think that including your Windows mount in the backup is a good idea. But bear in mind that YaST's System Restoration tool isn't very sophisticated and aims to restore files to their original locations. Because Windows mounts are usually read-only within SUSE Linux, that would prove impossible. It's therefore a better idea to back up your Windows files from within Windows itself.

If all of this sounds complicated, don't worry. Practically all the directories that you shouldn't back up will be included in the list automatically. However, if you've manually created a mount point for removable storage or your Windows directory, you should add it to the list so it isn't included. Just click the Add button, choose Directory, and type the full path to the mount (for example, `/media/windows/C`).

Regular expressions are used to define types of files not to be included. Regular expressions are described in Chapter 15, but it might be useful to know that you can avoid MP3 files being added to the backup job by clicking Add ➤ Regular Expression and typing `\.mp3$`. In this situation, you're effectively filtering by file extension. To exclude AVI movie files from the backup, type `\.avi$`.

Note Here's how the regular expression translates into plain English: The initial slash is an escape code, which is used to indicate that the period that follows shouldn't be interpreted as a search term but as a character in the search string. The dollar sign at the end indicates that the search term should be considered only if it appears at the end of the filename which, considering we hope to filter by file extension, is vital.

---

8. Click Next, and you'll be returned to the main System Backup window.

The backup job is defined and ready to be used. Now you can either start it manually or schedule the backup, as described in the following sections.

Tip As you might have realized, you can create more than one backup job. This might be useful if you wish to fine-tune the backup job for certain situations. For example, you might configure a "full" backup to run every month, but a "quick" backup covering only certain files to run every day. Follow the preceding instructions to create as many backup jobs as you wish.

Manually Running a Backup Job

After you've defined a backup job, you can start it manually using the YaST System Backup Tool. In the main window (see Figure 32-2), select your job and click the Create Backup button. The backup program will initially prepare a list of files to be backed up, and then it will make the backup, which may take a long time.

At the end, you'll see the Backup Summary window, as shown in Figure 32-4, which shows the number of files backed up, the size of the backup archive file, and its location. If you've followed the instructions in the preceding section, you should find the resultant backup file in your `/home` folder. Click OK to return to the main System Backup window.

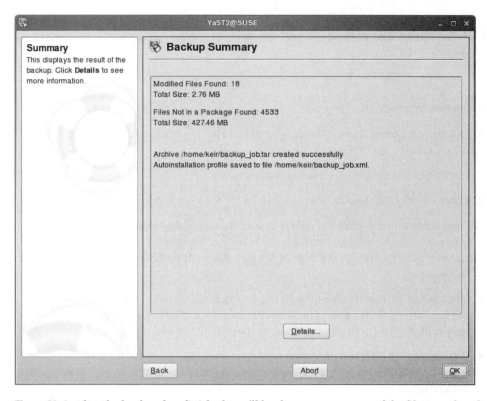

Figure 32-4. *After the backup has finished, you'll be shown a summary of the files saved and also the size of the backup file.*

The backup file created by System Backup is owned by root user and, as normal user, you will not have permissions to access it. This is to protect it from interference. The backup file is only meant to be restored by YaST's System Restoration tool, as described in the "Restoring a Backup" section later in this chapter.

■**Note** You might be wondering about the autoinstallation profile stored along with the backup. This is a file that can be used in certain circumstances to automate installation of SUSE Linux on new machines. The idea in the case of backup is that the file can be used to completely restore a system to a previous state. For more information about autoinstallation profiles and how they can be used, see www.suse.com/~ug/ AutoYaST_FAQ.html.

Scheduling a Backup Job

Backup jobs can be scheduled to occur daily, weekly, or monthly, and you can set precisely when the job should start. But keep in mind that creating a backup file is an intensive task, so any backups should be scheduled to occur while you're not at your computer.

■Tip The obvious time to schedule a backup to run is during a lunch break. It shouldn't take more than an hour to complete.

Here's how to schedule backup jobs:

1. In the main System Backup window (see Figure 32-2), click the Profile Management drop-down list, and then click Automatic Backup.

2. Put a check alongside Start Backup Automatically.

3. Choose from Daily, Weekly, and Monthly in the Frequency drop-down list.

4. Depending on your choice in step 3, choose the day of the week the backup should take place, the day of the month the backup should take place, and the hour and minute it should occur. Time is in 24-hour format. Setting 0 hour and 0 minute equates to midnight.

5. You can choose the number of old backups to keep. This refers to when automatic backups are made. It's always healthy to keep old backup files around, but realize that they're likely to be multiple gigabytes, so they will fill your hard disk quickly.

6. You can have the backup program send a system mail message to the root user when it has completed its job. This will inform the user of errors or success performing the backup job.

■Note System mail is not the same as the POP3 mail regularly used for e-mail. You need to use the command-line `mail` program to read system mail.

---

7. After you've make your choices, click the OK button.

You'll need to reboot your system for the new scheduling to take effect.

READING SYSTEM MAIL

In the old days of Unix, the system would automatically send messages to the root user to provide status reports when certain tasks had been run. This is a neat idea that has been carried across into Linux. However, modern Linux is highly automated, and it's not anticipated that the user will be as involved with the minutiae of the system, at least not when it comes to desktop Linux.

However, the System Backup tool can be set to automatically send mail to the root user to report on the outcome of the backup job. To read this message, you'll need to switch to the root user and use the command-line `mail` program, as follows:

```
su -
[Enter root password]
mail
```

You'll then see a list of messages. To read each one, type the number listed to its left. Messages are read in less, so type q when you've finished reading.

To delete the message, type d followed immediately with the message number. For example, d1 will delete message 1.

To quit the mail program, just type q and press Enter.

Burning the Backup File to CD/DVD

For safekeeping, you can burn your backup file to a CD or DVD. However, first, the file needs to be made readable by ordinary users. Ordinarily, it is only readable by the root user.

Making the Backup File Readable

To make the backup file readable, you need to change its permissions using the chmod command (see Chapter 14). Open a terminal window (in GNOME, click Applications ➤ System ➤ Terminal ➤ Gnome Terminal; in KDE, click K menu ➤ System ➤ Terminal ➤ Konsole), and type the following:

```
su
[Enter root password]
chmod +r backupfile.tar.bz2
```

Replace the filename backupfile.tar.bz2 with the name of your backup file.

GNOME: Burning the CD/DVD

Under GNOME, you can use Nautilus's CD/DVD burning mode to write the backup file to a writable CD or DVD of the appropriate size, as follows:

1. Click Applications ➤ Multimedia ➤ CD/DVD Burning ➤ Gnome CD/DVD Creator.

2. Click and drag the file onto the new Nautilus window.

3. Click the Write to Disc button.

4. Make sure the correct size disc is inserted, and then click the Write button in the dialog box.

KDE: Burning the CD/DVD

Under KDE, you can use K3b to write the backup file to a writable CD or DVD, as follows:

1. Click K menu ➤ Multimedia ➤ CD/DVD Burning.

2. Click the New Data CD Project or New Data DVD Project button at the bottom of the window, depending on which medium you're using.

3. In the file tree at the top left, navigate to the backup file, which should be in your /home directory.

4. Click and drag the backup file to the bottom of the K3b window.

5. Click the Burn button, and you'll see the dialog box shown in Figure 32-5.

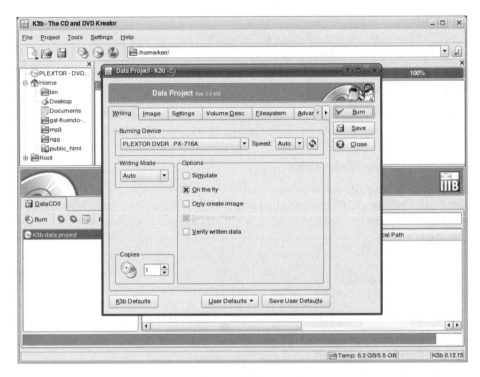

Figure 32-5. *Backup files can be burned to disc under KDE using the K3b program.*

6. Adjust the settings as necessary, and then click the Burn button in the dialog box.

■**Note** Bear in mind that CD-R/RW and DVD-R/RW discs don't last forever. In fact, some estimates put the typical life span of a disc as little as a few months! As always, quality matters. Buying more-expensive branded discs will produce far better results. Kodak estimates its Ultima CD-R discs will last 200 years, for example! Storage is also important. Store your discs in a location away from strong light and with average temperature and humidity levels.

Restoring a Backup

If you need to restore data, you can use the YaST System Restoration tool. You can either restore the entire backup file, which will effectively return the system to the time of the backup, or selectively restore files within the backup file.

■Note The YaST System Restoration tool works only with backup files made by the YaST System Backup tool.

Here's how to restore a backup:

1. Start YaST. Under GNOME, click Desktop ➤ YaST. Under KDE, click K menu ➤ System ➤ YaST. Enter your root password when prompted.

2. Click the System icon on the left side of the program window, and then click the System Restoration icon on the right.

3. Select the backup file you wish to restore. If the file has been burned to CD or DVD, insert the disc, wait a few seconds for it to be recognized, and then click the Removable Device radio button.

4. Make sure the removable storage device is selected in the Device drop-down list, and then click the Select button alongside the Archive Filename field to choose the actual backup file. If your backup spans several discs, insert the first disc and choose the first backup file.

■Note The System Restoration tool will mount the contents of the CD/DVD disc in the /tmp directory, rather than /media, as you might expect. Don't worry about this.

---

5. Click the Next button, and then wait a few moments while the backup file is scanned.

6. You'll be presented with a summary of the backup file, including the date it was created. You can take a look at the files in the archive by clicking the Archive Content button. You can also click Expert Options for some advanced options. These control whether the boot loader (GRUB boot menu) is rewritten during restoration and whether SuSEconfig, a program that rewrites some system files, is run. If you're performing a system restoration after a devastating loss of data, involving a complete reinstallation of SUSE Linux, these options should be activated. If you're aiming to selectively restore data files, the two options can be unchecked.

7. Click Next to continue. In the Packages to Restore window, shown in Figure 32-6, you can select which files to restore from the archive. All of the files are selected by default, which is indicated by a check alongside each entry in the list. Don't put a check in the Restore RPM Database box. This is designed to repair SUSE Linux's software installation tool after its database has become corrupt and should be used only in very specific situations by those who know what they're doing.

   - If you want to restore the system to the way it was previously, click Accept. The backup will then be restored.

   - If you want to restore particular files, click the Deselect All button. Then, assuming that the files you want to restore are personal data files, click the --No Package-- entry in the list, and then click the Select Files button. In the list, scroll down to your /home directory and put a check alongside the file(s) you want to restore. Then click Accept.

■**Caution** Finding the files you want to restore can be tricky because the list of files is long and all the hidden files that normally live in your /home directory are included, too. Also, the list of files to restore includes both directories and files, and there's no obvious way of telling them apart aside from common sense and experience. Be aware that putting a check alongside a directory will restore all the files in that directory. For example, putting a check alongside /home/keir on my test machine would restore all the files that were within /home/keir during backup, *overwriting any files currently there*! Remember what I said earlier in this chapter: Although capable of the task, System Restoration isn't really designed to restore individual files and doesn't make the task particularly easy.

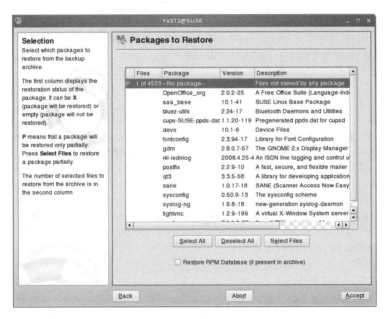

Figure 32-6. *Once you've selected the files you want to restore, click the Accept button to write them to disk.*

8. The file(s) will then be restored to their original location(s). This may take some time, depending on the number of files you want to restore. Once the restoration is completed, you'll see a summary of the restored files. Click the Finished button to close the System Restoration window.

Making Backups from the Command Line

Although the YaST backup tool allows the uninitiated to make quick backups, the tar program is preferred by Linux old-timers. This creates .tar files and is one of the original carryovers from Unix. tar stands for Tape ARchive and refers to backing up data to a magnetic tape backup device. Although tar files are designed for backup, they've also become a standard method of transferring files across the Internet, particularly with regard to source files or other installation programs.

A tar file is simply a collection of files bundled into one. By default, the tar file isn't compressed, although additional software can be used to compress it. tar files aren't very sophisticated compared to modern archive file formats. They're not encrypted, for example, but this can also be one of their advantages.

■**Note** Linux comes with a couple more backup commands, which you might choose to use. They are cpio and pax. Both aim to improve on tar in various ways, but neither is broadly supported at the moment. Examine their man pages for more details.

Creating tar Files

Perhaps unsurprisingly, tar files are created at the console using the tar command. Usually, all you need to do is specify a source directory and a filename, like so:

```
tar -cf mybackup.tar /home/keir/
```

This will create a backup called mybackup.tar based on the contents of /home/keir/. tar is automatically recursive so, in this example, it will delve into all subdirectories beneath /home/keir. The -c command option tells tar you're going to create an archive, and the -f option indicates that the filename for the archive will immediately follow. If you don't use the -f option, tar will send its output to standard output, which means that it will display the contents of the archive on the screen.

If you typed in a command like the preceding example, you would see this message:

```
Removing leading '/' from member names.
```

This means that the folders and files added to the archive will all have the initial forward slash removed from their paths. So, rather than store a file in the archive as this:

```
/home/keir/Mail/file1
```

the file will be stored as follows:

```
home/keir/Mail/file1
```

The difference between the two forms concerns when the files are later extracted from the archive. If the files have the initial slash, `tar` will write the file to `/home/keir/Mail/file1`. If there's already a file of that name in that location, it will be overwritten.

On the other hand, with the leading slash removed, `tar` will create a new directory wherever you choose to restore the archive. In this example, it will create a new directory called `home`, and then a directory called `keir` within that, and so on. Of course, if these directories already exist at that location, then `tar` will simply write the files to them.

Because of the potential of accidentally overwriting data by specifying absolute paths in this way, a better way of backing up a directory is simply to change into its parent and specify it without a full path. The following will back up my `/home` directory:

```
cd /home/
tar -cf mybackup.tar keir
```

When this particular archive is restored, it will create a new folder called `keir` wherever it's restored.

Compressing tar Archives

You can also compress the archive from within `tar`, although it actually calls in outside help from either `bzip2` or `gzip`, depending on which you specify.

To create a `tar` archive compressed using `bzip2`, the following should do the trick:

```
tar -cjf mybackup.tar.bz2 keir
```

This will create a compressed backup from the directory `keir`. The `-j` command option passes the output from `tar` to the `bzip2` program, although this is done in the background. Notice that I've changed the backup filename extension to indicate that this is a `bzip2` compressed archive. This is standard practice.

The following command will create an archive compressed with the older `gzip` compression:

```
tar -czf mybackup.tar.gz keir
```

This uses the `-z` command option to pass the output to `gzip`. This time, the filename shows it's a `gzip` compressed archive, so you can correctly identify it in the future.

■**Note** You might be wondering which you should use: `bzip2` or `gzip`? In nearly every case, `bzip2` is better. It will shrink files to a much higher degree. `gzip` is used when you might have to transfer files to a computer that does not have `bzip2` installed. This is very, very rare nowadays. However, many source code files are compressed using `gzip` because there's a chance they might be extracted on a Unix system without `bzip2`.

Extracting Files from a tar Archive

Extracting files using tar is as easy as creating them:

```
tar -xf mybackup.tar
```

The -x option tells tar to extract the files from the maybackup.tar archive.

Extracting compressed archives is simply a matter of adding the -j or -z option to the -x option:

```
tar -xjf mybackup.tar.bz2
```

■**Note** Technically speaking, tar doesn't require the preceding hyphen before its command options. However, it's a good idea to use it anyway, so you won't forget to use it with other commands.

Viewing tar Archive Information

To view the contents of a tar archive without actually restoring the files, use the -t option:

```
tar -tf mybackup.tar |less
```

This example adds a pipe into less at the end, because the listing of files probably will be large and scroll off the screen. Just add the -j or -z option if the tar archive is also compressed.

In addition, you can add the -v option to all stages of making, extracting, and viewing an archive to see more information (chiefly, the files that are being archived or extracted). Adding -vv provides even more information:

```
tar -cvvf mybackup.tar keir
```

This will create an archive and also show a complete directory listing as the files and folders are added, including permissions.

Saving a tar File to CD/DVD

Once the tar file has been created, the problem of where to store it arises. As I mentioned earlier, storing backup data on the same hard disk as the data it was created to back up is foolish, since any problem that might affect the hard disk might also affect the archive. You could end up losing both sets of data!

If the archive is less than 700MB, consider storing it on a CD. If it's less than 4.3GB, you could save it to a DVD. To do this from the command line, first turn the file into an ISO image, and then burn it.

To turn the archive into an ISO image, use the mkisofs command:

```
mkisofs -o backup.iso mybackup.tar.bz2
```

You can then burn the ISO image to a CD or DVD by using the cdrecord or cdrecord-dvd command, respectively. To use the command, you need to know which SCSI device number your CD or DVD drive uses. (All CD or DVD drives are seen as SCSI devices, even if they're not.) Issue the following command (as the root user—cdrecord accesses the system hardware directly):

```
su -
[Enter root password]
cdrecord -scanbus
```

Alternatively, if you're using cdrecord-dvd, type:

```
cdrecord-dvd -scanbus
```

You should find the device numbers listed as three numbers separated by commas. To burn the backup image, all you need to do is enter a command in this format (replacing cdrecord with cdrecord-dvd to burn a DVD image):

```
cdrecord dev=<dev number> speed=<speed of your drive> mybackup.iso
```

On a typical system, this might take the following form:

```
sudo cdrecord dev=0,0,0 speed=24 mybackup.iso
```

If you're using cdrecord-dvd, bear in mind that DVD drives currently write more slowly than CD drives. To find out the speed of your drive, consult its documentation.

Note Remember that you can use the man command to learn about any commands, including those detailed here. In the case of cdrecord in particular, this is worthwhile, because it's a very powerful piece of software.

Summary

In this chapter, we looked at making backups. First, you saw how to verify where your personal and other vital data is stored. Then we looked at how the YaST tools can be used to back up system configuration and personal data, and to restore data from your backup. Finally, you learned how to use tar at the command line to back up any kind of data.

In the next chapter, we'll look at how tasks can be scheduled to occur at various times under SUSE Linux.

■ ■ ■

## CHAPTER 33

Scheduling Tasks

In this book, you've learned about various tasks you can perform to keep SUSE Linux running smoothly. You may decide that you want some of these tasks to occur on a regular basis. For example, perhaps you want your /home directory to be backed up every day, or perhaps you want to clean the /tmp directory to ensure that you always have enough free disk space. You could carry out each task individually, but human nature would no doubt step in, and you would forget, or you might perform the action twice, because you've forgotten that you've already done it.

As you might expect, SUSE Linux is able to automate the running of particular tasks. They can either be run periodically at scheduled times or as one-time tasks. Using SUSE Linux's scheduling features is explained in this chapter.

Scheduling with crontab

Under SUSE Linux, the main way of scheduling tasks is via the cron service. This works on behalf of the user in order to schedule individual tasks, and it is also used by the system in order to run vital system tasks, although a different way of working is used in each case.

For cron to run user-scheduled tasks, it reads a file called crontab. Each user has his or her own version of this, which is stored in the /var/spool/cron/tabs directory. You should use a special command to edit this file in vi (the text editor covered in Chapter 15), rather than edit it directly.

■**Note** System-wide tasks are listed in /etc/cron.hourly, /etc/cron.daily, and so on, depending on when the tasks are meant to be run (every hour, day, and so on). The average user never needs to bother with system-wide cron jobs. These are handled by the internal system, and programs create their own entries as and when necessary.

The cron daemon starts at bootup and simply sits in the background while you work, checking every minute to see if a task is due. As soon as one comes up, it starts the task going, and then goes back to waiting.

Creating a Scheduled Task

Adding a scheduled task is relatively easily and is done via the shell. Entering the following command will cause your personal crontab file to be loaded into vi, ready for editing:

```
crontab -e
```

If this is the first time you've edited your crontab file, it will most likely be completely empty. However, don't be put off. Adding a new entry is relatively easy and normally takes the form of something like this:

```
01 12 15 * * tar -cjf /home/keir/mybackup.tar.bz2 /home/keir
```

Let's examine the line piece by piece. The first part—the numbers and asterisks—refers to when the task should be run. From left to right, the fields refer to the following:

- Minutes, from 0 to 59

- Hours, in 24-hour time, from 0 to 23

- Day dates, for the day of the month, from 1 to 31 (assuming the month has that many days)

- Months, from 1 to 12

- Day, for a particular day, either from 0 to 6 (0 is Sunday), or specified as a three-letter abbreviation (mon, tue, wed, and so on)

In the example, the task is set to run at the first minute at the twelfth hour (midday) on the fifteenth day of the month. But what do the asterisks stand for? They're effectively wildcards and tell cron that every possible value applies. Because an asterisk appears in the month field, this task will be run every month. Because an asterisk appears in the day field, the task will be run every day.

Note You might have noticed a logical contradiction here. How can we specify a day if we also specify a date in the month? Wouldn't this seriously limit the chances of the task ever running? Yes, it would. If you were to specify sat, for example, and put 15 in the date field, the task would run on only the fifteenth of the month if that happened to be a Saturday. This is why the two fields are rarely used in the same crontab entry, and an asterisk appears in one if the other is being used.

After the time and date fields comes the command itself: tar. As you learned in the previous chapter, tar is designed to back up your personal data, and the command in the line we're examining backs up my /home directory.

Only standard BASH shell commands can be used in the command section. cron isn't clever enough to interpret symbols such as the tilde (~) as a way of referring to your home directory. For this reason, it's best to be very thorough when defining a cron job and always use absolute paths.

Let's take a look at another example (shown in Figure 33-1):

```
59 23 * * 0-3 tar -cjf /home/keir/mybackup.tar.bz2 /home/keir
```

Figure 33-1. *Editing crontab lets you schedule tasks using the vi text editor.*

The first field says that this task will run at the fifty-ninth minute of the twenty-third hour (that is, one minute before midnight). The date and month field have asterisks, so this implies that the task should run every day and every month. However, the day field contains 0-3. This says that the task should run on only days 0 through to 3, or Sunday through Wednesday.

You can have as many cron entries as you like; simply give each a separate line. There's no need for them to be in date or time order. You can just add them as and when you see fit.

When you're finished, save the file and quit vi in the usual way (by entering :wq).

■**Note** SUSE Linux is unusual among Linux distributions in that it doesn't make use of another form of task scheduling called anacron. anacron is designed to periodically schedule system tasks, so that, for example, a maintenance task could be started every other day, regardless of the date. However, with SUSE Linux, cron is used to duplicate this functionality behind the scenes by monitoring when tasks were last run.

Using at to Schedule Tasks

What if you quickly want to schedule a one-time-only task? For this, you can use the at command. This relies on a daemon that isn't activated by default on SUSE Linux, so you'll need to add it first.

Adding at to the Current Run Level

You can use YaST to add at to the current run level. Start YaST, click System, and then click the icon marked System Services (Runlevel). The at daemon is called atd. Select it and click Enable. This will start it at run levels 2, 3, and 5 every time the system is booted, until it's disabled. (Don't worry if YaST reports an additional service must be started to support atd.)

Adding a Job with at

Adding a job with at is very easy, largely because the at command accepts a wide variety of time formats. For example, the following will run a job at lunchtime tomorrow:

```
at noon tomorrow
```

It really is as simple as that!

Alternatively, you can specify a time, date, and even a year:

```
at 13:00 jun 25 2008
```

This will run the job at 1 p.m. on June 25, 2008. The various time and date formats are explained in the at command's man page.

Once the at command containing the date has been entered, you'll be presented with a mock shell prompt. Here, you can type the commands you want to run. Many shell commands can be entered, one after the other; just press Enter between them. Then press Ctrl+D to signal that you're finished editing. At this point, at will confirm the time and write the task into its list.

■**Note** As explained in Chapter 17, pressing Ctrl+D sends an end-of-file (EOF) signal to various applications. at is one of the programs where this is necessary. By pressing Ctrl+D, you're telling it that there's no more data to enter.

You can view the jobs at any time by typing atq. This will show a list of numbered jobs. You can remove any job by typing atrm, followed by its atq job number. For example, the following will remove the job numbered 9 in the atq list:

```
atrm 9
```

Summary

In this brief chapter, we looked at how you can schedule tasks under SUSE Linux, which is essentially making programs run at certain times. We examined the cron facility, which can schedule tasks to run periodically, and we also examined the at service, which can schedule one-time tasks to run at certain times.

In the final chapter of this book, we will look at how you can access your SUSE Linux computer remotely—theoretically, from any Internet-equipped location in the world.

■ ■ ■

## CHAPTER 34

Accessing Computers Remotely

One area where Linux particularly excels is in its support for networking. If you wish to learn about how networks operate on a fundamental level, then Linux is an ideal choice, because it puts you in virtually direct contact with the technology.

The widespread integration and support for networking extends to several useful system tools, which let you access Linux across any kind of network, including the Internet. In fact, it's even possible to access a Linux machine running on a different continent, just as if you were sitting in front of it!

This chapter looks at the many ways you can access your SUSE Linux computer remotely. In addition, you'll discover how you can use SUSE Linux to access almost any other computers, including Windows PCs.

Using Secure Shell

The history of Unix has always featured computers connecting to other computers in some fashion, whether they were dumb terminals connecting to a mainframe computer or Unix machines acting as nodes on the fledgling Internet. Because of this, a wide variety of techniques and protocols were invented to allow computers to communicate and log in to each other across networks. However, while these still work fine over the modern Internet, we're now faced with new threats to the privacy of data. In theory, any data transmitted across the Internet can be picked up by individuals at certain key stages along the route. If the data isn't protected, it can be easily intercepted and read.

To counter such an occurrence, the ssh suite of programs was created. Although these programs started as open source, they gradually became proprietary. Therefore, several newer open source versions were created, including the one used on the majority of Linux distributions (including SUSE Linux): OpenSSH.

■Note This chapter provides a whistle-stop introduction to ssh. If you're interested in truly mastering this powerful tool, I would advise you read *Pro OpenSSH*, by Michael Stahnke (1-59059-476-2; Apress, 2005).

The goal of ssh is to create a secure connection between two computers. You can then do just about any task, including initiating a shell session so you can use the remote computer as if you were sitting in front of it, or copying files to and from the remote computer. ssh uses various techniques at both ends of the connection to encrypt not only the data passing between the two machines, but also the username and password.

■**Note** This chapter refers to *remote* and *local* machines. The remote machine is the computer you're connecting to across the network or Internet. The local machine is the one at your physical location. These two terms are widely used in documentation describing networking.

Logging In to a Remote Computer

The most basic type of ssh connection is a remote login. This will give you a command prompt on the remote computer, as if you had just sat down in front of it and opened a GNOME Terminal or Konsole window.

But before you can log in to any machine via ssh, you'll need to be sure that the remote computer is able to accept ssh connections. This means that it needs to be running the ssh server program (referred to as a *service*), and also that its firewall is configured to accept incoming ssh connections.

Preparing the Remote Computer

The two major components of OpenSSH are the client and server. The former makes connections, while the latter accepts connections from other machines.

Under SUSE Linux, both the client and server programs are installed by default. However, the firewall is configured not to let ssh connections through.

■**Caution** Some Linux distributions, such as Ubuntu, don't automatically install the server component. Therefore, extra software will need to be installed to connect to such a computer.

Chapter 9 describes setting up the SUSE Linux firewall. The following steps will be sufficient to allow ssh connections. These steps need to be undertaken on the *remote* machine; the local machine's firewall settings don't need to be altered.

1. Start YaST. Under GNOME, click Desktop ➤ YaST. Under KDE, click K menu ➤ System ➤ YaST. Enter your root password when prompted.

2. In the YaST window, click the Security and Users icon on the left, and then click the Firewall icon on the right side of the program window.

3. In the Firewall Configuration window, click Allowed Services in the list on the left. In the Service to Allow drop-down list, select SSH. Then click the Add button.

4. Click the Next button at the bottom right, and then click the Accept button in the next window.

Connecting to a Remote Machine via ssh

Initiating an `ssh` remote shell session with a remote machine is usually achieved by typing something similar to the following at a command prompt on the local machine:

```
ssh username@IP_address
```

In other words, you specify the login username and the IP address of the machine. If there's a fully qualified domain name (FQDN) for the system you want to access, you could specify that instead of the IP address.

Note In this context, an FQDN equates to the hostname of a system plus its Internet address, such as `mycomputer.example.com`. Unless you have had this function specifically set up for you by a system administrator, you'll probably need to connect via IP address. However, if you rent a web server, you might be able to `ssh` into it using a web site address.

When you log in for the first time, you'll see the following message:

```
The authenticity of the host <host IP address> can't be established
```

Figure 34-1 shows an example. This means that the remote computer's encryption key hasn't yet been added to your PC's store file. However, once you agree to the initial login, the encryption key will be added, and it will be used in the future to confirm that the remote computer you're connecting to is authentic.

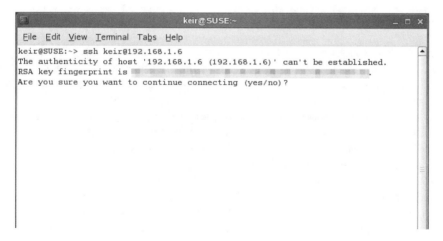

Figure 34-1. *When logging in via ssh for the first time, you'll need to confirm acceptance of the encryption key.*

■**Note** There's a fine line between security concern and paranoia. Connecting to a remote machine for the first time and accepting its `ssh` key is considered insecure by some people, because you cannot be 100% sure that the remote machine is the one to which you want to connect. It might have been swapped for a different machine by hackers (or some such theory). In addition, the key might be intercepted on its journey to you. Because of this, those who are highly security conscious can use the `ssh-keygen` program to create a key on the remote machine first, and then import it to the local machine via floppy disk before logging in. See the `ssh-keygen` man page for more details.

After confirming that you want to make the connection, you'll be invited to enter the password for the user account under which you initiated the `ssh` connection *on the remote computer*. Once this is done, you should find yourself with a shell login on the remote computer. You can run the same commands as usual and perform identical tasks.

The machine you're logged in to will show no symptoms of being used remotely. This isn't like the movies, where what you type on your local machine is somehow mirrored on the remote machine for all to see. However, if a user of the remote machine were to view her network connections using something similar to the `netstat` command, then she would see another computer attached via `ssh`.

To end an `ssh` session, simply type `exit`. This will log you out and return you to the command prompt on the local machine.

■**Tip** There's a version of the `ssh` client that runs on a variety of non-Linux operating systems, making it possible to log in to your SUSE Linux machine from a Windows computer. The program is called PuTTY and can be downloaded from `www.chiark.greenend.org.uk/~sgtatham/putty/`.

MANAGING REMOTE SESSIONS

Whenever you open any kind of shell to enter commands and run programs, you might have noticed that any commands you execute run only as long as the shell window is open. When the shell window is closed, any task running within it ends, too. This is because the shell is seen as the "owner" of the process, and when the owner quits, any processes it started also quit.

When using `ssh` to start a remote shell session, this also applies. Whenever you log out, any tasks you were running are ended. This can be annoying if, for example, you've started a lengthy download on the remote machine. Effectively, you must remain logged in via `ssh` until the download has finished.

To get around this, you can use the handy `screen` program. This program isn't specifically designed to be an aid to remote logins, but there's no reason why it cannot be used this way.

The `screen` program effectively starts shell sessions that stick around, even if the shell window is closed or the `ssh` connection is ended or lost. After logging in to the remote computer via `ssh`, you can start a `screen` session by simply typing the program name at the prompt:

```
screen
```

After pressing the spacebar as prompted to start the program, there won't be any indication that you're running a `screen` session. You won't see a taskbar at the bottom of the terminal window, for example. `screen` works completely in the background.

Let's consider what happens when you detach and then reattach to a `screen` session. To detach from the `screen` session, press Ctrl+A, and then Ctrl+D. You'll then be returned to the standard shell and, in fact, you could now disconnect from your `ssh` session as usual. However, the `screen` session will still be running in the background on the remote computer. To prove this, you could log back in, and then type this:

```
screen -r
```

This will resume your `screen` session, and you should be able to pick up quite literally where you left off. Any output from previous commands will be displayed.

To quit a `screen` session, you can either type `exit` from within it or press Ctrl+A, and then Ctrl+\ (backslash).

The `screen` program is very powerful. To learn more about it, read its `man` page. To see a list of its keyboard commands, press Ctrl+A, and then type a question mark (?) while `screen` is running.

Transferring Files Between Remote Computers

The `ssh` utility brings with it two basic ways of transferring files between machines: `scp` and `sftp`. `scp` is fine for single file transfers, but if you want to copy a lot of files, `sftp` is probably a better choice.

Using scp

Strictly speaking, `scp` is merely a program that copies files from one computer to another in a secure fashion using the underlying `ssh` protocol. You don't need to be logged in to another computer via `ssh` to use it. For example, if I were merely browsing my own computer and wanted to transfer a file to a remote computer, I could type this:

```
scp myfile keir@IP_address:/home/keir/
```

I would replace *IP_address* with the IP address of the computer to which I wanted to send the file. In other words, you must first specify the local file you want to copy across, and then provide the login details for the remote computer in the same format as with an `ssh` login. Then, after a colon, you specify the path on the *remote* computer where you would like the file to be copied.

■Note If it helps, consider the latter part of the `scp` command after the filename as one large address for connecting to the remote computer: first you provide your username, then the computer address, and then the path.

Using the command when you are logged in to another computer via ssh works in exactly the same way. This way, you can pass a file back from a *remote* computer to your *local* computer. Let's consider an example.

Assume there are two computers running SUSE Linux: A and B. I have a user account on each one. So sitting at the keyboard of A, I establish an ssh connection with B by typing the following:

```
ssh keir@computer_B
```

This lets me log in to B as if I were sitting in front of it. I spot a file called spreadsheet.xls that I want to copy to my local machine (A). I therefore issue the following command:

```
scp spreadsheet.xls keir@computer_A:/home/keir/
```

This will copy the file from computer B to computer A and place it in the /home/keir/ directory.

Then, assuming that I've finished, I can log out of computer B as usual by typing exit, and then access spreadsheet.xls on my local computer.

Tip With scp, you can copy entire directories, too. Simply add the -r command option, like so: scp -r *mydirectory <username>@<IP address>:/path/*.

Using sftp

To copy a lot of files to or from a remote computer, the sftp program is the best solution. If you've ever used a shell-based ftp program, you'll feel right at home, because sftp isn't very different.

You can initiate an sftp session by using this command format:

```
sftp username@IP_address
```

The same rules as when you're logging in with ssh apply, both in terms of formatting the login command and also confirming the encryption key if this is the first time you've logged in.

Tip With all the ssh login commands, if you omit the username, along with the @ sign, ssh will assume you're attempting to log in with your the username you're using on the local machine.

The sftp commands are fairly easy to understand. For example, to copy a file from the remote machine, simply type this:

```
get filename
```

This will copy the file into the directory you were in on the local machine before you started the sftp session.

By specifying a path after the filename, the file will be copied to the specified local directory:

```
get spreadsheet.xls /home/keir/downloaded_files/
```

Sending files from the local machine to the remote machine is just as easy:

```
put filename
```

By specifying a path after the filename, you can ensure the file is saved to a particular remote path.

One useful thing to remember is that any command preceded by an exclamation mark (!, called a *bang* in Linux-speak) is executed on the local machine as a shell command. So, if you wanted to remove a file or folder on the local machine, you could type this:

```
!rm -rf filename
```

Typing a bang symbol on its own starts a shell session on the local machine, so you can perform even more tasks. When you're finished, type exit to return to the sftp program.

For a list of popular sftp commands, see Table 34-1.

Table 34-1. *Common sftp Commands*

Command	Function
cd	Change the remote directory
lcd	Change the local directory
get	Download the specified file
ls	List the remote directory
lls	List the local directory
mkdir	Create a directory on the remote machine
lmkdir	Create a directory on the local machine
put	Upload the specified file to the remote machine
pwd	Print the current remote directory
rmdir	Delete the remote directory
rm	Delete the remote file
exit	Quit sftp
!command	Execute the specified command on the local machine
!	Start a temporary local shell session (type exit to return to sftp)
help	Show a list of commands

CLIENTS AND SERVERS

This chapter refers to *servers* and *clients*, two components of an end-to-end network connection.

A *server* is a computer program that offers resources that other computers can access, usually across a local area network or the Internet. For example, many office workplaces have file servers, which are simply computers that store files that many desktop computers can access. You might also have heard of web servers, which are the computers that store web sites so that all the computers on the Internet can connect and thereby access the sites.

Clients are the computers that connect to the server. In the case of a web server, all the computers that connect to view the web site can technically be referred to as clients. In the case of a file server, all the computers that connect to download or upload files are clients.

In the context of remote computing, the server is the software running on the remote computer that allows others to connect and take control of the system. The computer that connects in order to take control is referred to as the client.

Unfortunately, it gets a little confusing when we consider the X server, the graphical subsystem under Linux. In this context, the terms are turned around. In the case of an X server, the server runs on the *local* machine, and the programs that use it (appear on the screen) are referred to as clients. These client applications can run on the local machine alongside the server program, and this is the usual way of working for stand-alone computers. However, client programs can also be run on computers across the local area network or even the Internet; in which case, they can be told to connect to the server on the local machine.

In this chapter's coverage of how to use ssh so that graphical applications running a remote computer appear on the screen of a local machine, the applications are clients of the X server running on the local machine.

Accessing GUI Applications Remotely

So far, we've looked at connecting to a remote machine using tools that let you establish command-line shell sessions. But SUSE Linux is based around the graphical desktop. So, is there any way of running, say, a Nautilus file browser window so you can manipulate files on the remote machine? Yes!

The graphical subsystem of Linux, X, is designed to work across a network. In fact, if you run Linux on your desktop PC, X still works via a loopback network within your machine (meaning that network commands are addressed to the very same machine on which they originated). Because of this, it's possible to make programs on a remote machine run on a local machine's X server. The actual work of running the application is handled by the *remote* machine, but the work of drawing the graphics is handled by the *local* machine.

■**Caution** X connections across a network can be a little slow and certainly not as snappy as running the same application on the local machine. This lag can become irritating after a while.

Running X Applications Across a Remote Connection

Unfortunately, X server communications aren't normally encrypted, so if one machine were to simply connect to an X server over a network (or even the Internet), the data transfer would be unencrypted and open to eavesdroppers. But ssh once again comes to the rescue.

You can configure ssh so that X applications on the remote computer can be run on the local machine, with the data sent through the ssh connection. Doing so is simple. Log in to the remote machine using ssh and start a command-line session, but also specify the -X flag:

```
ssh -X username@IP_address
```

When you're logged in, you can simply start any graphical application by typing its name as usual. For example, you could start the Nautilus file browser by typing nautilus, or open GNOME Calculator by typing gnome-calculator. The program will then appear on the screen of the local machine, rather than on the remote machine, as shown in Figure 34-2.

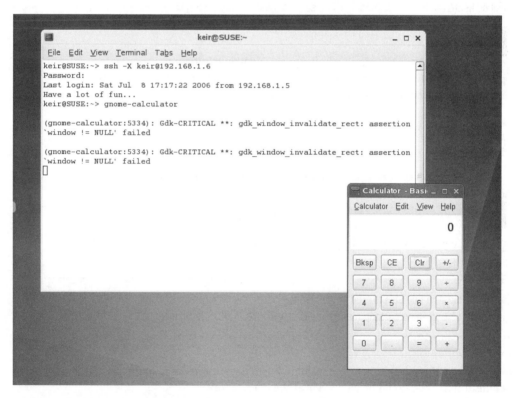

Figure 34-2. *Although the calculator application appears on the local computer's display, it's actually running on the remote machine.*

Using X across the Internet or even a local network isn't very fast, and you can expect delays when you open menus or if the screen must be redrawn frequently. However, it can prove very useful.

Running a Desktop Environment Across a Remote X Connection

It's even possible to run the entire GNOME and KDE desktops across an ssh connection. In other words, you can access the desktop environment of a remote computer as if you were sitting in front of it.

You can do this by starting a stripped-down X server shell on the local computer, then logging in via ssh, and then initiating the desktop on the remote computer. As before, all the applications will run on the remote computer but will be rendered on the local machine.

■**Note** If the remote computer is already running a desktop, yours will run in addition to it. Anyone using the remote computer won't be aware of what you're doing, unless they specifically look for evidence. However, X doesn't take care of sound, so any sounds normally made during GNOME startup, such as the jingle, will be heard on the remote machine. The same applies for any error noises, such as beeps.

On the local machine from which you would like to initiate the connection, close all open programs, and then exit the X server by switching to run level 3. To do this, open a GNOME Terminal or Konsole window and type the following:

```
su -
[Enter root password]
init 3
```

At the command prompt, log in using your username and password. Then type the following:

```
xinit
```

This will start a rudimentary X session, complete with an xterm shell window.

■**Note** You won't be able to type in the xterm window unless your mouse cursor is within its window. This is a quirk of X when no desktop manager, such as GNOME or KDE, is running.

You can then use the ssh command to log in to your remote machine, specifying that X communications should be allowed over the connection:

```
ssh -X username@IP_address
```

And then type the following to start a GNOME session:

```
gnome-session
```

Alternatively, if you want to start a KDE session, type the following:

```
startkde
```

After a few seconds, the remote computer's desktop will appear. Make sure you don't close the original xterm window, because this owns the `gnome-session` and `startkde` processes, so closing it would kill the desktop.

Once again, the remote desktop will be fairly slow to respond to mouse clicks and keyboard strokes, but it should be usable.

If you intend to do this regularly, it's worth booting into run level 3, which is text only. This will save you the hassle of killing a GUI each time. To do this, you'll need to modify the `/etc/inittab` file. The following commands will switch you to the root user, which is necessary to edit the file, and then load it into the Gedit text editor under GNOME:

```
su -
[Enter root password]
gedit /etc/inittab
```

Alternatively, under KDE, you can type the following to load the file into the Kate text editor:

```
su -
[Enter root password]
kate /etc/inittab
```

Look for the line that begins `id:5:initdefault:` and change it so it reads `id:3:initdefault:`. Then save the file and reboot.

Once you've logged in at the command prompt, you'll have the choice of either starting the X server shell for a remote connection, as described earlier, or starting your usual desktop environment on the local machine, by typing `startx`.

Accessing Remote Computers via VNC

SUSE Linux includes built-in Virtual Network Computing (VNC) components. Once activated, these allow users of practically any computer and operating system to access the SUSE Linux desktop, provided the remote computer has the correct client software installed. The good news is that VNC is open source, and the client software is therefore available free of charge.

In addition to client software, VNC servers are also available for practically all operating systems, which means that SUSE Linux can be used to control a Windows or Apple Macintosh computer, for example. (Using VNC to access a remote Windows machine is described in the "Connecting to Other Windows Computers" section later in this chapter.)

VNC is best described as remote control software. Unlike the remote X sessions described in the previous section, VNC sends actual images of the remote desktop across the network to the client computer.

This approach has some drawbacks. If you access a Windows computer's desktop using VNC, anyone standing in front of the remote computer will see you take control of the mouse, and will witness whatever happens on screen. Effectively, the desktop is shared.

Accessing a remote Linux computer running VNC is slightly different than accessing a Windows computer. In this case, an additional X session is started in the background, in addition to the one that might already be running on the remote computer, and this is transmitted via VNC. So the outcome is very much like accessing a remote computer's desktop via an X session, as described in the previous section. No one will be aware you're connected unless they specifically investigate.

Note Although the outcome of remote access with an X session and with VNC is the same, remember that radically different technologies are being used. With a remote X session, although the desktop applications run on the remote computer, the graphical interface is drawn by the local computer. In other words, the buttons, windows, and so on are rendered on the local computer in response to prompting by the remote computer. With a VNC session, the desktop applications run on the remote computer *and* the graphical interface is rendered on the remote computer too. However, images of it are passed to the client, and this is what you see in the VNC client window.

The biggest drawbacks of using VNC relate to security. The actual VNC data isn't sent encrypted. This means that it could be open to eavesdroppers while being transferred across the network/Internet.

Note There are some secure implementations of VNC, such as UltraVNC (`www.ultravnc.com`), but these aren't implemented by default under SUSE Linux.

Before you can use VNC to access a remote computer, you need to activate VNC on the computer you wish to access. Then you can connect to that remote computer using the GNOME or KDE desktop, a web browser, or even a Windows computer (after installing the VNC software on it). The following sections outline how to set up a SUSE Linux computer so it can be accessed using another computer in a remote location, and then how to connect to this computer.

The following items apply to the techniques described in the following sections:

- It's not a good idea to access a VNC session on a remote desktop if the remote computer is already logged in under the same username you intend to use. File corruption could result if two separate users attempt to access the same file. To avoid this problem, before you connect to the remote computer, make sure the user account you wish to use has been logged out on the remote computer.

- After connecting to the remote machine, you can select alternative desktop environments from the Session menu. For example, if the remote computer has both KDE and GNOME installed, you can choose between them.

Activating Remote Administration (VNC) on the Remote Computer

SUSE Linux doesn't make explicit reference to VNC. Instead, it refers to the technology as Remote Administration, and this can be activated using YaST, as follows:

1. Start YaST. Under GNOME, click Desktop ➤ YaST. Under KDE, click K menu ➤ System ➤ YaST. Enter your root password when prompted.

2. In the YaST window, click the Network Services icon on the left, and then click the Remote Administration icon on the right.

3. In the Remote Administration window, click the Allow Remote Administration radio button. Additionally, put a check alongside Open Port in Firewall, as shown in Figure 34-3 (otherwise, it will be impossible for computers across the network or Internet to connect to your computer). Then click Finish.

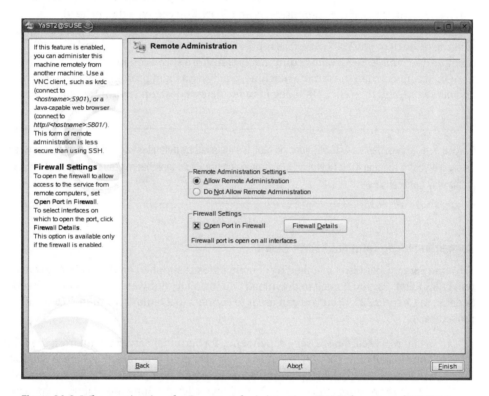

Figure 34-3. *When activating the Remote Administration (VNC) function of SUSE Linux, it's necessary to open the firewall so incoming connections can get through.*

4. You'll see a dialog box stating that a system service needs to be manually restarted. However, it is sufficient to simply reboot the computer, so click OK in the dialog box, quit all open programs, and then reboot.

GNOME: Accessing a Remote SUSE Linux Computer

To access the remote SUSE Linux computer from a local computer running the GNOME desktop under SUSE Linux, two options are available. You can either use a command-line program to connect or use the Terminal Server Client program, which must be downloaded and installed separately.

Connecting from the Command Line

To connect from the command line, open a GNOME Terminal window (Applications ➤ System ➤ Terminal ➤ Gnome Terminal) and type the following:

```
vncviewer IP_address:1
```

You should replace *IP_address* with the IP address of the computer to which you want to connect. Alternatively, if the computer has an FQDN, you can type that instead.

The :1 part of the command refers to the VNC server number. If the remote computer is running more than one VNC server, as is possible, you could type :2, :3, and so on. But in this example, the remote SUSE Linux computer is running a single session.

Once connected to the remote machine, you'll see a login prompt. Type your username and password, and then click OK to log in to the default desktop environment.

■**Note** vncviewer isn't a GNOME-specific tool. It's installed by default on all SUSE Linux systems, so can be used if you're running KDE. However, KDE provides a graphical tool that makes direct use of vncviewer in this way unnecessary.

Connecting Using Terminal Server Client

Terminal Server Client isn't installed by default and isn't supplied on the SUSE Linux installation DVD-ROM. So, you'll need to download and install it. (Software installation is described in detail in Chapter 29.) Then you can use it to connect to a remote computer. Here's the procedure:

1. Install rdesktop, a necessary dependency for Terminal Server Client, from the SUSE Linux installation DVD-ROM. (rdesktop is also used to connect to remote Windows computers.) Click Desktop ➤ YaST and enter your root password when prompted. Select the Software icon on the left, and then click the Software Management icon on the right. In the next window, type rdesktop in the Search field and click the Search button. In the results list on the right, put a check alongside rdesktop. Then click the Accept button at the bottom right. Once the software has installed, click No in the dialog box asking if you want to install more software.

2. Download the Terminal Server Client software. Visit www.gnomepro.com/tsclient/ and choose to download the RPM file of the latest release. Save it to your /home directory.

■**Caution** Make sure that you don't download the src RPM file. You should download the RPM file with i386 in its filename.

---

3. Open a GNOME Terminal window (Applications ➤ System ➤ Terminal ➤ GNOME Terminal) and type the following (replace *filename.rpm* with the name of the file you downloaded, and replace *username* with your username):

```
su -
[Enter root password]
rpm -Uvh /home/username/filename.rpm
```

4. To start Terminal Server Client, click Applications ➤ Internet ➤ More Programs ➤ Terminal Server Client.

5. To connect to the remote SUSE Linux computer using Terminal Server Client, enter *IP_addresss*:1 in the Computer text box (replace *IP_address* with the address of the remote computer). Alternatively, if the remote computer has an FQDN, you can type that instead. The :1 part of the command refers to the VNC server number. If the remote computer were running more than one VNC server, as is possible, you could type :2, :3 and so on. But in this example, the remote SUSE Linux computer is running a single session. Select VNC from the Protocol drop-down list, as shown in Figure 34-4. You don't need to fill in the other text boxes. Click Connect to continue.

Figure 34-4. *Enter the address of the remote machine, followed by the VNC server number. There's no need to enter any other details.*

6. Once connected to the remote machine, you'll see a login prompt. Type the username and password *for the remote machine*, and then click OK to log in to the default desktop environment, such as GNOME or KDE.

KDE: Accessing a Remote SUSE Linux Computer

Under KDE, you can use the Krdc software to connect to the remote SUSE Linux computer, as follows:

1. Click K menu ➤ System ➤ Remote Access ➤ Krdc.

2. In the Address text box, type vnc:/*IP_address*:1. Replace *IP_address* with the address of the computer to which you wish to connect. Alternatively, if the remote computer has an FQDN, that can be used instead. The :1 part of the command refers to the VNC server number. If the remote computer were running more than one VNC server, as is possible, you could type :2, :3, and so on. But in this example, the remote SUSE Linux computer is running a single session.

3. The VNC Host Preferences dialog box will appear. Here, you can select the connection type, which refers to the quality of the on-screen graphics and the overall responsiveness of the connection. If you're connecting across a slower connection, such as the Internet (even if you have broadband), you should select Medium Quality or Low Quality. If you're connecting via a local area network, the High Quality setting will work fine. Click OK.

4. Once connected to the remote machine, you'll see a login prompt. Type your username and password, and then click OK to log in to the default desktop environment, such as GNOME or KDE.

The Krdc session takes over the entire screen, but adds a toolbar at the top, as shown in Figure 34-5. To disconnect from the remote session, simply click the red X icon.

Figure 34-5. *Krdc will default to full-screen display of the remote computer's desktop. The toolbar is at the top of the window.*

Accessing a Remote SUSE Linux Computer Using a Web Browser

Any web browser on any computer that has the Java Runtime Environment (http://java.sun.com) installed can access the remote SUSE Linux machine. Simply type the following address:

```
http://IP_address:5801
```

You should replace *IP_address* with the address of the remote computer. Alternatively, if the computer has an FQDN, you can use that instead. The :5801 part of the address refers to the port number on the remote computer. When the VNC server is activated, the remote computer listens on port 5801. Note that the last digit refers to the number of the VNC server. If you have more than one server activated, then this number will increase—:5802, :5803, and so on. However, in this example, only one VNC server is running.

There's no need to type a password at the prompt. Simply click OK, and then you'll see a login prompt. Enter your username and password, and then click OK to log in to the default desktop environment, such as GNOME or KDE.

Accessing a Remote SUSE Linux Computer Using Windows

A Windows computer that has VNC software installed can also connect to the SUSE Linux desktop. TightVNC is one of the best variations of VNC around. Here's how to install and use it:

1. Go to www.tightvnc.com and download the self-installing package for Windows. During installation, you'll be asked which components of TightVNC you want to install. If you only want to connect to remote computers running VNC, you can remove the check from the box alongside the TightVNC Server entry in the list.

2. Once the software is installed, run the VNC Viewer program by clicking Start ➤ Programs ➤ TightVNC ➤ TightVNC Viewer.

■**Note** Three variations of the TightVNC Viewer program are available: Best Compression, Fast Compression, and Listen Mode. I suggest you use the Fast Compression mode, which offers the best trade-off of data speeds and visual quality.

---

3. When the program starts, enter *IP_address*:1 in the Connection Details dialog box. Replace *IP_address* with the address of the computer to which you wish to connect. Alternatively, if the remote computer has an FQDN, that can be used instead. The :1 part of the command refers to the VNC server number. If the remote computer were running more than one VNC server, as is possible, you could type :2, :3, and so on. But in this example, the remote SUSE Linux computer is running a single session. Click OK to connect.

4. Once connected to the remote machine, you'll see a login prompt. Enter your username and password, and then click OK to log in to the default desktop environment, such as GNOME or KDE.

Connecting to Remote Windows Computers

Windows XP or Windows 2000 computers use Remote Desktop Protocol (RDP), which allows other computers to connect to them and take control of their desktop. Some versions of Windows NT support RDP; check to see if Microsoft Terminal Services is installed on the computer. Windows Server products will also likely support RDP. Unfortunately, Windows XP Home, Me, 98, and 95 don't support RDP connections, which means that they aren't able to run an RDP server and allow other computers to access their desktops.

To connect to Windows XP or 2000 computers running RDP, you can use either the Krdc program, under KDE, or the Terminal Server Client, under GNOME. Additionally, the same VNC server technology used under SUSE Linux for remote access can be used under Windows.

Allowing RDP Connections

The Windows computer will need be configured to allow incoming RDP connections. To configure it, right-click My Computer, select Properties, click the Remote tab, and check Allow Users to Connect Remotely to This Computer.

The Windows computer to which you want to connect may also need to be updated with the latest service packs, particularly in the case of a Windows 2000 computer.

■**Caution** If you haven't set a password for your user account on the Windows machine, you won't be able to log in. This is a quirk of the Windows XP RDP system. The solution is simple: use the User Accounts applet within the Windows Control Panel to assign yourself a password.

GNOME: Connecting to Windows Using Terminal Server Client

Terminal Server Client is a graphical front-end to the rdesktop software that allows users to connect to Windows 2000 and XP computers that have RDP activated. Terminal Server Client isn't installed by default and isn't supplied on the SUSE Linux installation DVD-ROM, so you'll need to download and install it. (Software installation is described in detail in Chapter 29.) Then you can use it to connect to a remote Windows computer.

■**Note** You can skip steps 1 through 3 if you've already installed Terminal Server Client by following the instructions in the "GNOME: Accessing a Remote SUSE Linux Computer" section earlier in this chapter.

Follow these steps:

1. Install rdesktop, a necessary dependency for Terminal Server Client, from the SUSE Linux installation DVD-ROM. Click Desktop ➤ YaST and enter your root password when prompted. Select the Software icon on the left, and then click the Software Management icon on the right. In the next window, type rdesktop in the Search field and click the Search button. In the results list on the right, put a check alongside rdesktop.

Then click the Accept button at the bottom right. Once the software has installed, click No in the dialog box asking if you want to install more software.

2. Download the Terminal Server Client software. Visit www.gnomepro.com/tsclient/ and choose to download the RPM file of the latest release. Save it to your /home directory.

Caution Make sure that you don't download the src RPM file. You should download the RPM file with i386 in its filename.

---

3. Open a GNOME Terminal window (Applications ➤ System ➤ Terminal ➤ GNOME Terminal) and type the following (replace *filename.rpm* with the name of the file you downloaded, and replace *username* with your username):

```
su -
[Enter root password]
rpm -Uvh /home/username/filename.rpm
```

4. To start Terminal Server Client, click Applications ➤ Internet ➤ More Programs ➤ Terminal Server Client.

5. In the Computer text box, type either the IP address of the machine or its FQDN (if applicable). You don't need to enter the username, password, or any other details. Click Connect to continue.

6. You should see a new window with a Windows login prompt. Log in to Windows using your username and password. Eventually, you'll see the Windows desktop, as shown in Figure 34-6 (Windows XP Professional in this example).

Figure 34-6. *You can access remote Windows XP Professional machines using RDP and the Terminal Server Client program.*

If this is the first time you've accessed the Windows computer over an RDP connection, you might be wondering why the graphics look so bad. This is because they're heavily compressed in order to transmit efficiently across networks.

■**Note** When logging in via RDP, you will be literally sharing the same desktop as anyone who might be standing in front of the computer. Because of this, for privacy and security, the desktop on the remote Windows computer is blanked when you log in.

KDE: Connecting to Windows Using Krdc

With the KDE desktop, you can use Krdc to connect to Windows machines, as follows:

1. To start Krdc, click K menu ➤ System ➤ Remote Access.

2. In the Remote Desktop text box, type rdp:/*IP_address*. Replace *IP_address* with the IP address of the machine to which you want to connect.

3. You'll see a dialog box asking you to set the desktop resolution, color depth, and keyboard language. Simply select from the drop-down lists. In general, lower desktop resolution and color depth are better, because less data will be transferred across the network.

4. A Windows username and password box will appear. Enter the username and password for the Windows computer. Then the Windows desktop will appear.

KDE DESKTOP SHARING

KDE offers Krfb, also known as KDE Desktop Sharing, which allows others to connect to the currently running desktop and take control. Krfb is almost exactly the same as the Remote Assistance feature of Windows XP, which allows users to send out e-mail invitations for help and get responses from others.

As with the Remote Administration function of SUSE Linux, KDE Desktop Sharing uses VNC. However, Krfb isn't designed for remote access. Instead, it's designed to allow a user to get external help or to work collaboratively with another person.

To activate Krfb, click K menu ➤ System ➤ Remote Access ➤ Krfb. To invite someone to connect, click the Invite via Email button. This will start the default e-mail client, which will be KMail, unless you've changed it. Therefore, unless KMail is configured with a mail account, Krfb won't work. Chapter 8 describes how to set up KMail.

The e-mail you send will contain details of the your computer's IP address, including a special username and password for VNC. This is all the individual receiving the mail will need to be able to connect via VNC client software or even by using a web browser that has the Java Runtime Environment installed.

There are obvious risks to sending an e-mail message across the Internet because this vital information will be sent in plain text. It could therefore be intercepted along the way, giving a stranger all the information he needs to control your computer. Therefore, you should be careful when sending your invitations.

Each invitation lasts for an hour before it expires. You can manually prune the list of invitations by clicking the Manage Invitations button.

Connecting to Other Windows Computers

You can download a VNC server for just about any operating system—Windows, Linux, and Mac OS X are supported. A VNC server will run on any Windows computer, from 95 upward. Once it's installed, you can then use the Terminal Server Client or Krdc program to connect to that computer's remote desktop, as described earlier in the chapter.

Using a VNC server under Windows isn't perfect. It's fairly insecure because, by default, the screen isn't blanked on the remote computer, so anyone in front of the computer will be able to see what you're doing. But if you're prepared to accept this, you'll be pleased to hear that setting up the VNC server on the Windows machine is easy.

TightVNC, available from `www.tightvnc.com`, is one of the best VNC products around. You should download the self-installing package for Windows. During installation, you'll be asked if you want to register TightVNC as a system service. Click the check box alongside this option. This will activate the VNC server every time the computer starts, thus making it remotely accessible.

Once the program has installed, the server configuration program will appear. You should change the password by replacing the default in the Password field. If you fail to do this, the VNC server will refuse connections.

After the server is installed, follow the instructions in the "Accessing a Remote Computer via VNC" section of this chapter to connect to the Windows machine. Simply substitute the details of the SUSE Linux remote computer with those of the remote Windows computer.

Summary

In this chapter, we looked at how you can access your SUSE Linux computer remotely across the Internet or a local area network connection. We examined how you can access the computer as if you were sitting in front of it, using the `ssh` program. This allows you to start a command-line prompt and even run GUI programs on the remote computer.

In addition, we discussed how you can transfer files using the `sftp` and `scp` programs. Then we looked at how to use the VNC, Terminal Server Client and Krdc tools to access the desktop of remote SUSE Linux and Windows computers.

◼◼◼
Glossary of Linux Terms

This appendix provides brief explanations of common terms used in the Linux and Unix environments. These include technical terms, as well as conventions used within the Linux community. Due to space limitations, this glossary is somewhat selective, but still should prove a lasting reference as well as a helpful guide for those new to Linux.

Cross-referenced terms are highlighted in italics.

Symbols

.

Symbol that, in the context of file management, refers to the current directory.

..

Symbol that, in the context of file management, refers to the parent directory of that currently being browsed.

/

Symbol that, in the context of file management, refers to the *root* of the file system; also separates directories in a path listing.

~

Symbol that, in the context of file management, refers to a user's home directory.

|

Pipe symbol; used at the *command prompt* to *pipe* output from one *command* to another.

>

Symbol that, when used at the *command prompt*, indicates output should *redirect* into a file.

<

Symbol that, when used at the *command prompt*, indicates a *command* should accept input from a file (see *redirect*).

#

Symbol that, when it appears on the *command prompt*, usually indicates the user is currently logged in as *root*.

$

Symbol that, when it appears on the command prompt, usually indicates the user is currently logged in as an ordinary user. *SUSE Linux* is different in that a > symbol indicates the same thing; some versions of *Linux/Unix* use %.

?

Wildcard character indicating that any character can be substituted in its place.

*

Wildcard character indicating that zero or more characters can appear in its place.

*nix

Popular but unofficial way of describing the family tree that comprises *Unix* and its various clones, such as *Linux* and *Minix*.

A

administrator

Another word for either the *root* user or one who has adopted that user's powers temporarily.

AIX

IBM's *proprietary* form of *Unix* that runs on the company's proprietary hardware, as well as *commodity* hardware based around AMD and Intel processors. Nowadays, IBM is slowly deprecating AIX in favor of *Linux*.

alias

Method of creating a user-defined *command* that, when typed, causes another command to be run or a *string* to be expanded.

Apache

Popular *open source* web server software that runs on *Unix*, *Linux*, and other operating system platforms. Considered responsible in part for the rise in popularity of Linux in the late 1990s.

applet

Small program that, in the context of the *SUSE Linux* desktop, runs as part of a larger program and offers functions that complement the main program. The *KDE* and *GNOME* desktops incorporate several applets.

archive

Any file containing a collection of smaller files, compressed or otherwise (see also *tar*).

B

BASH

Bourne Again SHell. The most common *shell* interpreter used under *Linux* and offered as default on many Linux systems.

binary executable

Another way of referring to a program that has been compiled so that it is ready for general use. See also *compile*.

block device

How the *Linux kernel* communicates with a *device* that sends and receives blocks of data; usually a hard disk or removable storage device. See also *character device*.

BSD Unix

Berkeley Software Distribution Unix; form of *Unix* partially based on the original Unix *source code* but also incorporating recent developments. BSD is *open source* and free for all to use and share with practically no restrictions. There are various forms of BSD Unix, such as FreeBSD, NetBSD, and OpenBSD. BSD doesn't use the *Linux kernel*, but it runs many of the same programs. Some of the programs offered within the Linux operating system come from BSD.

bzip2

Form of file compression. Together with the older and less-efficient *gzip*, it is a popular form of file compression under *Linux* and the equivalent to Zip compression under Windows. Files employing bzip compression are usually given a `.bz2` file extension. See also *tar*.

C

C

Programming language in which much of the *Linux kernel* is written, as were later versions of *Unix* before it. C was created by some of the same people who created Unix, and its development mirrors that of Unix.

C++

Object-oriented programming language; originally designed to be an enhancement to *C*, but now seen as a popular alternative.

C#

Modern programming language, which uses similar syntax to *C*, created by Microsoft and re-created on *Linux* via the Mono project.

character device

How Linux refers to a *device* that sends/receives data asynchronously. For various technical reasons, this typically refers to the *terminal* display. See also *block device.*

checksum

Mathematical process that can be applied to a file or other data to create a unique number relative to the contents of that file. If the file is modified, the checksum will change, usually indicating that the file in question has failed to download correctly or has been modified in some way. The most common type of checksum program used under *Linux* is *md5sum.*

client

Shorthand referring to a computer that connects to a *server.*

closed source

The reverse of *open source*; the *source code* is not available for others to see, share, or modify. See also *proprietary.*

code

See *source code.*

command

Input typed at the *shell* that performs a specific task, usually related to administration of the system and/or the manipulation of files.

command-line prompt

See *shell.*

commodity

In the context of hardware, describes PC hardware usually based around Intel or AMD processors that can be bought off the shelf and used to create sophisticated computer systems (as opposed to buying specially designed hardware). One reason for *Linux*'s success is its ability to use commodity hardware.

community

The general term for the millions of *Linux* users worldwide, regardless of what they use Linux for or their individual backgrounds. By using Linux, you automatically become part of the community.

compile

The practice of creating a binary file from *source code*, usually achieved using the `./configure`, `make`, `make install` series of commands and scripts.

config file

Configuration file; any file that contains the list of settings for a program. Sometimes it's necessary to edit config files by hand using programs like *vi* or *emacs,* but often the program itself will write its config file according to the settings you choose.

copyleft

The legal principle of protecting the right to share a creative work, such as a computer program, using a legally binding license. Copyleft also ensures future iterations of the work are covered in the same way.

cracker

Someone who breaks into computer systems to steal data or cause damage. The term is not necessarily linked to *Linux* or *Unix* but was created by the *community* to combat the widespread use of hacker in this sense. The word *hacker* has traditionally defined someone who merely administers, programs, and generally enjoys computers.

cron

Background *service* that schedules tasks to occur at certain times. It relies on the crontab file.

CUPS

Common Unix Printing System; set of programs that work in the background to handle printing under *Unix* and *Linux.*

curses

Library that lets software present a semigraphical interface at the *shell*, complete with menu systems and simple mouse control (if configured). The version of curses used under *Linux* and *Unix* is called ncurses.

CVS

Concurrent Versioning System; application that allows the latest version of software packages to be distributed over the Internet to developers and other interested parties.

D

daemon

See *service.*

Debian

Voluntary organization that produces *distributions* of *Free Software* operating systems, including *Linux*.

dependency

A way of referring to system files that a program requires in order to run. If the dependencies are not present during program installation, a program might refuse to install.

device

Linux shorthand describing something on your system that provides a function for the user or that the system requires in order to run. This usually refers to hardware, but it can also describe a virtual device that is created to provide access to a particular Linux function.

directory

What Windows refers to as a folder; areas on a hard disk in which files can be stored and organized.

distribution

A collection of software making up the *Linux* operating system; also known as a distro. The software is usually compiled by either a company or organization. A distribution is designed to be easy to install, administer, and use by virtue of it being an integrated whole. Examples include SUSE Linux, Red Hat, and Ubuntu.

distro

Shorthand for *distribution*.

documentation

Another way of describing written guides or instructions; can refer to online sources of help as well as actual printed documentation.

E

emacs

Seminal text editor and pseudo-*shell* beloved by *Unix* aficionados; can be used for programming tasks, simple word processing, and much more. This editor has cultural significance as one of the core pieces of software offered by the *GNU Project*. Emacs was originally developed principally by *Stallman, Richard*. See also *vi*.

environment

Shorthand referring to a user's unique *Linux* configuration, such as variables that tell the *shell* where programs are located.

F

FAT32

File Allocation Table 32-bits; file system offered by Windows 98, Me, 2000, and XP. *Linux* can both read and write to FAT32 file systems. See also *NTFS* and *VFAT*.

Firefox

Web browser program offered under SUSE Linux and produced by the *Mozilla Foundation*.

FLOSS

Free, Libre, or Open Source Software; used within the *community* to describe all software or technology that, broadly speaking, adheres to the ethical approach of *open source* software and/or *Free Software*, as well as its legal guidelines.

FOSS

Free or Open Source Software; alternative term for *FLOSS*.

free

When used to describe software or associated areas of technology, "free" indicates that the project abides by the ethical (if not legal) guidelines laid down by the *GNU Project*. It doesn't indicate that the software is free in a monetary sense; its meaning is quite different from "freeware."

Free Software

Software in which the *source code*—the original listing created by the programmer—is available for all to see, share, study, and adapt to their own needs. This differs from the concept of *open source* because the right of others to further modify the code is guaranteed via the *GPL* software license (or a compatible license). For various reasons, Free Software sometimes does not include the source code (although the software can still be legally decompiled), but this is rare.

G

GCC

GNU Compiler Collection; programs used when creating *binary executable* files from *source code*.

GID

Group ID; numbering system used by the operating system to refer to a *group*.

GIMP

GNU Image Manipulation Program; high-powered image-editing program that runs under *Linux*, *Unix*, Windows, and other operating systems. Often preceded by the definite article: "The GIMP."

GNOME

GNU Network Object Model Environment; a *GUI*-based desktop environment offered by *SUSE Linux*, as well as several other *distributions*. It uses the GTK+ *libraries*. See also *KDE*.

GNU

GNU's Not Unix; see the *GNU Project, The*.

GNU/Linux

Another name for the operating system referred to as *Linux*. The name GNU/Linux gives credit to the vast quantity of the *GNU Project* software that is added to the *Linux kernel* within a *distribution* to make a complete operating system. As such, GNU/Linux is the preferred term of many *Free Software* advocates.

GNU Project

Organization created by *Stallman, Richard* in order to further the aims of *Free Software* and create the body of software comprising the *GNU* operating system.

GNU Public License

Software license principally created by *Stallman, Richard* in order to protect software *source code* against *proprietary* interests and ensure that it will always be shared. It does this by insisting that any source code covered by the GNU Public License (GPL) must remain licensed under the GPL, even after it has been modified or added to by others. The *Linux kernel*, as well as much of the software that runs on it, uses the GPL.

GPL

See *GNU Public License*.

grep

Global Regular Expression Print; powerful *shell command* that lets you search a file or other form of input using *regular expressions*. Because of the ubiquity of the grep program, many *Linux* and *Unix* users refer to searching as "grepping." To "grep a file" is to search through it for a *string*.

group

Collection of users under one heading (group name) to facilitate system administration.

GRUB

GRand Unified Bootloader; boot manager program that offers a menu from which you can choose which operating system you wish to boot. It's needed to load the *kernel* program and thereby initiate the *Linux* boot procedure.

GUI

Graphical user interface; describes the software that provides a graphical system to display data and let you control your PC (usually via a mouse).

guru

One who is experienced and knowledgeable about *Linux/Unix* and is willing to share his or her knowledge with others. In a perfect world, every *newbie* would have his or her own guru.

gzip

One of the two preferred forms of file compression used under *Linux*. Files employing gzip compression usually have a `.gz` file extension. See also *bzip2*.

H

hack

Ingenious and/or extremely efficient solution to a problem, particularly within the programming world.

hacker

Term used within the *community* to describe anyone who enjoys computers and possesses some skill therein, either in a professional capacity or as a hobby. This term is distinct from connotations of maliciously breaking into computers propagated by the media. See also *cracker*.

host

Shorthand referring to any computer that acts as a *server* to another computer. See also *client*.

HP-UX

Hewlett-Packard's *proprietary* form of *Unix* designed to work on its own hardware platform.

Hurd

Kernel being developed by the *GNU Project*. It's not associated with the *Linux* kernel in any way.

I

info page

Source of *documentation* accessible from the *shell*; an alternative to the more-established *man page* system. Also known as Texinfo.

init

The program that is automatically run after the *kernel* has finished loading, and therefore early in the boot procedure. It's responsible for effectively starting the operating system.

init.d

Collection of startup *scripts* that make up the components of a *run level*. Under *SUSE Linux*, these are found at /etc/init.d/. *Symbolic links* to selected init.d scripts are contained in folders within /etc/init.d that are named after *run level* numbers, such as rc0.d, rc1.d, rc2.d, and so on.

initrd

Initial RAM disk; system used by the *Linux kernel* to load *modules* that are essential for the kernel to be able to boot, such as disk controllers.

inode

Part of the usually invisible file system structure that describes a file, such as its ownership permissions or file size.

ipchains

Now deprecated component of version 2.2 of the *Linux kernel* that allows the creation of network security setups, such as firewalls or port-forwarding arrangements. Note that some *distributions* still prefer to use ipchains. See also *iptables*.

iptables

Component of versions 2.4 and 2.6 of the *Linux* kernel that allows powerful network security setups. Chiefly used in the creation of firewalls, but can be used for more elementary arrangements such as network address translation (NAT) routers.

J

job

How the *BASH shell* refers to a running program in order to facilitate administration by the user.

journaling

File system technology in which integrity is maintained via the logging of disk writes.

K

KDE

K desktop environment; *GUI* and set of additional programs used on various *distributions*, and is available under SUSE Linux. See also *GNOME*.

kernel

Essential but ordinarily invisible set of programs that run the computer's hardware and provide a platform on which to run software. In the *Linux* operating system, the kernel is also called Linux, after its creator, *Torvalds, Linus*.

kernel panic

Error message that appears when the *kernel* program in *Linux* cannot continue to work. In other words, a polite way of indicating a crash or, more often, a problem arising from user misconfiguration. This is most often seen when booting up after making incorrect changes to the system.

kludge

Community slang describing an inelegant way of making something work, usually not in a way that is generally accepted as being correct. Pronounced "kloodge."

L

LAMP

Acronym describing a series of programs that work together to provide a complete *Linux*-based web-hosting environment. Stands for *Linux*, *Apache*, *MySQL*, and Perl, PHP or Python (the last three in the list are scripting languages; see *script*).

LGPL

Lesser GPL; version of the *GNU Public License* (GPL) in which some use restrictions are slackened at the expense of various freedoms laid down by the main GPL. The LGPL is mostly used for *library* files.

library

General term referring to code that programs need to run and that, once in memory, is frequently accessed by many programs (leading to the phrase "shared library"). The most common and vital library is glibc (GNU C Library), created by the *GNU Project* and the fundamental building block without which *Linux* could not operate. *GNOME* relies on the GTK+ libraries, among others.

Libzypp

A *package management system* used to handle the administration of software *packages* under *SUSE Linux*. Libzypp works in conjunction with *RPM*. Libzypp manages *dependency* issues and relies on the RPM system to take care of the actual installation.

link

File system method of assigning additional filenames to a file; also known as a "hard link." See also *symbolic link*.

Linux

You mean you don't know by now? Linux is what this book is all about. It is a *kernel* program created by *Torvalds, Linus* in 1991 to provide an inexpensive operating system for his computer, along with other components. These days, Linux is used to describe the entire operating system discussed in this book, although many argue (perhaps quite rightly) that this is inaccurate, and use the term *GNU/Linux* instead.

local

Shorthand referring to the user's PC or a device directly attached to it (as opposed to *remote*).

localhost

Network name used internally by *Linux* and software to refer to the *local* computer, distinct from the network.

M

md5sum

Form of *checksum* software used commonly under Linux; utilizes the Message-Digest 5 (MD5) algorithm technology.

man page

Documentation accessible from the *shell* that describes a *command* and how it should be used.

Minix

Operating system that is a rough clone of *Unix*, created by Professor Andrew Tanenbaum. It was the inspiration for *Linux*.

module

Program code that can be inserted or removed from the *kernel* in order to support particular pieces of hardware or provide certain kernel functions. Drivers under Windows perform the same function.

mount

To add a file system so that it is integrated (and therefore accessible) within the main file system; applies to external file systems, such as those available across networks, as well as those on the *local* PC, such as the hard disk or CD/DVD-ROMs.

Mozilla Foundation

Organization founded by Netscape to create *open source* Internet software, such as web browsers and e-mail clients; originally based on the Netscape *source code*. At the time of writing, it produces the *Firefox* and Camino web browsers, the Thunderbird e-mail and Usenet client, the Bugzilla bug-tracking software, as well as other programs.

MySQL

Popular and powerful *open source* database application. See also *LAMP*.

N

newbie

Term used to describe anyone who is new to *Linux* and therefore still learning the basics. It's not a derogatory term! See also *guru*.

NFS

Network File System; reliable and established method of sharing files, printers, and other resources across a network of *Unix*-based operating systems. See also *Samba*.

NTFS

NT File System; file system offered by Windows NT, 2000, and XP. It can be read by *Linux*, but usually writing is prohibited because it is considered unsafe. See also *FAT32*.

O

OpenOffice.org

Open source office suite project created with the continuing input of Sun Microsystems and based on code Sun contributed to the open source *community*. Its commercial release is in the form of Star Office (although Star Office has several *proprietary* components added).

open source

(1) Method and philosophy of developing software whereby the source code—the original listing created by the programmer—is available for all to see. Note that open source is not the same as Free Software; describing software as open source doesn't imply that the code can be shared or used by others (although this is often the case).

(2) A community of users or any project that adheres to open source values and/or practices.

openSUSE

Community project that creates distrbiutions of *Linux*, called openSUSE, as well as Linux software used within the openSUSE distribution. openSUSE differs from commercial versions of *SUSE Linux*, released by *Novell*, because it uses only open source software and cutting-edge versions of software packages. However, commercial releases of SUSE Linux are built on previous openSUSE releases, and the two distros are virtually identical in terms of underlying software components.

P

package

A file that contains software that can be installed on a computer. Typically, a package file includes the software itself, in either *source* or *binary* format, plus any documentation and also several scripts to aid installation of the software. The installation of packages is handled by a *package management system*.

package management system

Software subsystem designed to handle the administration of software *packages*, including installation, removal, dependencies, and cataloging. Two interconnected package management systems are used under SUSE Linux: *RPM* and *Libzypp*.

partition

Subdivision of a hard disk into which a file system can be installed.

PID

Process ID; the numbering system used to refer to a *process*.

pipe

Method of passing the output from one *command* to another for further processing. Piping is achieved within the *shell* by typing the | symbol.

POSIX

Portable Operating System Interface; various technical standards that define how *Unix*-like operating systems should operate and to which the *Linux* operating system attempts to adhere.

PPP

Point-to-Point Protocol; networking technology that allows data transfer across serial connections like telephone lines. In other words, it's the technology that lets you connect to your Internet service provider using a modem.

process

The way the system refers to the individual programs (or components of programs) running in memory.

proprietary

Effectively, software for which a software license must be acquired, usually for a fee. This usually means the *source code* is kept secret, but it can also indicate that the source code is available to view but not to incorporate into your own projects or share with others.

R

Red Hat

Well-known company that produces distributions of *Linux*.

redirect

To send the output of a *command* into a particular file. This also works the other way around: the contents of a particular file can be directed into a command. Redirection is achieved within the *shell* using the left and right angle brackets (< and >), respectively.

regex

See *regular expression*.

regular expression

Powerful and complex method of describing a search *string*, usually when searching with tools such as *grep* (although regular expressions are also used when programming). Regular expressions use various symbols as substitutes for characters or to indicate patterns.

remote

Indicates a computer or *service* that is available across a network, including but not limited to computers on the Internet (as opposed to *local*).

root

(1) The bottom of the *Linux* file system directory structure, usually indicated by a forward slash (/).

(2) The user on some versions of *Unix* or *Linux* who has control over all aspects of hardware, software, and the file system.

(3) Used to describe a user who temporarily takes on the powers of the root user (via the sudo command, for example).

RPM

Red Hat Package Manager; system used to install and administer programs under *SUSE Linux*, as well as *Red Hat* and some other *distributions*. An RPM file, which usually has an .rpm extension, contains either the *binary executable* files that make up the program, or the *source code*. In addition, it often contains several *scripts* that check the operating system for compatibility and that, whever necessary, configure the system after installation.

RTFM

Read the f***ing manual/*man page*; exclamation frequently used online when a *newbie* asks for help without having undertaken basic research.

run level

Describes the current operational mode of *Linux* (typically, the *services* that are running). Under *SUSE Linux*, run level 1 is single-user mode (a stripped-down system with minimal running services); run level 3 provides a *command-line prompt*; run level 5 provides a *GUI*; run level 6 is reboot mode (switching to it will cause the computer to terminate its processes and then reboot); run level 0 is shutdown mode (switching to it will cause the PC to shut down). You can switch between run levels using the init command as *root*.

S

Samba

Program that re-creates under *Unix* or *Linux* the Microsoft *SMB*-based system of sharing files, printers, and other computer resources across a network. It allows Linux to become a file or printer server for Linux and Windows computers, and also allows a Linux client to access a Windows-based server.

SaX2

SUSE Advanced X configuration tool, version 2; *GUI*-based software by which the keyboard, mouse, display, and other aspects of *X* can be configured.

scalable

Term describing the ability of a single computer program to meet diverse needs, regardless of the scale of the potential uses. The *Linux kernel* is described as being scalable because it can run supercomputers as well as handheld computers and home entertainment devices.

script

Form of computer program consisting of a series of *commands* in a text file. Most *shells* allow some form of scripting, and entire programming languages such as Perl are based around scripts. In the context of the *Linux* operating system, Shell scripts are usually created to perform trivial tasks or ones that frequently interact with the user. Shell scripts have the advantage that they can be frequently and easily modified. The Linux boot process relies on several complex scripts to configure essential system functions such as networking and the *GUI*. See also *init*.

server

(1) Type of computer designed to share data with other computers over a network.

(2) Software that runs on a computer and is designed to share data with other programs on the same PC or with other PCs across a network.

service

Background program that provides vital functions for the day-to-day running of *Linux*; also known as a *daemon*. Services are usually started when the computer boots up and as such are constituent parts of a *run level*.

shell

Broadly speaking, any program that creates an operating environment in which you can control your computer. The *GNOME* desktop can be seen as a shell, for example. However, it's more commonly understood within *Unix* and *Linux* circles as a program that lets you control the system using *command*s entered at the keyboard. In this context, the most common type of shell in use on Linux is *BASH*.

SMB

Server Message Block; network technology for sharing files, printers, and other resources. See also *Samba*.

Solaris

Form of *Unix* sold by Sun Microsystems; runs on *proprietary* hardware systems as well as on *commodity* systems based on Intel and AMD processors.

source code

The original program listing created by a programmer. Most programs that you download are precompiled—already turned into *binary executables* ready for general use—unless you specifically choose to download and *compile* the source code of a program yourself.

SSH

Secure SHell; program that lets you access a *Linux*/*Unix* computer across the Internet. SSH encrypts data sent and received across the *link*.

SSL

Secure Sockets Layer; form of network data transfer designed to encrypt information for security purposes. It's used online for certain web sites and also within *Linux* for certain types of secure data exchange.

Stallman, Richard M.

Legendary *hacker* who founded the *GNU Project* and created the concept of *copyleft*, as well as the software license that incorporates it: the *GNU Public License* (GPL). See also *Torvalds, Linus*.

standard error

Linux and *Unix* shorthand for the error output provided by a *command*.

standard input

Linux and *Unix* shorthand for the *device* usually used to provide input to the *shell*. For the majority of desktop PC users, this refers to the keyboard.

standard output

Linux and *Unix* shorthand for the *device* usually used to display output from a *command*. For the majority of desktop PC users, this refers to the screen.

string

A word, phrase, or sentence consisting of letters, numbers, or other characters that is used within a program and is often supplied by the user.

sudo

Program that runs under *Unix* and *Linux* by which ordinary users are temporarily afforded *administrator* rights.

SUSE

Company owned by Novell that produces its own *distribution* of *Linux*, which is called *SUSE Linux*. SUSE stands for Software und System Entwicklung, a German phrase that translates as software and system development.

SUSE Linux

The distribution of *Linux* produced by *Novell*. This differs from *openSUSE* in that SUSE Linux releases are usually sold commercially and sometimes include proprietary software. However, they are based on *openSUSE* releases and incorporate software developed by the openSUSE project.

SVG

Scalable Vector Graphics; vector graphics technology. SVG is actually an XML markup language designed to create 2D graphics, increasingly used for *Linux* desktop icons and web graphics.

swap

Area of the hard disk that the *Linux kernel* uses as a temporary memory storage area. Desktop or *server* Linux differs from Windows in that it usually requires a separate hard disk *partition* in which to store the swap file.

symbolic link

Type of file akin to a Windows shortcut. Accessing a symbolic link file routes the user to an actual file. See also *link*.

sysadmin

Systems administrator; a way of describing the person employed within a company to oversee the computer systems. In such an environment, the sysadmin usually is the *root* user of the various computers.

System V

Variant of *Unix* used as a foundation for modern forms of *proprietary* Unix.

T

tainted

Describes a *kernel* that is using *proprietary modules* in addition to *open source* modules. Can also refer to insecure software.

tar

Tape Archive; software able to combine several files into one larger file in order to back them up to a tape drive or simply transfer them across the Internet. Such files are usually indicated by a .tar file extension. Note that a tar file isn't necessarily compressed; the *bzip2* and *gzip* utilities must be used if this is desired.

TCP/IP

Transmission Control Protocol/Internet Protocol; standard protocol stack used by most modern operating systems to control and communicate across networks and also across the Internet.

terminal

Another word for *shell*.

TeX

Method and set of programs for typesetting complex documents. Invented prior to word processors and desktop publishing software, and now considered a specialized tool for laying out scientific texts. An updated version of the program called LaTeX is also available.

Torvalds, Linus

Finnish programmer who, in 1991, created the initial versions of the *Linux kernel*. Since then, he has taken advantage of an international network of volunteers and staff employed by various companies who help produce the kernel. Torvalds himself contributes and oversees the efforts.

tty

TeleTYpewriter; shorthand referring to underlying *Linux* virtual *devices* that allow programs and users to access the *kernel* and thereby run programs.

Tux

The name of the penguin cartoon character that is the *Linux* mascot. The original Tux graphic was drawn by Larry Ewing.

U

UID

User ID; numbering system used by the operating system to refer to a *user.*

Unix

Seminal operating system created as a research project in 1969 by Kenneth Thompson and Dennis Ritchie at Bell Labs (later AT&T). Because it was initially possible to purchase the *source code* for a fee, subsequent revisions were enhanced by a variety of organizations and went on to run many mainframe and minicomputer systems throughout the 1980s, 1990s, and up to the present. Nowadays, Unix is fragmented and exists in a variety of different versions. Perhaps most popular is its *open source* rendition, *BSD Unix,* which has seen many developments since the source code was first released. This means that BSD Unix no longer exists but has instead diversified into a number of separate projects. *Proprietary* versions are also available, including *Solaris, HP-UX,* and *AIX.*

user

The way the operating system refers to anyone who accesses its resources. A user must first have a user account set up, effectively giving that user his or her own private space on the system. In addition to actual human users, an average *Linux* system has many other user accounts created to let programs and *services* go about their business. These are usually not seen by human users.

V

variable

A changeable value that stores a certain data type (such as a number, date, or *string*), remembering it for future reference by the system or *script* by which it is defined. Variables defined by and for the *Linux kernel* are vital to it.

verbose

Command option that will cause it to return more detailed output (or, in some cases, to return actual output if the command is otherwise "quiet"); usually specified by adding the -v command option.

VFAT

Virtual File Allocation Table; technical name of Microsoft's FAT file system offered under Windows and also on removable storage devices such as flash memory cards.

vi

Arcane text editor and pseudo-shell beloved by *Unix* aficionados that can be used for creation of text files or for creating programs. Traditionally, Unix users either love or hate vi; some prefer *emacs*.

W

Wine

Short for Wine Is Not an Emulator; software that re-creates the Windows Application Programming Interface (API) layer within *Linux* and lets users run Windows programs.

workspace

X terminology referring to a *GUI* desktop.

X

X

Short for X Window; software that controls the display and input devices, thereby providing a software foundation on top of which desktop managers like *GNOME* are able to run.

X11

Version 11 of the *X* software, currently in use on most desktop *Linux* systems.

XFree86 Project

Organization that creates *X* software. At one time, every *distribution* of *Linux* used XFree86 software, but most now use similar software from the *X.org* organization.

xinetd

The *service* responsible for starting various network servers on the computer.

X.org

Organization that produces the X Window software and, in particular, a set of programs called XFree86. XFree86 is used on most modern distributions of *Linux*. It is backed by a number of *Unix* and Linux industry leaders.

xterm

Simple program that allows you to run a shell under X. This program has the advantage of being available on most *Linux* systems that offer a *GUI*.

Y

YaST

Yet Another Setup Tool; principal system configuration tool within *SUSE Linux* by which the hardware and software systems are configured.

■■■

BASH Command Index

This appendix provides a whistle-stop tour of commands that can be used at the BASH shell. This is a highly selective listing, intended to provide a guide to commands that see day-to-day use on average desktop systems. In a similar fashion, although some command options are listed, they're strictly limited to those that receive regular deployment.

The descriptions of each command are deliberately simple. Note that the quantity of space a command is given is not an indication of its importance or usefulness.

Various conventions are used in the list:

- Commands that can and might be run by ordinary users are preceded with a dollar sign ($).

- Commands that require root privileges are preceded with a hash symbol (#).

- Commands that offer far more than features than hinted at by their brief description here have an asterisk after their name. In such cases, I strongly advise you to refer to the command's man page for more information.

- You should substitute your own details wherever italicized words appear.

Commands that present dangers to the system through misuse are clearly marked. Such commands should not be used without research into the command's usage and function.

Command	Description	Command Options	Example of Typical Use
$ alias	Create or display command aliases		alias *list*='l'
$ alsamixer	Alter audio volume levels		alsamixer
$ apropos	Search man pages for specified words/phrases		apropos *"word or phrase"*
$ bzip2	Compress specified file (replaces original file with compressed file and gives it .bz2 file extension)	-d: Decompress specified file	bzip2 *myfile*
		-k: Don't delete original file	
		-t: Test; do a dry run without writing any data	
$ bzip2recover	Attempt recovery of specified damaged .bz2 file		bzip2recover *myfile.tar.bz2*
$ cal	Display calendar for current month (or specified month/year)		cal *4 2005*
$ cat	Display a file on screen or combine and display two files together		cat *myfile*
$ cd	Change to specified directory		cd */usr/bin*
$ cdparanoia *	Convert CD audio tracks to hard disk files	-B: Batch mode; convert all tracks to individual files	cdparanoia -S 8 -B
		-S: Set CD read speed (2, 4, 8, 12, and so on; values relate to CD-drive spin speed; used to avoid read errors)	
# cdrecord *	Burn audio or CD-R/RW data discs (the latter usually based on an ISO image; see mkisofs)	-dev=: Specify the drive's device name, such as /dev/hdc	cdrecord *dev=/dev/hdc* *-speed=16 -v* *myfile.iso*
		-speed=: Specify the write speed (2, 4, 6, 8, and so on)	
		-v: Verbose output; obligatory for feedback on cdrecord's progress	

Command	Description	Command Options	Example of Typical Use
# cfdisk *	DANGEROUS! Menu-based disk-partitioning program		cfdisk /dev/hda
# chgrp	Change group ownership of a file/directory	-R: Recursive; apply changes to subdirectories	chgroup mygroup myfile
# chkconfig	Administer or display services running at the current run level		chkconfig servicename on
$ chmod	Change permissions of a file/directory (where a=all, u=user, g=group, r=read, w=write, x=executable)	-R: Recursive; apply to subdirectories --reference=: Copy permissions from specified file	chmod a+rw myfile
$ chown	Change file ownership to specified username	-R: Recursive; apply to subdirectories	chown username myfile1
# chroot	Change the root of the file system to the specified path		chroot /home/mydirectory
# chvt	Switch to the specified virtual terminal (equivalent of holding down Ctrl+Alt and pressing F1–F6)		chvt 3
$ clear	Clear terminal screen and place cursor at top		clear
$ cp	Copy files	-r: Recursive; copy subdirectories and the files therein -s: Create symbolic link instead of copying	cp myfile1 directory/
$ crontab	Edit or display the user's crontab file (scheduled tasks)	-e: Edit the crontab file (create/amend) -l: List crontab entries -r: Delete the crontab file -u: Specify a user and edit the user's crontab file	crontab -e
$ date	Display the date and time		date

Command	Description	Command Options	Example of Typical Use
$ df	Display free disk space within file system	-h: Human-readable; display sizes in KB, MB, GB, and TB, as appropriate	df -h
		-l: Restrict to local file systems, as opposed to network mounts	
$ diff	Display differences between specified files	-a: Consider all files text files (don't halt when asked to compare binary files)	diff myfile1 myfile2
		-i: ignore lowercase and uppercase differences	
$ diff3	Display differences between three specified files		diff3 myfile1 myfile2 myfile3
$ dig	Look up IP address of specified domain		dig mysite.com
$ dmesg	Display kernel message log		dmesg
# dosfsck *	Check and repair MS-DOS–based file hard disk partition (see also fsck)	-a: Repair without asking user for confirmation	dosfsck -rv /dev/hda4
		-r: Repair file system asking user for confirmation when two or more repair methods are possible	
		-v: Verbose; display more information	
$ du	Show sizes of files and folders in kilobytes	-h: Human-readable; produce output in MB, GB, and TB	du -h /home/myuser
		-s: Summary; display totals only for directories rather than for individual files	
$ eject	Eject a removable storage disk	-t: Close an already open tray	eject /media/dvd-rom
$ ex *	Start a simple text-editor program used principally within shell scripts		ex myfile.txt
$ exit	Log out of shell (end session)		exit
$ fdformat	Low-level format a floppy disk (this won't create a file system; see also mkfs)		fdformat /dev/fd0
# fdisk *	DANGEROUS! Hard-disk partitioning program	-l: List partition table	fdisk /dev/hda

Command	Description	Command Options	Example of Typical Use
$ fg	Brings job running in background to foreground		fg 1
$ file	Display information about specified file, such as its type		file myfile
$ find *	Find files by searching directories (starting in current directory)	-maxdepth: Specify the number of subdirectories levels to delve into, starting from 1 (current directory)	find -name "myfile"
		-name: Specify name of file to search for	
		-type: Specify file types to be returned; -type d returns directories and -type f returns only files	
$ findsmb	Search network for file sharing computers (Windows or Macs using SMB)		findsmb
$ free	Display information about memory usage	-m: Show figures in MB	free -m
		-t: Total the columns at bottom of table	
# fsck *	Check file system for errors (usually run from rescue disc)		fsck /dev/hda1
$ ftp *	FTP program for uploading/downloading to remote sites		ftp ftp.mysite.com
$ fuser	Show which processes are using a particular file or file system	-v: Verbose; detailed output	fuser -v myfile
$ grep *	Search specified file for specified text string (or word)	-i: Ignore uppercase and lowercase differences	grep "phrase I want to find" myfile.txt
		-r: Recursive; delve into subdirectories (if applicable)	
		-s: Suppress error messages about inaccessible files and other problems	
# groupadd	Create new group		groupadd mygroup
# groupdel	Delete specified group		groupdel mygroup
$ groups	Display groups the specified user belongs to		groups myuser

Command	Description	Command Options	Example of Typical Use
$ gzip	Compress files and replace original file with compressed version	-d: Decompress specified file	gzip *myfile*
		-v: Verbose; display degree of compression	
# halt	Initiate shutdown procedure, ending all processes and unmounting all disks	-p: Power off system at end of shutdown procedure	halt -p
# hdparm *	DANGEROUS! Tweak hard disk settings		hdparm */dev/hda*
$ head	Print topmost lines of text files (default is first 10 lines)	-n: Specify number of lines (such as -n 5)	head *myfile.txt*
$ help	Display list of common BASH commands		help
$ history	Display history file (a list of recently used commands)		history
$ host	Query DNS server based on specified domain name or IP address	-d: Verbose; return more information	host *65.19.150.100*
		-r: Force name server to return its cached information rather than query other authoritative servers	
$ hostname	Display localhost-style name of computer		hostname
$ id	Display username and group information of specified user (or current user if none specified)		id *myuser*
# ifconfig *	Display or configure settings of a network interface (assign an IP address, subnet mask, and activate/deactivate it)	down: Disable interface (used at end of command chain)	ifconfig *eth0 192.168.0.10* netmask *255.255.0.0* up
		netmask: Specify a subnet mask	
		up: Enable interface (used at end of command chain)	
$ info *	Display info page for specified command		info *command*
# init	Change current run level		init *3*
$ ispell	Spell-check specified file		ispell *myfile.txt*
$ jobs	Display list of jobs running in background		jobs
# kernelversion	Display kernel version number		kernelversion
$ kill	Kill specified process		kill *1433*

Command	Description	Command Options	Example of Typical Use
$ killall	Kill process(es) that have specified name(s)	-i: Confirm before killing process	killall *processnumber*
$ last	Display details of recent logins, reboots, and shutdowns	-v: Verbose; report if and when successful	last
$ ldd	Display system files (libraries) required by specified program		ldd */usr/bin/program*
$ less	Interactively scroll through a text file	-q: Quiet; disable beeps when end of file is reached or other error encountered	less *myfile.txt*
		-i: Ignore case; make all searches case-insensitive unless uppercase letters are used	
$ ln	Create links to specified files, such as symbolic links	-s: Create symbolic link (default is hard link)	ln -s *myfile1 myfile2*
$ look	Spell-check specified word		look *word*
$ lpr	Print file (send it to the printer spool/queue)	-V: Verbose; print information about progress of print job	lpr *myfile.txt*
$ lpstat	Display print queue		lpstat
$ ls	List directory	-a: List all files, including hidden files	ls -h *mydirectory*
		-d: List only directory names rather than their contents	
		-h: Human-readable; print figures in KB, MB, GB, and TB	
		-l: Long list; include all details, such as file permissions	
		-m: Show as comma-separated list	
# lsmod	Display currently loaded kernel modules		lsmod
$ lsof	Display any files currently in use	-u: Limit results to files used by specified user	lsof -u *username*

Command	Description	Command Options	Example of Typical Use
`$ mail`	Command-line `mail` client	-s: Specify subject prior to creating new mail	`mail user@mydomain.com`
`$ man`	Display specified command's manual		`man command`
`$ mc`	Semigraphical file-browsing program based on Norton Commander		`mc`
`$ md5sum`	Display MD5 checksum (normally used to confirm a file's integrity after download)		`md5sum myfile`
`# mkfs *`	DANGEROUS! Create specified file system on specified device (such as a floppy disk)	-t: Specify type of file system	`mkfs -t vfat /dev/fd0`
`$ mkisofs *`	Create ISO image file from specified directory (usually for burning to disc with cdrecord)	-o: Options; this must appear after command to indicate that command options follow -apple: Use Mac OS extensions to make disc readable on Apple computers -f: Follow symbolic links and source actual files -J: Use Joliet extensions (make ISO compatible with Windows) -R: Use Rock Ridge extensions (preferred Linux CD-ROM file system) -v: Verbose; display more information (-vv for even more info)	`mkisofs -o isoimage.iso -R -J -v mydirectory`
`# modinfo`	Display information about kernel module		`modinfo modulename`
`# modprobe`	Insert specified module into the kernel, as well as any others it relies on	-k: Set module's autoclean flag so it will be removed from memory after inactivity -r: Remove specified module as well as any it relies on to operate	`modprobe modulename`
`$ more`	Interactively scroll through text file (similar to less)		`more myfile.txt`

Command	Description	Command Options	Example of Typical Use
# mount *	Mount specified file system at specified location	-o: Specify command options, such as rw to allow read/write access; various types of file systems have unique commands	mount /dev/hda4 /mnt
$ mv	Move (or rename) specified files and/or directories	-b: Back up files before moving -v: Display details of actions carried out	mv myfile mydirectory/
$ netstat *	Show current network connections		netstat -a
$ nice	Run specified command with specified priority	-n: Specify priority, ranging from the highest priority of -20, to 19, which is the lowest priority	nice -n 19
$ nohup	Run specified command and continue to run it, even if user logs out		nohup command
$ passwd	Change user's password		passwd
$ ping	Check network connectivity between local machine and specified address	-w: Exit after specified number of seconds (such as -w 5)	ping mydomain.com
$ printenv	Display all environment variables for current user		printenv
$ ps *	Display currently running processes	a: List all processes (note that command options don't require preceding dash) f: Display ownership of processes using tree-style graphics u: Limit results to processes running for and started by current user x: Include processes in results not started by user but running with the user ID	ps aux
$ pwd	Display current directory		pwd
# reboot	Reboot computer		reboot
$ renice	Change a process's priority while it's running (see nice)		renice 19 10704

Command	Description	Command Options	Example of Typical Use
$ rm	Delete single or multiple files and/or directories	-r: Recursive; delete specified directories and any subdirectories	rm -rf *mydirectory*
		-f: Force; don't prompt for confirmation before deleting (use with care!)	
# rmmod	Delete module from kernel		rmmod *modulename*
# route *	Add and create (or view) entries in routing table (see ifconfig)		route add *default gw* 192.168.1.1
# rpm *	Red Hat Package manager; installs, removes, and otherwise administers specified package	-e: Uninstall specified package	rpm -Uvh *packagename*
		-h: Graphically indicate progress when installing/uninstalling	
		-i: Install package	
		--nodeps: Ignore dependency errors (use with care!)	
		-qa: Display listing of installed packages	
		-qp: Display details of specified package	
		-U: Upgrade package (will install package if not already installed)	
		-v: Verbose; display detailed output	
# sax2 *	Configure Xorg, including input devices and display(s)	-V: Specify initial resolution and refresh rate, such as -V 800x600@60	sax2
$ screen *	Program that runs pseudo shell that is kept alive regardless of current user login	-ls: Display list of currently running screen sessions	screen
		-R: Reattach to already running screen session or start new one if none available	

Command	Description	Command Options	Example of Typical Use
$ sftp *	Secure Shell FTP; like FTP but running over an ssh connection (see ssh)		sftp username@192.168.1.14
$ shred	Overwrite data in a file with gibberish, thereby making it irrecoverable	-u: Delete file in addition to overwriting -v:Verbose; show details of procedure -f: Force permissions to allow writing if necessary	shred -fv myfile
$ sleep	Pause input for the specified period of time (where s=seconds, m=minutes, h=hours, d=days)		sleep 10m
$ smbclient *	FTP-style program with which you can log in to an SMB (Windows)–based file share		smbclient //192.168.1.1/
$ sort	Sort entries in the specified text file (default is ASCII sort)		sort myfile.txt -o sorted.txt
$ ssh *	Log in to remote computer using secure shell		ssh username@192.168.1.15
$ startx	Start GUI session when in run level 3 (at shell login)		startx
$ su	Temporarily log in as specified user; log in as root if no user specified (provided root account is activated)	-: Adopt user's environment variables, such as $PATH	su
$ sudo	Execute specified command with root privileges (requires root password)		sudo command
# SuSEconfig	Update system according to settings in SUSE Linux–specific config files		SuSEconfig
$ tac	Display specified text file but in reverse (from last to first line)		tac myfile.txt
$ tail	Display final lines of specified text file	-n: Specify number of lines to display (such as -n4)	tail myfile.txt

Command	Description	Command Options	Example of Typical Use
$ tar *	Combine specified files and/or directories into one larger file, or extract from such a file	-c: Create new archive -j: Use bzip2 in order to compress (or decompress) files -f: Specify filename (must be last in chain of command options) -r: Add files to existing archive -x: Extract files from existing archive -z: Use gzip to compress (or decompress) files	tar -zcf myfile.tar.gz mydirectory
$ tee	Display piped output and also save it to specified file		ls -lh| tee listing.txt
$ top *	Program that both displays and lets the user manipulate processes		top
$ touch	Give specified file current time and date stamp; if it doesn't exist, create a zero-byte file with that name		touch myfile
# traceroute	Discover and display network path to another host		traceroute 192.168.1.20
$ umask	Set default permissions assigned to newly created files		umask u=rwx,g=r,o=
# umount	Unmount a file system		umount /media/cdrom
$ unalias	Remove specified alias	-a: Remove all aliases (use with care!)	unalias command
$ uname	Display technical information about current system	-a: Display all basic information	uname -a
$ unzip	Unzip a Windows-compatible zip file	-l: Display archive content but don't actually unzip	unzip myfile.zip
$ uptime	Display uptime for system, as well as CPU load average and logged-in users		uptime
# useradd	Add new user	-m: Create home directory for user	useradd -m username

Command	Description	Command Options	Example of Typical Use
# userdel	Delete all mention of user in system configuration files (effectively deleting the user, although files owned by the user might remain)	-r: Remove user's home directory	userdel -r *username*
$ vi *	Text editor program		vi
$ wc	Count the number of words in a file		wc *myfile.txt*
$ whatis	Display one-line summary of specified command		whatis *command*
$ whereis	Display information on where a binary command is located, along with its source code and man page (if applicable)	-b: Return information only about binary programs	whereis -b *command*
$ xhost	Configure which users/systems can run programs on the X server	+: When followed by a username and/or system name, gives the user/system permission to run programs on the X server; when used on its own, lets *any* user/system use the X server	xhost +
		-: Opposite of +	
# xinit	Start elementary GUI session (when not already running a GUI)		xinit
# yast *	Start the YaST system configuration program (if in run level 3, or GUI is otherwise not started, command will start YaST command-line version)	-i: Install specified RPM	yast
$ zip	Create Windows-compatible compressed zip files	-r: Recursive; includes all subdirectories and files therein	zip -r *myfile.zip mydirectory*
		-u: Updates zip file with specified file	
		-P: Encrypts zip file with specified password	
		-v: Verbose; display more information	
		-#: Set compression level (from 0, which is no compression, to 9, which is highest)	
$ zipgrep	Search inside zip files for specified text string		zipgrep *"search phrase" myfile.zip*

■ ■ ■

Getting Further Help

So you've read through this book and have a good working knowledge of Linux. SUSE Linux is running exactly as you want it to, and things are going okay. But then you hit a brick wall. Perhaps you want to perform a task but simply don't know how. Or maybe you know roughly what you need to do but don't know the specifics. Although this book tries to be as comprehensive as possible, it can't cover every eventuality.

You need to find some help, but where do you turn? Fortunately, many sources of information are available to those who are willing to help themselves. Linux contains its own series of help files in the form of man and info pages, and these are good places to start. In addition, some programs come with their own documentation. If none of these sources provide the help you need, you can head online and take advantage of the massive Linux community around the world.

Read the Manual!

Before asking for help online, it's important that you first attempt to solve your problems by using Linux's built-in documentation. If you go online and ask a question so simple that it can be answered with a little elementary research, you might find people reply with "RTFM." This stands for Read the darned Manual (language toned down to protect the innocent). In other words, do some basic research, and then come back if you're still stuck.

It's not that people online don't want to help. It's that they don't like people who are too lazy to help themselves and expect others to do the hard work for them. Although not all Linux people you encounter will take such a hard line, doing a little homework first can provide answers to a lot of questions, removing the need to ask others. This is particularly true when it comes to the fundamentals.

Documentation typically comes in three formats: man pages, info pages, and README files.

man Pages

man pages are the oldest form of Unix documentation. In the old days, once an individual had created a piece of software, he would write a brief but concise man page in order to give others a clue as to how to operate it. The programmer would come up with a few screens of documentation that could be called up from the command prompt. This documentation would outline what the software did and list all the ways in which it could be used.

Nowadays, depending on the software package, man pages are usually created by technical writers, but the concept of providing essential information still applies. man pages under

Linux provide all the information you need about how to use a particular command or piece of software.

Sounds great, doesn't it? Alas, there's a problem: man pages are written by software engineers *for* software engineers. They expect you to already understand the technology being discussed. This is illustrated very well by the man page for cdrecord, software that can be used to burn CD images to disc. You can view this man page by typing man cdrecord at the command prompt.

The first line of the man page states, "Cdrecord is used to record data or audio Compact Discs on an Orange Book CD-Recorder or to write DVD media on a DVD-Recorder."

Most of that is clear, but what do they mean by "Orange Book"? They don't explain. (If you're curious, head over to http://searchstorage.techtarget.com/sDefinition/0,,sid5_gci503648,00.html).

Further down in the man page, you see, "Cdrecord is completely based on SCSI commands. . . Even ATAPI drives are just SCSI drives that inherently use the ATA packet interface as [a] SCSI command transport layer."

What's SCSI, or ATAPI for that matter? Again, the man page doesn't explain. (They're methods of interfacing with storage devices attached to your computer.)

But why should man pages explain as they go along? Their function is to describe how to use a piece of software, not to provide a beginner's introduction to technology. If they did that, a single man page could run to hundreds of pages.

In other words, man pages are not for complete beginners. This isn't always the case and, because Linux sees widespread usage nowadays, man pages are sometimes created with less-knowledgeable users in mind. But even so, the format is inherently limited: man pages provide concise guides to using software. Luckily, there are some tips you can bear in mind to get the most from a man page. But before you can use those tips, you need to know how to read a man page.

How to Read a man Page

To read a man page, you simply precede the command name with man. For example, to read the man page of cdrecord, a piece of software used to write ISO images to CD-R/RW discs, type the following command:

```
man cdrecord
```

This opens a simple text viewer with the man page displayed. You can move up and down line by line with the cursor keys, or move page by page using the Page Up and Page Down keys (these are sometimes labeled Pg Up and Pg Down). You can search by hitting the forward slash key (/). This will highlight all instances of the word you type. You can search for other examples of the word in the document by hitting the / key again and pressing Enter.

The average man page will include many headings, but the following are the most common:

Name: This is the name of the command. There will also be a one-sentence summary of the command.

Synopsis: This lists the command along with its various command options (sometimes known as *arguments* or *flags*). Effectively, it shows how the command can be used. It looks complicated, but the rules are simple. First is the command itself. This is in bold, which indicates it is mandatory. This rule applies to anything else in bold: it must be included when the command is used. Anything contained within square brackets ([ ]) is optional, and this is usually where you will find the command options listed. A pipe symbol (|) separates any command options that are exclusive, which means that only one of them can be used. For example, if you see [apple|orange|pear], only one of apple, orange, or pear can be specified. Usually at the end of the Synopsis listing will be the main argument, typically the file(s) that the command is to work on and/or generate.

Description: This is a concise overview of the command's purpose.

Options: This explains what the various command options do, as first listed in the Synopsis section. Bearing in mind that command options tell the software how to work, this is often the most useful part of the man page.

Files: This lists any additional files that the command might require or use, such as configuration files.

Notes: If this section is present (and often it isn't), it sometimes attempts to further illuminate aspects of the command or the technology the command is designed to control. Unfortunately, Notes sections can be just as arcane as the rest of the man page.

See Also: This refers to the man pages of other commands that are linked to the command in question. If a number appears in brackets, this means the reference is to a specific section within the man page. To access this section, type man <section no> command.

Although there are guidelines for the headings that should appear in man pages, as well as their formatting, the fact is that you may encounter other headings, or you may find nearly all of them omitted. Some man pages are the result of hours if not days of effort; others are written in ten minutes. Their quality can vary tremendously.

Tips for Working with man Pages

The trick to quickly understanding a man page is decoding the Synopsis section. If you find it helps, split the nonobligatory command options from the mandatory parts. For example, cdrecord's man page says that you *must* specify the dev= option (it's in bold), so at the very least, the command is going to require this:

```
cdrecord dev=<something or other> filename
```

Then you should skip to the Options section and work out which options are relevant to your requirements. While you're there, you'll also need to figure out what the dev= command option requires.

Although the command options contained in square brackets in the Synopsis section are, in theory, nonobligatory, the command might not work satisfactorily without some of them. For example, with cdrecord, I use the -speed command option, which sets the burn speed, and also the -v option, which provides verbose output (otherwise, the command runs silently and won't display any information on screen, including error messages!).

Another handy tip in decoding man pages is understanding what standard input and standard output are. In very simple terms, standard input (stdin) is the method by which a command gets input—the keyboard on most Linux setups. Standard output (stdout) is where the output of a command is sent, which is the screen on most Linux setups. (See Chapter 15 for more details about standard input and standard output.)

Often, a man page will state that the output of a command will be sent to standard output. In other words, unless you specify otherwise, its output will appear on screen. Therefore, it's necessary to specify a file to which the data will be sent, either by redirecting the output (see Chapter 17), or by specifying a file using a command option. For example, the mkisofs command can be used to create ISO images from a collection of files for subsequent burning to CD. But unless the -o option is used to specify a filename, mkisofs's output will simply be sent to standard output—it will appear on the screen.

Finally, here's the best tip of all for using man pages: don't forget that man has its own man page. Simply type man man.

info Pages

man pages date from the days of relatively primitive computers. Back then, most computers could only display page after page of text, and allow the user to scroll through it. In addition, memory and disk space were scarce, which is why some man pages are incredibly concise— fewer words take up less memory!

The *Texinfo* system is a valiant attempt by the GNU Project to overcome the shortfalls of man pages. Often, this is referred to as info, because that's the command used to summon Texinfo pages (normally, you type info *command*).

For starters, info pages are more verbose than the equivalent man pages, and that gives the author more space to explain the command or software. This doesn't necessarily mean that info pages are easier to understand, but there's a better chance of that being the case.

Secondly, info pages contain hyperlinks, just like web pages. If you move the cursor over a hyperlinked word, which is usually indicated by an asterisk (*), and hit Enter, you can proceed to a related page. In a similar sense, pages are linked together so that you can move back and forth from topic to topic.

The bad news is that the man page system is far more popular and established than Texinfo. If a programmer creates a new application, for example, it's unlikely he'll bother with an info page, but he will almost certainly produce a man page.

In fact, in many cases, typing info *command* will simply bring up the man page, except in the software used to browse info pages.

However, nearly all the GNU tools are documented using info pages, either in their own pages or as part of the coreutils pages. For example, to read about the cp command and how to use it, you can type this:

```
info coreutils cp
```

To browse through all sections of the coreutils pages, type this:

```
info coreutils
```

Because man pages are so established, everyone expects to find one for every utility. So most utilities that have info pages will also have man pages. But in such a case, the man page will state near the end that the main documentation for the utility is contained in an info page and you may find it more fruitful to use that instead.

Navigating through info pages is via keyboard and is something of an art. But, as you might expect, there's a highly user-friendly guide to using info: just type info info. Remember that words preceded with an asterisk are hyperlinks, and you can jump from link to link using the Tab key.

README Files and Other Documentation

Some programs come with their own documentation. This is designed to give users the information they need to get started with the program (as opposed to the man page, which is a concise and complete guide to the software). Alternatively, program documentation sometimes gives a brief outline of the program's features.

The files are usually simple text, so they can be read in any text editor or word processor, and are normally called README. Under SUSE Linux (and most versions of Linux), these documents are usually stored in a program-specific directory within /usr/share/doc/packages/.

Not all programs are friendly enough to provide README documentation, but even so, you'll still find a directory for the software in /usr/share/doc/packages/. This is because the directory may contain installation notes, designed for those installing the package from source code. Alternatively, it may simply contain copyright information about the program. Usually the best policy is just to take a look in the directory corresponding to the package you're interested in and see what you can find.

Also within the directory you'll probably find a CHANGELOG document, which is a text file listing features that have been added to each release of the software. The directory might contain some other files, too, detailing where to send information about bugs, for example.

Viewing the README documentation is easy. For example, to view the cdrecord documentation, you could type this:

```
cd /usr/share/doc/packages/cdrecord
less README
```

Sometimes, the README documentation is in a compressed tarball, in which case it will have either a .tar.gz or a .tar.bz2 file extension. However, less is clever enough to realize this and extract the document for reading.

Sometimes, as with the SUSE Linux official documentation, the file is an HTML document. To read this, simply use Firefox or Konqueror, depending on your browser preferences:

```
firefox filename.html
```

or

```
konqueror firename.html
```

Getting Help Online

If you can't figure out the answer by referring to the documentation, then you have little choice other than to look online.

Generally speaking, there are three ways to get help online:

Official documentation: Linux benefits from a massive community of users, all of whom are usually willing to help each other. SUSE Linux is particularly blessed in this regard and benefits from documentation generated by the openSUSE community.

Forums: Often the best way to get help is to visit a forum. Here, you can post messages for others to reply to. The advantage is that not only do you receive a personal service but you can also continue to ask questions if the original answer proved difficult to understand, or perhaps inadequate for your needs.

Mailing list: A nice alternative to the online documentation and forms is to sign up for a mailing list. This is a way of sending e-mail to several hundreds, if not thousands, of people at once. Any individual can then reply. Mailing lists often have the benefit of allowing personal attention and interaction, but this comes at the expense of each subscriber receiving a whole lot of mail.

Official Documentation

SUSE Linux benefits from online documentation produced both by Novell, which owns SUSE Linux, and the community of users that constitute the openSUSE project.

■**Note** The openSUSE project is a worldwide grouping of community volunteers as well as Novell employees who develop the various versions of SUSE Linux that go on to form full releases. You can learn more at `http://en.opensuse.org`.

You can find Novell's official documentation at `www.novell.com/documentation`. The topics are arranged in alphabetical order and cover the components of SUSE Linux as well as the complete operating systems. Novell's documentation is thorough and formal, having been written by professional technical writers, and is supplied in PDF form, so it is ideal for printing.

In addition to desktop computing, it covers many server-based aspects of SUSE Linux use, and this can sometimes make it confusing to find the information you need. In addition, the documentation can lag behind the very latest releases of SUSE. However, Novell's documentation is undoubtedly the first place to look online if you're seeking help on a particular matter.

The openSUSE documentation, which can be found at `http://en.opensuse.org/documentation`, benefits from being cutting edge. It often covers beta (testing) versions of SUSE Linux, for example. The only issue is that it's hosted on a *wiki*, a form of web site that anyone can edit. Because of this, the openSUSE documentation is constantly updated. This can mean that pages move or are deleted in favor of updated versions hosted elsewhere on the site, and this can be slightly confusing (particularly if you bookmark a page).

In general, however, the openSUSE community documentation offers a more down-to-earth guide to SUSE Linux, written by people who use it on a daily basis and are looking to help others overcome particular hurdles that they've encountered. It's recommended for this reason alone.

Forums

The parent company of SUSE Linux, Novell, hosts a number of newsgroups that you can subscribe to if you have a suitably equipped news reader (and your ISP allows NTTP traffic).

Under the GNOME desktop, you can use the Pan program to access newsgroups (Applications ➤ Internet ➤ Usenet News Reader ➤ Pan). Under KDE, you can use KNode (K menu ➤ Internet ➤ Usenet News Reader ➤ KNode).

You can access a newsgroup as a forum by visiting http://support.novell.com/forums/ 2su.html, where you'll also find the names of the newsgroups that you'll need to search for and subscribe to in Pan or KNode.

The benefit of these newsgroups/forums is that your inquiry may well receive the attention of an official Novell support staff member (although other forum members are, of course, permitted to answer queries and often do).

Several third-party web sites also provide forums for SUSE Linux users to seek help, or simply to chat with other users:

www.suseforums.net: This site hosts a wide variety of forums covering practically every aspect of SUSE Linux configuration, from software to hardware and even including topics such as gaming. In addition, you'll find a handful of forums covering community issues, including a "soapbox" forum, where you can make your personal views about Linux known!

http://forums.suselinuxsupport.de: If you find Suseforums.net bewildering, Suselinuxsupport.de might be for you. It offers only a handful of forums, covering all aspects of SUSE Linux use, but these forums are extremely busy and frequented by many knowledgeable users.

http://groups.yahoo.com/group/suselinuxusers: This is a Yahoo Group for users of SUSE Linux. As with all Yahoo Groups, it's built around a mailing list, but the various postings can be read online and there's an extensive archive of past postings. If you're already a member of Yahoo Groups, this could be a good place to visit.

Tip If English isn't your first language, visit http://en.opensuse.org/Communicate, where you'll find links to forums in a variety of other languages.

Before you can post on most forums, you need to register by providing an e-mail address. This is designed to keep down the quantity of unwanted junk postings to the forum.

You might think it fine to post a new question immediately after registering, but don't forget the simple rules mentioned at the beginning of this appendix: if you don't do elementary research first and try to solve your own problem, you may elicit a hostile response from the other posters, especially if your question is one that comes up time and time again, and has been answered several times.

So, first make use of the comprehensive search facility provided with the forums. For example, if you're looking for advice on getting a Foomatic D1000 scanner working, use this as a search term and see what comes up. The chances are that you won't be the first person who has run into problems with that piece of hardware, and someone else may have already posted a solution.

Often, you'll need to read the full thread to find an answer. Someone may start by asking the same question as you but, with the help and guidance of the forum members, they might find a solution, which they then post several messages later.

In addition, some individuals write their own HOWTO guides when they figure out how to do something. These are normally contained in the Customization Tips & Tricks forum.

If you're unable to find a solution by searching, consider posting your own question. Keep your question simple, clear, and concise, because no one likes reading through acres of text. If possible, provide as many details about your system as you can. You will almost certainly want to provide the version number of the Linux kernel you're using, for example. You can find this version number by typing the following in a terminal window:

```
uname -sr
```

In addition, any other details you can provide may prove handy. If you're asking about hardware, give its entire model name and/or number. Don't just ask for help with a Foomatic scanner. Ask for help with a Foomatic D1000 scanner, model number ADK1033, Revision 2. If you're asking about a piece of software, provide its version number (click Help ➤ About).

Sometimes in their replies, other forum members may ask you to post further details or to provide log files. If you don't understand the question, simply ask the poster to give you more details and, if necessary, instructions on what to do. Just be polite. Explain that you're a newbie. If you think the question is extremely obvious, then say so. Apologize for asking what may be a stupid question, but explain that you've tried hard to answer it yourself but have failed.

Mailing Lists

Mailing lists have a number of advantages and disadvantages. The advantages are that a mailing list provides an excellent way to learn about SUSE Linux. All you have to do is read through the e-mail messages you receive in order to partake of a constant information drip-feed. In addition, some mailing lists are designed to make public announcements, so you'll find it easy to learn about the latest happenings in the SUSE Linux community.

Mailing lists also have a terrific sense of community. They offer a neat way of getting to know other SUSE Linux users and talking to them. E-mail messages often drift off topic into humor and general discussion.

The disadvantages of mailing lists are that you can easily receive in excess of 200 messages a day, depending on which mailing list you join. Even if you have a moderately fast Internet connection, that quantity of messages can take a long time to download. In addition, you'll need to sort out any personal or business e-mail from the enormous quantity of mailing list traffic (although the mailing list messages usually have the list title in square brackets in the subject field; you can therefore create a mail rule that sorts the mail according to this).

You can learn how to sign up to the SUSE Linux mailing lists at http://lists.suse.com. Here you can also browse past messages. Bear in mind that there are many, many mailing lists. Before subscribing to one, it's a good idea to read past messages to get an idea of typical postings.

Index

Find it faster at http://superindex.apress.com/

Find it faster at http://superindex.apress.com/

Find it faster at http://superindex.apress.com/

Find it faster at http://superindex.apress.com/

You Need the Companion eBook

Your purchase of this book entitles you to buy the companion PDF-version eBook for only $10. Take the weightless companion with you anywhere.

We believe this Apress title will prove so indispensable that you'll want to carry it with you everywhere, which is why we are offering the companion eBook (in PDF format) for $10 to customers who purchase this book now. Convenient and fully searchable, the PDF version of any content-rich, page-heavy Apress book makes a valuable addition to your programming library. You can easily find and copy code—or perform examples by quickly toggling between instructions and the application. Even simultaneously tackling a donut, diet soda, and complex code becomes simplified with hands-free eBooks!

Once you purchase your book, getting the $10 companion eBook is simple:

❶ Visit **www.apress.com/promo/tendollars/**.

❷ Complete a basic registration form to receive a randomly generated question about this title.

❸ Answer the question correctly in 60 seconds, and you will receive a promotional code to redeem for the $10.00 eBook.

2560 Ninth Street • Suite 219 • Berkeley, CA 94710

eBookshop

THE EXPERT'S VOICE™

Apress®

Apress License Agreement (Single-User Products)

THIS IS A LEGAL AGREEMENT BETWEEN YOU, THE END USER, AND APRESS. BY OPENING THE SEALED CD PACKAGE, YOU ARE AGREEING TO BE BOUND BY THE TERMS OF THIS AGREEMENT. IF YOU DO NOT AGREE TO THE TERMS OF THIS AGREEMENT, PROMPTLY RETURN THE UNOPENED DISK PACKAGE AND THE ACCOMPANYING ITEMS (INCLUDING WRITTEN MATERIALS AND BINDERS AND OTHER CONTAINERS) TO THE PLACE YOU OBTAINED THEM FOR A FULL REFUND.

DISCLAIMER OF WARRANTY

NO WARRANTIES. Apress disclaims all warranties, either express or implied, including, but not limited to, implied warranties of merchantability and fitness for a particular purpose, with respect to the software and the accompanying written materials. The software and any related documentation is provided "as is." You may have other rights, which vary from state to state.

NO LIABILITIES FOR CONSEQUENTIAL DAMAGES. In no event shall Apress be liable for any damages whatsoever (including, without limitation, damages from loss of business profits, business interruption, loss of business information, or other pecuniary loss) arising out of the use or inability to use this product, even if Apress has been advised of the possibility of such damages. Because some states do not allow the exclusion or limitation of liability for consequential or incidental damages, the above limitation may not apply to you.